SAM ANDERSON
DR 3 - 7334

1:30 ANY WED

MONEY AND BANKING

MONEY
AND
BANKING

by

CHARLES L. PRATHER, Ph.D., Pd.D.

Professor of Banking and Finance
The University of Texas

SIXTH EDITION

1957

RICHARD D. IRWIN, INC.

HOMEWOOD, ILLINOIS

SIXTH EDITION

First Printing, April, 1957

Library of Congress Catalogue Card No. 57–8542

PRINTED IN THE UNITED STATES OF AMERICA

To

K. F. P.

AN INSUFFICIENT ACKNOWLEDGMENT

PREFACE

THIS BOOK is the sixth edition of *Money and Banking*, first published in 1937. As was true of the original and subsequent editions, the author's primary purpose has been to set forth the elementary principles of money and banking with emphasis on current problems as these have changed through the years. In this edition, use has been made of the flow-of-funds system of national accounts with resulting enrichment of the subject matter.

The central theme of money and banking is an explanation of changes in the value of money or general prices. With the exception of an introductory chapter, monetary and banking theories are discussed along with the topic to which they are applicable rather than in a separate section of the textbook. The author's assumption is that theory should be introduced where it will be most helpful. In this way, it is hoped that principles will cease being abstractions divorced from their application and will become tools to be used in arriving at an understanding of ever-changing conditions.

Of the thirty-two chapters in this book, the first eight deal primarily with "money," that is currency, deposit currency or checkbook money, monetary reserves, and the theory of the value of money. While some instructors prefer to have the chapter entitled "An Introduction to the Theory of the Value of Money" in the first part of the textbook, others feel that this material should be presented later. The author is inclined to the first point of view because most students have had a course in the principles of economics as a prerequisite to one in money and banking; but he assumes that instructors will assign this material so as to meet the needs of their students. The other seven chapters in this section are: "The Nature and Functions of Money," "Qualities of Money," "Commercial Banks—A Source of Money," "Clearing and Collection of Checks," "Paper Currency, Coins, and Gold," "The Gold Standard," and "The History of Monetary Standards and Currency in the United States."

The dual role of commercial banks—as a source of money on one hand and as a source of loanable funds on the other—has necessitated the presentation of certain banking activities in the first section of this book. However, the money creation and loanable funds functions of a commercial banking system cannot be separated as long as the United States has the fractional reserve system. The last chapter in this section, "History of Monetary Standards and Currency in the United States," is followed by two chapters which deal with the history of commercial banking in the United States.

As a background for the chapters dealing more specifically with the mechanics, management, and theory of commercial banking is the chapter entitled "Credit and Credit Instruments." The quality of bank management as well as the differences among individual banks because of size are reflected in their financial statements. So the first of the next six chapters dealing with the problems of individual banks is entitled "Bank Management and the Bank Statement." The next four chapters: "Commercial Bank Deposits," "Management of Bank Funds," "Bank Loans and Discounts," and "Commercial Bank Investments," point out the differences in the problems faced by bankers due to differences in the nature of deposits, loan demands, location, and size of individual banks. In point of numbers, about 85 per cent of commercial banks in the United States have deposits of $10 million or less; but the 215 banks each with deposits of $100 million or more (only about 1.6 per cent of all banks) hold 60 per cent of all commercial bank deposits. The last chapter in this section, dealing with the techniques of foreign exchange and financing foreign trade, appears here in sequence with other chapters dealing primarily with commercial banking. Not only does this arrangement of material permit tying in the mechanical aspects of foreign exchange to commercial banking but it also links the foreign exchange market to the money market and central bank policy.

Any modern book on "Money and Banking" will stress the need for wise monetary management, which must be provided in the United States by the Federal Reserve authorities and the United States Treasury. The effects of national monetary and credit policies are reflected first in the money market and later in the capital market. Therefore, the first of the seven chapters that deal with monetary and fiscal policies is "The Money Market," which includes, in addition to the older segments of the money market, a discussion of the market for federal funds. The next two chapters present a summary of the organization of the Federal Reserve System and the operations of the Federal Reserve banks. The remaining four chapters in this section are entitled "Member Bank Reserves and Treasury Monetary Policy," "Credit and Monetary Policy," "Fiscal Policy," and "Economic Stabilization."

Chapters XXV and XXVI treat the broader aspects of international finance, and they seem to follow logically the discussion of monetary and fiscal policies which emphasize domestic growth and economic stability. It is felt that a further advantage of this arrangement is that by the time students have covered the material on policy, they will be better able to absorb the intricacies and implications of international financial relations involving balance-of-payment problems and postwar international co-operative efforts to solve them.

Now the importance of capital markets in explaining economic growth is generally recognized. Therefore, as in all preceding editions, this book continued to stress the role of noncommercial banks and other financial institutions in our economy. Among these specialists are investment bankers and brokers, life insurance companies (which now dominate the new corporate securities market), trusts and pension funds, savings institutions, urban and rural mortgage financing institutions, and consumer financing institutions. The last chapter, "Foreign Banking Systems," presents a survey of the banking systems of Canada, Great Britain, and France with comparisons to the United States banking system.

Over the last twenty years, the list of those to whom the author is indebted for their assistance in writing this edition and preceding editions has become so long as to prevent adequate individual acknowledgment. His debt to the staffs of the Board of Governors of the Federal Reserve System, the Federal Reserve banks, the Federal Deposit Insurance Corporation, and other agencies as well as to the teachers of money and banking who have used earlier editions of this textbook is hereby acknowledged.

In the preparation of this edition, the author is particularly indebted to his colleagues Professor Irving O. Linger and Mr. Albert H. Cox, Jr., who were most generous with their time and helpful with their suggestions, as were the following for earlier editions: Professors D. H. Bellemore, F. S. Doody, and A. C. Neal of Boston University, Dr. Charls E. Walker of the Federal Reserve Bank of Dallas, Professor J. W. Bell of Northwestern University; Professors R. A. Graves and J. W. Stehman of the University of Minnesota; and Dr. J. K. Langum, vice-president of the Federal Reserve Bank of Chicago. In preparation of this volume, as for all preceding editions, the author is deeply indebted to his wife, Katherine F. Prather.

C. L. P.

THE UNIVERSITY OF TEXAS
September, 1956

TABLE OF CONTENTS

LIST OF CHARTS, MAPS, AND TABLES

CHARTS

MAPS

TABLES

Chapter 1 | NATURE AND FUNCTIONS OF MONEY

IN MODERN economics, money is anything which is customarily used as a medium of exchange or means of payment and as a standard or measure of value. In this chapter consideration is given to (1) the things used as money, (2) the significance of money, (3) the functions of money or the job that money is expected to do, and (4) the role of banks in supplying money.

The central problem around which all other economic problems tend to cluster is money. In modern industrial society, money is used as a device for measuring the expenses and returns from business. Production is planned and carried on with the objective of making a money profit. Although money income is the prime motive of economic effort, the prices at which this money income can be converted into goods, services, and securities are of equal importance. The concept of price is closely associated with the more general concept of exchange value, that is, the ability of one good to command a second in exchange. Instead of comparing the value of one good in terms of the second, it is customary to compare prices—the exchange value of the two goods expressed in terms of money.

THINGS USED AS MONEY

In our definition of money as anything which is customarily used as a medium of exchange and as a standard of value, the word "customarily" suggests that what is considered to be money by one generation or within one country may not be thought of as money by a different generation or in a second country. In the earlier stages of economic development the thing used as money was usually some commodity that had value in use as well as value in exchange. Articles used as money have included those used for ornament and display, such as beads, gold, and silver; consumable necessities, such as salt, grains, cattle, and skins; capital goods, such as knives, nails, pots, and weapons; and tokens, such as pieces of leather and furs. These articles were passed from hand to hand in exchange for other things, thus

1

circulating as a means of payment (hence the use of the name "commodity currency" in all cases except that of tokens).

The use of tokens suggests the possibility of having a commodity as the standard that does not circulate as money. The word "pecuniary," which is synonymous with "monetary," is derived from the Latin word *pecuniarius* originally meaning property in cattle (from *pecus* or cattle). In an agrarian age, cattle probably were used more as a standard of measuring wealth than as circulating money.

As some commodities circulated as money, a preference for metals, particularly precious metals, emerged gradually because these commodities are durable, possess great value in small bulk, are easy to recognize, and can be divided and reunited without loss in value. Precious metals were first used in commodity or bullion form, and each exchange transaction in which they entered entailed weighing and testing the metals. Later, goldsmiths, bankers, and early rulers aided trade by marking the weight and quality of metals passing through their hands; this process permitted ready identification and increased the acceptability of pieces of metal. Modern coinage gradually developed from this system of marking metals.

While coins are still a convenient medium of exchange for transactions involving small amounts, they are of secondary importance as compared to paper money and checking accounts when total transactions are considered. When computed on a per capita basis, there is about $11 in coins, $172 in paper money, and $630 in checking accounts in the United States. Perhaps of equal or greater significance is the estimate that checks are used in 90 per cent of each business day's transactions of over $8 billion and that about 30 million checks are written an average business day. One New York bank has handled checks valued at $1 billion on a single day.[1] The extent to which the American people have adopted the "banking habit" is suggested by the fact that there are over 47 million checking accounts in commercial banks in the United States.[2]

In most countries, such as the United States, the general public does not use all of the different kinds of currency (see Table 1); instead, some kinds are held by central banks or governments for use in international transactions or for reserve purposes (which may be

---

[1] Chase Manhattan Bank, *Report to Stockholders for the Annual Meeting, December 6, 1955*, p. 4.

[2] The "banking habit" refers to the practice of keeping demand deposits in commercial banks and writing checks on them.

TABLE 1

KINDS OF UNITED STATES CURRENCY OUTSTANDING AND IN CIRCULATION*

[On basis of compilation by United States Treasury. In millions of dollars]

| KIND OF CURRENCY | TOTAL OUT-STANDING, MAY 31, 1956 | HELD IN THE TREASURY | | | HELD BY F.R. BANKS AND AGENTS | CURRENCY IN CIRCULATION† | | |
		As security against gold and silver certificates	Treasury cash	For F.R. Banks and agents		May 31, 1956	Apr. 30, 1956	May 31, 1955
Gold	21,772	21,118	653‡	.....	.....	.....	.....	.....
Gold certificates	21,118	.....	.....	18,269	2,816	34	34	35
Federal Reserve notes	26,993	.....	75	.....	1,065	25,853	25,602	25,419
Treasury currency—total	5,030	2,417§	51	.....	353	4,626	4,575	4,555
Standard silver dollars	489	216	32	.....	5	235	233	221
Silver bullion	2,200	2,200	.....	.....	.....	.....	.....	.....
Silver certificates and Treasury notes of 1890	2,417§	.....	.....	.....	259	2,158	2,124	2,161
Subsidiary silver coin	1,317	.....	13	.....	51	1,253	1,241	1,192
Minor coin	462	.....	2	.....	9	451	448	430
United States notes	347	.....	2	.....	27	318	315	320
Federal Reserve Bank notes	150	.....	‖	.....	2	148	149	164
National Bank notes	65	.....	‖	.....	‖	64	65	67
Total—May 31, 1956	¶	23,535	779	18,269	4,234	30,513	.....	.....
Apr. 30, 1956	¶	23,505	783	18,235	4,442	.....	30,210	.....
May 31, 1955	¶	23,427	828	18,172	4,132	.....	.....	30,009

* Source: *Federal Reserve Bulletin* (July, 1956), p. 721.

† Outside Treasury and Federal Reserve banks. Includes any paper currency held outside the continental limits of the United States.

‡ Includes $156,039,431 held as reserve against United States notes and Treasury notes of 1890.

§ To avoid duplication, amount of silver dollars and bullion held as security against silver certificates and Treasury notes of 1890 outstanding is not included in total Treasury currency outstanding.

‖ Less than $500,000.

¶ Because some of the types of currency shown are held as collateral or reserves against other types, a grand total of all types has no special significance and is not shown.

thought of as a special aspect of the medium-of-exchange or store-of-value functions of money).

In the United States, the development of money has been along specialized lines to meet the varying needs of the economy. Currency (pocket money or all legal coins and paper money) is used chiefly in retail trade. Checking accounts (demand deposits in commercial banks) are used chiefly in business transactions and when obligations are paid by mail. Gold is held chiefly by central banks and governments for reserve purposes and is used in foreign exchange operations when obligations cannot be settled more economically in other ways. In the United States, silver bullion held by the Treasury is used as a reserve for silver certificates. Current gold certificates and gold credits are used as a means of payment among the twelve Federal Reserve banks and between the United States Treasury and the Federal Reserve banks in transactions in gold.

While gold, gold certificates, and silver bullion are held by the

Treasury and the Federal Reserve banks as reserve money, ordinary commercial banks hold their reserves in the form of central-bank credit, currency, and/or balances with correspondent banks. Reserves are cash items kept by banks to meet minimum legal reserve requirements (legal reserves) and to meet normal daily recurring debt obligations and other demands (working reserves). Federal Reserve bank credit, either in the form of member banks' reserve accounts (book credit) or in the form of paper money (Federal Reserve notes), is normally the chief source of new bank reserves. At times, as in the 1930's, the chief source may be gold.

Standard money is the kind of money, established by custom or law, to which the value of other kinds of money in the monetary system is linked. The current standard in the United States is gold, the dollar being defined by law as $\frac{1}{35}$ of an ounce of pure gold troy weight or $15\frac{5}{21}$ grains of standard gold (which is $\frac{9}{10}$ fine). However, gold is not now minted into coins in the United States and private ownership of gold bars is illegal except in small amounts or under license (issued for manufacturing and other legal purposes). Nevertheless, gold is the standard because all kinds of money are being kept equal in value to a gold dollar, legally defined as a weight unit of gold.

Statistics of United States currency outstanding and in circulation are shown by kinds in Table 1. Since some kinds of money are held in whole or part as reserves or collateral against other kinds, the total of all kinds of currency is not significant. For illustration, duplicating dollar amounts are represented by gold certificates and such gold bullion as is held in trust for the owners of gold certificates; the same is true for silver certificates and silver bars and/or silver dollars held in trust for them. The United States Treasury holds (1) $156,039,431 in gold bullion as reserves for United States notes and Treasury notes of 1890; and (2) an equal amount of standard silver dollars as reserves for the relatively small amount of Treasury notes of 1890 still in circulation. Treasury notes of 1890, Federal Reserve bank notes, and national bank notes are in process of retirement; and gold certificates are being withdrawn from circulation. The statistics of currency in circulation (Table 1) include some in the hands of foreigners and some in banks other than Federal Reserve banks.

Statistics of bank credit used as money refer mainly to demand deposits in commercial banks. Although time deposits are considered to be money by some, they are more accurately referred to as *near money* because they must be converted into currency or transferred to checking accounts before they can perform the medium of exchange function. The most accurate estimate of the amount of checking accounts used by the general public as money is *demand deposits adjusted*—total demand deposits minus cash items in process of collection, interbank deposits, and United States government deposits. The banking practice of commercial banks is to give depositors immediate credit for checks, drafts, and similar claims on other banks; so, the statistics of total demand deposits in banks will include such items twice until the drawers' accounts have been debited. Duplication also results when one bank redeposits funds in a second bank (called interbank deposits or bankers' balances). United States government deposits are deducted because emphasis is on the amount of money in the hands of the general public. (Before such government deposits are spent, they are customarily transferred from commercial banks to Federal Reserve banks wherein the United States Treasury keeps most of its checking accounts.) After the foregoing adjustments, the amount of money in the form of checking accounts is between three and four times (over $100 billion) the amount of currency in circulation.

SIGNIFICANCE OF MONEY

Money is merely a tool that helps man to do his economic job more efficiently. Although money does not clothe or feed man, it permits job specialization, the use of machinery, and other things that enable man to enjoy a higher standard of living. From the viewpoint of economics, production is the creation of economic value; and its correct purpose is to provide man with the necessities, conveniences, and luxuries of life (not the aggrandizement of the state).

In modern industrial society, money is used as the device for measuring expenses of and returns from business—an accounting function of money that even the totalitarian governments use. Production is planned and carried on with the view of making a money profit. Money, and the economy it presupposes, permits businessmen to concentrate on producing for the market place, rather than on meeting production quotas as set by some government control agency. While the profit motive may be criticized, no effective substitute has been found in a free economy. In a world plagued by a conflict of ideologies the use of money and credit permits individual planning and freedom of action. In addition, it permits a degree of specialization, division of labor, and co-operation not possible in any other type of economy except the most autocratic wherein all phases of production are specified by the government.

The seemingly disjointed, unrelated, and individualistic economic activities of specialists are made effective through the market place. Undirected co-operation is found among those who work upon a good in the different stages of production, from the raw material to the finished product. The need for co-operation among these independent producers increases with the increase in the quantity and variety of products, the number of specialists, the size of the market, and the number of productive steps between the producer and the ultimate consumer. The producer, keeping in mind not only his own plans but also those of his competitors, must estimate the quantity and quality of goods consumers will demand. Thus, while specialization and division of labor increase "the productivity of labor on the technical side," the money economy "tremendously increases the problems of finance and management."

The present structure and productive efficiency of American business bear witness to the ability of financiers and entrepreneurs to solve these problems. Now the gross national product, that is, the gross value of the current output of goods and services, is the greatest per capita in history. Estimates suggest that the rate of growth in the national output has been over 3 per cent per year, which is about twice the rate of growth of the population. At the same time, there has been a decline in the number of work-hours per week in the private economy. Over the long run, industrial progress not only has reduced the toil of work for producers but also has raised living standards for consumers.[3]

Producers are also consumers and most consumers are workers, future workers, or ex-workers. Thus, those who are workers have a dual role in the economy—receiving money payments for their services (of course, there are exceptions) and using their money income to buy goods and services to fulfill their needs and wants. In a democracy, consumers have a major role in determining what is produced. By buying more of certain goods, they cast dollar votes for increased production of these goods. The consumption problem of the individual is to budget his liquid money income in order to care for his immediate and future needs to the best advantage. In making decisions, his choice is determined primarily by the size of his money

[3] Frederick C. Mills, "The Role of Productivity in Economic Growth," *American Economic Review Supplement*, Vol. XLII (May, 1952), p. 557.

income and the quantity and quality of goods that can be bought with it. Although the obtaining of money income is the prime motivator of economic effort, the price at which this money can be converted into goods and services is of equal importance. The welfare of a community is dependent upon the size of its "real income" (goods and services that money will buy).

The use of money permits the consumer to shift purchases from one commodity to a second, to buy certain goods today or to postpone purchases, to buy in one community or a second, or to buy from one merchant or another. The consumer's time and place options are important to buyers and sellers. Much of modern advertising is explainable only in terms of this liquid purchasing power, which is always limited in amount and shiftable from goods to goods, from the present to the future, and from market to market.

In modern economics there is an increasing recognition of the importance of consumption in determining the size of the national income—that is, the aggregate earnings of labor and property which arise from current production.[4] Since one man's expenditure may be another man's income, what is spent in one time period by the community tends to determine the size of the community's income in the period that follows. Of the two types of expenditures—for consumption and for investment—the first is the larger and therefore the more important. On the other hand, the amount of investment may fluctuate violently, which means that it may be an important factor affecting employment and the amount of consumer spending. To stress consumption—so as to encourage investment and production—and to stress investment and production—so as to increase income and encourage consumption—represent two approaches to the ever-present problem of increasing the quantity and quality of goods and services which are essential to the improvement of the well-being of society.

Since money is used in the exchange process, production continues only if goods and services are bought and sold. Effective demand (desire accompanied by the ability to pay) means "spending" or the use of money in the exchange process. Once spent, money is in new hands where it is available for further spending. In general, the purchasing power that it represents is not exhausted but merely transferred to new owners. The continuous flow of money is just as

[4] National income is expressed in terms of current dollars, being the total amount of money received during a year from all sources by the members of a country (including primarily wages, salaries, interest, dividends, rents, royalties, corporate savings, and government payments).

essential to the well-being of society as the continuous flow of the blood stream is to the well-being of the human body.

FUNCTIONS OF MONEY

Money, like so many other things in everyday use, is defined in terms of its functions; that is, in terms of what it does or is expected to do. Practically all definitions of money emphasize its primary functions; namely, its use as a medium of exchange and as a standard of value. In addition, consideration is usually given to the use of money as a store of value (for savings), as a standard of deferred payments, and other secondary functions. However, these functions of money are merely special aspects of the use of money as a medium of exchange or as a standard of value.

Medium of Exchange. In a barter transaction, goods and services are exchanged directly for goods and services; but, when money is used as a medium of exchange, it is the means by which goods and services are exchanged indirectly for goods and services. Sales are made for money, and money is used to purchase goods. Two transactions are necessary instead of one, as in the case of barter. The second exchange may be delayed, transferred to a second market, or used to purchase any one of a large number of goods, services, or securities. This option to choose the time, the place, and the thing or service to purchase is a valuable privilege resulting from the use of money as a medium of exchange.

Measure or Standard of Value. Money is used much more frequently as a measure of value than as a medium of exchange because (1) values are often measured many times before exchange takes place; (2) the standard-of-value function is present in barter, that is, when eggs are traded for groceries, old cars are traded in, and bills and commissions are traded out at stores; and (3) the standard-of-value function is used to measure values or to compare prices even though no purchase is made. Money, as a standard of value, provides a unit for measuring the relative value of all exchangeable goods. In modern economies, the value of goods and services is expressed in terms of price. Without the use of some value-measuring device, it would be necessary to compare the value of each good to all others appearing in the market.[5] By using money as the standard

---

[5] Without a standard for measuring value in a market wherein there are but 10 commodities, there would be 45 exchange ratios instead of 10 prices. The first commodity would have to be measured against the other 9, the second against the next 8, and so on throughout the list. In a market wherein there are 100 commodities, there would be 4,950 exchange ratios instead of 100 prices.

of value, only prices need to be compared. By "price" is meant the number of monetary units, or fractions or multiples thereof, for which a good will be exchanged. Whenever price tags are attached to goods, price lists are posted, or purchase offers and sale offers are made, money is used as a standard of value.

In an economy dominated by private enterprise, most economic planning is done in terms of the monetary unit. The dollar, or a similar unit, is used in weighing the importance of past and current activities and in setting up future goals. In order for the record of achievement and the plans for the future to mean more than illusory dollar figures, the monetary unit must be fairly stable in value. A standard of value which is an elastic measuring device is no more satisfactory than would be an elastic standard of weights and measures.

As a standard of value, money is more than a common denominator for expressing exchange ratios as prices. It provides businessmen and others with a standard unit to use in planning future production (budgeting), in measuring current costs and receipts (cost accounting), and in reporting on the income and assets of business enterprises (financial accounting).

Store of Value. Money may be thought of as a claim check on the economy, for it represents purchasing power. When one accepts money as payment for goods or services, as proceeds from a loan transaction, as a gift, as a pension payment, or as the result of any other transaction, he has what is called *general purchasing power.* This claim check may be used immediately to obtain goods or services; it may be invested in securities or real property; it may be deposited in a bank or some other financial institution (such as a savings and loan association) which may lend it to someone who will spend it; or it may be held idle as a cash balance for future needs. Money may be held as a cash balance to meet anticipated payrolls and tax obligations; to care for weekly, monthly, or seasonal purchases of goods; to make planned investments; or to have ready purchasing power in order to take advantage of bargains expected in the future. Cash balances may also include hoarded money which is held for fear that it will not be obtainable when needed later. Hoarded money does not flow back into the income stream during the period in which it is obtained. The effect of hoarding is to reduce the income velocity and the velocity of circulation of money with similar effects on national income and total monetary expenditures (see Chapter III).

At any particular moment, actually very little of the money in the United States is being spent; therefore, most of it is being held as cash balances that may be thought of as stores of value. Those who hold money as a store of value should have the right to expect that its purchasing power will remain unchanged during the interim between its receipt and spending for goods, services, and investments. If money were expected to decline in value (prices are expected to increase), people would be reluctant to hold it as a store of value because the dollars saved would have less value, that is, they would purchase less in the future. This means that money must be stable in value in order to serve satisfactorily as a store of value.

Until government and law gave every man some guarantee of his rights to property, and prior to the creation of negotiable instruments, money was almost the only store of value of a generally exchangeable nature. Today, the chief advantage of holding money is that it provides ready purchasing power. The modern saver normally keeps his store of value in the form of money just large enough to provide needed "liquidity" (ready purchasing power) because money hoards bring in no income. However, when the value of money is increasing (prices are falling), people tend to hold money because any loss in interest which could be obtained from investments may be more than offset by the increase in purchasing power of money held as a store of value. This withholding of money from the market place tends to cause a decrease in national income, an increase in unemployment, and a further decline in general prices.

Low interest rates on savings deposits, government bonds, and other investments reduce the penalty (loss of interest) for keeping funds idle. On the other hand, maintenance of fairly stable interest rates on government obligations and provisions for redemption of savings bonds in cash at par have given these credit instruments greater liquidity and have made them more like money. Because of the existence of large amounts of these near-money types of assets, the problem of monetary management has been made more difficult.

Standard of Deferred Payments. Money serves as a standard of deferred payment when obligations to make future payments are expressed in terms of money. To an increasing extent, modern business involves written or implied contracts to deliver goods, including capital goods, and services in the future. These contracts may involve the leasing of land for ninety-nine years (as in the case of that on which Rockefeller Center in New York is build); the leasing of a railroad to complete a "line" between two metropolitan areas; the building of a dam or battleship that will take years to complete; the supplying of electricity or water for twenty or thirty years; or merely the purchasing of raw materials, finished goods, or labor that will be paid for within days or weeks, or, in some cases, even before delivery is made. In these transactions the recipients of the goods and services assume an obligation, and there must be some way to determine how the debt will be paid. While the contracts may take the form of repayment in kind (as between governments in the case of silver and other lend-lease goods during World War II), usually the creditor wants to receive payment in money or promises to pay money that can be used to buy things other than those sold. Thus, money facilitates business transactions by being the thing promised in payment; but whether this promise means little or much depends in part upon the future value of money, as well as upon the keeping of these promises to pay money.

The need for a stable standard is increased by the fact that so much of modern financial administration is linked to the past and projected into the future by the use of borrowed funds. The words "borrow" and "lend" suggest a transaction in which something is borrowed or lent on the condition that the same or its equivalent will be returned in the future. Instead of borrowing the things needed, governments, corporations, individuals, and others find it more convenient to borrow money with which to buy things. Thus, money is used as a loan medium, as well as the standard of deferred payment. Usually the lender contracts to receive a given sum of money in the future, and the debtor contracts to pay the same sum of money in the future (with or without interest).

Not all deferred payments involve lending of money. Many purchases are made on "time," and in these credit transactions payment for things is deferred. In order to facilitate planning, contracts for goods and services are projected into the future. Contracts made by management and labor union leaders, through collective-bargaining agreements, illustrate the use of money in a capacity which might be called a "standard of future payments."

In modern society, contracts to pay money resulting from delivery (or promises of delivery) of goods and services are of secondary importance compared to those in which money or bank credit is the "commodity" that first changes hands. In this case, money is at the same time the thing borrowed, the thing lent, and the thing in which the contract to pay in the future is drawn. The mere possession of money and bank credit would be meaningless if these could not be exchanged for goods and services. So, governments sell bonds, businessmen borrow from banks, and consumers borrow from personal finance companies to secure "cash" with which to purchase goods and services. Today, the gross public and private debt in the United States is more than $768 billion; and most of this debt resulted from the borrowing and lending of money.

The chief criticism of money as a standard of deferred payment is that its value does not remain stable. This dissatisfaction is illustrated by the fact that an increasing number of wage agreements include the principle that money wages must be linked to the cost-of-living index of prices (called the "escalator" clause). This means that when prices of things that labor must buy increase, the money wages of labor must be increased in order that labor's purchasing power will be maintained.[6] In addition, there are many long-term business contracts and leases that are adjusted automatically to compensate for changes in costs as measured by a wholesale commodity price index number.[7] Recently, considerable attention has been given to the merits and demerits of issuance of government bonds, the value of which would be guaranteed in terms of purchasing power.[8] There is considerable support for plans providing variable retirement annuities.

There is danger that the support of those groups which are protected by the "escalator" clause will be lost to the broader movement to obtain fairly stable prices. Technically, the "escalator" clause would reduce money income during falling prices. This means that such contracts would have disturbing effects during both rising and falling price periods—more spending during rising prices and less spending during falling prices. The ideal is to have money whose purchasing power is fairly stable.

THE ROLE OF BANKS

Banking is defined as the business of a bank or banker. Of the many services performed by a commercial bank, the one which

[6] For an illustration, see press descriptions of the May, 1948, wage agreements between General Motors Corporation and United Automobile Workers. Acceptance of the principle that wages should be tied to the cost-of-living index is not new, having been adopted by a number of cities and other local governments including St. Paul, Minnesota; Madison, Wisconsin; Portland, Oregon; and Duluth, Minnesota. Wide use of this principle in Sweden has given labor relations in that country a degree of stabilization not achieved in the United States. In France and Australia the basic wage is "anchored" to the cost-of-living index.

[7] Many types of contracts are tied to the wholesale commodity price index number of the U.S. Bureau of Labor Statistics. They include public-utility rates (Florida), cost of maintaining elevators in buildings, ship construction and other types of building contracts, long-term leases, and care of the insane (Alaska).

[8] Joint Committee on the Economic Report, *Monetary Policy and the Management of the Public Debt* (Washington, D.C.: U.S. Government Printing Office, 1952), Part 1, pp. 142–45 *passim*.

necessitates its being studied along with the subject of *money* is the use of checking accounts by the general public as a means of payment. To a bank, deposit accounts are promises to pay (debts); and, by their lending and investing operations (giving deposits for promissory notes or bonds), banks can "create" money. Conversely, they may "destroy" money in their everyday operations by reducing the volume of bank loans and investments. This ability of a single commercial bank to "create" or "destroy" money is small, but it is very large when all the 13,700 commercial banks as a group are considered (see also Chapter IV).

The ability of commercial banks to create and destroy money within certain limits is not a recent development. At one time, all commercial banks issued paper promises to pay in convenient denominations ($1, $5, $10, etc.) which circulated as money. Then borrowers from banks, in exchange for their promissory notes, received paper money which they, in turn, used to buy goods and services and to meet other business or personal obligations. Today, in the United States and most foreign countries, paper money is issued only by the central banks and/or national governments.

A central bank not only issues paper money but also acts as a bank for commercial banks and the national government. In the United States, the twelve Federal Reserve banks are the central banks which function as a team under the general supervision of, and regulations issued by, the Board of Governors of the Federal Reserve System in Washington, D.C. If one were to identify in a sentence the principal function of a central banking system it would be to see that the economy that it serves has the right amount of money at all times (a difficult task to which more attention is given in later chapters).

Commercial banks, in addition to handling the checking accounts of their customers, provide loanable funds, accept savings or time deposits, manage trust funds, and provide their communities with many other services. These activities are shared with other financial institutions and are discussed in separate chapters with titles such as savings institutions, trust banking, consumer financing institutions, and real estate lending.

The United States government has in many ways become closely connected with our monetary and credit system. It not only regulates practically all phases of the modern financial structure but also participates directly or indirectly in many of them either as an investor or as a lender. Governmental influence is exercised through (to name only the more important) the United States Treasury, the Federal

Reserve System, the Comptroller of the Currency, the Federal Deposit Insurance Corporation, the Farm Credit Administration, Housing and Home Finance Agency, Department of Agriculture, and the Securities and Exchange Commission. The role of each of these governmental agencies, or its subdivisions, is treated as part of the subject matter to which it is most appropriate.

SUMMARY

A modern economy is characterized by division of labor which necessitates the use of a medium of exchange and a standard of value called "money." Exchanges may and do take place without the use of money, but it is difficult to visualize how a free economy could function without the use of money. Money is used more frequently as a measure of value than as a medium of exchange. As a standard of value, money is a common denominator for expressing exchange ratios as prices, and it furnishes businessmen and others with a standard or unit of account which is indispensable in budgeting, cost accounting, financial accounting, and all phases of financial planning.

During earlier stages of economic development things used as money commonly had value in use as well as in exchange. Articles used as money have included those used for ornament and display, consumable necessities, capital goods, and tokens. The use of tokens suggests the possibility of having a commodity as the standard that does not circulate as money. Modern money includes coins, paper money, and bank checks; and the relative importance of bank checks in the United States is shown by the fact that about 90 per cent of each day's business transactions are consummated with the use of checks.

Money serves as a store of value representing purchasing power. Under normal circumstances, the modern saver keeps his store of value in the form of money only large enough to care for his need for ready purchasing power because idle cash balances represent loss of interest. On the other hand, those who hold idle cash balances have the right to expect that the purchasing power of the money held as a store of value will not decline during the interim between receipt and spending for goods, services, or securities. This means that, in order to serve satisfactorily as a store of value, money must be stable in value.

The need for a stable standard is increased by the fact that so much of modern financial administration is linked to the past and projected into the future by the use of borrowed funds. Money

QUALITIES OF MONEY

CHAPTER I dealt with the nature and functions of money; that is, what money is and what we expect it to do. Logically, two questions follow: (1) What qualities must money and the monetary system possess in order to perform these functions properly? and (2) How well does money perform its functions? To describe the functions of money is to suggest, at the same time, the qualities that money must have in order to perform these functions. To serve as a medium of exchange, money must be generally acceptable; and to serve as a store of value, as a standard of value, and as a standard of deferred payments, money should be stable in value.

ACCEPTABILITY OF MONEY

The use of anything as a medium of exchange depends upon the willingness of people to accept it as payment for goods, services, and other things which they have for sale. This willingness to accept something in payment depends upon the confidence that sellers have that others will accept it when they wish to purchase goods, services, and other things. While almost anything which is generally acceptable may be used as money, it has been found that the functions of money are best performed when money units appear in different denominations (1 cent, 5 cents, 10 cents, etc.) with identical units within each denomination.

Suitable Denominations. In any modern economy, there are varying types of transactions wherein a particular unit of money may be acceptable on one occasion and not on a second. For illustration, 1-cent coins may be acceptable in buying a postage stamp but may not be acceptable in payment of fees or tuition or for an automobile. Since things bought and sold in the market have various values, the monetary system must include a series of related units or values, that is, a denomination system.

In the United States the basic or primary unit is the dollar. At the present time the dollar is defined as $15\frac{5}{21}$ grains of gold $\frac{9}{10}$ fine

17

(or 13.71 grains of pure gold). The gold dollar is not coined, and the unit exists only in bullion or bar form. However, it has many substitutes in the form of paper money, coins, and credit instruments.

The United States is fortunate in having a decimal system wherein the secondary denominations are multiples or fractional parts of the dollar, varying from 1 cent to $10,000. The banking system makes possible much larger units, for checks of millions of dollars may be written.

Money-of-Account System. The varying values of things bought and sold in a modern economy necessitates different units in which to express prices and to keep accounts. In the United States, the standard unit in which records are kept is the dollar but there are also smaller units—the cent and the mill (one tenth of a cent). Although the mill is not coined, it is the unit in which many state and local governments express the tax rate on personal and/or real property. To this extent, the United States money-of-account system (units used to express or compute financial or monetary transactions) is more inclusive than the currency system with its emphasis on dollar and cent units.

Physical Convenience. Because money is being moved continually from place to place in making sales and purchases, convenience with reference to the physical shape and size of the various units is necessary. Although one may think that the physical forms of checks, paper money, and coins is unimportant, the government, central banks, and commercial banks are giving a great deal of consideration to this problem. By way of illustration, major attention is being given currently to the development of checks that may be handled by machines (for example, the Electronic Recording Machine Accounting, "Erma," developed by the Bank of America National Trust and Savings Association).

Currency is kept on hand as a store of ready purchasing power and is held by banks and business firms as "till" money and for reserve purposes. Therefore, it must have considerable value in small bulk in order to reduce the burden of transporting and the space necessary for storing. Most modern coins are circular disks of uniform size for each denomination. They are easy to handle, stack, and store. The silver dollar, sometimes called a "cartwheel," is so large that many people refuse to accept it; and when the gold dollar and the $2.50 gold coins were in circulation, even the latter proved too small for convenient handling. (Both are valuable collectors' items.) The need for convenience in size is recognized for paper money as well as for coins. The paper currency issued since 1929 measures $6\frac{5}{16}$ by $2\frac{11}{16}$ inches, which is the same size as the standard bank check. It fits into a business envelope without folding and is easy to handle in packages.

Durability. Money should possess the quality of indestructibility in order to serve as a medium of exchange and a store of value. In the tropics, where paper money tends to deteriorate because of climatic conditions, coins are preferred. Originally, coins were made of pure metals; but, because gold and silver are soft, coins made therefrom were subject to a large amount of abrasion. This problem was solved by adding an alloy to give the coin hardness. The early coins bore a design on only one side, which made it possible to clip or file off a part of the metal. This weakness was corrected by stamping a design on both sides. To prevent clipping (cutting the edges), coins were milled, that is, the edges were furrowed. All United States coins except the 1-cent and 5-cent pieces have these edges. A slight rim raised around the edge of all coins facilitates stacking and prevents the weight from resting on the whole surface of the coin. This rim reduces abrasion and protects the design, thereby adding not only to the life of the coin but also to its cognoscibility.

The government's main problem is that of making durable paper money. On the average, all paper currency in circulation must be replaced once every year, and $1.00 bills must be replaced every six months. The paper used for checks need not be of the same high quality as that used for paper currency because checks are not expected to remain in circulation. When a merchant accepts a check in payment or cashes one for a customer, he usually deposits it in his bank promptly; then the check is sent to the bank on which it is drawn where the drawer's account is debited for the amount and the check is cancelled. (See also Chapter V.)

Ease of Recognition. Money will be more acceptable, and therefore a better medium of exchange, if it is easily recognized. A great deal of thought has been given to designing coins that will be difficult to imitate but easy to recognize. The technique in the manufacture of coins now has reached such a high standard that the problem of cognoscibility largely has been replaced by that of making paper money which cannot be imitated by counterfeiters. Fraudulent currency must be kept at a minimum in order to prevent loss to the public. The existence of even a small percentage of counterfeit bills may lead to a decrease in confidence in all paper money and a loss in its acceptability.

Protection of Money and Government Obligations. In the United States money is protected by laws covering the conditions under which coins, paper currency, government checks and other obligations may be reproduced (Section 474 of Title 18 of the United States Code). Advertisers recognize the fact that pictures of money are sure to attract the attention of the public—everyone seems to be interested in money. In 1951 the law covering the reproduction of currency was changed to permit photographing and printing pictures of coins (Public Law 79, Eighty-second Congress, approved July 16, 1951). By special regulation, the Secretary of the Treasury sometimes allows pictures of savings bonds and stamps to be used to increase their sales; but such pictures are required to be off-size. Although it is permissible to photograph paper money so that it will not be "in the likeness" of genuine money, it is safer to refrain from photographing paper money, checks, or governmental obligations (violaters may be subject to a maximum penalty of fifteen years in prison and/or a fine of $5,000).

Paper currency is protected from counterfeiting by secret processes in the manufacture of the paper, secret designs, and special texture of paper. In spite of these safeguards, imitations of the official currency appear frequently. As a result, secret-service men are kept busy running down counterfeiters, and bank clerks constantly are on the alert for the appearance of the counterfeit bills. In order to obtain greater uniformity and thereby minimize counterfeiting, the Treasury Department placed new designs on all United States paper currency on July 10, 1929. The portraits assigned to different denominations and other ways of identification are shown in Table 2.

TABLE 2

PAPER CURRENCY: DENOMINATIONS AND IDENTIFICATION

PORTRAIT

$ 1	Washington	$ 100	Franklin
2	Jefferson	500	McKinley
5	Lincoln	1,000	Cleveland
10	Hamilton	5,000	Madison
20	Jackson	10,000	Chase
50	Grant		

SEALS AND BACKS

The backs of the new currency are printed uniformly in green; the faces in black; and the Treasury seals and the serial numbers in the following colors:

United States notes	Red
Silver certificates	Blue
Federal Reserve notes	Green

Even greater cognoscibility would be achieved if paper money varied in size with the size of the denomination (as is true of English and French currency) and if the denominations varied in color, as has been proposed by two Treasurers of the United States (both women). Although it is a good idea, it has not been adopted by the government at this writing.

In 1871, George La Monte invented a "national safety paper" to help prevent widespread check raising and forgeries which made businessmen and others wary of accepting checks. During subsequent years improvements have been made;[1] and now, national safety paper is in demand not only for checks and drafts but also for railroad, bus, and airplane tickets, gift certificates, cash slips, notes, and other special documents. It has been suggested that La Monte's invention of national safety paper should rank with developments such as the telephone and telegraph; without it, the current extensive use of check currency, as noted in Chapter I, would not exist.

Uniformity in Value. The need for different denominations and different kinds of money will be met only by a monetary system in which all forms of money have relatively equivalent value. One hundred pennies, ten dimes, one paper dollar, and one gold dollar all must have the same purchasing power. If two kinds of money have equal nominal value but unequal value in terms of demand, the inferior type tends to drive the preferred type out of circulation. When money has uses that are more attractive than that as a domestic medium of exchange (including uses in foreign exchange, hoarding, or as a commodity), it will tend to be used where its value is greatest. The generalization explaining the tendency for the less valuable money to drive the more valuable out of circulation is called "Gresham's law," so named for Sir Thomas Gresham, who explained this monetary principle to Queen Elizabeth in 1558.[2] It seems a strange contradiction that the best articles capture the market in most lines, whereas in the case of money alone the poor is used more than the good as a medium of exchange. The reasons for this situation are obvious after one reviews his own experience and considers what is meant by the demand for money. Assume that a person has a new one-dollar bill and an old one. Most people will spend the old

[1] The paper currently used has dyes that are applied with a protective coating and in designs, both on the front and back of the check, which makes it impossible to alter checks either by mechanical or chemical means without leaving a white spot.

[2] H. D. Macleod first named this principle "Gresham's law" (*The Elements of Economics* [New York: D. Appleton & Co., 1881], Vol. I, pp. 270–72).

one and keep the new one. The same tendency is noticed in spending coins; the worn ones are spent first, and the new ones are held back from active circulation. If this situation exists when there is no difference in value, it is evident that it would be far more pronounced when two moneys differ in value.

As noted above, money is used not only as a medium of exchange but also as a store of value. At any particular time, most of the money outside of the issuing agencies, "in circulation," will be held as cash balances. It is this store-of-value or "cash-balance" market which is captured by the more valuable of two kinds of money. In domestic trade the buyer usually decides which form of legal-tender money he will use, and self-interest results in the use of the cheaper form; but in international trade, not covered by the domestic legal-tender law, a buyer may find it advantageous to use the dearer kind of money (in fact, he may have no option because sellers naturally prefer the more valuable type of money). If the cheaper money exists in sufficient quantity, it will replace the more valuable money in domestic trade; and the more valuable money will be exported or hoarded.

LEGAL QUALITIES OF MONEY

The history of monetary legislation in the United States indicates that money may be made (1) legal tender, (2) lawful money, and/or (3) receivable for specified purposes.[3] While Congress alone may specify the kinds of money that have the legal-tender quality, a state may legislate on what kinds of money are to be lawful for legal reserves of state nonmember banks and/or acceptable in payment of state taxes, debts, and other obligations due it.

Legal Tender. "Legal-tender" money is that money which the law requires debtors to offer and creditors to accept when tendered in payment of money obligations. In disputed cases over money values, some method must be provided to fix conclusively when a debt is paid. The mere offering of legal-tender money, without acceptance by the creditor, does not discharge the debtor's obligation. If the court decides that the amount offered was the proper sum and that it was legal tender, the amount must be paid but no interest may be charged from the time the tender was first made.

Before 1933, currency in the United States was classified as full legal tender, limited legal tender, and "optional" money. Gold, gold

[3] See also Arthur Kemp, *The Legal Qualities of Money* (New York: Pageant Press, Inc., 1956).

certificates, and silver dollars were full legal tender. United States notes were legal tender for everything except import duties and interest on the public debt. Small silver coins were legal tender for amounts not exceeding ten dollars in one payment, and nickels and pennies were legal tender for amounts not exceeding twenty-five cents in one payment. Federal Reserve notes, Federal Reserve bank notes, national bank notes, silver certificates, and "deposit currency" were optional money (without legal-tender qualities). In 1933, Congress made all types of United States currency (all legal coins and paper money) legal tender; but checks and drafts are "optional" money.

Lawful Money. The term "lawful money" is used here in the technical sense to mean those types of money that may be used by banks to meet their legal-reserve requirements; it is not used, as in the popular sense, to mean money which has been issued lawfully. For illustration, gold certificates and gold credits are the only types of money that may be used by the Federal Reserve banks for legal-reserve purposes. Banks that are members of the Federal Reserve System are required to keep their legal reserves as credit balances (deposits) with their Federal Reserve banks. Although all kinds of circulating money have the legal-tender quality, they may not be counted in meeting the legal-reserve requirements of Federal Reserve banks and member banks. Furthermore, under current laws, gold certificates may not be lawfully held by individuals, firms, or corporations other than the Federal Reserve banks. It is not surprising that there is confusion in regard to the rights of individuals and the obligations of the monetary authorities when reserves must be kept in a specified form that cannot be used for the purposes for which the reserves are kept. Later more attention will be given to this and other inconsistencies in our current laws. (See also Chapter VI.)

Receivable for Specified Purposes. Governments may specify the kinds of money that may be used for special purposes. Most commonly, such legislation has specified the kind of money acceptable in payment of obligations due the government. The legal quality thereby given this type of money is called government tender. On the other hand, the legal provision may specify the kind of money that the government may use to meet its obligations to individuals and others. For illustration, Section 23 of the National Bank Act of 1863 as amended in 1864 permitted the United States government to use national bank notes to pay salaries of its employees and to pay other obligations. Finally, governments may designate the kinds of money that is to be receivable when payments are to be made between persons and banks or other corporations. For illustration, the right of "offset" or "set-off" allows one who is both a debtor and creditor of another person to use the credit due him to cancel an equal amount of the indebtedness held against him.

VALUE OF MONEY

Because money is used to buy things, its value is commonly referred to as its purchasing power; that is, the amount of things that each monetary unit (dollar in the United States) will buy. If money were used to buy but one thing (gold for illustration), its value would be determined by the value of this one commodity. The fact that money is used as a medium of exchange means that its value must be considered in terms of things for which it is commonly exchanged, and they number in the thousands or millions. Thus, the value of money is its purchasing power over goods and services in general, and not over any particular good.

Interest Rate. Sometimes the value of money is confused with the price paid for the use of funds—the interest rate. In its broadest sense, interest is money paid for the use of loan funds spent for capital equipment, land, consumption goods, and even to acquire cash balances. There are several theories of why interest may and must be paid which are considered in later chapters.

Stability in Value. The value of money is stable when its purchasing power (the amount of things a monetary unit such as the dollar will buy) is fairly constant over a period of time. When prices in general are increasing, the value of money is decreasing; and, when prices in general are decreasing, the value of money is increasing. Therefore, stability in the value of money is synonymous with stability in the general price level.

The major criticism of modern money is that it lacks stability in value. Although the record of the United States dollar has been better than that of most foreign monetary units, it has had this same fault as indicated by Chart 1 which shows that there has been a sharp increase in prices during war periods. Such upward movements in general prices are commonly referred to as "inflation" (meaning that general prices are inflated). The opposite movement is illustrated by the period from 1920 to 1933. Such downward movements in prices are commonly referred to as "deflation" (meaning that general prices are deflated).

In recent years, primary attention has been given to the effects

CHART 1

WHOLESALE PRICES

Bureau of Labor Statistics Index, 1947–49 = 100

Annual Averages

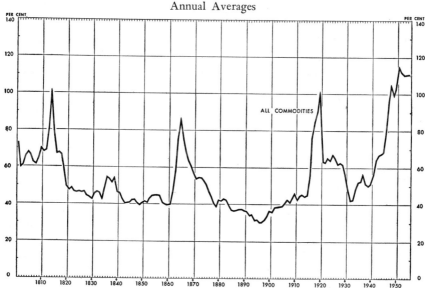

Source: Board of Governors of the Federal Reserve System, *Federal Reserve Charts on Bank Credit, Money Rates, and Business, Historical Supplement*, September, 1956, p. 105.

of inflation on our economy. Experience shows that inflation may be remedied by decreasing spending and/or increasing production. The problem is one of keeping in balance two continuing flows through our economy in opposite directions—the stream of money payments to the market place to match the stream of goods and services resulting from current production and other transactions. There is a financial demand for money that results from the purchase and sale of land, outstanding securities, old buildings, and other things not currently produced. As a result, the Federal Reserve System has developed the flow-of-funds system of national accounting to picture more vividly the strategic role played by monetary and credit developments (see Chapter III).

The monetary approach to the problem of preventing inflation is not only to increase the cost and reduce the availability of credit but also (most important) to prevent further increases in the money supply and if necessary to bring about a decline. The fiscal approach to the problem of preventing inflation is for governments to reduce their spending and/or to plan their financing so as to cause a reduction in private spending. Under different circumstances, the flow of money payments may be such that there will be a decline in prices, in employment, and in national income. These and other associated problems will be considered in later chapters.

Measurement of the Value of Money. In a modern economy the exchange value of things is expressed in terms of money (as prices), but to say that a "dollar is worth a dollar" is meaningless. As every housewife knows, the volume of things that a dollar will buy has declined during the last ten years, and those with the longest memories may say that the current dollar will buy no more than twenty-five cents did in 1900. It is apparent to all that, when prices in general are increasing, the value of money is decreasing; and when prices in general are decreasing, the value of money is increasing. But, at any one time, some prices may be increasing, others may be decreasing, and others may be unchanged. In order to take the guesswork out of whether the value of money is increasing or decreasing, price index numbers are constructed.

Price Index Numbers. Price index numbers are statistical devices for comparing groups of prices and for measuring their changes. In the United States the two most widely used price index numbers ("Consumers' Price Index for Moderate Income Families in Large Cities" and "Wholesale Prices, by Groups of Commodities") are constructed and published by the United States Bureau of Labor Statistics. Although more specialized index numbers are available, either of the above is satisfactory for measuring changes in the value of money. The one used depends on the special problem involved. For illustration, the consumers' price index number (popularly known as the "cost-of-living" index) is widely used as a basis for adjusting money wages; and the wholesale commodity price index number is used as a basis for adjusting rents and other non-wage money contracts.[4]

Measurement of Changes in the Value of Money. At any particular time a dollar is worth a dollar. Statements to the contrary have no meaning unless reference is made to some preceding period when the purchasing power of the dollar was more or less in terms of things in general (or in terms of gold). The importance of the value of money at any particular time is minor compared to the significance of changes in the value of money over a period of time. Therefore, measuring changes in the value of money is a major problem.

[4] Since methods used in constructing index numbers are covered in textbooks on statistics, they are omitted here.

Since index numbers are used for comparative purposes, they usually have a base year (or base period) to which a figure of 1.00 or 100 is assigned. Since the current situation is emphasized, an index number with a fairly recent base is not only desirable but usually more accurate. In addition, with the change in the base period, there are changes in the specific commodities included and weights assigned to individual commodities so as to make the current index number representative of the current price structure as a whole.

Use of Index Numbers. To compute changes in the value of money over a period of time, one simply takes the price index

CHART 2

CONSUMER PRICES

INDEX, 1947-49 = 100

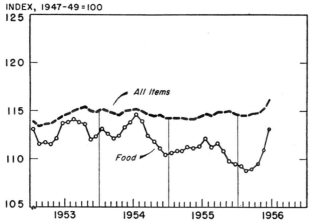

Source: U.S. Department of Commerce, Office of Business Economics, *Business Statistics, A Weekly Supplement to the Survey of Current Business* (July 27, 1956), p. 1.

numbers of the two periods being compared and divides the one for the earlier date by the one for the more recent date. For illustration, the consumer price index for 1933 was 92.4 and that for 1951 was 185.6, and so the value of the dollar in 1951 in terms of 1933 dollars was 92.4 divided by 185.6, or 49.8. This means that the 1951 dollar would buy, in terms of the 1933 dollar, about 50 cents' worth of goods and services as measured by the consumers' price index number. In June 1956, the consumers' price index of all items was 116.2 in terms of 1947–49 dollars (1947–49 = 100). (See Chart 2.)

The value of one's salary may be compared over a period of time simply by dividing the year's current income by the current price index number which would give one the current value in terms of the base period. Similar computations may be made for other dollar figures, including those for rent, interest, total national income, the gross national output, and wealth.

The experiences of the present generation have been primarily with rising prices; but the experts have projected price index numbers back over a hundred and fifty years. Although the scarcity of price data for these earlier years may lead one to question the accuracy of the index numbers, they do indicate that general prices decrease as well as increase and that the twin evils—war and inflation—go together (see Chart 1).

Inflation and Deflation. Sometimes inflation is defined as "a disproportionate and relatively sharp and sudden increase in the quantity of money and credit relative to the amount of exchange. Inflation produces a rise in the price level." According to this definition, the excessive increase in the quantity of money is the disease, and the increase in the level of prices is the symptom. But, inflation is more commonly defined as "a rise in the general price level." While a sharp increase in the quantity of money is recognized as being inflationary, a rise in prices may not follow if the money is not spent. So, if the increase in the price level is "inflation," a fall in the general price level is "deflation." A "disproportionate and relatively sharp decrease in the quantity of money" would be deflationary.

EFFECTS OF CHANGES IN THE VALUE OF MONEY

If mystic rays were to shrink the length of our yardstick and everything else by 50 per cent, no one would be the wiser. But if some plants, animals, geographic formations, and human beings were reduced 5 per cent, others 25 per cent, and others 80 per cent, making the average 50 per cent, the results would be tragic. So it is with changes in the value of money. If all prices and money contracts changed equally, a change of 50 per cent in their value would not be significant. It is because prices and money contracts do not change equally that changes in the general price level are so disturbing and of such wide importance.

Problems created by changes in the value of money involve: (1) redistribution of wealth among creditors and debtors; (2) reallocation of real income among fixed-income receivers and fluctuating-income receivers; (3) production of goods and services; and (4) decline in social morality, cultural development, and respect for law and order.

Redistribution of Wealth. In order to illustrate how inflation redistributes wealth, it is assumed that (1) long-term promises to pay were equal to one half of the wealth (all material and transferable economic goods) in the United States in 1940; (2) although production increased from 1940 to 1950, all of the increase was used for war purposes and therefore the total amount of wealth remained about the same; and (3) wholesale commodity prices increased 100 per cent during this period. In 1950 the value of claims of creditors would be the same in dollars but would be equal to one fourth the wealth of the United States, as compared to one half in 1940. Although these assumptions are not accurate, they illustrate what took place during the postwar inflation.

Throughout much of the history of the United States, when creditors were few and debtors were many, exploitation of creditors by price inflation had popular support. In addition, Biblical teachings—that lending should be regarded as a form of charity, that mercy must be shown in the case of loans to the poor, and that debts should be forgiven every seven years—have influenced the attitude toward debts. With the increase in ownership of savings accounts and bonds by the masses, the development of social security, the creation of private and public old-age retirement plans, and the widespread purchase of life insurance and annuities, the problem of maintaining the future value of money contracts, in terms of purchasing power, has become one which involves practically every family in the United States.

Advances in medical science have added years to the life expectancy of the average American. To have ten years added to one's life, on one hand, and to be faced with compulsory retirement at the age of sixty-five, on the other, makes the problem of maintaining the value of future money-income contracts something more than a theoretical one to an increasing number of people. From the viewpoint of the beneficiary, the ideal credit instrument or future income contract would be one which provides for an income adjusted to changes in the cost of living.

While an increase in the general price level reduces the purchasing power of money represented by fixed income obligations, a decrease in the general price level has the opposite effect. However, this "gain" is not assured because defaults on obligations are common during these periods. In a credit (debt) economy operating on a fluctuating monetary unit, "the cards seem to be stacked" against the creditor. In fairness to both creditors and debtors, neither an increase nor a decrease in general prices is desirable.

Income and Price Changes. Of the current national income, more than two thirds is accounted for as compensation of employees; one eighth as income of proprietors of farms, proprietors of nonfarm businesses, and those in the professional services; about one eighth went to corporations; and the remainder was accounted for as rental income to persons and net interest. (The aggregate earnings of labor and property are different from the gross national product "in that it is computed after deduction of indirect business taxes and of depreciation charges and other allowances for business consumption of durable capital goods.") During inflation the problem is to keep one's money-income rising, after payment of taxes, so as to meet the higher cost of living; during deflation, the problem is one of having sufficient money income to spend (due to unemployment, etc.).

During an inflationary period the loss of purchasing power of the dollar falls heaviest on those whose incomes are most stable in terms of the number of dollars received. These include pensioners and those dependent on income from bonds and other fixed-income contracts (hospitals, private colleges, and other endowed institutions). In addition, this category includes those who work for salaries that are adjusted infrequently or not at all (teachers, public employees, and other white-collar workers). Most labor groups tend to gain from rising prices until full employment is achieved because of steadier employment (after allowance for loss of work due to strikes), overtime pay, and supplements to wages and salaries including bonuses, payments in kind, commissions, holidays with pay, and social security benefits.

Although the wage-rate changes tend to lag behind price changes, labor contracts are frequently revised, and many contain "escalator" clauses. Organized labor is seemingly in a position to keep its standard of living from deteriorating during inflation. About one third of all wage and salary earners are members of labor unions. Others are in, or closely related to, occupations where unions are strong, and it may be that over one half of wage earners are in a position to obtain wage adjustments to keep pace with the rising cost of living.

Although earnings differ widely among industries and among different corporations within the same industry, stockholders' incomes tend to rise as fast or faster than the rise in cost of living during inflationary periods. Farmers, small business firms, doctors, and those in other professional groups tend to have the same experience as stockholders because their gross receipts tend to increase faster than their expenses. Where there is no rent control, landlords tend to belong to this group.

During deflationary periods the unemployed suffer the greatest loss in purchasing power (offset only in part by payments of unemployment benefits), and others may be placed on a part-time work basis. The wage rate tends to be cut and overtime pay to disappear. Teachers, public servants, and other white-collar workers also face unemployment and wage cuts.

During periods of falling prices, dividends on stocks are usually reduced and sometimes omitted. Businessmen sustain losses because of a decline in the value of inventories, a decline in the volume of business, and a tendency for gross receipts to decline more rapidly than expenses. Professional men are in the same position as proprietors of small businesses and farmers. While many farmers are protected from price declines by the government's price support program, they tend to find it more difficult to meet payments for interest, principal, taxes, and other fixed charges. Those who are in a position to collect fixed incomes are the chief beneficiaries during periods of falling prices. While most individuals belong primarily to one group or another, some individuals belong to two or more classes mentioned above (for illustration, both bondholders and stockholders), and their gains and losses tend to offset each other. However, it should not be forgotten that over two thirds of the national income is accounted for as compensation to employees.

Production and Price Changes. Monetary instability is of grave social and economic concern not only because of its effects on the real income of debtors, creditors, and fixed-income groups but also because of its effects on production. Production for markets is speculative enough; but when fluctuations in general prices are added to the other hazards, business ventures become doubly speculative in nature.

To reach decisions, businessmen need to make dependable estimates of expected costs and expected receipts. During deflationary periods, standard accounting practices tend to overstate costs and understate profits; during inflationary periods, the opposite tends to be true. During 1946–48 this tendency to overstate profits placed corporations in an unfavorable position with reference to stockholders (who wanted more dividends), the government (which wanted more taxes), and organized labor (which wanted more wages, based on the principle of ability to pay). Actually, many corporations may have been using their capital when paying taxes, higher wages, and dividends.

Although the injustices resulting from inflation are widely recognized, rising prices are popular because they are usually associated with prosperity (rising money wages for workers, rising money profits for the businessman, and rising money income for the farmer and professional man). During rising-price periods, production is increased because management (1) is able to make a profit on selling goods produced during the previous lower-cost period and (2) expects to sell current output at still higher prices. In order to increase production, employment is increased. As the money income of labor increases, the demand for things increases. This new demand further stimulates production. Thus, rising prices are closely associated with increasing employment and rising incomes for the masses.

Capacity operation of plants permits spreading of overhead costs and lowering of per unit costs of goods. During World War II the use of plants and machinery "around the clock," seven days per week, was an important factor in the so-called "miracle of production." In retailing and in the service industries, as well as in manufacturing, the spread of overhead costs contributes to the increase in output per worker. These factors explain in part why profits and wage increases run ahead of price increases.

Based upon the above analysis, it might be assumed that production may be expanded to ever-higher levels by continuously inflating prices. If this followed, China, Greece, Hungary, and other countries that have recently experienced hyperinflation would be enjoying the greatest increase in production. However, the limits to production are not determined by prices but by the volume of productive resources—labor, capital, and land. Once these resources are fully utilized, further increases in general prices can have no further stimulating effects on production.

In practice, because of the development of bottlenecks in key industries, the ill effects of higher prices become evident even before full employment is reached. Rising prices discourage saving and increase the demand for consumer goods. This diversion of productive resources, from creation of producer goods to creation of consumer goods, causes curtailment in future production. Rising prices also encourage strikes and the withholding of goods from the market. In extreme cases, merchants might prefer to close their stores rather than to sell inventories that can only be replaced at higher prices or with fewer goods. The loss in value of the monetary unit reduces the incentive to hold money as a store of value and leads to more rapid spending, which causes more inflation. All these factors reduce the incentive to produce and to sell for money; this strikes at the heart of the modern economic system based on private initiative. During the early and middle stages of an inflationary period, the good effects of rising prices seem to outweigh the ill effects; but during the later stages, the opposite is true.

Social Effects of Price Changes.   During inflationary periods there is a transfer of wealth and income among individuals and groups that adversely affects the political, the social, and the cultural development of a nation. The stability of a government may be undermined by penalizing those who save and invest directly or indirectly in governmental obligations (Series E and similar bonds). Price control may be introduced which encourages the development of black markets and disrespect for law. The "fixer," the "expeditor," and the seller of political influence appear. To some, speculation (the holding of things for capital gain) seems more attractive than working for a living. The legislator is reluctant to vote more taxes, and the construction of schools is delayed. Private schools, hospitals, and other institutions have difficulty in meeting their needs for funds.

The hardships associated with rising prices seem minor compared to those associated with sharply falling prices. A sharp decline in prices brings with it a decline in production, in employment, and in the volume of things to consume. It means more bankruptcies, longer bread lines, makeshift work projects, and other types of social relief. No party in power can survive such catastrophes.

SUMMARY

In a modern economy, money is expected to serve as a medium of exchange, a store of value, a standard of value, and a standard of deferred payments. In order to perform its function as a medium of exchange, money should be generally acceptable, exist in suitable denominations, have suitable physical characteristics, and be uniform in value. The legal-tender quality adds to its acceptability during times of financial uncertainty.

Governments make provisions for the creation of money and decide which types must be accepted by creditors at face value in payment of debts (legal tender) and specify which types may be used for special purposes (lawful money). When monetary demands fall upon one commodity, it is imperative that this commodity shall have the quality of divisibility in order to permit both division into small pieces and reunification without loss in value. This quality is possessed by all metals and explains, in part, why metals have been used for money. The use of paper money and checks has lessened the importance of this physical quality because paper money may be printed in any denomination and checks may be written for any amount.

In addition to making provisions for a denomination system, governments have provided for currency which has the physical characteristics of convenience, durability, and cognoscibility. At the same time, steps have been taken to keep the value of all kinds of money relatively equivalent in order to prevent the operation of Gresham's law from driving one or more kinds out of circulation.

While the legal status given to money by governments has increased its use, no government guarantees the purchasing power of any type of money. Therein lies the chief weakness of all modern monetary systems.

Changes in the value of money affect the current and future well-being of those dependent on fixed money income—those participating in private and/or public retirement or pension plans and holders of fixed-income securities or obligations such as savings accounts, savings bonds (and other types of government securities), life insurance policies, and other investments that have their greatest appeal to the conservative savers. In somewhat the same category are the injustices suffered by debtors or creditors, depending on whether prices are decreasing or increasing.

Perhaps the most serious effects of changes in the value of money are those that are reflected in production and the free competitive economy. To an increasing extent, it is being recognized that money which is stable in value promotes the economic, political, and other goals of society by increasing the incentives to save, lend, invest, and produce. The concept of stabilized general prices assumes flexibility within the general price structure due to changes in supply and demand. Instead of encompassing the concept of monopoly prices, the advocates of monetary stability stress the fact that a generally stable price structure will discourage the creation of monopolies. They call attention to the fact that restrictions on output are most common during periods of depression; and after recovery, many of the monopolies of products and of labor are permitted to remain. They also note that governmental restrictions and/or aids to businessmen, laborers, and others are encouraged by price and income instability; and that once a group has acquired a vested interest in governmental aid, it is difficult for a democratic government to disengage itself.

QUESTIONS AND PROBLEMS

1. Identify: (*a*) primary monetary unit, (*b*) denomination system, (*c*) mill, and (*d*) "cartwheel."
2. How does the existence of a denomination system affect the acceptability of money?
3. What physical qualities should hand-to-hand money have to enhance its acceptability?
4. Is Gresham's Law in operation at all times or only during periods of financial disturbances? Why?
5. Explain what is meant by (*a*) legal tender money, (*b*) optional money, and (*c*) lawful money.
6. What is meant by the "value of money"? How are changes in the value of money measured? If prices increase 100 per cent, how much does the value of money decrease? Is there an inflationary bias in price index numbers?
7. What justification is there for the world-wide tendency to tie money wages to cost-of-living index numbers? What would constitute a better solution for this problem? Why?
8. How does inflation cause a redistribution of wealth? Income?
9. Since the purchasing power of a dollar increases during falling prices, why do not laborers tend to gain? Explain.
10. Explain the effect of price changes on (*a*) income, (*b*) production, and (*c*) competition.
11. Analyze: "Reports of new price boosts have figured prominently in the business news for some time now. Puzzling to many, in the face of this, is the continued stability of the major price indexes. The consumer index—the most comprehensive indicator of price activity at the retail level—has shown no perceptible response." (Federal Reserve Bank of Chicago, *Business Conditions*, January, 1956, p. 8.)
12. "Full employment, rising incomes, and a stable dollar have been cherished goals of our society. The practical attainment of these ideals during 1955 was the year's great economic achievement." (From letter of transmittal of the President to Congress accompanying the *Economic Report to Congress*, January 24, 1956.) Do you agree? Why?

13. "Some people feel that chronic mild inflation is the way to perpetual prosperity as it is to easing debt burdens. The truth is that inflation is a tax on the savings of the poor, an impediment to orderly forward planning, and the harbinger of crisis and depression." (First National City Bank of New York, *Monthly Letter, Business and Economic Conditions*, January, 1956, pp. 6–7.) Do you agree? Why?

Chapter III

INTRODUCTION TO THE THEORY OF THE VALUE OF MONEY

MONEY has properties which render it useful and desirable; therefore, it has value. The most important of these properties is purchasing power, the utility which enables it to satisfy human wants. Obviously, there are many reasons why money is desirable and why it is in demand. For anything to have value, it must be limited in supply—otherwise it would be a "free good"; but, in the case of money, the need for having the supply limited is not always obvious to individuals.

Monetary theory that explains the value of money is but a statement of tendencies. An individual's desire for an unlimited amount of things—usually associated with general purchasing power (money), on one hand, and the ease with which modern banks and governments create or destroy money, on the other hand—makes it important for all citizens to understand the theory of the value of money.

In this chapter the immediate causes of changes in the value of money are emphasized. These include the elementary principles that have guided monetary authorities in handling monetary problems. By following these principles, one may better understand the arguments for and against such controversial subjects as limiting the supply of money by making it exchangeable for a fixed quantity of gold, increasing the control of the Board of Governors of the Federal Reserve System over commercial banks' lending and investing policies, and co-ordinating monetary policy and government fiscal policies (taxation, debt, and spending policies).

SUPPLY OF MONEY AND THE QUANTITY THEORY

As pointed out in the preceding chapter, there are two continuing flows of things in opposite directions in our economy: (1) the flow of goods and services, and (2) the flow of money payments for these goods and services. The size of the money stream depends upon the number of dollars and the number of times each

37

dollar is spent over a period of days, weeks, months, or years. In explaining the value of money, attention is given first to how changes in the supply (quantity) of money tend to influence its value (the simplest approach to the study of any problem of value determination).

The value of money, like that of any commodity, is influenced by its supply. The supply of money affecting the price level is properly thought of as hand-to-hand money and deposit currency used by the general public for spending. An increase in the money supply would encourage spending; and increased spending would tend to increase general prices or to decrease the value of each monetary unit (each unit would buy less). Obviously a decrease in the money supply would discourage spending; and decreased spending would tend to decrease general prices or to increase the value of each monetary unit (each unit would buy more).

Although the amount of emphasis varies among monetary economists, all recognize the supply of money as a factor in determining the general price level. John Stuart Mill wrote emphatically: "That an increase in the quantity of money raises prices, and a diminution lowers them, is the most elementary proposition in the theory of currency. . . ."[1] As stated by the late Dr. E. W. Kemmerer, "The difference between the supporters of the quantity theory and its opponents" amounts to "differences in the relative importance attributed to certain factors entering into the determination of the general price level."[2]

While the mere existence of money may have certain psychological effects, in order to be effective money must be spent. Since modern money has little or no intrinsic value, it is logical to assume that most of it will be spent some day. However, if the money supply is increased, the amount by which it is increased may be held temporarily as idle cash balances; or it may be matched by an increase in the supply of things. Thus an increase in the supply will not necessarily cause an increase in general prices. The least that may be claimed for the relationship between changes in the quantity of money and changes in the general price level is that the former is a factor which conditions spending and therefore the general price level. The quantity theory is merely a principle

---

[1] J. S. Mill, *Principles of Political Economy* (5th ed.; New York: D. Appleton & Co., 1895), Vol. II, p. 33.

[2] E. W. Kemmerer, *Money and Credit Instruments in Their Relations to General Prices* (New York: Henry Holt & Co., 1909), p. 2.

which emphasizes the importance of the possession of money and the willingness to spend it among the factors which affect prices.

TRANSACTION VELOCITY OF MONEY

Meaning of Transaction Velocity of Money. The transaction velocity of money is the rate at which money passes from hand to hand as a medium of exchange during a period of time, usually a year. The rate is usually called the "turnover" or "velocity" of money and is equal to a figure found by dividing the total number of dollar transactions by the average number of dollars owned by the general public (currency outside of banks and demand deposits adjusted).[3] This concept of the velocity of money includes money transfers between individuals, corporations, and others, whether in connection with consumers' purchases, producers' purchases, financial transactions, or other purchases not falling in the above classes.

If the monetary units that make up the money supply were spent regularly, an increase or decrease in the money supply would be reflected immediately in the volume of money payments. In practice, this is not true; therefore, the economy is subject to changes both in the amount of money and in the rate of spending. Statistics are available, in the form of debits to deposit accounts, which indicate changes in the rate of spending. Although such statistics are not all-inclusive because pocket money leaves no record of the number of times it is spent, they are significant because deposit currency is used in about 90 per cent of all money transfers.[4]

Banks' books show the number of checks written and the amounts for which each checking account has been debited. Often photographic records of checks paid, canceled, and returned to the drawer are kept for future reference. Since the basic factors causing changes in the velocity of hand-to-hand money are the same as those causing changes in the velocity of deposit currency, the assumption may be made that changes in the velocity of pocket money will be approximately the same as changes in the velocity of deposit currency. This does not mean that the two circulate at the same

---

[3] The term "demand deposits adjusted" means total demand deposits minus cash items in process of collection, interbank deposits, and government deposits.

[4] See current and past issues of the *Federal Reserve Bulletin,* published monthly by the Board of Governors of the Federal Reserve System. The series showing the turnover or velocity of bank deposits includes: (1) annual rate of turnover of total deposits, except interbank and government, for (*a*) New York City, and (*b*) other reporting cities; and (2) annual rate of turnover of demand deposits, except interbank and government, for (*a*) New York City, and (*b*) other leading cities.

rate but merely that, during normal times, changes in the velocity of each will tend to be at about the same rate.

It is obvious that a $1.00 bill moving rapidly from hand to hand in payment for things will do as much exchanging as a $20.00 bill moving with only one twentieth the rapidity. This fact is illustrated by the old English axiom: "A nimble six-pence will do the work of a lazy crown." Thus a change in velocity tends to have the same effect on general prices (or the value of money) as a change in the supply of money—an increase tends to increase general prices (to reduce the value of each monetary unit) and a decrease tends to lower general prices (to increase the value of each monetary unit). This relationship is illustrated by developments following the outbreak of war in Korea in 1950 when an increase in prices resulted from an increase in spending in anticipation of war scarcities without any substantial increase in the money supply.

Control of Velocity of Money by Individuals. In analyzing the reasons for changes in the velocity of money, it is necessary to examine what individuals do "to retard or advance the rate at which they spend their cash balances." Velocity is the "simple resultant of the decisions which the individuals in charge of the administration of cash balances make with respect to the size of the cash balance that they choose to keep relative to outlay."[5] This means that all individuals who have funds to spend are responsible for the rate of spending and therefore the velocity of money. If an individual delays purchases on one occasion or speeds up purchases on another, to that extent he decreases or increases the velocity of money.

Relative Size of Cash Balances. The size of an individual's cash balance, relative to his total monetary transactions, will depend in part on the nature and size (both actual and anticipated) of his money supply, the source of which may be money income, borrowed funds, gifts, and/or receipts from the sale of assets. If one's money income is small and received weekly, it will be spent more or less regularly throughout the week; and throughout the year the average size of his cash balance will be small compared to total expenditures. If one's money supply is large and received irregularly, more budgeting is necessary; and throughout the year the average size of his cash balance will be large relative to total expenditures.

During periods of prosperity, the absolute size of cash balances

[5] A. W. Marget, *The Theory of Prices* (New York: Prentice-Hall, Inc., 1938), Vol. I, p. 419 *passim.*

tends to be larger because money incomes increase; however, the relative size of cash balances tends to decrease during these times because individuals tend to spend more freely. During periods of depression, the absolute size of cash balances tends to be smaller because money incomes decrease; however, the relative size of cash balances tends to increase during these periods because individuals tend to spend less freely. This means that the velocity of money, or rate of spending, tends to be high during periods of prosperity and low during periods of depression.

Nature of the Credit System. The factors that influence the relative size of cash balances include, in addition to variations in income and the business cycle, the nature of the credit system. The ability to buy on credit, to borrow from financial institutions, and to convert liquid assets (savings bonds and other government securities, savings or time deposits, etc.) into money help to explain why some business firms and individuals tend to keep lower cash balances than do other business firms and individuals.

In an economy dominated by cash sales, large cash balances are held. The need for holding cash balances is greater in commercial and industrial regions than in agricultural sections wherein more of the needs of the people are cared for without the use of money. Today the greater dependence on the market place for goods and services tends to cause people to hold larger amounts of money relative to money income. However, improvements in the banking and credit system permit businessmen and others to borrow or to sell assets when money is needed; and the amount of money kept as cash balances tends to be less relative to total monetary expenditures.

Reasons for Holding Money. One reason for holding cash balances is to care for current transactions of a business or personal nature (the transaction motive). Obviously, cash is held between receipt and spending; and the amount held depends on the amount of one's income, spending habits, prices of goods and services (current and expected), and many other factors.

A second reason for holding cash balances is to meet contingencies (the precautionary motive). Whether considered from a personal or business viewpoint, these are merely "reserves" for outlays of an unusual, infrequent, or irregular nature. From the viewpoint of personal finances, these would include cash balances held to meet sickness or accident expenses, the cost of a vacation, a semiannual payment on a home mortgage, or the payment of a yearly insurance premium.

Rather than to hold idle cash balances to meet contingencies, the current practice is for individuals to invest in savings bonds or to keep funds in savings accounts with banks, savings and loan associations, or other financial institutions (such assets are called "near money"). This is also true to some extent for business firms that hold "near money" in different forms (such as government securities) to meet taxes and to fund other accounting reserves.

A third reason for holding cash balances is to care for future investments. Although there may be exceptions, the chief reason for postponing investments is because the holders of cash balances expect more favorable prices at a later date. That is, individuals and others prefer to hold cash balances if prices are expected to decline; and they prefer to hold things if prices are expected to rise. Since speculation is acting with the expectation of making profits from price fluctuations, the motive for holding relatively large or small cash balances is sometimes called the "speculative motive."

VOLUME OF THINGS

In the preceding paragraphs emphasis was on changes in the volume of money payments and how they tend to affect the general price level or the value of money. The other half of the problem includes the flow of things to the market place, the items for which money is spent, and how a change in the volume of things tends to affect the general price level or the value of money.

If the money supply and the rate of turnover remain the same, an increase in the volume of goods, services, and securities offered in the market will depress prices. An increase in the volume of things offered may be due to an increase in production or may result from "bearish" sentiments (anticipation of falling prices). In order to sell things, price reductions will be in order. Conversely, a decrease in the volume of goods, services and securities offered in the market will tend to increase prices. In order to buy things, buyers will have to compete more actively with others, with a "bullish" effect on prices. A decrease in the volume of things offered may be due to a decrease in production or may result from anticipation of higher prices. So, an increase in the number of things offered will tend to lower general prices and a decrease in the number of units offered will tend to increase prices.

During a year the supply of securities, real estate, and other things does not change very much; therefore, if there are changes in the volume of transactions or trading, they are traced primarily to turnover in the ownership of things rather than to changes in the volume of things. When goods and services are considered, the volume of production tends to be more influential in affecting the general price level. So, one cure for higher prices is an increase in output which will tend to offset any increase in prices. The mere fact that prices are higher will also tend to lessen the demand for things, which likewise will tend to check further inflation. Conversely, decreased production will tend to check deflation; and the mere fact that prices are lower will tend to increase demand which likewise will tend to check further deflation.

If the flow of money payments is kept equal to the flow of items to the market place, the two flows will be in balance with each other and there will be no great change in prices or the value of money. However, the problem of keeping these two flows in balance is not an easy one because of the changing nature of the economy. Among the factors which make this problem difficult are: the increase in number of workers, changes in methods of production, fickleness of consumers' preferences, and variations in the rate of spending.

If the flow of money payments fails to keep pace with the increase in the flow of items, there will be a tendency for prices to decline, employment to decrease, national income to fall, and other symptoms of depression to appear. Conversely, if the flow of money payments increases more rapidly than the flow of items, there will be a tendency for the symptoms of boom to appear (redistribution of wealth and income, substitution of speculation for production, decline in real income, and so forth).

EQUATIONS OF EXCHANGE

Sometimes the relationship among the different factors which determine the value of money is presented in the form of an equation, known as the equation of exchange, which is "nothing more or less than shorthand expressions designed to indicate the nature of the variables whose operations can be shown to influence prices."[6]

Transaction Equation of Exchange. The best known among the equations of exchange is $MV = PT$, called the "transaction" equation because it emphasizes total transactions. In this equation MV stands for the total money expenditures during a period of time, usually a year; and PT stands for the money value of things for which money is spent. P represents the average price of things

[6] *Ibid.*, p. 91. Italics in the original are omitted.

exchanged, and T represents the total volume of transactions. During a year, goods, services, securities, and other things may be sold more than once; and so the total volume of transactions will be larger than the physical volume of things. M represents the supply of money in the hands of the general public, and V represents transaction velocity or the average number of times a dollar is exchanged for things during the period of time.

Cash Balance Approach. Certain monetary economists emphasize the importance of holding money rather than spending money in explaining the value of money. Thus the supply of money (M) is defined as money held as a cash balance. The total demand for money at a particular time is merely the sum of individuals' demands to hold money (which in terms of dollars must equal the supply). The holding of cash balances may be thought of as the "store-of-value" demand for money. An increase in this demand for money will tend to increase its value (lower general prices), and a decrease in this demand will tend to decrease the value of money (increase general prices).

For those who stress the use of money as a store of value, it seems more logical to use the equation $M = KTP$, called the cash-balance equation of exchange. The symbol M represents money outside of banks and demand deposits adjusted, and KTP represents the money value of things over which the purchasing power is held in the form of money (supply equals demand). KT stands for the physical volume of things over which people wish to hold command in the form of money, and P is the average price of each unit of these things. T is the physical volume of trade to be effected with money during a year, and K equals the length of time or fraction of a year during which control of future spending is held in the form of money. This means the length of time it takes, on the average, to spend the cash balance once. If K equals one tenth of a year, it means that the velocity of money (V) is ten times per year.

Assuming the money supply equals $100 million, the volume of transactions equals 1,000 million, the average price per unit equals $1.00, and the length of time during which control over transactions is held in the form of money equals one tenth of a year, the two equations may be illustrated as follows: $M = KPT$ or $\$100,000,000 = 1/10 \times \$1 \times 1,000,000,000$; $MV = PT$ or $\$100,000,000 \times 10 = \$1 \times 1,000,000,000$. The transaction equation may be written $M = \dfrac{1}{V}TP$.

The similarity between the two equations may be illustrated as follows: $P = \dfrac{MV}{T}$ and $P = \dfrac{M}{KT}$.

As in the transaction equation, the symbols used in the cash-balance equation are subject to different definitions. K can be defined as the proportion between total transactions, income transactions, or any other outlay, and the cash balance held against that outlay. In effect, K is the coefficient which brings the two sides of the equation into balance.

Income Equation. In the income approach, national money income and how it is related to output and employment are emphasized. National income is the total amount of money received during a year from all sources by the residents of a country (plus a relatively small amount of undistributed corporate profits). Not included in national income (sometimes called net national income) are payments for depreciation and obsolescene (replacement savings) and business taxes. The value of goods entering into all intermediate business transactions as well as those in land, old buildings, second-hand goods, stocks and bonds, and many others are excluded. Emphasis is on values of goods and services currently purchased as measured by the amount paid at the end of the production process, by consumers for consumers goods, by businessmen for new capital which excludes replacement capital, and by the government for both consumer and producer goods (and strictly speaking, a small amount by foreigners not included in the preceding).

The income equation may be written $MV' = PO$, which means that the total money income (MV') received during a period of time is equal to the money value of the current output of goods and services (PO). In the income approach, the flow of money income is stressed on the money side of the equation; while in the transaction approach, total monetary expenditures are stressed.

Money income (MV') equals the money supply (M) times income velocity (V'). Income velocity (V') refers to the average number of times a dollar is used during a year in income transactions (that is, in purchasing the end-products of goods and services as previously defined). The annual rate of income velocity for an economy is found by dividing the national income by the average amount of money supply in use during the year. (In the transaction approach, each time a dollar is spent it is counted; and, therefore, the velocity of money will be several times greater than its income velocity.)

While the flow of all money transfers is recognized in the transaction approach, the income approach considers only the prices and volume of goods currently produced. The transaction approach considers prices, volume, and transfer of all things—new and old, goods, services, land, securities, and all other things not included in the above. So the total dollar value of quantities appearing on each side of the income equation of exchange will be a small fraction of the quantities appearing in the transaction equation.[7]

The income equation could be written in terms of the cash-balance equation, $M = KPO$; but K would need to be defined as the fraction of real income (not physical volume of things) over which people wish to hold command in the form of money, and P would carry the narrower connotation noted above (prices of goods currently produced).

FLOW-OF-FUNDS SYSTEM OF NATIONAL ACCOUNTS

In order to fill in a major gap in statistical information, the Division of Research and Statistics of the Federal Reserve System, in co-operation with others, developed a comprehensive system of national accounting for the flow of funds through the economy. The Federal Reserve System released the first major publication on the flow-of-funds system of national accounting in December, 1955, which gives substance to the more inclusive approach to problems of monetary management (total money expenditures–total transactions approach).[8]

The authors of the flow-of-funds system recognize that the study of national income and the spending thereof is valuable to an understanding of the production and distribution processes in the economy; but that it is inadequate to an understanding of an economy having as complex a financial structure as that of the United States.

Changes in the level and pattern of income expenditures for and prices of the current output of goods are included in the flow-of-funds system; but, in addition, other things are included that reflect changes in total expenditures and total output. These include such financial factors as the volume of currency and deposits, gold, and United States Treasury currency, bank loans other than mortgages, federal, state, and local obligations, corporate securities, mort-

[7] While gross national product or gross national income was estimated to have been $350.9 billion in 1953, total expenditures as presented in the Flow-of-Funds Accounts was $1,332.7 billion. *Federal Reserve Bulletin*, October, 1955, p. 1089.

[8] *Flow of Funds in the United States, 1939–1953* (Washington, D.C.: Board of Governors of the Federal Reserve System, December, 1955).

gages, trade credit, and miscellaneous financial assets and liabilities. Students of money and banking as well as the monetary authorities, businessmen, and others are and always will be interested in these factors as long as our present monetary and credit system exists.

In addition, the flow-of-funds national accounting system presents on the other side of the balance sheet as nonfinancial transactions, the types of goods and services exchanged or the immediate purpose served by the exchange. In the nonfinancial categories the following items appear: payroll, interest, rents and royalties, dividends, net withdrawals of funds by proprietors, insurance premiums, insurance benefits, grants and donations, taxes, tax refunds, real estate transfers, and other goods and services.

The flow-of-funds national accounting system helps to answer questions such as: "How did consumers as a group make purchases of goods and services amounting to 238 billion dollars (including 64 billion for new and old houses and consumer durables), provide for insurance, retirement, and gifts to the extent of 23 billion, pay taxes to the amount of 41 billion, and add nearly 13 billion to their cash and other financial assets—a grand total of 314 billion dollars?"[9]

Part of the answer to this question is found in statistics of personal income. The cash wages and salaries available to consumers amounted to approximately three fifths of $314 billion; another one fifth of the expenditures were made out of investment income of various kinds; and the remaining one fifth of the expenditures were from receipts from the sale of capital assets (houses and other real estate, automobiles, etc.), insurance benefits, pension receipts, gifts, public and private aid, and tax refunds, and borrowings (consumer mortgage debt increased by $6 billion and other consumer debt by about $5 billion).

The flow-of-funds system of national accounts is also helpful in answering questions such as: "How did the Federal Government finance payments of 85 billion dollars when its tax receipts were 65 billion?" "What sources of funds financed the 38 billion dollars of business capital investments?"[10]

SUMMARY

During a given period of time in the market there is a "man-directed" flow of money payments for a stream of things including goods, services, and securities. Within a given time period the money

[9] *Ibid.*, p. 3.
[10] *Ibid.*, p. 5.

value of the two flows will be equal because the dollar value of money given for things must equal the money value of the things given for money (five dollars given for a book equals the money value of a five-dollar book).

The size of the money stream is the product of two factors—the number of monetary units multiplied by the velocity at which they circulate. Money is different from things for which it is spent in that it is designed for continued use in the markets. It is this repeated use of money which explains why so much trade can be carried on with a relatively small supply of money. Therefore, in influencing the size of the money stream, changes in the rate of spending (velocity) may be at least as important as changes in the amount of money.

The physical flow of things varies during a given time period. Services of teachers, doctors, barbers, and others appear once, only to be replaced by new services on the following days; goods are withdrawn from the markets to be consumed by individuals; and new securities are purchased by investors to be held for income or appreciation in value. In addition to the number of units of things, the turnover of things in the market is a factor to be reckoned with in explaining the total volume of transactions. For example, a bushel of wheat that appears ten times in the market has the same effect as ten bushels which appear but once. Things are sold for money, and the total money value of things sold will be matched by the total money payments.

Those who criticize the transaction theorist by claiming that he is overlooking the fact that money may not be spent (except in the long-run) are ignoring the fact that the transaction theorist does recognize changes in the relative size of cash balances in the concept of velocity of circulation of money and the flow of money payments. Thus any drastic or sudden shift in the desire to hold money is recognized in the transaction theory as well as in the cash-balance or income approach. The transaction or cash-spending theory does not assume any causal relationship among changes in the quantity of money, the velocity of circulation of money, prices, and the volume of transactions. The equation of exchange may be written $PT = MV$.

Prices (actual and anticipated) will tend to influence the volume of production and the amount of already existing things placed on the market. Prices (actual and anticipated) will have an effect also upon the flow of money payments. Thus P in the equation of exchange may be an active, as well as a passive, factor because of the influence of prices on the amount of borrowing M, on the rate of spending V, and on the output of goods and the volume of sales T.

The fact that the symbol T includes a multitude of transactions of all types during a specified period of time must be recognized. Instead of there being one price level, there are many price levels to be considered in breaking down total transactions. These price levels include those for goods, services, and securities. Each of these may be subdivided in turn. Therefore, an increase or decrease in the amount of money spent for things will have varying effects, depending upon whether the outlays are for goods, services, or securities. Because of the large number of variables involved, the effects of a change in one of the factors in the equation of exchange are not predictable without knowledge as to changes in the others. Causes of changes in the value of money (P) may originate in M, V, or T; but most frequently changes in the value of money result from concomitant changes in all three factors.

The transaction theory, sometimes called the "cash-spending theory," and certain versions of the cash-balance theory center attention on the use of money in all transactions—financial, producers', consumers', governments', and intermediate transactions of all types. Recognition is given to financial markets, raw material markets, wholesale and other intermediate markets, secondary markets for old houses, secondhand car markets, and other things not currently produced. In monetary management, these are not neglected as shown by certain regulations of the Board of Governors of the Federal Reserve System—for illustration, Regulation X (real estate credit) and Regulations T and U (speculative credit). A major contribution has been made toward a better understanding of our monetary and credit system by the publication of the Board of Governors of the *Flow of Funds in the United States, 1939–53.*

QUESTIONS AND PROBLEMS

1. (*a*) What is the conflict between social and individual interests suggested by the statement: "In the case of money, the need for having the supply limited is not so obvious to individuals"?

   (*b*) May the destruction of paper money in the hands of an individual ever promote social interests? Explain.

2. (*a*) What is the quantity theory of money? Explain, giving necessary qualifications.

   (*b*) Compare to the transaction theory.

3. Comment on the statement: "Behind demand lies the money supply.

And basically it is the excessive supply of money in relation to goods and services which is at the root of our inflation." (Federal Reserve Bank of Philadelphia, *The Business Review*, July, 1948, p. 75.)

4. (*a*) What is meant by the transaction velocity of the circulation of money?

   (*b*) Compare to income velocity of the circulation of money.

5. (*a*) What is one of the first indicators that the growth in monetary expenditures is increasing more rapidly than the increase in the growth of goods and services?

   (*b*) May a too rapid expansion in monetary expenditures be reflected in markets other than for goods and services?

   (*c*) Do your answers suggest guides to monetary action? Why?

6. Distinguish between "cash balances" and "relative cash balances."

7. Explain the differences among (*a*) volume of transactions, (*b*) volume of things, and (*c*) velocity of circulation of goods.

8. Explain: "During a given period of time in the markets, a flow of money payments equals the money value of the flow of things."

9. Variations in the value of money (P) may originate in M, V, or T, but most frequently they result from concomitant changes in all three. Discuss, bringing in the fact that it is individuals who are responsible for spending.

10. "So long as there is unemployment, *employment* will change in the same proportion as the quantity of money; and when there is full employment, *prices* will change in the same proportion as the quantity of money." (J. M. Keynes, *The General Theory of Employment Interest and Money* [New York: Harcourt, Brace & Co., 1936], p. 296.) What does this mean?

11. Identify each of the three equations of exchange as given in the text book.

12. (*a*) What is the flow-of-funds system of national accounting?

    (*b*) How does it differ from income analysis system of national accounting?

13. "The money supply . . . continued last year the increase that began with the recovery of business activity during the latter half of 1954." However, the "demands by businesses and consumers for bank loans last year in the face of Federal Reserve credit restrictions resulted in the average demand deposit dollar being spent more often." (*New York Times*, January 3, 1956, p. 101.) Do these quotations indicate that the money supply and the rate of spending are important? Are special problems of monetary management suggested? Explain.

14. "To judge from the latest available information, it appears that gross national product . . . totaled about $387 billion in 1955. This is some 7 per cent above the total a year earlier, and it easily eclipses the previous annual record of $384½ billion achieved in 1953." (The Guaranty Trust Company of New York, *The Guaranty Survey*, January, 1956, p. 4). Since the normal growth in the economy is

at the rate of 3 per cent per year, may one properly consider 1955 as a year in which the economy had but partly regained preceding losses?

15. "The man in the overalls and the man in the business suit often try, by purchasing insurance, to build up some security to leave to their wives and children in the event of untimely death. It is a terrible thing to have the purchasing power of his insurance . . . cut nearly in half in the short period of just 15 years." (George M. Humphrey, "What Makes America," *Tax Outlook*, January, 1956, p. 11.) What is your solution? Why?

16. "Life insurance companies generally have been reluctant to enter this field ["variable annunity" plan]. Up to now their operations have been confined entirely to fixed dollar contracts." (Chester C. Nash, "The Contribution of Life Insurance to Social Security in the United States," *International Labour Review*, Vol. 72, No. 1, July, 1955, p. 36. Analyze the position of life insurance companies as suggested by this quotation.

Chapter IV | COMMERCIAL BANKS—A SOURCE OF MONEY

MONEY is defined to include things used as a means of payment; in the United States these include *checkbook* currency. Although a check is an order to pay a certain sum of money, usually to a specified party, it may not be necessary for the bank on which it is drawn to pay currency to this party. In many cases, the bank simply charges the amount against the drawer's account and credits it to the payee's account. For example, if a check is given to the electric light and power company, the drawer's account with the bank will be debited and the company's account will be credited for the amount.

A check might be drawn on one bank and deposited in a second bank. This necessitates settling between the two banks. In this case, payment is usually made by offsetting claims and then paying only the difference by debiting the "checking" or "reserve" account of the debtor bank and crediting the account of the creditor bank at their Federal Reserve bank. Although this description does not cover all of the clearing and collection procedures in use in the United States, it includes the most important ones. (See Chapter V.)

This chapter deals with commercial banks as a source of bank paper money and checkbook money or deposit currency including the distinguishing characteristics of each, the development of deposit currency, creation of bank deposits, limits on bank-credit expansion, and problems pertaining to the control of the volume of deposit currency.

BANK PAPER MONEY AND DEPOSIT CURRENCY

During the history of commercial banking in the United States, the public has been sold on the idea of using bank credit as a means of payment either in the form of bank paper money or bank deposits. In return for permitting the use of bank credit, banks have obtained valuable assets from their customers. In doing so, bankers are but following the practices of businessmen and others who buy things on credit. When banks issue paper money or new deposit currency, they create liabilities; and if they do not get equal value in return, they will not be in business long. Below, the two forms of bank credit—bank paper money and deposit currency—are compared.

Physical Forms. Deposits and bank notes or bank paper money are credit instruments or contracts, but their physical forms are different. Bank notes are engraved on durable pieces of paper, while bank deposits are bookkeeping accounts which may be transferred by the order of the owner to others by means of bank checks. Obviously, bank notes are expected to remain in circulation for a long period, while checks are not expected to be exchanged more than once or twice before they are returned to the banks for cancellation.

Homing Power. In the United States, checks are tested, in effect, as soon as they are presented for payment; but bank notes are seldom tested as to convertibility. The homing power of checks is great compared to that of bank notes. This is true for a number of reasons, among them the ever-present question as to the credit standing of the drawer and sometimes that of the bank. In addition, a check customarily is drawn for the exact amount of payment involved, which is usually some odd figure rather than the convenient denominations of bank notes; this condition makes the check inconvenient for further use. A check usually is made out to a specific person, who must endorse it before it can be transferred legally. In order to limit his contingent liability to as short a period as is possible, the holder of a check usually presents it for payment immediately after endorsement.

Legal practice now demands that checks be presented for payment within a reasonable period. This varies according to a number of factors, but the courts realize that a successful deposit-currency system rests upon prompt presentation and payment of checks. The longer a check remains in circulation, the greater becomes the danger of fraud and forgery. Furthermore, a check may be good at the time it is written; but it may be invalidated by removal of the deposit, failure of the bank, or refusal of the bank to honor it. Usually, if the check is not presented within a reasonable period, the drawer is discharged from the liability of loss caused by the delay.

Government Protection. The chief hazard assumed by a depositor is the possibility of the failure of the bank whose receiver is unable to liquidate assets in amounts sufficient to pay the depositor in full. The creation of the Federal Deposit Insurance Corporation has eliminated this hazard for small depositors of insured banks, but it remains as one that must be faced by noninsured banks' depositors and by large depositors (over $10,000).

Before the Civil War, bank-note circulation was more important than deposit currency; and, then, as now, the government's statutory provisions for protection of banks' creditors favored noteholders over depositors. Professor C. F. Dunbar suggested that the special protection given to noteholders may be due to the failure of legislators generally "to perceive the similarity of the two kinds of liability. . . ."[1] If this is true, most bank noteholders are unaware that they are creditors of banks because legislators generally reflect the knowledge of the people they represent.

At the present time the Federal Reserve banks have a monopoly of issuing bank notes which the government guarantees. In addition, the Federal Reserve agent of each Federal Reserve bank must hold collateral (government obligations, commercial paper and/or gold certificates) equal to 100 per cent of all notes issued. The gold certificate portion of this collateral may also be counted as part of the 25 per cent minimum gold certificate reserve that each Federal Reserve bank must hold against Federal Reserve notes in circulation. If this treatment of promises to pay of the Federal Reserve banks is justified, may not depositors claim similar protection?

Circulating Hazards. Checks are safer than currency when payments are made by mail because most checks cannot be negotiated unless they are endorsed. A thief may forge the signature of the payee, but the bank which cashes the forged check must take the responsibility for the loss. Stolen currency is difficult to recover because it passes into the hands of innocent persons. Checks that are burned, destroyed, or lost may be replaced with little difficulty.

Under certain conditions, checks give protection to drawers if errors are made. When a purchaser discovers (immediately after a transaction) that a mistake has been made in quantity or quality, he may have difficulty in recovering his money if the payment was made with currency; but, if a check was used for payment, he may request his bank not to honor the check when it is presented. In all cases where such "stop payments" are to be made, immediate action is necessary.

Canceled Checks as Receipts. When a check is presented, the bank pays the sum designated to the holder; and, later, it cancels

---

[1] C. F. Dunbar, *The Theory and History of Banking* (4th ed.; New York: G. P. Putnam's Sons, 1922), p. 63.

the check and returns it to the drawer to serve as a receipt. This permanent evidence of payment is valuable in case a dispute should arise. If cash was used in making a payment and the payee dies, the payer has no protection unless he has a written receipt or made the payment in the presence of witnesses. If a check was used, the canceled check may be submitted as evidence; and, if the purpose for which it was drawn is written upon its face, its value as evidence of payment is increased. The use of machines to photograph checks and bank statements has added to the value of checks as records of payment of obligations. Canceled checks may be used also as an aid in keeping accounting records of expenditures and in making out income-tax statements.

Acceptability. Although there are many advantages in using deposit currency, its use is usually impractical in making small payments and it is not always acceptable. Because checks cannot be used conveniently in making some purchases, such as postage stamps and bus tokens, there always will be a place for small coins and paper money in the monetary system. However, the most serious limitation on the use of deposit currency is its lack of general acceptability.

Checks are personal credit instruments, and their acceptability is closely related to the credit standing of the individual user. Their acceptance is limited to business circles where there is knowledge of the drawers and endorsers. There may be doubt as to the authenticity of any check not drawn in the presence of the one who is asked to cash it. Even though the signature of the drawer is genuine, doubt may remain as to the value of the check because of lack of knowledge as to the size of the drawer's account and as to the credit standing of the names of the others on the check (payee and endorsers) who are secondarily liable.

A check may not be paid if the date is incorrect, if the signature differs from that on the depositor's signature card, if it has been altered after having been written by the drawer, or if it has not been presented within a reasonable period of time (a "stale" check). The hazards of accepting a counterfeit coin or bill are negligible compared to those of accepting worthless or otherwise troublesome checks.

DEVELOPMENT OF DEPOSIT CURRENCY

The existence of deposits is as old as banking, but the practice of transferring title to these deposits by orders written by individuals is a fairly recent development. It resulted logically from the practice of banks in using bank drafts to transfer funds between domestic centers and between foreign countries.

Fairly early in the history of exchange, funds were transferred by written orders drawn by one individual on an agent near the center where payment was to be made. These bills of exchange were used by private bankers, merchants, and agents of the Catholic church.[2] The use of bills of exchange made it possible to transfer title to funds within and between communities, without the dangers of confiscation by robber barons and others. The popularity of the bills of exchange was due partly to the practice of discounting them, a means used to circumvent the church usury laws, which prevented the taking of all interest for loans. But the legitimate use of bills of exchange increased with the growth of trade in medieval and early modern times.

About 1722 a private banking firm in London, Messrs. Child & Co., "began to supply their customers with printed cheque forms which they might complete as drafts for any amount and payable to any of their creditors."[3] These personal checks became very popular and marked the beginning of the present, modern deposit-currency system.

In what is now the United States, instruments similar to checks were used in connection with some of the embryo banks that were established during the Colonial period. Our chartered commercial banking system originated during the post-Revolutionary War period and with it came deposit currency. By 1850 the importance of deposit currency as a means of payment about equaled that of bank notes. During the decade following the Civil War the development of deposit currency was accelerated by restricting the privilege of note issue to national banks. The amount of paper money that each national bank could issue was limited to its capitalization, and state-chartered banks were denied this privilege altogether. Therefore, in order to carry on a profitable banking business, it was necessary for banks to develop deposit banking as distinguished from note-issue banking. "Pay by check" became the advertising slogan of commercial banks.

By 1875 the volume of payments completed with the use of checks and similar instruments was approaching the present dominant percentage. The development of the local clearinghouse system fa-

[2] W. S. Jevons, *Money and the Mechanism of Exchange* (New York: D. Appleton & Co., 1875), pp. 293–97.
[3] H. E. Evitt, *Practical Banking* (London: Sir I. Pitman & Sons, Ltd., 1935), p. 5.

cilitated this movement, and since 1915 the Federal Reserve par collection system has made the check a national instrument of exchange. The current emphasis on demand-deposit banking has a parallel in the early history of American banking, when there was a tendency to identify commercial banking with note-issue banking. Then, as now, the typical bank did much more than provide a means of payment; but this money function always has been the most important characteristic of commercial banks.

Demand deposits are banks' debts payable on call or order; and, in this respect, they do not differ from "call loans." It is the way in which banks' book promises to pay are used that makes them more significant than other similar contracts. The owners of demand deposits make their banks responsible for delivering money to those with whom they trade or to whom they are indebted. In making payments the depositor may write checks which, in effect, order his bank to transfer funds to the payees. This convenience in making payments accounts for the development of the "banking habit." This use of deposit currency might be very inconvenient to a bank if all payees insisted on being paid in hand-to-hand money. However, payees usually prefer to leave the checks with banks as deposits. When payees leave checks on deposit with their banks, they shift to their banks the responsibility for collecting funds in the same way as the drawers of the checks shift to their banks the responsibility for paying money. Thus banks serve as collectors and paymasters for their depositors, and the cost of these services and others given to depositors represents between 50 and 75 per cent of banks' operating expenses.

Depositors give life to the present commercial banking system by leaving their rights to money with banks rather than by cashing them; and what depositors give, they also may take away. Without depositors' funds to work with, even the strongest bank would be out of business in a matter of days. Thus, one may conclude that the future of the commercial banking system is dependent on the continuing good relationship between the 13,700 odd banks and their millions of owners of demand deposits (estimated to be as many as 45,000,000—this number includes considerable overlapping because many firms and individuals have several accounts in two or more banks).

DEPOSITS AS THE RESULT OF THREE TYPES OF TRANSACTIONS

The types of transactions which create bank deposits are: (1) exchanging coins and paper money for the right to draw upon the bank; (2) leaving checks, drafts, and other credit instruments with the bank with the understanding that the proceeds are to be credited to the account of the customer; and (3) borrowing from the bank, the proceeds of the loan being credited to the deposit account of the borrower. Considered from the viewpoint of the individual bank, the second type is the most important. It has been estimated that, in some sections of the country, 98 per cent of bank deposits are made in the form of checks. But, considered from the viewpoint of the banking system as a whole, the third type is the most important.

When a bank accepts coins, paper money, and credit instruments, it is apparent that the depositor is surrendering title to these assets in exchange for the bank's promise to pay, another type of personal asset. It should be equally apparent that, when a bank accepts an asset from a depositor, it also assumes a liability, which is formally recognized by entries in its books. The mere act of giving a depositor credit on the bank's books means that the bank is creating a deposit. However, this does not mean that the total means of payment is increased by this act of creating a deposit.

In case of deposits of coins and paper money, there is an exchange of one kind of means of payment for a second—currency for deposit currency. Similarly, when deposits of checks and other cash items are collected, there is a shift of title to already existing means of payment. This banking process may result in some increase in total bank deposits, if credit is given for cash items in process of collection (float), because there is some time lag between the entry of the credit on one bank's books and the cancellation of the same amount of credit on the second bank's books. Although these transactions (exchanging currency for deposit currency and exchanging checks and other credit instruments for currency) are of major importance to individual depositors and to individual banks, they have little effect upon day-to-day changes in the volume of deposit currency.

A typical bank loan transaction involves the exchange of the borrower's promise to pay for the bank's promise to pay. From an accounting viewpoint, the bank secures an asset which will appear under the general heading of "loans and discounts" and creates a liability which will appear under the general heading of "deposits." Since the borrower usually has an immediate need for cash, the bank expects him to "check out" all or most of this new deposit. If the borrower withdraws cash, the new deposit is canceled, and the bank has exchanged a nonearning asset (cash) for an earning asset (the borrower's interest-bearing promise to pay).

A more typical illustration of modern banking is a lending

transaction in which the deposit is used as money and is not with-drawn immediately (as cash) from the banking system. Both assets and liabilities are increased at the time of the loan transaction. If the borrower writes but one check in favor of a second depositor of the bank, and the payee deposits it in the bank, the borrower's account is debited, and the second depositor's account is credited. In this case, cancellation of the check would entail no change in the total deposits of the bank, no loss of cash, and no change in total assets.

If, in a closed economy, there were but one bank, the individual banker would be in a position to observe a close relationship between an increase in his lending activities and an increase in the volume of deposits at the time of the original lending transaction and later. If there were no legal-reserve requirements to meet, his problem would be one of keeping enough cash on hand to meet the demands of depositors. Since the daily flow of money to the bank tends to be about the same as the flow of money away from the bank, this cash reserve would need be only a small percentage of the total deposits. Instead of there being but one bank, there are thousands in the United States; and so an individual bank must anticipate demands for cash from other banks, as well as from its own depositors.

If a borrower writes only one check on a deposit resulting from a lending operation, and the payee deposits this check in a second bank, or if several checks are written and deposited in one or more banks other than the lending bank, the lending bank must be in a position to transfer funds to other banks. The books of the lending bank will show a decrease in assets (cash) and a decrease in liabilities (deposits), thus re-establishing the bank's original position in so far as total assets and liabilities are concerned (but cash has been decreased and loans have been increased). What this bank gives up in the form of cash and what the receiving banks assume in the form of liabilities (deposits) represents a redistribution of assets and liabilities but not cancellation of deposits. Therefore, deposits traceable to the increase in lending by a bank are not destroyed; the checks written on the borrower's deposit merely transfer the deposit to other accounts in the lending bank or to accounts in other banks.

LIMITS ON BANK CREDIT EXPANSION

Since bankers desire to make profits from lending and investing, what is there to prevent them from lending too much credit? In answering this question, the first thing to consider is banks' dependence on keeping the confidence of their depositors. To maintain this confidence, paying deposits on demand is imperative. Whenever depositors prefer currency to their deposits, there will be a drain on the reserves of the banking system as well as on those of individual banks. In the management of bank assets, bankers anticipate this development not only by holding currency and demand deposits in other commercial banks and/or the Federal Reserve banks but also by holding earning assets that may be converted into cash without loss or delay.

A second limiting factor in the expansion in the amount of bank credit is the fact that banks are required by law and custom to have reserves equal to a certain percentage of their deposits. Then, further expansion is dependent on excess reserves on hand or new reserves that may be obtained.

The three sources of new reserves for the commercial banking system are: (1) Treasury currency; that is, new issues of government coin and paper money; (2) increases in the gold stock; and (3) increases in the amount of Federal Reserve bank credit. While an expansion in any one of these forms of money tends to increase the amount of member-bank reserve balances, other institutions as well as the public compete with member banks for these new funds. For illustration (1) nonmember banks, foreign governments, foreign central banks, the United States Treasury, and certain government agencies may increase their deposits with Federal Reserve banks; (2) business firms, individuals, commercial banks, and other corporations may increase their holdings of coin and paper money; and (3) the United States Treasury may increase its holdings of inactive gold and currency. Since all of these factors are considered in more detail later, it is sufficient to note here that an increase in the amount of new or existing funds held by any one of the above would tend to reduce the amount of member-bank reserves.

In conclusion, in order to have the right amount of money, the Federal Reserve System must vary the amount of Federal Reserve credit in use so that member banks' reserve accounts are adjusted to offset (1) changes in production of things, and (2) losses or gains of reserves due to changes in (*a*) the amount of gold supply and Treasury currency, (*b*) the amount of money in circulation, (*c*) the holdings of Federal Reserve bank balances by the United States Treasury and others, and (*d*) the holdings of cash by the United States Treasury.

Multiple Expansion of Bank Credit on New Reserves. Member banks, that is banks that are members of the Federal Reserve System, are required by law to keep their required or legal reserves in Federal Reserve banks. In form, these reserves are similar to the checking accounts kept by individuals with their banks. In addition, member banks (which hold about 85 per cent of all checkbook money) also hold coin and paper money so that they may cash checks and meet the needs of retailers and others for currency. For business reasons, member banks also keep deposits with banks other than their Federal Reserve banks, and have certain cash items in process of collection. As a result of these uses of assets, the typical commercial bank may be in a position to lend or invest no more than 80 per cent of new deposits.

If Bank A receives a new deposit of $10,000,000 due to an import of gold, the amount of its reserves (as well as its deposit liabilities) will be increased by $10,000,000. Under the current fractional-reserve system, Bank A must hold a certain per cent of this amount as a reserve, assume 20 per cent for illustration; and, when it lends the remainder, its statement will show new deposits of $8,000,000 and a new offsetting loan of $8,000,000. Now assume that the sum is checked out and deposited in Bank B. Bank A cancels a deposit and releases cash equal to $8,000,000, leaving Bank B with its original deposit of $10,000,000 and cash of $2,000,000 and an earning asset (loan) of $8,000,000.

Now Bank B repeats the same process with its new $8,000,000 deposit, setting aside a 20 per cent reserve ($1,600,000) and lending $6,400,000, which is promptly withdrawn and deposited in Bank C. Bank B is left with an $8,000,000 deposit liability, $1,600,000 in cash, and $6,400,000 as an earning asset. This process is then repeated by Bank C, then D, and so on throughout the banking system, with results as shown in Table 3. In simplified form, Table 3 shows the theoretically possible expansion based upon new reserves and illustrates what tends to happen in the banking system. In practice, banks other than Bank B (including A) may share in the first withdrawal of cash from Bank A and so on for others.

Banks Also Destroy Deposits. When a bank loan is repaid with currency, the bank's reserves are increased and its earning assets are decreased. However, bank loans (except small ones) are usually paid with checks. Customarily the borrower builds up his deposit account during the loan period and, when the promise to pay comes due, he either writes a check on his account or requests the bank to debit it for the amount due (even without such instructions, a bank may charge a borrower's account because of the right of off-set). The banking process is one of canceling the note (thereby reducing the bank's assets) and debiting the depositor's account (thereby reducing the bank's liabilities—deposits). So, when earning assets of a commercial bank are liquidated, there is usually a decrease (at least temporarily) in the volume of checkbook currency.

TABLE 3

HYPOTHETICAL MULTIPLE EXPANSION ON NEW BANK RESERVES

Bank	Additional Deposits Received 100%	Additional Loans Made 80%	Additional Reserves Retained 20%
A.	$10,000,000	$ 8,000,000	$ 2,000,000
B.	8,000,000	6,400,000	1,600,000
C.	6,400,000	5,120,000	1,280,000
D.	5,120,000	4,096,000	1,024,000
E.	4,096,000	3,276,800	819,200
F.	3,276,800	2,621,440	655,360
G.	2,621,440	2,097,152	524,288
H*.	2,097,152	1,677,722	419,430
I.	1,677,722	1,342,178	335,544
J.	1,342,177	1,073,742	278,435
Total—first 10 banks...	$44,631,291	$35,705,033	$ 8,926,258
All other banks in turn.	$ 5,368,709	$ 4,294,967	$ 1,073,742
Total.	$50,000,000	$40,000,000	$10,000,000

* Figures for remainder of banks rounded to dollars.

The destruction of checkbook money also takes place when loans are repaid with checks drawn upon other banks—the banks upon which the checks are drawn lose deposits and cash and the banks whose loans are repaid gain cash and lose earning assets. If the liquidation of loans and deposit currency stopped here, the results would not be serious; but the banks on which the checks are drawn lose reserves as well as deposits. The problem faced by them is one of obtaining new reserves because they have lost not only the 20 per cent reserve kept against the transferred deposit but also additional assets kept as reserves for other deposits.

When some commercial banks reduce their loans and/or investments, it may cause other banks to lose cash and deposits. If bankers, in general, are taking a bearish (pessimistic) view of future business conditions, there may be set in motion a series of events that may be described as the multiple contraction of check currency due to the loss of bank reserves. For illustration, behind the liquidation of checkbook currency during 1932–33 there was a loss of confidence in banks and a withdrawal of deposits in the form of currency (which meant a dollar-for-dollar loss in bank reserves). However, such calamities may be avoided if the central banking system has the power to replace any losses of bank reserves due to hoarding of currency or to other factors.

Normally, the banking process entails making and collecting loans and investments simultaneously. Thus both "deposit-creating" and "deposit-destroying" activities are going on at the same time and the monetary problem is one of maintaining a balance between the supply of money and its uses and the changes in the volume of things offered for sale in the market. Solving this problem requires the co-operation of everyone, but the burden falls most heavily on central bankers and Treasury officials.

FACTORS COMPLICATING THE CONTROL OF MONEY

Competition. In the United States, competition among business firms and corporations (including banks) generally is considered to be advantageous to the general public. This philosophy has led to a policy of freely incorporating banks in order to prevent the development of a monopoly. At the present time the existence of some 13,700 commercial banks (competing for business) complicates the problem of control, since each bank is a place where new means of payment are created whenever a loan or investment is made. Similarly, means of payment are canceled whenever earning assets (debts of the government, individuals, business firms, and others held by commercial banks) are liquidated.

Banks are dependent chiefly upon income from earning assets (loans and investments) as the source of revenue out of which to meet expenses and to pay dividends on capital stock. At the same time, businessmen, firms, corporations, governments, and others are dependent upon banks for loanable funds. This makes bank lending and investing mutually attractive to lenders (banks) and borrowers. This further complicates the problem of control over the volume of deposit currency in that any repressive measure taken by the control authorities may arouse the antagonism of both lenders and borrowers

Dual Position of the Government. The most ironical aspect of the problem of control over deposit currency appears when the control agency (government) is controlling banks that are lending chiefly to the control agency (government). This situation brings into sharp conflict the interests of the government as the control authority, on the one hand, and as the chief borrower from the commercial banks, on the other. Can the government restrict the volume of deposit currency in order to protect the value of money and still depend upon commercial banks as a source of abundant and "cheap money" (low interest rates)? The mere fact that government securities now represent a dominant part of the earning assets of commercial banks at home and abroad suggests how important governmental policies of borrowing, spending, and debt-retiring may be in determining the volume of deposit currency.

Profit Motive. The fact that commercial banks are private corporations dominated by the profit motive is a third factor complicating the control over the money supply. Businessmen borrow and bankers lend when it is profitable to do so; therefore, bankers increase lending during periods of rising prices when doing so gives promise of earnings for their banks and when collections present the least problem. During periods of falling prices, the ability of borrowers to pay debts diminishes because dollar receipts decline; therefore, businessmen are reluctant to borrow and bankers to lend.

At the present time, although bankers may shift their banks' funds from loans to investments to keep the volume of bank assets and deposits stable, the decline in loans tends to have a deflationary effect because of its effect on the rate of spending. Before the growth in the national debt, the volume of safe investment outlets for commercial banks' funds was limited; and as a result, during earlier periods of falling prices a decline in the rate of spending was accompanied by a decrease in the volume of commercial banks' assets and liabilities.

The economic effects of a loan made when there is unemployment and one made when there is full employment are different. As pointed out previously, when there are unemployed resources, an increase in spending may be offset by an increase in production; but, when there is full employment, an increase in spending means that more dollars are chasing the same quantity of goods (resulting in price inflation). Asking businessmen and commercial bankers to refrain from borrowing and lending during inflationary periods and to increase borrowing and lending during inflationary periods is not the solution to the problem of keeping income and other expenditures in balance with production and other transactions without inflationary or deflationay pressures. The responsibility for keeping the United States economy on an even keel belongs to the Federal Reserve System and the United States Treasury.

Fractional Reserve System. A fourth factor that complicates the problem of control over the money supply is the existence of our fractional reserve system. When the economy needs more money, the central banks may provide the commercial banks with additional reserves but there is no assurance that these reserves will be used as a basis for an expansion of bank credit. When the economy needs less money, there is no doubt of the ability of central banks to reduce the supply by withholding new bank reserves or by contracting the existing supply. To use the old analogy, "While one may check a dog with a chain, one can not push him with it."

Cash Drain. A fifth factor to keep in mind is that the general public may increase or decrease its holdings of currency. If the public is holding 20 per cent of the money supply as currency today, it may hold 25 per cent tomorrow and 15 per cent the next day. As noted previously, an increase in the amount of money outside of the United States Treasury and Federal Reserve banks tends to cause a loss of member-bank reserves equal to the increase in the amount of money withdrawn; and conversely, a decrease in the amount of money outside the Treasury and Federal Reserve banks will tend to increase member-bank reserves. When there is an increase in the amount of currency held by the public, commercial banks will have to draw on their reserve accounts at their Federal Reserve banks to replace their loss of till money needed for day-to-day operations. Normally, banks pay out and take in currency simultaneously; but, if the outflow increases and the inflow decreases, they must obtain new currency or face a situation wherein they cannot meet liabilities (deposit claims) on demand. (In the latter case, they may be closed by regulatory agencies.)

The loss of member-bank reserves arising out of an increase in money in circulation is called the cash or internal drain (as distinguished from Federal Reserve banks' losses following exports of gold). In computing new reserve needs, the monetary authorities must consider that new Federal Reserve funds may be needed not only to care for expanding needs of member banks but also the demands of others—banks, other corporations, the United States Treasury, individuals, etc. for till money, vault cash, and/or pocket money. While a cash drain tends to reduce member-bank reserves dollar for dollar, a reverse cash drain tends to increase member-bank reserves dollar for dollar.

Assume that there is an increase in the amount of member-bank reserves of $10,000,000, then an allowance would have to be made for a cash drain depending on the ratio of currency in circulation to the volume of demand deposits adjusted. If this ratio is one to five, then the expansion of deposit currency as computed in Table 3 (p. 62) will need to be adjusted downward by about 20 per cent and available reserves will be but $8,000,000.

Whether the general public holds currency or demand deposits depends primarily on the habits of people in meeting their obligations, on the convenience of location of banks, and on the cost and

CHART 3

CURRENCY IN CIRCULATION*†

December 29, 1948—December 28, 1949

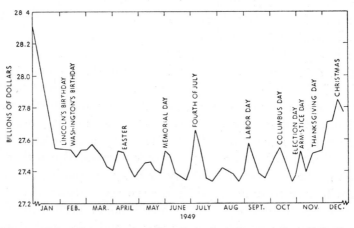

* Source: Federal Reserve Bank of New York, *Bank Reserves, Some Major Factors Affecting Them* (1951), p. 23.
† Outside U.S. Treasury and Federal Reserve Banks; Wednesday dates.

efficiency of banks' services. Although the volume of both demand deposits and the volume of currency tend to rise together in the long run, the relationship between changes in deposits and money outside of banks is not a constant one.

During periods when there is doubt as to the safety of banks, currency outside of banks tends to increase sharply, and bank runs are likely to occur. During the early 1930's banks' excess reserves were depleted and banks were forced to call loans, to sell assets, and to borrow. Deposits declined despite the fact that Federal Reserve credit was expanded in excess of the cash drain.

During World War II the volume of both bank deposits and currency in circulation increased; but the latter increased more rapidly. (The reason for the greater increase in the amount of currency in circulation was traced to the demands of those in the Armed Forces, operators in the black market, and individuals who wanted to conceal their incomes for purposes of tax evasion.) About one third of the increase in the money supply during World War II was in the form of currency which absorbed member-bank reserves dollar for dollar. The increase in member-bank reserves to meet the new reserve requirements resulting from expanded net demand deposits was $6.8 billion; but new reserve money absorbed by the increase in money in circulation was almost $20 billion.

From 1947 to June 1950, there was a reverse drain, and member banks had ample reserves even though the volume of Federal Reserve credit declined by almost $4.5 billion (due chiefly to a decline in money in circulation). It is easier to anticipate the changes in relative amounts of currency outside of banks and demand deposits when the changes are due to holiday, weekly, and seasonal demands. From past experiences, banks are able to chart the time of deposit withdrawals. Currency in circulation usually increases over the Labor Day week end and when the Fourth of July falls on Saturday or Monday. Currency tends to flow away from banks in larger amounts on Friday and Saturday to meet the demand for week-end shopping and weekly payrolls whether paid by check or in currency. Businessmen return receipts promptly to their banks; and, as a result, the return flow tends to exceed the outflow during the first part of the week and after holidays.

Since 1947 the volume of deposits has been subject to seasonal changes, shrinking during the first half of each year and expanding sufficiently during the second half to more than offset the losses during the first half of the year. The differences between the first and second halves of the years have been considerably greater than those of two decades ago because of the seasonal nature of loan demands of businessmen and consumers and the receipts and expenditures of the federal government.

Demand deposits and currency in circulation tend to reach a seasonal peak in December, and both decline in January. Demand deposits continue to fall until February or March, while the amount of currency in circulation tends to level off. The seasonal rise in demand deposits usually starts in June, but the seasonal rise in amount of currency is circulation starts much later, generally noticeable in November and December (see Chart 3).

From 1947 to 1956 the average annual rate of growth of deposits in all banks in the United States was at a rate of 3.9 per cent. If projected into the future, this means that the volume of deposits (and also assets) will be double in about 20 years. This expansion of

CHART 4

GROSS NATIONAL PRODUCT AND THE MONEY SUPPLY*

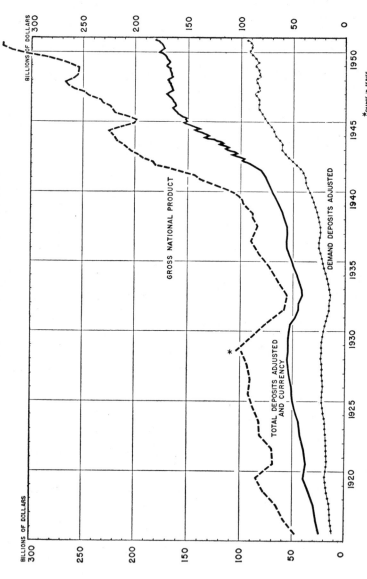

* Source: Joint Committee on the Economic Report, *Monetary Policy and the Management of the Public Debt* (Washington, D.C.: U.S. Government Printing Office, 1952), Part 1, p. 525.

NOTE.—Total deposits adjusted and currency include demand deposits adjusted, time deposits, and currency outside banks. Deposits are for all banks in the United States. Demand deposits adjusted exclude United States government deposits and interbank deposits and items in process of collection. Time deposits include deposits in Postal Savings System and in mutual savings banks.

bank deposits is closely related to the growth in the economic life of the nation. Since deposits are the chief means of payment used by individuals, business firms, and others, any decline in the rate of growth of deposits necessitates a decline in the rate of spending or a change in the habits of people. Since people's habits change but slowly, the growth in the volume of bank deposits is necessary for the continuing growth in the economy. However, this growth must be at a reasonable rate; if it is too rapid, it may invite a too-rapid increase in the money supply, too much spending, and price inflation, with disastrous disturbances to the economy. (See Chart 4.)

Chart 4 indicates the changes in the money supply from 1919 to 1952. The greatest increase took place after 1939, and the chief reason for this rise has been the increase in banks' investing and lending activities. This expansion of the money supply has been greater than the increase in production of goods. While part of the available money supply was held as idle cash balances, most of the excess was used to bid up prices of goods, real estate, and other things. The most significant fact brought out by Chart 4 is the effect of war financing on the money supply. Banks created deposits in connection with their purchases of United States government securities during World War II; and, as a result, loans and investments of all commercial banks increased from $50 billion to $124 billion, and the money supply more than doubled. (See Chart 4.)

SUMMARY

In the United States the most important means of payment (in terms of dollars) is deposit currency or checkbook money. This type of money originates in transactions which create bank deposits. Technically, banks create deposits when they give depositors bank credit on their books for hand-to-hand money, checks, and other credit items. Banks cancel deposits when they cash checks for depositors and otherwise settle for checks and other cash items with money that is withdrawn from the banking system. In addition, banks not only create bank deposits but also increase the volume of means of payment when they increase their holdings of earning assets. Similarly, banks decrease the volume of means of payment by decreasing their holdings of earning assets.

There are several factors which limit the amount by which a bank may expand bank credit. Banks must maintain the confidence of their depositors in the ability of the bank to pay their deposits on demand, and this requires them not only to hold currency and demand deposits in other banks but also to hold earning assets which may be converted into cash without loss or delay. Banks are required by law and custom to have reserves equal to a specified percentage of deposits. Then, when their excess reserves are used up, further bank credit expansion must cease unless new reserves are available.

The three sources of new reserves are Treasury currency, gold stock, and Federal Reserve bank credit. An increase in any one of these items tends to increase the amount of member-bank reserves, and a decrease tends to decrease member-bank reserves.

In the United States, the problem of control of money is complicated by many factors including (1) competition among business firms and corporations including banks; (2) the dual position of the government as an important "monetary authority," on one hand, and the chief "bank debtor," on the other; (3) the profit motive in business and commercial banking; (4) the fractional reserve system; and (5) cash drain which affects member-bank reserves. This summary suggests a number of problems which will be considered when the credit policy of the Federal Reserve System is described and the problems of fiscal and monetary policy are analyzed.

QUESTIONS AND PROBLEMS

1. Enumerate and explain the differences between deposit currency and bank notes. Do they have characteristics in common? Explain.
2. Identify: (*a*) checkbook money, and (*b*) a check.
3. Identify the three types of transactions which create bank deposits. Which type is most important to an individual bank? To the banking system as a whole? Why?
4. Under what circumstances may the check canceled and paid represent deposits which are withdrawn from the banking system?
5. "Since bankers desire to make profits from lending and investing, what is there to prevent them from lending too much credit?"
6. Comment on the following: ". . . people who discuss the 'creation of deposits' as if it were a highly valuable privilege of the banks, think of bank deposits as an asset; and they therefore believe that the banks can create assets for themselves. . . . In fact, . . . a bank deposit is . . . a liability so far as the bank is concerned." (G. F. Towers, *Bank of Canada*, radio address, December 1, 1938.)
7. Cycles "in banking follow closely those in business and industry. This appears elemental as banks cannot create deposits but must await receipt of funds or customers who . . . are willing to borrow. . . ." (N. M. McKernan, *Changing Banking Conditions* [Cambridge,

Mass.: Bankers Publishing Co., 1947], p. 6.) Is this true in a general way? In a technical way?

8. "As bank loans expand or contract, the volume of deposit liabilities and the reserve requirements of commercial banks change correspondingly." (H. V. Roelse, "The Money Market," *Money Market Essays* [New York: Federal Reserve Bank of New York, 1952], p. 5.) Explain. May there be exceptions?

9. "Banks have been in the spotlight because they are an *instrument* of inflation and because some people have confused the instrument with the *cause* of inflation." (Federal Reserve Bank of Philadelphia, *The Business Review*, April, 1948, p. 35.) Analyze this statement. What is the cause of inflation?

10. Explain why borrowing by businessmen from banks is inflationary. May the increase in money be offset by an increase in the volume of goods and services?

11. "To say that inflation threatens is alarming. But to say that bank deposits are rapidly increasing is not alarming at all. Most people fear the first statement and applaud the second, yet these words mean exactly the same thing." (Elmore Peterson, *Banking*, Sec. 2, October, 1935, p. 1.) What does Dean Peterson mean?

12. "The greatest factor in regulating banking operations is the confidence of the depositor. The depositor is our greatest control, for without him the system could not function." (James Muir, *The Canadian Banking System* [Toronto: The Royal Bank of Canada, 1948], p. 23.) Is this true in the United States, which, alone among the nations of the world, has deposit insurance?

13. It seems improbable that large changes in bank reserves are needed to maintain a stable growing stock of demand deposits. If wide changes in the volume of Federal Reserve credit are needed, it would be due to changes in the volume of paper money. Explain.

14. Analyze: "The significance of long-run growth in bank assets and deposits at rates approximating the average of recent years" . . . of 4.1 per cent "is to be regarded as normal and desirable, just as is similar growth in the nation's physical wealth and productive capacity." (*Annual Report of the Federal Deposit Insurance Corporation for the Year Ended December 31, 1954*, Washington, D.C., 1955, pp. 35–36.)

Chapter V   CLEARING AND COLLECTION OF CHECKS

PERSONAL checks, bank drafts, and similar orders to pay are widely acceptable as a means of payment even though they do not have the legal tender quality. The present general acceptability of check currency in the United States is due in part to the efficient check collection system, legal codes (all states have "bad check" laws), custom, and confidence in those who sign the orders to pay.

A commercial bank accepts demand deposits subject to the regulations prescribed by its board of directors and the bank is under moral obligation to investigate the character of each depositor. It is generally understood that the use of a checking account is a privilege reserved for those who are willing to abide by the rules pertaining thereto and these rules are formulated to insure the quality of the check currency system. Prompt presentation of all checks is the only way that good checks may be separated from bad ones—those written by individuals having no checking accounts or whose accounts are insufficient to cover the checks. This chapter deals with the clearing and collection of checks and other interbank transactions, as practiced in the United States.

DEPOSITS AND INSTRUMENTS OF TRANSFER

A check is most commonly defined as "a bill of exchange drawn on a bank payable on demand." The drawee must be a bank but the drawer may be an individual, a government, a corporation, or a bank. Checks drawn by one bank on another bank are called bank drafts; and they may be further identified as "on London," "on New York," and so on, or as "Federal Reserve bank drafts" as distinguished from those drawn on commercial banks. When the cashier of a bank draws a check on his own bank, it is called a "cashier's check."

Checks are but the instrument of transfer of title (the "bill of lading" and not the goods); it is bank credit that is transferred. When a check is canceled and the account debited, it usually means that the bank credit has been transferred to someone else rather than that the bank credit has been liquidated. Ordinarily, the payee prefers bank credit to coins and paper currency; and he leaves the check with his bank to be collected and credited to his checking account.

"Checkless" transfers of bank credit can and do take place. Telegraph, mail, cable, and wireless facilities are often used to transfer instructions to pay without the use of written credit instruments. For illustration, a request may be sent to the Chase-Manhattan Bank of New York by the Republic National Bank of Dallas to deposit a stated sum of money to the account of the Humble Oil Company with such additional instructions as are necessary. The Dallas bank, by using the wire services of the Federal Reserve System (described later in this chapter), will have funds with the Chase-Manhattan Bank which will be transferred to the account of the Humble Oil Company. Sometimes the instructions to transfer funds are sent by regular or air mail; and such transfers of funds without the use of negotiable credit instruments are common not only between banks in different cities of the United States but also between banks in cities in foreign countries.

Within banks, transfers of titles to deposits may take place without the use of checks or bank drafts. Banks commonly debit deposit accounts for service charges, rent on safe deposit boxes, and other amounts due to the banks. Institutions and corporations sometimes follow the practice of paying their employees by arranging with their banks to credit their employees' accounts with the appropriate monthly salaries and to debit the employers' accounts with the gross amounts transferred.

CLEARING AND COLLECTION OF CHECKS

Clearing Operations. When a check is written and deposited with a bank, the procedure which follows entails a payment or clearing operation and a collection operation. In order to economize in the use of funds in making payments, banks have developed a system of clearing—exchanging checks and other items held against each other, whereby credits and debits of the local banks are balanced and canceled and only the differences are settled. Sometimes the term "clearings" is used to refer to the gross value of items so exchanged.

Collection Operations. The individual items included in the gross value of clearings are not collected until each one is debited against the account of the drawer of the check. Usually, some items must be returned to the payees because some checks may be incorrectly drawn, the drawer may have no account with the bank drawn upon, or the deposit account may not be large enough to cover the amount of the check. The bank on which these dishonored checks are drawn will have a claim against the banks that presented them for payment; and such claims will be adjusted according to a prior arrangement.

Of the checks deposited with a bank, some may be drawn on the bank itself, others upon other local banks, and the remainder upon out-of-town banks; and all must be collected. Those drawn on the bank itself are sent to the bookkeeping department, where they are credited to and charged against individual accounts. The checks drawn on local banks are sent to the clearinghouse division to be arranged and prepared for the local clearinghouse. The checks drawn on out-of-town banks are sent to the transit department to be sorted and mailed to correspondent banks and/or to the district Federal Reserve bank.

Clearinghouse. A clearinghouse is an association of banks which is established to promote the interest of its members. The primary function of a clearinghouse is to facilitate the exchange of checks and other items (as agreed upon by members) and to settle any resulting balances. Of course, each bank could exchange all items directly with all the other banks in the community; but, in a community having ten banks, this would necessitate forty-five clearing and settling operations (nine for the first bank, eight for the second bank, and so on). If the ten banks participate in a clearinghouse arrangement and regard all their claims as being against the clearinghouse, the number of operations is reduced from forty-five to ten.

Clearing Process. In preparing for a clearing, each bank sorts and packages all clearinghouse items according to drawee banks, computes the total for each bank, and adds these figures to arrive at the sum due from the clearinghouse. At the appointed time, a clerk or messenger from each bank arrives at the designated office where the clearing is to take place and gives the clearinghouse manager a statement showing the total amount the clearinghouse owes his bank. After the manager adds the figures presented by the messengers, he will have the total of claims on the clearinghouse (total clearings). In the meantime, each bank's messenger will exchange his bank's clearinghouse items for each of those of other banks (the packages of checks and other items) and will add the figures he received. Then each messenger notifies the clearinghouse manager as to the amount his bank owes the clearinghouse. The manager adds these figures and checks the total against the claims on the clearinghouse. The total of the amounts (claims on) the clearinghouse must be the same as the total of the amounts owed to the clearinghouse. (Reading down under total credits or across for total debits in Table 4, gives the same amount.)

While the total "claims on" and "amounts owed to" the clearinghouse must be the same, this is not the case with individual banks; and ordinarily, the differences must be settled with money. While the manager is computing the total owed by the clearinghouse, each bank clerk will compute the "credit" or "debit" position of his bank by comparing the amount his bank owes to the clearinghouse to the total of his bank's claims against the clearinghouse. The total of "net credits" and "net debits" must be equal. (See Table 4.) In practice, the

TABLE 4

HYPOTHETICAL ILLUSTRATION OF CLEARING

Bank	1	2	3	4	5	Total Credits	Net Credits
1...................	....	$400	$350	$250	$200	$1,200	$100
2...................	$350	....	200	250	300	1,100	50
3...................	250	100	....	300	400	1,050	....
4...................	300	250	350	....	100	1,000	....
5...................	200	300	200	400	....	1,100	100
Total debits....	$1,100	$1,050	$1,100	$1,200	$1,000	$5,450	....
Net debits..........	....	....	$ 50	$ 200	....	....	$250

clearing operation is very simple and it usually takes but a few minutes.

Settling Process.   The task of settling is given to the clearinghouse manager who uses the method previously agreed upon by the members. One of the most popular methods is to use the facilities of the district Federal Reserve bank. Since all banks which are members of the Federal Reserve System must keep reserve deposits with their district Federal Reserve banks and since many nonmember banks keep "clearing balances" with these banks, these balances may be credited or debited according to a memorandum, letter, or simply a certified copy of the clearinghouse settling sheet sent to the Federal Reserve bank by the clearinghouse manager.

If balances are not settled through the Federal Reserve bank, the manager may be authorized to draw checks in favor of the creditor banks upon the debtor banks which are settled in currency or bank drafts. In some clearinghouse associations, members keep balances in the clearinghouse bank; the manager uses these balances to settle claims by crediting and debiting the accounts of banks according to the day's settlement-sheet record. The recommended practice is to settle the net amount owed or due on the books of the Federal Reserve bank or a correspondent bank on the same day.

Payment of Individual Items. As soon as the clearing process is completed (the settling process being left to the clearinghouse manager), the messengers return to their banks with the checks and other items received from other banks. These are taken to the bookkeeping department to be debited against the accounts of the appropriate depositors. If an item has been mis-sent, an account overdrawn, or any other mistake has been made, it is adjusted at a second clearing held later the same day. All dishonored checks and mis-sent items are sent back to the banks which presented them at the first clearing.

Trade Association Activities. In addition to clearing and settling functions, clearinghouse associations act on problems common to members. (Some so-called regional clearinghouse associations have been organized for purposes exclusive of clearing and settling.) Clearinghouse associations usually take action on many routine problems, such as the establishment of (1) banking hours, (2) clearinghouse meeting hours, (3) holidays, (4) methods of analyzing checking accounts for service charges, (5) amount of service charges and fees, and (6) basis for computing interest payments for time deposits and the rate to be paid.

Frequently clearinghouse associations operate credit bureaus in order to improve credit practices. In the past, clearinghouses frequently examined member institutions; but this practice has become less common because of the costs involved and the superior facilities of other bank-examining agencies. During money-market panics, these associations issued clearinghouse certificates, an emergency type of currency. (See accompanying illustration.)

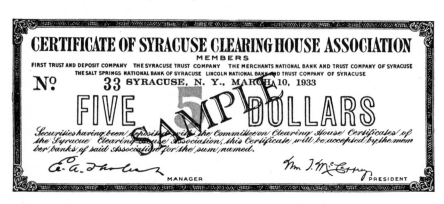

Clearinghouse associations have adopted policies governing the relationship of local banks to the public. They have adopted rules controlling methods and extent of advertising. In some communities, they have eliminated the "buying" of business by offering gifts, donations, and prizes. Mutual resistance has been made against "drive" committees and other pressure salesmen, and maximum donations have been fixed by clearinghouse rules. Educational work done by clearinghouse groups includes sponsoring thrift clubs and distributing home modernization plans, income-tax instructions, household budgets, and educational materials to school children and the public.

Cost of Operations Is Small. The clearing principle is hundreds of years old, but the first clearinghouse in the United States was not established until 1853. There may or may not be a clearinghouse building, although the term "clearinghouse" is commonly used to describe the place where the clearing is done. In many communities the place of the clearing is rotated among the members. A centrally located office may be rented when a number of nonclearing functions are to be performed. In Boston all the clearing functions for the clearinghouse are performed by the Federal Reserve Bank of Boston. The New York Clearinghouse owns its building, but hundreds of clearinghouses have little or no property other than the necessary office equipment, books, and stationery. Fees vary with the size of banks, volume of clearings, and amount of trade association activities, or nonclearing functions.

Control of the clearinghouse is placed in the hands of an executive committee. Officers—president, vice-president, secretary, treasurer, and manager—are elected or appointed. With, perhaps, the exception of the manager, they serve without pay. The president, vice-president, and members of the executive committee are usually key men in the banking community where the clearinghouse is located. Membership in clearinghouse associations is voluntary, but, in order to make the rules effective, the constituent banks' boards of directors agree, by resolution, to abide by its rules. Rules of the association provide that any penalty inflicted on a member bank becomes an enforceable claim against the bank.

Nearby Clearings. All local banks should participate directly in local clearings instead of depending on a clearinghouse member, as is done by some local banks. Since over 30 per cent of the out-of-town checks received by country banks for collection are drawn upon banks within a radius of twenty-five miles, many areas have set up a central clearing arrangement through which checks are presented to the drawees with settlement through a Federal Reserve bank or a correspondent bank. In other cases, where the volume of checks on nearby banks is large, the checks are mailed directly to the drawee banks for settlement. Direct presentation not only reduces the number of times that checks are handled but also speeds up the collection process. For most out-of-town checks direct routing to the drawee banks is impractical and so banks depend upon either their correspondent banks or the Federal Reserve bank to collect most of their out-of-town checks.

CORRESPONDENT BANKING

A correspondent bank is one which maintains reciprocal business relations with a bank in another city. Although the two banks participating in a correspondent banking relationship may be approximately the same size, usually one bank is much larger than the other and located so as to give financial services desired by the smaller bank. This means that services given by the larger bank tend to be dominant in the mutual arrangement and that the smaller bank usually reciprocates by keeping a deposit with the larger bank. Among the services most commonly given are (1) handling checks and other credit instruments on a reciprocal basis, and (2) other interbank transactions in which the larger bank acts as a bankers' bank for the smaller bank.

Clearing and Collection of Out-of-Town Checks. The basic need of banks for out-of-town banking services is traced to the desire to give customers better banking services.[1] When a business firm buys goods outside the community, its bank is called upon to settle for checks deposited in out-of-town banks. At the same time, a bank customer expects his bank to collect all checks and other items deposited which are drawn on banks located in other communities. Therefore banks are confronted with the problem of collecting checks drawn upon banks located in distant places as well as those drawn upon local banks.

The clearing and collection of out-of-town items require sorting of items by the transit department and mailing them to correspondent banks according to previously made arrangements covering credits,

---

[1] Before the Civil War, banks kept balances with New York and other metropolitan banks and used their services to collect checks and bank notes, to make call loans, and to purchase open-market commercial paper. In lending, banks sometimes gave borrowers drafts drawn on New York (or Boston, Philadelphia, etc.) banks rather than bank notes or bank credit; and, when these loans came due, the banks insisted on being paid with New York (or Boston, Philadelphia, etc.) drafts.

minimum balances, fees, and other charges (these are similar to rules covering deposits of ordinary business firms). Obviously, it is important to present checks and other items promptly to the banks on which they are drawn. Without this prompt testing of checks, there would be a deterioration of the quality of the money supply, for it would contain worthless checks and other items for weeks or months. Today, many large banks keep their transit departments functioning day and night; and, in some small communities, groups of banks are doing the same thing on a co-operative basis.

When a bank sends a check to a correspondent bank for collection, it usually receives immediate credit even though the check will not be paid by the drawer's bank until later. (This is similar to the immediate credit for checking purposes that most individuals are given when they deposit checks in their banks.) The correspondent bank may present the item to the drawer's bank indirectly through the clearinghouse if drawn on a local bank. However, if the drawer's bank is located in another city, the correspondent may deposit the check with the Federal Reserve bank for collection, mail it to its correspondent in the area where the drawer's bank is located, or send it directly to the bank on which it is drawn for payment.

Noncollection Functions. A bank may keep a deposit with a second bank for the same reasons that any depositor keeps an account with his bank—as a means of payment. A bank in Austin, Texas, may write checks (bank drafts) on its deposit in a New York bank in order to buy bills, notes, government bonds, and other types of assets; or the Austin bank may sell bank drafts on its account with the New York bank to customers. In many communities there are individuals and business firms that have obligations to meet in other cities. Their personal checks may or may not be acceptable; in the latter case, they may obtain bank drafts from their local banks. Thus, a merchant in Austin who has an obligation of $100.00 in New York, could obtain a draft from his Austin bank by paying $100.10, the 10 cents being an exchange charge.

A correspondent bank may provide its customer-bank with services other than those associated with clearing and collecting checks. Among these services are (1) giving advice on investments, loans, collection procedures, insurance protection, advertising, accounting and auditing practices, pension and profit-sharing plans, job analysis, equipment, taxes, and other bank problems; (2) acting as agent in making loans and investments; (3) providing credit information on firms that borrow in the open market; (4) providing foreign exchange facilities, including commercial and travelers' letters of credit and travelers' checks;[2] and (5) providing funds (loans) in case of need.

Today New York banks are acting as correspondents for banks in hundreds of other cities; and some of them hold deposit accounts of hundreds of customer banks. Banks in other large cities are acting as correspondents for banks in smaller cities; and those in small cities are acting as correspondents for banks in towns and villages. In practice a bank may be keeping bankers' balances, also called interbank deposits, with several different banks at the same time. As a result, a complex voluntary working relationship among banks blankets the country; and since certain metropolitan banks (sometimes called "international" banks) have extended these arrangements to include banks in foreign countries, the correspondent banking system has become international in scope of operations.

CLEARING, COLLECTION, AND TRANSFER SERVICES OF THE FEDERAL RESERVE SYSTEM

The Federal Reserve System, in addition to its responsibility for the flow of money expenditures, helps to improve the quality of money by providing for economical and prompt clearing and collection of checks and noncash items (which include matured notes, drafts, and matured securities except government obligations which are handled by the Federal Reserve banks as fiscal agents for the government). The Federal Reserve System's procedure for settling balances among banks has practically eliminated the need for shipping currency.

Par Collection of Checks. A Federal Reserve bank may receive checks for collection from member banks and clearing nonmember banks if such checks are collectible at par in funds acceptable to the Federal Reserve banks. This means that a bank using the collection services of the Federal Reserve System must remit at par for checks in funds acceptable to the System when the checks are presented by mail as well as when presented over the counter.

Before the existence of the Federal Reserve System, it was a common practice for banks to remit (pay) less than the stated amount for checks presented by mail. If a check for $100.00 was presented, the drawer's account was debited for that amount but only $99.90 was remitted to the presenting bank in payment. The drawer's bank

---

[2] Commercial and travelers' letters of credit and travelers' checks and their uses are discussed in Chapter XVII.

kept the 10 cents, calling it an exchange charge, and the payee's bank charged the 10 cents to the payee's account (in some cases, the payee's bank absorbed the charge). The important thing to note is that merchants and others who accepted checks drawn on nonpar banks were paid in inferior money—money at a discount from face value.

Nonpar Banks. Although the Federal Reserve System has made a great deal of progress in eliminating all money circulating at a discount in the United States, there are still 1,775 small banks on the nonpar list. (These banks hold about 2 per cent of all commercial bank deposits.) Since regulations of the Board of Governors of the Federal Reserve System do not permit the Federal Reserve banks to handle checks of nonpar banks, all banks using the collection services of the System are provided with the names of all nonpar banks. Since 1938, member banks have been prohibited from absorbing the discount on checks. In order to protect businessmen and others, some states have enacted laws forbidding banks to remit at less than par. To protect themselves, some businessmen stamp their statements to out-of-town customers "Payable only in New York exchange or checks cleared at par" (but when sellers receive checks on nonpar banks, they may hesitate to refuse them for fear of losing customers).

The adverse effects of nonpar remittance for checks include: (1) increasing the costs of sorting, routing, and handling checks; (2) forcing some banks to forego, in part, the use of the free collection and clearing services of the Federal Reserve System; and (3) lowering the quality of checkbook money by placing a burden on those receiving nonpar checks. The correct procedure for any commercial bank to follow is to remit at par and then to adopt a system of service and collection charges to compensate for the loss in revenue.

More Direct Check Routing. The Federal Reserve System has improved the quality of checkbook money not only by working toward the reduction in the number of nonpar banks but also by eliminating a great deal of time-consuming check routing. Perhaps the need that existed for more direct check routing is best shown by the illustration which appeared in Volume VI of the publications of the National Monetary Commission:

The check, which was for $43.56, was drawn by Woodward Brothers, of Sag Harbor, N.Y., and paid to Berry, Lohman & Rasch, of Hoboken, N.J., who deposited it in the Second National Bank of Hoboken. This bank sent it to Harvey Fisk & Sons, of New York, who, having no regular correspondent in the neighborhood of the bank on which it was drawn, sent it, along with other collections, to their Boston correspondent, the Globe National Bank. The Globe National Bank of

Boston, for reasons that are not apparent, sent it, presumably with other items, to its correspondent at Tonawanda, N.Y., viz, the First National Bank of that city. The Tonawanda bank, evidently realizing that the check had wandered far out of its course, and in an effort to get it nearer home, transmitted it to the National Exchange Bank of Albany, which institution, pursuing the same commendable policy, remitted it to its correspondent at Port Jefferson. The First National Bank of Port Jefferson, which thus got possession of the check, again diverted its course by inclosing it to the Far Rockaway Bank. The Far Rockaway Bank sent it back to New York, to the Chase National Bank, and thus this much-traveled check made its second call in the metropolis. The Chase National Bank, it would appear, endeavored to correct the wanderer's course, and so dispatched it to Riverhead, to H. M. Reeve.

Mr Reeve, either because he really knew where to send it for collection, or because of a lucky hit, forwarded it to the Queens County Bank of Brooklyn, which finally sent it home to the Peconic Bank of Sag Harbor, on which it was drawn. . . . The reader may estimate for himself the volume of correspondence which this check caused . . . and the amount of postage and cost of clerical work expended upon it.[3]

Intra- and Interdistrict Collection. Today, member banks and others using the Federal Reserve System collection facilities route their checks so that they usually go directly to the district Federal Reserve bank or one of its branches. A check may be drawn on a bank located in the same Federal Reserve district or on one located in a second Federal Reserve district. Checks received by a Federal Reserve bank which are payable in its own district are ordinarily forwarded or presented for payment directly to the banks on which they are drawn (intradistrict). Checks drawn on banks in a second Federal Reserve district are ordinarily forwarded for collection to the Federal Reserve bank of the district in which they are payable (interdistrict).

Sometimes arrangements are made whereby the Federal Reserve banks sends interdistrict checks directly to the banks on which they are drawn, with the second Federal Reserve bank being advised of the transaction. This type of direct routing appears most commonly when the drawer's bank is located in adjacent territory (as from the Federal Reserve Bank of New York directly across the district line to a bank located in northeastern Pennsylvania). This direct routing saves both time and handling by a second Federal Reserve bank.

By using air shipments between Federal Reserve banks and their

[3] J. G. Cannon (National Monetary Commission), "Clearing Houses," *Clearing Houses and Credit Instruments* (Washington, D.C.: U.S. Government Printing Office, 1911), Vol. VI, pp. 70–74.

branches, most interdistrict checks are presented to the second Federal Reserve bank (weather permitting) within hours after they have been forwarded by the first Federal Reserve bank. However, there still remains the problem of forwarding or presenting the check to the drawer's bank for payment as in the case of an intradistrict check.

Since checks written daily number in the millions, any possible reduction in the number of times checks are handled is a boon to banking. Increasing emphasis is being placed on even more direct routing of checks than that already provided by the Federal Reserve and other banks. Among the suggestions made which pertain to intradistrict checks are (1) where volume justifies doing so, send items directly to drawer's banks in adjacent areas of adjoining districts; (2) make direct air shipments of checks to financial centers where there is no Federal Reserve bank or branch; and (3) use the Federal Reserve System to collect all interdistrict items.

For intradistrict items, it has been suggested that checks drawn on commercial banks in a Federal Reserve city be sent to the correspondents of the country banks in that city for collection through the clearinghouse. For other intradistrict checks, it is proposed that checks be sent to the Federal Reserve banks with the privilege of crediting the proceeds to the account of a correspondent bank if the sending bank so desires.[4]

Time Schedules and Availability of Credit. Federal Reserve banks give either immediate credit or deferred credit for checks received according to time schedules, which are based on broad geographical areas where the items are collectible. Each Reserve bank and branch has its own schedule, which indicates when checks will be credited to the reserve balances (or clearing accounts of nonmember banks) of the banks that deposit them for collection.

As a rule, checks that are drawn on banks in cities where the collecting Reserve bank or branch is located are given immediate credit and others are given deferred credit. Some items that are automatically given immediate credit according to the time schedule will not be collected immediately. Therefore, "cash items in process of collection" is larger than "deferred availability cash items." Part of this difference is due to the fact that the time schedule is not realistic since it gives deferred credit for no longer than two days. For illustration, checks deposited in the Federal Reserve Bank of Dallas, which are collected through a second Federal Reserve bank, cannot be collected in two days.

[4] "Speeding Up Check Collection," *Banking* (January, 1956), pp. 42–43.

The American Bankers Association has developed symbols, printed on most checks, that aid in sorting and collection. The symbol is a fraction with the denominator being the routing part. When there are three digits in the denominator the first one indicates the Federal Reserve districts 1 through 9, and when there are four digits the first two indicate Federal Reserve districts 10, 11, and 12 (10 for Kansas City, 11 for Dallas, and 12 for San Francisco). The next digit (second if there are three digits, third if four) indicates the Federal Reserve bank office (1 for the head office, 2 to 5 for branches arranged alphabetically, and 5 to 9 designate special collection arrangements). The last digit indicates immediate (0) or deferred credit (1 to 9). Since credit is given within two days, numbers beyond 2 are not significant. Thus, if the denominator if 220, the check is drawn on a bank located in the Second Federal Reserve district (New York), is collectible at the Buffalo branch, and will receive immediate credit. The part of the fraction above the line (numerator) is the transit number that identifies the bank. A routing symbol is assigned to each bank using the collection services of Federal Reserve banks.

While most of the difference between the "cash items in process of collection" and "deferred availability cash items" is traceable to unrealistic time schedules, part of this difference may be due to delays in remittance for local items for which immediate credit is given. While ultimately most collection items are settled by debiting the drawer's bank account at the Federal Reserve bank after the drawer's bank remits in payment, any delay in remitting increases the spread or "float." (On December 28, 1955 because of weather conditions and delayed train and airplane schedules, the excess of "uncollected cash items" over "deferred availability cash items" reached the unusual figure of about $1.9 billion.)

Remittance for Checks. When a Federal Reserve bank collects checks it may accept in payment drafts, authorizations to charge, or other orders drawn on the drawer's bank's balance at the Federal Reserve bank.[5] Ordinarily, all remittances are settled ultimately by debiting the account of the drawer's bank. (The drawer's bank, in turn, will debit the account of the drawer.) Each check collected through the district Federal Reserve bank for banks within that district will increase one bank's balance and decrease a second bank's balance. This

---

[5] Banks are requested to remit payment on date of receipt and are provided with special stamped envelopes for this purpose. Amounts are deducted from the preceding remittances for items returned the next day. The Federal Reserve bank will "charge" the account of the endorser for the items not paid and return them to the endorser. There is no protest on items less than $500, and policy varies for larger amounts.

means that each Federal Reserve bank acts as a clearinghouse and paying center for clearing banks within its district.

Interdistrict Settlement.   Ordinarily, when a Federal Reserve bank receives a check drawn on a bank in another Federal Reserve district, the receiving Reserve bank will send it directly to the Federal Reserve bank or branch of the district where the drawer's bank is located. The depositing bank (usually the payee's bank or its correspondent bank) will receive "deferred" and then "immediate" credit, according to the time schedule of the first Federal Reserve bank as noted above. The second Federal Reserve bank will forward the check to the drawer's bank and collect as noted above. This Federal Reserve bank now owes the first Federal Reserve bank the amount of the check. Instead of remitting drafts in payment for this and other items that create obligations among the twelve Federal Reserve banks, they are settled through the facilities of the Interdistrict Settlement Fund (also called the Gold Certificate Fund).

The Interdistrict Settlement Fund is managed by the Board of Governors in Washington and is financed by the twelve Federal Reserve banks. It was created in 1915, and each Reserve bank placed a minimum of $1,000,000 in the Fund. The Federal Reserve banks and the clearing branches are linked to the Board of Governors by a private wire system.

At the close of each business day, each Federal Reserve bank and its clearing branches notify the Interdistrict Settlement Fund of the net amounts due to the accounts of each of the other Federal Reserve banks and their branches as a result of clearings on that day. The accounts of the other banks are credited and that of the sending bank is debited. Wires are received from the other Federal Reserve banks and branches, and these are treated similarly. Although all wires are sent at the close of business, they arrive at different hours in Washington because of different time zones.

In accordance with the telegrams received, each Federal Reserve bank's share in the total of the Interdistrict Settlement Fund will be changed; and, before the start of the next business day each bank and branch will be notified by wire as to the amount paid to it by each of the others. Branches do not actually participate in the Fund and their position is netted along with the head office in making final settlement. Settlement is made by transferring ownership of gold certificates on the books of the Interdistrict Settlement Fund. While an agent of the Board of Governors of the Federal Reserve System keeps the books, the gold-certificate fund is held by the Treasurer of the United States for the Federal Reserve banks. The share of each Reserve bank is counted as part of its legal reserve maintained against its deposit liabilities and Federal Reserve notes outstanding.

The Interdistrict Settlement Fund, in addition to being the agency through which the settlement of balances resulting from the interdistrict collection of checks is effected, is used to settle other interdistrict payments resulting from (1) wire and mail transfers of both Federal Reserve banks' and commercial banks' balances; (2) the collection of noncash items such as maturing notes and acceptances, state and municipal warrants, drafts, and orders on savings deposits, maturing bonds and coupons other than United States government obligations which are redeemed by Federal Reserve banks in their capacity as fiscal agents for the United States government; and (3) United States Treasury transfers.

If the United States Treasury receipts from borrowing and/or taxes in one Federal Reserve district are in excess of expenditures and the Treasury desires to transfer them from one district to another, the movement is effected by the transfer of gold certificates from the account of one Federal Reserve bank to the credit of the second Federal Reserve bank on the books of the Settlement Fund.

Any member bank or clearing nonmember bank may make arrangements with a Reserve bank to draw drafts against it. These drafts may be used to meet collection charges and other obligations at the Reserve banks. A member bank may also sell "Federal Reserve exchange drafts," which will be accepted by any Federal Reserve bank or branch. In using such a draft the issuing bank notifies its Federal Reserve bank on a special form prepared for this purpose, and the Reserve bank immediately debits the account of the bank for the amount sent.

Federal Reserve banks transfer money by telegraph at the request of their member banks. All Reserve banks are linked by their own wire system, and this service is available without cost if the amounts transferred are in round numbers of $100 or multiples thereof. For example, if Chicago Bank A wants to send $1,000,000 to New York Bank B, it will notify the Reserve Bank of Chicago to debit its account and transfer the sum to the Reserve Bank of New York for the credit of Bank B. The transfer takes but a few minutes, and funds which otherwise would be idle may be put to work immediately. These transfers are made by code in order to lessen the dangers of fraudulent transfers and payment of funds to the wrong party.

Federal Reserve banks also use commercial wires to transfer odd or even amounts for the accounts of banks, individuals, firms, or corporations. They make no charge other than the cost of the necessary telegram. Thus, merely by paying for the commercial wire, a member bank may make specific and immediate transfers of funds for its customers to distant places within the United States. Additional transfers are made over the private wire facilities of commercial banks and over those of commercial companies.

Collection of Noncash Items. The Federal Reserve System may also collect noncash items which include practically all matured credit instruments except (1) those handled as cash items, (2) checks and drafts drawn on and payable by nonmember banks which do not remit at par in funds acceptable to the Federal Reserve banks, and (3) obligations of the federal government and agencies which are redeemed by the Reserve banks as fiscal agents. In handling noncash items, Reserve banks act as agents. Usually items payable in other districts are collected through the Federal Reserve bank of that district. The form of payment may be cash, checks, bank drafts, transfers of bank credit, or other forms of remittance acceptable to the collecting Reserve bank. Reserve banks may collect for their expenses and for any losses sustained. This service is given to member banks, clearing nonmember banks, other Federal Reserve banks, and the United States Treasury and government agencies (under fiscal agency arrangements).

Postal Money Order Procedure. On July 1, 1951, a plan to handle money orders like checks became effective. These orders, not drawn on any particular post office, may be cashed at any post office or bank within one year after the date of issue. After being cashed these orders are deposited with a Federal Reserve bank or branch, where they are processed and the amounts are charged to the account of the Treasurer of the United States; and then they are sent to the regional accounting office of the Post Office Department in the Federal Reserve city of that district.

In the collection procedure, punch-proof machines designed and installed for this purpose are used. Orders are printed on "card" checks, prepunched with a serial number and the number of the twelve Post Office regions (which conform generally to Federal Reserve districts). The operator feeds a machine which lists the amount on tape, punches the amount in the order, and sorts the orders by Post Office regions.

SUMMARY

Clearinghouses were first organized as laborsaving associations; but they soon became the agencies through which banks co-operated on problems of common interest. By the very nature of banking, this covered not only problems among bankers themselves but also most of those associated with their contacts with the general public. In many fields, federal legislation leaves the final decisions to local bankers. This is illustrated by interest rate regulations, wherein federal legislation has defined deposits eligible for receiving interest and the maximum rates that may be paid; but the actual rate paid is usually decided by local clearinghouse members.

Commercial banks, in co-operation with each other and with the Federal Reserve banks, have contributed to improving the deposit currency system of the nation. Banks clear and collect checks and other items through local clearinghouses, correspondent banks, and the Federal Reserve banks. As a result, the personal check is a means of payment that is cleared at par anywhere in the United States, except for a small number of banks whose checks circulate at a discount in distant places because these banks do not remit at par.

The contribution of the Federal Reserve System in providing the country with better currency and greater mobility of credit includes such services as accepting, handling, and forwarding for collection cash items such as checks, matured drafts and government coupons, and noncash items such as promissory notes, bankers' acceptances, bonds, and other credit instruments.

By the use of the Federal Reserve exchange services, funds may be transferred among banks either in the form of items to be sent by mail or orders sent by wire. Each Federal Reserve bank acts as a regional settlement center for paying credit instruments; and the Board of Governors operates two settlement funds—the Federal Reserve Agents Settlement Fund, and the vastly more important Interdistrict Settlement Fund which settles balances resulting between Reserve banks. The use of the Federal Reserve System's wire service permits the transfer of large sums almost instantaneously anywhere in the United States.

QUESTIONS AND PROBLEMS

1. Define: (*a*) bank draft, (*b*) cashier's check, (*c*) checkless transfer, and (*d*) dishonored checks.
2. Identify: (*a*) clearing operations, (*b*) collection operations, (*c*) clearinghouse, and (*d*) correspondent banking.
3. What items are cleared through a clearinghouse? How are balances settled? Why must total credits and debits balance? Why must "net credits" and "net debits" balance?

4. What is meant by "member bank reserves are credited items rather than collected items"?

5. Distinguish between (*a*) par collection and nonpar collection, (*b*) cash items and noncash items, and (*c*) district and interdistrict clearing and collection of checks.

6. Identify: (*a*) transfer items, (*b*) "card checks," and (*c*) Interdistrict Settlement Fund.

7. Distinguish between exchange charges and collection charges. Compare to service charges on deposit accounts.

8. What specific regulatory functions are performed by clearinghouse associations? Other associations of banks?

9. "The establishment of the Interdistrict Settlement Fund of the Federal Reserve System and the provision for daily inter-regional settlements through the Fund have made it possible for commercial banks to effect almost immediate telegraphic transfer of funds across the country for their own accounts or for the accounts of their customers." (Joint Committee on Economic Report, *Monetary Policy and Management of the Public Debt* [Washington, D.C.: U.S. Government Printing Office, 1952], Part 1, p. 529.) Explain.

10. "Acting in their capacity as fiscal agents of the United States, on July 1, 1951, the Reserve Banks began processing punch card postal money orders, using specially designed equipment. They handled approximately 175 million money orders during the last six months of the year." (*Thirty-eighth Annual Report of the Board of Governors of the Federal Reserve System Covering Operations for the Year 1951* [Washington, D.C., 1952], p. 46.) What does this mean?

11. Customarily commercial banks give depositors immediate credit for checks. Do you think the Federal Reserve System's policy of giving "deferred credit" for the same items is justified? Why?

12. "In this period [1939–1952] the number of checks written annually grew from an estimated 3.5-billion to nearly 8-billion a year. Should the trend of this period continue, 14-billion would be written in 1960, and by 1970 check volume would be 22-billion." (John A. Kley, "Mechanization of Check Handling," *Banking*, February, 1956, p. 60.) What are the suggested solutions for this problem?

13. "Mr. Willis (vice-president of the Federal Reserve Bank of New York) said: 'We could never handle the number of checks we do— 3,000,000 some days this week—without the check routing symbol. . . .'" *New York Times*, June 26, 1956, p. 37. What is the check routing symbol? Explain each digit of a typical symbol.

Chapter VI ⎰ PAPER CURRENCY, COINS, AND GOLD

PRIOR TO 1933, exchangeability or convertibility of all kinds of money in gold or its equivalent was one of the most generally accepted tests of a good monetary system. Owing to the experiences of the United States during the early 1930's, the current emphasis seems to be on a monetary system which provides for the exchangeability or convertibility of checkbook money in currency (legal tender money). Demonetization of gold coins and liberalization of the conditions under which new currency and commercial bank reserves may be obtained seem to support this conclusion. The chief advantage of the new monetary system is that the liquidity of banks is assured, but the inherent danger is that the money supply may be expanded far more rapidly than production with inflationary effects on the economy. But, under any circumstances, considerable importance must be attributed to the conditions under which new currency is provided and old currency is replaced—the subject matter of this chapter.

DISTRIBUTION OF CURRENCY

Individuals, businessmen, and others receive paper money and coins in payment of goods and services, as gifts, or in payment for checks cashed. When an additional amount of currency is needed for payrolls, trade, etc., such funds are supplied by commercial banks.

During each business day, there is a flow of currency to and from banks. All commercial banks offer regular depository services during banking hours, and most banks have installed night depositories to give their customers a satisfactory means of protecting their cash receipts after banking hours. So most of the currency in the United States passes in and out of banks regularly, and the currency coming into banks is sorted and the worn pieces are sent back to the Federal Reserve banks along with those types of currency which are being retired.

Member banks are encouraged to send all redundant currency

back to the Federal Reserve banks because the latter pay all the costs of shipping currency to and from them. (For illustration, after the Christmas holidays, millions of dollars in currency are sent back to the Federal Reserve banks.) Of course, the member banks' legal reserve positions are enhanced when currency shipments are received and the amounts credited to their reserve accounts. Throughout the year, Federal Reserve banks accept deposits from member banks, clearing nonmember banks, the United States Treasury, certain governmental agencies and corporations, and foreign governments and central banks; and some of these deposits are in the form of coins and paper money. As in the case of commercial banks, there is a normal flow of currency in and out of the Federal Reserve banks. This raises the question: "Where do the Federal Reserve banks get new currency to replace worn-out currency and to meet the demand for additional coins and paper money?"

Sources of New Currency. New currency comes from two sources: (1) the United States Treasury and (2) issues of Federal Reserve notes by the Federal Reserve banks. When the United States Treasury issues additional coins or silver certificates, they are customarily deposited in Federal Reserve banks for credit to the account of the Treasury. When there is a general demand for additional currency, this Treasury currency may be used. If paper money is requested by the commercial banks, the supply of new silver certificates may not be adequate; and so the Reserve banks will issue Federal Reserve notes—our most important type of paper money in circulation.

Federal Reserve notes make up about 85 per cent of the currency in circulation, other forms of paper money (chiefly silver certificates) make up about 9 per cent, and coins make up about 6 per cent. Although these percentages change throughout the year, they represent what tends to be the average, with a tendency for Federal Reserve notes to be relatively more important and the other forms relatively less important.

FEDERAL RESERVE NOTES

Provisions for Issue and Retirement of Federal Reserve Notes. In Chart 5 the procedure for issue and retirement of Federal Reserve notes is illustrated. Federal Reserve notes, printed by the Bureau of Engraving and Printing, are kept in Treasury vaults; and, within the Treasury Department, the Federal Reserve Issue and Redemption Division of the Office of the Comptroller of the Currency acts as custodian for the notes. This division issues the notes to the Board of

Governors, where they are held until requisitioned by the Federal Reserve agent of the Federal Reserve bank for which they were printed. The Federal Reserve agent is responsible for the notes which he issues to his Federal Reserve bank in exchange for 100-per-cent collateral in the form of gold certificates, United States government securities, and/or commercial paper eligible for discount by the Federal Reserve banks.[1] The Reserve banks then use these notes to meet member banks' requests for currency. Member banks put them into circulation when they cash checks, make up payrolls, provide merchants with cash, and otherwise meet the demand of customers for currency.

Retirement of Federal Reserve notes involves the steps outlined above in reverse. When the notes are returned to their Federal Reserve banks by the member banks, they are sorted as "fit" and "unfit" currency. As is indicated by Chart 5, "unfit" notes are sent to the Office of the Comptroller of the Currency for redemption.

Each Federal Reserve bank must keep a sum of gold certificates sufficient, in the judgment of the Secretary of the Treasury, for the redemption of its notes in Washington. In no event may the sum of gold certificates be less than 5 per cent of the total amount of notes issued less the amount of gold certificates held by the Federal Reserve agent as collateral security. However, these gold certificates are also counted as part of the 25-per-cent gold certificate reserve that the Federal Reserve bank must keep against its Federal Reserve notes in circulation.

Prior to 1954, any Federal Reserve bank that paid out notes of a second Federal Reserve bank was subject to a 10-per-cent tax on such notes.[2] This necessitated sorting all notes received according to the name of each Federal Reserve bank and shipping those of other Federal Reserve banks to the banks of issue or to the Redemption Fund in Washington. The provision for this tax was repealed by Congress

---

[1] Eligible paper consists of notes, drafts, bills of exchange or acceptances, acquired under provisions of Section 13 of the Federal Reserve Act, and bills of exchange endorsed by a member bank or bankers' acceptances purchased under provisions of Section 14 of the Federal Reserve Act.

[2] While this provision was in effect, there was only one case wherein a Federal Reserve bank willingly issued notes of other Federal Reserve banks and paid the penalty tax for doing so. In 1953, the Federal Reserve Bank of Kansas City made available $600,000 in notes of all twelve Federal Reserve banks as demanded by the kidnappers of Bobby Greenlease and paid a penalty tax of $57,000 (a mere formality because most of the earnings of Federal Reserve banks are paid to the United States Treasury). The kidnapped boy was murdered and the kidnappers were caught and executed and about one half of the ransom money was recovered.

CHART 5

ISSUE AND RETIREMENT OF FEDERAL RESERVE NOTES

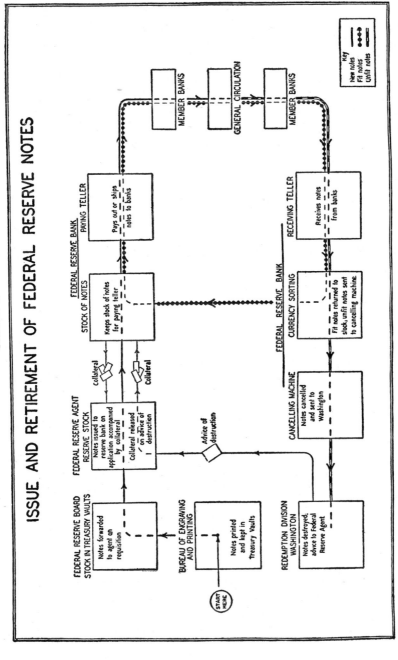

Source: *The Federal Reserve System Today* (New York: Federal Reserve Bank of New York, 1936), p. 27.

in 1954; and, now Federal Reserve banks may pay out the notes of other Federal Reserve banks without being penalized. Originally, the restriction on using the notes of one Federal Reserve bank by another Reserve bank was considered to be an anti-inflationary device to force the redemption of paper money; but, in effect, it was not and it served no useful purpose.

In the United States inflation tends to come from an overexpansion of deposit currency with the volume of currency in circulation tending to increase with the volume of deposit currency; but the increase in currency in circulation tends to follow the increase in deposit currency rather than to precede it. Expansion in the volume of member banks' credit is based upon reserve deposits in the Federal Reserve banks; and, since a demand by the public for more hand-to-hand money tends to reduce these reserves, an increase in the amount of money in the hands of the public tends to reduce the volume of deposit currency. In a country such as the United States, the monetary authorities give primary attention to the management of deposit currency and allow the volume of hand-to-hand currency to expand and contract without interference.

Federal Reserve Agents' Settlement Fund. The repeal of the 10-per-cent tax on paying out notes of a second Federal Reserve bank has reduced the daily shipments of Federal Reserve notes among Federal Reserve banks, but there will always be a problem of settling claims of Federal Reserve banks arising out of the redemption of worn or "unfit" Federal Reserve notes. The need for a central redemption center led to the creation of the Federal Reserve Agents' Fund in Washington, where daily settlement is made by crediting and debiting each Federal Reserve agent's account. Sums involved are much smaller than those in the Interdistrict Settlement Fund discussed in the preceding chapter.

Federal Reserve Agents' Accounts. Federal Reserve notes are properly regarded as central bank currency, but they are also promises to pay of the United States government. In placing the notes in circulation, the Board of Governors of the Federal Reserve System (also called the Federal Reserve Board) acts for the government. The Board has a Federal Reserve agent in each Federal Reserve bank to act for the Board of Governors. Each agent must hold 100 per cent collateral for all Federal Reserve notes released to his Federal Reserve bank. The combined statement of notes issued to the Federal Reserve banks and the collateral held against them appears as Table 5 (called "Federal Reserve Agents' Accounts"). These statements are attached to the Statements of Condition of Federal Reserve banks which are published in the *Federal Reserve Bulletin*.

Table 5 indicates how unimportant eligible paper is as collateral for Federal Reserve notes. Originally, it was assumed that this type of collateral would be most important, but now the portfolios of the Federal Reserve banks are dominated by federal government direct

TABLE 5

FEDERAL RESERVE AGENTS' ACCOUNTS FOR FEDERAL RESERVE BANKS
(In millions of dollars)
June 30, 1956

Item	Amount
Federal Reserve notes issued to Federal Reserve banks	$27,178
Collateral held:	
Gold certificates	11,478
Eligible paper	79
United States government securities	16,935
Total held	$28,492

Source: *Federal Reserve Bulletin*, July, 1956, p. 719.

obligations which are used as collateral. Gold certificates count both as collateral security and as reserves. Since the current legal reserve requirement is 25 per cent, over one half of the gold certificates could be freed in case of need by substituting other collateral for gold certificates. The Federal Reserve agents hold the government securities in trust and all income on them is paid to the Federal Reserve banks. (Securities may be pledged without transfer of title.)

Changes in Collateral Requirements. Prior to February, 1932, the only collateral the Federal Reserve agents were permitted to accept in exchange for Federal Reserve notes was gold or gold certificates and eligible paper. Because the volume of eligible paper in the hands of the Federal Reserve banks was small during the 1930–33 business depression, the banks were using gold and gold certificates as collateral; therefore, much of the gold stock was tied up and could not be used as a basis for new issues of Federal Reserve notes or as reserves for member-banks and other deposits with the Federal Reserve banks. In February, 1932, the law was changed to permit the use of government securities as collateral for Federal Reserve notes; but a great deal of harm had already been done because the Federal Reserve banks did not have free gold reserves to use as a basis for central bank credit expansion.

Changes in Reserve Requirements. The original Federal Reserve Act required each Federal Reserve bank to keep a 40-per-cent reserve against Federal Reserve notes in circulation in the form of gold and/or gold certificates and a 35-per-cent reserve against deposits in the form of lawful money (interpreted to mean all forms of United States currency except national bank notes, Federal Reserve notes, Federal Reserve bank notes, and subsidiary silver and minor coins). Congress, by the Act of June 12, 1945, provided that

Every Federal Reserve bank shall maintain reserves in gold certificates of not less than 25 per centum against its deposits and reserves in gold certificates of not less than 25 per centum against its Federal Reserve notes in actual circulation. . . .

The changes in minimum reserve requirements for Federal Reserve banks were made during World War II and they were obviously a war measure designed to remove the restraining influence of the larger reserve requirements previously in effect. The provisions for the redemption funds held by the Treasury to redeem Federal Reserve notes were not changed and they still contain the words "gold certificates or lawful money."

The word "reserves" customarily means assets which may be used to meet specific liabilities when and if necessary. As the law now stands in the United States, gold certificates, which are the basic reserves for deposits and notes of the Federal Reserve banks, may not be used legally to meet the domestic obligations of the Federal Reserve banks. Other kinds of United States currency, which cannot be counted as legal reserves of the Federal Reserve banks, are used to meet domestic obligations. Gold is used by the Federal Reserve banks to meet demands of foreign governments and foreign central banks (see Chapter VII).

The present reserve situation is both confusing and illogical. It could be corrected by (1) requiring each Federal Reserve bank to redeem its demand liabilities in gold certificates, gold coins, or gold bars; (2) permitting each Federal Reserve bank to hold its legal reserves in the form of gold and United States Treasury currency (see next section); or (3) adopting an inconvertible paper money standard and requiring each Federal Reserve bank to keep its minimum required reserves in some type of legal tender money printed and distributed by the United States government.

UNITED STATES TREASURY CURRENCY

Federal Reserve notes are issued in denominations of from $5 to $10,000; and the need for smaller denomination currency is met by United States Treasury issues of coins and paper money. In addition to silver certificates, United States notes, and coins, the statistics of Treasury currency include remnants of obsolete but not extinct forms of currency, namely national bank notes, Treasury notes of 1890, Federal Reserve bank notes, and gold certificates.

United States Subsidiary Coins. During the early history of the United States, both gold and silver coins were full-bodied money; but today gold coins have been demonetized and silver coins are subsidiary money. In most foreign countries, silver is merely one of the metals used in making subsidiary coins; but, in the United States because of the political forces behind the monetary use of silver, silver bars and silver certificates as well as token or subsidiary coins are used as money. When the United States Treasury purchases a twenty-five-pound bar of silver, it may be coined into 10-, 25-, and 50-cent coins worth about $415, into silver dollars worth a little over $385, or the silver may be retained in bar form to be used as a reserve for silver certificates worth a little over $385. In addition to silver subsidiary coins, the United States coinage system includes 1-cent and 5-cent coins to which the term *minor coins* is applied.

Subsidiary Coinage Principles. A subsidiary or token coin is an authorized coin whose value as bullion at the time of issuance is less than its value as money. Therefore, subsidiary coins are issued in limited amounts and are convertible (in reasonable amounts) into standard money or some other form of money that may be lawfully held. Since gold coins are no longer authorized, all kinds of coins in circulation in the United States are subsidiary or token coins. Prior to 1933, United States subsidiary coins had the desirable quality of limited legal tender; but they now have full legal-tender quality (money that the law authorizes a debtor to tender and requires a creditor to receive in payment of money obligations).[3]

In the United States, the government purchases silver which is minted into coins in amounts sufficient to care for trade and other needs. This means that coinage is "limited" rather than "free" (open to anyone who wants to bring metal to the mint to be coined). The coins are sold to banks which put them into circulation. By making the nominal or face value of coins greater than their bullion value, jewelers, silversmiths, and others will find it cheaper to purchase the metal in the open market than to melt down silver coins. When the

[3] Because of the nuisance factor, it would be better if coins were made limited legal tender in payment of a single transaction, as was the case prior to 1933 when fractional silver coins were limited legal tender in one payment for no more than $10.00 and minor coins (1-cent and 5-cent coins) for no more than 25 cents.

supply of a particular type of coin or coins becomes excessive and when coins become worn, the United States Mint must repurchase them at their token value, usually in amounts of $20 or more.

Silver Bars. For over twenty years, as provided for in the Silver Purchase Act of 1934, it has been the declared policy of the United States government to buy silver until the proportion of silver to gold in the United States monetary stock is one to three or until the market price of silver is $1.2929 per ounce. (Since 1941 the Secretary of the Treasury has not been able to purchase foreign silver under conditions considered to be advantageous to the United States.) Other acts of Congress have required the United States mints to buy all newly mined domestic silver offered to them at the statutory price (currently $1.29 per ounce minus a seigniorage charge of 30 per cent, which means that the net price is 90.5 cents per fine ounce).[4]

The Secretary of the Treasury is required to monetize silver purchased to the extent necessary to pay the one selling it; and the President of the United States may authorize the Secretary of the Treasury to issue silver certificates against any silver in the Treasury which is not held as security for silver certificates. The Secretary of the Treasury may sell silver not otherwise obligated for no less than 90.5 cents per fine ounce (called "free silver").

The most important aspect of the silver-buying policy is that our economy has been deprived of the use of over $2 billion worth of silver that might be used more economically in manufacturing, industry, and the arts. Silver certificates in circulation could be replaced with some other type of paper money and the silver held in the Treasury could be sold to the advantage of the nation. The sentiment for silver and the political aspects surrounding the monetary use of silver date back to the early part of our national history when the United States had a bimetallic standard (see Chapter VIII).

Silver Dollar. One of the provisions of the Act of February 12, 1873, was for a "trade dollar" weighing 420 grains of standard silver; but the act made no provisions for the coinage of the so-called standard silver dollar of 412.5 grains of standard silver that had been included in the coinage laws prior to that date. Because of the worldwide decline in the price of silver and the political aspects thereof, Congress made provisions for the reissuance of the standard silver dollar in 1878 when the Secretary of the Treasury was authorized to purchase not less than $2,000,000 or more than $4,000,000 of silver

---

[4] See Acts of July 6, 1939 (31 U.S.C. 312 c) and July 31, 1946 (31 U.S.C. 316 d).

bullion each month and to mint it into legal-tender silver dollars. He was also authorized to accept silver dollars in exchange for silver certificates which were not legal tender. Later the amount of silver to be purchased was increased as noted in Chapter VIII and later in this chapter.

Experiences with the standard silver dollar suggest that convenience is more important than legal-tender quality in maintaining the acceptability of money. Generally silver certificates displaced the standard silver dollar despite the fact that they did not have the legal-tender quality until 1933. This has been true even though the United States government has tried at different times to increase the general use of silver dollars (by discontinuing the issuance of United States notes in denominations of less than five dollars, paying salaries and other obligations in silver, and paying the costs of shipping silver dollars to different parts of the United States).

Silver Certificates. Silver certificates are a form of money certifying that silver in like amount is deposited in the United States Treasury and is payable to the bearer on demand. As originally authorized, in 1878, silver certificates were backed unit for unit by silver dollars; but experience demonstrated that the minting of all the silver reserves held specifically against silver certificates was not necessary. So, most of the silver, against which silver certificates are issued, is in bar form. The description of silver certificates suggests that they should be classified as representative money, which would be correct, considered from a legal viewpoint. But because the value of silver certificates—like the value of the silver money which they represent—depends in part on the credit of the United States government, they are classified as credit money.

Treasury Notes of 1890. The Sherman Act of 1890 provided for not only an increase in the amount of silver to be purchased by the United States Treasury but also the issuance of legal-tender Treasury notes which were to be used by the Secretary of the Treasury to pay for the 4,500,000 ounces of silver to be acquired each month. The Act also directed the Secretary of the Treasury to redeem these notes at his discretion in gold or silver coins. Most of the notes issued during the time the purchasing provision of the Sherman Act was in effect (from 1890 to November, 1893) have been retired.

United States Notes. United States notes were first issued by the United States Treasury in 1862 and 1863 to help finance the Civil War. They are promises to pay of the United States government; but, originally, they circulated at a discount in terms of gold.

In 1879 they were made convertible into gold; and since that time they have been at par with gold except in 1933–34, when all currencies were at less than par in terms of the then current gold dollar. Among the three current kinds of paper money, the United States note is least important. In addition to being a direct obligation of the government, these notes are protected by gold reserves of about 45 per cent of the total amount authorized.

National Bank Notes. National bank notes were issued by banks chartered under the National Bank Act of 1863. The bank notes were obtained from the Comptroller of the Currency in exchange for specific issues of United States bonds which Congress indicated could be used as collateral. The last of the bonds, eligible for security for national bank notes, was redeemed in 1935. The Treasury Department has assumed responsibility for national bank notes still outstanding, which explains why they are now called *Treasury* currency.

Federal Reserve Bank Notes. The Federal Reserve Act of 1913 originally authorized the issuance of Federal Reserve bank notes to replace national bank notes. Since Federal Reserve bank notes were issued originally under the same provisions as those relative to national bank notes, they are sometimes referred to as national currency. The Pittman Act of 1918 authorized additional issues to be used to replace silver certificates; and the Act of March 9, 1933, authorized additional issues as emergency currency. At the beginning of World War II, the supply of Federal Reserve bank notes on hand was released; but the total volume of these notes in use at any one time was relatively small. In 1945, Congress provided for their withdrawal from circulation and made the Treasury responsible for those outstanding; therefore, like national bank notes, Federal Reserve bank notes are known as *Treasury* currency.

GOLD MONEY

Gold Dollar. In the United States, the Secretary of the Treasury is required by law to maintain the value of all United States money at parity with the gold dollar.[5] The gold dollar is now defined as $1/35$ of an ounce of gold (troy weight) or $15\frac{5}{21}$ grains of standard gold (standard gold is $9/10$ fine). So, each ounce of gold in the United States Treasury is called $35.00. This means that the 600 million ounces of gold (using round numbers) in the United States Treasury are $21 billion.

---

[5] See Gold Standard Act of 1900 and the Act of May 12, 1933 (31 U.S.C. 314).

Gold Coins. Prior to the passage of the Gold Reserve Act of 1934, there were legal provisions for the free coinage of gold. The Coinage Act of April 2, 1792, defined the gold dollar as 24.75 grains of pure gold. In 1834, this weight was reduced to 23.2 grains of pure gold; and, in 1837 it was increased to 23.22 grains of pure gold. This weight was retained until January 30, 1934, when it was changed to 13.71 grains of pure gold; but no gold coinage is permitted under the current law. Old United States gold coins are prized by collectors, hoarders, and others; and the quantity of such coins scattered throughout the world is unknown.

Gold Certificates. Except during financial emergencies, the American people prefer paper money or deposit currency to gold coins; and, in the Act of March 3, 1863, Congress authorized the Treasury to issue gold certificates in exchange for gold coins or gold bars (the gold certificates being called representative money). Gold certificates were acceptable in payments to the government (government tender) until December 24, 1919, when they were made full legal tender. Today, gold certificates issued prior to March 4, 1933, are being retired from circulation and those being issued currently may be owned legally only by the Federal Reserve banks.

Gold Bars. Since 1933, the United States Treasury has followed the policy of not minting gold coins and of melting down those withdrawn from circulation into gold bars. Although some gold coins are still outstanding, they are not considered to be part of the money supply and they do not appear in the Treasury statement of *Currency in Circulation.* While gold bars may not look like money, as one normally thinks of money, they are the most acceptable means of payment among central banks, national governments, and international agencies (such as the International Monetary Fund and the Bank for International Settlements). If the current gold standard were an unrestricted type of standard, the demand for these bars would be even greater.

Government Ownership. In the United States and most foreign countries, private ownership of monetary gold is illegal; but gold bars may be obtained for legal purposes, such as for use in dentistry and in the manufacture of jewelry.[6] This means that gold which is mined in the United States, imported from abroad, or reclaimed from melting jewelry or other things made of gold must be sold to the United

[6] The Secretary of the Treasury prescribes the conditions under which gold may be acquired and held as provided for in the Gold Standard Act of 1934 as amended.

States Mint at the price fixed by law ($35.00 per fine ounce, minus a charge of ¼ of 1 per cent, that is 8¾ cents per fine ounce).

An Increase in Gold Stock. Because the average person does not see the gold in our monetary system and has little or no knowledge of the part it plays, he is likely to consider it to be nonessential. He may be interested to know that changes in the gold supply affect the total money supply in about the same way today as it did before 1933. Let us assume that a gold bullion dealer acquires gold bars; as required by law, he sells them to the United States Treasury which pays for them with a Treasury check drawn upon its account at a Federal Reserve bank. The following will result if the gold is monetized by issuing gold certificates or gold credits: When the seller of the gold deposits the Treasury check in his commercial bank, the supply of money is increased. The bank sends the check to its Federal Reserve bank which settles for it by giving the commercial bank credit in its reserve account. Thus, both the deposits and reserves of the bank are increased by the same amount.

The Federal Reserve bank charges the checking account of the Treasury at the same time that it credits the reserve account of the commercial bank. In the meantime, the Treasury customarily will use gold as a reserve for gold certificates or gold credits which are deposited in the Federal Reserve bank.[7] The offsetting items are an increase in gold certificate reserves of the Federal Reserve bank and an increase in the Treasury's checking account (matching the amount of the check given in payment for the gold). Although the gold is now owned by the United States government, it must be held in trust for the Federal Reserve bank which holds the gold certificates or gold credits.

When all the bookkeeping is completed, an import of $1,000,000 in gold would ordinarily increase each of the following by $1,000,000: the money supply, member-bank reserves, and Federal Reserve bank reserves. This effect is similar to that which occurred before 1933; but then, there was a possibility that the gold might have been hoarded, used as collateral for gold certificates, or minted into gold coins with little or no effect on the amount of member-bank reserves or Federal Reserve bank reserves.

The fact that the Treasury must purchase gold when offered means that the money supply and member-bank reserves will be increased with an increase in the monetary stock. However, the Treas-

---

[7] For convenience, the Secretary of the Treasury usually gives the Federal Reserve banks gold credits on the books rather than printing and delivering gold certificates to them.

ury is not required to issue gold certificates or gold credits; and, so the volume of gold certificate reserves of Federal Reserve banks may or may not be increased with an increase in the monetary gold stock. In other words, the Treasury may keep the gold in its vaults without monetizing it; in which case, there would be no increase in the gold certificate reserves of the Federal Reserve banks. In this second procedure, which is the exception rather than the rule, the new gold is reported as "Treasury cash."[8]

A Decrease in Gold Stock. When gold is exported or released at home for use in industry, dentistry, or the arts, the results are usually as follows: The Treasury accepts a check in payment for the gold, deposits the check in a Federal Reserve bank, and uses the funds to redeem previously issued gold certificates or gold credits. The buyer of the gold has his deposit account debited, which reduces the money supply; and the Federal Reserve bank, being the collection agency, debits the reserve account of the bank on which the gold buyer's check was drawn and credits the account of the Treasury. In brief, the money supply, the amount of member-bank reserves, and the amount of gold certificates or gold credits will be reduced in an amount equal to the gold exported or released for nonmonetary purposes.

In some cases, the gold sold by the Treasury may be delivered out of "Treasury cash" without affecting the gold certificate or gold credit reserves of the Federal Reserve banks. Of course, the gold buyer would still pay with a check; and the Federal Reserve bank, as the collection agency, would charge the reserve account of the buyer's bank and credit the checking account of the Treasury. The supply of Treasury cash would be reduced but the Treasury's checking account at the Federal Reserve bank would be increased.

Whether considered from the viewpoint of gold imports or gold exports, the conclusion is the same—changes in the monetary gold stock have a direct influence on the amount of the money supply and the volume of member-bank reserves. Ordinarily, changes in the monetary gold stock have similar effects on the volume of Federal Reserve bank reserves; but sometimes the United States Treasury may not monetize gold imports and/or may meet the export demand out of United States Treasury stock without changing Federal Reserve banks' gold certificate reserves.

Gold and Federal Reserve Credit. Federal Reserve banks are

---

[8] Treasury cash includes currency as well as free gold. Of the Treasury cash in the form of gold ($655,000,000), $156,039,431 is held against United States notes and Treasury notes of 1890.

required to keep a minimum reserve of 25 per cent in the form of gold certificates against their deposits and Federal Reserve notes in circulation.[9] If the volume of deposits is $20 billion and the amount of Federal Reserve notes in circulation is $28 billion, the Federal Reserve banks must have at least $12 billion in gold certificate reserves.

Originally, the gold certificate, first authorized in 1863, was a form of paper money issued by the Treasurer of the United States given in exchange for voluntary deposits of gold. Each certificate stated on its face that the number of gold dollars indicated on the certificate was being held on deposit in the Treasury and was payable to the bearer on demand. Although not obligatory, many holders of gold coins exchanged their coins for gold certificates; and as a result, gold certificates (yellow backs) were one of the most popular forms of circulating money. In 1933, the federal government required holders of gold certificates to surrender their certificates to banks; consequently most of them were retired from circulation. Now gold certificates may not be owned legally by individuals or private institutions in the United States other than the Federal Reserve banks (which are practically public banks even though their stock is owned by member banks).

It has been proposed that the gold certificate reserve system be abolished because it is confusing to both Americans and foreigners. This confusion would be eliminated if Congress were to repeal the laws providing for the issuance of gold certificates and permit the gold they represent to be used directly by the Federal Reserve banks as reserves. The United States Treasury licenses all gold exports and regulates conditions under which gold may be obtained for legal purposes at home. The result is to further confuse the status of the gold standard as it is today in the United States. If the Federal Reserve banks were given title to the gold stock and permission to buy and sell gold freely at fixed prices, the United States would have a gold bullion standard (as the present standard has been called in some government publications).[10]

Earmarked Gold. The United States is an important monetary center wherein foreign governments and central banks customarily

[9] The Board of Governors of the Federal Reserve System may suspend the 25 per cent requirement for short periods, subject to certain penalties. Usually, the amount of gold certificates or gold credits held as Federal Reserve bank reserves is considerably above the one-to-four ratio required by law, having been between 40 and 50 per cent during recent years.

[10] See Joint Committee on the Economic Report, *Monetary Policy and the Management of the Public Debt* (Washington, D.C., U.S. Government Printing Office, 1952), p. 38.

keep all or part of their gold stock for safekeeping and for other reasons. Although this gold is in the United States, it is earmarked (physically tagged) to indicate the owner. Such gold does not belong to the United States government; and the amount is not included in statistics of the gold stock of the United States.

SUMMARY

The burden of distributing currency among users in the United States falls on the Federal Reserve banks and commercial banks. The expenses associated with transporting currency to and from commercial banks are paid by the Federal Reserve banks; and the burden of handling currency within the commercial banks is borne by these banks (they sometimes charge customers for cashing checks, making up payrolls, packaging currency, and so on). The sources of new as well as replacement currency are the United States government and the Federal Reserve banks. Under current laws, the quantity of coins, silver certificates, and Federal Reserve notes may be increased but the amount of United States notes is fixed by law and the other types of paper money are being retired from circulation.

The most important type of circulating paper currency in the United States is the Federal Reserve note, which is issued in denominations of $5 to $10,000. The provisions for the issue and retirement of Federal Reserve notes were designed to give the United States an elastic currency system which would expand and contract in accordance with the needs of the economy. At the present time, the collateral held by the Federal Reserve agents against Federal Reserve notes issued to Federal Reserve banks is made up as follows: 40 per cent in gold certificates, over 59 per cent in United States government securities, and the remainder in eligible paper. Although gold certificates are used as a reserve for Federal Reserve notes, these certificates may not be used to meet the domestic obligations of the Federal Reserve banks but may be used to acquire gold to meet demands of foreign governments and foreign central banks.

United States Treasury currency includes subsidiary coins, silver bars, silver dollars, silver certificates, Treasury Notes of 1890, United States notes, national bank notes, and Federal Reserve bank notes. Of these types of currency, Treasury notes of 1890, national bank notes, and Federal Reserve bank notes are being retired and are sometimes classified as obsolete but not extinct currency.

United States gold money appears in bar form in the vaults of the government and central banks; but title to the gold rests with the United States government. Most of the gold is held as reserves for gold certificates or gold credits which are owned by the Federal Reserve banks. The Federal Reserve banks are required to keep a 25-per-cent gold certificate or gold credit reserve against their deposits and Federal Reserve notes in circulation. When the United States monetary gold supply increases, the money supply and member-bank reserves increase and either central bank reserves or United States Treasury cash increase. Conversely, a decrease in the United States monetary gold supply decreases the money supply and member-bank reserves and either central bank reserves or Treasury cash. Earmarked gold is owned by foreign central banks or governments, and it is not part of the United States monetary gold stock.

QUESTIONS AND PROBLEMS

1. How do the Federal Reserve banks meet the daily requests for currency received from member banks? Where do the Federal Reserve banks obtain the currency which they use?

2. Outline the provisions for the issuance and retirement of Federal Reserve notes. What are the merits and demerits of the present system?

3. Assume that depositors were to demand additional currency for but 10 per cent of their funds on deposit with banks (about $180,000 million). How would it affect the Federal Reserve Agents' Accounts as they appear in Table 5?

4. "Its [the central bank's] primary duty is to see that at any given moment in the development of its country's economy there is the right amount of money in existence, neither too much, nor too little." (G. F. Towers, *Bank of Canada*, radio address, November 17, 1938.) How can central bankers and others tell whether there is too little or too much money? Explain.

5. What is meant by the statement that silver money is "token" money?

6. Identify the token coinage principles. Is the current silver-buying program essential to the proper functioning of the subsidiary coinage system of the United States? Explain.

7. Identify the kinds of money classified as United States Treasury currency.

8. Identify: (*a*) standard money, (*b*) gold certificate, (*c*) gold credits, (*d*) "mint" price of gold, and (*e*) earmarked gold.

9. How does the import of gold affect the money supply? Member-bank reserves? Federal Reserve bank reserves?

10. In *Public Resolution No. 63*, 74th Cong. (approved August 27, 1935), appears: "Holders of the coins or currencies of the United States shall be entitled to exchange them, dollar for dollar, for other coins or currencies which may be lawfully acquired. . . ." What

does this mean as to convertibility of United States currency? With reference to the statement on Federal Reserve notes that they are redeemable in "lawful" money?

11. Analyze the following statement: "To a very important degree . . . changes in the money supply reflect the public demand for money and credit. This is clearly so in the case of currency. . . . So far as bank deposits are concerned . . . , their movement reflects changes in the loans and investments of the banking system, which in turn responds to the demand for credit on the part of business and government." (The Bank of Nova Scotia, "The Supply of Money," *Monthly Review* [Toronto], March-April, 1952, no page number.)

12. Discuss the following, which appear as recommendations of Subcommittee on Monetary, Credit, and Fiscal Policies of the Joint Committee on the Economic Report, Congress of the United States, *Monetary, Credit and Fiscal Policies* (Washington, D.C.: U.S. Government Printing Office, 1950): (*a*) "We recommend that the United States Government cease buying silver for monetary purposes" (p. 40); (*b*) "We believe that to restore the free domestic convertibility of money into gold coin or gold bullion at this time would militate against, rather than promote, the purposes of the Employment Act, and we recommend that no action in this direction be taken" (p. 41).

13. As reported in the press (September 4 and 5, 1947), British Foreign Secretary Bevin said: "My own conviction is that she [the United States] handicapped herself and caused high taxation in her own country by failure to redistribute the Fort Knox gold. If you find another gold mine in the world it would assist you . . . but there is gold which has already been mined and it is doing nothing." What does gold used as reserves ever do that the Fort Knox gold is not doing? Should "redistribution" be permitted by coining gold and converting paper money into gold coins? Is the United States Treasury willing to sell gold freely to Great Britain? Did Mr. Bevin mean this kind of "redistribution"? From whom was the Fort Knox gold bought in the first place?

14. Analyze: "The international gold market during 1955 showed considerable stability. As demand for hoarding largely disappeared, the central banks acted as the main purchasers of newly mined gold, and also bought some dishoarded gold." (International Monetary Fund, *International Financial News Survey*, February 3, 1956, p. 238.)

15. "The gold and dollar holdings of countries outside the United States, which had increased by $2.6 billion in 1953 and by $1.9 billion in 1954, rose further—by $1.6 billion—in 1955; at the end of the year they totaled $26.6 billion." (International Monetary Fund, *International Financial News Survey*, February 24, 1956, p. 261.) Does this mean that the gold stock of the United States can be regarded as an asset of the United States alone? Why?

Chapter VII

THE GOLD STANDARD

ONE OF the functions of money was identified as being its use as a standard of value; and the dollar was recognized as the standard monetary unit in which exchange values or prices are expressed in the United States. This chapter deals with the gold standard, the most popular among the full-bodied kinds of monetary standards. In the United States the standard unit is the gold dollar, defined as $15\frac{5}{21}$ grains of gold $\frac{9}{10}$ fine (standard gold). This monetary unit is a fixed weight of gold, which means that gold is the monetary standard.

INTERNATIONAL GOLD STANDARD

The current gold standard is sometimes referred to as an international gold standard. By an "international gold standard" is meant an international system wherein all participating countries have legally (1) prescribed the gold value of their respective monetary units (dollar, franc, pound sterling, etc.), and (2) established a mechanism whereby their local currencies are kept equal in value to gold and to each other.

Monetary Units Defined in Terms of Gold. In 1944 at Bretton Woods, New Hampshire, arrangements were made for the establishment of an international organization, the International Monetary Fund, which has the primary purpose of facilitating the operation of an international monetary system wherein the value of the currency of each participating country is to be linked to gold. The International Monetary Fund Agreement requires that "the par value of the currency of each member should be expressed in terms of gold as a common denominator or in terms of the United States dollar of the weight and fineness in effect on July 1, 1944." About sixty countries have so defined the value of their monetary units.[1]

The size and weight of the standard unit of a country is signifi-

---

[1] Copies of the current *Schedule of Par Values* may be obtained from the International Monetary Fund, Washington, D.C.

cant because it determines the number of dollars, francs, etc., that may be made from an ounce of gold and, therefore, the exchange ratio with all other countries on the gold standard. A country that selects as its monetary unit one weighing $\frac{1}{70}$ of an ounce of fine gold establishes an exchange ratio of 2 to 1 with a second country whose monetary unit weighs $\frac{1}{35}$ of an ounce of fine gold. Since the latter weight is that of the United States dollar, the parity price of the former is fifty cents. The selection of the size of a country's monetary unit is of great importance to all countries now on the gold standard and to all others planning to adopt it, because the exchange ratio influences the relative purchasing power of one currency in terms of all others in international trade.

In order to have meaning to the average American, prices quoted in terms of foreign money must be converted into dollars and cents. The price of an English automobile quoted at 750 pounds sterling may be compared to domestic prices of automobiles when 750 is multiplied by $2.80, the par rate of exchange. The exchange rate is the monetary link between the economies of two countries. When on an unrestricted gold standard, there is an upper and lower limit beyond which the sight rate of exchange cannot go (called the export-import points for gold).

Prior to the organization of the International Monetary Fund, it was assumed that any nation had the right to change its monetary unit at will, even though such action had worldwide effects upon the economies of other nations with which it carried on trade and had financial transactions. By accepting the International Monetary Fund Agreement, nations adopted a code of behavior which, among other things, involved the surrender of a part of the freedom to modify their monetary units and to impose exchange restrictions.

Convertibility of Currency in Gold. If defining a country's monetary unit in terms of gold is to have significance, some provisions must be made whereby those who have rights to currency may convert them into gold or gold equivalent on demand. The International Monetary Fund Agreement does not require countries to make provisions for domestic convertibility in gold, but it does anticipate the ultimate international convertibility in gold or gold exchange. The smooth functioning of a domestic monetary system depends on the free interchange of all kinds of money at par throughout the areas served; and, although the problems are more complicated, an international monetary system must have this same interchangeability of currencies at or near par.

The free interchange of currencies linked to gold and the elimination of tariffs and other artificial trade barriers would tend to have the effect of securing, to some degree, a common level of prices throughout the gold standard area. If all currencies are kept equal to gold in value, they will be equal to each other because things equal to the same thing are equal to each other. As logical as this seems, there may be enough inflexibility in different national economies to cause prices to be artificially high or low in one country as compared to prices in a second country.

Regulator of the Balance of Payments. If countries accept the rules of the international gold standard, a country losing gold because its value is lower at home (general prices are higher) than abroad will follow policies that will tend to lower the domestic price level; and a country gaining gold will follow policies that will tend to raise its domestic price level. The automatic adjustments that would follow the export of gold in one country and the import of gold in the other would tend to bring the respective price levels into equilibrium. For illustration, if Great Britain is losing gold when on the gold standard, the automatic regulatory aspects of the standard may be implemented by central-bank policy. Thus the Bank of England would raise its discount rate or curtail investment in the open market so as to reduce the amount of its credit in use. Since central-bank credit is used as bank reserves, the following would tend to happen: (1) interest rates would increase, (2) borrowing by business firms and others would decline, (3) spending would decline, and (4) prices would fall (value of money would rise).

If, at the same time, the United States is gaining gold, the Federal Reserve System would implement the automatic regulatory aspects of the gold standard by reducing the discount rate and by increasing open-market purchases of government securities. Thus, bank reserves would be increased by more than the increase in gold stock and the following would tend to happen: (1) interest rates would fall, (2) borrowing by business firms would increase, (3) spending would increase, and (4) prices would rise (the value of money would decline).

Higher interest rates in Great Britain would attract investments from the United States, where interest rates have been depressed by the influx of gold and the expansion of Federal Reserve bank credit. The price decline in Great Britain would stimulate exports and discourage imports. Great Britain's more favorable investment and trade balance would decrease pressure on its gold reserves—reducing the need for exporting gold. At the same time the opposite would tend to take place in the United States.

According to this formula, countries gaining gold were to lower the discount rate so as to lower interest rates in the market, increase borrowing and spending, and raise general prices. Lower interest rates in one country were expected to encourage a flow of investment funds to countries having higher interest rates, and higher prices were expected to encourage purchasing abroad where lower prices prevailed. The resulting flow of funds away from the economy gaining gold to the country losing gold would help correct the situation which led to the original gain of gold in one case and the loss of gold in the other.

The breakdown in the nineteenth century type of gold standard came in the 1920's and 1930's when central banks adopted policies which tended to insulate their national economies from the deflationary and inflationary effects of gold movements. When the influx or efflux of gold was offset by the withdrawal or increase of central bank credit, changes in interest rates, spending, and prices did not follow. Lack of adjustments in these economies meant that the levels of prices and interest rates were not consistent with the equilibrating nature of a truly international monetary system.

In a modern economy, even without central bank interference, there is no certainty that adjustments would be along the lines anticipated when gold flows out of a country. Money wages and other costs of production tend to be fairly rigid, making it difficult to lower prices in response to the influence of higher interest rates. Instead of lower prices the result may be a decline in employment, production, and exports. The depressed economy may be less attractive to investment funds; and higher interest rates may fail to attract capital.

The loss of gold, gold credits, and foreign balances may be evidence of the development of a serious situation in the country's international financial position. It means that cash reserves abroad are being spent more rapidly than they are being replaced. A continuance of this situation would tend to result in the depletion of foreign cash reserves, depreciation in the value of the country's currency unit in terms of foreign money, deterioration of its international credit position, and other adverse events. Since the close of World War II, the world press has used the rise and fall in Great Britain's gold and other exchange balances as a barometer of her international financial position. Present-day economists no longer visualize the international gold standard as an automatic gold standard; but the principles under which it operated do have an important place in the International Monetary Fund Agreement and the type of international monetary system anticipated therein.

GOLD AS THE REGULATOR OF THE CURRENCY

Monetary economists have emphasized the importance of limiting the supply of circulating money in order to maintain its value. "Too much money," like too much of anything else, means a decline in its value. Since governments, central banks, and commercial banks are responsible for supplying circulating money, one would assume that they would create monetary systems wherein the supply of currency would be regulated so as to prevent fluctuations in its value. But banks are in business to make profits from lending and investing; governments are under pressure to spend, which is so great that there seems to be no safeguard against overspending; and central banks are in a position wherein they seemingly must "go along" with the financial policies of their governments. It is feared that monetary authorities will permit the creation of money in such amounts as to bring about more and more inflation.

The severest critics of paper money and monetary management favor the return to some system which would provide an automatic check on the supply of money. They consider an automatic check to be the only means of achieving price stability, without which the system of free enterprise is in danger. They associate the instability in the value of money with economic and political chaos, strikes, and the growth of socialism and communism.

One device suggested to limit the supply of money is that of making all types of money redeemable or convertible, directly or indirectly, in gold which is limited in amount. Emphasis is on the need for limiting the amount of money rather than on the need for backing; because money, clothed in the legal-tender quality, will be acceptable even though it is declining in value. While no restrictions are placed on the supply of gold money (other than by nature and effective demand for nonmonetary purposes), other types must be limited; otherwise, the government or central bank may be confronted with a situation of having claims to gold money in circulation that cannot be met on demand.

The mechanism used to maintain parity between currency and gold has varied from time to time and from place to place. In order to maintain parity, provisions may be made for (1) free coinage of gold and interchangeability of gold coins and circulating money,

(2) interchangeability of gold bars and circulating money, or (3) interchangeability of local currency for foreign currency which is interchangeable for gold bars or gold coins. One, two, or all of these devices may be used at the same time. Furthermore, parity may be achieved by acts of the monetary authorities without any specific statutory provisions. This may be done by never refusing to give gold or its equivalent at a fixed price for domestic currency and vice versa.

The mechanism whereby countries make provisions to keep the value of their currencies equal to the value of their gold units permits the classification of gold standards as gold-coin standards, gold-bullion standards, and gold-exchange standards. This classification is for convenience in discussion; and it does not mean that, at any one time, any country adheres exclusively to the practices that are described.

TYPES OF GOLD STANDARDS

Gold-Coin Standard. A country operating on a gold-coin standard makes provisions for gold coins at established weights and gold contents. If the standard unit, such as the gold dollar, is not coined because it would be too small to be practical, multiples of the standard unit are coined. Free coinage of standard metal is permitted, and gold bullion may be left at the mint by the public for coinage into gold coins with or without mintage and/or seigniorage charges. The relationship between gold coins and gold is fixed; and credit money is redeemable in gold coins. Gold coins are made legal tender, but this legal compulsion to accept gold coins is not necessary. People are free to do as they please with their gold coins or gold bullion—it may be hoarded, used in business, exported, and so on.

Gold-Bullion Standard. A country operating on a gold-bullion standard makes provisions for an established gold unit which is not coined but has a fixed weight and gold content by legal definition. The government buys and sells all gold offered or asked for at fixed prices; however, because gold is usually in bar form having relatively large values, the public is limited in its ability to acquire gold. Once gold is acquired, it may be hoarded, used for industrial purposes, exported, used to meet obligations, and so on. The government gives gold for credit money and vice versa, and thus the value of the two are kept equal.

Gold-Exchange Standard. A country operating on a gold-exchange standard makes provisions for a gold unit or merely declares that its monetary unit, whatever its physical form, is to be kept equal in value to that of some foreign money. Its money is redeemed in drafts drawn on a bank in a foreign country which is on the gold-coin or gold-bullion standard. These drafts are claims on gold or money in the latter country. The government buys drafts on foreign banks; and so there is a two-way movement of domestic currency (1) to the government when it sells foreign gold drafts and (2) away from the government when it buys gold drafts. Since the government buys and sells gold drafts at fixed prices, the value of domestic money is fixed with reference to the foreign gold money. Since there are no restrictions on the domestic gold market, the public is free to acquire gold, to hoard it, to export or import it, and otherwise to use it freely.

The basic requirement of a gold-exchange standard is the right to buy and sell gold exchange freely in unlimited quantities at established prices. As in the case of the gold-bullion standard, the central bank or government must assume responsibility for selling gold exchange if and when it cannot be obtained more cheaply elsewhere and buying gold exchange if and when it cannot be sold more dearly elsewhere.

In order for a central bank or government to play its role as a seller of gold exchange, it must have or be able to obtain gold or gold exchange. The sale of a bank draft drawn on a foreign bank may be covered by a shipment of gold, by an existing bank deposit held abroad, or by borrowing (or liquidating an investment in the foreign market) and depositing the funds in the bank on which the draft is drawn. The lender may be the International Monetary Fund, the government, central bank, or some financial institution in the market where the gold draft is payable.

Restricted Gold-Bullion Standard.   Because of the various restrictions placed upon acquisition and private ownership of gold, it is apparent that none of the three traditional types of gold standard is current in the United States. The United States does permit foreign central banks and governments to acquire gold from the United States Treasury, and the United States Treasury does buy all gold offered at its fixed price.

Gold produced in the United States may be taken to any mint or assay office of the Treasury, where it is paid for with a check drawn on the Treasury's account in a Federal Reserve bank. Under the regulations of the Secretary of the Treasury, the Director of the Mint sells gold to those having a license to obtain it for professional, industrial, or other legitimate purposes (and in small amounts—$200 —without a license). The amount of gold used annually for non-monetary purposes is considerably in excess of the amount produced at home or reclaimed from melting down fabricated gold. So the commercial demand for gold is met in part by using monetary gold. The selling and buying price of gold is uniformly $35.00 plus or minus a handling charge of one fourth of 1 per cent.[2] (Some of the gold brought to assay offices must be refined to remove impurities; in this case, a charge is made to cover all costs.)

WHY THE GOLD STANDARD?

Gold became the standard metal at a time when the emphasis was on full-bodied money; and the use of gold as the standard was made possible by the development of subsidiary coinage, paper money, and deposit currency as circulating media. These substitutes for gold, which made operating on the gold standard possible, have grown to such proportions that they have destroyed most of the meaning of the gold standard as visualized by those who created it during the nineteenth century.

Historical Background. During the early history of monetary systems, emphasis was on full-bodied money—gold and silver. Silver, in addition to having many of the same qualities as gold, is more suitable for use as circulating money because it is less valuable and physically more abundant than gold. Gold, because of its greater value in small bulk, is more convenient for use as a reserve and as a means of international payment. Long after the Western nations were using token coins, paper money, and deposit currency as circulating media, the masses of Asia still preferred circulating money which had commodity value as well as money value. While the standard money of the East (silver) was still being used both as the medium of exchange and as the standard of value, the West had developed a more complicated monetary system in which it was not necessary for the standard money to serve both as the medium of exchange and as the standard of value.

Although England had been operating on the gold standard since the close of the Napoleonic War, most Western nations retained both gold and silver as standard metals in their bimetallic systems until about 1870. When the bimetallic standard became unworkable in practice, they chose gold, rather than silver, for the

---

[2] This charge of 8¾ cents per ounce is made when gold is earmarked for the account of a foreign government or central bank. If gold is exported, there is in addition freight, packing, and insurance charges. These add up to about 16 to 18 cents per ounce for gold bars when gold is moved from New York to London. This means that the price of gold in London would need to be at least $35.25 per ounce before gold movements from New York to London would be justified.

monetary standard (see Chapter VIII). In making this selection the
leaders in commercial countries were influenced by the fact that
many of their international commercial and financial transactions
were with merchants and bankers in London. When financial transactions were in terms of the English unit the money used was gold
or its equivalent.

As an increasing number of commercial nations adopted the
gold standard the attractiveness of the gold standard increased. Considered from an international viewpoint the chief advantage of
adherence to the gold standard was that it provided a uniform basis
(after allowance for obstacles to trade) for comparing commodity
and security prices. This uniform monetary basis facilitated the expansion of foreign trade and investment; and, as a result, gold became the international medium of exchange and standard of value
until World War I. Since that time, gold has been used intermittently
as the international medium of exchange and standard of value.

Qualities of Gold. As a commodity, gold has value for orna-
mental and industrial purposes; and, like all metals, it has the qualities
of indestructibility, homogeneity, and divisibility. Being a precious
metal, gold has great value in small bulk, giving it the quality of
portability. As evidenced by exhibits of coins, thousands of years
old, metallic money is almost indestructible. These qualities of gold
make it suitable for coinage and for use as reserve money; the
economic quality of stability in value, relative to other commodities,
made it desired as standard money.

Gold Mining. Since the value of any commodity tends to be
influenced by changes in its supply, stability in supply tends to contribute to stability in value. Gold is a durable commodity and a
large percentage of the gold mined throughout the ages is still in
existence. Since the average annual output of newly mined gold
is only 3 to 4 per cent of the existing gold stock, an increase of
even 100 per cent in the annual output would have but little effect
on its value. On the other hand, if the world's annual output of
wheat were increased by 100 per cent, there would be a very noticeable and immediate effect on its value.

Because the price of gold is fixed by law, gold is produced
under conditions that tend to stabilize its value. When general prices
and costs of production are high, gold production is depressed; and
when general prices and costs are low, gold production is stimulated.
In addition, like other extractive industries, gold mining operates
under the law of increasing per unit cost. New mines may be

opened, cheaper ores may be exploited, and deeper shafts may be dug; but with each intensive or extensive development unit costs increase, thereby intensifying the depressing effects of rising prices on the gold-mining industry. With no offsetting increase in the price of its product, the gold-mining industry cannot expect to offset higher costs by increasing the volume of its product.

When the general price level is falling, gold production is stimulated while production in other industries may be curtailed. With the price of gold fixed and the costs of production decreasing, it becomes profitable to reopen abandoned gold mines, to extract gold from cheaper ores, and to mine other deposits of ore more intensively. Profits beckon, and the sourdoughs head for the hills. The resulting increase in the amount of new gold produced is socially beneficial because an increase in the amount of new standard money will tend to check the contraction in currency and the fall in general prices.

Because gold has been given money qualities, the peak and low points in profits of companies in the gold-mining industry tend to follow a contracyclical pattern, while those of other closely allied industries tend to follow a cyclical pattern. Some gold-mining companies mine two or more ores in addition to gold; as a result, their losses and gains on different products tend to offset each other during the business cycle. Others are not so fortunate, and it is from them that pressure arises for gold subsidies and higher gold prices— not during periods of depression but during periods of high prosperity.

An analysis of the factors influencing gold production, when the price of gold is fixed, leads to the conclusion that gold is produced under conditions which tend to stabilize its value. If governments are to follow a plan of stabilizing the value of gold by controlling gold production, the principles to be followed would be designed to implement this natural tendency—suppressing gold production during rising prices and stimulating it during falling prices.[3]

Nonmonetary Demands for Gold. Not all the world's gold supply is used as money; and, therefore, the size and value of the monetary gold stock is influenced by the nonmonetary demand for

[3] An ambitious plan of this type was proposed by Professor Lehfeldt of Johannesburg, South Africa. His plan was never given much serious consideration because of (1) the difficulties that would be encountered in organizing producers so as to limit production during high prices and in getting commitments from governments to subsidize the industry during depressions; and (2) a growing appreciation of the fact that the value of gold is determined to a greater extent by the money supply rather than the other way around.

gold. The commercial or industrial demands for gold include those for gold plating, for gilding, for manufacturing processes, for dental and surgical purposes, for architectural effects in churches and other buildings, and, most important, for jewelry. Any increase or decrease in the commercial demand for gold tends to have a corresponding effect on its value.

During periods of rising and high prices the value of gold is low (being money, the value of gold is low when general prices are high) and nonmonetary demands increase, thereby reducing the relative supply of gold money and tending to check the upward price trend. During periods of falling prices, just the opposite conditions exist. Purchases of luxuries, including gold articles, decrease and gold is freed for monetary purposes. If the depression is severe, there may be a movement of old gold from the arts to the monetary field.

The second nonmonetary demand for gold is the traditional hoarding demand of the Far East and Middle East, particularly India. Technically, most of this gold is hoarded only in the sense of being held in the form of ornaments. Because of inadequate banking facilities, together with religious and social customs, India has taken about 14 per cent of the world's annual output since the discovery of America.[4] Because orthodox Mohammedans are prohibited from receiving interest, they buy ornaments as investments. The Hindu laws of inheritance make women ineligible for receiving any share in immovable and real property, and so considerable capital is invested in ornaments for their inheritance.

The investment demand for gold is linked to national income. As a result of the depression beginning in 1929 and the increase in the world price of gold following England's departure from the gold standard, the annual amount taken by India not only decreased but much of the so-called "hoarded" gold was attracted to the monetary market. War and postwar restrictions have prevented large gold imports and improvements in banking, and other changes in India's economy have decreased the traditional hoarding demand for gold.

In recent years gold has been bought and sold at a large premium in the Bombay bullion market (one of the most important

[4] During this same period it was estimated that America and Europe consumed 30 per cent of the gold output for nonmonetary purposes. When it is recognized that India contains 20 per cent of the world's population, the hoarding demand for gold of 14 per cent of the world's output is not excessive. (S. G. Panandikar, *Banking in India* [New York: Longmans, Green & Co., 1934], pp. 331–33.)

in the world). However, this market has been isolated from the London and other gold markets since rigid restrictions were placed on the import and export of gold by the Indian government. Although the Oriental demand for gold is but a small part of the total demand, it tends to be greatest when the value of gold is lowest and to be smallest when the value of gold is highest. In economic terminology, there is an elastic demand for gold; and the more elastic the demand for gold, the more stable its value tends to be.

Monetary Demands for Gold. Most of the gold supply is used for monetary purposes, and it is this demand which explains most of the current value of gold. At present most of the monetary stock of gold is in bar form in the vaults of central banks and governments. Among the changes which have reduced the supply of gold money relative to other means of payment are: (1) the withdrawal of gold coins from circulation and their replacement with other means of payment; (2) the use of central bank credit as reserves for banks within countries; (3) the use of foreign exchange as reserves for central banks; (4) the restrictions placed on the use and ownership of gold; and (5) the establishment of judicial procedures and legal codes that encourage investment in things other than gold as stores of value. Any development that would destroy confidence in paper money and token coins, in commercial and central banks, and/or in governments would tend to increase the monetary demand for gold. This explains much of the hoarding in western Europe since the 1920's.

It is the hoarding type of monetary demand associated with financial disturbances which has caused so much criticism of the gold standard. Usually, it is lack of confidence in domestic currency which causes individuals to hoard gold, and this lack of confidence may arise during depressions as well as during boom periods. While the withdrawal of gold reserves for hoarding and the resulting multiple contraction of the money supply may be helpful in checking inflation, a similar withdrawal during depression periods, having the same effects on the money supply, may be disastrous. Thus, the chief strength of the gold standard is, at the same time, its chief weakness.

If a country is operating on a paper standard and general prices are inflated, gold hoarding will decrease the store-of-value demand for currency and thereby will tend to decrease its value. If the central bank is deprived of gold reserves, the prospects for stabilization of the currency will be dimmed; this would further reduce confidence in the currency. Although trading in Beirut, Brussels, Zurich, and London gold markets has been at or near par in terms of the gold price of $35.00 per fine ounce, for the most part, only gold bars and wholesale markets are involved. In retail markets, wherein gold coins are being bought and sold (such as Paris, Zurich, Milan, and Beirut) for hoarding, the premium on gold is as much as $5 per fine ounce. With the spread of free gold markets now underway, differences in prices of gold in the wholesale markets will soon disappear.

COMMODITY THEORY OF MONEY

According to the commodity theory of money, money has value because it is made of some generally acceptable commodity that has "use" value as distinct from money value. With the appearance of subsidiary coins, paper money, and deposit currency, the commodity theorists explained that their value was derived from the value of the commodity used to "back" and to "redeem" them. They recognize the existence of other types of money as factors in explaining the value of money only in so far as their existence affects the supply and demand for the standard commodity. When general prices increase or decrease, it is explained in terms of changes in the demand for or supply of the commodity out of which standard money is made.

The commodity theorists (known as "bullion theorists" when the commodity standard is metal) had difficulty in explaining the value of irredeemable credit paper money but finally concluded that its value is based on anticipated future redemption in the standard commodity. Now it is recognized that money may have value independent of the value of any standard commodity.

The chief difference between the pure commodity-standard system, at one extreme, and the fiat-paper standard, at the other, is that in the former the supply of money is determined by the supply of the standard commodity; and in the latter the supply of money is regulated artificially. Under a fiat-paper standard, the movement of things, including gold, across national boundaries is regulated; foreign exchange prices are fixed; and there is usually price control, rationing, and allocation of productive resources within the economy. The monetary systems of countries behind the "iron curtain" would best illustrate what is meant by pure fiat-money systems.

Although practices associated with managed fiat-money systems are antithetical to the free enterprise system, the democracies have used them during war and reconstruction periods.

The development of monetary systems has involved an increasingly greater use of subsidiary coins, paper money, and deposit currency, which means that these systems have become less and less pure types of commodity-standard systems. While management is necessary, it should be of the type that sets the stage on which the forces of free enterprise play. Needed policies are general in nature and work through the mechanism of free markets (interfering the least with private enterprise). So long as a link remains between currency and some commodity, such as gold, a commodity-standard factor remains. Since most of the world's gold stock is now used for monetary purposes, one may ask: "How much commodity value now resides in gold?" In other words: "What would be the value of gold if it were not used as money?" The answer is: "Not very much." Today, it is the value of money—specifically the United States dollar—that determines the value of gold. Now the "tail wags the dog."

OTHER PROPOSED COMMODITY STANDARDS

The historical development of monetary standards has been away from the pure-commodity-standard system. It has been proposed that a monetary system be created which would be based upon many commodities rather than upon one commodity (gold) or two commodities (gold and silver). The theoretical advantages of such a system are (1) greater stability in the value of money and (2) greater stability in the prices of the basic commodities used as standard commodities.

Multiple Commodity Standard. By issuing a type of "commodity certificate" to serve as money, this plan would permit each of the standard commodities to be monetized in the same way that gold and silver are monetized in bimetallism of the bullion type. Congress would have to decide (and herein lies a serious problem) how many commodity certificates would be given for each of the standard commodities (corresponding to mint-buying prices of metals). Similarly, Congress would have to provide for the convertibility of the commodity certificates (corresponding to mint-selling prices of metals). The result would be the establishment of a fixed price for each standard commodity. This might be $35.00

per ounce for gold, 90 cents per ounce for silver, $2.20 per bushel for a particular grade of wheat (with variations in price for other grades), and so on for all the standard commodities.

In effect, this system would provide a minimum price for each standard commodity in the same way that bimetallism provides minimum prices for gold and silver. This mint or government price might not always be the market price because the mechanics of the system would permit market prices to rise above mint prices. This situation would make profitable the conversion of commodity certificates into commodities and would result in a flow of commodities from government warehouses to the market, where the increased supply would tend to check the rise in prices in the market. At times, the government would be without certain standard commodities (as happened in bimetallism), which would increase the monetary importance of those remaining. The conversion of commodity certificates would decrease the quantity of money, and this would tend to have a stabilizing effect on prices.

During falling prices, the increase in the monetizing of standard commodities would increase the quantity of money, and this would have a stabilizing effect on general prices. Since these shifts of standard commodities in and out of the government's warehouses and the commercial market would take place automatically, there would be no need for monetary management except of the ministerial type. It would provide automatically for the stabilization of prices of certain basic commodities and the storage of these commodities during depressions. This is in keeping with recent emphasis on the federal government policies of the "ever-normal granary" and "storage of strategic materials."

Composite Commodity Standard. A modification of the multiple commodity standard is one which would provide for a standard composed of a composite of staple commodities. This system would necessitate the delivery to the monetary agency of all commodity units in their fixed proportion, as provided by law, in the same way that both gold and silver would be presented in symmetallism. Similarly, the government or central bank would be required to deliver the composite commodity units when the holders of the commodity certificates sought to redeem them. The owners of wheat and other standard commodities would find this system less convenient than the multiple commodity system. The composite commodity standard would have the same advantage over the multiple commodity standard that symmetallism would have over bimetallism: no standard commodity would disappear from the monetary system.

The currency-issuing authority could either hold the stock of commodities that had been monetized or leave the commodities with private traders and accept title documents (as do banks when they make loans on warehoused goods). In the latter case, the traders, in effect, would be receiving interest-free loans but they would have to pay the storage, insurance, and other costs which otherwise would be paid by the currency-issuing authority.

Some degree of discretion may be left to the currency-issuing authority, which would watch the prices of the commodities included in the list; and, if their combined price were to fall by a specified percentage such as 5 per cent, the currency-issuing authority would start buying them in the specified proportion. Payment would be made with new issues of currency which would increase the amount of money outstanding. Conversely, if the combined price were to increase 5 per cent, the currency-issuing authority would sell commodities in the specified proportion. The currency received in payment would reduce the money supply and the sale of commodities formerly in storage would tend to reduce their prices.

There is a possibility that some goods may become so scarce as to necessitate substitution. However, if possible, alterations in the list of commodities used as the base for the currency should be avoided. If the plan were adopted on an international basis, changes in the list might be left to the discretion of a World Court; but if adopted on a national basis, decisions as to changes in the list might be made by the proper authority, such as the Supreme Court of the United States. Only one type of currency would be permitted and commercial banks could accept deposits provided all of those used as checking accounts were backed unit for unit in commodity currency (see also the 100-per-cent-reserve plan). Among the advantages claimed for an international commodity-based currency system are that it would (1) prevent recessions and unemployment, (2) provide markets for farm surpluses, (3) help underdeveloped countries to obtain capital, and (4) help stabilize general prices.[5]

Compensated Dollar Plan. The Compensated Dollar Plan is a proposed system in which the weight of the gold dollar would be adjusted automatically with changes in general prices. If prices were rising, the weight of the gold dollar would be increased; and, if prices were falling, the weight of the gold dollar would be decreased. Since changes in the weight of the gold dollar mean changes in the mint price of gold, the sponsors of this plan propose to secure a more stable price level by substituting a variable mint price for gold for the present fixed-price system.

The Compensated Dollar Plan would influence the general price level through its effect on the available amount of reserve money, as does the gold standard today. Changes in the standard unit would take place after the index number of prices used as the guide had changed, and so the corrective effects of changes in the quantity of reserve money would be delayed. On the other hand, no forecasting in anticipation of future developments would be necessary, and this would lessen the need for discretionary management.

Actually, when the weight of the dollar is being increased in order to check rising prices, the foreign exchange rate of the dollar in terms of foreign currencies would tend to increase. International bankers might anticipate such changes by shifting funds to New York, thereby increasing the volume of funds in the money market at the time when the operation of the plan should have decreased the volume of funds. During falling prices, when the operation of the plan would be expected to increase the volume of funds, international banks might anticipate changes by withdrawing funds from New York to avoid losses.

The price that would be paid for operating under the Compensated Dollar Plan—fluctuating exchange rates—would be small if the broader objectives of a stable price level and a stable economy could be assured. Today, although no country is seriously considering the adoption of the plan, the International Monetary Fund Agreement recognizes the need for adjusting the weight of monetary units by individual countries or in unison by all countries.

SUMMARY

Countries accepting the International Monetary Fund Agreement are committed to the adoption of the international gold standard. They have voluntarily accepted a "code of behavior" covering the conditions under which they may change the weight of their standard gold units, buy and sell gold, and buy and sell foreign exchange. The mechanism whereby they keep the value of money equal to gold at home may be the adoption of the gold-coin, gold-bullion, or gold-exchange standard.

There are strong arguments in favor of the gold-coin standard. During inflation the hoarding of gold coins would mean a loss of bank reserves, forcing a decline in bank lending and investing. This tightening of credit would tend to curtail spending which would put a check on rising prices. Thus, the gold-coin standard would act as a sort of "policeman" of the monetary authorities. This same argument is applicable to the gold-bullion standard and to the gold-exchange standard, but to a lesser degree because of the inconvenience of holding gold bullion or gold exchange. The weakness of this argument is the assumption that the wise man hoards gold only during inflation. Deflation may stimulate gold hoarding, and during 1929–33 gold hoarding was one of the many factors contributing to the deflationary forces at work in the United States and abroad.

In reconstructing monetary systems by placing them on a gold-exchange standard basis, governments are individually and co-operatively (1) strengthening the use of the gold bill of exchange as the chief instrument of international payments; (2) limiting the use of monetary gold to settling accounts among governments and/or central banks; and (3) developing domestic exchange systems wherein trade is carried on with token coins, paper money, and deposit currency.

The development of monetary systems has involved an increasingly greater use of subsidiary coins, paper money, and deposit currency, which means that these systems have become less and less pure types of commodity-standard systems. While management is necessary, it should be of the type that sets the stage on which the forces of free enterprise play. Needed policies are general in nature and work through the mechanism of free markets (interfering the least with private enterprise). So long as a link remains between currency and some commodity, such as gold, a commodity-standard factor remains.

QUESTIONS AND PROBLEMS

1. Identify: (*a*) standard money, (*b*) international gold standard, and (*c*) a gold monetary unit.
2. Does defining the value of a country's standard monetary unit in terms of gold mean that the country has a gold standard? Explain.
3. What is meant by the statement that gold is the "regulator of the balance of payments"?
4. Analyze the statement that "gold serves as the regulator of the currency."

5. What factors in gold production tend to make its value more stable than the value of other commodities?

6. Analyze the following statement: "To argue that a rise in the commodity price level should be followed by an increase in the price of gold is a version of the economics of perpetual inflation." (M. A. Kriz, *The Price of Gold*, Essays in International Finance, No. 15, International Finance Section, Department of Economics and Social Institutions, Princeton University [Princeton, N.J., July, 1952], p. 26.)

7. Does the nonmonetary demand for gold tend to stabilize its value? Can the same be said for the monetary demands for gold? Explain.

8. In 1955 gold production outside the Soviet Union amounted to about $1 billion, of which $700 million remained outside the gold reserves of central banks and governments. Comment on the effects of such hoarding on the value of money in countries on (a) a paper standard, and (b) a gold standard. Do these statistics suggest that gold has lost its appeal as a store of value or as money?

9. What are the chief characteristics of (a) the gold-coin standard, (b) the gold-bullion standard, and (c) the gold-exchange standard?

10. Since a central bank may cover sales of gold exchange by shipping gold out of its own vaults, is it necessary for a central bank to keep gold balances abroad in order to operate on the gold-exchange standard?

11. Is one justified in describing the current monetary standard in the United States as a gold-exchange standard? Why?

12. "The 'commodity' argument [favoring subsidization of gold mining because of costs] contradicts the accepted function of gold, which is to act as a deflationary influence when increasing costs tend to reduce production." (*New York Times*, August 24, 1952, p. F1.) What does this mean? Do gold miners lose or gain from the use of gold as money when the mint price of gold is fixed? Assume that governments and central banks were to reverse their current hoarding policies, would the results be beneficial to gold miners?

13. What justification is there for the assumption that a commodity-based currency would tend to stabilize general prices and reduce unemployment?

14. What is the Compensated Dollar Plan? Would gold or the prices of commodities be the important factor in determining the money supply?

Chapter VIII

HISTORY OF MONETARY
STANDARDS AND CURRENCY
IN THE UNITED STATES

THROUGHOUT the history of the United States, the monetary unit has been the United States dollar; but, at different times, there have been different monetary standards. The first important monetary standard legislation in our history was the passage of the Coinage Act of 1792 which provided for a bimetallic system. The next major change in the standard situation occurred during the Civil War period when there was a shift from a commodity standard to a paper standard. Following the Reconstruction Period, the gold standard was adopted and lasted until 1933. Since 1933, the United States has had a restricted type of gold standard. Following a historical introduction, these periods are discussed in this chapter.

HISTORICAL INTRODUCTION

The United States monetary system, as established in 1792, was based on the best monetary principles of that time. Those responsible for its establishment showed a preference for full-bodied money (full-weight gold and silver coins which had a commodity value equal to their exchange value). This preference for hard money was a natural reaction to experiences with inflation due to overissues of paper money by the colonies, states, and the Continental Congress. To the founding fathers, it seemed improbable that there would ever be too much money if money were made of gold and silver.

Colonial Currency. Early in the history of the American colonies, commodities (beads, corn, tobacco, shot, pelts, and gunpowder) were used as money; and for a short time they were made government tender. Although the colonists were familiar with English coins, most of those which they brought with them were exported to pay for goods. Other coins were imported, chiefly from the Spanish colonies. Since the colonists thought of banking primarily as a source of paper money, they sought to solve their monetary problem—scarcity of money—by establishing banks of issue.

The conditions under which paper money was issued varied, but three types of notes or bills were authorized by the same or different colonial governments at different times and at different places: (1) government bills of exchange, which were to be redeemed out of public revenue after a year or more; (2) paper money issued by government banks and lent at interest (notes were to be redeemed when the loans were paid, usually on an annual installment plan); (3) bills issued by chartered private banks, which were backed by deeds to land and commodities. Although all of these types of paper money provided for ultimate redemption, no provisions were made for current convertibility.

Some of the colonial banking ventures were successful, and their note issues had a beneficial effect on the economy wherein they circulated. In other cases, overissuance of notes was followed by depreciation, postponement of redemption, and sometimes repudiation. Finally, England prohibited the issuance of paper money in the colonies.

Continental Currency. One of the first tasks of the Second Continental Congress was to provide means for financing the Revolutionary War. Because the new government's credit was too poor to permit borrowing and the colonists were opposed to heavy taxes, paper money was issued. On May 11, 1775, Congress authorized the issuance of notes equivalent to 2,000,000 Spanish milled dollars. The process was repeated many times during the next few years, and more than $240,000,000 were issued.[1] The notes purported to be credit money—a promise of the Continental Congress to pay coins; but, since there were no coins for this purpose, the notes were irredeemable paper money. Depreciation was rapid, and those who accepted and held the notes suffered heavy losses. In 1780 there was an unsuccessful attempt to redeem "old tenor" currency in "new tenor" currency. By 1781 "old tenor" notes ceased to circulate as money and were bought up by speculators at rates of from 400 to 1 to 1,000 to 1.[2] During this period and later, things that were considered valueless were referred to derisively as "not worth a Continental."

State Issues. After the outbreak of the Revolutionary War in 1775, without waiting for any Declaration of Independence, the states authorized the issuance of paper money for war financing

[1] D. R. Dewey, *Financial History of the United States* (11th ed.; New York: Longmans, Green & Co., 1931), pp. 36–44.

[2] Ten years later about $6,000,000 was turned in to be redeemed at a rate of 100 to 1; and it is inferred that the remainder was destroyed.

and other purposes. Every one of the thirteen states issued bills of credit during 1775; and, for several years, new issues appeared in most states. In 1778 the Continental Congress appealed successfully to the states to cease issuing paper money in order that the value of the continental currency might be maintained. But in 1780, following the announcement by Congress that it would replace the old continental currency with a "new tenor" issue and would authorize no new paper-currency issues, new state issues appeared. Within two years the country was flooded with new state issues.[3]

Specie. Most of the $4,000,000 in coins which had been in the country at the outbreak of the Revolutionary War was hoarded as a result of the depreciation of paper money. But new coined money came from three sources: (1) Great Britain, which paid for supplies and services (including troop pay) in coins; (2) France, which sent gold and silver directly to the United States and also followed the practice of paying for goods and services in specie; and (3) Spain and the Spanish colonies, which had an unfavorable balance of trade with the United States. By 1780 the supply of specie was sufficient to permit the national government to make its payments in "hard money."

Because the shortage of fractional currency continued, some states gave approval to private coinage projects. Many specimens of brass, copper, and tin coins appeared; and some states issued paper money in fractional denominations. Merchants in Boston and New York imported small coins of various descriptions (more than forty tons of one design reached New York). This situation was bound to cause trouble; and, in 1782, several states prohibited the circulation of private coins.

This background helps to explain the provisions in the United States Constitution giving Congress the power "to coin money, regulate the value thereof, and of foreign coins . . . ."[4] and forbidding any state "to coin money; emit bills of credit; make anything but gold and silver coin a tender in payment of debts. . . ."[5]

BIMETALLISM

The Coinage Act of 1792. The Coinage Act of 1792 provided for a United States mint, "full-bodied" gold and silver coins, token copper coins, a mint ratio of 15 to 1 for silver and gold

[3] Ralph V. Barlow, "Aspects of Revolutionary Finance, 1775–1783," *American Historical Review*, Vol. XXXV, p. 68.

[4] *The Constitution of the United States*, Article 1, Section 8.

[5] *Ibid.*, Article 1, Section 10.

for monetary purposes, free coinage of gold and silver, and legal tender for all United States gold and silver coins. At the same time, all persons, corporations, and other legal entities had the right to own, hoard, import, and export both metals. In effect, Congress provided for two competing standards—a gold-coin standard and a silver-coin standard—with silver having been dominant until 1834 and gold thereafter until the Civil War, when the paper dollar became the standard.

Silver Overrated at the Mint. The free coinage of both gold and silver provided "pegs" below which their market prices would not fall (minor allowances must be made for the cost of moving metals, mintage, and other charges). For illustration, if one could not sell silver in the market for $1.29+ or gold for $19.39+ per fine ounce, one could take it to the mint and have it minted into silver and gold coins, as provided for by the free coinage privilege.

As a matter of record, the Coinage Act of 1792 overrated the value of silver and underrated the value of gold, which meant that Gresham's Law operated to drive or keep gold out of circulation. Spain had a 16 to 1 ratio; and, after 1800, France had a 15½ to 1 ratio. Silver tended to flow to the more favorable monetary market in the United States, where only 15 ounces of silver were needed to obtain one ounce of gold (as compared to 16 or 15½ elsewhere); and gold was sold abroad or used at home for purposes other than as money. This left the United States on a silver standard, even though the law provided for both gold and silver standard coins.

The Theory of Bimetallism. Those who favored the bimetallic system assumed that the mechanism of the bimetallic standard would keep the market ratio of gold and silver in line with the mint ratio, thus maintaining the double standard. The principle of bimetallism assumes that the shift of the monetary stock of the underrated metal into the commercial market will decrease its market price because of the increase in supply. At the same time the increase in monetary work thrown on the metal overrated at the mint and the withdrawal of bullion from the commercial market will increase its value. These two movements, one working so as to decrease the value of the metal underrated at the mint and the other working so as to increase the value of the metal overrated at the mint, are expected to keep the mint and market ratios in balance.

Shifting the monetary demand in part from one metal to the other was expected to give the economy a more stable price level than would result from having a single commodity as the standard. At the same time, the commodity base for the monetary system was expected to be broader with less fluctuations in the volume of the two metals than would be true if one metal were used. The need for small- as well as large-value coins was also recognized, and it was felt this would be met more readily from silver than from gold.

If all countries had established the same mint ratio, the bimetallic system might have worked as expected; but this need for a common mint ratio and international co-operation was recognized too late. During the third quarter of the last century, the problem of a common mint ratio was discussed at a number of international monetary conferences. In 1865 the Latin Monetary Union was formed by Belgium, France, Italy, and Switzerland (later Greece joined the Union). This was an international bimetallic system which had the same mint ratio and interchangeable coins, but it was in operation for only a few years. After the Franco-Prussian War, Germany received an indemnity of five billion gold francs, and this gold furnished the basis for the shift of Germany from a silver to a gold standard. Fearing a flood of silver released from Germany, France and other members of the Latin Monetary Union discontinued the free coinage of silver.

Token Money, Foreign Coins, and Bank Notes.   Although Congress showed a preference for full-bodied money, concessions were made in favor of token coins and paper money. Congress not only provided for a small quantity of copper coins and made certain foreign coins legal tender but also chartered the first Bank of the United States, which was given the right to issue paper money in an amount equal to its capital ($10,000,000). However, the greatest divergence away from full-bodied money resulted from the chartering of banks by state governments. The notes and demand deposits of these state banks were used as money. Many of these banks issued small fractional notes as well as notes of larger denominations. In addition, paper money was issued by the three banks chartered by the national government, the Bank of North America, and the first and second Bank of the United States. These cheaper means of payment tended to drive all coins out of circulation.

The Gold Bill of 1834.   In the Act of June 28, 1834, sometimes called the "Gold Bill," Congress reduced the gold content of the dollar from 24.75 grains of pure gold to 23.2 grains without altering the silver content of silver coins. This changed the coinage ratio from 15 to 1 to about 16 to 1. In 1837 gold and silver coins were made $\frac{9}{10}$ fine (previously $\frac{11}{12}$ fine); and the gold content of the dollar was increased slightly to 23.22 grains, thus creating a ratio of slightly less than 16 to 1 (the mint price of gold was $20.67 and that of silver remained at $1.29+).

Congress expected changes made by the Acts of 1834 and 1837 to attract gold to the mint; and its expectations were realized, especially after the discovery of gold in California. However, Congress did not anticipate the gradual disappearance of full-weight silver coins. The Coinage Act of 1834 (and as amended in 1837) underrated the value of silver, and bankers found it profitable to sell their silver bullion and larger silver coins abroad in exchange for gold bullion and gold coins. Thus, gold became the standard money. Although some small fractional American coins and debased Spanish pieces continued to circulate, the small-coin situation became progressively worse.

Silver Subsidiary Coinage Act of 1853. In the Act of February 21, 1853, sometimes called the "Silver Subsidiary Coinage Act," Congress departed farther from the full-bodied or "hard-money" principle and made all fractional silver coins token money. The free-coinage principle, as applied to silver, had not provided the economy with a satisfactory coinage system; and it was replaced by "limited" coinage.

All silver coins, except the silver dollar, were made lightweight. Bullion was purchased by the mint in the market and struck into coins which were sold at their "face" or token value. While the deposit of silver for coinage into silver dollars was permitted, fractional silver coins were minted only on the account of the United States. Soon after the passage of this law, the United States had an adequate supply of domestic coins; and, in 1857, all acts making foreign coins legal tender in the United States were repealed.

PAPER STANDARD OR THE GREENBACK PERIOD

From the beginning of its history, the United States currency system included paper money. The Republic was launched on a flood of irredeemable paper. Because the powers of the federal government were delegated powers and no specific powers were granted to issue paper money, the Fathers of the Constitution assumed that no government credit paper money would be issued after the adoption of the Constitution. Before 1861 three banks were chartered by the national government and hundreds by state governments (see Chapter IX), and paper money soon became an important form of pocket money. Although most of the state-banking legislation of the pre-Civil War period was directed at making paper money issues of banks safe, the results were unsatisfactory from a national viewpoint. Nevertheless, when Congress authorized the issuance of irredeemable legal-tender paper money fairly early in the Civil War (February, 1862), it came as a shock.[6]

Greenback Issues. During the Civil War, Congress provided for three issues of United States notes (greenbacks). Almost all of the $450,000,000 authorized was issued; and, by July, 1864, they had depreciated to such an extent that $100 in greenbacks was worth $35 in gold (partly due to speculation in gold). Because of war spending and inflationary financing, prices rose sharply; and, by 1864, they were more than double their 1861 level. Between July, 1864, and the spring of 1865, the discount on greenbacks, in terms of gold, fell by 50 per cent; but general prices declined less than 5 per cent.

Although the people in California refused to accept United States notes, these notes were the standard money for the remainder of the country from 1862 to 1879. After 1866 the currency situation was simpler and, in some respects, sounder than it had been prior to the Civil War. Greenbacks, fractional paper money, and national bank notes had replaced specie and hundreds of different kinds of state bank notes of the prewar years.

Following the Civil War, prices dropped sharply and continued downward for several years. The volume of national bank notes was carefully limited, state bank notes had been taxed out of existence, and Confederate currency had disappeared. The West had borrowed large sums in order to develop its agricultural resources, and the South borrowed heavily in order to reconstruct the war-devastated communities. Because greenbacks were only slightly below par and could be used to meet debt contracts, certain political leaders considered them to be the solution to the country's monetary problems and wanted more of them in order to stimulate business and to raise prices.

The Act of January 14, 1875, known as the "Resumption of Specie Payments Act," provided for the redemption in specie of all

---

[6] On February 24, 1815, Congress authorized the issuance of noninterest-bearing Treasury notes in denominations as low as $3.00. Although they lacked any legal tender quality, these notes, as well as the War of 1812 issues of interest-bearing Treasury notes, were made receivable in payment of customs duties and taxes. Perhaps, if this war had continued, Congress would have authorized issues of legal-tender paper money.

greenbacks presented to the Treasury on and after January 1, 1879. In addition, the act provided that the total circulation was to be reduced to $300,000,000; but, in 1878, Congress amended this provision and fixed the volume of greenbacks at the number then outstanding ($346,681,016, where it has remained to this day). In December, 1878, the premium on gold in terms of United States notes disappeared; and on January 1, 1879, the shift to a convertible basis was made with no internal or external drain on gold reserves in the Treasury.

National Bank Notes. From the viewpoint of the general public the most significant change in the currency system during the late 1860's was the replacement of hundreds of state-bank-note issues of varying quality and degrees of discount by national bank notes. National bank notes were obligations of the issuing bank fully supported by United States government promises to pay. Every national bank was required to accept at par "any and all notes" issued by national banks organized under the provisions of the law. This prevented these notes from circulating at a discount when far from the place or origin. During the half century that followed, the importance of the monopoly of bank-note issue given to national banks was largely offset by the increasing use of deposit currency.[7]

End of Legal Bimetallism. In addition to the provision for redemption of greenbacks in gold, Congress made plans to replace the silver and other coins which had been melted during the Civil War. A bill providing for a revision and codification of scattered coinage laws was passed by Congress and became law in 1873. By omitting the standard silver dollar from the list of United States coins, this law eliminated the last remnant of the original free-coinage privilege as it applied to silver.[8] Thus ended legal bimetallism in

[7] The Act of March 3, 1865, implemented the National Bank Act by placing a tax of 10 per cent on the amount of notes of any state bank or banking association paid out by every national bank, state bank, or state banking association after July 1, 1866. If this had been made applicable to notes and bills of exchange, the national bank monopoly of supplying bank money would have been complete.

[8] The silver dollar was being used in the trade with China, where it passed by weight. When the standard silver dollar was dropped in 1873, provisions were made for a "trade" dollar containing 6.75 more grains of silver than the old silver dollar. Three years later Congress changed the status of the "trade" dollar by withdrawing its legal-tender quality, and the Secretary of the Treasury was authorized to limit its coinage "to such an amount as he may deem sufficient to meet the export demand for the same." (National Monetary Commission, Sec. 2 of "Joint Resolution of July 22, 1876," *Financial Laws of the United States 1778–1909* [Washington, D.C.: U.S. Government Printing Office, 1910] Vol. II, p. 576.) In 1887 Congress repealed all laws and parts of laws that provided for the coinage of

the United States as provided for in 1792. Since the country was on a paper standard, this change meant nothing at the time; but a few years later it came to be very important.

Two developments which began in 1874 made the Act of 1873 of political significance. One was the discovery of rich silver mines in Nevada, and the other was the fall in the market price of silver below the old mint price. The new silver interests soon discovered that if the free coinage of the silver dollar were permitted they could take their silver bullion to the mint and dispose of it at the mint price of $1.29+ per fine ounce. The drive for the restoration of the bimetallic standard and the return of the standard silver dollar began. Although the silverites have secured many concessions from Congress, including the return of the standard silver dollar, they have not secured a law permitting the free coinage of silver and the return of the bimetallic standard.

The Act of February 28, 1878, popularly known as the "Bland-Allison Act," required the Secretary of the Treasury to purchase from $2,000,000 to $4,000,000 worth of silver each month at the market price and to coin it into standard silver dollars having full legal tender. The Treasury purchased the minimum amount provided for. This was limited coinage, not free coinage, and the silver dollars were but token coins. The amount of silver purchased was expected to equal the output of domestic mines, and the owners of silver dollars could exchange them for silver certificates which could only be issued when secured by silver dollars.

THE GOLD-COIN STANDARD

When the United States began redeeming the United States notes (greenbacks) in 1879, it was moving into a twenty-one-year era during which bank paper money and subsidiary coins were redeemable in lawful money, United States notes and gold certificates were redeemable in gold coins, and silver certificates were redeemable in "standard silver dollars." But what was the status of the standard silver dollar? For all practical purposes the country was on a gold standard; but the uncertainty of the status of the silver dollar caused this period to be known as that of the "limping" gold standard, or gold standard with a "peg-leg" made of silver.

----

trade dollars; authorized the Treasury to accept those outstanding, for a six months' period, in exchange for other silver coins; and provided for the melting-down of trade dollars and recoinage into other coins. (See *ibid.*, "Act of March 3, 1887," p. 588.)

The Sherman Act. The Act of July 14, 1890, popularly known as the "Sherman Act," added to the complexity of the monetary system in two ways: (1) it required the monthly purchase of silver to be increased to 4,500,000 ounces per month at the prevailing market price, which doubled the quantity of silver bullion purchased; and (2) it required that the silver purchased be paid for with Treasury or "Sherman" notes (eliminating the delay in obtaining payment by sellers who previously had to wait until the silver bullion was coined). Now the Treasury went through the procedure of buying silver bullion, paying for it with paper money called "Treasury notes," coining silver into silver dollars, issuing silver certificates to retire the Treasury notes, and retaining the silver dollars as a reserve against the silver certificates.

Panic of 1893. The effect of increasing the amount of silver in the monetary stock was to lessen confidence in the ability of the United States to remain on the gold standard. Several domestic and foreign factors account for the panic of 1893, but the silver issue played an important part. On November 1, 1893, Congress repealed the silver-purchase clause of the Sherman Act. From 1893 to 1897 the government had great difficulty in keeping the United States on the gold standard. It was not until the end of the presidential campaign of 1896 that general confidence in the monetary system returned, and with it the pressure upon the country's gold reserves was decreased. Although the candidate of the party favoring the free coinage of silver was defeated in the campaign of 1896, the legal position of the silver dollar was not settled until the passage of the Gold Standard Act of 1900.

Gold Standard Act of 1900. The Act of March 14, 1900, did what the Coinage Act of 1873 failed to do—it recognized the gold dollar as the "standard unit of value" and provided that "all forms of money issued or coined by the United States shall be maintained at a parity with this standard" and made it the duty of the Secretary of the Treasury "to maintain such parity." The act provided for creation and maintenance of a reserve fund of $150,000,-000 in gold coin and bullion to be set aside for the redemption of United States notes and Treasury notes of 1890. The redeemed notes could be reissued in exchange for gold;[9] but, if the fund fell below $100,000,000, the Secretary of the Treasury was required to restore it to $150,000,000 by selling government bonds.

---

[9] Previously, United States notes that were redeemed had to be reissued, permitting an "endless chain" drain on the gold stock during panics.

When the price level turned upward in 1896, it reversed a deflationary trend that had been current in the United States since 1865 and in the world since 1873. The influx of gold from the Yukon and South Africa increased the base on which to expand the volume of credit and currency. Although the United States now had a gold-coin standard, most of the gold was held by banks and the government; and gold circulated primarily in the form of gold certificates.

Gold Certificates. Gold certificates were first authorized in the Act of March 3, 1863. Although gold was being mined in large quantities in California, it was flowing either out of the country, or into gold hoards, except in California where the people refused to use United States notes as money.[10] In the remainder of the country the only compulsory uses for gold were in payment of custom duties and interest on the federal debt (greenbacks were not government tender for these purposes). The government's receipts of gold were in excess of Treasury needs for interest payments; and this led to the policy of selling gold in the market at the market price, which fluctuated from day to day. The provision for gold certificates was for the convenience of the users of gold, and this reflected the preference for paper money over "hard money."

After 1879 the volume of gold coins and gold certificates in circulation increased steadily until the organization of the Federal Reserve System in 1914. The volume of gold and gold certificates represented but one eighth of the currency in circulation during the low point in the 1870's and one half in 1914.

After the establishment of the Federal Reserve banks, the Federal Reserve System began its policy of absorbing the gold stock of the nation. Although some gold was received in payment for the capital stock of the Reserve banks, a larger percentage came in when member banks transferred part of their reserve balances from their own vaults to the Federal Reserve banks. In June, 1917, legal-reserve requirements of member banks were reduced; but member banks were required to keep all their required reserves as balances with the Reserve banks. This led to an additional shift of gold from member banks' vaults to the Reserve banks.

---

[10] Congress not only permitted this situation to exist but also authorized the formation of "gold banks," which were no different from others except that their national bank notes were redeemable in gold instead of greenbacks. This distinction became unimportant in 1879, when the greenbacks were made convertible into gold. The Act of February 14, 1880, authorized the conversion of "national gold banks" into ordinary national banks.

Federal Reserve Notes. The Federal Reserve Act provided for Federal Reserve bank notes (which were to replace national bank notes) and Federal Reserve notes, which were to be the "elastic currency." Since Federal Reserve notes were obtained in exchange for commercial paper, it was thought that the amount of these notes would fluctuate with the needs of trade. However, instead of using Federal Reserve notes to reclaim matured paper held by the Federal Reserve agents as was expected, gold and gold certificates were used. This meant that Federal Reserve notes remained in circulation and that the amount was not related to the volume of commercial paper held by the Federal Reserve banks.

All types of currency flow through the Federal Reserve banks; and, by retaining gold certificates and paying out Federal Reserve notes, the Federal Reserve banks impounded most of the gold and gold certificates. During the 1920's, a gold reserve ratio of 80 per cent for Federal Reserve banks was common, reflecting both the Federal Reserve System's policy of impounding gold and the influx of gold from abroad. The Reserve banks used much of this gold as collateral for Federal Reserve notes in place of commercial paper (which meant that these notes had the same security as gold certificates).

From 1930 to February, 1932, the 100 per cent collateral requirement in the form of gold certificates and eligible paper was the chief depressing factor in the issuance of additional Federal Reserve notes. The Federal Reserve banks lacked a sufficient supply of eligible paper to obtain Federal Reserve notes, and so they used gold certificates not only as collateral for Federal Reserve notes but also to meet the demand for currency. This situation was rectified in 1932 (by the Glass-Steagall Act) when the Reserve banks were permitted to obtain Federal Reserve notes from the Federal Reserve agents in exchange for United States government direct obligations. In 1934, the Gold Reserve Act provided for the withdrawal of all gold certificates from circulation.

Federal Reserve Bank Notes. The original intent of Congress in providing for Federal Reserve bank notes was for them to replace national bank notes, but the currency demands during World War I interferred with this objective and national bank notes continued to circulate. National bank notes were secured by United States government bonds designated for this purpose; and, when the last of these bonds was retired on August 1, 1935, new issues of these notes ceased and the United States Treasury assumed responsibility for those outstanding.

In the Bank Emergency Act of 1933, the collateral base for Federal Reserve bank notes was broadened to include commercial paper and any type of government direct obligation. Although there was no gold reserve requirement, the need for this type of currency was less than expected and only a small percentage of the Federal Reserve bank notes printed were placed in circulation. At the beginning of World War II (December, 1942) this stock of printed notes was used as an economy measure.

The Pittman Act of 1918 authorized the retirement of $350,-000,000 in silver certificates and their replacement with Federal Reserve bank notes, and provided that the silver dollars they represented be melted down and the bullion sold to Great Britain to pay for purchases from India during World War I (some of the bullion was recoined into U.S. subsidiary coins). The act also provided that this silver, which was sold for one dollar per ounce, must be replaced at the same price by purchases of domestically mined silver. After the price of silver fell, the silver bullion reserve was replaced, and Federal Reserve bank notes were replaced by silver currency. This episode illustrates how easy it would be to retire outstanding silver certificates and thereby to release the silver held as a reserve against them for use in industry. The power of the Federal Reserve banks to issue Federal Reserve bank notes was withdrawn by Congress on June 12, 1945; and the United States Treasury was made responsible for the Federal Reserve bank notes in circulation.

RESTRICTED GOLD-BULLION STANDARD

Beginning on March 4, 1933, there began a series of events that led to the adoption of the current restricted gold-bullion standard. When Franklin D. Roosevelt became President of the United States on March 4, 1933, one of his first official acts was to declare a national banking holiday.

Suspension of Gold Payments. In addition to suspending banking activities (except those authorized by the Secretary of the Treasury), the national banking holiday proclamation contained provisions forbidding the hoarding of gold and gold certificates and the exportation of gold. When Congress met on March 9, it passed the Emergency Banking Act of 1933. In Title I the emergency steps taken by the President were confirmed, and the emergency powers of the President and the Secretary of the Treasury over gold and other financial transactions were strengthened. In effect, convertibility of currency into gold was suspended for the duration of the national emergency.

During the crisis in the United States, transactions in the dollar ceased in some foreign markets; and trading was limited in others. After the crisis was over, the Secretary of the Treasury followed a fairly liberal policy in issuing licenses permitting the export of gold; and the price of the dollar remained at or near par in the foreign exchange markets of gold standard countries.

A New Monetary Policy. On April 19, 1933, the Treasury announced that gold export licenses for all ordinary purposes would be suspended. Gold was sequestered in the Treasury, and all United States coins and paper money were to be legal tender. In addition, the President and the Secretary of the Treasury admitted publicly that the United States was not on a gold basis.

In May, 1933, considerable light was thrown upon the future credit and money policy of the United States government by the President in a radio address to the American people. He stated: "The Administration has the definite objective of raising commodity prices to such an extent that those who have borrowed money will, on the average, be able to repay that money in the same kind of dollar which they borrowed. . . . We do not seek to let them get such a cheap dollar that, in effect, they will be able to pay back a great deal less than they borrowed."

Thomas Inflation Act. Emphasis was to be on raising of commodity prices by monetary action. In this same talk the President referred to certain powers which were then in the process of being granted to him. They appeared as Title III of the Agricultural Adjustment Act of May 12, 1933, and this part of the Act is known as the Thomas Inflation Act. The most important aspect of the law is that the powers granted the President were discretionary powers. Some of these powers were never used, and others were used only in part.

The Thomas Inflation Act gave the President the power to (1) reduce the weight of the gold dollar by as much as 50 per cent, (2) re-establish bimetallism by authorizing the free coinage of gold and silver, (3) accept silver from foreign governments in payment of their current and past-due debts in an amount of $200,-000,000 only, at a price of 50 cents an ounce, (4) authorize the

Secretary of the Treasury to issue $3,000,000,000 in United States notes if the Secretary could not persuade the Federal Reserve authorities to increase central bank credit by purchases of United States government obligations in the open market, and (5) approve requests of the Federal Reserve Board to make emergency changes in the minimum reserve requirements of member banks.

Silver Purchase Act of 1934.   The greatest subsidy to the silver industry abroad resulted from the passage of the Silver Purchase Act of 1934, which provided for the purchase of silver by the Treasury at prices not in excess of $1.29 per fine ounce. The law also stated that the silver was to be purchased until the money value of silver in the monetary stock held by the government was equal to 25 per cent of the total value of gold and silver stock (now it is about 10 per cent of the total). Domestic silver that has been acquired under the provisions of this and other acts now exceeds 100,000 tons. This is a tragedy, since silver is in large demand for industrial purposes.

Gold Purchase Plan.   On October 22, 1933, in another radio address, the President restated his price program and announced his new plan to secure it—governmental purchases of gold at higher prices. The assumption was that since each increase in the price of gold would increase the number of gold dollars represented by the gold stock, general prices would rise correspondingly. Three days later the Reconstruction Finance Corporation announced that it would purchase all domestic gold at $31.36 per ounce, and the following day governmental purchases were extended to foreign markets through the facilities of the Federal Reserve Bank of New York. Subsequently, gold buying prices were increased.

The gold buying plan aroused a storm of protest from the first. It was not understood by businessmen; and the resulting uncertainty was enough to prevent its successful operation, assuming that it had been scientifically correct in its concept. The fact that the mint price of gold is increased and more paper money (gold certificates) is printed and deposited in Federal Reserve banks, is no guarantee that the supply of money will increase. Even if the supply of money does increase, the price level or volume of transactions or both will not increase if businessmen and others hold more funds and spend relatively less. A decrease in velocity of money may even cause a decline in general prices. The main result of the gold buying policy was to prepare the country for the devaluation of the gold dollar, which became effective on January 31, 1934.

Gold Reserve Act of 1934. The Gold Reserve Act of 1934 changed the emergency status of most of the preceding monetary changes and greatly expanded governmental control over the monetary system. The three most important changes provided for in the act were: (1) the transfer of the nation's gold stock from the Federal Reserve System to the government; (2) the placement of responsibility for domestic and foreign gold transactions in the Treasury Department, under the President; and (3) the creation of a $2,000 million stabilization fund to be used by the Treasury to stabilize foreign exchange rates. These changes made the Secretary of the Treasury responsible for the international monetary policies of the United States.

The act prohibited coinage of gold into United States coins and demonetized those outstanding. The minimum reserve requirements of the Federal Reserve banks were changed to the general effect that gold certificates were to be substituted for gold. However, these gold certificates could not be owned legally by the public; and this created the peculiar situation wherein gold certificates were required to be held for reserves against Federal Reserve notes but they could not be used to meet the obligations of the Federal Reserve banks.[11] Federal Reserve notes carry the legend "redeemable in lawful money at the United States Treasury, or at any Federal Reserve bank." What is meant by "lawful money" for this purpose has never been defined by Congress.

The remaining provision in the act amended the Thomas Inflation Act by specifying that the new gold dollar could not be more than 60 per cent of its former weight. Since the Thomas Inflation Act specified that the President could reduce the weight of the gold dollar by not more than 50 per cent, this meant that the President was permitted to make a selection somewhere between 50 and 60 per cent of the dollar's former weight.

Devaluation of the Gold Dollar. After the close of business on January 30, 1934, the President issued a proclamation fixing the weight of the gold dollar at $15\frac{5}{21}$ grains of gold $\frac{9}{10}$ fine, making the mint price $35.00 per fine ounce troy weight. The new weight

[11] Sec. 6 of the Gold Reserve Act reads in part: "Except to the extent permitted in regulations which may be issued hereunder by the Secretary of the Treasury with the approval of the President, no currency of the United States shall be redeemed in gold: *Provided, however,* that gold certificates owned by the Federal Reserve banks shall be redeemed at such times and in such amounts as, in the judgment of the Secretary of the Treasury, are necessary to maintain the equal purchasing power of every kind of currency of the United States; . . . ."

was 59.06 per cent of the former weight, and this is the basis for reference to the "59-cent dollar."

As a result of the policy of counting one ounce of gold as $35.00, the number of gold dollars held by the government was "written up" from approximately $4,000 million to $6,800 million. Thus far, only bookkeeping changes have been described. For these changes to mean anything the Treasury had to buy gold at $35.00 per fine ounce and/or use the "new dollars" created by devaluation as a basis for currency that could and would be spent.

Treasury Regulations of Gold Transactions. Immediately following the devaluation proclamation, the Treasury issued regulations that provided for a gold buying policy at $35.00 per fine ounce, minus a handling charge of one fourth of 1 per cent. The Treasury has followed this policy to date, with the exception of war years when the source of gold offered was carefully investigated. Although the Treasury has followed a policy of selling gold to selected foreign central banks and governments, an element of uncertainty is created by the fact that the Treasury must give would-be purchasers permission to buy gold. Sales of gold at home have been regulated carefully, with the negative purpose of keeping the general public from using gold as a store of value or for the positive purpose of keeping gold in the hands of the government to be held as reserves against paper money (chiefly gold certificates, which serve as reserves for obligations of Federal Reserve banks).

Although the power to change the weight of the gold dollar by executive decree has expired, the Treasury's control over gold transactions has been a source of international confusion. For illustration, in mid-August, 1947, reports were current in London that the Secretary of the Treasury would increase the buying price of gold from $35.00 to $50.00 per fine ounce. The reports were so widespread that official denial from the Secretary of the Treasury was required.

In the Bretton Woods Agreements Act of July 31, 1945, Congress forbade the President or any person or agency acting for the United States to propose or agree to any change in the par value of the United States dollar as defined in terms of gold. Although the wording of the Gold Reserve Act of 1934 seems to give the Secretary of the Treasury unlimited discretionary power over the price paid by the Treasury, the price of gold cannot be changed without affecting the "par value of the United States dollar as defined in terms of gold." The Articles of Agreement of the International Monetary Fund also limit unilateral changes in the price of gold without consultation; and, if the changes are for more than 10 per cent, without prior approval. Further clarification of the gold-standard situation would follow if the gold-certificate mechanisms were eliminated, and the gold represented by gold certificates were transferred to the Federal Reserve banks.

Stabilization Fund. The Gold Reserve Act of 1934 provided for a $2,000 million Stabilization Fund to be administered by the Secretary of the Treasury. The basic function of the Fund was to stabilize the international value of the dollar. However, the dollar did not need such support because of the strong economic position of the United States and because the dollar, after devaluation, was undervalued in terms of foreign currencies. Only 10 per cent of the $2,000 million allocated to the Stabilization Fund was placed on deposit with the Federal Reserve Bank of New York. The Treasury carried the remainder as "inactive gold" in the Treasury statement of cash holdings until 1945, when Congress authorized that it be used as part payment of the United States quota of $2,750 million due the International Monetary Fund.

Sterilization Policy. Although the creation of the Stabilization Fund did prevent most of the profits from devaluation from being "monetized" immediately, the new price of gold made the United States a favorable market in which to buy goods. First, preparations for war and then the outbreak of war magnified the demand for United States products. But even prior to these developments the influx of gold caused a disturbing inflationary situation at home.

As noted earlier, gold imports tend to increase the volume of member-bank reserves on which the volume of deposit currency may be expanded. On December 24, 1936, the Treasury inaugurated its "sterilization" policy. Gold imports were kept as "inactive gold," and the increase in member-bank reserves resulting from the Treasury's purchase of gold was neutralized by Treasury borrowing in the open market. In 1937, following the break in security and commodity prices and the decline in business and national income, this policy was reversed.

Other Treasury Powers. In the Silver Purchase Act of 1934, Congress committed the United States to a policy of buying silver until silver is one fourth of the metallic monetary stock, or until the market price of silver reaches $1.29+ per fine ounce. In addition, the Treasury is required to accept all of the current output of domestic silver mines offered at a net price of 90.5 cents per fine ounce.

In the Act of June 12, 1945, Congress changed the minimum Federal Reserve banks' reserve requirements to 25 per cent in gold certificates for Federal Reserve notes and deposits, terminated all the powers with respect to the issuance of Federal Reserve bank notes,[12] and eliminated the provision in the Thomas Inflation Act permitting issuance of $3,000 million in United States notes. Although these changes reduced the authority of the President and the Treasury, they are minor compared to the increase in the Treasury's power resulting from the increase in the size of the national debt and the debt-management policies associated with it. These and other aspects of fiscal policy are linked closely to Federal Reserve policy, and they are described in more detail in later chapters.

SUMMARY

This very brief monetary history of the United States shows the development away from the use of full-bodied money. The first coinage act passed by Congress under the new constitution provided for a bimetallic standard including both gold and silver full-bodied coins. Provisions were also made for a small quantity of token coins, bank credit money (bank notes issued by the Bank of the United States), and deposit currency.

Although their constitutionality was challenged, many banks were chartered by state governments; and these banks were given the right to issue paper money. They also accepted demand deposits which many depositors used as means of payment. Thus, from the beginning of the history of the United States, full-bodied money had to compete with less expensive forms of bank credit money and a small quantity of token coins. It was expected that the bank notes of state banks would be used locally and that most of the money in circulation on a national basis would be "hard" or full-bodied money.

The bimetallic standard worked poorly because of the failure to appraise accurately the market ratio prevailing between gold and silver. In 1853 all silver coins except the standard silver dollar were made token coins. In 1873 provisions for the coinage of standard silver dollars were discontinued; and, in 1878 when recoinage of silver dollars was provided, restrictions were placed on the amount,

[12] The amount of Federal Reserve bank notes in circulation was increased under provisions of the Bank Emergency Act of 1933, first in 1933 and again in December, 1942, when the President made use of the stock on hand to conserve labor and material during the war period.

and they were made token coins (the commodity value of their silver content was less than their face value). The fact that silver certificates were introduced to replace the silver dollars which did not circulate illustrates the preference of the general public for paper money during normal times.

During the Civil War era, United States notes were issued: and they became the standard money from 1862 to 1879. State bank notes were eliminated and replaced by new national bank notes which provided the nation with a uniform and safe bank-paper-money system for the first time in its history. The convertibility of United States notes into gold ended the paper standard era in 1879. Although the silver dollar was being coined under a limited coinage law, the situation was confused because (1) no provisions were made to keep these coins at par with gold, and (2) there was no specific declaration by Congress that the gold dollar was the standard coin. This situation was clarified in 1900 when the gold dollar was made the "standard unit of value," and the Secretary of the Treasury was required to maintain the value of all coins at par with the gold dollar.

The Federal Reserve Act led to fundamental changes in the currency and banking situation of the United States. The Federal Reserve note became the most important kind of currency in circulation, replacing gold coins, gold certificates, and national bank notes. Steps taken to simplify the currency structure have been offset somewhat by the successful "pressure" of the silver lobby that led to the purchase of large quantities of silver bullion and issues of silver certificates. But the greatest monetary changes have taken place in the standard situation. The monetary standard was changed from a gold-coin standard to a restricted gold-bullion standard as a result of the passage of the Gold Reserve Act of 1934 and administrative policies subsequently adopted.

QUESTIONS AND PROBLEMS

1. Identify (*a*) colonial currency, (*b*) continental currency, (*c*) state issues of paper money, and (*d*) "private" coins.
2. What are the two monetary provisions in the Constitution of the United States? What is the significance of each?
3. What are the chief provisions of the Coinage Act of 1792? Was too much expected of "free enterprise"? Explain.
4. What mistake, made in the Coinage Act of 1792, was overcorrected in 1834? How was the mistake made in 1834 corrected in part in 1853?

5. Summarize the changes made in the currency system of the United States from 1861 to 1870 (standard, coins, and paper money). What steps were taken to reconstruct the standard and the currency system from 1873 to 1879?

6. Explain what is meant by the "limping" gold-coin standard. What act brought to an end this period in United States monetary history? What are the chief provisions of the act?

7. To what extent may the gold-coin standard (1900–33) be considered a gold-bullion standard in international transactions and a gold-certificate standard in domestic transactions?

8. What is meant by the statement that the different silver-buying acts (1878, 1890, and 1934) did not provide for a bimetallic standard? What were the chief provisions of the three major silver-buying acts?

9. "Since Federal Reserve notes were obtained in exchange for commercial paper, it was thought that the amount of these notes would fluctuate with the needs of trade." Explain.

10. Outline the main provisions of the "Gold Reserve Act of 1934." As it is being operated today, what is the gold-standard situation in the United States?

11. Trace the history of the shift away from emphasis on full-bodied money as found in the Coinage Act of 1792.

Chapter IX

COMMERCIAL BANKING
BEFORE THE CIVIL WAR

THE STORY of commercial banking is linked to money because commercial banks are an important source of means of payment—in earlier times, bank paper money, and now, checkbook money. The stress on the money function of commercial banks dates from colonial times when the colonists regarded a bank as little more than a source of currency. But another line of analysis is to treat commercial banks in terms of other functions, such as a source of loans and as agencies for the distribution of savings, the collection of credits, and the payment of debts.

SPECIAL CHARTERING OF BANKS

When the Declaration of Independence was signed, there was not a single incorporated bank in the United States. At that time, this situation was not extraordinary because the century of commercial banking was still around the corner. To be sure, the "Old Lady of Threadneedle Street" (the Bank of England) had been in existence since 1694, but banking was still in its pioneer stage. Merchant princes, private bankers, pawnbrokers, and goldsmiths dominated the poorly developed financial machinery of the period.

Significance of Incorporation. Until the end of the eighteenth century, most business enterprises, including banking, were carried on chiefly by single proprietors or by firms consisting of a few partners. A few charters were granted for the purpose of giving a monopoly or making a concession to certain individuals or groups of individuals.[1] Later, corporations developed into legal entities, separate and apart from the owners themselves; and, as such, limited liability usually was given to shareholders. While the organizers of banks found incorporation advantageous, the government used bank incorporation as an aid in limiting the number of banks and in es-

---

[1] For illustration, note the monopoly given to certain colonizing and trade companies famous in American history (London Company, Plymouth Company, Dutch West India Company) and the charters given to individuals (Sir Walter Raleigh, Roger Williams, Lord Baltimore, and William Penn).

tablishing banking standards. Incorporation also facilitated supervision because failure to meet charter provisions or statutory requirements could lead to revocation of charters. Charters of the early banks usually were granted for a limited number of years, a limitation which forced owners to submit to periodical review by chartering authorities before being granted a new charter.

Varied Experiences in the United States. According to popular thinking, banking was originally synonymous with paper money issuance; therefore, the desirability of having banks was not "accepted as the matter of course that it has become today."[2] As a result, the chartering policies varied widely, not only in point of time but also among the various chartering authorities (federal and state governments). At different times, in certain states, there had been (1) no banks, (2) only unincorporated private banks, (3) banks organized under special charters issued by the legislative bodies, (4) banks organized under general legislation applying to all corporations, or (5) banks organized under general legislation applying to all banks. In other words, in the past, banking has been prohibited, practiced as a private monopoly, practiced as a public or semipublic monopoly, or free to all under supervision of the government.

Note-Issue Banking. Most of the early American banks either operated under special chartering laws or were unincorporated. The chartered banks were of greatest importance because, almost without exception, they issued paper money.[3] This means that banks printed bank notes on which customarily appeared the name and location of the bank, the denomination of the note, and a promise to pay gold or silver on demand (the country had a legal bimetallic standard). Denominations were as low as 5 cents and as high as $10,000. Banks used this money in their day-to-day activities, that is, to pay salaries of employees, to purchase supplies, to lend to customers, and to pay claims of depositors. Since the initial cost of the issuing bank was the cost of printing the notes, it was much easier to start a bank with the note-issue privilege than without it.

The continued success of a bank of issue depends upon its ability to keep its notes in circulation, for, if note circulation is impossible, the bank must use funds provided by the owners (capital)

---

[2] H. E. Miller, *Banking Theories in the United States before 1860* (Cambridge, Mass.: Harvard University Press, 1927), p. 19.

[3] Bagehot justifies the use of the note-issue privilege as follows: "No nation as yet has arrived at a great system of deposit banking without going first through the preliminary stage of note issue. . . ." (Walter Bagehot, *Lombard Street* [14th ed.; London: John Murray, 1915], p. 88.)

and by depositors. In the early history of banking a sole reliance upon capital and deposits would have limited seriously a bank's lending operations; thus, each bank was desirous of having as many people as possible using its notes as "cash balances." The ideal note-issue transaction, from the viewpoint of the bank, would have been one that involved the lending of bank notes that never came back to the bank. More practically, the larger the amount of bank notes outstanding relative to a bank's capital, the more profitable the bank tended to be.

The interest of each individual bank in keeping its notes outstanding also explains why a monopoly of note issue would have been important to a bank. While this monopoly might not mean that the total volume of bank paper money would be less, it does mean that the volume issued by a single bank would be more. If there are two or more banks, it is to the interest of each to have fewer of the other banks' notes in circulation. Furthermore, if the existing banks can keep the note-issue field to themselves (subject to their own tug of war for volume), so much the better; hence the continuous unsavory political pressure on legislative bodies of this period not to charter new banks and not to renew the charters of existing banks (other than those of the banks exerting the pressure) when old charters expired. But, in the long run, banks did find it profitable (and healthy) to associate with each other in a mutual protective movement against all would-be newcomers and all outsiders.

One of the fundamental factors behind the note-issue system, on which early American banking depended, was the willingness of the people to accept and use these promises to pay as a store of value and as a medium of exchange. In this respect, the accepting, holding, and spending of bank notes was to the bank-note system what the "banking habit" is to the current deposit-currency system. Since coins were scarce in many communities, this statement of the situation does not mean that the noteholders always had a choice between holding bank notes and holding specie.

Technically, bank notes and specie always were interchangeable; but, in practice, this was not the case because of the inconvenience of remitting notes to the place of issue and the unwillingness or inability of certain individual banks to pay specie on demand. Nonconvertibility by local banks had popular support, especially when requests for conversion came from outside the community. The inconvenience of remitting notes to the place of issue usually meant that these notes were at a discount in terms of local currency. When wildcat banks were located in the wilderness (banking laws required them to have some nominal place of business), this inconvenience of location was exploited in a ruthless way. However, this was not the only trick resorted to by some banks to keep notes from being returned. Innkeepers, being channels through which notes could be distributed widely, were preferred borrowers of local banks. Borrowers who would accept small-denomination notes were preferred to those who requested large-denomination notes because the former stayed in circulation longer; and borrowers who spent notes outside the community were preferred to those who spent them locally. However, it does not follow that all banks were specialists in these practices.

By 1820 many banks in cities were more dependent upon deposits for funds (with which to operate) than upon the assets which could be secured by issuing their own promises to pay. This means that they were guided by the same motives, in regard to location, as those which cause modern bankers to make their banks as accessible as possible to depositors.

The First Chartered Banks. The Articles of Confederation (the first United States constitution) did not mention banking. Robert Morris, the Superintendent of Finance, led the movement to secure a federal charter for a semipublic bank. Arguments used in support of the request for the bank were the needs of the federal government and the advantages to commerce and industry. In 1781 Congress passed a special act providing for the Bank of North America. Although this federal charter was "unlimited" or "indeterminate" as to time, the officials later secured special state charters from the states of Pennsylvania, New York, Massachusetts, and Delaware. Prior to 1864,[4] the Bank of North America operated chiefly under the Pennsylvania charter.[5] The bank was financed chiefly with government funds. Part of the stock allotted to the government ($250,000 of the total capital stock of $400,000) was paid for with silver obtained from France. The government did borrow about

---

[4] In 1863 the Bank of North America entered the National Banking System, without changing its name, claiming that it already had a national charter. This position was not seriously challenged by the Comptroller of the Currency.

[5] In 1785 the state of Pennsylvania repealed this chartering act (in favor of a Bank of Pennsylvania which had a more liberal loan policy), and for two years the bank operated under its federal charter. The debates over the merits of banking in general and the Bank of North America in particular are valuable to students of banking history. When this bank made plans to move, the mercantile and other interests in Philadelphia secured a second charter from the state.

$1,250,000 from the bank, which it later repaid partly with cash and partly with that part of the bank's own stock owned by the government. The government had no voice in the management of the bank; and, throughout its history, the bank was operated primarily as a private institution. The Bank of North America differed from the two Banks of the United States in being local rather than national in geographical scope of operations. In this respect, it was similar to the state-chartered institutions that soon were created by special state chartering acts.

New York, Massachusetts, and other states imitated Pennsylvania in making provisions for state-chartered institutions. The Bank of New York, founded by Alexander Hamilton and others, operated for seven years as a joint stock company and then, in 1791, received a state charter. In 1784 the Bank of Massachusetts was chartered by the state government, and in 1790 the state of Maryland chartered the Bank of Maryland. The Providence Bank of Rhode Island followed, and soon there was at least one bank in each state. These banks had large capitalizations, the average having been $1,000,000. Although most of the stock of these banks was privately owned, the banks provided many free fiscal services for their state governments. Even when the banks were owned in part by their state governments, they operated under private management with little governmental interference.

All of the early chartered banks were banks of issue. They supplemented the specie currency in circulation with paper money which was generally acceptable in the area served by the issuing bank. There were no minimum reserve requirements, and the bank notes were secured by the general assets of the banks. The assets of the banks chiefly were in the form of commercial loans, including bills of exchange arising out of the financing of both foreign and domestic trade. In addition to lending their credit in the form of notes, these banks accepted deposits. These early banks had successful careers, and most of them are still in existence either under their original names or under one that has been changed as a result of merger, reincorporation under national law, or addition of a trust business.

After 1800, banks were chartered more freely by their state governments; but the existing banks made common cause against the proposed new banks and were able to defeat many new special chartering bills as they came before the state legislatures. In addition, by playing upon the prejudices of the "state-rights" school and "hard-money" advocates, they were able to bring to an end, in turn, the first and second Bank of the United States.

FIRST AND SECOND BANK OF THE UNITED STATES

First Bank of the United States.   In a special chartering act in 1791, the federal government provided for the Bank of the United States.[6] It was given a charter that was to expire on March 4, 1811; and, during this period, no other banking instituiton was to be chartered by the federal government. The bank had a capital of $10,000,000, of which $8,000,000 was open to public subscription and the remaining $2,000,000 was subscribed by the federal government.[7] The bank could issue notes in an amount equal to its capital. The notes were not legal tender; but, as long as they were redeemable in gold and silver, they were receivable for all payments due to the United States government (government tender).

Part of the capital stock was paid for with government securities, which the bank was authorized to sell. However, the bank was forbidden to "purchase any public debt whatsoever"; but it was permitted to make loans to the federal and state governments and (with prior approval of Congress) to foreign princes and foreign states.[8] The bank was permitted to sell commodities taken on bad loans; otherwise it was forbidden to deal in anything except bills of exchange and gold and silver. The organizers' aim was to establish a commercial bank to serve as a fiscal agent for the government, a source of loanable funds (short term) for the federal and state governments, a bank of issue, and a bank of discount. The activities of the bank are reflected in its statement of condition (balance sheet) appearing as Table 6.

The first Bank of the United States was governed by a board of twenty-five directors, all of whom were required to be citizens of the United States.[9] Foreign shareholders were not allowed to vote

[6] See National Monetary Commission, "Act of February 25, 1791," *Financial Laws of the United States 1778–1909* (Washington, D.C.: U.S. Government Printing Office, 1910), Vol. II, pp. 269–76.

[7] This investment was profitable to the government, which subsequently sold its shares to private investors, many of whom lived in England and other foreign countries. The last sale was made in 1802 to the investment banker, Sir Francis Baring, who retailed the stock to English investors.

[8] The loans to the federal government were limited to $100,000, but subsequent acts increased this amount to $800,000 in 1793, $1,000,000 in 1794, and $2,000,000 in 1798. The maximum loan permitted to each state was $50,000.

[9] The privilege of voting was on a degressive basis, with the maximum per "person, co-partnership, or body politic" being thirty votes. Sixty shareholders, holding two hundred shares, had the right to call a meeting at any time.

by proxy, and this restriction guaranteed American control of the bank, even though, as later happened, 18,000 of the 25,000 shares were held abroad.[10] The Secretary of the Treasury was given the

TABLE 6

STATEMENT OF THE FIRST BANK OF THE UNITED STATES, JANUARY, 1811

RESOURCES (IN MILLIONS)		LIABILITIES (IN MILLIONS)	
Loans and discounts	$14.6	Capital	$10.0
United States 6 per cent and other		Surplus	0.5
United States stock	2.8	Circulation	5.0
Due from other banks	0.9	Individual deposits	5.9
Real estate	0.5	United States government de-	
Notes of other banks	0.4	posits	1.9
Specie	5.0	Due to other banks	0.6
		Unpaid drafts outstanding	0.2
Total	$24.2	Total*	$24.2

Source: *Annual Report of the Comptroller of the Currency*, 1916, Vol. II, Table 93, p. 912.
* Individual items total less than $24,200,000 because of rounding.

power to call for reports (not oftener than once a week) and to inspect the affairs of the bank. The head office was located in Philadelphia; and the directors were permitted "to establish offices wheresoever they shall think fit, within the United States, for the purposes of discount and deposit only. . . ."[11] Subsequently, eight branch offices were opened in the leading cities of the country.

Judging from available reports, the relationship between the bank and the government was very satisfactory. The bank transacted most of the fiscal business of the government and lent money to the Treasury in anticipation of tax revenues. It acted as the custodian of public funds and transmitted them from place to place through its branch-banking system.

Although the Bank of the United States had a powerful following, its federal charter was permitted to lapse on March 4, 1811. A rechartering bill, which had the support of Secretary of the Treasury Albert Gallatin and powerful leaders in Congress, did not pass.[12]

[10] Six directors and the president constituted a board large enough to conduct business transactions. Directors were elected for one year; and not more than three fourths, other than the president, were eligible for re-election.

[11] National Monetary Commission. "Act of February 25, 1791," *Financial Laws of the United States 1778–1909* (Washington, D.C.: U.S. Government Printing Office, 1910), Vol. II, p. 274.

[12] In February, 1811, Congress chartered the Bank of Washington, Farmers Bank of Alexandria, Bank of Potomac, and Union Bank of Georgetown. Later, more bank charters were granted to groups in the District of Columbia. Congress also approved of the acts of legislative assemblies in the territories which provided for the organization of banks.

The old bugaboo of unconstitutionality, politics, opposition of more than eighty state-chartered banks, fear of a money trust, and foreign ownership of stock have been given as reasons for not renewing the bank's charter. When the bank's assets were liquidated, shareholders received a bonus of $34.00 on each share. Individuals purchased the goodwill and assets of the main office and of some of the branches.

The liquidation of the Bank of the United States was followed by a trying war period (1812–15), during which (1) the banks suspended specie payments and expanded severalfold the volume of bank paper money; (2) the government issued noninterest-bearing Treasury notes in denominations as low as $3.00; (3) specie disappeared from circulation, and barbers, bartenders, manufactures, and others issued fractional paper money; (4) there was more than 100 per cent inflation of prices; and (5) the government had all the difficulties in tax collection and borrowing that are associated with a confused currency and banking situation. Most of these difficulties could have been avoided if the Bank of the United States had been rechartered.

Second Bank of the United States. Following the financial debacle of the War of 1812, one of the most important reform measures taken by Congress was the chartering of the second Bank of the United States in 1816.[13] The charter of this bank was similar to that of the first, but there were a number of differences which showed the development of banking principles during the intervening period. All deposits, as well as notes, were to be redeemed in legal-tender money. While it had been the prevailing conception that notes should be redeemed in specie, little consideration had been given to deposits. As a result, even when banks were operating on a specie basis, depositors often were paid in bank notes which sometimes were at a discount. In 1790, deposits were unimportant; but, by 1816, they had become important, particularly in cities.

Notes were to be issued in denominations no smaller than $5.00, and post notes were limited to denominations of $100.00 or more and to maturities of sixty days or less. Post notes—time promises to pay—were a means of borrowing from the public with or without interest. They were used widely at this time, but often they were issued in such small denominations that the recipients mistook them for demand notes.

[13] National Monetary Commission, *Financial Laws of the United States 1778–1909* (Washington, D.C.: U.S. Government Printing Office, 1910), Vol. II, pp. 295–310.

The government reserved the right to subscribe for the same percentage of the bank's stock, one fifth; but, in addition, required the bank to pay a franchise tax of $1,500,000. It also reserved the right to appoint five of the twenty-five directors. The amount of capital stock ($35,000,000) was three and one half times that of the first bank, and the growth of the country necessitated the establishment of twenty-four branch offices. The law also provided in greater detail, for inspection and supervisory regulation by both the Secretary of the Treasury and either house of Congress, and for the fiscal relationship between the bank and the government. Thus, the bank was made generally accountable to both Congress and the Secretary of the Treasury. Later, laws were passed that had the general effect of increasing the role of the bank as fiscal agent of the government. The bank's first and third presidents (William Jones and Nicolas Biddle) were selected from among the government directors. Under the first president, the management of the bank was reckless, if not dishonest. In 1819, under Langdon Cheves, the bank's condition became sound and its president unpopular in the process. He was replaced (November, 1823) by Nicholas Biddle, who remained in charge for the remainder of the bank's history as a national institution.

In 1831 a bill providing for the rechartering of the bank was passed by Congress but was vetoed by President Andrew Jackson. However, conditions were not beyond repair until the bank became an issue in the presidential campaign of 1832. Jackson's reelection was followed by a removal of the government's deposits from the bank in 1833 and the elimination of any remaining hope for a renewal of the federal charter. The bank received a Pennsylvania charter in 1836 and continued to operate as a state institution until it suspended payments in 1839 and was liquidated in 1841. While creditors were paid in full, the stockholders lost about 25 per cent of the value of their assets (as will be noted later, modern bank creditors and stockholders rarely fare as well when their banks are suspended).

Central-Banking Functions. Before the Civil War the term "public bank" was preferred to "central bank," but this difference should not cause one to lose sight of the fact that the first and second Bank of the United States performed central banking functions. Although both banks shared the note-issue privilege with others, the notes of the first and second Bank of the United States were accepted nationally and were used by state-chartered banks to redeem their bank notes. Both banks acted as fiscal agent for the federal government, lent money to the government in anticipation of tax receipts, handled refunding of debts, accepted government deposits, and transferred funds from place to place through their branch-banking systems. Out of the acceptance of government deposits, there developed the central-bank function of regulator of the currency, which is now considered one of the most important functions of a central bank.

Regulation of Currency. Alexander Hamilton stressed the monetary advantage of having a bank which would provide paper money that would be widely acceptable, but the two banks of the United States did much more. When the banks received tax receipts in the form of bank notes of other banks, they became the creditors of these banks (in contrast to the present situation in which the Federal Reserve banks are debtors to member banks). Possession of these notes, coming in a fairly steady stream as a result of collection of import duties and other indirect taxes, gave the "public bank" a simple and effective device whereby it could influence the policies of other banks. These notes could be and were returned to the issuing banks for redemption. Thereby the issuing banks were kept under pressure to keep notes of the Bank of the United States and gold and silver reserves on hand and also to limit the volume of their notes (debts) within their ability to pay on demand.

The state-chartered banks, and some private banks that were issuing notes, resented the regulation of currency by the Bank of the United States. They wanted the privilege of paying their creditors, including the Bank of the United States, if and when they pleased.[14] They found support from the agrarian interests who wanted an abundant supply of cheap money, from those who felt that the sovereign rights of the states were being violated, and from those who believed in hard money and opposed all banks that issued paper money.[15]

[14] Legal attacks were made on the bank, and Maryland attempted to tax the Baltimore branch out of existence. The Supreme Court upheld the constitutionality of the chartering act (1819) and also stated that without the consent of Congress a state could not interfere by taxation or otherwise with the operation of a bank chartered by Congress (1824). See *McCulloch* v. *Maryland*, Wheat 316; and *Osborne* v. *United States*, 9 Wheat 738. It was contended that states, as well as the national government, did not have the legal right to charter banks issuing paper money; and it was not until 1837 that the power of states to do so was confirmed by the Supreme Court.

[15] For a reappraisal of the controversy over rechartering of the Bank of the United States, see Bray Hammond, "Jackson, Biddle, and the Bank of the United States," *Journal of Economic History*, Vol. VII, No 1 (May, 1947), pp. 1–23.

Even though Congress failed in an attempt to pass a rechartering bill over President Jackson's veto, a strong sentiment remained in and out of Congress for a public bank. Even some of the eastern state banks recognized the merits of such an institution. When President Martin Van Buren was defeated for the Presidency in 1840, the reform party (Whigs) gained control of both Congress and the Presidency. One of the first bills passed by Congress was a special chartering act providing for a third Bank of the United States. But the death of President William Henry Harrison, one month after his inauguration, elevated John Tyler to the presidency and he vetoed the bill.[16]

STATE BANKING EXPERIENCES UNDER SPECIAL-CHARTER BANKING

Throughout the history of the first and second public banks, banking was carried on within the several states under special state chartering acts. During the interim between the two public banks (1811–16), the rapid growth of state banks was due to (1) war financing, (2) state banks' holdings of government deposits, (3) export of specie to pay foreign shareholders of the Bank of the United States (leaving room for state banks' notes), and (4) withdrawal of the stabilizing effect (redemption influence on state banks' note issues) of the Bank of the United States. Since all periods of bank-credit inflation are due to a demand for loanable funds, the basic cause of this inflationary period (1812–18) was war financing and postwar business expansion. The easy profits that resulted from investing in government bonds attracted promoters of all types. Following the suspension of specie payments (August, 1814), banks had the privilege of note issue without the responsibility of redemption. By accepting these notes, the government in effect acquiesced to this breach of common law that requires banks and others to fulfill their obligations (in this case, promises to pay gold or silver on demand). After the war, boom conditions made it easy to lend; and these conditions continued until the bubble burst in 1818. Most of the banks west of the Appalachian Mountains failed, and the record of those in the South was almost as bad.

Gradually, legal and other changes were made with the purpose of checking various abuses prevalent in banking. After 1820, some states passed laws which penalized banks that failed to redeem their notes in specie, other states limited the note issue of each bank

[16] Tyler was a Democrat who had been placed on the ticket to secure the votes of discontented members of his party.

to some specific proportion of its capital and deposits, and other states limited bank note issues to denominations of $5.00 and over because the homing power of these notes is greater than that of smaller denomination notes. In all cases, the ultimate purpose was to limit the amount of bank notes in circulation. Although bank notes were convertible at par over the counter, they often circulated at a discount in distant places because the holders did not want to bear the cost of sending them back to the issuing bank for redemption. Private bankers, "money brokers," and (later) chartered banks made a profit by buying these notes at a discount with local currency and then collecting them at par. This business was speculative because often there was doubt as to the ability and willingness of the issuing bank to redeem its notes.

Suffolk Banking System. In 1818 the merchants of Boston organized the Suffolk Bank, which announced that it would accept and pay only the notes of the out-of-town banks which maintained redemption deposits with it. The Suffolk Bank offered to give the country banks the discount on their notes. Although this plan did not remove the discount on notes, it increased competition for the notes and reduced the risk involved. In 1824 the Suffolk Bank introduced a plan wherein each country bank was requested to keep a permanent deposit with it and an additional current deposit sufficiently large to redeem at par all the notes received by the Suffolk Bank. In return, the Suffolk Bank received the notes and gave credit for them on the day following their receipts. Notes of country banks were held subject to order of the issuing bank and were sent home for redemption unless the country bank arranged for redemption in Boston. The expenses of operating the plan were cared for (as is true of modern correspondent banking) by fees on overdrafts and by income earned from lending the deposits of the banks.

Originally, many interior banks refused to join the Suffolk Banking System; but, after the other seven Boston banks agreed to participate, the interior banks were forced to join. The forcing process used was simple. The notes of interior banks not in the system were promptly sent back for redemption. If the notes were reissued, the process was repeated promptly. By 1825, virtually all New England banks were in the system; and, from then on until the Civil War, the notes of New England banks circulated at par throughout that section. Moreover, they were in considerable demand in other parts of this country and in Canada.

The Suffolk system of note redemption continued in revised

form[17] until the notes were taxed out of existence by the federal government in 1866, when national bank note currency replaced state bank notes. The principles involved were used later by the national government in providing for central redemption of national bank notes in Washington, D.C. The Suffolk Banking System recognized the importance of convertibility not only at the bank of issue, but also in a central redemption center. At the same time, the Suffolk Bank facilitated the settling of banks' claims against each other. In a banking system made up of a few banks with a large number of branches, serving a small geographical area, provisions for convertibility at the branch and head offices may be sufficient; but, where there are hundreds of local banks, central redemption is necessary if a discount on notes is to be prevented. This same principle is applicable to checks or deposit currency, and this desirable quality has been obtained for most checks through development of correspondent banking relations and later through the Federal Reserve System. While the Suffolk Banking System provided a dramatic illustration of how one weakness of the early bank paper money system was corrected in New England, the collection policy of the Bank of the United States also was tending to reduce the discount on bank notes. In addition, banks (voluntarily, in some cases, and because of legal requirements in others) made arrangements through correspondent banks to redeem their notes in distant cities at or near par.[18]

Safety Fund System. Before the Civil War, bank notes became worthless, on the average, at the rate of 5 per cent each year. While these losses were greatest during the years of severe depression and bank failure (1818–21 and 1837–42) and varied widely among states, the results were sufficiently serious to justify the taking of special protective measures to prevent bank failures and to reduce the losses of banks' creditors if failures did take place. Among the latter

[17] In 1858 a group of banks in Boston organized the Bank for Mutual Redemption, which paid interest on banks' deposits and otherwise offered more attractive services (from the viewpoint of costs) to the country banks than did the Suffolk Bank. However, the Suffolk Bank was able to hold part of its business with other banks because of well-established banking contacts. The Bank for Mutual Redemption was less effective than the Suffolk Bank. In 1862 the Bank Commissioners of Massachusetts began a long series of lawsuits against it.

[18] In May, 1840, the New York State legislature required all banks outside of New York, Brooklyn, or Albany to appoint an agent and to open an office in Albany or New York for the purpose of redeeming their notes at no more than one half of 1 per cent discount. R. E. Chaddock (National Monetary Commission), "The Safety-Fund Banking System in New York State, 1829–1866," *Banking in United States before Civil War* (Washington, D.C.: U.S. Government Printing Office, 1911), Vol. IV, p. 307.

type of protective measures was the Safety Fund Banking System of New York.[19]

In brief, the plan was managed by the state; but this does not mean that the state guaranteed the liabilities of banks. It called for a yearly assessment of one half of 1 per cent of each bank's capital until 3 per cent was paid. If the fund's assets became depleted, additional contributions could be requested at a rate of one half of 1 per cent. Since the banks were paying dividends in excess of 7 per cent, it was assumed that the burdens would not be excessive. Although the debates on the bill emphasized bank notes, the law was so drawn that depositors, as well as noteholders, were covered.

The system was tested severely as a result of bank failures (1837–42), and the claims were so great that the fund was bankrupt in 1842. Then, the law was changed, limiting the future protected liabilities to notes and freezing future claims until all pending ones were met. By 1866, all banks in the system had secured new charters either under the state General Banking Act of 1838, or under the National Bank Act of 1863, as amended. In the final accounting, all claims presented to the Fund were met, and there was a surplus of $13,000 given to the New York treasury. However, this does not mean that all creditors were paid in full, because some of the notes of banks were never presented and depositors of the four banks suspended after 1842 were not covered by the guarantee of the Fund. The system should have either excluded deposits in the beginning or should have increased the contributions. The basis of the contributions (capital) tended to penalize banks that had the largest capital-liability ratio and to favor the more speculative type of bank with the smaller capital-liability ratio. If protection had been limited to noteholders and the charges had been based on notes, the assets of the fund would have been sufficient for prompt payment of insured liabilities.[20]

State Ownership of Bank Stock. In nearly all states the government subscribed for a portion of the stock of new banks. In the East, where banking needed little encouragement, the chief desire was to participate in the large profits which the banks were expected to earn. In 1816 practically all the older states, with two or three exceptions, owned bank stock. In most cases, the expectation of profits was justified. A second reason for purchase of stock was to

[19] Chaddock, *ibid.,* pp. 227–388.

[20] When Ohio (1845) made provisions for a safety fund system, it insured only notes and made assessments proportional to the amount of notes outstanding.

give the states, through ownership, participation in the management of the banks. Stock purchases also placed the states in the position of favored customers when they desired to borrow.

In the South and West, the chief reason for government banking was the scarcity of private capital. In the South, planters were expanding their plantations, and most of their assets were invested in slaves and land. The money interests of the country would not lend on such security, and the planters had great difficulty in securing private credit. Numerous government banks were established to meet their needs. The states had no money for this purpose, but they were able to borrow it. Similar conditions existed in the West.

Most of the banks which were, in part, state-owned were managed privately. Their records varied like those of all privately managed banks; but, in general, they were better than those of private institutions. When the government not only owned the banks but managed them as well, their records were poor. This was due in part, at least, to the fact that some of these banks were started near the peak of the business boom and had invested their resources in internal improvement projects of various types (canals, turnpikes, bridges, etc.) or in farm mortgages. However, the records of some of the other banks were no better; and noteholders were no better (if as well) protected by state-owned institutions than they were by privately owned and managed institutions.

Louisiana Banking Act of 1842. Although the period from 1836 to 1860 has been referred to as one in which wildcat banking was dominant, a great deal of progress was made in some states in achieving better banking. During the panic of 1857, the banks in Louisiana were among the few that did not suspend specie payments. This situation attracted national attention; and, when an explanation was sought, it was found that the Louisiana banks were operating under the strictest banking code applicable to any privately managed banks.

In 1842 the Louisiana state legislature passed a banking act that made no provisions for new banks, and this was sufficient to check a tendency to create too many banks during business booms. This law forced banks to protect both noteholders and depositors, recognizing that both were fundamentally the same sort of obligation. The unusually high standard set for minimum reserve requirements provided for 100 per cent backing for notes and deposits, one third in specie and two thirds in short-term paper. The law also provided for quarterly examinations by state officials, monthly publication of bank statements, and weekly settlement of interbank balances. It also prohibited banks from paying out notes other than their own, and this necessitated sending notes to banks that had issued them; thus, testing their ability to redeem them.

TRANSITION FROM SPECIAL-CHARTER TO FREE BANKING

All sections of the country were affected by the speculative boom that preceded the panic of 1837, and many new banks were established in the East, as well as in the South and West. The number of banks increased about threefold, note issues increased in proportion, and loans increased about fourfold. When the collapse came, the banks suspended specie payments; and, during the next four years, more than one third of them failed. The misery and hardships resulting from bank failures were so great that some states outlawed banks. While depositors suffered along with noteholders, only the latter were given special protection in reform measures which resulted.

Until 1838 a special act of a state legislature was necessary before a charter for a new bank could be obtained, and even the purchase of new bank stock was subject to government supervision. The history of banking in New York State illustrates the conditions which resulted. Prior to 1804, there were only six banks in the state, and they made common cause against all applicants for bank charters. By lavish expenditures of funds, however, bank charters could be secured. The new bank charters invariably went to friends of the political party in power. White summed up the situation as follows: "In short, politics, monopoly, and bribery constitute the key to banking in the early history of the state."[21]

In 1838, New York joined in the nation-wide condemnation of banking. An antimonopoly legislature met and passed a general banking law under which charters could be obtained without a special act of the legislature. This law permitted banks to be organized under its "free-banking" provisions and required them to deposit collateral with the state Comptroller in amounts equal to the volume of notes issued. If a bank failed, the collateral was sold and the proceeds were used to pay its noteholders. At first, mortgages and bonds were used as collateral; but later, higher standards were set, resulting in the development of a safe note-issue system.

The democratic nature of the free-banking system and the pos-

[21] Horace White, *Money and Banking* (5th ed.; Boston: Ginn & Co., 1914), p. 303.

sibilities of abundant paper money appealed to the public. Within a short time, fourteen additional states had adopted similar laws.[22] With the growth of democracy and the western movement, there was a change in attitude toward banks and banking from that existing during the first years of chartered banking. New banks were chartered as private business enterprises, with little or no consideration for the needs of commerce. From the beginning of our national history, farmers and others challenged the theory that commercial-bank credit should be advanced only to finance commerce.

The period from 1836 to 1860 has been referred to as one in which wildcat banking dominated; but this was true only in certain sections of the country. As a result of boom conditions, the number of banks increased from 500 in 1834 to 900 in 1840; and the number declined to less than 700 by 1843. By 1861, there were 1,600 banks, and the states which had adopted free-banking laws contributed most of this increase in number. The ease of opening banks is illustrated by the following quotation: "The speculator comes to Indianapolis with a bundle of bank notes in one hand and the stock in the other; in twenty-four hours he is on his way to some distant point of the union to circulate what he denominates a legal currency. . . ."[23]

The chief criticism of free banking is that it sometimes results in unsound banking. However, not all of the banking difficulties of the period from 1836 to 1860 resulted from free-banking laws, because the majority of the banks still were operating under charters granted prior to the enactment of these laws. Specific criticisms made of the activities of individual banks included: (1) operating with faulty or inadequate capital structures; (2) holding too small a percentage of reserves against notes and deposits; and (3) making too large investments (or loans) in speculative and nonliquid assets.

During 1832 and 1833 the Secretary of the Treasury, acting on instructions of the President, shifted government deposits from the Bank of the United States to certain state-chartered banks. Jackson's purpose in giving this order was to lessen the shock upon the credit and currency systems which was expected to result from the

[22] While the free-banking law was being considered by the New York State legislature, Michigan passed a general bank incorporation act. Prior to 1860, the following additional states had passed similar laws: Connecticut, Florida, Illinois, Indiana, Iowa, Louisiana, Ohio, Massachusetts, New Jersey, Pennsylvania, Tennessee, Vermont, Virginia, and Wisconsin.

[23] A. M. Davis (National Monetary Commission), "The Origin of the National Banking System," *The National Banking System* (Washington, D.C.: U.S. Government Printing Office, 1910), Vol. V, p. 20.

liquidation of the second Bank of the United States with the lapse of its federal charter. This brought the Treasury into direct contact with the problem of the varying values of bank notes. In 1835 the Treasury brought pressure to bear on banks to redeem their notes either in specie or in bank credit of banks that were redeeming their obligations in specie. This was followed by the issuance of the "specie circular" to land agents directing them to accept nothing except specie or notes of specie-paying banks in payment for public land. These measures emphasized the importance of convertibility of bank notes in specie, brought on the panic of 1837, and demonstrated the importance of fiscal policy when applied to such a routine matter as determining which form of currency is government tender.

During the panic of 1837 and the depression which followed, the government (along with others) suffered from the inconveniences of inconvertibility, loss of deposits in suspended banks, and loss due to holding paper money of suspended banks. Temporarily in 1840 and again in 1846, Congress made provisions for the safekeeping of its own funds in its own vaults. It provided for subtreasuries in various cities and for the collection and payment of amounts due to or owed by the government in specie. Thereby the sponsors expected to keep a large supply of coin in the country, to reduce the volume of paper money, to prevent the expansion of bank currency based on government deposits, and to provide for safety of government funds. This so-called Independent Treasury System (independent of banks) had to be modified during the Civil War, but it was adequate while the receipts and expenditures of the Treasury were small.[24] However, it was no substitute for a public bank as a regulator of currency (as some of its sponsors argued that it would be).

Ohio (1845), Indiana (1855), and Iowa (1858) chartered privately owned banks that were state-wide in their operations. These "central" banks were capably administered and provided their states with a healthy banking core in spite of the deep inroads of "free banking." The development of correspondent banking was making New York the money market of the nation, with New York banks holding the bulk of the gold reserves of the nation. In 1853 the New York Clearinghouse was organized (incorporated the next year with $1,000,000 contributed by the five largest banks). The Boston Clearinghouse was organized in 1855, and the next year others were organized in Philadelphia, Baltimore, and Cleveland.

[24] After the Federal Reserve banks took over the subtreasury functions, Congress abolished the Independent Treasury System (1920).

EARLY PRIVATE BANKING IN THE UNITED STATES

To assume that the history of banking can be outlined without some consideration of nonchartered banks (called "private banks") is to ignore the role of banking houses, which often have been dominant in the banking affairs of the nation. In most countries and communities, private banking is much older than chartered banking. During the early history of the United States, conditions were favorable to the development of private banking. There is a place for the private banker, the broker, the speculator, and the promoter, where chartered banking is inadequate or unreliable or handicapped by governmental regulations, where currency is in a state of confusion, and where business is expanding rapidly.

One group of private bankers was indigenous in origin, and another traces its origin to the financing of international trade and international lending. The first group of private bankers (1) accepted deposits; (2) dealt in domestic exchange; (3) issued paper money in convenient denominations, which circulated as money even though sometimes it was disguised as a bill of exchange; (4) bought bank notes of chartered banks at a discount and presented them to the issuing banks for payment; and (5) sold gold and silver at a premium during periods of banks' suspension of specie payments. Many of these private bankers were operators of country stores, carrying on both a mercantile and banking business. It was natural for the frontier merchant to carry on limited deposit banking, to extend credit, and to participate in the financing of local ventures such as turnpikes, railroads, and canals. Too often the frontier-chartered banks were formed solely for the purpose of issuing paper money, and the more modern type of banking was left to the merchants and private bankers.

A second group of private bankers developed a banking business as a result of foreign trade contacts and the need for funds in foreign centers to pay for goods obtained from abroad. Merchant-bankers purchased American securities and sent them abroad to financial centers. When these securities were sold to foreign bankers, the American merchant-bankers were given bank credit to use in purchase of goods. Some of the merchant-bankers set up their own branch offices in foreign centers so as to sell securities directly to investors. Later, some of these firms gave up their mercantile businesses to specialize in the purchase and sale of securities, foreign exchange credit instruments, and gold and silver. Others carried on a more general banking business, including, in addition to the above, the acceptance of deposits, the issuance of paper money disguised as orders to pay and/or as shop notes and commercial-loan and discount operations.

SUMMARY

The chief weakness of the banking system as it existed before the Civil War was the fluctuation in the volume of money—overexpansion during boom periods and overcontraction during depressions. Basically, the cause of these difficulties was a failure to recognize the relationship between lending functions of commercial banks and fluctuations in the volume of means of payment. Even today this combining of lending and money-creating or money-destroying activities in the same institution is a major source of trouble.

A second major weakness of the banking system was the absence of uniformity in the value of bank notes—varying from those that were as "good as gold" to those that were worthless.[25] Bank notes (having been a product of 1,600 chartered banks operating under 34 different state laws) varied as to design, size, and other physical characteristics; and this made recognition difficult and counterfeiting easy and profitable. This situation decreased the acceptability of all bank notes. At places far from the place of issue, often even good notes either were not accepted or were at a discount because of the cost of returning them to the place of issue. Added to the public loss due to worthless bank notes and counterfeit currency was this annual toll of millions of dollars taken in the form of discounts (a type of exchange charge) on paper money. Equally important were less direct costs such as difficulties of travelers, loss of trade due to nonacceptability of money, and inconvenience of checking on notes as they were presented for payment.

Following the closure of the second Bank of the United States, a third major weakness of the banking system was the absence of some type of central bank and a well-organized money market. Even before the Civil War the New York banks were receiving deposits from interior banks. The interior banks regarded these deposits as reserve funds and withdrew them in case of need. Unfortunately, the New York money market was not well enough organized to stand the strain of heavy withdrawals of funds. This situation remained to plague the United States until (1) a central bank system was created where new reserves could be obtained in case of need;

[25] Davis, *op. cit.*, pp. 12–26.

and (2) a money market in government securities and commercial bills was developed to supplement the call loan market and the open market for commercial paper. In addition, the government needed a central bank to provide it with banking and other services. Finally, there was a need for a "regulator of the currency" that would hold the gold reserves of the nation. For these reasons, some regard the failure of the federal government to recharter the second Bank of the United States as one of the most serious mistakes made in our early monetary and banking history.

The government met these problems, in part, by (1) specifying that only specie (or its equivalent) would be accepted in payment of import duties and for public lands; and (2) providing for the Independent Treasury System. Some of the banks attempted to solve these problems by co-operative action, as in New England, and by co-operative action under governmental pressure, as in New York State. Later, in these and other states, emphasis was on more governmental regulation.

As banking abuses were exposed, two lines of action were taken: (1) In some states, special-charter banking laws were replaced by general-charter banking laws, which included special features to protect noteholders (in the form of deposits of collateral with a governmental agency). However, newer emphasis on deposit banking made this method of improving the quality of banks' liabilities relatively less important than it would have been at the beginning of state banking systems. (2) In many states the government made provisions for detailed regulation of opening, operating, and liquidating banks. The main contribution to banking during this period prior to the Civil War was the development and testing of banking principles. Many of these principles were incorporated in the National Bank Act of 1863.

QUESTIONS AND PROBLEMS

1. How is incorporation of banks advantageous to both bankers and the government?
2. Distinguish between "special" chartering of banks and "general" chartering of banks. In what sense is the latter "free banking"?
3. What relationship is there between changes in earning assets of note-issue banks and changes in amount of paper money in circulation? Does this mean that bank-note lending is more inflationary than lending by an individual? Why? Is this true of deposit banking?
4. The "best way to diffuse banking in a community is to allow the banker to issue bank notes of small amount that can supersede the metal currency. This amounts to a subsidy to each banker to enable

him to keep open a bank till depositors choose to come to it."
(Walter Bagehot, *Lombard Street* [14th ed.: London: John Murray,
1915], p. 82.) Was this method used in the United States? Was it
successful?

5. Who decides whether the proceeds of a loan are to be taken in the
form of deposits or bank notes? Why were bank notes preferred before 1850?

6. How did the frontier demands for credit affect the traditional policy
of expansion of bank credit on commercial paper and other short-
term assets? Was this good for business and banking in the short
run? In the long run?

7. It has been estimated that not more than $500,000, or 5 per cent of
the capital of the first Bank of the United States was paid in specie.
Does this suggest that specie is unimportant in operating a note-
issue bank? What does the statement of condition of this bank (see
Table 6) suggest as to the type of banking business conducted by it?

8. The first mistake of a monetary nature was made "when Congress
refused to renew the charter of the first Bank of the United States
in 1811." (E. C. Jerome, *Governments and Money* [Boston: Little,
Brown & Co., 1935], p. 172.) Was this a serious monetary mistake?
Why?

9. Explain how the first and second Bank of the United States acted as
"regulator of the currency." Were they debtors or creditors of other
banks?

10. "In the infancy of Banking it is probably much better that a Government should as a rule keep its own money." (Walter Bagehot,
op. cit., p. 99.) Do the experiences of the United States from 1836
to 1846 justify this conclusion?

11. What banking principle of note issue was emphasized by (*a*) the
Suffolk Banking System, and (*b*) the Safety Fund System of New
York.

12. Many early bankers issued notes far beyond their ability to redeem
them. They "hoped that the notes would fly so far that they would
never find their way home." Why? Was "home" made as accessible
as possible? Why were some of these early banks called "wildcat"
banks?

13. What were the chief reasons for state ownership of banks and of
bank stock in the East? In the West?

14. "During the panic of 1857, the banks in Louisiana were among the
few that did not suspend specie payment." Explain this record.

Chapter | COMMERCIAL BANKING

X | SINCE THE CIVIL WAR

ALTHOUGH many members of the first Civil War Congress favored chartering a third Bank of the United States, the principle of free banking was accepted when Congress authorized the establishment and operation of nationally chartered banks under the supervision of the Comptroller of the Currency. The Act of 1863 (revised in June, 1864) permitted the organization of thousands of small banks under national law as a substitute for the big bank idea. The Act supplemented states' legal provisions for the organization of banks, but did not replace them (thereby providing for a dual banking system in each state).

The Federal Reserve Act, passed in 1913, provided for a modified kind of central banking system with new paper money and made important changes in banking activities as carried on by the nationally chartered banks. Twenty years later, Congress provided for the Federal Deposit Insurance Corporation in an amendment to the Federal Reserve Act. The congressional plans for central banking and deposit insurance were drawn so as to include both national and state-chartered banks, thus preserving the dual banking system.

THE NATIONAL BANKING SYSTEM

National Bank Act. The need for a uniform currency system was apparent long before the Civil War, and the suggestion that government bonds be used as a basis for national currency appeared as early as 1815. In his annual report of December 31, 1861, Secretary of the Treasury Salmon P. Chase urged Congress to pass a national banking act. Events during 1861 had impaired the relationship between the Treasury and the banks. While the banks readily agreed to underwrite $150,000,000 of the Treasury's first major issuance of war bonds, they requested that the Treasury keep the banks' advances on deposit with the lending banks and that the Treasury draw on these deposits by checks. However, Secretary Chase insisted on specie payments; and the war-bond issue was not a success. Consequently, the

Treasury began to make payments with small demand notes, which the banks refused to accept in exchange for their own notes or gold. By the end of the year, banks went even further and stopped redeeming their own notes in gold. During 1862 and 1863 the Treasury issued United States notes (greenbacks), and the relationship between the Treasury and the banks further deteriorated. In his report at the end of 1862, Secretary Chase renewed his request for the passage of a national banking act, and this time he got prompt action—the passage of a bill which became law on February 25, 1863.

Comptroller of the Currency. The Currency Act of 1863, popularly known as the National Bank Act of 1863, created a special bureau in the Department of the Treasury to supervise national banks and to be responsible for the issuance, redemption, and retirement of national bank notes. This bureau was placed under the control of the Comptroller of the Currency, who was to be appointed by the President, with the consent of the Senate, for a term of five years. The Office of the Comptroller of the Currency was the first administration agency created by Congress.[1]

Now the most important duties of the Comptroller of the Currency are: (1) to supervise the organization, expansion (through amalgamation or establishment of branches), operation, and liquidation of national banks; (2) to perform comparable functions with respect to all banks and certain credit unions in the District of Columbia; (3) to operate an issue and redemption division to handle the engraving and destruction of Federal Reserve notes; (4) to make annual reports to Congress on the condition of national banks; (5) to make legislative recommendations; and (6) to make detailed decisions involving administrative interpretation of the law.[2]

Purposes of the Law. The Act of 1863 was revised in 1864 and has been amended as to details by more than sixty different acts. Originally, it was a war measure, enacted in order to create a safe and uniform note-issue system and to provide a new and continuing market for government bonds. The Act authorized the organization of new banks and the reincorporation of old banks under a national banking law. It required the banks to buy government bonds, which they were permitted to deposit with the federal government as collateral for national bank notes. State banks, operating under liberal

[1] See Guy H. Fox, *Regulation of Banking by the Comptroller of the Currency* (unpublished dissertation, The University of Texas, 1948).

[2] The Comptroller is an ex officio member of the board of directors of the Federal Deposit Insurance Corporation and was formerly a member of the Federal Reserve Board.

state note-issue laws, were lukewarm toward the national banking system until 1866, when their note-issue privilege was made unprofitable by a 10 per cent tax on their circulation. After 1866 the new national banking system gained recruits from among state-chartered banks, as well as from private banks.

Jay Cooke, able financier of the Civil War, was responsible for the organization of three national banks, including the First National Bank of Philadelphia, which received Charter No. 1 on July 11, 1863.[3] Members of the sales organization that Cooke built up to sell government bonds were instrumental in organizing many national banks, particularly in the West, which was more friendly than the East toward the new system.

Weaknesses of State Note Issues and Their Correction. In providing for conditions of circulation of national bank notes, Congress took steps to correct two weaknesses of the state-bank note-issue system—lack of safety and lack of uniformity in value throughout the country. These weaknesses were corrected by requiring each bank (1) to deposit bonds (with the Comptroller of the Currency) to be used to protect noteholders in case the bank failed, (2) to redeem its notes over the counter and also in Washington, and (3) to accept the notes of other banks at par. The first provision insured the safety of bank notes; the other two insured their circulation at par throughout the United States, irrespective of the distance from the issuing bank. Although safe and uniform in value, national bank notes lacked elasticity, one of the characteristics of a good note-issue system. Beginning in 1914, their circulation was supplemented by note issues of Federal Reserve banks; and, in 1935, provisions were made to withdraw national bank notes from circulation.

Growth of Deposit Banking. The chief reason for the original shift of banks to incorporation under national law was the desire for the then valuable note-issue privilege. Although deposit banking rivaled or exceeded note-issue banking in importance in metropolitan centers by 1840, banks in pioneer communities, where transportation facilities were poor and daily or weekly contacts with banks were impossible, still found a demand for bank notes rather than for deposit currency. The increase in regulation of state banks' note issues, following disastrous bank failures from 1837 to 1841, hastened the movement toward deposit banking; but the shift from note-issue to deposit banking was most rapid after the Civil War.

[3] H. M. Larson, *Jay Cooke, Private Banker* (Cambridge, Mass.: Harvard University Press, 1936), p. 139.

Deposit banking meant that banks were lending their credit in the form of promises to pay deposits on demand instead of lending their credit in the form of bank notes. National banks, as well as state banks, were interested in this type of lending because there was no legal limit to the deposit-capital ratio; while note issue was limited to the capital of the issuing bank. After 1866 bankers discovered (as English bankers had discovered during the second quarter of the nineteenth century) that deposit banking may be just as profitable as note-issue banking. Both state and national banks, by emphasizing the advantages of checking accounts, encouraged depositors to allow funds to be used by the banks, pending withdrawals.

New Types of Banking Services. The development of deposit currency lessened the importance of the note-issue privilege and eliminated the near monopoly of commercial banking which national banks enjoyed during the first decade of their history. In the settlement of the West, one of the first business enterprises to be established in a new town was a bank. Although the note-issue privilege was desired, there were other factors which often led the sponsors to favor a state-chartered institution.

In the West and South the minimum-capital requirements for a state-chartered bank were less than those for a national bank. Formerly, in ten states, there were no minimum-capital requirements; and, in others, it was as low as $5,000. In addition, the states required less rigid examination, or no examinations, and fewer restrictions on loan and investment policies. State charters gave banks much broader banking privileges than national charters; and it was customary for many state banks to combine the banking business with the farm mortgage, fire insurance, life insurance, and real estate businesses. Savings, safe deposit, and trust banking were added later.

Growth of Correspondent Banking. An unexpected effect of the passage of the National Bank Act, as amended, was the strengthening of correspondent banking in the United States. The Act, as amended, required banks located in New York and, after 1887, in Chicago and St. Louis to hold all their required reserves against deposits in their own vaults in the form of lawful money (all kinds of currency except national bank notes). Other banks, however, were permitted to carry part of their required reserves with other banks as "bankers' balances" or deposits. As early as 1870, about two fifths of the banking reserves of the country was in the form of bankers' balances; of these reserves, a large percentage was with the nine "super-banks" in New York. From that date to 1914, these large New York banks, with thousands of correspondents, were the chief institutions responsible for determining national credit policies.

Acceptance of "Free Banking." Since the National Bank Act provided for the incorporation of banks under a general banking act, it, in effect, committed the states to a similar policy. The provisions of the National Bank Act were applicable to all states—"free-banking" states, "prohibited-banking" states, "monopoly" or "semimonopoly" states, and states that permitted banks to be formed under general incorporation acts which applied to banking, manufacturing, mining, and other business ventures. By 1890, while some state banks were being organized under these laws, most new state banks were being organized under general banking laws.

Weaknesses of the Banking System. In its report to Congress in 1912 the National Monetary Commission preceded its recommendations for banking and currency reform with a summary of the principal defects in the banking system.[4] The Commission stressed the lack of provisions for mobilizing cash reserves for use in time of trouble, the legal restrictions on the use of bank reserves and on the lending power of banks in the presence of unusual demands, and the absence of adequate means whereby banks could replenish or increase their reserves to meet unusual or normal demands for bank credit. The Commission also criticized the inelasticity of the national bank-note circulation.

While recognizing the services of clearinghouse organizations, the Commission pointed out the need for "means to insure such effective co-operation on the part of banks as is necessary to protect their own and public interest in times of stress or crisis." The Commission also noted the need for an agency for making the domestic and foreign exchange systems more effective.

The character of the commercial credit market was criticized because of (1) the lack of commercial paper of an established standard; (2) the flow of bank credit to New York for use of brokers, dealers, and buyers of stocks; (3) the placement of "farmers and others engaged in productive industries at a great disadvantage in securing" credit; and (4) the "lack of equality in credit facilities between different sections of the country." These conditions could be met, in part, by an agency which would aid "in securing greater uniformity, steadiness, and reasonableness of rates of discount in all parts of the

[4] National Monetary Commission, *Letter from Secretary of the National Monetary Commission Transmitting, Pursuant to Law, The Report of the Commission* (Washington, D.C.: U.S. Government Printing Office, 1912), Vol. XXIV, pp. 6–9.

country;" and "provide adequate banking facilities for different regions promptly and on reasonable terms to meet the ordinary or unusual demands for credit or currency necessary for moving crops or for other legitimate purposes."

The provisions for bank regulation and supervision were criticized because there was "no power to enforce the adoption of uniform standards with regard to capital, reserves, examinations, and the character and publicity" of bank reports. Attention was also called to the need for "American banking institutions in foreign countries" and the inability of national banks to make mortgage loans to farmers and others. The functioning of the Independent Treasury System was criticized because it meant "irregular withdrawals of money from circulation and bank reserves in periods of excessive Government revenues" and the "return of these funds . . . in periods of deficient revenues." The attempts to modify this situation by depositing funds "among national banks have resulted, it is charged, in discrimination and favoritism in the treatment of different banks."

Recommendations of the National Monetary Commission. The Commission recommended, among other things, the incorporation of a "National Reserve Association of the United States" with fifteen district branches and local associations of participating banks. Because of the change in political control of the federal government, this plan was not adopted; but the administration recognized the need for banking reform in the Federal Reserve Act which became law on December 23, 1913.

In many respects the Federal Reserve System was similar to the plan proposed by the Commission. The most important differences were: (1) the provision for a greater degree of decentralization, which has been largely nullified by subsequent changes in the System; (2) the provision for a more liberal currency and reserve system, which has been criticized because it has meant excessive expansion of the money supply; and (3) the divorce of the Federal Reserve System from control by member banks.

The Federal Reserve System was certain to have far-reaching effects on the American banking system in the long run; but the outbreak of war in Europe in 1914 and the series of economic, military and political events that followed made the Federal Reserve System one of the foremost financial powers among central banks in the world in less than five years. It was fortunate that the Federal Reserve System was established in time to help finance the United States and her allies during World War I.

COMMERCIAL BANKING SINCE THE ESTABLISHMENT
OF THE FEDERAL RESERVE SYSTEM

The framers of the Federal Reserve System had as their purpose the strengthening of the existing banking structure without changing fundamentally the existing unit-banking system. National banks were authorized to accept savings deposits, to undertake a limited mortgage banking business, to perform trust functions under rules and regulations of the Federal Reserve Board, to grant acceptance credit, and to carry on foreign finance business. In subsequent legislation the further liberalization of many of these powers was directed at improving and enlarging the services offered by individual banks. However, in order to have a good banking system, it is equally important to have co-operation among banks; and this is the central idea of the Federal Reserve System.

Mobility of Credit. One of the requisites of a good banking system is its ability to provide mobility of capital, that is, its ability to move credits from place to place according to the varying requirements of business. The banking system of the United States is basically local in nature. Most of the units are local in organization and management and are not national or even regional in scope of operations. In the United States the nearest counterpart of the branch banking systems of foreign countries is in the investment-banking field. Most of the large bond or investment houses have branch offices scattered throughout the United States. In addition, large commission houses or brokerage firms, and small-loan and sales-finance companies, have branch offices in the leading cities of the country.

In the United States, some mobility of credit is provided by correspondent banks and by facilitating organizations which take credit instruments of local origin and sell them in the money market. In this group are included the acceptance dealers, bill brokers, commercial-paper houses, cattle-loan associations, and a few mortgage dealers and brokers. It is primarily because of the local nature of financial institutions in the United States that the Federal Reserve System's facilities are so important. Now Federal Reserve bank credit is made available throughout the nation at practically uniform rates. The differences in interest rates in different markets are explainable in terms of differences in size of loans, in risks, and in the amount of competition prevailing in different local markets.

Elastic Credit System. In addition to geographical mobility of credit, the banking system should provide an elastic credit system, that is, one capable of expanding and contracting in volume as the credit needs of business expand and contract. With perfect elasticity, two undesirable developments would be avoided—an expansion which outruns the need and causes inflation and a contraction which causes businessmen to liquidate assets and to postpone or curtail production. The index of the efficiency of an elastic credit system is the absence of sharp fluctuations in interest rates in the money market.

(3) *Efficient Collection System.* A good monetary system embodies a mechanism whereby bank reserves may be transferred among depositors and converted into currency at their request. Although banks had developed a system of correspondent banking for out-of-town clearing and collection of checks and other items, the Federal Reserve System has largely assumed responsibility for the nation-wide development of this function.

Unsolved Banking Problems. The Federal Reserve Act left unsolved many problems which had faced the people of the United States since before the Civil War. There remained the problem of weak, poorly managed, small local banks. Bank failures were not eliminated, and banking codes and government regulation were as fruitless in protecting the creditors of banks as they had been before 1914. Branch banking still was restricted or prohibited. Every community thought it necessary to have its own locally owned and locally operated bank; as a result, there were "too many banks and not enough bankers." There was a tendency to lower banking standards, and apparently too much reliance was being placed upon mere membership in the Federal Reserve System.[5] The popular expression which indicates this attitude was "members of the Federal Reserve System cannot fail." Even the belief that money panics were impossible under the Federal Reserve System proved to be false in February and the first three days of March, 1933.

Bank Failures. The most important banking phenomenon between 1921 and 1934 was the large number of bank failures. Before 1930, failures were generally in the agricultural sections of the country; the mortality rate having been particularly high among small banks located in communities with populations of less than 1,000. Between 1930 and 1934, failures were so widespread that most com-

[5] Professor J. H. Williams sums up this situation as follows: "Nevertheless, many of our people undoubtedly regarded the Reserve Act of 1913 as a complete and final answer to our banking troubles. In their view, it was to mark the end of banking crises and bank failures in this country." (J. H. Williams, "The Banking Act of 1935," *American Economic Review, Supplement,* Vol. XXVI [March, 1936], p. 105.)

munities had suffered from at least one bank suspension. The wide-spread banking panic led to a local, then to a state, and finally to a national banking moratorium. About 11,000 banks failed between 1920 and 1933, and over 4,000 more were suspended during 1933. From a peak of approximately 29,500 banks in 1921, the total number of chartered commercial banks declined to less than 14,000 in 1933. During this period, many new banks were organized, some were merged with unit banks, and others were absorbed by other banks and operated as branch banks in those states where branch banking was legal. But the fact that stands out is that much of this decline was due to the large number of bank failures.

After the national banking holiday of March, 1933, there were two classes of banks—licensed and unlicensed. There were 13,500 of the former and 4,500 of the latter. Many banks in the second group were considered hopelessly insolvent; and, during 1933 and 1934, more than 2,000 of them were placed in receivership, and practically all of the remainder were reorganized with the financial assistance of the Reconstruction Finance Corporation.

Reconstruction Finance Corporation's Aid to Banks. By the end of 1934 the Reconstruction Finance Corporation's investment in banks amounted to $850,000,000. Additional stock purchases and capital loans were made during 1935 and part of 1936, until the time that the head of the Corporation announced that such investments soon would be discontinued. Refinancing with funds provided by the Corporation included some transactions consented to by banks in order to remove the stigma that otherwise might have been associated with the sale of capital-account items by financially weak banks. For this reason, some of the most conservative banks sold capital-account items to the Corporation in 1933 and in 1934. In the city of New York, some of the largest banks were the ones "to break the ice"; and, in other communities, the clearinghouse association members agreed that if one bank sold stock or capital notes to the Reconstruction Finance Corporation all members would do likewise. When the financially strong banks sold stock or capital notes, usually they were liquidated promptly. In all, the Reconstruction Finance Corporation invested an aggregate of more than $1,000 million in more than 6,000 banks.

BANKING REFORM ACTS OF 1933 AND 1935

In Canada, banks are chartered for but ten years; and, before a general rechartering act is passed, the banking codes and banking practices are reviewed. Outside experts are employed, hearings are held, and recommendations are made to Parliament. In the United States, most major banking-reform legislation follows or takes place during some national emergency. Following the banking collapse of 1933, two major reform banking acts were passed—the Banking Act of 1933 and the Banking Act of 1935.

Banking Act of 1933. This Act was passed by Congress in order (1) to correct specific abuses uncovered by the Senate investigating committee, (2) to increase the control of the supervisory authorities over the volume of bank credit, and (3) to provide for a federal deposit insurance plan. These provisions are explained more fully where the specific banking problem is discussed.

For the convenience of the reader, it may be noted that the Act (1) provided for the separation of investment and deposit banking; (2) required holding companies, under certain conditions, to submit to examination and to follow certain financial practices; (3) placed limitations on and provided for regulation of banks' investments; (4) prohibited interest payments on demand deposits; (5) authorized the Federal Reserve Board to fix the maximum interest rates paid on time deposits; (6) permitted national banks to establish branches under the same territorial rules as those applying to state-chartered banks; (7) enlarged the membership provisions of the Federal Reserve System to include Morris Plan and mutual savings banks; (8) increased minimum-capital requirements of national banks located in communities of 3,000 and less from $25,000 to $50,000; (9) permitted national banks to charge interest on loans and discounts at the legal rate, as provided by state law, or 1 per cent above the Federal Reserve banks' discount rate for ninety-day commercial paper, or a different maximum rate if applicable to state banks, whichever is the higher (if there is no legal rate in a state, it shall be deemed to be 7 per cent); (10) limited the number of directors to twenty-five; (11) provided for removal of directors and officers under certain conditions; and (12) provided for federal insurance of deposits.

The Banking Act of 1933 provided for the temporary insurance of deposits up to $2,500 for six months. Before the six months had expired the coverage was increased to $5,000, and the temporary plan was extended for a year. The permanent plan provided for in this Act was modified by the Banking Act of 1935. The Federal Deposit Insurance Act of 1950 increased insurance coverage to $10,000.

Banking Act of 1935. There are three major subdivisions of the Banking Act of 1935. Title I provided for the organization of the Federal Deposit Insurance Corporation, practically as it exists today. Title II amended the Federal Reserve Act, providing for the reorganization of the Federal Reserve Board and the Federal Open Market Committee. It renamed the Board the "Board of Governors of the Federal Reserve System" and increased the powers of both the Board and the Open Market Committee. Title III provided for many technical changes in the banking laws. Among the forty-six sections in this title are several hundred detailed changes in the statutes, covering every aspect of banking.

Failure to Correct Structural Defects. The banking acts of 1933 and 1935 were of the "patching" and "propping" variety of legislation, not going far enough in the correction of certain structural defects in the banking system. There can be no quarrel with the two basic aims of the acts, even though they were antithetical. (1) Congress sought to improve the banking system by eliminating certain specific abuses, by strengthening bank management, and by providing for better supervision. If successful, depositors would be adequately protected against loss due to bank failures. (2) In providing for deposit insurance, Congress seemingly questioned the effectiveness of the above provisions; and this action suggests that the provisions for banking reform in the banking acts of 1933 and 1935 are inadequate.

Banking Facilities. The decline in the number of commercial banks since 1921 has been partly offset by an increase in the number of branch offices. However, when compared to English or Canadian banking facilities, the American public is not being as well served, on a per capita basis, as are residents of these countries. Compared to 1930, the reduction in the number of banking offices has been partly offset by improvements in banking facilities, including more convenient location of banking offices, improved layout of offices, greater mechanization of operations, popularization of banking by mail, and "drive-in" and "escalator" banking.

The increase in urban population and the improvement in means of transportation have brought more people within areas served by banks. However, the congestion in downtown areas is testing the ingenuity of bank management, particularly those in states wherein opening branch offices is not permitted. The growing practice of using expensive land as space for parking and "drive-ins" means more expensive banking.

If the growth of cities continues to follow the present trend of decentralization (as with community shopping centers, etc.), banks will either have to open branch offices or lose an increasing volume of business to competing institutions (savings banks, savings and loan associations, check-cashing offices, etc.). Most suburbanites are in the middle-income group requiring banking services of all kinds—checking accounts, safekeeping facilities, and real estate, consumer, and small business loans. While the volume of business in each suburb may not justify a new unit bank, it may be more than sufficient to meet the cost of a branch office (called "cubbyhole" banking).

Since 1945, banks have been faced with rising costs of operations traced to higher salaries and rising costs of equipment; at the same time, they have not been in a position to increase interest rates because the level of interest rates is determined by factors largely beyond their control. Therefore, in order to offset rising costs, banks must depend primarily on economies in operation and increases in the volume of business. After expansion, banks are usually able to cut their per-unit costs by spreading overhead, using mechanical and electronic equipment more efficiently, and bidding more successfully against trade and industry for highly qualified personnel.

The rapid growth in industrial production during and since World War II has led to the formation of business firms having plants and/or distribution outlets throughout the country and even throughout the world. Such business firms need banking services of all kinds and, because of their size, their loan requirements can be met only by co-operation among banks in the areas served and by major banks in metropolitan areas. These loan demands are now coming from business firms in many fields (such as petroleum, metals, chemicals, etc.), and only large banks can afford to employ the specialists needed to handle them (geologists, atomic physicists, chemists, and engineers).

MULTIPLE OFFICE BANKING

The increase in the need for retail banking services by individuals and small business units, and for wholesale banking services by large business firms, might lead one to assume that there has been a large increase in the number of new banks; however, since the end of 1949, only 350 new banks have been organized and more than 675 banks have merged with others (representing about 4.5 per cent of the number of banks and 8 per cent of total bank assets). Since many merged banks are operated as branch offices, the total number of banking outlets may not have changed materially; in fact, the merged institution is usually in a position to enlarge existing facilities and to open new offices which would tend to result in an improvement in banking services in the community.

Branch Banking. Many Americans have looked with envy at the record of chartered banking in Canada and in Great Britain. In these countries, as in most foreign countries, banking is conducted by a few large banks with many branches. Most of the work of supervision over banking consists of internal supervision of branches by the main or regional offices, with the government entering the field at the main-office level. The advantage of this system is apparent when it is noted that there are but ten chartered commercial banks in Canada and fifteen in Great Britain. In Canada, four fifths of the banking is done by the four largest commercial banks; and in Great Britain the Big Five handle about three fourths of the banking business.

Branch banking consists of a system of branch offices emanating from a single bank or corporation. The territory served may be world-wide, state-wide, district-wide, or only within the city in which the bank is located. Branch managers direct the affairs of local branches in accordance with regulations of the main office. The branches carry on the same kind of activities performed by a unit bank or a member of a group system similarly located. Large loans must be approved by the head office, where most of the credit work is done. Trust and other types of specialized banking are limited to the head office and larger branches.

Under provisions of the Banking Act of 1933, national banks— in states allowing branch banking—are permitted to establish branches under conditions similar to those under which the state banks operate. Now a national bank may establish branches outside the head office city, provided it has capital at least equal to the aggregate amount which would be required if each of its branches were unit banks similarly located. State-member banks must meet similar requirements as provided by state law for capital and surplus for each city involved.[6] Thus the future of the branch-banking movement is in the hands of forty-eight state governments.

Now, more than 6,500 branches and offices are operated by about 13,700 banks which accept demand deposits. (Because of bank mergers, closures, and the establishment of new banks or branches, the number changes weekly.)[7] California leads the states in the

[6] *Federal Reserve Bulletin,* July, 1952, pp. 773–74.
[7] *Ibid.,* August, 1955, p. 945.

branch-banking movement, and New York is second. With the exception of Montana and West Virginia, all states are participating in some form of branch-banking movement. Since the above statistics include banking offices at military reservations and other government establishments (about 160), some states which prohibit branch banking are reported as having "additional banking offices." As almost 70 per cent of the branch banks are located in the main-office city or county, branch banking is "neighborhood-wide" in the United States as compared to the nation-wide systems of branch banking in Canada and Europe.[8]

There are many arguments in favor of branch banking, the most important being the claims of superiority as to (1) flexibility in structure, (2) management, (3) diversification of assets, (4) geographical mobility of funds, (5) uniformity in interest rates, (6) economy in reserves, (7) clearing and collection services, and (8) deposit and lending services for retail and other firms which have ceased being local in nature. After a study of the growth of branch banking in California, the conclusion was drawn that branch banks (1) were able "to make banking facilities available in areas where unit banks could not survive," (2) "have produced a larger volume of loans per dollar of assets than unit banks as a group," and (3) "have demonstrated economies of scale and of structure which are not available to unit banks generally."[9]

The chief argument against branch banking is that it is monopolistic in nature. This argument fails to recognize that there may be competition between branches of different banks in the area, as well as between unit banks, and that often the opening of a branch bank in a town has broken the monopoly formerly enjoyed by the local unit bank. The second argument is that the main office would neglect the needs of small communities. This argument is hard to substantiate in view of the experiences with branch banking in California and other western states. Any good banker desires to make profitable loans, irrespective of the domicile of the borrower; and this desire does not exclude those located in small communities. If one banker fails to make these loans, a rival branch-office manager will.

In banking, there is no substitute for good management; and it is not guaranteed by any type of structural organization. If managers

[8] Branch banking is permitted in thirty-five states, and on a state-wide basis in eighteen of these states. It is prohibited in ten states, and four states have no legislation as to branch banking. (The District of Columbia is counted as a state.)

[9] D. A. Alhadeff, *Monopoly and Competition In Banking* (Berkeley and Los Angeles: University of California Press, 1954), p. 232.

of single-office banks are more efficient than those of branch-office banks, they have nothing to fear from a federal law which would permit branch banking on a state-wide or Federal Reserve district basis. In addition to commercial banks, mutual savings banks and savings and loan associations are opening branch offices for the convenience of their customers. However, it must not be forgotten that the price society pays for greater efficiency and other advantages of branch banking is concentration of financial power. Perhaps for political, social, or other reasons, society may not choose to pay this price. Although it may mean little or much, the fact is that the United States and India are the only important countries wherein branch banking does not dominate.

Group Banking. Group banking exists when two or more banks are controlled by a corporation or some similar type of company. The group-banking movement started about 1900; but nearly all of the now-known groups were organized during the last few months of the period of speculation preceding the stock-market crash of October–November, 1929, and some did not complete their organization until after the panic.

Group banking developed because of legal obstacles and local prejudices against branch banking; and the movement has been most widely developed in those states where branch banking has been prohibited or restricted. While branch banking is usually limited to head-office cities or counties, groups may cut across state lines and include units in several states. In states having no branch-banking laws, such as Texas, there has been growing opposition to group banking. At the same time, many states have liberalized their branch banking laws and some group banking systems have been replaced in whole or part by branch banking (merging units and operating them as branches).

Since the holding company is not a bank, it does not come under the general banking laws of states or the national government. Numerous states have passed laws providing for some control, and the Banking Act of 1933 and the Bank Holding Company Act of 1956 contain provisions for federal regulation. Before the holding company can vote the shares of a member bank, it must secure a voting permit from the Board of Governors of the Federal Reserve System; and, before the permit is granted, the holding company must agree to submit to examination, to build up a surplus equal to 25 per cent of its holdings of bank stock, and gradually to dispose of its non-banking business (there are a number of exceptions).

The same arguments used to justify branch banking are used to justify the organization of group banking. But a system made up of unit banks cannot have the economy in operation or the flexibility in structure (opening and closing of offices) that characterizes branch banking. In practice, holding companies that are expanding seem more interested in gaining control of existing successful unit banks than they are in organizing new banks. Their higher cost of operation may be more than offset by avoiding loss of goodwill that might follow the substitution of a branch office for a local unit bank.

Chain Banking. Chain banking exists when two or more banks are controlled by one or more individuals rather than by a corporation or similar company. "Chains" are more numerous than "groups," but they are smaller both in the number of banks and in the size of the unit banks controlled.

The arguments in favor of chain banking are similar to those in favor of group banking, but such "chains" tend to be unstable since control is in the hands of an individual or group of individuals. The chain type of organization avoids the regulations and requirements applicable to bank holding companies and similar organizations. However, neither "group" nor "chain" banking is the solution for the need for more banking facilities in certain areas.

Foreign Branches and Subsidiaries of American Banks. Since the purpose of the passage of the Federal Reserve Act was to correct the weaknesses of the banking system, provisions were made for the establishment of American banking institutions abroad. The Federal Reserve Act authorized national banks with capital and surplus of $1,000,000 or more to establish, with the permission of the Board of Governors, foreign branches. In addition, a national bank may invest an amount not exceeding 10 per cent of its paid-in capital and surplus in banks or corporations which are chartered either by the United States or any state and which are engaged principally in international or foreign banking. (For illustration, the American Overseas Corporation which commenced business in June, 1955 had as its first shareholders the Chase-Manhattan Bank, New York; Chemical Corn Exchange Bank, New York; First National Bank of Boston; Mellon National Bank and Trust Company, Pittsburgh; and National Bank of Detroit.)

Banks may organize foreign banking corporations under the laws of certain states, such as New York. Of course, such institutions must meet the statutory requirements of the countries in which they operate. The growth in size of American business units, many of which are international in scope of operations, has increased the problem of obtaining adequate banking services to care for international receipts and payments and international financing (made more difficult by exchange control, licensing of imports, quota systems, and fluctuating currencies).

Most of the international business of American banks is conducted through facilities offered by foreign correspondent banks; but major American banks have more than 110 foreign branches, agencies, or offices in foreign countries (compared to 500 such units operated by banks located in the United Kingdom). The First National City Bank of New York operates 61 overseas branches; but, although American banks have expanded their overseas facilities, this expansion has not kept pace with the increase in the volume of their financing of foreign trade, foreign travel, and other international transactions.

Concentration in Banking. An analysis of banks by size reveals the extent to which banking is now concentrated in the hands of a few banks. Over 5,000 of the commercial banks in the United States "have deposits of $2 million or less," and their combined assets are "less than 4 per cent of the assets of all insured commercial banks. On the other hand, there are 18 banks . . . which hold 26 per cent of the assets of all insured commercial banks."[10]

In some quarters the growth in size of banking units has caused alarm because of potential adverse effects on competition, but the answer to this problem seems to lie in more adequate regulation rather than prohibition of mergers and combinations of different types. As has been obvious since the beginning of chartered banks in the United States, one objective of public supervision has been the prevention of destructive competition among banks. The money-creating function of commercial banks is of public interest; and, if we are to have sound money, banks must be sound. While the merger of two or more banks does not insure a sounder bank and an improved banking system, it may be a step in that direction. Furthermore, the competition faced by a bank is not limited to that offered by other banks because the money and capital markets include not only commercial banks but also insurance companies, savings banks, discount or finance companies, savings and loan associations, governmental agencies of many kinds, and other lenders. In order to meet the needs of our

[10] *Annual Report of the Federal Deposit Insurance Corporation for the Year Ended December 31, 1954* (Washington, D.C.: U.S. Government Printing Office, 1955), p. 61.

growing economy, even larger banking units may be required (but public officials should see that competition is not unduly restricted).

SUMMARY

In this chapter major attention has been given to structural changes in the commercial banking system of the United States since 1865. Equally or more important have been the changes in the nature of the assets held by commercial banks. Before 1920 major emphasis was on self-liquidating commercial loans secured by commodities; but, following the sharp break in commodity prices in 1920, emphasis shifted more and more to loans secured by securities. Consequently, safety and the ability to regain funds depended on the functioning of the securities markets. With the break in security prices in 1929, practically all banks in the United States became "problem" banks. Since 1933 commercial banks have emphasized investment in government securities or loans guaranteed by some governmental agency. Although commercial bank lending increased after World War II, it has not regained the relatively important position it occupied prior to 1930.

The conditions under which Federal Reserve credit may be created and borrowed have been liberalized. Federal Reserve banks' minimum-reserve requirements have been reduced to 25 per cent, and the current gold policy has freed the Federal Reserve banks from the fear of the crippling effects of an internal or external drain of gold. As collateral for loans from the Reserve banks, member banks may pledge government securities, eligible commercial paper, and other paper (with the latter loans being subject to a penalty rate of one half of 1 per cent above the regular discount rate). At present, banks' investments in government securities seem sufficiently large to care for any emergency need for Federal Reserve bank credit.

QUESTIONS AND PROBLEMS

1. What would have been the effect on the development of commercial banking if the National Bank Act as amended in 1864 had forbidden any bank other than a national bank to make a contract to pay money on demand?
2. What are the duties of the Comptroller of the Currency? What state official may be compared to him?
3. Monopoly of bank-note issue was the chief reason for the early success of the National Banking System. Explain.
4. Distinguish between note-issue banking and deposit banking.

5. The National Bank Act rejected the big bank idea and enthroned the local bank system. Explain.

6. "I have tediously insisted that the natural system of banking is that of many banks keeping their own cash reserve, with the penalty of failure before them if they neglect it." (Walter Bagehot, *Lombard Street* [14th ed.; London: John Murray, 1915], p. 310.) Is this view accepted today? Explain.

7. What were the weaknesses of the banking system in 1912, as reported by the National Monetary Commission? What congressional action did the Commission recommend? What action did Congress take?

8. What have been the main contributions of the Federal Reserve banks and federal regulatory authorities to better banking in the United States? Have they been sufficient? Why?

9. What are the advantages claimed for branch banking over unit banking? What are the arguments against it?

10. The 15,000 banks "seems to me a sufficient number of banks to provide ample banking facilities for the nation. The rest of the world manages to get along with less." (Jacob Viner, "Recent Legislation and the Banking Situation," *American Economic Review, Supplement*, Vol. XXVI [March, 1936], p. 111.) Does the United States have too many banks? If the number is reduced, must branch banking be extended? Why?

11. Professor J. H. Williams writes: "Our chief need is not reform of the Federal Reserve system but the much more fundamental reform of our commercial banking structure, organization, and practice." ("The Banking Act of 1935," *American Economic Review, Supplement*, Vol. XXVI [March, 1936], p. 104.) Why? In what other way than by providing deposit insurance is the Federal Deposit Insurance Corporation fitting into the reform plan?

12. Comment on the following: "It is agreed by all competent observers that unusually complex problems will demand the attention of our banking authorities in the not-too-distant future. The question therefore arises whether even the most skillful administration can cope with such problems successfully under the limitations set by our antiquated and unreformed banking system." (H. L. Reed, "Principles of Banking Reform," *American Economic Review*, Vol. XXXVII, No. 2 [May, 1947], p. 277.)

13. In the United States a proposed bank must have a charter. Why?

14. Legally, is it more difficult to open a new bank than a new branch?

Chapter XI | CREDIT AND CREDIT INSTRUMENTS

THE DIFFERENT kinds of credit, credit instruments, and other securities are dealt with in this chapter along with certain legal principles which are basic for understanding the mode of operation of our credit institutions and credit system.

BASIC CONCEPTS

Credit. The word "credit" has many meanings, but in economics it usually refers to the ability to obtain something of value in the present in return for a promise to pay for it at some future time. The thing received may be goods, securities, services, or money. The thing which is promised to be paid in the future may take the form of goods, securities, services, or money. In any credit transaction, there are two parties involved: the creditor, who surrenders the thing borrowed; and the debtor, who assumes the obligation to pay. Usually, ownership, as well as possession, is transferred. Otherwise, the renting of houses, where possession alone is transferred, would have to be considered a credit transaction.

A credit transaction differs from a money transaction in that the former leaves something to be done before the transaction is completed. This is true even though payment may be made with a check, since this transaction is not complete until the check is "collected." Although such a transaction usually is regarded as a cash transaction, a deferred payment is involved; this time element is the distinguishing characteristic of a credit transaction. In banking and allied fields (with the exception of the stock market, where stocks are borrowed daily), a credit transaction usually involves either a promise or an order to pay a definite sum of money. These are the largest and most important of all credit transactions.

Credit Instruments. If the obligation of the debtor and the rights of the creditor are written, the paper is called a "credit instrument." Certain types of credit contracts must be in writing if they are to be enforceable at law; but there are others, based on oral agreements alone, that are legally binding on both parties. In the latter case, there is no credit instrument although the value of the thing borrowed may be large, as is true when brokers on organized exchanges deal with one another. Credit instruments vary according to purposes, customs, and the statutes of the states in which they originate. In some fields of credit, considerable uniformity in credit instruments has resulted from the adoption by states of uniform laws, from the influence of federal legislation, and from the decisions of the courts.

Under a more primitive social order, property (things having economic value) was chiefly in the form of personal ornaments, clothing, rude shelters, stores of food, and implements. But even in primitive society there is evidence that credit instruments were in use, for promissory notes in baked clay have been discovered. However, until modern times, credit instruments accounted for only a small fraction of all forms of property: today, they are equal to more than one half of all forms of wealth (all economic goods that are material and transferable) in the United States. A highly specialized and complex financial structure and legal machinery have been developed to handle transactions in credit instruments and other instruments of finance.

Credit System. The term "credit system" is used to include credit, credit instruments, credit agencies, and laws and customs pertaining to the granting of credit and to the collecting of obligations. The credit system is growing in complexity and size because of the trend in production which is placing more and more emphasis upon indirect rather than direct production of consumer goods.

The basis for the development of a credit system is a high sense of business morality, which gives creditors, who give up present wealth or rights to wealth, assurance of repayment in the future. The growth of the credit system has been aided by custom and law. Owners of surplus funds are more willing to lend their funds when they know that they have a legal right of action against debtors if the latter default on their obligations. While credit instruments do represent a legal right of action against debtors, the future of the credit system depends primarily upon the debtors' willingness and ability to repay and upon wise management on the part of those who are responsible for grants of credit. In general, the credit system has had its greatest development in those countries where customs and laws exact the highest moral and business standards not only from debtors but also from creditors. The shyster lawyer, the fraudulent stock salesman, and the Shylock type of small-loan dealer are as harmful to the credit system as are the "dead beat," the forger, and similar characters. Legitimate dealers in credit fully appreciate this situation, and they have been the leaders in promoting blue-sky, antifraud, and small-loan laws.

ADVANTAGES AND DISADVANTAGES OF CREDIT

Credit has been described by Daniel Webster in the following glowing terms: "Credit is the vital air of the system of modern commerce. It has done more, a thousand times more, to enrich nations than all the mines in the world." However, credit is not wealth, nor does it create wealth, since no more goods, no more capital, and no more wealth exist after credit is granted than before. Credit is the agency of transfer. Total wealth, total income, and total well-being are increased by credit only to the degree that land, labor, and other goods may be utilized more efficiently and pleasurably.

Credit enriches consumption by permitting consumers to possess homes, cars, electrical equipment and appliances, and other types of durable consumer goods in the present in return for promises to pay in the future. Credit enables individuals to purchase goods and services to meet the emergency financial needs that accompany births, sickness, and death. Credit is used also in the retail field because it is convenient for both sellers and buyers to charge things purchased.

Credit aids in production by contributing to a general increase in size and efficiency of production units. Credit may be said to have made possible our modern productive system because few businessmen possess the necessary funds with which to purchase land, build a plant, equip it with modern machinery, buy raw materials, and pay labor. An honest and capable businessman may obtain these factors of production on a large scale if he has credit. Inactive businessmen, small savers, widows and orphans lend him funds with which to carry on his business activities. Thus, credit makes it possible to shift capital into the hands of those who are able and willing to use it. Most credit is used for productive purposes, thus making more goods available for exchange. More goods make possible more credit, and the cycle continues unless there is a breakdown in confidence.

Credit serves as an aid in making payments by serving as a substitute for money. By stimulating exchange, it contributes to the general efficiency of production, making possible specialization, division of labor, and production for the market. This advantage of credit has been considered first under the heading of currency and later under the title of checkbook currency.

Much has been written about the advantages of credit but little about the disadvantages. The justification of credit depends upon how wisely it is used. Possession of credit—that is, the ability to borrow—may prove to be a curse, as well as a blessing. The debtor mortgages his future income. But the pleasure of having consumption goods ahead of income may be offset by the burden of forced savings and loss of consumption in the future. The expected profits from increased production may not materialize, thus leaving the proprietors with large obligations. Governments that borrow may be forced to decrease future activities because a large part of their revenues must be used to pay interest and to repay loans. From 1930 to 1933 this situation was serious for state and local governments because relief demands on their budgets were large; and, as a result, defaults on their interest and principal payments were common. In the case of the federal government the situation was different because the government was in a position to resort to measures that monetized its credit on a scale sufficiently large to meet the emergency.

Those who extol the virtues of credit sometimes forget that every credit obligation is also a debt obligation. The more freely credit is used, the deeper becomes the indebtedness of the members of society. The two problems, credit and debt, should not be studied separately, for they are parts of the same problem. When considered from the viewpoint of monetary management, the growth of debt, particularly short-term debt, has made it more difficult to achieve and to maintain a high level of employment and to keep in balance monetary expenditures and the volume of items sold without inflating or deflating general prices. Now, short-term obligations of business firms and individuals are larger in the aggregate than their long-term obligations. Short-term debts are particularly troublesome because their voluntary or forced repayment in large amounts within a short period of time tends to cause sharp changes in spending, national income, prices and the volume of employed resources. Thus, the development of credit, with all of its advantages, must be weighed carefully against the disadvantages of debt—another way of regarding the same problem. Although it may seem unrealistic, the proposal has been made that business firms should do all their financing with capital provided by owners; but if debt financing is to be used, long-term debt would be preferable to short-term debt, and the preferred obligations would be those having no maturity date (such as the British consols).[1]

[1] Henry C. Simons, "Rules Versus Authorities in Monetary Policy," *Readings In Monetary Theory* (New York: Blakiston Co., 1951), pp. 343–46.

THE THREE "C'S" OF CREDIT

Since payment for value received in the present is to be made in the future, the creditor must have confidence in the willingness and ability of the debtor to pay. In the case of individuals or corporations, this faith is based upon the character, the capacity, and the capital of the borrower. These three "C's" of credit are the most widely used bases on which to form a judgment of the merits of an applicant for credit.

Character. The first "C," character, refers primarily to one's determination to pay. It is reflected by a person's past business record, such as bankruptcies and reputation for honest dealing. It involves one's personal habits and activities, such as social affiliations, associates, gambling tendencies, style of living, and political and social ambitions. All borrowers, to be essentially sound credit risks, must possess good character; and this same requirement holds for nations and business firms as well as for individuals.

Capacity. The second "C," capacity, refers primarily to the measure of one's ability to use wisely and well the control over wealth that has been granted him. This depends in part on one's age, business experience, education, common sense, and shrewdness. In granting credit to corporations and other large borrowers of funds, special attention is given to credit ratios. These include the ratio of current assets to current liabilities, merchandise to receivables, net worth to fixed or noncurrent assets, sales to receivables, and sales to fixed or noncurrent assets. Although many credit men take the position that these ratios do not show the ability of the applicants, others regard them as excellent indexes of the ability of management. If ratios are constructed for a period of years, the resulting comparative ratios give an excellent statistical picture of the history of the corporation. There are, however, other important factors, such as the geographical location of the business, nature of the enterprise, and general economic conditions.

Capital. The third "C," capital, usually is considered by the uninitiated as the most desirable and practically the only quality needed in order to obtain credit. This belief is common in spite of the numerous testimonies of lenders to the contrary, as well as the innumerable experiences of men who possessed only character and ability but who have obtained fame and fortune. Too often those who applied for credit have lacked not only capital but also those other characteristics necessary for credit. However, the reader should not draw the conclusion that capital is not a desirable basis for credit. Perhaps a perfect credit applicant would be given 40 per cent for character, 30 per cent for capacity, and 30 per cent for capital. Of course, one may argue that in the final analysis only character, under its broader meaning, need be considered in determining a sound credit risk. This assumption is grounded in the belief that a borrower of good character will not seek credit beyond his capacity and capital.

The basic requirement in business, in so far as credit worthiness is concerned, is good management. Good management is based primarily on the character and capacity of the individuals responsible for the formulation and execution of policies. There are various ways of classifying the causes of business failures—those due primarily to poor management and those in which the quality of management played little or no part. Studies of the causes of failures suggest that inexperience and incompetence, lack of capital, extravagance, neglect, and fraud are the chief causes of business failures. All these reasons, even the lack of capital, suggest the importance of character and capacity in management. When one considers the more specific causes of failures of small business concerns, two are of primary importance: too large an investment in merchandise or inventory and too liberal grants of credit to customers. The two chief causes of failures of large business concerns are overexpansion of plant and too many fixed or long-term debts.

Usually, large business firms are reorganized when they cannot meet their obligations; but, if they are liquidated, it usually means that their assets are sold to more efficient business firms to the advantage of the economy as a whole. If the social objective is to prevent business failures, there should be general approval of cartels or monopolies—voluntary associations of private business firms to reduce competition by price-fixing, division of marketing territory, limitations on production, and/or pooling of profits.

CLASSIFICATION OF CREDIT AND CREDIT INSTRUMENTS

Public and Private. Students of public finance and investments emphasize the nature of the recipients of credit. There are, under this classification, two chief types of credit—public and private. Public credit includes all grants of credit to governments: federal, state, local, and foreign. Because of the government's powers of taxation, this type of credit usually has the highest credit rating in the market. Public credit may be used either for short-term or for long-term financial requirements.

Private credit involves all grants of credit to individuals, partnerships, and private corporations. It may or may not be secured by specific pledges of assets as backing for the obligations. The credit ratings of private credit instruments vary widely, depending upon the nature of the business and credit record of the borrower, the financial structure of the corporation if incorporated, the phase of the business cycle, and the financial hazards of the money and capital markets.

Secured and Unsecured. A second classification of credit is according to the presence or absence of a special lien on property or a property right pledged as security. Only when credit rests upon some specifically segregated thing, legally set aside to guarantee payment of an obligation, it is classified as being "secured." The thing pledged may be real property (land and improvements attached to land), tangible personal property (merchandise, machinery, raw materials, household property, automobiles, etc.), and intangible personal property (stocks, bonds, royalties, and patent rights).

Pledging assets that belong to the debtor does not increase the debtor's debt-paying ability, but it does give the secured creditor a preferred claim to assets over that of the unsecured creditors. However, if the assets pledged are owned by a second party, the base for the general credit of the borrower has been broadened. The borrower's credit may also be improved if a second party endorses his promissory note, guarantees his obligations, or otherwise places his debt-paying ability behind that of the obligor.

Technically, an unsecured loan is one for which the borrower has not pledged specific assets. Usually, the credit rating of the individual or business firm that borrows in this way is better than the credit ratings of those who are required to pledge specific assets as security. The basic security for a sound loan is the earning power of the borrower. If security is accepted in lieu of a satisfactory earning power, the assets pledged may prove of little value when the borrower's earnings are not sufficient to service the loan. In the past, the payment record has been better for unsecured loans than for secured loans. Security is often required by lenders because it may be used as a device for disciplining borrowers, it is customary in the type of lending, and/or it permits granting a larger loan. (See also Chapter XV.)

Use Classification. Credit and credit instruments may be classified according to the use made of the funds borrowed. Short-term credit extended to business firms is usually classified as commercial credit; and credit extended on a long-term basis is classified as investment credit. Commercial credit is used to finance current operations, such as the purchase of goods and payment of wages. Investment credit is used to finance durable or fixed forms of capital goods, such as the purchase of equipment plant, etc. Real estate credit is a special type of investment credit which is secured by land and buildings (agricultural, industrial, and residential). Mercantile credit is that extended to business firms by other business firms, and retail credit is that extended by stores and dealers to consumers and others who buy from them. Bank credit, as noted previously, relates to the obligations of banks to pay (appearing on banks' books as deposit accounts).

Credit extended to finance speculation in goods, foreign exchange, and securities is called "speculative credit." The degree of risk assumed is greater than in other types of credit transactions. Usually, speculators buy and sell because they expect changes in prices. They seek to gain profits from differences in prices at different times rather than to secure income from their investments. Most margin buyers of securities and commodities are speculators. The mere fact that they are buying or selling more in the present than they can pay for or deliver is evidence that they are expecting a rise or fall in prices. The obtaining of funds for speculative purposes usually involves short-term credit transactions.

Credit extended to consumers to finance purchases of goods and/or services to be used for personal consumption is called "consumer credit." Funds may be borrowed to pay for either a birth or a funeral and for every want intervening between these two events. Consumer credit normally does not increase the borrower's income; therefore, liquidation of the debt involves a curtailment of future spending.

Time Classification. One of the simplest ways of classifying credit and credit instruments is according to the time period involved in the credit contract. If the credit period is less than a year, it is called "short-term" credit; if five or more years, it is called "long-term" credit; and if it is one year and less than five years, it is called "intermediate" credit.

The Office of Business Economics in the Department of Commerce uses but two time classes of debts: (1) short-term, which has an original maturity of less than one year from the date of issue; and (2) long-term, which has an original maturity of one year or more from the date of issue. When this classification is used, the short-term debts of private business corporations are one third larger than their long-term debts. The increase in relative importance of short-term debts has been a feature of all sectors of the American economy— agriculture, business, consumer, and even the federal government. This growth in debts having shorter maturities is due not only to changes in production and consumer buying habits but also to the ease of financing both producers' and consumers' goods. These changes in debt maturities are reflected in the earning assets of banks and other financial institutions.

INSTRUMENTS OF LONG-TERM FINANCE

Stock Certificate. A stock certificate is the written or printed evidence of ownership of shares of capital of a corporation. A certificate may be issued for any number of shares to indicate a stockholder's total ownership in a corporation; but, if shares are purchased at different times, several stock certificates may be issued to one individual. If the stock is listed on the New York Stock Exchange, certificates are usually not issued for more than 100 shares.

All shareholders are proprietors or owners rather than creditors of their corporations. A stockholder receives a share in the earnings, which is called a "dividend." In general, dividends are paid only when earned and voted by the board of directors. Most stockholders of large corporations have little to say about the policies of their corporations; and, if they vote at all, it is by proxy. In deciding to buy stock, such investors are guided by investment rather than by managerial motives.

There are many ways of classifying shares of stock, but the two most general classes are "preferred" and "common." Preferred stockholders have prior claims to earnings and, in the event of liquidation, usually to assets. In return for this preferred position, preferred stockholders usually accept a limited rate of return and surrender voting rights except when their rights and privileges are involved (such as issuance of new preferred stock with equal or superior rights, cancellation of accrued dividends, voluntary dissolution of the company, and so on). If preferred stock dividends are omitted for a stated period, preferred stockholders may be authorized to vote for all or to elect a specified number of directors. Unless specified to the contrary, preferred stockholders have the same voting rights as common stockholders. Preferred stock is called a hybrid security because it has characteristics of both stocks and bonds (see below).

Preferred stock may be cumulative or noncumulative, participating or nonparticipating. If it is 6 per cent cumulative participating stock, it means that, if dividends are only 3 per cent one year because of low earnings, an equal amount becomes an obligation due preferred stockholders which must be paid before dividends are paid to common stockholders. If earnings are above 6 per cent, the participating preferred stockholders may share (depending, of course, upon the participation clause) in the excess earnings on the same basis, or some other basis, as common stockholders.

The common stock certificates of a corporation represent the claims of stockholders after creditors and preferred stockholders have received interest and dividends. They may have a definite face or par value, or they may be issued without par value. Owners have a residual claim to earnings and assets. Thus, common stock differs from borrowed capital; it is proprietary, ownership, or equity capital, which means that: (1) the business firm using equity capital is not legally bound to pay any income return to those who provide it; (2) there is no stated time when the funds provided by owners must be returned; and (3) those who provide it are responsible, at least in theory, for the control and management of the business enterprise.

In addition to the risk assignable to the nature of the business, there may be an added financial risk assumed by common stockholders owing to the financial structure of the corporation. This risk is determined by the relationship between fixed charges and the income available, after taxes, to meet these fixed charges. If one assumes that a corporation has outstanding $200,000 in 3 per cent bonds, 1,000 shares of 5 per cent preferred stock with a par value of $100, and 1,000 shares of common stock with a par value of $10, the fixed charges on the bonds will be $6,000; and dividends on the preferred stock will be $5,000.

TABLE 7

LEVERAGE OF CAPITAL STRUCTURE

Type of Security	Capital	Earnings			
		3%	4%	5%	6%
Bonds (3%).............	$200,000	$6,000	$ 6,000	$ 6,000	$ 6,000
Preferred stock (5%)......	100,000	3,300	5,000	5,000	5,000
Common stock...........	10,000	.....	1,400	4,500	7,600
Total.............	$310,000	$9,300	$12,400	$15,500	$18,600

The effect of changes in earnings assignable to common stock are illustrated in Table 7. If one assumes that the preferred stock is noncumulative and nonparticipating, when the corporation is earning

3 per cent, after taxes, no income is available for common stock; and dividends on preferred stock are covered only in part. However, an increase in earnings to 6 per cent, after taxes, means that $7.60 is available for each share of common stock. This method of financing with senior securities (bonds and preferred stock) is called "trading on equity" (but only in a nontechnical sense because preferred stock also represents equity in the legal sense). Any increase in earnings is passed through the senior securities and pyramided into a wide fluctuation of earnings assignable to common stock. In financial circles, this resultant intensified swing in common stock is called "leverage."

The danger in the use of borrowed capital is that the corporation will overborrow during good times and will have too large a fixed debt to be serviced when returns on capital are very low. In the past, this has been one of the primary reasons for the failure of railroads and other large corporations. Following financial difficulties during the 1930's, corporations began to finance to a greater extent with retained earnings, preferred and common stock, short-term bonds, and other bonds with callable features. Currently, the pressure to finance with debts is considerable because, in computing the base for payment of federal corporate income taxes as well as many state income taxes, interest on debts is deductible. When corporate taxes are taking more than half of the taxable income, the savings that result from financing with debts rather than common or preferred stock are great.

Subscription Warrants. A stock subscription warrant is a written or printed document that authorizes the owner to subscribe to new stock under the conditions stated therein (price, method of payment, time period, and so on). Sometimes warrants are attached to bonds to enhance their salability, but more often such warrants are issued to represent the pre-emptive rights of old stockholders to buy new issues of stock or bonds convertible into stock. Stock purchase rights are prorated among existing stockholders according to the number of shares owned; but, if they are not used within the time specified, the privilege lapses. Arrangements whereby *rights* may be sold to others are usually made by listing the rights on a stock exchange or by arranging for their sale through investment banking houses.

Sometimes corporations give their officers stock-purchase options at or near the market price of the stock when the options are issued. Customarily, such options are for periods of from ten to twelve years from the date of issue; if the company prospers and the market price of the stock increases, the options may be exercised at the price stated in the option. Usually such stock-purchase options are issued under "executive incentive plans."

Bonds. A bond is a written or printed acknowledgment of debt or a contract to pay money, and it is usually one of a number of similarly issued instruments. Usually, a bond is a long-term obligation at the time of issuance. The modern practice of the federal government and business corporations is to classify similarly issued credit instruments running for from one to five years from the date of issue as notes (but notes may be for longer terms, and a 5-year note may be considered long-term for one borrower and short-term for a second borrower or one in a different industry). Corporate bonds are classified in many ways, the most common being as debenture bonds, mortgage bonds, collateral trust bonds, and guaranty bonds.

Debenture bonds are unsecured promises to pay, "dignified by a formal indenture, the interposition of a trustee, and marked by the participation of many individual creditors. . . ." The indenture agreement, which is held by a trustee, describes the rights and remedies of holders of bonds for broken promises given by the debtor. In general, limitations are placed upon (1) the issuance of new bonds, (2) dividend payments when working capital is depleted, (3) procedure to be followed by trustees when agreements are violated, and (4) the use of funds raised by the bond sale. As in all types of bond issues, many creditors are participating in advances of funds to but one corporate debtor.

Mortgage bonds differ from debenture bonds in that they are promises to pay secured by special liens upon tangible property. The mortgage is held and supervised by a trustee, who acts for the holders of the bonds. The original type of mortgage bonds (with rigid provisions for foreclosure in case of failure to pay interest and taxes, to maintain insurance, and to meet installment-principal payments) has been modified by law and court actions. For these reasons, the indenture agreements now used in this type of financing, as well as for debenture bonds, are of increasing importance.

The collateral trust bond is similar to the mortgage bond, but it is secured by pledges of other securities, which are held by a trustee. As in the case of mortgage bonds, there is a supplementary agreement obliging the debtor to pay if the pledged property is insufficient. Collateral trust bonds most often are issued by holding companies and investment trusts which have chiefly stocks and bonds to offer as security for public borrowing.

From the viewpoint of security, guaranty bonds stand between debenture bonds and those secured by liens on real or personal property. They include bonded debts of one of the other classes of bonds which have been assumed, guaranteed, endorsed, or otherwise protected by the credit of a second corporation, as sometimes happens in case of railroad mergers. Sometimes bonds are the individual and joint obligation of two or more corporations, as illustrated by the bonds of the federal land banks and the federal home loan banks.

Many minor classes of bonds have appeared as corporation finance has become more complex. Bonds may belong to an open-end or to a closed-end issue. If open-end, additional bonds may be issued under certain specified conditions under the indenture agreement, mortgage, and/or collateral trust agreement. If closed-end, no new bonds of the same lien as those already outstanding may be issued. Bonds may be issued with or without convertible features. If convertible, the holder can, under certain conditions, exchange them for shares of stock. The bonds may be callable or noncallable. If callable, the debtor company may call them under certain stipulated conditions. Bonds may be registered both as to principal and as to interest, or they may be registered as to principal only. If bonds are not registered as to principal, they are payable to bearer.

Bonds are also classified according to the provisions made for repayment of the principal. If a certain quantity of the total borrowed is repayable annually or at definite periods, the bonds are called "serials." Serial bond issues are common among public issues, particularly those of local governments. If all bonds are due on a particular date, they are called "term bonds." The term bonds are paid either out of a sinking fund that has been built up over the life of the bond issue for this purpose or with proceeds of a new security sale. If the bonds are put out for a definite period (for example, twenty years) but are callable after a fixed period (say, ten years), they are known as "callable term bonds." This type is common among the federal issues. Perpetual bonds, with no maturity date, are common among government issues in foreign countries.

With one exception, bonds call for interest payments at stated intervals (usually every six months); but the payment of interest on income bonds depends on net profits of the issuing corporation. These bonds are sometimes called "adjustment bonds" because they are used widely in adjusting fixed interest debts of bankrupt corporations. Since the payment of interest is dependent on earnings, they are similar to preferred stock in this respect; and they are also called "preference bonds." Because of the tax advantage, preference bonds might be used more commonly in place of preferred stock.

Long-Term Notes. Long-term notes, as distinguished from those used in financing intermediate credit needs, appear most commonly in the form of real estate or mortgage notes (promises to pay secured by mortgages on specific real property of the makers). In recent years, insurance companies and banks have been supplying corporations with funds in exchange for installment notes. (An installment note is one in which the principal is payable in specified installments at specified times together with interest until the note is paid in full.) Sometimes, serial notes are used. Loans to business firms for one year or longer are called "term loans" to distinguish them from short-term debt contracts (usually associated with commercial bank lending). In granting term credit, the lender usually requires the borrower to sign a "loan agreement." The loan agreement is similar to a bond indenture which governs the relationship between lenders and creditors when financing with bonds.

INSTRUMENTS OF SHORT-TERM CREDIT

Charge Accounts. A charge account is an arrangement whereby one receives credit when making purchases without giving a promissory note or other credit instrument. In the strict sense of the term a charge account is not a credit instrument, but it is an important instrumentality of credit. It is used by bankers, retailers, wholesalers, and others in granting or receiving credit. As noted in preceding chapters, when banks receive credit from depositors, they indicate their obligations in depositors' passbooks or on deposit slips (which are held by depositors) and by book entries on the ledgers of the banks. Proceeds of bank loans to customers usually are placed to the credit of the borrower in this form, subject to withdrawal on order. Department stores and other mercantile institutions cater to on-account customers; and, where best collection practices exist, bills are presented at the end of each month. In turn, merchants buy on account from wholesalers, jobbers, and manufacturers.

Promissory Note. A promissory note is a credit instrument consisting of a written promise to pay a sum of money on demand or on a definite future date to a designated person or bearer. The person making the promise is called the "maker," the one to whom the promise is made is called the "payee." The maker and the payee may be the same person or firm. Promissory notes may be single name or double name, interest-bearing or noninterest-bearing, payable upon demand or at the end of a specified period, and secured or unsecured by the pledge of some specified collateral.

Numerous legal documents are used in connection with short-term and intermediate-term promises to pay. In case of tangible personal property, the legal document used to pledge title may be a chattel mortgage (similar to a real estate mortgage); a trust receipt (which means that the property has been transferred in trust); a conditional sales contract (which means that certain things are to be done in the future); a warehouse receipt (which serves as a receipt, a contract and a document of title of the goods it represents); or a bill of lading (which is similar to a warehouse receipt but is issued by railroad companies, steamship companies, and other public carriers). Since stocks, bonds, insurance policies, and other forms of intangible property may be delivered to banks, title is pledged by a collateral note that customarily combines the promise to pay, the consent to pledge, the right to call for more collateral, the right to "sell off" in case of nonpayment, and the right to use the depositor's bank account to settle the obligation (the right to set-off counter claims).

Bill of Exchange. A bill of exchange is defined in the Uniform Negotiable Instruments Act as "an unconditional order in writing addressed by one person to another, signed by the person giving it, requiring the person to whom it is addressed to pay on demand or at a fixed or determinable future time a sum certain in money to order or to a bearer." The personal check is the most common type of order to pay. Others, which also are used as means of payment, include various types of bank checks or drafts (cashier's checks, registered checks, and bank money orders), express money orders, telegraphic money orders, and postal money orders.[2] In these orders to pay, "money" qualities dominate rather than credit qualities. There are other orders to pay in which credit qualities predominate.

Trade drafts are orders to pay drawn by the sellers on the buyers. These drafts may be time or demand and secured or unsecured. If the order to pay drawn by the seller of goods on the purchaser of such goods is accepted by the purchaser, it is called a "trade acceptance." Bankers' acceptances are similar to trade acceptances ex-

---

[2] Specific forms of checks are certified checks, travelers' checks, and checks drawn under provisions of a traveler's letter of credit. A certified check is a personal check that has been certified by a bank officer, and the amount has been charged against the account of the drawer, which makes the check an obligation of the bank. Travelers' checks are sold by banks and the American Express Company, and they must be signed and cashed by the owners. Travelers' letters of credit authorize the drawing and cashing of a special type of personal check at certain banks in distant places.

cept that the orders to pay are drawn upon banks by the sellers of the goods. (A bank may purchase the rights of the seller of goods and act as the drawer.) The seller usually receives authority to draw upon the bank in a formal letter, called a "commercial letter of credit," which is arranged for by the buyer of the goods.

The conditions covering the financing of goods may specify: (1) that the bill of exchange is payable on "sight," on "arrival" of the goods, or thirty days, sixty days, or some other number of days after sight or date; (2) that certain documents are to be attached to the "bill"; and (3) that title to goods will be released when the "bill" is paid (D/P bill), or when it is accepted (D/A bill). If payment is required, the bill of exchange is canceled; but, if acceptance is required, the credit instrument may be in existence for thirty days, sixty days, etc., from the date of acceptance (thirty, sixty, etc., sight bills) or from the date on which it was drawn (depending on the terms of credit).

The accepting process consists of writing or stamping on the face of the "bill" the word "accepted," followed by the date of acceptance and the signature of the drawee. This corresponds to the endorsement on a promissory note with this important difference: the acceptor is primarily liable for the credit instrument, while the endorser is only secondarily liable. At the end of the credit period, the bill of exchange is presented to the drawee a second time—this time for payment.

NEGOTIABILITY, ENDORSEMENT, AND PRESENTMENT

The wide use of credit instruments has resulted in legal rules covering their purchase and sale and the rights of owners. One of the most important legal features which pertains to them is the quality of negotiability. Ordinary transfers of wealth or property rights pass by assignment, since most types of property possess the legal qualities of salability and transferability. The buyer (assignee) is subject to all the defenses that may exist between original parties. Any defect in the title is passed along from the assignor to the assignee. For example, if a man purchases a stolen car, the original owner may reclaim it by proving that he is the legal owner. The assignee may sue the assignor, if he can find him; but he has no adequate defense against the legal owner. Most forms of credit instruments have the legal qualities of salability and transferability, but in addition they also may possess the legal quality of negotiability.

Negotiability. The legal title of negotiable instruments is transferred by endorsement and delivery or by delivery only. The transferee obtains a good title, provided that he is a purchaser for value and has no notice or knowledge of any infirmity or defect of the instrument. This is true even though the title of the transferer is defective, which is different from the ordinary contract wherein the assignee is subject to all the defects and defenses that may exist between the original parties. It is intended that negotiable instruments be transferred from hand to hand like money. So the Uniform Negotiable Instruments Act aims to free owners from defenses that earlier holders may have asserted and therefore from claims of other parties.

Originally, the rules governing the transfer of promissory notes and bills of exchange were developed by merchants. Their incorporation into law helps to explain why bankers and others purchase billions of dollars worth of negotiable instruments annually without being forced to assume risks that would have prevented the organization of financial markets as we know them today. In contrast, every buyer of real estate must make or have a title search made (which normally costs from $25 to $75) before he completes his plans for assuming ownership and the financial obligations involved in the transfer of the title to real property to his name.

All credit instruments do not possess the quality of negotiability because they do not meet the legal conditions provided for in the Uniform Negotiable Instruments Act, which has been adopted by all the states. In order to be negotiable, the instrument must (1) be in writing and signed by the maker or drawer; (2) contain an unconditional promise or order to pay a certain sum of money; (3) be payable on demand or at a fixed or determinable future time; (4) be payable to order or to bearer; and (5) name the drawee, if addressed to him, or otherwise indicate him with reasonable certainty. Negotiability depends upon following certain legal procedures, including proper endorsement, and presentation.

Endorsements. Endorsement is the technical act of signing one's name, with or without qualification, to an instrument for the purpose of transfer. To complete the endorsement, there must be delivery of the instrument. Endorsement is necessary whenever a credit instrument is an order or promise to pay to a specified party. Endorsement may be special, in blank, restrictive, qualified, or conditional. The first type—special—specifies to whom or to whose order the instrument is to be paid. For example, Jones receives a check from Smith endorsed as follows: "Pay to John Jones or order," Signed "Henry Smith." Jones's endorsement is necessary for further negotiability. An endorsement in blank specifies no endorsee, being in the foregoing case simply "Henry Smith." When Henry Smith restricts his endorsement to some special purpose, such as "for deposit to the account of," "for collection only," or "pay to John Jones only," further negotiation of the instrument is limited, and the endorsement is restrictive.

A qualified endorsement may be made by adding to the endorsement the words "without recourse." The holder who signs an obligation in this way refuses to assume any financial responsibility for the check. This type of endorsement may impair the acceptability of the check but not the negotiability. Conditional endorsement makes payment of the credit instrument conditional on some happening. Thus, a father may endorse a check "Payable to my son, John Smith, when he finishes college," signed "Henry Smith"; or a businessman may endorse a credit instrument "Pay to the order of John Smith on the next arrival of the S.S. *United States* in New York," signed "Henry Smith."

Presentment. The act of handing to the maker or drawee a matured note, draft, or bill of exchange is known as "presentment." The word also applies to the act of handing to a drawee a time bill of exchange for acceptance. Presentment must be made at the place and time specified in the credit instrument. If payment or acceptance is refused, the instrument has been dishonored. If the obligation involves a party in a second state or foreign country, it must be protested in order to hold endorsers responsible in event of nonpayment, unless the collecting bank (or other endorser) marks it "no protest" or "protest waived." In doing so, the endorser accepts secondary liability without the requirement that the credit instrument be protested. Inland or domestic bills (within states) may be protested. The protest consists of a formal statement sent to endorsers and to the maker or drawer that a demand for payment or acceptance has been made and that the credit instrument has been dishonored. It is signed by a notary public. The purpose of the protest is to hold all primary and secondary parties liable. Notice of dishonor may be waived by makers, drawers, and endorsers. When the waiver is embodied in the instrument, it is deemed binding upon all parties. The costs of protesting are added to the amount of the credit instrument which has been dishonored.

Uniform Stock Transfer Act. Under common law, stock certificates are not credit instruments; and transfer of their title is not covered by the Uniform Negotiable Instruments Act. Now, in all states, they are negotiable under a statute known as the Uniform Stock Transfer Act. Title may be transferred by endorsement and delivery or by a separate written assignment and delivery. Both the stock certificate and the written agreement may be endorsed in blank or to a specified party. If, after endorsement in blank, a stock certificate comes into the hands of an innocent party for value, the innocent person has a good title, as in the case of negotiable credit instruments.

SUMMARY

The extent to which credit has been used in the United States is sufficient evidence of the importance of this system of transfer of goods and services. Practically every adult in any one month uses some type of credit instrument. Primary responsibility for the correct use of credit remains in the hands of the bankers, but every user or grantor of credit shares in the responsibility. On the economic side, the growth of credit is due: (1) to the change in the nature of modern production, which calls for the accumulation of large savings in order to finance public and private buildings, railroads, manufacturing plants, machinery, and equipment; (2) to more stable and democratic governments, which permit them to borrow and to tax in order to finance routine and socialized activities; (3) to the existence of a productive system that makes it possible to accumulate a surplus which may be invested in capital goods; and (4) to the development of financial institutions which specialize in the business of accumulating, handling, and investing the savings of society.

QUESTIONS AND PROBLEMS

1. Identify: (*a*) credit, (*b*) credit instruments, and (*c*) credit system.
2. Discuss the advantages and disadvantages of credit.
3. Show why all three "C's" of credit must be present in most credit transactions.
4. Distinguish between (*a*) public and private credit, (*b*) secured and unsecured credit, (*c*) commercial and investment credit, and (*d*) short-term and long-term credit.
5. Identify the chief "instruments of long-term finance."
6. During the period of 1927–29, banks were charged with overemphasizing the importance of collateral in making loans. Do you think this criticism is justified? Was capacity, as evidenced by individual

earning power, neglected? Were similar mistakes made in 1918–20? What is the situation at the present time?

7. What are the chief current advantages to large corporations of financing with debts?

8. Identify the chief ways in which short-term credit is made available.

9. What is meant by "accepting" a bill of exchange? Compare to an endorsement on a promissory note. What is meant by a "thirty-day-sight bill"?

10. Explain carefully the conditions necessary to render a credit instrument negotiable. May a credit instrument be transferable without being negotiable? Illustrate.

11. Assume that you have received in change a five-dollar bill which is later identified by a friend as a Federal Reserve note that he has lost. What are your rights to the note?

12. Assume that you have rented an apartment and have purchased the furniture from the former occupant. You later receive a notice that an installment payment on the furniture is due to a furniture store. Are you liable?

13. Assume that you have checks and want to endorse them in order to accomplish the following purposes. Write out your endorsements: (a) to make the check negotiable without further endorsements; (b) to limit your financial responsibility; (c) to prevent anyone except your bank from collecting; (d) to make it necessary for the party to whom you give the check to endorse it, thereby making it easier to trace payments.

14. Distinguish between the Uniform Negotiable Instruments Act and the Uniform Stock Transfer Act.

15. Classify the following credit instruments into two or more groups: (a) three-year United States Treasury note; (b) demand promissory note given by a stock exchange broker to a New York bank; (c) ninety-day endorsed bill or acceptance; (d) 1955–57 Treasury bonds; (e) Great Northern Railway Company thirty-year 3½ per cent general mortgage bond; (f) Boston Metropolitan District one to twenty-five years 2¼ per cent serial bond issue; (g) federal intermediate credit bank one to nine months' debenture; (h) bank draft drawn by Lincoln National Bank on Austin National Bank; (i) personal check which has been written by M. C. Jones on his bank; and (j) stock certificate of Chase-Manhattan Bank of New York.

Chapter | **BANK MANAGEMENT AND**

XII | **THE BANK STATEMENT**

IN THE United States, banking is a licensed and highly regulated business. All new banks must incorporate, either under state or federal law; and, after incorporation, they must operate within limits as provided by law. The purpose of requiring incorporation is to facilitate better bank administration in the interest of stockholders, depositors, and the general public. However, in the final analysis, the success of a bank depends upon its management as reflected in its financial statements.

This chapter deals with (1) the steps involved in the incorporation of a bank; (2) bank management and personnel; and (3) the bank statement, earnings and expenses, and certain problems pertaining to them.

ORGANIZATION OF A NATIONAL BANK

Since the procedures for organizing banks under state and national laws are similar, the latter will be used as an illustration of bank chartering in the United States. Although there is general acceptance of the free-banking principle, obtaining bank charters is not as easy as it would seem because administrative action prevents the organization of many proposed banks. Only commercial banks are incorporated under the national banking act, but both commercial and savings banks are chartered by states. The federal government, under certain statutes, provides for specialized banks such as the twelve Federal Reserve banks and federal land banks.

Request for Title. The National Bank Act provides that five or more natural persons may make application to the Comptroller of the Currency for a national bank charter. The first formal step is for a member of the group to write to the Comptroller stating the intent of the group and giving the proposed title, location, and capitalization of the bank to be organized. Ordinarily, the proposed title will be reserved for the bank provided the word "national" is included and no other bank in the community has the same name.

209

Action on Application to Organize a National Bank. If the request for title is approved, the organizers will make formal application for a charter on a form entitled "Application to Organize a National Bank." In the spaces provided, there must be given the name and location of the bank; its proposed capital, surplus, and undivided profits; considerable information about the applicants; and other information about the plans for setting up the bank (renting or erecting a banking house; salaries to be paid to various officers and employees; expenditures to be made for furniture, fixtures, stationery, supplies, vaults, etc.).

When the Comptroller of the Currency receives the application, his office instructs the chief national bank examiner of the district to make an investigation. In addition to checking the details contained in the application, the examiner will investigate the character, standing, and business experience of the applicants and others who are to take an active part in managing the bank; and he will appraise the banking needs of the community, the probable earnings of the proposed bank, the adequacy of existing banking facilities, and the expected effects of the bank on existing institutions.

The examiner's report is sent to the Organization Division of the Comptroller's Office in Washington, where it is checked to see that statutory requirements have been fulfilled. An assistant chief examiner, the chief national bank examiner, and three deputy comptrollers of the currency then review the application on its merits. The final decision is made by the Comptroller of the Currency, who will have obtained reports from the Federal Reserve agent of the district Federal Reserve bank and from the Federal Deposit Insurance Corporation.[1] Although further investigation may be made, if there is any disagreement among the three agencies, the final decision rests with the Comptroller of the Currency.

Articles of Association and Organization Certificate. When the Comptroller of the Currency approves the application for a charter, he sends the organizers two forms, the "Articles of Association" and "Organization Certificate." The stock of the bank is offered for sale at a price that will provide the necessary capital and a paid-in surplus equal to at least 20 per cent of the capital. The shares must have a par value of not more than $100, of which one half must be paid in cash prior to opening the bank and the remainder

---

[1] Formerly, the opinions of political figures (mayors, congressmen, and others) were obtained; but, for obvious reasons, the Comptroller prefers other channels of information on the character of the applicants. The Comptroller may check with state banking authorities on the community's need for the bank and on other questions.

within six months. The stockholders must meet and elect at least five but not more than twenty-five directors; and the directors, in turn, must meet and select officers for the bank, including at least a president, vice-president, and cashier. Then the two forms will be completed and signed, preferably by the same five persons who signed the application for the charter, and copies will be sent to the Office of the Comptroller of the Currency.

The articles of association repeat in final form much of the tentative information found in the preliminary papers filed with the Comptroller and also certain specific information with reference to the organization of the bank. The organization certificate is merely an attestation as to the purposes of the organization. It gives the title, location, and capital stock of the bank, and also the names, net financial worth, and residence of each shareholder, and number of shares held by each.

The Bank Charter.   The bank may not commence business until the Comptroller issues a "Certificate of Authority to Commence Business," which banks commonly refer to as the "charter." Before the Comptroller issues the charter, the bank must certify that it has subscribed to stock of the district Federal Reserve bank in an amount equal to 6 per cent of its capital stock and surplus and that it has already paid an amount equal to one half of its subscriptions. An "Affidavit of Publication of Charter" is sent along with the charter. The former must be signed by the publisher of the newspaper in which the charter has been published for at least sixty days (as required by law). The bank is requested to inform the Comptroller when it commences business. Although the bank may open with 50 per cent of the stock paid for, the remainder is due in five monthly installments after the bank opens.

In 1927, national bank charters were made indeterminate, that is, perpetual unless terminated by legislative action, dissolved by shareholders, forfeited by the bank for violation of the law, or closed voluntarily or by regulatory authorities because of insolvency.

Effects of Administrative Action on the Number of Banks. Although free banking remains as a statute, it can be seen readily that many proposed charters are rejected by administrative action. The record of successful applicants is high, but this may be due in part to the fact that many would-be organizers are discouraged informally before applications are made. In recent years, among the most common reasons given for rejecting applications for charters are: (1) lack of community need; (2) unsatisfactory character, experience, or financial standing of applicants; and (3) insufficient capital.[2] Since 1946 unsuccessful applicants have been given reasons for the denial of their applications; but, prior to this time, this information usually could be obtained informally from the district examiner.

Today, the protection provided by the Federal Deposit Insurance Corporation is so highly regarded as to cause applicants for bank charters (both state and national) to seek the Corporation's approval for insurance coverage of deposits before organization of the banks. Although the Corporation has no legal control over the issuance of charters, it may have veto power in effect. The Corporation cannot deny a new national bank deposit insurance; but, under certain conditions, it can withdraw this deposit insurance. In the case of state banks, it may issue deposit insurance but it is not required to do so; and, unless a state bank's deposits are insured or are to be insured, it is not eligible for membership in the Federal Reserve System.

When a request is made to the Comptroller for a national bank charter by the directors of a state bank, with the approval of stockholders owning at least 50 per cent of the stock of the bank, the procedure followed is identical to that already outlined for securing a national-bank charter. Mergers of two or more banks may be completed under either state or national law.

Minimum-Capital Requirements. While minimum-capital requirements are fixed by law, in practice considerably larger amounts of capital funds are needed. At the time of organization the chartering authorities may insist that more capital be provided, and operating banks may increase their capital with the approval of the proper banking authorities. The current minimum-capital requirements for new national banks are contained in the National Bank Act, which was drafted to meet economic and other conditions as they existed in 1864. A new national bank must have a minimum capital of $100,000, except in cities having less than 6,000 population where minimum capital required is $50,000.[3] Where the population exceeds

[2] Among the most common reasons given by the Comptroller of the Currency for rejecting 144 applications for authority to organize national banks from 1941 to 1950 inclusive were: (1) insufficient need, 104; (2) earning prospects unfavorable, 57; and (3) unsatisfactory management, 33. Since two or more reasons may be given for rejection, the total was more than 144. See Joint Committee on the Economic Report, *Monetary Policy and the Management of the Public Debt* (Washington, D.C.: U.S. Government Printing Office, 1952), Part 2, p. 930.

[3] From 1900 to 1933, in communities of 3,000 or less, a new national bank could be organized with capital of $25,000; and some banks so capitalized are still in existence.

50,000 the bank customarily must have a minimum capital of $200,-000. In the last case the Comptroller may waive this requirement for banks located in outlying districts of a city where a state law permits state banks to be organized with a smaller amount of capital ($100,000 if state banks are permitted to organize with $100,000 or less).

BANK OWNERSHIP AND MANAGEMENT

Practically all activities of banks are subject to regulation by some governmental agency. Although detailed banking regulations emphasize the protection of depositors, the rights and privileges of shareholders have not been neglected.

Certain Characteristics of Bank Stock. Unlike most other corporations, banks are permitted to issue only stock having par value; and now the par value figure of $20.00 seems to be the most common. Since 1933 banks have been authorized to issue preferred stock as well as common stock; but, with the exception of those banks that obtained financial aid from the Reconstruction Finance Corporation, very little use has been made of this power. Most of the preferred stock previously owned by the Reconstruction Finance Corporation has been sold to others or liquidated.

Shareholders may be assessed with their consent to restore the capital of a bank whose capital has been impaired by losses; but, if the bank is placed in liquidation under the national and most state laws, shareholders are not subject to assessment to cover losses of depositors and other creditors in amounts up to 100 per cent of the par value of each share held.[4]

As a substitute for double liability, generally the commercial banks are required by state or national law to retain earnings until surplus at least equals common stock capital. The percentage distribution of capital accounts for insured commercial banks is: surplus, 48 per cent; undivided profits and reserves, 22 per cent; and capital, 30 per cent (including 0.3 per cent of preferred stock, capital notes, and debentures); and so it is apparent that bank management has done considerably more than merely provide for a surplus account equal to capital.

[4] In 1953, Section 22 of the Banking Act was amended to authorize the Comptroller of the Currency to take steps necessary to terminate the double liability of shareholders of national banks that had not acted to do so. The Comptroller acted promptly by publishing the required notice in the case of five banks; and, as of January 5, 1954, the double liability of shareholders of all national banks was terminated.

Duties and Rights of Stockholders. Ownership of a bank is divided into shares of capital stock evidenced by certificates held by shareholders. At the time of organization, bank stock may be owned only by natural persons; but, later, this stock may be acquired by corporations. Stockholders have a right to vote, in person or by proxy, for directors, on matters of policy, and on other issues brought before the stockholders' meeting. Usually, a stockholder of record is entitled to one vote for each share held. However, in electing directors each national-bank stockholder has the privilege of cumulative voting. Thus if a stockholder owns five shares and there are twenty directors to be elected, he may cast a maximum of one hundred votes for one candidate, fifty votes for two candidates, etc., rather than five votes for each of twenty candidates as would be the case under noncumulative voting rules. Bills have been introduced in Congress that would abolish cumulative voting in the election of directors of national banks; but, at this time, such bills have failed to pass.

Shareholders' approval must be obtained in order to change the bank's capital stock, to assess shareholders, and to liquidate the bank if it is solvent. In case a bank is insolvent or has been operating illegally, final action rests with the appropriate governmental supervisory agency. Bank stockholders also have the right (1) to be notified of the time and place of stockholders' meetings; (2) to inspect the books of the bank at "all reasonable times, and for all proper purposes"; (3) to receive prior right to subscribe to new stock; (4) to sue directors for malfeasance in office; (5) to receive dividends, properly declared and made payable by the board of directors; (6) to share in stock dividends; and (7) to share in the surplus, if any, upon liquidation of the bank.

Requirements for Directors. A national bank is required to have a board of directors of not less than five or more than twenty-five members. Each director is elected for a term of one year and serves until his successor has legally qualified to serve in his position. All directors must be citizens of the United States; three fourths of them must have resided in the community for at least a year prior to election;[5] and each director must own stock in the bank equal to at least $1,000 par value, except where the bank's capital

---

[5] Local residence is defined as residence in the state, territory, or Federal Reserve district in which the national bank is located or within fifty miles of the bank regardless of state or district lines. In order to help individuals in or near metropolitan areas to qualify, it has been proposed in Congress that residential requirements be changed to include an area of 100 miles.

is $25,000, in which case the minimum is $500. Directors must take an oath that they will "diligently and honestly administer" the affairs of their bank. Usually men and women are selected as bank directors because of their professional or business standing in the community.

Responsibilities of the Board of Directors. The president of the bank or an officer known as the "chairman of the board of directors" presides over meetings of the board of directors. The cashier of the bank or some special officer serves as secretary. Between meetings, most of the work of the board of directors is done by committees, the most important of these being the "executive" and the "loan" or "discount" committees. A bank's board of directors is responsible for the satisfactory operation of the bank. It formulates major policies and selects the officers. The board supervises the officers, reviews their actions, audits their accounts, enacts bylaws, and otherwise controls the bank's operations.

Directors are subject to common-law penalties, both civil and criminal. They are liable for neglect of duty and lack of ordinary diligence in supervising their banks. When cases come before the court the test is "the degree of care which ordinarily prudent and diligent men would exercise under similar circumstances" (the "prudent-man" theory). There is necessity for different interpretations under varying conditions, but among the things for which directors have been held liable for losses are failure (1) to examine or audit (or cause to be audited) their banks regularly; (2) to examine or audit (or cause to be audited) their banks accurately; (3) to make a reasonable effort to collect substandard assets; (4) to appoint "loan" and "examining" committees; (5) to require officers and employees to be bonded; and (6) to charge off assets and to follow other instructions of the Comptroller of the Currency.

In addition to common-law penalties, bank directors (and also officers and employees) are liable under national law for criminal prosecution. Among these prohibited acts are: (1) accepting a fee or commission for making a loan; (2) embezzlement in any form; (3) falsely certifying any check; (4) making false entries in books, reports, etc.; (5) making loans to a bank examiner having authority to examine the bank; (6) lending to or borrowing from any director, officer, or employee of any funds held in trust by the bank; and (7) permitting their bank to make a "contribution" in connection with any election to any political office.

Space does not permit a discussion of all the legal responsibilities of directors; but enough has been presented to show the intent of Congress, which is to protect the general public from losses due to illegal or careless operations. However, no law or series of laws can insure proper and profitable operation of any bank. This is the function of bank management. Not being a professional banker, a director is expected to act as the "prudent man" would act under similar circumstances; but being a bank director involves substantially more risk than being a director of any other type of business corporation.

Officers. Officers are selected by boards of directors to manage their banks, and so the relationship between officers and directors is that of employees to employers. The chief officers are known as "president," "vice-president," and "cashier," or by similar titles; and their duties may be defined in the bylaws formulated by the board of directors and adopted by the shareholders. Usually, the chief officers are members of the board of directors and are large stockholders; and, therefore, they often are in the multiple position of employer, employee, and owner.

1. The president is selected by the board from among its own members. He is elected to serve for one year, but usually is re-elected from year to year. The president may be a trained banker, developed by years of experience in banks; or he may be a businessman active in the bank's affairs. Today, the first type is most common. In a city bank, he may give all his time to the bank's affairs; but in a rural community, he may leave the operation of the bank to the cashier and devote only a small part of his time to the bank's business. However, in either case, the president must sign certain documents and attest to reports to supervisory officials.

2. The national and most state banking codes require that each bank have at least one vice-president. If there are two or more vice-presidents, one is designated as the senior or first vice-president in order to fix responsibility for the president's duties when the latter is not present. The specific duties of vice-presidents depend primarily on their assignments, and these in turn depend on the size and organization of the bank. Customarily, a vice-president is placed in charge of each major department (see Chart 6) and in charge of large branch offices, if the bank has branch offices.

3. Each national bank is required to have a cashier, who usually is a trained banker with years of banking experience. In practice, he is the "executive officer," second only in importance to the president in the administration of the internal affairs of the bank. In small

banks, he assumes all the nonstatutory functions of the president. He is classified as a senior officer and may hold the title of vice-president in addition to that of cashier (usually "treasurer" in trust companies and "secretary" in savings banks).

Unless the responsibility is otherwise delegated, the cashier is responsible for the bank's funds, the safekeeping of earning assets,

CHART 6

BANK MANAGEMENT—ORGANIZATION CHART*

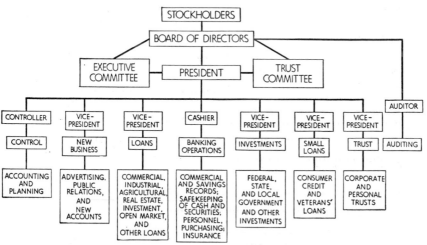

* This chart is based on the organization of a medium-sized commercial bank and is presented to show the channels of administrative responsibilities of the chief officers. The number of departments will vary according to the volume of business of the bank. There may be added foreign exchange, bond, real estate, savings, branch management, legal, and other departments as needed. In small banks all the activities of the bank may be in the banking operations department.

the employment of the junior members of the staff, the purchase of supplies, and the arrangement for insurance. He also serves as secretary for the bank, making out and signing (along with the president) the important papers of the bank. He signs certificates of stock, takes charge of the stock ledger and dividend books, and has charge of the bank's correspondence. He signs cashiers' checks, bank drafts, and vouchers; and he has charge of the transactions when his bank sells securities, borrows money, or rediscounts paper. He endorses notes and drafts before they are sent to other banks for collection. The cashier is primarily responsible for all the actual transactions after lines of policy have been determined by the president and the board of directors.

4. Many large banks have added an officer known as the "chairman of the board of directors." His duties customarily are defined by resolution of the board of directors or in the bylaws of the

bank. He may be the chief administrative officer; but, usually, his activities are less routine than those of the president, being in the nature of "policy forming," "public relations," and "new business." In all cases the chairman's personality, business and social contacts, ability, and "power" within and outside the bank will determine his banking activities.

5. The National Bank Act gives the board of directors the power to appoint other officers in addition to the president, vice-president, and cashier. Titles and duties are not uniform, but next in rank are the assistants to the chairman of the board, to the president, to the vice-president, and to the cashier. These titles give no indication as to their functions, but among the junior officers are tellers, chief clerks, and head bookkeepers; and among the employees are accountants, stenographers, typists, file clerks, machine operators, junior clerks, and many others.

Since 90 per cent of the customers of a bank never come into contact with the senior officers of a bank, it is the employees who are responsible for the impression that the general public has of the bank. This is recognized generally by those who select new employees, and consequently neatness and personality are emphasized. Since most bank jobs are routine or technical in nature, the qualities of accuracy, dependability, and speed also are essential in employees. Those employees who can see things to be done are the best officer material.

Promotion from within the ranks of any organization is a basic requirement in any sound personnel policy, and banking is no exception. Most of the current banking leaders have risen through the ranks, and surveys made of bank officers' training and experience support the conclusion that most of them have had many years of banking experience (but not necessarily with the same bank). At present, there are about 500,000 bank officers and bank employees of whom about one third are women; and salaries and wages paid for their services are the chief cost of operating banks. Banking, like teaching, is handicapped in obtaining personnel because of its reputation for paying low salaries and for giving little opportunity for advancement.

The chief advantages of working for a bank are security, pleasant surroundings, and the prestige associated with the job. However, salaries paid to bank employees are about the same as those paid to other office employees and above those paid in retail stores; but, if relative responsibilities are considered, they may be below those paid in industry. Gradually, the salaries of bank officers and employees are being increased; and now, the average yearly salary of bank officers is $7,700 and of bank employees, $3,000. These figures understate the amount of compensation because they include salaries of part-time employees and exclude "fringe" benefits such as payments into pension funds and for hospitalization insurance. Because of the nature of banking, there is an absence of the sharp division between management and labor found in industry; this may help to explain the absence of organized labor in banks, outside of some metropolitan areas and parts of the West Coast.

CAPITAL ACCOUNT ITEMS

A bank statement is a report setting forth the financial condition of a bank. It is submitted to the proper federal and/or state banking authorities, to depositors, and to the general public. The type of bank statement prepared depends on the purpose for which it is to be used. There are three types—the condensed, the nontechnical, and the uncondensed. The condensed (see Table 8) and nontechnical

TABLE 8
THE AUSTIN NATIONAL BANK STATEMENT OF CONDITION
As of June 30, 1956*

ASSETS		LIABILITIES		
Loans and discounts (net)	$27,356,627.18	Capital stock		$ 1,250,000.00
U.S. government bonds, etc.	19,936,838.17	Surplus		1,250,000.00
		Undivided profits		910,516.01
Municipal bonds, etc.	851,640.11	Reserved for contingencies		523,266.92
		Reserved for accrued expenses		143,484.11
Stock of Federal Reserve bank	75,000.00	Dividends payable July 2, 1956		62,500.00
		Other liabilities		10,328.71
Banking house	925,041.63			
Furniture and fixtures	343,149.77	Deposits:		
		Individual demand	$34,186,898.66	
Other real estate	2,424.25	Individual time	5,932,851.28	
		Correspondent banks	6,383,711.23	
Other assets	71,861.21	U.S. government	3,813,816.62	
		Other public funds	10,585,980.41	
Cash and due from banks	20,682,118.40	Other deposits	5,191,346.77	66,094,604.97
Total	$70,244,700.72	Total		$70,244,700.72

* Courtesy of George K. Meriwether III, Public Relations Officer of the Austin National Bank.

types are the ones most widely distributed. The uncondensed type is the most complete, and it is the form used in making reports to supervisory agencies.

The capital stock, surplus, undivided profits, and any other proprietary claim combined represent the equity of the stockholders. This figure divided by the number of shares of stock gives the book value of each share. The total of these proprietary items is but a small percentage of total liabilities, and this only emphasizes the importance of other sources of funds.[6] However, proprietors' investments or capital funds are legally necessary to start a bank, to act as shock absorbers in case of losses, and to form a factor of safety for depositors. Each of the capital items has certain features that distinguish it from the others.

Capital. The capital of a bank is the amount of capital as stated in the bank's charter. Unlike other corporations in the United States and banks abroad, American banks usually sell all of their capital stock at the time of organization. Shares are carried at par value, and the total par value of all shares is the capital of the bank. The capital of a bank has been described as a trust fund for depositors that must be kept unimpaired at all times. Hence, depositors are assured that stockholders always will have a financial stake in their bank equal to the capital item. If, for any reason, this stake is impaired by losses, regulatory officers are responsible for such action as will protect the community, the depositors, and the bank. In co-operation with other governmental agencies the directors and officers of the banks and others in the community may raise new capital funds to keep the bank functioning or may close it and later either reorganize it or liquidate it. Under common law, directors of any corporation must take action to protect the interests of stockholders and creditors.

Surplus. Surplus is an accounting item representing both an amount in excess of the par value of stock paid in at the time of organization and/or the earnings of the bank which have been retained by the management. It differs from the capital stock in that it may be impaired by losses without making the bank subject to reorganization. When banks are formed, it is customary to sell the capital stock for more than par value, thereby giving the banks funds with which to assume some losses without affecting the capital. Furthermore, some of the additional funds thus obtained are used to acquire bank premises, fixtures, and equipment, and to make investments and loans so as to obtain income to help cover operating costs.

Undivided Profits. The undivided profits account is an accounting item showing earnings that have not been paid out as

---

[6] Many years ago Walter Bagehot wrote that "the main source of profitableness of established banking is the smallness of the requisite capital. Being only wanted as a 'moral influence,' it needs not be more than is necessary to secure that influence." (Walter Bagehot, *Lombard Street* [14th ed.; London: John Murray, 1915], p. 232.)

dividends, placed in surplus, or placed in one of the reserve accounts that banks keep to offset losses or some expenses that are certain. In rare cases it even includes funds paid into a bank in excess of capital and surplus at the time of organization. When retained earnings are accounted for in the undivided profits account, management has much greater freedom of action than when they are accounted for in the surplus account; and, therefore, the undivided profits item is becoming more important on bank statements. The funds accounted for in the undivided profits account may be transferred to the surplus account, added to one of the reserve accounts for contingencies, or paid out to stockholders as dividends. Most banks prefer to have a stable dividend policy, which means that the undivided profits account will be built up during good years and paid out during lean years.

Other Capital Account Items. Other capital account items represent earnings that have been earmarked to care for taxes, interest, and other accrued expenses. An account may be set up to care for dividends by the board of directors but not paid as of the date of the bank statement. The policies in regard to "reserves for contingencies" depend upon bank management, the financial positions of individual banks, the outlook for future profits, the attitude of regulatory officials, and sometimes the source of the profits. For example, if a bank has a large trading profit on investments, it probably would set aside a large "reserve for contingencies" to offset possible future trading losses.

Many banks, particularly small ones, treat losses and charge-offs on assets that have declined in value as direct expense items to be charged against current income; but a growing number of banks are making such charges against valuation reserves previously set aside from earnings. When this practice is followed, banks may deduct the transfers from reported earnings, in amounts approved by the Internal Revenue Service, before computing corporate income taxes. The amount of such valuation reserves for losses on loans is limited, but the Internal Revenue Service rule permits banks to use a loss ratio based on any consecutive twenty-year period since 1927 (including the years when losses were greatest, 1930–34).

Banks' Capital Position. Except in the outlying sections of metropolitan areas and in small communities, national banks' minimum-capital requirements are only of academic interest, because banks having assets worth millions of dollars would not try to operate with the mere $200,000 capital required for national banks. Bankers, supervisory officials, and students of banking emphasize the relationship between total capital accounts and total assets or total deposits. In 1945, the total capital accounts of insured commercial banks was less than six per cent of their total assets (the lowest percentage on record). Although their assets have increased since that time, the growth in their total capital accounts has been more rapid; and now the total capital accounts amount to more than seven per cent of total assets of insured commercial banks.

Capital-Deposit Ratio.   Throughout the history of banking in the United States, the ratio of capital accounts to deposits has been declining. Those who oppose the establishment of a minimum capital accounts to deposits ratio point to the past when even higher ratios did not protect depositors from losses. From 1869 to 1938 the average loss taken by depositors in suspended banks was 30 per cent of the deposits involved, plus loss of interest during the liquidation period. Today, there are few bank suspensions; and depositors in insured banks are protected by the Federal Deposit Insurance Corporation's policy of merging or reorganizing financially distressed banks and guaranteeing the assets and thereby the deposits involved. This practice shifts the burden to the Corporation, which is supported fully by all insured banks and, if and when necessary, by government credit.

Capital-Risk Assets Ratio.   In the final analysis the safety of bank deposits depends on the quality of bank assets. Today supervisory authorities stress not only the ratio between capital accounts and total assets (or total deposits) but also the ratio between capital accounts and total assets minus cash items and government securities (called the "ratio of capital accounts to risk assets"). A bank having a low capital account to deposits ratio, but having no risk assets, may be a far safer bank than one having a high capital accounts to deposits ratio but having a large amount of risk assets.

In analyzing the protection provided by total capital account items (equity protection), bank management must recognize the fact that a bank's capital must not be impaired. This means that the amount of "reserves," "undivided profits," and "surplus" must be large enough to absorb all losses. From this viewpoint the practice of capitalizing retained earnings (distributing a stock dividend and charging surplus, undivided profits, and/or reserves) tends to weaken a bank's capital position even though the total equity protection provided depositors remains the same.

LIABILITIES

Deposits. The largest item on a bank statement is the one representing "total deposits" or simply "deposits." From the viewpoint of depositors, this item indicates money that they left with or lent to the bank. Although these funds pass beyond the control of depositors and become the property of the bank, depositors retain the right to demand the equivalent in dollars at such time and under such conditions as were agreed upon when the deposits were made. Usually, they may be withdrawn on demand, at the end of a specified number of days or so many days after notice of intention to withdraw has been given. These agreements give rise to the popular classification of deposits as "demand," "time," and "savings," a subject which is discussed more fully in the next chapter.

The average annual rate of growth of deposits and assets of all banks for the last ten years has been about 4 per cent (which would tend to double them in about eighteen years). The increase in the rate of growth of demand deposits has been somewhat less than that of total deposits and total assets. Such a rate of growth is normal and desirable, being similar to the rate of increase in the physical output of goods and services (gross national product).

Others. If a bank is financing domestic and foreign trade, travel, or some other transactions with letters of credit or grants of acceptance credit, the items "liabilities on letters of credit," "liabilities on acceptances outstanding," or similar accounting items may appear on the bank's statement. The statement also may show borrowing from its Federal Reserve bank, correspondent banks, and others.[7] Under miscellaneous items there may appear "income collected but not earned" (discounts), "expenses accrued and unpaid," "officers' checks," and others, with the number of miscellaneous items increasing with the size and complexity of the bank's business.

ASSETS

Cash and Due from Banks. The item "cash and due from banks" includes: (1) coins and paper money kept on hand by banks in order to care for the needs of depositors; (2) reserve accounts

---

[7] Borrowings include the total borrowed on (1) banks' own promissory notes, (2) certificates of deposit, (3) bills and notes rediscounted, and (4) any other instrument given for the purpose of borrowing money. It also includes loans and securities sold under repurchase agreements and "federal funds." See Board of Governors of the Federal Reserve System, *Banking and Monetary Statistics* (Washington, D.C., 1943), p. 70.

kept by member banks with their Federal Reserve banks to meet
their legal reserve requirements; (3) balances kept with correspondent banks; and (4) "cash items in process of collection." Cash items
in process of collection are items collected in one, two, or more
days; they are "virtually cash" and, hence, are included in the total
primary reserves of banks.

Securities. Since good bank assets represent the chief protection of depositors, the second major class of items on the asset side
of a condensed bank statement usually is United States government
securities. These securities vary according to maturity and yield,
with banks placing greater emphasis on short-term obligations than
is true of ordinary institutional investors. Other investments include:
(1) obligations guaranteed by the United States government (now
of minor importance), (2) obligations of government corporations
not guaranteed by the United States government, (3) obligations of
states, (4) obligations of subdivisions of the state, (5) obligations of
private institutions, and (6) stock.

Loans. Bank loans are reported according to purposes for
which the funds are used. These classes are: (1) commercial loans,
including open-market paper; (2) agricultural loans; (3) brokers'
and dealers' loans and other loans to purchase or carry securities;
(4) real estate loans; (5) consumer loans; and (6) others.

Other Assets. The items "bank premises owned" and "furniture and fixtures" represent the book value given to these physical
assets. The item "other real estate owned" usually is the result of
bad real estate loans and subsequent foreclosures which have become
necessary in order to protect banks from greater losses. In other
cases, "other real estate owned" may have resulted from purchases
of property by a bank planning to move to a new site, to open
a branch, or otherwise to expand its operations. Sometimes a bank's
real estate investments take the form of holdings of securities of a
subsidiary company which has been formed to hold the titles to
the bank's premises and other real estate owned by the bank.

The item "customers' liability on acceptances" represents claims
of the bank against customers for whom they have made grants of
acceptance credit. Most of these claims arise out of the financing
of foreign trade and are discussed in the chapter dealing with that
subject. The item "income accrued but not yet collected" is an
accounting item showing income earned during the accounting period but which has not come due and is not payable until some-
time later. "Other assets" is the catchall classification found on any

balance sheet, and it includes all items which have not been covered in other classes of assets.

While national banks must publish statements of condition four times a year and state banks are subject to similar requirements, individual banks possess wide discretion in appraising their assets. Supervisory officials are primarily concerned with the safety of depositors, and they seldom object when assets are left out or appraised at less than market value. For illustration, most banks carry the value of their premises at a nominal figure, although they may be worth millions of dollars. Supervisory agencies permit banks to carry investments in government bonds at the original purchase price, less equal annual amortization of the premium paid if purchased above par; but, over a period of time, there is no obligation to show "paper" profits or losses due to market fluctuations. Loans previously "written down," or "charged off," may become collectible. In good times, banks like to accumulate hidden reserves, and this means that the book value of bank stock is usually understated; and, during depressions, the book value of bank stock may be overstated.

EARNINGS AND EXPENSES

Over a period of years a sound bank must earn enough to pay all its expenses, to cover its losses, and to provide a reasonable return on its capital accounts. Otherwise, it is only a question of time until losses eliminate all capital account items that provide the cushion between claims of depositors and other creditors and the capital of the bank. This suggests the importance of profit and loss statements, as well as earnings statements, in appraising the financial position of banks. Although banks seldom publish statements of earnings and expenses, these statistics are made available to supervisory agencies which publish them. A commercial bank's chief source of operating income is interest derived from loans and from investments in United States government obligations and other securities. Other sources of income include service charges and fees on bank loans, service charges on deposit accounts, other commissions and fees, exchange and collection charges, and earnings of trust departments.

The sources of nonoperating income of banks include profits from the sale and/or redemption of securities and profits due to accounting changes, such as transfers from reserve accounts and recoveries on loans and investments that previously had been "written down" or "charged off" as losses. Conversely, there are nonoperating expenses of the same sort; and, during the years 1931–34, these adjustments accounted for the unsatisfactory earning position of banks.[8]

In arriving at net current operating earnings, current operating expenses must be deducted from current operating earnings. These current operating expenses include: (1) salaries and wages paid to officers and employees; (2) interest on time and savings deposits and on borrowed money; (3) taxes other than net income taxes; (4) recurring depreciation on banking house, furniture, and fixtures; and (5) other items. Now, the earnings of insured commercial banks classified by major sources are a little more than 50 per cent from

TABLE 9

SOURCES AND DISPOSITION OF TOTAL INCOME, INSURED BANKS IN THE UNITED STATES
(Continental U.S. and Other Areas), 1947, 1954, and 1955

ITEM	AMOUNTS (IN MILLIONS)						PER CENT OF TOTAL, 1955†	
	Insured Commercial Banks			Insured Mutual Savings Banks*			Commercial banks	Mutual savings banks
	1955	1954	1947	1955	1954	1947		
Total Income....................	$6,617	$6,405	$3,360	$846	$781	$475	100.0%	100.0%
Sources								
Loans.......................	3,697	3,263	1,282	536	454	153	55.9	63.3
U.S. government obligations.......	1,334	1,273	1,080	151	156	185	20.2	17.8
Other securities.................	351	325	179	99	96	24	5.3	11.7
Service charges on deposits........	340	312	148	......	......	......	5.1	......
Other current income‡...........	656	601	409	28	28	13	9.9	3.3
Recoveries, etc.§...............	240	631	262	33	47	100	3.6	3.9
Disposition								
Salaries and wages..............	1,896	1,762	947	75	71	45	28.7	8.9
Interest and dividends on deposits..	678	618	298	536	466	181	10.2	63.4
Other current expenses‡..........	1,386	1,258	737	83	83	49	20.9	9.8
Charge-offs, etc.‖...............	707	553	295	56	51	112	10.7	6.6
Income taxes ¶...................	794	907	302	9	11	6	12.0	1.1
Dividends to stockholders**.......	566	517	315	......	......	......	8.6	......
Additions to capital accounts......	590	790	466	87	99	82	8.9	10.3

Source: *Annual Report of the Federal Deposit Insurance Corporation for the Year Ended December 31, 1955* (Washington, D.C., 1956), p. 36.

Note: Due to rounding differences, components may not add precisely to the totals.

* Because of changes in 1951 in the method of reporting, data for 1954 and 1955 are not strictly comparable with those for 1947 nor with those for commercial banks.

† Percentages are computed from unrounded data.

‡ For mutual savings banks in 1954 and 1955 includes amounts classified as "nonrecurring" income or expenses.

§ Recoveries from assets previously charged off except those credited to valuation reserve accounts, profits on assets sold, and transfers from valuation reserve accounts.

‖ Losses and other charge-offs except those charged to valuation reserve accounts, and transfers to valuation reserve accounts.

¶ For mutual savings banks, includes franchise taxes computed on an income basis.

** Includes interest on capital notes and debentures.

[8] Member banks' net current earnings expressed as percentages on total capital accounts for the six years beginning with 1931 were: 7.9, 7.2, 7.7, 7.8, 7.3, and 7.7, which would seem to indicate a stable and satisfactory situation. Following adjustments for net charge-offs, net profits were as follows: 0.2, −4.5, −7.3, −4.4, 4.1, and 8.9.

loans, about 25 per cent from securities, and 25 per cent from all other sources.

Net profits before income taxes will be net current operating earnings plus or minus nonoperating earnings. Since 1947, as a result of a favorable ruling of the Internal Revenue Service, banks have been making large transfers to reserve accounts; and this has been an important reason why reports of nonoperating expenses have been more than nonoperating earnings. As compared to 1945 and 1946, the peak years in war financing, there has been a sharp decline in profits on securities sold and/or redeemed. Like other business corporations, commercial banks are subject to federal income taxes and, in some states, also to state income taxes. Net profits, after income taxes, may be retained by banks or used to pay dividends. The relative importance of earnings, expenses, and dividends of commercial banks are indicated in Table 9.

SUMMARY

In the United States the federal and most state governments are still committed to a free banking policy because the privilege of organizing a new bank technically is open to all qualified individuals. In practice, many groups are denied charters because of insufficient need, unfavorable earning prospects, and for other reasons. Since deposit insurance is generally regarded as necessary for successful operation of a commercial bank, many would-be organizers of new state banks are hesitant about preceding with plans without assurance by the Federal Deposit Insurance Corporation that the bank's deposit accounts will be insured. This permits the Corporation to play an important role in determining conditions under which new state banks are to be opened.

Management and operation of banks is subject to much detailed regulation, and bank directors and officers are held to a higher legal code of behavior than corresponding officials of other business corporations. The managerial policies of bankers are reflected in their banks' financial statements, of which the two most important are: (1) statement of condition or balance sheet, and (2) statement of earnings, expenses and dividends, or profit and loss statement. Currently, the financial statements of banks indicate a healthy condition. In general, banks' financial positions reflect general business conditions fairly accurately, being sensitive to any change from depression to prosperity or from prosperity to depression.

QUESTIONS AND PROBLEMS

1. Outline briefly the procedure involved in incorporating a national bank.

2. Analyze: "However, one of the fundamental tenets of our views and actions on applications for charters and branches is the desirability of competition wherever possible. We believe that sound and healthy competition between banks redounds favorably to the public welfare through increased adequacy of credit facilities, fair rates of interest, and the prevention of undue concentration of monetary and economic power." (Reply of the Comptroller of the Currency in Joint Committee on the Economic Report, *Monetary Policy and Management of the Public Debt* [Washington, D.C.: U.S. Government Printing Office, 1952], Part 2, p. 929.) Does this appear to be "free banking"?

3. What steps may be taken by shareholders and directors of a bank when it is threatened by insolvency? What government agency may order the liquidation of a state bank? A national bank?

4. Stocks of banks in metropolitan centers customarily sell for less than their book value. "On the face of it, the market seems to appraise private commercial banks, especially in large metropolitan centers, as worth more dead than alive." (R. E. Speagle, "Bank Stocks at a Discount," *Harvard Business Review*, Vol. XXIX, No. 1 [January, 1951], p. 99.) Is this situation due to the earning record of commercial banks? Fear of depreciation? Conservative dividend policy? Preference for industrial stocks as a hedge against inflation? Unsatisfactory nature of "book value" as a guide to investments?

5. What are the principal duties of (*a*) directors and (*b*) stockholders of banks? Do depositors share in the responsibility for their banks? Explain.

6. What are the principal duties of the (*a*) president, (*b*) vice-president, and (*c*) cashier of an average-size bank?

7. Under what circumstances may the same person be in the multiple position of employer, employee, and owner of a bank? Are these circumstances unusual? Explain.

8. "For a junior officer trying to balance his budget on $8,000 to $10,000 a year, the wait for promotion can seem to be everlasting." ("The Bankers," *Fortune*, Vol. XXXVIII, No. 5 [November, 1948], p. 120.) Comment.

9. Since 90 per cent of banks' customers never come into contact with senior officers, what bank personnel problems are involved?

10. Using Table 9 as a reference, what are (*a*) the chief sources of operating income for insured commercial banks for each of the selected years, and (*b*) the chief operating expenses?

11. Using Table 9 as a reference, have insured commercial banks been (*a*) following a stable dividend policy? (*b*) earning a satisfactory

return on total capital accounts? (*c*) allocating net profits after income taxes conservatively? and (*d*) depending considerably upon service charges on demand deposits as a source of income?

12. Analyze: "The second quality for banking leadership, after knowledge, is vision and imagination, or a receptiveness to new ideas. It is the opposite of smugness, a disease against which bankers are not entirely immune." (Homer J. Livingston, "Executive Leadership Depends Upon Self-Development," *Banking*, September, 1955, p. 138.)

Chapter XIII | COMMERCIAL BANK DEPOSITS

DEMAND deposits in commercial banks are classified as money because checks drawn on such deposits are used as a means of payment. From the viewpoint of an individual banker, giving depositors the privilege of drawing checks on deposit accounts is one of the inducements offered to secure assets (primary deposits). The funds acquired from depositors are used by banks in their lending and investing operations. When bank deposits increase, bank assets also increase.

In an earlier chapter the implication was made that the banking system as a whole is primarily responsible for the volume of bank deposits because of its policies of credit expansion and contraction. It is true that the banking system may expand credit provided (1) there is a demand for loans, (2) the public is willing to hold bank deposits in place of currency, and (3) the required legal reserves are available or may be created. This means that in order to have an expansion in bank credit, the process must usually be concurred in by the public, the commercial banks, and the Federal Reserve System. After deposits are created by a lending or an investing operation, it does not follow that the deposits will remain in the bank that created them, because banks compete with each other for deposits and collectively they must convince the public that checkbook money is safer and more convenient than currency in most transactions.

This chapter deals with the interrelationships among depositors, commercial banks, and the Federal Deposit Insurance Corporation. It may help to think about the problems to be discussed from the viewpoint of an individual depositor on one hand and from the viewpoint of his bank on the other hand.

KINDS OF BANK DEPOSITS

Deposits are classified according to (1) provisions for withdrawal, as demand or time deposits; (2) presence or lack of special protective features, as secured or unsecured; (3) insured status, as insured or uninsured; (4) ownership, as public or private; and (5) origin, as primary or derivative.

Demand and Time Deposits. Demand deposits are those which may be drawn upon or transferred at any time without previous notice of withdrawal. Most frequently they appear as deposits in checking accounts in banks. Time deposits are those which may be withdrawn (*a*) after the elapse of a specific period of time, as evidenced by certificates of deposit; (*b*) on a specific date, as in the case of deposits in Christmas, vacation, tax, and other so-called "savings" clubs; and (*c*) after thirty or more days following previous notice of intent to withdraw (but, under normal conditions, banks waive this requirement). Time deposits also include the savings deposits of the United States Postal Savings System which have been redeposited in banks (see Chapter XXIX). An analysis of banks according to size, as determined by total deposits, indicates that demand deposits make up about 75 per cent of total deposits of both the smallest and the larger banks, and 63 per cent of the total deposits of banks holding deposits of from $10,000,000 to $25,000,-000.

Secured and Unsecured Deposits. Secured deposits are similar to other secured credits in that something has been pledged specifically to assure their payment. The two most common kinds of secured deposits are "trust" and "public" deposits. This means that public deposits (federal, state, city, county, and other subdivisions of the state) and trust funds left on deposit are secured by a special lien on the bank's assets, earmarked for this purpose. Like preferred creditors of any debtor, these creditors have preferred claims to the pledged assets which, in case of failure of the bank, places their rights (to what are usually the best assets of the bank) ahead of the Federal Deposit Insurance Corporation and other unsecured creditors.

Unsecured deposits are all deposits which are not secured by something specifically pledged to assure their payment. If and when a bank is liquidated, the unsecured creditors as a group will lose to the extent that the secured creditors gain. While this situation does not present a special problem to small depositors ($10,000 or less) as long as the Federal Deposit Insurance Corporation continues to guarantee their accounts, it is a problem to the Corporation and to large depositors. The reason for the discrimination in favor of certain types of depositors is that the laws covering the deposit of these funds require this special protection. So, there are two ways to regard the advertisement "depository for federal [state, city, etc.] funds": (1) the bank is so strong that the government has selected it as a depository; or (2) the bank gives less protection to my deposit than it does to government and trust deposits. Seemingly, if public and trust funds require special protection, it should be provided by means other than by increasing the risks assumed by general depositors and the Federal Deposit Insurance Corporation.

Insured and Uninsured Deposits. Insured deposits are those protected against loss resulting from bank failure or insolvency by a second corporation or agency. In business finance, sometimes one corporation will guarantee the liabilities of a second corporation in whole or part, thus placing the debt-paying ability of the two corporations behind the debts of the first corporation. Between 1907 and 1918, eight states made statutory provisions for insurance of deposits; but, before 1930, these laws had become inoperative.

Between 1933 and 1943, New York, Connecticut, and Massachusetts established insurance funds for mutual savings banks; and Texas made provisions for guarantee of bank deposits. Of the state insurance funds, only those of Connecticut and Massachusetts are in operation. Now insured deposits are thought of as those in banks insured by the Federal Deposit Insurance Corporation. Legally, the protection given each depositor in one bank is limited to $10,000. (Savings accounts in savings and loan associations may be insured by the Federal Savings and Loan Insurance Corporation; but, since these accounts are not technically deposits, they are considered in a later chapter.) Uninsured deposits are those which are not protected against loss resulting from bank failure or insolvency by a corporation or agency. Legally, they include not only deposits in uninsured banks but also that part of any account in an insured bank not covered because of the size of the individual account (over $10,000).

Public and Private Deposits. Public deposits are those owned by the federal government, state governments, political subdivisions of states, or foreign governments. As previously noted, deposits of American governments are protected by specific pledges of assets as required by national or state law. Private deposits are those owned by individuals, partnerships, private corporations, and other private institutions. In reporting to supervisory agencies, most banks classify their private deposits as (1) interbank; and (2) individuals, partnerships, and corporations. An interbank deposit is one owned by another bank; and deposits reported as "individuals, partnerships, and corporations" include all deposits except "public" and "interbank."

When classified by ownership, business and personal deposits are relatively more important to the largest banks and relatively less important to the smaller banks. Government deposits represent between 11 and 12 per cent of total deposits of all sizes of banks up to those holding deposits of $500,000,000; but for banks holding deposits in excess of $500,000,000, government deposits represent between 8 and 9 per cent of total deposits. The relative importance of interbank deposits increases with the increase in size of banks, representing 0.3 per cent of total deposits of the smallest banks and 15.5 per cent of deposits of banks holding deposits in excess of $1 billion.[1]

Primary and Derivative Deposits. Primary deposits are those which result from the collection of cash items or deposits of currency. They are traced to deposits of checks, drafts, interest coupons, and currency, and to collection of mail and wire transfers, notes and other obligations which are due. The significant fact to recognize is that primary deposits give an individual bank new funds to invest or to lend. A bank usually gains primary deposits when its competitive position is improving and/or when the banking system as a whole is expanding.

Derivative deposits are those which result from the lending and investing operations of the bank, being derived from the bank's credit-granting activities. When bank customers borrow, they usually take the proceeds of their loans as "checking accounts." So the bank's deposits will be increased. When banks purchase government obligations, they may be permitted to make payment by crediting the government's account. However, banks' lending and investing activities depend on their holdings of cash reserves. Therefore, they tend to increase derivative deposits when their primary deposits are increasing; and, conversely, to decrease derivative deposits when their primary deposits are decreasing.

Although deposits are considered "cash in the bank" by their owners, the fact is that deposits are but liabilities of the bank; and only a fraction of these liabilities will be offset by "cash" in the bank. Banks do hold a small amount of currency for the convenience

[1] See Table 43 in the *Annual Report of the Federal Deposit Insurance Corporation for the Year Ended December 31, 1954* (Washington, D.C.: U.S. Government Printing Office, 1955), p. 74.

of their customers; and they also keep checking accounts with their correspondent banks and/or with their district Federal Reserve banks, if they are member banks, which they draw upon with bank drafts to settle obligations. However, most of a bank's assets are in the form of loans and investments because our fractional reserve system permits the banking system to support deposits in amounts far in excess of cash reserves. The relationship between the depositor and his bank is that of creditor and debtor; and, as creditors, depositors are protected by the earning power and all of the assets of their banks, not merely by the small percentage of banks' assets represented by reserves (cash and funds due from other banks).

Time Deposits, Open Accounts. The term *time deposits, open accounts* includes those accounts covered by written contracts that permit the depositor to withdraw all or part of his deposit by check or otherwise before the maturity of the account, subject however to the thirty-day rule (as determined on the date of deposit or written notice of the intent of withdrawal). Such deposit accounts are associated with Christmas and vacation clubs and others that are arranged to meet some anticipated expenditures. Usually they necessitate periodic deposits by the participants over a period of three months or longer with all deposits made available on a specified date according to prior contractual arrangements.

Certificate of Deposit. Business corporations and others sometimes make time deposits which are evidenced by certificates of deposit. A certificate of deposit is a receipt and also a promise to pay to bearer or any specified person or his order. For each deposit, a new certificate of deposit is drawn showing the date, name of depositor, amount of the deposit, interest rate, and date due. The certificate of deposit may be so drawn as to make it negotiable or nonnegotiable.[2]

Classification of Deposits for Reserve Purposes. The Federal Reserve Act, as amended, permits member banks to keep a lower minimum legal reserve against time deposits than against those classified as demand deposits; and state laws are similar for state nonmember banks. The distinction made between a time and a demand deposit, for reserve purposes, depends upon the terms or conditions under which the deposit is made.[3] If a deposit is evidenced by a

---

[2] J. C. Teevan and L. Y. Smith, *Business Law* (St. Paul, Minnesota: West Publishing Co., 1949) pp. 336–37.

[3] Reserves of member banks are based on "net demand deposits" (that is, total demand deposits minus items in process of collection and balances in domestic banks which are withdrawable on demand) and total time deposits.

passbook, the terms of which specify that withdrawal is subject to notice of thirty days or more, or by a certificate of deposit drawn for thirty days or more, it is classified as a "time" deposit.

Criticism of Administration of Deposits. While the federal law places the dividing line between time and demand deposits at thirty days, there were, prior to 1933, no legal checks on banks "waiving notice" or cashing certificates of deposit before maturity. As a result, many depositors, including business corporations, classified their funds as "time" deposits in order to draw interest paid on such deposits without fear of having their funds temporarily frozen awaiting maturity. Competition among banks was keen; and this practice of classifying deposits as "time," rather than as "demand," was not only condoned by bankers but encouraged by them. The banks profited, to a minor extent, by having more assets "freed" for lending and investing because the minimum percentage reserve requirement against time deposits was smaller than for demand deposits.

The practice of paying interest on "reclassified demand deposits" meant that banks' lending and investing operations were geared to the high expenses that went with the payment of interest on these deposits; and, as a result, too often yield rather than safety was stressed in banks' lending and investing operations. Another practice which drew criticism was that of giving preference to some depositors by cashing their time deposits while others were placed on notice. If the bank failed in the interim, the depositors who had been placed on notice, in addition to being deprived temporarily of the use of their funds, faced the loss of part of their assets.

The banking acts of 1933 and 1935 prohibited banks from paying time deposits before maturity, except under conditions and in accordance with rules and regulations prescribed. Finally, banks were prohibited from waiving requirement of notice before withdrawal of savings deposits unless this waiver applied to all similar deposits. Since these provisions are applicable to all insured banks, most savings and time deposits are involved. (Many state noninsured banks are covered by similar state laws.)

Emphasis on Proper Classification. To check the tendency to classify commercial and other business accounts as savings deposits, the definition of a savings account permits only individuals and certain nonprofit organizations (religious, charitable, educational, fraternal, and other philanthropic institutions) to open savings accounts. Business corporations may and do open interest-bearing time accounts. Thus, a corporation which has created a "reserve account" for some purpose may "fund" it by depositing cash with a bank. These time deposits may not be withdrawn before maturity unless undue hardship can be shown. When the deposit matures, the deposit must be reclassified as a demand deposit or redeposited as a time account.

Interest Payment Regulation. The arguments in support of legislation prohibiting the payment of interest on demand deposits in member banks and other banks insured by the Federal Deposit Insurance Corporation are summarized as follows: (1) the payment of interest on demand deposits is unwarranted because depositors are compensated for the use of their fund by banking services; (2) interest payments decrease net earnings out of which accounting reserves and special funds are created to protect the bank and depositors; and (3) the nonpayment of interest would reduce banks' incentives to lend or invest excessively in assets wherein large credit risks are present. (It may be argued that the increase in net profits will be paid out as dividends rather than retained to strengthen the bank; however, during the last twenty years, the capital positions of most commercial banks have been improved substantially by the practice of retaining earnings.)

The objective in the regulation of interest payments on time and savings deposits is to prevent excessive interest payments. Because savings and time depositors are not given the services associated with checking accounts, it is appropriate that they be paid interest on their deposits. Other arguments in support of the payment of interest on such deposits include: (1) legal reserve requirements are less, which permits a larger percentage of time and savings deposits to be invested; (2) bookkeeping, overhead, and other costs assignable to savings and time accounts are less; and (3) savings and time deposits remain in the banks for longer periods of time and may be invested in less liquid assets on which yields are usually larger than on shorter-term more marketable assets.

The maximum rates on time deposits in all insured banks, by classes of time deposits, as fixed by federal agencies, are: (1) savings deposits, 3 per cent; (2) postal savings deposits, 2½ per cent; and (3) other deposits payable in (*a*) six months or more, 3 per cent, (*b*) ninety days to six months, 2½ per cent, and (*c*) less than ninety days, 1 per cent.[4] Most banks are paying less, usually as a

---

[4] The current permissive interest rates became effective for all insured banks at the beginning of 1957, when they were increased ½ per cent for savings deposits and other time deposits except those payable in less than ninety days.

result of action taken by clearinghouse associations, state supervisory agencies, and/or individual banks.

The tenacity of the system of paying interest on deposits is due to the fact that banking is carried on under the law of decreasing per-unit costs. If higher interest payments for deposits by one bank result in redistribution of funds among the banks in the community, the banks which lose deposits will have to contract loans; and this will tend to increase their per-unit costs. So these banks will have two reasons for increasing interest paid on deposits: loss of loanable funds and increase in per-unit costs. The resulting cut-throat competition—a characteristic of commercial banking during periods when there is a demand for loans—tends to go to excess unless curbed by co-operative action among banks or by government control.

CHECKING ACCOUNTS AND RELATED SERVICES

In selecting a bank the depositor usually considers convenience of location and the bank's reputation for friendly and efficient service. A newcomer in a community is usually influenced by professional and business associates in selecting his bank. Although there are exceptions, a personal introduction is usually insisted upon by bank officers when they are opening a checking account; but this is rarely true when opening savings and other nonchecking accounts.

Although there is a tendency for the general public to assume that opening a deposit account is a right rather than a privilege, banks may and do refuse to open deposit accounts for individuals, partnerships, and corporations including the government. Among the reasons for refusing to accept deposits are: (1) the account would fail to meet some technical requirements such as maintaining a mimimum balance; (2) the prospective depositor's reputation may be such as to lead the bank's officers to conclude that having the account would be harmful to the bank; and (3) the nature of the account would make it difficult for the bank to service it properly and/or profitably.

A New Checking Account. Usually, the prospective depositor arranges for an introduction to an officer of the bank. The officer in charge of new accounts explains the bank's requirements and regulations and answers questions. The prospective depositor is then asked to fill in a "new account" card containing spaces for answering questions which will help to identify the depositor. These include: (1) depositor's name, names of his parents, and sometimes names of grandparents; (2) current address and previous address; (3) previous bank accounts and present accounts in other banks, if any; and (4) business or other connections. If this information is satisfactory, the prospective depositor is asked to sign a "signature card." Then a passbook is issued, and the account is opened. This is usually followed by an introduction to officers and members of the bank's staff.

Partnership accounts are opened on the same basis as individual accounts, except that filing a copy of the partnership agreement is required. In the case of a corporation's account the bank customarily requires the board of directors of the corporation (1) to authorize the opening of the account by resolution, (2) to specify those authorized to sign checks and other credit instruments, (3) to indicate who may endorse credit instruments and sign promissory notes, and (4) to certify that there is nothing in the corporation's bylaws or charter which would impair or limit the authority conferred in the resolution. Banks have printed forms which cover these requirements; and, when these are properly filled in and signed, the account is opened.

Banks accept cash, properly endorsed checks, sight drafts, and matured interest coupons. Ordinarily, a deposit slip is prepared according to the directions thereon and presented over the counter or by mail. Usually, the bank keeps the original deposit slip and provides the depositor with a "machine-printed" receipt. After the original deposit, entries may be made in the depositor's checking-account passbook; but this is rarely done.

Monthly Statements. Ordinarily, a bank prepares a monthly statement for each depositor. This statement shows transactions which affect the account—deposits made, withdrawals, bank charges against the account, and the amount on deposit at the beginning and at the end of the period. The depositor should check this statement for errors; and, if any are found, they should be reported to the bank immediately. This reconciliation is fairly simple for an individual account but more difficult for a business account. Although errors are seldom made, the depositor's full co-operation is helpful in disclosing unauthorized withdrawals, raised checks, and forgeries.

Service Charges. Ordinarily, banks operate on the principle that each checking account must pay its own way. An account may be unprofitable because it is too small relative to the number of checks written, the number of deposits made, and the overhead costs involved. To facilitate computing service charges, individual accounts are usually charged a flat amount per month ($0.75 to $1.00) as an overhead charge and a per-item charge for each check written (4 to 6 cents) and for each item deposited (3 to 5 cents). Special charges may be made for returned items, stop-payment orders, and other special services such as mailing the monthly statement. These service charges may be offset, in whole or part, by an "earning credit" which may be fixed arbitrarily at 10 or 15 cents for each $100 in the minimum or average balance, or calculated more scientifically in terms of what the bank may earn on the available balance (the amount left after cash reserves and uncollected items are subtracted). Ease of administration has popularized the so-called "meter" system of calculating service charges, wherein the "minimum" rather than the "average" or "available" balance is used as a basis for computing earning credit.

No-Minimum-Balance Plan. Many banks offer a popular kind of checking account in which no minimum balance is required. This consists of selling a book of checks with the depositor's name on each check. As now used by banks in most large cities, there is no minimum-balance rule but each depositor pays a service charge each month (recently changed from 25 cents to 50 cents in New York) and 10 cents for each check. From the viewpoint of the bank, this type of checking account has much to recommend it because it reduces the cost of sorting, eliminates the need for analyzing checking accounts, and brings new customers to the bank. When this plan was introduced in the larger cities, it proved popular immediately. One bank in New York reported the opening of more than 250,000 new accounts of this type. Each account earned about 70 cents per month, about one half of which was net operating profit. Experience with these so-called "thrifty checking accounts" has been about the same as with regular checking accounts insofar as "insufficient funds" are concerned. The social implications resulting from the pay-as-you-go checking plans are far-reaching. Many individuals who cannot afford regular checking accounts now may have these services at a small cost which varies directly with the use of the services. The chief cost of handling checks is traced to the time required to sort them. This may cause banks in the future to offer only a type of checking-account service wherein the name of the drawer is imprinted on the checks. There has been a steady increase not only in the volume of checks written but also in service charges made for providing this service.

Collection Services. When presented by old customers, banks usually give immediate credit for checks and United States government-bond coupons; but a great many noncash items are accepted for collection only. These items include promissory notes, trade drafts, acceptances, and bond coupons other than those on United States government obligations. Banks may be requested to collect these items because they are payable at only one place, such as the place of business of the debtor; or they may have documents attached which are surrendered on payment or acceptance of the draft. Local collections are made by the bank's own messengers, and out-of-town collections may be made through correspondent banks or the Federal Reserve System. Collection fees charged for these services are nominal and seldom cover the cost of the services involved.

Safekeeping Services. Since depositors leave funds with banks for safekeeping, it is only natural for them to expect their banks to keep other things of value such as jewelry, silver, securities, and other valuable papers. Most banks are equipped with safe-deposit boxes and vaults which are rented to customers at an annual fee. This fee varies according to the location of the bank, the size of the box, and other variables. (The smallest and most popular box rents for about $5.00 per year plus federal tax.) Some banks also keep valuables in their vaults for customers. Fees vary for this service, the most common being $2.00 per year plus 25 cents for each access to the envelope (in excess of from four to six) in which the valuables are kept. Some banks limit the contents of envelopes to nonnegotiable government bonds and insurance policies; others place no restrictions on the contents.

Bank Drafts, Money Orders, etc. A bank draft is a check drawn on one bank by another bank. A cashier's check is a check drawn by the cashier of a bank on his bank. These checks and bank drafts are purchased by individuals and used in making payments, usually by mail and/or when personal checks would be unacceptable. Many banks also sell money orders, using a special form bearing the words "money order." Basically, a bank money order is a cashier's check; but a stub has been added which is filled in and given the purchaser as a receipt. The "registered check" is a copyrighted remittance service used by some banks. The customer fills in the blanks of the registered check as if it were a personal check; then the bank teller collects the amount plus a fee (usually 10 cents) and imprints the amount on the check, on its stub, and on a prenumbered credit slip, which is kept by the bank for accounting purposes until the check is paid. Travelers' letters of credit and travelers' checks, offered by banks, are similar to those sold by the American Express Company. Both are used by travelers to secure cash on the spot and are not used for mail remittances.

IMPORTANCE OF DEPOSITORS TO BANKS

In advertising for deposits, banks are stressing not only the service that touches more customers than does any other but also the function of banking on which their business is based. Depositors are recognized as the chief source of funds with which individual banks operate, and all important bank policies are based on this fact. If the organizers of a bank planned to use only their own capital resources, the proper procedure would be to lend and invest in various types of mortgages, bonds, and stocks in order to secure an income. Instead, the organizers invest much of their capital in a bank building and banking equipment, which provide no income. As an added expense, they use part of their funds to employ personnel. The only reason for such an allocation of capital resources is that the organizers expect the bank to attract depositors who will leave funds with the bank in amounts many times the organizers' original investments.

Customarily, when a commercial bank makes a loan, the proceeds thereof appear as an increase in the borrower's deposit account. Although the bank merely lends its promise to pay, such promises must be supported 100 per cent by assets, a part of which may be in the form of money to meet the bank's legal and other reserve requirements. So, there is nothing illogical in banks' emphasis on acquiring new funds (primary deposits) even though they customarily lend their credit. Nevertheless, sight must not be lost of the fact that banks do create new money (derivative deposits) when they lend and invest.

In the operation and management of banks, increasing attention is being given to the solution of problems which not only will increase the efficiency of banks but also will make them more attractive to customers. This is reflected in the layouts of banks, the elimination of the grille work and high screens around tellers' windows, and the replacement of high counters with low ones. In addition, emphasis has shifted from dark woodwork and furniture, massive columns, and high ceilings to brighter interiors marked by better lighting, more attractive fixtures, and pleasantly colored drapes and walls.

For quite a number of years, banks have been using the "unit-teller" system whereby the same teller will receive and pay deposits.

This relieves the customer from the necessity of going first to one window to make a deposit and then to a second to cash a check. Banking by mail has been encouraged; and banks provide a special mailing envelope, a portion of which serves as the deposit slip. This slip is stamped by the bank and returned to the depositor along with a fresh envelope for the next deposit. In addition, special coin-deposit envelopes are furnished to commercial depositors; and banks provide night depository services accessible through a special chute from the outside of the building. In addition, drive-in facilities are being provided by an increasing number of banks throughout the country.

Since tellers may be the bottlenecks in banks during rush hours, emphasis has been on ways and means whereby their work may be done more rapidly and efficiently. Thus, by introducing "coin cashiers," the amount of time saved in cashing a check is estimated to be 35 per cent. Where coins are received in large amounts, coin sorting and packaging machines are timesaving devices. A window machine for receipting deposits not only is timesaving but also provides the depositor with a printed receipt for his deposit, thus tending to eliminate use of duplicate deposit slips and passbooks. Tellers also are being provided with "portable teller units," which give them greater control over the cash items for which they are responsible. These units may be locked during lunch hours, or when the teller must leave his cage, and rolled away from the counter when there is desk work that can be done best away from the counter; and extra ones may be rolled to the counter when there is need for more "teller help." Also, "split windows" are used whereby the teller receives the check on one side of a vertical panel and delivers the currency and coins on the other side. (This keeps the customers moving.)

Depositors now receive better service because of bookkeeping machines, mechanical devices, and procedures that speed up the collection of checks. These include photographing checks, omitting checking on endorsement on small items, using new check routing symbols, and, in some cases, eliminating "protest." Now some banks are introducing the imprinted check (with the name of the drawer printed on it), and the government, some corporations, and individuals are using "card" checks (with holes to facilitate machine sorting). These checks may be prepunched to show the number of the depositor's account, the routing symbol, and other information that facilitates sorting. After a check is drawn and presented, it may be punched with the cash amount.

Some of the changes made by banks in handling depositors' accounts have spread certain types of the work of the staff—staggered plan for computing monthly balances and sending out monthly statements. The mechanization of banking involves the use of machines designed particularly for banks. Among proposed changes that would assist banks in keeping up with the increasing volume of business are standardization of checks, greater use of the American Bankers Association routing symbols, organization of additional clearinghouses in local areas, elimination of nonpar banks, and greater use of the collection and settlement services offered by the Federal Reserve System.

INSURANCE OF BANK DEPOSITS

Among the most important contributions made to a sounder money and banking system in the United States has been the organization and operations of the Federal Deposit Insurance Corporation.[5] The Corporation is an instrumentality of the federal government, organized under the authority of the Banking Act of 1933; and it began operations on January 1, 1934. Originally, legal provisions for deposit insurance appeared as an amendment to the Federal Reserve Act; but now they appear in a separate law known as the "Federal Deposit Insurance Act of 1950."[6]

The Federal Deposit Insurance Corporation is managed by a board of three directors—one is the Comptroller of the Currency and the others are appointed by the President with the consent of the Senate. All of the original capital stock ($289,000,000) of the Corporation has been retired. Although the Corporation has no capital stock, it does have an earned surplus of more than $1,500,000,-000 and substantial additions are made to it each year. The Federal Deposit Insurance Act of 1950 increased the maximum insurable deposit in one name in one bank from $5,000 to $10,000; and it has been estimated that over 55 per cent of total deposits in insured banks are protected under the $10,000 maximum rule.[7] This means

[5] For a history of guaranty or insurance of bank deposits see *Annual Report of the Federal Deposit Insurance Corporation for the Year Ended December 31, 1950* (Washington, D.C., 1951), pp. 61–101.

[6] Public Law 797, 81st Cong.; 64 Stat. 873; 12 U.S.C. 1811–31.

[7] At irregular intervals, the Corporation estimates the number of deposit accounts; and, on September 21, 1955, there were 130,000,000 deposit accounts of which 98.2 per cent had balances of $10,000 or less.

that the owners of small deposits are fully protected, but that large depositors must continue to exert a restraining influence on bank management.

TABLE 10

NUMBER AND DEPOSITS OF ALL BANKS IN THE UNITED STATES (CONTINENTAL U.S. AND OTHER AREAS), DECEMBER 31, 1955

ITEM	NUMBER OR DEPOSITS			PERCENTAGE OF TOTAL	
	Total	Insured banks	Non-insured banks	Insured banks	Non-insured banks
Number of banks—total.............	14,284	13,457	827	94.2%	5.8%
Banks of deposit...................	14,225	13,457	768	94.6	5.4
Commercial....................	13,697	13,237	460	96.6	3.4
Mutual savings.................	528	220	308	41.7	58.3
Trust companies not regularly engaged in deposit banking...............	59	....	59	....	100.0
Deposits (in millions)—total..........	$221,392	$212,226	$9,166	95.9%	4.1%
Banks of deposit..................	221,325	212,226	9,099	95.9	4.1
Commercial....................	193,138	190,989	2,149	98.9	1.1
Mutual savings.................	28,187	21,237	6,950	75.3	24.7
Trust companies not regularly engaged in deposit banking*..............	67	....	67	....	100.0

Source: *Annual Report of the Federal Deposit Insurance Corporation for the Year Ended December 31, 1955* (Washington, D.C., 1956), p. 27.
* Deposits of these companies consist of uninvested trust funds and special accounts.

Participating Banks. All banks that are members of the Federal Reserve System are required to insure their deposits with the Federal Deposit Insurance Corporation, and qualified nonmember banks may do so. Now, more than 94 per cent of all banks of deposit in the United States and possessions have insured their accounts with the Corporation. These insured banks hold almost 96 per cent of total deposits. (Included in the remaining 6 per cent of banks, classified as noninsured, are the mutual savings banks in Connecticut and Massachusetts whose accounts are insured in their own insurance systems.)

Insurance Costs. In practice, deposit-insurance assessment is most accurately described as a special type of proportional property tax levied upon deposits of insured banks by a public corporation with the specific purpose of protecting depositors in amounts not exceeding $10,000 per depositor per bank. The annual deposit-insurance assessment rate is $1/12$ of 1 per cent of total deposits adjusted for certain cash items in process of collection. In order to arrive at the dollar amount of deposits on which premiums are paid semi-annually, the average of deposits on only two base dates is used (end of March and June for the first six months, and the end of September and December for the second six months). This replaces the daily average for all deposits for each six-month period that had been required prior to the passage of the Federal Deposit Insurance Act of 1950.[8]

Although most of the insurance premiums are collected from large banks, these banks pass along the costs to their depositors when they estimate service charges on checking accounts. Since many of these depositors are large corporations, the burden of the cost of deposit insurance is more widely diffused than the source of collection of the premiums would suggest. Originally, one argument used to support the basing of costs on total deposits was that smaller banks would be contributing indirectly because of the prohibition placed on interest payments on demand deposits including bankers' balances held with the larger banks. (In fact, the reductions of interest payment to depositors have been more than the cost of insurance.) Another argument was that, if insurance premiums were to be based on insured deposits, the assessment rate would be so high that small banks would find it impossible to participate in the plan.

Assessment Credit.   In 1950 considerable pressure was brought to bear on Congress by large banks to eliminate all insurance assessments, and a compromise was evolved. The annual assessment rate of $\frac{1}{12}$ of 1 per cent was retained, but insured banks receive credit on their next assessment equal to 60 per cent of the "net assessment income" (which is equal to total assessment income minus the Corporation's losses and expenses). In addition to retaining 40 per cent of the "net assessment income," the Corporation has substantial income from its investments in United States government obligations and from other sources. Of the total insurance assessment of $148,000,-000 for 1955, over one half (almost $88,800,000) was credited pro rata to insured banks.

Action to Protect Depositors.   Since its organization the Federal Deposit Insurance Corporation has given financial assistance to 429 insured banks to protect their depositors from losses. This help has been provided in two ways: (1) the payment by the Corporation of the amount due to depositors when banks were closed, and (2) the guarantee of assets of insolvent banks whose deposit liabilities were assumed by a second bank in the same or a nearby community. The second method was made more flexible in 1950,

[8] See "Rules and Regulations of the Corporation, Amendment of Assessments and Other Provisions," *Annual Report of the Federal Deposit Insurance Corporation for the Year Ended December 31, 1954* (Washington, D.C., 1955), pp. 87–96.

when Congress authorized the Corporation to make loans to, purchase assets from, or make deposits in any insured bank in danger of closing. This change permits the Corporation to help financially weak insured banks in "one-bank" towns and where mergers cannot be arranged. In effect, when an insolvent bank is absorbed by another insured bank, all the deposits in the insolvent bank are fully protected even though they may exceed the maximum specified by law. Between 1944 and 1955, no insured bank was placed in the hands of a receiver; before May, 1944, there were 245 and 4 in 1955.

Receiver. The Federal Deposit Insurance Corporation not only assumes responsibility for paying insured depositors but also acts as receiver for insolvent national banks and for insured state-chartered banks when designated as receivers by the appropriate state authority. As the chief claimant to the funds obtained from liquidation, the Corporation is more interested in economical liquidation than is an individual receiver whose primary interest may be his salary and/or fees. In addition, the Corporation is in a position to obtain the maximum returns from liquidation of assets because it has a trained staff to perform this function. The Corporation may hasten the liquidation process by buying the residue of the assets of a suspended bank at a competitive public sale.

Reports and Examinations. Fortunately, the Federal Deposit Insurance Corporation does not have to "sit on the sidelines" and watch banks become insolvent. The Corporation has the power to examine insured banks that are not members of the Federal Reserve System and, under certain conditions, to terminate the insurance status of any insured banks for "continued unsafe or unsound banking practices." The Federal Deposit Insurance Corporation receives reports from all insured banks. Its own examiners make regular annual examinations of each insured bank which is not a member of the Federal Reserve System and entrance examinations of operating banks and proposed banks. It receives copies of reports of examinations of other insured banks made by the Comptroller of the Currency and by the Board of Governors of the Federal Reserve System, and it may make a special examination of any insured bank to determine the insurance risk if such action is deemed advisable.[9]

[9] From 1936 to 1955, the Corporation has taken action to terminate the insurance status of 170 insured banks for unsafe, unsound, and/or illegal banking practices. On or before the date set for termination of their insurance status, most of these banks corrected the banking practices criticized and/or merged with other banks. Most of the others have been closed (suspended) but a few cases are awaiting final action. Only three banks have tried to continue operation after the loss of

Supervisory Activities. In order to improve the quality of bank management and to keep insured banks sound, the Federal Deposit Insurance Corporation was granted many technical or routine powers already possessed by national and state regulatory officers. States' experiences with deposit insurance emphasized the need for strict control over participating banks, if any guarantee system was to be successful. In its supervisory activities the Corporation (with assistance from regulatory bodies and bank leaders) has sought to prevent deposit insurance from being a "cover" for poor bankers and lax banking practices. Well-managed, sound banks should not be placed in a position which will force them to pay for the mistakes of poor bankers. One of the most encouraging developments (which might have taken place even without the establishment of the Corporation) has been the movement among bankers to improve bank management.

General Aspects of Deposit Insurance. It is a common misconception that deposit insurance in the United States is government insurance. Many think that the Federal Deposit Insurance Corporation is financed by the government, but now the Corporation is completely financed by banks' past and current contributions (and earnings thereon). The Corporation paid to the United States Treasury an amount equal to its original capital, which included subscriptions by the government of $150 million and by the Federal Reserve banks of $139 million. In case of need, the Corporation has the right to borrow up to a maximum of $3,000 million from the Treasury.

Some of the claims made for the Federal Deposit Insurance Corporation are reminiscent of those made for the Federal Reserve System, such as "a member bank cannot fail" and "the Federal Reserve eliminates all money panics." Most important among present-day claims is the claim that the Corporation has ended the danger of "runs" on banks. This is not true because the position of large depositors has changed very little, and their interest in keeping funds in strong banks and avoiding weak ones has not been affected by deposit insurance. In the future, as in the past, the most disturbing presuspension withdrawals of bank deposits will be those of large depositors.

Concentration of Bank Deposits. Periodically the Federal De-

---

their insurance status, and one of these was suspended four months later. *Annual Report of the Federal Deposit Insurance Corporation for the Year Ended December 31, 1955* (Washington, D.C., 1956), pp. 4–6.

posit Insurance Corporation makes special calls for deposit information; and, among the findings from the reports of September 21, 1955, are the following: (1) the 13,498 insured banks reported 130,-000,000 deposit accounts and total deposits of $203,000,000,000; (2) more than 98 per cent of the deposit accounts had balances of $10,000 or less (being fully protected while the remainder were insured for but $10,000); and (3) insured deposits on the survey date totaled $112,000,000,000 or slightly more than 55 per cent of all deposits in insured banks.

The 1955 survey of deposits confirmed previous conclusions that most deposit accounts are fully insured; but the proportion of deposits covered varies inversely with the size of the bank. At one extreme are the six large banks with assets of $2,500,000,000 or more which have but 33.8 per cent of their deposits insured, and at the other extreme are the twenty-five banks with deposits of less than $250,000 which have 91.8 per cent of their deposits insured. However, the six large banks (fewer than one twentieth of 1 per cent of all insured banks) held insured deposits of about $9,000,000,-000, or more than five times the Corporation's deposit insurance fund. Furthermore, the largest 2 per cent of insured banks hold 45 per cent of insured deposits.

As might be expected, more than one half of the insured deposits are located in cities with populations of 100,000 or more (in fact, 16 per cent of insured deposits are located in New York City); and more than two thirds of insured deposits are in 16 states in the northeast and north central section of the country. Since the large banks are the chief holders of interbank deposits, a failure of one such bank would have more serious effects than the failure of another bank holding an equal amount of total deposits. Since these large banks are either national banks or state member banks, they are not examined regularly by the Federal Deposit Insurance Corporation; therefore, the Corporation is confronted with a concentration of risks involving large banks in large cities which are not examined regularly by the Corporation.[10]

The Federal Deposit Insurance Corporation is stressing the need for providing greater protection for depositors by increasing capital accounts of individual banks. This need has increased because a larger proportion of depositors' funds is being invested in earning assets that carry more risks than do government obligations. Al-

[10] See also *Annual Report of the Federal Deposit Insurance Corporation for the Year Ended December 31, 1955* (Washington, D.C., 1956) pp. 47–96.

though the assets of the Corporation seem large ($1,700,000,000), they are small compared to the $116,000,000,000 of insured deposits (being about 1.41 per cent), and to total deposits of $203,000,000,-000 in insured banks (0.77 per cent).

In carrying out its duties the Federal Deposit Insurance Corporation has tended to make banks more mindful of their responsibilities to depositors and less considerate of borrowers. In view of the distress and financial embarrassment accompanying the 1930–34 banking debacle, deposit insurance may be a small price to pay if panics thus may be avoided.[11] In considering the successful record of the Corporation to date and in forecasting its future, the significance of insured banks' holdings of government obligations and insured assets should not be ignored. To the extent that banks' assets are in the form of government securities or securities guaranteed by a governmental agency, solvency is assured; and there is little need for deposit insurance. The fine record of the banking system since 1934 has been due in part to the improved liquidity of the economy, the annual growth in the output of goods and services, and the improvement in bank management.

Assuming most ideal circumstances, the need for the Federal Deposit Insurance Corporation could be eliminated by wise management of banks by bankers themselves. While supervisory officials may assist, the burden of preventing deposit insurance from attracting poor bankers and fostering lax bank management rests primarily on bankers. During the next twenty years, the volume of assets in our banking system should double. The important question is "Do banks, in their selection of new personnel and in their in-the-bank training programs, fully realize the need for future officers qualified to manage this expanded volume of assets?"

SUMMARY

Bank deposits are classified in various ways; but the one most important to banks and to the general public is according to the provisions for withdrawal, as demand and time deposits. Although the use of demand deposits as money is purely incidental from the viewpoint of bankers, it is of major significance from the viewpoint

---

[11] From July 1, 1864, to June 30, 1934, 16,000 commercial banks failed. Total deposits involved were $9,000 million, with loss to depositors of $3,000 million, which does not include loss of use of funds while banks were in the hands of receivers. Two thirds of these losses occurred during the four years ending June 30, 1934. See testimony of Leo T. Crowley before a subcommittee of the Committee on Banking and Currency, U.S. Senate, 74th Cong., 1st Sess., on "Banking Act of 1935" (S. 1715 and H.R. 7617).

of the public. It is the desire on the part of Congress to protect the circulating medium (deposit currency) of the country that justifies the detailed regulation of banking as described in this and subsequent chapters. The creation and functioning of the Federal Deposit Insurance Corporation have increased the confidence of depositors in banks, raised banking standards, and increased the soundness of the banking system. Although this has meant better currency for the nation, the supervisory agencies and the Corporation alone cannot assure the nation of a safe currency system because basic responsibility rests with banks and their depositors.

QUESTIONS AND PROBLEMS

1. Distinguish between (*a*) public and private deposits, (*b*) secured and unsecured deposits, (*c*) primary and derivative deposits, and (*d*) insured and uninsured deposits.

2. In what ways are the differences between secured and unsecured deposits of interest to depositors? To the Federal Deposit Insurance Corporation?

3. What is the relative importance of time and demand deposits in commercial banks?

4. "When the government prohibited interest payment on demand deposits, it necessitated the placing of restrictions on time-deposit withdrawals from banks." Do you agree? What other factors led to regulation of time-deposit withdrawals?

5. If you have a checking account, compare your experiences with those outlined in the text (noting reasons for selecting your bank, experiences in opening the account, minimum balance and service charge rules [if any], and monthly reconciliation of your account).

6. What relationship, if any, exists between increases in service charges and increases in the amount of money in circulation? Is it true that service charges "drive people out of banks"?

7. Analyze the statements: "Due to the preponderance of large accounts in big banks, the proportion of insured deposits is relatively low. Since assessments are based on total deposits, it is claimed that the big banks carry more than a proportionate share of the costs of deposit insurance. . . . On balance, we do not favor amending the deposit-insurance law to provide full insurance for deposits as the disadvantages, in our opinion, substantially outweigh the advantages." (Reply of Federal Deposit Insurance Corporation to Joint Committee on the Economic Report, *Monetary Policy and the Management of the Public Debt* [Washington, D.C.: U.S. Government Printing Office, 1952], Part 2, p. 952.)

8. What other services of banks are related to the deposit function? How are banks compensated for these services?

9. What changes were authorized by Congress in 1950 that have re-

duced the cost of deposit insurance to banks participating in the Federal Deposit Insurance System?

10. When insured banks are placed in receivership, how does the Federal Deposit Insurance Corporation protect depositors (*a*) fully covered under the $10,000 maximum rule, and (*b*) not fully covered under the $10,000 maximum rule?

11. Present the arguments in favor of and opposed to the Federal Deposit Insurance Corporation's policy of merging banks to prevent them from being suspended. What added flexibility in administering this policy was authorized by Congress in 1950?

12. What is the Federal Deposit Insurance Corporation's power in regard to: (*a*) chartering banks, (*b*) terminating insurance of a bank, and (*c*) refusing to insure national banks and state banks which have been admitted to the Federal Reserve System?

13. What justification is there for assuming that banks prize membership in the Federal Deposit Insurance Corporation more than membership in the Federal Reserve System? Explain your answer.

14. The assets of the Federal Deposit Insurance Fund are $1.7 billion, and the volume of total insured deposits may be $116 billion (it changes daily). Does this mean that the Corporation's position would be hopeless if an epidemic of bank failures should occur? Is the Corporation's position analogous to that of fire insurance companies in the United States (some of which have been functioning successfully for more than a hundred years)?

Chapter XIV

MANAGEMENT OF BANK FUNDS

BANK management is primarily responsible for the safety of banks, which, because of the nature of banks' liabilities and the thin layer of their equity, is a challenging problem. Some students attribute the excellent safety record of banks during recent years, as indicated by the small number of bank failures, to the functioning of the Federal Deposit Insurance Corporation; however, equally or more important factors were the increase in the liquidity of the economy and the improvement in bank management.

In considering the problems of American banks, it is important to remember the extremes in size to be found among banks in the United States. For illustration, of the 13,400 insured commercial banks in the United States, 5,000 have deposits of $2,000,000 or less per bank and 11,438 (about 86 per cent) have deposits of $10,000,-000 or less per bank. The 11,438 smaller banks hold about 20 per cent of the total deposits in insured banks. One may conclude that on a numerical basis the typical bank in the United States is one in a small community which emphasizes agricultural, real estate, and consumer loans in that order.

At the other extreme in size are the eighteen largest banks each holding deposits of more than $1 billion and holding among them about 25 per cent of total deposits of all insured banks. On the basis of loans granted, one may conclude that any one of these large banks is typical because in the aggregate they make about 40 per cent of all the commercial and industrial loans of all insured banks. In addition, they hold the largest percentage of "loans for carrying securities," almost 20 per cent of real estate loans, and about 16 per cent of "other loans to individuals" (chiefly consumer loans).

In between the large number of smallest banks and the few largest banks are 1,944 other insured commercial banks holding deposits varying between $10,000,000 and $1 billion per bank. The loans of these banks are more evenly distributed among loans classified as commercial and industrial, real estate, consumer, agricultural, and for carrying securities. (See also Chapter XV.)

RISKS OF BANKING

The fact that commercial banks have most of their liabilities in the form of demand deposits makes these banks particularly vulnerable to public loss of confidence, adverse criticism, or anything that may reflect on the integrity of the bank. Thus a bank must be in a position to care not only for the ordinary demands for money by its depositors but also for abnormal demands for money. A bank is in a liquid position when it can convert its assets into cash without any considerable loss or delay.

Theories of Liquidity. (1) The traditional theory is that a bank's liquidity is assured if its earning assets are in the form of short-term promissory notes and orders to pay (bills) which have resulted from financing the processing of goods and their movement from producers through the market into the possession of the ultimate consumers. The proceeds of the sale of goods are used to retire the debt owed to the bank. Thus, loans and discounts are converted into cash as the result of the "normal course of trade."

In the past, banks had difficulties with their loans and discounts when goods did not move readily into the "channels of trade," and banks' assets were congealed or "frozen." Under these circumstances, it was sometimes possible for an individual bank to shift its holdings of paper to correspondent banks or to sell this paper in the open market; but at times, practically all banks were in the position of sellers with no buyers. Before 1913 these experiences with nonshiftability of bank assets heightened the interest of bankers in the development of a "bill" market to care for normal shifts in banks' holdings of bills and in the establishment of a central banking system to provide new funds to care for seasonal and extraordinary needs. This emphasis on the shiftability theory of bank liquidity has been strengthened by the growth in the volume of government obligations, particularly Treasury bills and other short-term government obligations. During the 1920's, when loans were based on securities, shiftability depended on the normal functioning of the securities market.

(2) At present the liquidity of assets of banks, which are in the form of "term" loans to business, loans to consumers, and loans to homeowners, depends on borrowers' meeting installment payments out of income. These types of lending have given rise to a third

concept of liquidity of bank assets, <u>one based on anticipated income.</u>
All of these concepts of liquidity have their place in modern banking;
but, during extraordinary times, the liquidity of the banking system
as a whole depends on the existence of a central banking system
which permits banks to use any sound assets to obtain cash from the
central banks. Today, a member bank may obtain cash from its Federal Reserve bank by the sale, discount, or rediscount of assets, or by
using such assets as security for loans or "advances" of credit.

Need for Safety. Banks must take the usual lenders' risks—
the possibility of nonpayment of funds lent or invested and a loss in
market value of assets. However, the losses taken by a bank may be
particularly embarrassing because the capital margin on which a bank
operates is smaller than that of any other major business enterprise.
The loss in market value of assets has an important bearing upon the
position of the bank because of the legal requirement that a bank's
capital must not be impaired. This requirement means that a bank
must meet harsher tests of safety than those which must be met by
other business organizations.

Need for Fidelity Insurance. Banks are subject also to such
risks as illegal appropriation of funds by officers and employees,
"honest mistakes" that may occur in any organization, and robbery.
Approximately one fourth of the 400 banks that the Federal Deposit
Insurance Corporation "has assisted because of financial difficulties
have been placed in this unfortunate position because of defalca-
tions."[1] A book published in 1947 describes 210 methods used by individuals to defraud banks;[2] however, bank losses due to dishonesty
of officers and employees are only about 1 per cent of those of
American business concerns as a whole. Compared to the value of
property and property rights handled by banks, the losses are in-
finitesimal.

A bank may protect itself from loss due to defalcation by adequate fidelity insurance; but this type of protection merely shifts the
burden from the bank to the insurance or bonding company, which,
in turn, is supported by the banks and others as a group. Many difficulties may be avoided by improvements in bank administration,
such as using better protective equipment, clarifying the duties of
officers and employees, and improving auditing systems. The
last includes continuous checking (pre-auditing), staff co-operation,

[1] *Annual Report of the Federal Deposit Insurance Corporation for the Year
Ended December 31, 1947* (Washington, D.C., 1948), p. 9.

[2] See L. A. Pratt, *Bank Frauds, Their Detection and Prevention* (New York:
Ronald Press Co., 1947), pp. 221–32 (Appendix).

and frequent post-audits. However, no accounting or auditing system can prevent an individual from being dishonest if he is so inclined; and so the best that can be done is to control the opportunities and to shorten the time between commitment of an offense and exposure.

Runs on Banks. If a bank does not have cash and cannot secure it quickly and without great loss, it is nonliquid. Such situations arise when depositors are requesting cash in place of deposits. These requests may be made at the tellers' windows (as illustrated by the old-fashioned "run," occasionally pictured in the movies); or these requests may be made by mail or through the clearinghouses, giving rise to the "clearinghouse" type of run in which depositors (particularly large depositors) write orders on their accounts and deposit them with other banks. Even bankers may lose confidence in a correspondent bank and shift their accounts from it to other correspondent banks or to their Federal Reserve banks. Depositors who have lost faith in all banks may convert their deposits into currency. This conversion may take place over a period of time, which means that banks lose funds because of "seepage" of cash rather than because of "runs."

Insolvency Most Troublesome. At the present time, because of the existence of central banks, the dangers of nonliquidity are minor compared to the dangers of impairment of capital. Therefore, bank management is giving more attention to this problem than was true in the past. Emphasis on solvency is synonymous with emphasis on the quality of assets. In addition, more attention is being given to "accounting reserves," which can be used to absorb losses on assets.

The history of banks shows that losses tend to be highly concentrated in a few years. To bank management this means that, during years of good business, years of bad business must be anticipated by writing off current losses and building up accounting reserves to absorb future losses. While substandard assets may be avoided, losses do occur. During an emergency, local loans may be the least liquid of a bank's assets; and long-term investments may be liquidated only at great loss. Because the management of a bank's assets presents no difficult problems during inflationary periods, the test of good management comes during deflationary periods. This is true of all types of management, but the test that bankers must meet is the most rigorous of all.

When losses wipe out a corporation's capital (stock, surplus, undivided profits, and liabilities reserves—net worth), its assets are less than its liabilities, and the firm is insolvent. Unless pressed into bankruptcy, the corporation may continue in business and regain its solvency. But banks are expected to be solvent at all times; and, in addition, the appraised value of their assets must equal not only the appraised value of liabilities but also the capital stock. This is what is meant by the statement that "a bank's capital must not be impaired."

PRIMARY ASSET RESERVES

Liquidity and Earnings. If the liquidity of a bank is to be maintained, bank management must secure the proper allocation of assets among primary reserves, secondary reserves, loans, and investments. While recognizing the problem of liquidity, sight must not be lost of the fact that banks must "live." Although there may be disagreement as to the proper size and source of profits, those who believe in private ownership of banks do not question the desire of bankers to secure earnings large enough to pay all expenses of their institutions and to provide a reasonable return on the capital that has been invested in them.

Banks obtain earnings to meet operating expenses from service charges on deposit accounts and from fees, commissions, and other charges made for special services performed by the banks for their customers. Important as these charges are, in the aggregate they represent only a small percentage of the income earned as "interest and dividends on securities" and "interest and discounts on loans" (about 75 per cent of total earnings). It is readily apparent that the earning assets of banks are the most important source of earnings; without them, our banking system as we know it could not exist.

Another aspect of banking, reflecting the traditional desire of bankers to build up their own communities, is the desire of management to accommodate local businessmen and others. This involves much more than emphasis on making temporary or emergency loans because bankers realize that the future of their banks depends upon the well-being of the communities in which they are located. This complicates the problems of management because local loans may be the bank's most nonliquid assets. Factors which bring on a local crisis will affect both depositors and borrowers; and, therefore, the bank is forced to go outside the community to obtain cash with which to meet requests for money by depositors and borrowers.

Primary Reserves. Primary reserves are assets that make up a bank's first line of defense. They include coins and paper money, cash items in process of collection, and deposits with the Federal Reserve banks and with correspondent banks. A bank holds cash in its own vaults to meet day-to-day requests for currency. These reserves are small because the flow of currency out of a bank usually is matched by new deposits of currency. Thus the amount of cash on hand will not average more than 1½ per cent of total deposits; this percentage will be smallest in cities where Federal Reserve banks or branches are located and largest where these facilities are least accessible. Cash items in process of collection appear as primary reserves; they represent near cash for which credit is given by the collecting bank on or before collection. The items are canceled after collection, but other similar items take their place. At any particular time, the volume outstanding depends on business conditions and payment practices, and at the end of each calendar year they represent between 4 and 5 per cent of the total assets of insured commercial banks.

Member banks must keep reserve accounts with their Federal Reserve banks and may also keep deposits with their correspondent banks. Nonmember banks may keep their required reserves in their own vaults, with their correspondent banks, and/or as clearing balances with the Federal Reserve banks. Since these primary reserves are nonearning assets, bankers are interested in keeping them at the lowest level possible. At the same time, bankers are aware of their banks' responsibilities to depositors as well as of their need for meeting legal reserve requirements.

Among the assets of insured commercial banks classified according to total deposits, primary reserves tend to be fairly uniform percentagewise, ranging from 19.5 to 24.1% of total assets. Banks holding deposits of from $250,000,000 to $1 billion hold relatively more of their assets as primary reserves (24.1 per cent) than do banks in other groups; banks holding deposit of from $10,000,000 to $25,000,000 hold the smallest percentage of their assets as primary reserves (19.5 per cent); and the average for all insured commercial banks is 21.9 per cent.[3]

Legal Reserve Requirements. From the viewpoint of an individual bank, legal cash reserves are assets which may not be lent or invested but which may be used as a means of payment. Member banks' legal reserve requirements vary according to class of deposits, geographical location of the bank, and the form in which the re-

---

[3] *Annual Report of the Federal Deposit Insurance Corporation for the Year Ended December 31, 1954* (Washington, D.C., 1955) p. 68, Table 40.

serve is kept. For illustration, the Federal Reserve Act provides for different reserve percentages not only for demand and time deposits but also for banks classified geographically as central reserve city banks, reserve city banks, and country banks. The Federal Reserve Act also permits the Board of Governors of the Federal Reserve System to change reserve requirements within percentage limits as fixed by law (see Table 11). Today, the legal reserves of all member banks must be in the form of credited balances at their district Federal Reserve banks.

TABLE 11

MEMBER BANK RESERVE REQUIREMENTS

CLASS OF BANK	PERCENTAGE FOR DEMAND DEPOSITS			PERCENTAGE FOR TIME DEPOSITS		
	In Effect	Maximum	Minimum	In Effect	Maxi-mum	Mini-mum
Central reserve city.......	20	26	13	5	6	3
Reserve city.............	18	20	10	5	6	3
Country................	12	14	7	5	6	3

Source: *Federal Reserve Bulletin*, July, 1956, p. 716.

The reserve requirements for nonmember state banks are similar to those for member banks of the Federal Reserve System, but the percentages in effect correspond most closely to those applicable to member banks classified as country banks. Most state banking laws provide for classification of deposits as demand and time deposits, and some provide for geographical classification of banks for reserve purposes (such as, California, Massachusetts, and New York). The laws of about one half of the states permit the state banking authorities to change reserve requirements within limits fixed by law. Perhaps the most important difference between reserve requirements of member and nonmember banks is the form in which the legal reserves may be kept.

In general, legal reserve requirements of nonmember banks may be met either with balances in depository banks or vault cash; in other words, their reserve requirements are smaller than those of member banks because they use vault cash and demand deposits in other banks in computing their legal reserve positions. If there are two competing banks, a member bank and a nonmember bank, faced with a 12 per cent legal reserve requirement, the member bank must have vault cash and balances with correspondents (which usually represent from 8 to 10 per cent of total assets) in addition to the

12 per cent reserve that both banks must keep. At various times, proposals have been brought before Congress that would result in greater uniformity in legal reserve requirements. These proposals include requiring all commercial banks to be members of the Federal Reserve System, eliminating the geographical classification of member banks, and changing the form in which legal reserves may be kept.

The classification of member banks for reserve purposes according to the cities in which they are located originated in the National Bank Act;[4] and the breakdown into the time and demand deposit classification was provided for in the Federal Reserve Act. The variations in reserve requirements, between time and demand deposits and among banks according to geographical location, were justified because of different rates of turnover of deposits. Normally, deposits of new cash will offset withdrawals of cash but, if deposits decrease and withdrawals increase, the results will be most serious where the movements are the most rapid.

Banks' most volatile deposits are those of other banks; therefore, banks in New York and Chicago—the chief holders of interbank deposits—are required to keep higher reserves against demand deposits than are other banks. In practice, individual country banks may have more interbank deposits than have individual banks in reserve cities. Similarly, individual banks in reserve cities may have more interbank deposits than have individual banks in central reserve cities. Actually, the proportion of total deposits represented by interbank deposits has decreased, interbank deposits now being 7.5 per cent of total deposits of all banks. One suggestion for rectifying these injustices is to base reserve requirements on the nature of the deposits held, irrespective of the location of the bank. This solution would mean adoption of a uniform reserve requirement for bankers' balances, another for other demand deposits, and the continuance of the existing uniform reserve requirement for time deposits.

In recognition of the varying needs for till money, member banks should be permitted to hold part of their legal reserves as cash rather than exclusively as balances with their Federal Reserve

[4] The designation of cities for reserve purposes was according to a plan adopted by the Board of Governors in 1947, as follows: banks in New York and Chicago are classified as central reserve city banks; banks in Washington and those in cities where main offices and branches of Federal Reserve banks are located (except New York and Chicago) and in fifteen other cities are classified as reserve city banks (nine because of their holdings of interbank balances and six because they are permitted to retain reserve city classification on written request of the banks involved); and all other member banks are classified as country banks.

banks.[5] Finally, if the same reserve requirements are made applicable to all banks (nonmember as well as member banks), the stage will be set for the use of minimum reserve requirements as a device for credit control on a more equitable basis than exists today.

The effect of changing reserve requirements on banks' assets is readily apparent. If the Board of Governors of the Federal Reserve System establishes a higher ratio, it means that the minimum amount of assets that must be kept as primary reserves is increased and earning assets are decreased; and, if the Board lowers the ratio, the situation is reversed. In one case member banks will have relatively less money to lend and invest; and, in the other, they will have relatively more money to lend and invest. Furthermore, changes in reserve requirements increase or decrease the potential expansion of credit in the banking system based on new reserves. Thus an increase from a 20 to a 25 per cent reserve requirement would mean a potential reduction of bank credit based on new reserves from a 5-to-1 ratio to a 4-to-1 ratio (assuming no adjustment for cash drain).

From the viewpoint of the banking system, required reserves are an important device for controlling the money supply; but, from the viewpoint of the individual bank, these reserve accounts may be used as a sort of checking account to meet adverse clearing balances and their customers' demands for currency. Like an individual who wants to avoid paying service charges on his checking account, banks must keep minimum balances as prescribed by law and/or regulation. And like individuals, banks usually have some excess reserve balances.

MANAGEMENT OF RESERVE POSITION

Member banks must maintain reserve balances at least equal to their required minimums over a prescribed period of time (semimonthly for country banks and weekly for all other member banks). In order to maintain a bank's legal reserves at its Federal Reserve bank at the correct level, the one in charge is concerned with his bank's actual daily position which entails matching the reserve balance with required reserves. Although there is no penalty if the reserves fall below the minimum required legal balance, the one in charge must see that the account averages at or above the amount

[5] Member banks located in Federal Reserve bank or branch cities are in a position to replenish their supply of till money within minutes; so they usually carry a smaller percentage of their assets in the form of till money than banks less fortunately located.

required in relation to the bank's deposits during the bank's reserve accounting period.

On the first day of each reserve accounting period and every day thereafter, the officer in charge of the bank's reserve position (also called the money or cash position) receives a statement of the amount of reserves needed as based upon total time deposits and net demand deposits (total demand deposits minus cash items in process of collection and demand deposits in other banks except Federal Reserve, foreign, and unincorporated banks) as they appear on the records on opening the bank for business; and the reserve balance with the Federal Reserve bank as of the close of the preceding day. Now, the officer knows how much his bank's reserve requirements are for the day; but he will not know whether he has a deficiency or excess of reserves until the end of the day. On the second day of the reserve period he will have the same information as above plus a statement of how much excess or deficiency in reserves was carried over from the preceding day. This computation is carried on throughout the reserve accounting period with excesses offsetting deficiencies and vice versa; and, if adjustments needed to average up to the required reserves are not made before the end of the reserve period, they must be made on the last day.

In larger banks, in order to make a preliminary estimate of what the bank's reserves will be at the end of the day, the officer in charge of the money position of the bank keeps a record on a work sheet of all current transactions that will increase the bank's reserves. These include a favorable clearinghouse balance (settled by crediting the bank's reserve account) and other clearing and collection transactions payable in Federal Reserve bank funds (checks on out-of-town banks collected through the Federal Reserve banks and available that day); collections of United States Treasury checks, matured United States government securities, and other obligations of the United States government and its agencies; and deposits by customers of credits and receipts resulting from wire transfers over the Federal Reserve System telegraphic transfer system, and collection of any other credits payable in federal funds.

At the same time that the bank is receiving items which are payable in Federal Reserve funds for which it is given reserve credit, there will be other items that must be settled in federal funds and must be deducted. These include checks and other cash items presented for payment by the Federal Reserve bank, withdrawals from the Treasury tax-and-loan deposits with the bank, withdrawals of currency, and customers' loans, wire transfers, and any other debits payable in federal funds.

A bank may adjust its reserve position at any time by buying federal funds if it has a deficit, or selling them if it has a surplus. To correct a deficiency, it may borrow from its Federal Reserve bank and/or sell Treasury bills or other government obligations in the open market for cash delivery with payments in federal funds. (Regular delivery against federal funds would take one day, and regular delivery against a clearinghouse check would take two days.)

SECONDARY ASSET RESERVES

Secondary Reserves. By "secondary" reserves are meant highly liquid earning assets that may be converted into cash with little or no delay and at practically no loss. This definition, when considered from the viewpoint of the banking system, eliminates all long-term bonds and all short-term paper that may have to be sold at a loss either because of credit or money market risks (see below). Even self-liquidating short-term loans are excluded because so many of them are uncollectible (frozen) during a depression. Since the term "secondary reserve" is a functional one, it does not appear in a bank's statement of condition. It is used in the same way as "primary reserves"; that is, it refers to a group of assets making up the second line of defense of a bank.

Secondary reserves are income-producing assets held by banks to provide primary reserves whenever the latter become depleted. Two general situations may be involved—seasonal and emergency. Banks are subject to seasonal losses of primary reserves because of seasonal lending and withdrawal of deposits. Since both of these movements tend to come during the last half of the year, secondary reserves must be arranged to meet these needs. In addition, banks must be in a position to meet emergency and other withdrawals of deposits, some of which may not be predictable. Finally, bank management must meet interest payments due time depositors and cash dividends on stock when declared by the board of directors.

Secondary reserves of the seasonal type usually are selected from (1) the trade and bankers' acceptances or the bill market, (2) the open market for commercial paper, (3) the call-loan market, and (4) the short-term government security market. Interior banks are practically excluded from some of these divisions of the money market because of the prevailing low discount rates, the fees charged by correspondent banks for placing funds in the market, and the ability of metropolitan banks to supply all the funds required by borrowers in the market. But the abundance of short-term government obligations makes it possible for banks to hold all the secondary reserves desired in any scientifically planned portfolio. About 34 per cent of insured commercial banks' total assets are in the form of federal government securities, of which almost 75 per cent have maturities of five years or less.

Secondary reserves of the nonseasonal type may be selected from the promises to pay of the federal, state, and local governments and of public utility and similar types of corporations. All of these assets must have two characteristics: prime quality and a maturity of less than four or five years. By careful spacing of the maturities of secondary reserves, a bank may have a continuous return of funds to meet unexpected demands for primary reserves. If a bank regards its secondary-reserve account as a revolving fund to be reinvested in similar securities as they mature, it will be able to maintain the liquidity of its portfolio and still show satisfactory earnings on these assets.

Under normal conditions, a bank will have an inflow of funds from (1) depositors; (2) borrowers, who are meeting payments on loans; and, (3) issuers, who are repaying bonds and other forms of debt as they mature; as well as an outflow to meet demands for funds. However, if banks are managed wisely, they will be prepared to meet not only normal but also emergency demands for funds; and, since their primary reserves are kept as low as feasible, most of their demands for cash will be met by changes in secondary reserves. The secondary-reserve policies of individual banks should be adjusted according to the character of deposit liabilities, capital structure, the nature and soundness of other assets, and the business cycle.

Influence of Deposits. Fewer secondary reserves will be required when deposits have great stability, and this stability depends upon the type and size of the deposits and the location of the bank. Time deposits are more stable than demand; small deposits are more stable than large; and deposits in country banks are more stable than those in city banks. Although commercial banks are, to some extent, savings institutions, experience shows that their time deposits are more volatile than those of savings banks. During panics, the distinction between time and demand deposits in commercial banks is more artificial than real. The most unstable deposits are interbank and public deposits, and a bank may find it expedient to keep an amount equal to these volatile deposits in primary and secondary reserve assets.

Capital-Deposit Ratios. The capital-deposit ratio is important in planning a lending and investing program because a bank that has a relatively small amount of equity (assume a 1–20 ratio of capital to deposits) may have its capital impaired by a loss equal to two or three per cent of deposits and may be made insolvent by a loss equal to more than five per cent of deposits. For a second bank having a relatively large amount of equity (assume a 1–10 ratio of capital to deposits) similar losses would be serious but the danger of impairment of capital and of insolvency would be greatly reduced. A general rule is that the lower the percentage of capital accounts relative to deposits, the higher the secondary-reserve position of the bank must be.

Nature of Loans and Investments. The nature of a bank's loans and investments is also important in determining a sound bank's secondary-reserve position. A bank whose loan and investment account is dominated by real-estate loans, capital loans, and long-term bonds must of necessity keep a higher secondary-reserve position than a second bank whose loan and investment portfolio is dominated by short-term commercial loans and highly marketable investments. The first bank must be in a position to avoid losses on security sales when security prices decline and be able to acquire new cash when real estate and other loans become frozen.

Business Cycle. At the beginning of boom periods, secondary reserves should be at their peak; and, insofar as conditions permit, the bank's investment account should have been shifted gradually in the direction of shorter maturities in anticipation of higher interest rates and lower market prices of government obligations, particularly long-term government securities. Later, security-market conditions permit banks to improve their investment portfolios by increasing government-bond holdings, the prices of which tend to be lowest at or near the peak of the business cycle and highest at or near the bottom of the cycle. One of the criticisms that has been made of the investment policies of commercial banks is that they acquire securities when business is dull, interest rates are low, and bond prices are at their peak and then liquidate them at a loss when loan demand increases, interest rates advance, and bond prices decline.[6] When banks

---

[6] For illustration, in 1955 insured commercial banks' allowances for losses on assets disposed of or revalued were $707,000,000 of which $240,000,000 was offset by capital gains or cancellation of loss allowances.

switch from one type of earning asset to another there are usually offsetting advantages such as higher yields on loans to compensate for losses on investments.

LOANS AND INVESTMENTS

The lending and investing of a bank's funds should not be thought of as a water faucet that is shut off when no new cash is coming into the bank and turned on only when new deposits or cash from repaid loans and investments are available. What actually happens is that the faucets are always open, with the rate of flow regulated so as to keep stable the level of funds in the cash reservoir. (See Chart 7.) However, it must be emphasized that in the use of

CHART 7

FLOW OF BANK FUNDS

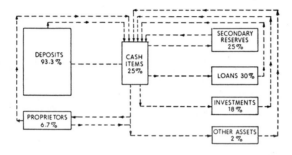

bank assets, bankers may use their discretion only within the limits as provided by law and rules of supervisory officials, and then only insofar as local and general economic conditions permit. In some communities, banks may be highly selective in making loans because of the loan demand; in other communities, banks must go outside of their communities to find investment or loan outlets for their loanable funds.

Preference for Lending. Lending is the most profitable activity of commercial banks. Not only is the rate of earnings on bank loans greater than on investment but lending is also more profitable because borrowers keep deposit balances at their banks and use other services offered by them. On the other hand, the costs entailed in lending are greater than those in investing; therefore the difference in gross yields does not represent the net gain. A bank's loan policy involves questions as to the percentage of assets to be placed in loans and discounts after its primary and secondary reserve requirements have been met. If the demand for loans from acceptable prospective borrowers is adequate, there is no reason for not lending the remaining available funds.

The responsibility for determining loan policies of a bank rests with its board of directors. The board of directors should answer questions as to the following: (1) area within which the bank will confine its lending activities; (2) types of loans the bank should make—term, installment, consumer, etc.; (3) volume of loans to be made in each category; (4) maximum terms as to maturities; (5) interest rates (maximum and minimum); and (6) limitations as to the power of officers to commit the bank without prior approval of the loan committee and/or the board of directors.

Investment Risks. After caring for primary and secondary reserves and meeting demands for acceptable loans, banks place their remaining funds in investments. A bank's board of directors is responsible for determining the bank's investment policies which should be planned so as to provide safety and income. When a bank invests, it assumes two kinds of risk: credit risk, the risk that the creditor will default on the obligation; and money risk, the risk that interest rates will change causing the market prices of investments to change. Contrary to popular opinion, banks assume risks when they invest in government securities; and the decline in prices of government securities in 1954–56 indicates that this money risk is substantial. Low interest rates create a dilemma for bankers; their continuance means low earnings, while an increase would tend to mean capital losses. Over a period of time, banks do profit from an increase in money rates because they receive greater returns from investments; but, if they are forced to sell their securities, they may suffer large capital losses. If bankers follow the accounting rule of "the lower of cost or market" in evaluating their banks' investments, they may find their banks to be insolvent (assets less than liabilities) even though their investments have not been sold.

The price of any bond is determined by the credit-standing of the obligor and the level of money rates in the market. Where there is practically no question of the credit-standing of the debtor, bond-price fluctuations are dominated by money-market risks—the higher the money rates of interest, the lower will be the prices of bonds; and conversely, the lower the interest rates, the higher will be the prices of bonds. When a twenty-year $100 government bond has a rate of 2.5 per cent and the market rate is similar, the bond will be selling at par ($100); but, if the market rate increases to 2.6 per cent, the market price will be $98.45. If the market rate were to decline to 2.4 per cent, the market price of the bond would rise to $101.58. The influence of money market rate changes on investment values is greater on long-term than on short-term obligations. (Where the credit risk is large, the market price of a bond will be influenced more by changes in economic conditions of the debtor, the industry, and the country than by changes in interest rates.)

Banks could limit the "money risk" by restricting their investments to short-term obligations on which the yield is usually lower than on longer maturities. Since the risks on long-term investments appear excessive and the yields on short-term obligations are inadequate, banks have been diversifying by "spacing maturities."

Maturity Arrangement of Loans and Investments. In buying securities, banks may arrange maturities so as to avoid destructive capital losses even if market prices decline. In order to be able to provide depositors or new borrowers with funds, without disturbing their bond portfolios, banks may arrange the maturities of their loans and investments so that a percentage of these assets mature each year. In other words, banks may integrate their investment and loan programs. If a large portion of their loans is in the form of real estate mortgages on homes and other forms of real property, use of the installment plan of repayment of principal will provide the banks with funds to lend or invest.

A bank may have a policy of placing one tenth of its investment account in government obligations of six-year maturities, another one tenth in seven-year maturities, and so on. This would give the bank an investment portfolio of government bonds with average maturities of ten and one half years. At the end of each year, obligations having maturities of five years would be reclassified as secondary reserves; and the cash obtained from the matured bills and other securities would be used to buy bonds of fifteen-year maturities if such funds were not needed to meet loan demands or to care for deposit withdrawals. The bank would be investing in the "long-end" of the government securities market where interest rates are usually higher than in the "short-end."

The "spaced maturity" program tends to increase the average yield on banks' investments and reduces the "money risk" assumed in holding long-term securities. The policy of arranging maturities to provide funds automatically implies that banks have perpetual lives. If government bonds decline in market price temporarily, they will be at par at maturity and so may be retained in the bank's portfolio without capital loss.

Investments in state and local government securities are influenced by their high ratings and the tax-exemption feature they possess. Usually, they appear in serial form, which gives the banks an opportunity to select the maturities that fit into their investment programs. When a bank or investor is in the 52 per cent income tax bracket for marginal income, tax exemption on a 2 per cent bond means that its interest equivalent on a taxable bond is over 4.16 per cent (2.00 ÷ (1–0.52) per cent).

Other securities held by banks include corporate bonds, notes, and debentures. Usually, they are of longer maturity than those of the federal and other governments. Most corporations, whose credit standings warrant bank purchases of their securities, raise their long-

TABLE 12

DISTRIBUTION OF ASSETS OF BANKS IN THE UNITED STATES, DECEMBER 31, 1955
(Percentage of Total Assets)

Item	All Insured Banks*	All Insured Commercial Banks
Cash and balances with other banks.............	20.4	22.3
United States government obligations (direct and guaranteed)...........................	28.7	29.1
Other securities.............................	8.3	7.8
Loans and discounts........................	41.2	39.4
Other assets...............................	1.4	1.4
Total.............................	100.0	100.0
Total capital accounts......................	7.3	7.2

* Includes mutual savings banks.
Source: *Annual Report of the Federal Deposit Insurance Corporation for the Year Ended December 31, 1955* (Washington, D.C., 1956), pp. 128–29.

term capital by selling bonds with callable features. Because credit risks may be great, this group of securities presents a more difficult portfolio management problem than do other types of investments; and the volume of such bonds held by commercial banks is relatively small. Today, commercial banks are unimportant buyers of corporate bonds, the corporate bond market being dominated by other institutional investors chiefly life insurance companies. The way in which the funds of commercial banks are administered is reflected by the distribution of their assets (see Table 12).

SUMMARY

As substantiated by the history of business and bank failures, the risks involved in banking are greater than those of other businesses. This greater risk is due to a number of factors, including:

(1) the nature of banks' liabilities, (2) the thin layer of equity capital on which banks operate, and (3) the high standards of safety set by law and supervisory agencies. Since commercial banks create and destroy money, banking is regulated in greater detail than any other business.

In managing their affairs, commercial bankers must protect their depositors while earning enough to meet the costs of operating their banks. As a result, banks hold more idle cash funds (primary reserves) than all other business firms combined. In addition, a large percentage of their earning assets are invested in securities having a low rate of return (secondary reserves). Banks, like other lenders, must assume risks. Their greatest risks as well as their most profitable source of earnings are represented by loans to local businessmen, consumers, and others. However, banks also assume risks in buying long-term government securities—the risk of capital loss if interest rates increase.

QUESTIONS AND PROBLEMS

1. Distinguish among the "traditional," "shiftability," and "anticipated income" theories of the liquidity of banks' assets. During serious financial disturbances, upon what does the liquidity of banks' assets depend?

2. Explain "risks of banking." How do they differ from those assumed by other business enterprises? What is meant by a "run" on a bank? "Clearinghouse run"?

3. During depressions, which is more troublesome to banks, remaining liquid or remaining solvent? Distinguish between the two problems that are involved.

4. What is meant by the statement "a bank's capital must not be impaired"?

5. Identify: (a) primary reserve and the bank items that are included; (b) secondary reserves and the bank items that are included. What are the functions of primary and secondary reserves?

6. Are businessmen who borrow from commercial banks better than average credit risks? How does their credit standing compare with the credit standing of those who borrow in the money and capital markets?

7. Do banks prefer lending to investing? Why?

8. What is meant by the flow of bank funds? Which of the different items in the chart showing the flow of bank funds are relatively "active" and which are relatively "passive"? Explain.

9. In well-managed banks, explain how the amount of secondary reserves will be influenced by (a) a low capital-deposit ratio, (b) a relatively large amount of interbank and public deposits, and (c) a relatively large amount of local loans.

10. Analyze the following statement: "If the price declines [of government securities] were sharp they could have highly unfavorable repercussions on the functioning of financial institutions and if carried far enough might even weaken public confidence in such institutions." (*Thirty-second Annual Report of the Board of Governors of the Federal Reserve System Covering Operations for the Year, 1945* [Washington, D.C., 1946], p. 7.)

11. Analyze the following statement: "A banker's ability in his profession is most clearly revealed in the composition of the bank's portfolio, for it is in the bank portfolio that the conflicting demands of profitability and safety of a bank must be reconciled." (D. A. Alhadeff, "Monetary Policy and the Treasury Bill Market," *American Economic Review*, Vol. XLII, No. 3 [June, 1952], p. 333.)

12. Must banks forego profits in order to have liquidity? Explain. How do banks meet this problem?

13. Explain: "As a means of obtaining reserves to expand their loans, member banks liquidated a portion of their holdings of securities . . . and resorted to heavier and more sustained borrowing from the Federal Reserve bank. In the process, there was a decline in the liquidity of the banking system. . . ." (Federal Reserve Bank of Dallas, *Monthly Business Review*, March 1, 1956, p. 39.)

Chapter XV | BANK LOANS AND DISCOUNTS

DETERMINATION of the policies of a bank is the primary responsibility of the bank's board of directors and execution of these policies is the responsibility of the bank's president and other officers. This chapter deals with the loan and discount policies and practices of commercial banks.

BASIC CONCEPTS

Loans and Discounts. Technically, a loan transaction is one wherein interest is paid either at the end of the loan period along with repayment of the principal or periodically throughout the loan period. In a discount transaction, interest is deducted from the principal amount at the time the credit is arranged. Usually, only short-term loans are discounted; but, before one concludes that it would be impractical to make long-term loans on this basis, note that the federal government borrows on a discount basis when Series E savings bonds are sold. For all practical purposes, a discount transaction is a special type of loan transaction, and it is so treated. Usually, a banker prefers a discount transaction because the yield thereon is higher than would be the yield on a loan carrying the same rate of interest.

Secured and Unsecured Loans. A bank customer may borrow from his bank by giving a promissory note with or without specifically pledging something as security for the loan. Thus the loan may be either secured or unsecured, depending on the presence or absence of pledged assets. The promissory note may have only the name of the maker, or it may be endorsed by a second party. Thus it may be single-name or double- or two-name paper. Technically, the second name may appear in the form of a guarantee of the obligation which would place the debt-paying ability of the guarantor behind the obligation.

Although secured loans are more numerous in the business field, unsecured loans are more important in the aggregate because the average unsecured loan is larger than the average secured loan. This is due in part to the fact that large borrowers keep better financial records of their firms' business affairs than do small ones, and one maxim of bank lending is that all loans above a specified figure (determined by the board of directors) must be made against adequate financial statements or pledges of assets. Most loans are negotiated over the counter, and the factors that determine the terms include custom, the credit standing of the borrower, and conditions in the money market. However the ability to provide acceptable collateral tends to expedite bank lending whether loans are large or small.

The range of collateral accepted by banks includes most types of tangible and intangible property (staple commodities, inventories, equipment, oil runs, real property, mortgages, stocks, bonds, life insurance policies, accounts-receivable, royalties, assignments of claims, and others). The use of these types of property as collateral necessitates various legal instruments, such as bills of lading, warehouse receipts, trust receipts, conditional sales contracts, chattel mortgages, real estate mortgages, consents to pledge, and assignment forms of different types.

A bank usually wants collateral for the protection given to loans, but sometimes security may be requested because it may be used as a means of disciplining the borrower. Threats of seizure and sale of mortgage or assigned property may cause the debtor to make an extra effort to meet his obligation. In comparison, legal proceedings to collect for nonpayment of an unsecured note may be less effective. In other cases, a bank may request collateral so that it may lend an amount in excess of the limit fixed by the 10 per cent rule, an amount fixed at 10 per cent of a bank's capital and surplus. This means that a bank having unimpaired capital and surplus of $1,000,-000 could not legally lend more than $100,000 to one name on an unsecured basis. Often banks with capital and surplus of $1,000,000 have total assets of $20,000,000 or more; for them, individual loans of $200,000 to $500,000 would not be excessive. Loans in excess of the amount fixed by the 10 per cent rule may be made when certain types of securities are pledged (for illustration, 25 per cent of a bank's unimpaired capital and surplus may be lent to one name if the loan is secured by United States government securities).

Short-Term and Long-Term Loans.   Other things being equal, a commercial bank prefers to make short-term loans because the shorter the term of a loan the smaller is the risk involved. The traditional bank loan is a short-term loan drawn for less than a year. In principle, this necessitates an annual "clean-up" of loans. In spite of the fact that borrowers may insist that they are "good" for the loan and that the bank is denying itself income when it insists on payment, bankers may want a periodic demonstration of the customer's ability to pay. Lacking funds at maturity, some borrowers may either borrow from a second bank to repay the first or secure renewals of their loans, in whole or part. Some advantage results from the first alternative—the borrower is forced to submit to credit analysis by the second bank. The second alternative has led to the wider use of "term" loans.

Term Loans. A so-called "term" loan is defined as a loan to a business firm that is repayable after the lapse of a year or more. Such a loan usually runs from one to five years (but it may be longer) and it is usually repayable periodically during the life of the loan. Loans of this type are well adapted to financing the credit needs of a business whose ability to repay is related to its anticipated earning power. Most of the funds obtained from term loans are used to increase working capital, purchase equipment and machinery, and expand or purchase facilities.

Since the risks assumed by the lender increase as the length of time increases, a number of things that the creditor must do, and may not do, are embodied in the term-loan agreement. A clause in the agreement makes the loan due and payable if any one of these provisions is violated (the acceleration clause). By specifying these provisions in detail in the loan agreement, the bank is seeking to protect both the lender and the borrower.

In addition to provisions covering interest and repayment of principal, other provisions commonly found are those prohibiting (1) pledging or mortgaging any of the assets of the company to anyone else, (2) merging with another company, (3) guaranteeing or assuming obligations of another company, (4) paying excessive dividends and salaries, (5) borrowing from other sources, (6) discounting receivables, and (7) using funds borrowed for purposes other than those prescribed in the agreement. The borrower usually agrees to (1) maintain certain minimum current ratios, (2) keep plant and equipment in good repair, (3) include property hereinafter acquired in the covenant (the after-acquired property clause), and (4) provide the lender with complete financial information. Similar provisions are found in the indenture agreements that are used in open-market financing when bonds are sold to investors.

Call and Time Loans. A call loan is one repayable at the option of either the lender or the borrower at any time during a business day. Such loans have been associated with the financing of the securities markets. Many brokers and dealers in securities and commodities borrow on "call," and many buyers of securities finance their purchases on margin with funds obtained with loan contracts containing no specific maturity. At the peak of the stock market boom in 1929, the volume of call loans was in excess of $10 billion. However, it would be a mistake to assume that the call or repayment option cannot be inserted in any loan contract. In practice, many business, consumer, and real estate mortgage loans have or have had this clause.

Time loans are those made for a definite or determinable period of time. Those for less than a year are usually classified as short-term, and those for a longer period, as long-term. Sometimes an intermediate classification is used covering loans made for a period of from one to three, four, or five years. The loan agreement may specify that if certain general or specific things happen the loan may be called at the option of the lender. In making a loan the bank is usually given the right of "set-off"—debiting the borrower's deposit account and crediting his debt to the bank. The borrower has the same common-law right which is important to him if his bank is closed because of insolvency or for other reasons.

Single-Payment and Installment-Payment Loans. A single-payment loan is one wherein the loan agreement provides for the payment of the principal in one sum, while an installment-payment loan is one wherein the principal is repaid in installments. Ordinarily, consumer loans, real estate loans, and term loans to businessmen are repaid periodically throughout the life of the loan. Repayment terms are based upon the anticipated income of the borrower, and so the anticipated income theory is used to justify this type of lending.

Over-the-Counter and Open-Market Loans. Although most bank loans are negotiated over the counter between bankers and borrowers, sometimes borrowers obtain funds through intermediaries— commercial paper houses, bill brokers and dealers, mortgage loan brokers and dealers, and other specialists. Banks finance borrowers through these intermediaries by purchasing the borrowers' promises to pay (as in the case of the operation of commercial paper houses and mortgage loan brokers) or by buying (discounting) trade and bankers' acceptances.

Open-Market Commercial Paper. Open-market commercial paper consists of promissory notes of large business firms, which usually have maturities of from thirty to ninety days. The dealer (commercial paper house) does not endorse the promises to pay, so they are single-name paper unless endorsed by a second party at the time the notes are drawn (which would be unusual). The size of an issue of commercial paper may be millions of dollars, and the issue may contain hundreds of promissory notes. The denominations of notes are not standardized, and they may be drawn in amounts varying from a few hundred to tens of thousands of dollars. Often the dealer will have an "if and when issued" sales agreement with buyers during the period of negotiation, and these commitments will influence the final arrangements as to the form of the notes to be delivered by the issuer to the dealer.

Today, five sales-finance companies act as their own agents in selling promissory notes in the open market. Since their needs for new funds are related to the expansion in the volume of consumer credit, the amount of promissory notes now sold directly by them is about four times the volume handled by dealers. The terms of the promissory notes sold directly by finance companies are more variable than those sold by dealers, varying in maturity from as long as 270 days to a few days according to the requests of investors. In the aggregate, the volume of commercial and finance paper is in excess of $2.5 billion; but this amount is small when compared to the $33.5 billion of commercial and industrial loans made by banks (see also Chapter XVIII).

Commercial Bills. Domestic bills and time bills of foreign exchange include bankers' acceptances and trade acceptances. Bankers' acceptances are those which have been accepted by a financial institution, while trade acceptances are those which have been accepted by a business firm other than a bank or financial institution. Bills usually have maturities of from 30 to 180 days, and they are used most commonly in financing foreign trade. A businessman may sell (discount) a bank or trade bill to his bank over the counter before or after acceptance; but, if it is offered in the open market, it has usually been accepted previously by the party drawn upon or has been endorsed by a bank. Commercial bills are important in financing foreign trade (see Chapter XVII); but the amount of acceptances outstanding during most of a current year will average only about $650,000,000.

STATISTICS OF COMMERCIAL BANK LOANS

The statistics of commercial bank loans are usually presented according to the type of borrower; but they are also presented, to some extent, according to the purpose for which funds are used. By an interagency agreement, the Federal Deposit Insurance Corporation gathers and publishes the most complete series of statistics for all operating banks in the United States including the continental United States and other areas (Alaska, American Samoa, Puerto Rico, and Virgin Islands). Although almost 500 commercial banks are not participating in the Federal Deposit Insurance Corporation, their deposits make up only 1.2 per cent of the total deposits of commercial banks; therefore the loans of insured commercial banks are used to illustrate commercial bank lending.

Commercial and Industrial Loans. Among the loans made by commercial banks, the most important are those classified as commercial and industrial (37.5 per cent of total loans and discounts). Of course, these statistics include traditional short-term loans as well as term loans of banks. At different times, estimates have been made of the proportion of business loans which are term loans; and these estimates vary between one third and one half of all business loans (expanding when credit conditions are easy and contracting when they are tight).[1]

Agricultural Loans. Although banks are subject to more competition from federal governmental agencies in the field of agricultural credit than in other fields, insured commercial banks are the chief source of credit of farmers. However some governmental agencies assist banks in making agricultural loans (as well as competing for them). At the end of 1955, over $1.1 billion of the over $4 billion agricultural loans (excluding real estate loans) were guaranteed by the Commodity Credit Corporation. The volume of such loans fluctuates widely because of variations in the amount of farm crops in storage under provisions of the federal government's agricultural price support program.

Loans for Carrying Securities. Banks' loans made for the purpose of purchasing and carrying securities include those made to individuals and others who are speculating in securities as well as those made to investment houses, security dealers, and others who are underwriting and distributing securities. Investment bankers, like merchants and others, use their inventories as security for loans. It is the customary practice for commercial banks to make such loans on a secured basis. The volume of loans secured by stocks and bonds is

---

[1] In October, 1955, term loans to business accounted for 34 per cent of member banks' business loan portfolios. Nearly 40 per cent of such loans were confined to two major industry groups: (1) transportation, communications, and other public utilities; and (2) coal, chemicals, and rubber. See also *Federal Reserve Bulletin* (April, 1956), pp. 332–34.

small compared to the amount of trading in securities on the New York Stock Exchange and other stock exchanges and in the over-the-counter market. Most of the current purchases of securities are paid for with cash and, when funds are borrowed for this purpose, the margin (collateral) requirements are high.

Real Estate Loans.   Among the loans made by insured commercial banks, those classified as real estate loans have shown the steadiest growth since the end of World War II. Real estate loans made by insured commercial banks include those on farm land ($1.2 billion) as well as those on other types of property ($19.5 billion). Commercial banks have shown a slight preference for nonconventional real estate loans (those insured by Federal Housing Administration and insured or guaranteed by the Veterans' Administration) on residential properties which aggregated $8.1 billion, as compared to $7.5 billion of conventional residential real estate loans at the end of 1955. Commercial banks also make real estate loans based on other properties ($3.8 billion).

Other Loans to Individuals.   The category "other loans to individuals" is made up for the most part of consumer loans which may be subdivided as follows: (1) retail automobile installment paper, (2) other retail installment paper, (3) repair and modernization installment loans guaranteed by Federal Housing Administration, (4) installment cash loans, and (5) single-payment loans. Among the first four classes of consumer loans, the installment principle of repayment is used. The first three classes relate the amount of credit advanced to the goods or services being financed. (See Chapter XXXI.) When the statistics of financing consumers are added to those of real estate financing, the fundamental changes in the nature of commercial bank lending become apparent.

All Other Loans.   The category "all other loans" includes loans to other banks and overdrafts (checks drawn in excess of the drawers' deposits, which have been honored by the bank) and others which have not been classified. Today, banks are using the resources of the Federal Reserve banks more freely than in the past to acquire new loan credit; and the relatively small amount of loans of this type, as reported by insured commercial banks, are those made by them to nonmember banks for the most part. In European countries it is a common practice to honor checks when deposit accounts do not cover them; but, in the United States, this practice is considered to be poor banking and the amount of bank credit advanced in this way is relatively small.

TABLE 13

PERCENTAGE DISTRIBUTIONS OF LOANS AND DISCOUNTS WITHIN SIZE GROUPS OF INSURED COMMERCIAL BANKS, JUNE 30, 1954

LOAN ITEM	ALL BANKS	BANKS WITH DEPOSITS (IN MILLIONS OF DOLLARS) OF—										
		1 or less	1 to 2	2 to 5	5 to 10	10 to 25	25 to 50	50 to 100	100 to 250	250 to 500	500 to 1,000	More than 1,000
Loans and discounts, net.................	98.5%	99.5%	99.4%	99.1%	98.8%	98.7%	98.5%	98.5%	98.5%	98.6%	98.5%	98.2%
Valuation reserves..................	1.5	.5	.6	.9	1.2	1.3	1.5	1.5	1.5	1.4	1.5	1.8
Loans and discounts, gross.............	100.0	100.0	100.0	100.0	100.0	100.0	100.0	100.0	100.0	100.0	100.0	100.0
Commercial and industrial loans.......	38.3	7.6	10.8	14.3	18.8	23.2	29.6	36.5	39.2	46.6	52.3	54.4
Agricultural loans (excluding real estate).......	7.5	45.7	37.6	25.6	13.5	6.0	4.4	4.6	4.0	3.9	3.6	2.3
Loans to farmers directly guaranteed by Commodity Credit Corporation.......	2.8	10.9	9.9	6.7	3.7	2.0	2.3	2.4	2.4	3.0	2.5	1.3
Other loans to farmers (excluding real estate)....	4.7	34.8	27.7	18.9	9.8	4.0	2.1	2.2	1.6	.9	1.1	1.0
Loans for carrying securities.........	5.4	.3	.4	.6	.9	1.4	2.2	2.3	4.4	5.9	7.6	11.1
Loans to brokers and dealers in securities.........	3.6	*	.1	*	*	.1	.7	.5	2.1	2.3	5.6	9.1
Other loans for carrying securities.........	1.8	.3	.3	.6	.9	1.3	1.5	1.7	2.3	3.6	2.0	2.0
Real estate loans.........	25.2	25.1	30.0	36.0	38.8	38.3	33.2	25.4	22.1	20.6	15.9	17.1
On farm land..............	1.7	9.9	9.1	7.1	3.9	1.8	.9	.6	.4	.3	.3	.3
On residential properties:												
Insured or guaranteed by FHA or VA.......	10.2	3.0	4.6	7.4	10.2	11.9	12.0	10.3	10.9	10.1	8.8	11.2
Not insured or guaranteed by FHA or VA....	8.9	9.5	12.8	16.3	18.0	17.1	12.8	8.1	6.7	6.1	3.8	3.8
On other properties.......	4.4	2.7	3.5	5.2	6.7	7.5	7.5	6.4	4.1	4.1	3.0	1.8
Other loans to individuals.............	21.2	19.9	20.1	22.4	26.8	29.8	28.9	29.0	26.5	20.3	18.2	11.9
Retail automobile instalment paper........	6.4	6.8	6.9	7.6	9.1	10.1	9.6	8.2	6.9	5.1	6.4	3.1
Other retail instalment paper........	2.9	2.0	2.3	2.9	3.6	3.6	3.5	3.4	3.8	3.0	2.6	1.9
Repair and modernization instalment loans........	2.5	.2	.5	.9	1.9	3.5	3.0	4.1	3.3	3.1	2.4	1.9
Instalment cash loans.........	3.0	2.9	2.9	3.3	4.3	4.6	4.3	4.9	3.2	1.9	1.5	2.0
Single-payment loans.........	6.4	8.0	7.5	7.7	7.9	8.0	8.5	8.4	9.3	7.2	5.3	3.0
Loans to banks..................	.3	*	*	*	*	*	*	.1	.2	.1	.1	.7
All other loans..................	2.1	1.4	1.1	1.1	1.2	1.3	1.7	2.1	3.6	2.6	2.3	2.5
Number of banks..................	13,400	2,002	3,084	4,340	2,012	1,189	369	189	123	50	24	18
Amount of total gross loans (in millions)........	$68,002	$605	$1,872	$5,308	$5,229	$6,680	$4,700	$5,023	$6,782	$6,670	$6,109	$19,024

Source: *Annual Report of the Federal Deposit Insurance Corporation for the Year Ended December 31, 1954*, p. 70.

* Less than .05 percent.

DISTRIBUTION OF LOANS BY DIFFERENT SIZE BANKS

Of the numerous studies made by the Federal Deposit Insurance Corporation, one of the most important to an understanding of the lending problems of different size banks has been that published in the Corporation's annual report for 1954. For the convenience of the reader, who may not have a copy of this publication available, one of the summaries of the findings of the author of this study is reproduced as Table 13.

Among the more important facts to be noted from Table 13 are that:

(1) Commercial and industrial loans tend to increase in relative importance as banks increase in size, being only 7.6 per cent of the total loans for banks in the smallest size group (deposits of $1,000,000 or less) and more than 54.4 per cent for banks with deposits of more than $1 billion.

(2) Agricultural loans, other than real estate loans, tend to decrease in relative importance as banks increase in size, comprising 45.7 per cent of total loans for banks in the smallest size and only 2.3 per cent for banks holding deposits of $1 billion or more. Only since 1933, when the Commodity Credit Corporation began selling certificates of interest in pooled agricultural paper, have agricultural loans had any significance for larger banks.

(3) Loans made for the purpose of purchasing and carrying securities make up an insignificant percentage of the loans of banks in the smallest size group; but such loans increase in relative importance with the increase in size of banks, accounting for 0.3 per cent of loans for banks with deposits of $1,000,000 or less and 11.1 per cent for banks with deposits in excess of $1 billion. The concentration of loans to brokers and dealers in the portfolios of larger banks is not surprising because these banks are located in financial centers where most loans of this type are made.

(4) Real estate loans do not follow a bank-size pattern; but generally they are relatively more important to banks in the smaller and middle-size groups than to larger banks. Of course, the real estate loans based on farm land are relatively more important to the smaller banks than to the larger ones. Usually the real estate loans made by the larger banks are insured or guaranteed loans while more of those made by smaller banks are conventional loans. However real estate loans are more important to banks with deposits of from $2,000,000 to $50,000,000 than either commercial and industrial loans or agricultural loans.

(5) Other loans to individuals (chiefly consumer loans) are relatively more important to banks in the smaller and middle-size groups than to the larger banks. For banks with deposits of from $5,000,000 to $50,000,000, they are second in importance to loans on real estate; and for banks with deposits of from $50,000,000 to $1 billion they are second

in importance to commercial and industrial loans (with the exception of the $250,000,000 to $500,000,000 deposit group). The breakdown in Table 13 suggests the popularity of the different types of consumer credit to banks in different size groups (see also Chapter XXXI).

(6) Loans to banks are relatively unimportant but most of such loans are made by the larger banks.

(7) All other loans include overdrafts, sales of "federal" funds (see Chapter XVIII) and all other unclassified loans.

BANK LENDING PRACTICES

The lending practices of commercial banks are determined by many factors and they differ with the type of loan. When a bank makes loans to consumers and homeowners, it uses techniques which are similar to those used and developed by competing specialized institutions (see Chapters XXIX and XXX). To avoid repetition, the discussion in this section is limited to lending practices of commercial banks in regard to business loans.

Lines of Credit. In order to avoid costly delays when faced with the need for funds, many large borrowers with adequate credit standing secure lines of credit from their banks at the beginning of their fiscal years. A "line of credit" is an informal understanding between the borrower and his bank as to the maximum amount of credit which the bank will provide at any time; but it is not a guarantee that the amount of credit arranged for will be available when requested. A bank usually honors a line of credit, but the amount may be reduced sharply or the line cancelled if the financial position of the firm or industry deteriorates. Before granting a line of credit, the credit position of the borrower is analyzed; and the amount of the line of credit is fixed by the bank's loan committee and/or the board of directors. Usually, a line of credit is opened at the request of the borrower; but, in some cases, lines of credit are established by a bank in order to build up its loan business or merely to serve as a guide to its loan officers (with or without the borrowers being notified).

The amount of a line of credit will be determined by the size of the company, its past and anticipated earnings, current and anticipated general business conditions, and other factors that are considered when the work of the credit department is described. A line of credit may provide for granting credit with or without security. In the fall of 1955, in a survey conducted by the Federal Reserve System, it was found that only 56 per cent of the banks examined extended lines of credit.[2] In general, the use of this method of lending was more general

[2] *Federal Reserve Bulletin* (June, 1956), p. 574–75.

among large banks than small ones; and the chief holders of lines of credit are companies with high credit standings engaged in lines of business wherein repayment could be anticipated within the year. Although a line of credit is customarily open for but one year, it usually leads to a revolving type of credit arrangement between the borrower and his bank that runs from year to year. One of the qualifications for this type of credit accommodation is the ability of the customer to keep a substantial deposit balance with his bank.

Compensatory Balances.   After having been granted a line of credit, the borrower may or may not use it; but, in order to keep it open, he is usually expected to keep a "compensatory balance" on deposit with his bank (10 to 20 per cent of the line of credit or of the amount borrowed or of both). From the viewpoint of the bank, this balance is an indirect compensation for making credit available in case of need; from the viewpoint of the customer, it is an "asset reserve" which strengthens his financial position. Business firms customarily keep a part of their working capital (cash) in the form of deposits in banks and the minimum balance requirement merely encourages them to keep such funds in the banks wherein they have established lines of credit. If the minimum balance is in excess of the amount the borrower would normally need, it would have the same effect as a higher interest rate. Although minimum balances are not insisted upon by all banks, the usual deposit balance of a borrower is taken into account when fixing the interest rate on loans.

The application of the minimum-balance rule varies from bank to bank, being used by 90 per cent of banks holding deposits of over $500,000,000 and by only 5 per cent of the banks holding deposits of less than $20,000,000.[3] Some banks apply the minimum-balance rule to all customers who have been granted lines of credit; other banks apply it only to certain classes of customers (such as sales-finance companies). Banks usually enforce the minimum-balance rule more rigidly when general credit conditions are "tight" and less rigidly during periods of "easy" money.

The loan needs of some business firms are so uncertain and irregular as to make line-of-credit arrangements impractical; and such firms usually apply for loans when the need arises. A business firm of this type whose financial affairs are sound, as shown by financial statements, usually keeps a deposit balance with its bank in about the same proportion to its loans as would a line-of-credit customer.

Loan Commitments.   Sometimes, businessmen arrange for loan

[3] *Ibid.*, p. 576.

commitments from their banks in order to avoid the uncertainties associated with lines of credit. Generally, loan commitments are binding legal agreements between the customers and their banks, the terms of which are so drawn as to meet varying needs and circumstances. (For illustration, during World War II, loan commitments were made in anticipation of government war contracts.) Loan commitments involve the payment of fees based on the size of the anticipated loans and payment of interest if and when loans are made. A loan commitment may be obtained from a bank in anticipation of purchasing new equipment, remodelling buildings, improving facilities, or meeting many other anticipated needs.

Usually commercial banks prefer to adjust other parts of their loan and investment portfolios rather than to disturb their loan relationships with their business customers. The large earnings on short-term commercial loans make their acquisition and retention desirable; and so, during periods of tight credit conditions, banks may liquidate their investments, collect commercial bills and open-market paper, and withdraw in part from the money market in order to make loans to their customers. For illustration, during 1955 the business loans of commercial banks increased by $6.2 billion while their investments in United States government securities declined by $7.3 billion.[4]

Small business enterprises usually borrow from but one bank; but, for a number of reasons, large business firms have little choice but to borrow from several banks. For illustration, a national bank is prohibited from making an unsecured loan to one name in excess of 10 per cent of its unimpaired capital and surplus. Many banks prefer to spread the risk entailed in a large loan among different borrowers in order to diversify their loan portfolios, many businessmen want to spread their loans among different lenders so as to secure a greater amount of financial independence, and business firms which are national in scope of operations find it advantageous to borrow from banks in different sections of the country.

Term Lending. Some banks prefer to use the short-term loan contract despite the fact that the borrower may negotiate for a renewal when the note matures. On the other hand, many borrowers prefer to finance with loans having maturities of one year or longer; and the lending policies of most banks are flexible enough to meet such requests. A term loan, one having a maturity of one year or longer, is negotiated between the borrower and lender, and about one half of these loans are secured. If the funds requested are un-

[4] *Federal Reserve Bulletin* (February, 1956), p. 99.

usually large, two or more banks and sometimes life insurance companies may participate in the loan.

When a loan is syndicated, this is, divided among several lenders, one of the lenders administers the loan—handles repayments, collects interest, sees that clauses in the loan agreement are followed, and prorates receipts among the lenders. This syndicate manager is usually compensated by a service fee paid by the borrower. In the credit analysis work that precedes term lending, more emphasis is placed on investment factors pertinent to anticipated earnings than is the case in credit analysis preceding short-term lending wherein liquidity or marketability of inventories and other assets is more important. Interest rates on term loans are usually higher than on short-term loans, and many term loan contracts contain the escalator clause (interest rates increase as the Federal Reserve bank or some other specified interest rates increase).

In the survey conducted by the Federal Reserve System of business loans made by member banks, it was found that term lending is least popular with business firms having relatively few fixed assets (such as sales-finance companies, commodity dealers, and firms in the wholesale trade) and most popular with firms having large amounts of fixed assets (such as public utility, transportation, and communications companies, and producers or manufacturers of petroleum, chemical, coal, and rubber products). Larger companies are the chief users of term credit but the relative importance of term borrowing by small companies is increasing.[5]

CREDIT DEPARTMENT AND GOVERNMENT REGULATION

When banks lend or invest, they must assume risks. If banks are too exacting in their requirements, they may lose income by refusing to make certain loans or investments; if they are too careless in selecting borrowers or investments, they may suffer large capital losses.

Credit Department. Every commercial bank has a credit department or division or some officer who is responsible for assembling, recording, and analyzing credit information. While a small bank is not in a position to have many specialists on its staff, someone must be responsible for these activities. But, in making loans, the responsibility rests with the bank's board of directors, loan committee, and senior officers.

Most of the work of a bank's credit department consists of gathering information about actual and potential borrowers in order

[5] *Federal Reserve Bulletin* (April, 1956), pp. 332–34.

to assist the lending officers and to answer inquiries from correspondent banks and others. In addition, the credit department may be asked to check on nonborrower-customers, to analyze checking accounts, and to compute service charges. Analyzing a checking account is not as far out of line with the primary function of the credit department as it may seem because such an analysis is an excellent source of credit information. Analyzing an individual's account reveals a great deal about the depositor's sources of income and his spending and saving habits, and analyzing a business account may be equally illuminating. When a borrower draws a check in excess of his deposit, the bank should investigate his credit position immediately.

Sources of Credit Information. Sources of credit information include borrowers themselves, credit-reporting agencies, and others. In making bank loans, current information about borrowers is essential, and this must come from the borrowers directly or indirectly. This necessitates a close relationship between the borrower and his bank, with the former (in the case of a business loan) providing the bank with signed financial and operating statements, submitting to specific and general questioning (orally or by correspondence) as to accounting and other items, and permitting the bank to investigate the plant or business firm. The bank checks with other banks having had experience with the borrower as well as making trade checks.

Investigation within the borrower's trade area usually reveals how he meets his obligations. Failure to take cash discounts usually is a danger signal that calls for immediate investigation. It may reflect lack of cash or ignorance—both unfavorable credit factors. When used to supplement other sources of information, reports of mercantile agencies are of value in giving the history and background of the borrower. Mercantile agencies or attorneys may make special investigations for banks; and other information may be found in public records (transfers of property, judgments rendered, and suits pending) and in newspapers, magazines, circulars, government bulletins, and trade-association and other directories.

Credit Analysis. An analysis of the credit standing of a large business firm usually includes the construction of comparative balance sheets for five years or more and the computation of important credit ratios. Among the ratios used are: (1) current assets to current debts (current ratio), (2) annual net profits to annual net sales, (3) tangible net worth to annual net sales, (4) net receivables to annual net credit sales (average collection period), (5) current debt to tangible net worth, and (6) total debt to tangible net worth. A separate folder or file is kept on each borrower; and subsequent information on each name is assembled, recorded, and analyzed methodically, so that the credit file on each active borrower is kept up to date. A credit file consists of a large number of small items which, to the expert, gives a picture of credit-worthiness of the borrower or potential borrower.

The terms of bank loans (maturities, interest, and other charges, provisions for repayment, and the thing pledged as security) are influenced by law, the regulations of and examinations by banks' supervisory agencies, and, if guaranteed, the rules of the guaranteeing agency.

Interest Rates. As a general rule, national banks and branches in foreign countries are permitted to charge the same rate of interest (or discount) as that authorized by the state or country in which the bank or branch is located. When no rate is fixed by law of the state, territory, or district, national banks may charge a rate not exceeding 7 per cent per annum. However, during periods of high interest rates, even these rates may not be the maximum, because the law also specifies that a bank's maximum rate may be 1 per cent in excess of the discount rate on ninety-day commercial paper in effect at its district Federal Reserve bank. The penalty for "taking, receiving, reserving, or charging a rate" in excess of the legal maximum is "deemed a forfeiture of the entire interest which the note, bill, or other evidence of debt carries with it . . ."; and, if greater interest has been paid, the person paying it may recover twice the interest paid, provided action "is commenced within two years from the time the usurious transaction occurred."[6]

There are special acts which fix the amount of interest that may be charged on loans made under their provisions. For illustration, originally the maximum that banks could charge on veterans' loans was 4 per cent (raised to 4½ per cent in 1948). On homeowners' loans insured by the National Housing Administration, the maximum legal rate is generally 5 per cent, with a maximum rate of 6 per cent permitted under certain circumstances. However, the rate in effect is fixed by the Housing Administrator plus over-all costs of making the loan. For other loans insured by or participated in by a federal agency, such federal agency usually is given the power to determine the interest rate charged borrowers.

[6] *United States Revised Statutes*, Sec. 5198; *United States Code*, Title 12, Sec. 86.

Loan Limitations. The national banking code places many limitations on loans in order to insure the quality of bank assets. The original 10-per-cent rule (10 per cent of a bank's capital was the maximum that could be lent to one name) was modified; under the present rule, the maximum loan to one name is 10 per cent of a bank's capital and surplus. In addition, the list of major exceptions to this rule was enlarged.

There are no loan limits to one borrower, in terms of a bank's unimpaired capital and surplus, applicable to (1) discounts of drafts or bills of exchange drawn in good faith against actually existing values; (2) discounts of two-name commercial or business paper, given by the purchaser to the seller in payment for a commodity, provided it is negotiable and bears the full recourse endorsement of the actual owner; (3) discount of one-name paper secured by goods in process of shipment; (4) discount of bankers' acceptances of other banks; (5) loans on obligations secured or covered by guarantees, agreements, or other contracts to purchase, within sixty days after request, made by a Federal Reserve bank or the United States government including a department, bureau, or other institution or agency of the government; and (6) loans to a receiver, conservator, or supervisor in charge of a bank when approved by the Comptroller of the Currency.

National banks may also make secured loans to one borrower in excess of the amount computed by the 10-per-cent rule but not in excess of a percentage provided by law. These maximum percentages in terms of unimpaired capital and surplus are (1) discounts of two-name paper other than commercial and business, 25 per cent; (2) discounts of notes and drafts secured by liens on livestock, 25 per cent; (3) loans secured by United States government direct and fully guaranteed obligations, 25 per cent; and (4) discounts of notes and drafts secured by readily marketable nonperishable staples, when additional security is provided, 50 per cent.

Executive officers of member banks are prohibited from borrowing from their own banks in amounts in excess of $2,500; and, if an executive officer of a member bank borrows from a second bank, he must make a written report to the directors of his own bank. Banks are prohibited from making loans secured by their own bank stock, unless it is necessary to prevent loss on debts previously contracted in good faith. Banks are also prohibited from making loans to bank examiners.

SUMMARY

Loans and investments are the chief sources of a bank's income. Bank loans are classified as secured and unsecured loans, short-term and long-term loans, call and time loans, single-payment and installment-payment loans, and over-the-counter and open-market loans. Banks are required to report their loans according to the purposes for which funds are used: commercial and industrial, agricultural, real estate, for carrying securities, other loans to individuals, and all others. (See Table 13.)

Lending practices of banks involving business loans include the use of lines of credit, loan commitments, loans made in participation with others, loans guaranteed in whole or part, and loans made by different departments of a bank to one name. A bank's lending is influenced by information made available by its credit department and is limited by governmental regulations. The primary purpose of each is to safeguard the quality of bank assets. A secondary purpose of governmental regulation is to prevent the exploitation of borrowers, and this aspect of regulation stresses interest rates that may be charged by banks.

QUESTIONS AND PROBLEMS

1. Distinguish between (a) secured and unsecured loans, (b) short-term and long-term loans, (c) call and time loans, (d) single-payment and installment loans, (e) over-the-counter and open-market loans, and (f) reporting classes of loans.

2. Account for the fact that the average size unsecured loan is larger than the average size secured loan.

3. How has the pattern of commercial bank lending changed since the 1930's?

4. In term lending, the business firm's "ability to repay is related to its anticipated earning power." Discuss.

5. Identify the types of loans included in each of the items in Table 13.

6. For insured commercial banks in the United States, what is the relative importance of (a) commercial and industrial loans? (b) real estate loans? (c) other loans to individuals which are chiefly consumer loans?

7. "As banks increase in size, as measured by the volume of deposits, commercial and industrial loans and loans for carrying securities become increasingly more important both absolutely and relatively while agricultural loans decrease in importance." Explain.

8. Identify: (a) lines of credit, (b) "proportionate balances," (c) credit

department of a bank, (d) guaranteed loans, (e) loan commitments, (f) participation loan, and (g) 10 per cent rule.

9. Identify: (a) acceleration clause, and (b) escalator clause.

10. "Analyzing a checking account is not . . . far out of line with the primary function of the credit department." Explain.

11. What are the chief sources of credit information available to a commercial bank?

12. What justification is there for calling a modern commercial bank a "department store of finance"?

Chapter XVI | COMMERCIAL BANK INVESTMENTS

IN ECONOMIC analysis the word "investment" is used broadly to include the application of economic resources to the production of producers' and consumers' goods. In a purely financial sense, investments refer to funds placed in enterprises for a relatively long period of time in order to obtain a regular return with a maximum of safety. Traditionally, the concept of lending carries with it the idea of permitting the use of something on the condition that it or its equivalent will be returned; and the concept of investing carries with it the idea of committing or laying out money for the purpose of obtaining an income or profit.

Insofar as bankers are concerned, lending includes those transactions in which borrowers come to the bank for funds (over-the-counter transactions), while investing generally includes those transactions in which bankers take the initiative (open-market transactions). In a loan transaction the bank is usually the only creditor, but in an investment transaction the bank is usually one of many creditors. Although certain open-market transactions of commercial banks are exceptions, this rule generally holds. Finally, banks' lending transactions are usually evidenced by promises or orders to pay, while investments may be evidenced by both credit instruments and stock certificates.

IMPORTANCE OF COMMERCIAL BANK INVESTMENTS

As compared to the years prior to 1930, there has been a decline in the relative importance of commercial loans and an increase in the relative importance of noncommercial loans and investments of commercial banks. Now, perhaps no more than 10 per cent of the earning assets of commercial banks would fall within the traditional concept of commercial bank lending—granting self-liquidating, short-term loans to finance seasonal working capital needs of farmers, wholesalers, retailers, and manufacturers.

Among the changes in business and banking practices that have been factors in reducing the demand for traditional bank loans are: (1) the growth in volume of cash sales; (2) the increase in the number of specialized institutions which finance accounts and installment notes receivable; (3) the decline in size of business firms' inventories made possible by improvements in transportation facilities and in inventory management; (4) the reduction in business losses due to improvements in credit analysis and collection techniques; (5) the increased use of retained earnings to finance new needs of business firms; (6) the increased willingness of banks to invest their assets in longer term loans to business firms; and (7) the over-all increase in liquidity of the economy. Perhaps only the last of these factors needs to be discussed here; of the remainder, some are obvious and the others are discussed elsewhere.

Development of Liquidity. At one time the liquidity of the economy was measured primarily in terms of the money supply; but today the development of many kinds of near money has resulted in making the volume of these assets as large as or larger than the money supply. The kinds of near money include: (1) time and savings deposits in banks; (2) shares in savings and loan associations and credit unions; (3) credit balances with brokers and other financial institutions which are payable on demand or after short notice; (4) credit instruments which are readily marketable without loss of principal, such as bankers' acceptances, United States Treasury bills, Series E savings bonds, and other short-term obligations of the government; (5) lines of credit with business suppliers; and (6) many readily marketable stocks and bonds. Modern markets of all kinds have given liquidity to assets and have reduced the need for short-term bank loans.

Liberalization of Federal Reserve Policy. Changes made in the laws under which the Federal Reserve System and other monetary authorities operate have liberalized Federal Reserve policy, and this has resulted in greater liquidity for many kinds of near money. These changes include (1) substituting a limited or restricted gold standard for the gold-coin standard, (2) reducing Federal Reserve banks' legal reserve requirements, (3) authorizing the use of United States government securities as collateral for Federal Reserve notes, (4) liberalizing conditions under which Federal Reserve credit may be borrowed, and (5) increasing commercial banks' reserve funds through the Federal Reserve System's open-market operations (investment activities).

Emphasis on Security. Throughout the history of the United States there has been a search for sound money. This is reflected in the original adoption of the bimetallic standard with its stress on hard money, the opposition to chartering commercial banks, and the limitations placed on the investments of banks, life insurance companies, and other financial institutions. Since the depression of the 1930's, there has been a desire on the part of bankers, businessmen, and consumers to keep their business and personal assets in a liquid condition. Low interest rates have lessened the penalty for keeping funds idle—loss of income. The guarantee or insurance of loans by federal agencies (Federal Housing Administration, Veterans' Administration, Commodity Credit Corporation, and so on) has encouraged banks to expand their earning assets (and therefore the money supply).

The Federal Debt. Perhaps the most important factor in the increased liquidity of the economy is the expansion that has taken place in the size of the federal debt and the fact that this new debt was financed in part with bank credit. The impact of the federal debt on the money supply can not be measured solely in terms of commercial banks' investments because the demand for liquidity has necessitated an increase in the supply of currency, chiefly Federal Reserve notes, which has been matched by an increase in the Federal Reserve System's investments in government obligations. The increase in the federal debt is also reflected in the investments of savings banks and other institutions whose obligations and shares have been classified as near money.

Relative Importance of Banks' Investments. The relative importance of commercial banks' investments as compared to their total earning assets (loans and investments) did not change very much between 1914 and 1930, investments having been 22.5 per cent of total earning assets in June, 1914, and 29.1 per cent in June, 1930. However, by June, 1935, investments were 56.9 per cent of total earning assets; by 1945, they reached 79.3 per cent. Since 1945 the percentage has declined, and the present figure is about 46 per cent (the percentage changes daily).

Classes of Securities. The investments of commercial banks are classified as follows: (1) United States government obligations, (2) obligations of states and their subdivisions, (3) other bonds, notes, and debentures, and (4) corporate stocks. Although the percentage of banks' investments in United States government obligations varies from day to day, these securities comprise about 80 per cent of banks' investments (declining during boom periods and increasing during slack periods).

Commercial banks' investments in obligations of states and their subdivisions are increasing with the growth in this form of debt; but, generally, these securities account for about 15 or 16 per cent of the investments of banks. Other bonds, notes, and debentures are chiefly obligations of business corporations that are financing in the open market. While the gross long-term debts of business corporations have increased from $45.3 billion in 1945 to $111.1 billion in 1955, most of these debts are held by insurance companies and pension funds. The contribution of commercial banks toward meeting the long-term credit needs of business is largely in the form of term loans. The amount of corporate stock held by commercial banks is less than 1 per cent of their total investments. The holding of stock by commercial banks is traced for the most part to investments of member banks in stock of Federal Reserve banks or to acquisitions of stock to prevent losses on loans.

UNITED STATES GOVERNMENT OBLIGATIONS

United States government obligations are attractive to banks because they have the qualities of (1) safety, there being no danger of any modern national government's defaulting on obligations payable in its own currency; (2) stability in price, particularly as long as the Federal Reserve System guarantees an "orderly" market; (3) preferred treatment by supervisory officials and bank examiners who permit banks to carry them at cost (less reserves for amortization of premium if purchased above par) irrespective of market value; (4) acceptability as collateral for loans at Federal Reserve banks (recently more than $1 billion was borrowed at one time); and (5) availability in almost any desired maturity.

There are many classes of United States government obligations; but those owned by commercial banks include four major classes: (1) United States Treasury bills, which are issued by the Treasury, sold on a discount basis, payable at par, and issued regularly with maturities of ninety-one days; (2) certificates of indebtedness, which are promises to pay and which usually have maturities of one year or less; (3) Treasury notes, which may be either coupon or registered obligations and which usually have maturities of from one to five years; and (4) Treasury bonds (similar to Treasury notes), which usually have maturities of from five to twenty-five years.

Usually, bonds are callable at the option of the Treasury on or after an original call date.

Treasury Bills. Originally, Treasury bills were regarded as credit instruments to be used to bridge the gap between expenditures and receipts on quarterly federal income tax dates or to care for interim financing between issues of long-term bonds. Now there are thirteen issues outstanding, of which one matures each week. As one issue matures, it is retired with funds obtained from the sale of a new issue. In effect, the entire amount of bills outstanding will be replaced with new bills within a period of thirteen weeks or ninety-one days (a one-day adjustment may have to be made if the due date falls on a holiday).

The "roll over" of the United States Treasury debt in the form of bills permits some flexibility because a new issue may be larger or smaller than the issue retired. The volume of bills has not varied greatly; but when the amount of a new issue is changed, it is usually upward. In 1952, the outstanding issues varied from $1.1 billion to $1.4 billion, and currently each issue is $1.6 billion (the total being $20.8 billion). Apparently, this type of weekly financing is to continue indefinitely.

The Federal Reserve banks, as fiscal agents of the government, handle the details of financing with Treasury bills. Offers to buy are submitted by the public, chiefly commercial banks, every Monday for bills to be paid for on Thursday (the same day that the Treasury must pay for maturing bills). While this refinancing is in process, the Treasury prepares the next week's issue with the amount and date (the next Thursday) announced on Thursday, with the repetition of the invitation to submit tenders for a specified amount of such bills on or before two o'clock the following Monday. On Monday night, the Treasury determines the extent to which tenders are accepted and releases the details for publication the next morning—total bills applied for, total accepted, average price, and high and low bids accepted (different buyers pay different prices). The Treasury's policy is to accept all bids up to $200,000 at the average price of accepted bids from large investors. This is most helpful to country banks and other small investors, who otherwise might be squeezed out of the market by the higher bids of large investors. After distribution, Treasury bills may be bought and sold in the open market.

The yield rate on Treasury bills fluctuates widely, having been as low as ½ of 1 per cent and over 3 per cent during the last two years. The use of Treasury bills permits the government to finance inexpensively, and they are purchased by commercial banks and others because they are the most liquid of available credit instruments.

Certificates of Indebtedness. Certificates of indebtedness are promises to pay which are customarily issued at par by the United States Treasury. Usually their maturity is one year or less, and the entire interest is payable at maturity. The interest rates on certificates of indebtedness reflect the market rates at the time of issuance but later the certificates may sell above or below par.

Treasury Notes. United States Treasury notes are promises to pay having maturities of from one to five years at the time of issue. Customarily, they are issued at par with provisions to pay interest semiannually (except when the last interest payment date is close to the maturity date, in which case it is payable at maturity as in the case of certificates of indebtedness). The sixteen issues outstanding at the present time total about $35.1 billion, and individual issues vary from $22,000,000 to more than $12 billion. The use of Treasury notes permits financing in the market wherein intermediate term obligations are preferred, and this market is broader than that for short-term obligations.

Treasury Bonds. United States Treasury bonds are similar to Treasury notes except that their maturities are in excess of five years at the time of issue. The longest term bond issued in recent years (1955) was one having a maturity of forty years. Treasury bonds are issued with a first optional call date which means that the Treasury may elect to pay off the issue at par (in which case, it would make the announcement one quarter in advance). This privilege may then be exercised on any interest payment date thereafter until the final maturity date. The Treasury usually uses the call privilege if it is advantageous to do so; therefore, the best rule to follow in estimating the maturity date is to use the first optional call date if the bond is selling at or above 100 (par) and the maturity date if it is selling below 100. The 25 bond issues outstanding at the present time total about $82 billion.

Other United States Obligations. Many government securities are issued under special conditions which limit their marketability; these include the various classes of savings bonds, tax and savings bills, notes and certificates, special issues sold to government agencies and trust funds, and one bond issue which is not marketable but which is convertible into short-term obligations which are negotiable. When the investments of commercial banks are considered, marketable issues are their chief interest; but commercial banks may buy other types of government securities in relatively small amounts for their customers and for trust and pension funds which they manage.

Maturity Classification. Today, commercial banks hold government securities in their investment portfolios primarily to meet secondary reserve needs. Of their current investments in marketable United States government obligations amounting to $51 billion, about 12 per cent mature in less than one year, more than 50 per cent mature in less than five years, and more than 90 per cent mature in less than ten years. Banks have increased their investments in obligations of states and their subdivisions chiefly because of tax benefits (see below); but the maturities of these investments have been limited for the most part to those of five or six years. Many banks still hold long-term bonds because their sale would entail substantial losses. The decreasing emphasis by commercial banks on the purchase of government bonds for income is linked to the rising loan demand but this trend may be reversed overnight. However, banks will continue to hold short-term United States government securities to meet their secondary reserve needs; and this will be the case particularly for smaller banks.

Rights Value of Government Securities. Usually those holding government securities, except Treasury bills, are permitted to exchange obligations at maturity for new obligations of a like issue because most government issues outstanding are refunded (not paid off with tax receipts). The interest rate and other provisions of the new issue may be made so attractive that the right to exchange maturing obligations will be valuable. When this happens, the old issue may be selling at a premium just before the exchange date becomes effective. Thus, the maturing issue is said to have a "rights" or option value as indicated by the premium price even though the exchange for the new issue is on a par-for-par basis.

MUNICIPAL AND OTHER SECURITIES

Obligations of States and Their Subdivisions. Second in importance to United States government securities among the investments of commercial banks are obligations of states and their political subdivision. While the amount of banks' investments in such issues is small compared to their holdings of federal issues, it has shown a steady growth since 1946. This growth reflects not only the increase in debt financing by these governments but also the attractiveness of these issues to investors due to their tax-exemption quality.

Banks must compete with wealthy individuals and other investors for municipal securities; and, as a result, the tax-exemption quality is reflected in their prices. Securities issued by school and improvement districts, towns, cities, and counties are often purchased by local banks motivated by the desire to support their communities. This may mean that the local bank is duplicating its loan portfolio in its investment account and thereby depriving itself of geographical diversification for its earning assets.

Other Bonds, Notes, and Debentures. Other bonds, notes, and debentures are promises to pay other than those of the federal, state or local governments. These obligations may include those of business corporations, foreign governments, schools, churches, hospitals, and other nonprofit organizations. In general, all such obligations are eligible for bank investment provided they are marketable and have investment qualities. Although the terminology is not standardized, bonds usually are long-term secured promises to pay that are bought and sold in the open market, notes are similar to bonds except for shorter maturities, and debentures are unsecured long-term promises to pay.

Corporate Stock. Investment by commercial banks in stock is generally prohibited, but commercial banks do own corporate stock. Among the special situations that account for stock ownership by commercial banks are:

(1) Member banks are required to purchase stock of their Federal Reserve banks in an amount equal to 3 per cent of their capital stock and surplus. (Dividends of 6 per cent are paid on such stock; and dividends are cumulative.) The stock is not transferable; and, if a member bank is liquidated or withdraws from membership, the stock held by the bank is canceled.

(2) Banks are usually permitted to own stock in a corporation organized to own the building in which the bank is located; but, without the prior approval of the Comptroller of the Currency, a national bank may not invest in the stock or obligations of such a corporation or make loans thereto in amount in excess of the bank's capital stock. The creation of a subsidiary corporation to hold title to a bank's building limits the liability of the parent bank to its investment (which means that creditors may not seize the general assets of the bank in case of default on the obligations of the subsidiary corporation).

(3) Banks may own stock in a safe-deposit company which it has organized. The reasons for incorporating this business are the same as those which lead a bank to organize a real estate company to own its bank building—to limit the risks assumed by the bank because a bank never knows when the court may hold it liable for some claim of a

renter of a safe deposit box. The amount that a national bank may invest in the stock of a safe-deposit company is limited to 15 per cent of its capital stock and surplus.

(4) If a national bank has a capital and surplus of $1,000,000, it may receive permission of the Board of Governors of the Federal Reserve System to invest no more than 10 per cent of its capital stock in a corporation or corporations formed under state or national laws to engage in foreign banking or other financial transactions.

(5) All banks may hold corporate stock for a "reasonable" time which has come into their possession as the result of default on loans. Without this privilege, banks would be unable to protect themselves when stock has been pledged as collateral for bank loans which are in default.

(6) Some state laws permit state-chartered banks to own special types of corporate stock (such as savings and loan association shares in Texas) or limited amounts of preferred stock of some companies.

INVESTMENT DEPARTMENT AND REGULATION OF INVESTMENTS

In addition to investing its own funds, a bank is responsible for investing trust and pension funds under its control. As agents, banks may purchase bonds, stocks, and other securities for their customers. Commercial banks may participate in underwriting obligations issued by state governments and their political subdivisions and by the International Bank for Reconstruction and Development (World Bank). The metropolitan banks also give investment advice to their correspondents and their other customers.

A large bank usually has an investment department which gathers, records, and analyzes data pertaining to investment securities and makes this information available to the officers and others. Periodically, it reviews the securities in trust funds and in the bank's own portfolio. (Usually the trust department handles its own investments.) Although a small bank may not have a separate investment department, one or more of its officers will be responsible for the work pertaining to the bank's investments. A bank may limit its investments to United States government obligations and a few others, in which case its investment analysis work would be small compared to its credit analysis work.

The ultimate responsibility for administering the investment program of a commercial bank lies with the bank's board of directors. The objectives of an investment program should be (1) to assure the safety of the bank's funds, (2) to balance the loan and investment program with the nature of deposit liabilities and the bank's capital structure, and (3) to secure income for the bank. After an investment program has been formulated, it should be written up in a form that will permit some discretionary action on the part of the chief investment officer.

A commercial bank's written investment program will cover items such as the goal of the program, the amount of securities to be acquired for secondary reserve needs, and the use of other funds remaining after primary reserve requirements and loan demands have been met. A written program will also state the principles and practices of management of investments as to quality and diversification (as to maturity, issuer and geographical location), and the policies as to trading (buying and selling for profit) and accounting for profits and losses resulting from the portfolio as a whole. (Are they to be regarded as regular income and expenses, or will the gains and losses be credited to or charged against a special valuation reserve account in full or up to a certain amount?) Finally, provisions should be made for administering the investment portfolio and its periodic review by the board of directors. Commercial banks' investments must also meet the standards set by regulatory agencies.

Regulation of Commercial Banks' Investments. Banks may invest in securities in two categories—regulated and nonregulated. In the Banking Act of 1933, Congress authorized member banks to purchase "marketable obligations evidencing indebtedness" in the form of "bonds, notes, and/or debentures," which are "commonly known as investment securities." In other acts of Congress, certain securities are automatically classified as investments and not subject to regulation. They include: (1) obligations of the United States government, including those guaranteed as to principal and interest; (2) general obligations of states and their political subdivisions; and (3) obligations of certain public and semipublic banks and agencies.[1]

In the Banking Act of 1935 the Comptroller of the Currency was authorized to define further the term "investment securities." His regulation of July 1, 1938, defines "marketable" to mean that, under ordinary circumstances, the security in question is salable at a fair value and with reasonable promptness. This, in turn, depends on public distribution and the conditions and terms of the issue that would assure a fair value. The security must be one in which in-

[1] In this category of securities, automatically classified as investments, are also included: (1) federal land bank bonds; (2) federal intermediate credit bank debentures; (3) federal Home Loan Bank bonds and debentures; (4) notes, bonds, debentures, and other such obligations of National Mortgage Associations; and (5) certain mortgages and debentures resulting from financing low-cost housing under Sections 204 (*d*) and 207 of the National Housing Act.

vestment qualities predominate; and, if there is any doubt, the banker may check the ratings in two or more investment rating manuals. (The security must be rated within the four top classes.) These findings are not final because the responsibility for judicious investing rests with the bank's directors.

Banks may hold securities which do not qualify as investments if they had so qualified at the time of acquisition. They may also hold substandard stocks and bonds acquired in good faith—through foreclosure on collateral, by way of compromise of a doubtful claim, and/or to avert an apprehended loss on a debt previously contracted. Real estate mortgages are thought of as investments but banks classify them as loans.

BANK SUPERVISION IN THE UNITED STATES

Bank Supervision. The chief purpose of bank supervision is to obtain and maintain sound banks. Supervisory officials stress the financial condition and management of individual banks, and this means that monetary aspects of banking may be secondary to them. During the early and middle 1930's, there was an apparent conflict between examining policies and general credit policies. While the national policy was one of "easy credit," supervisory officials were holding to the principle that participation of banks in lending and investing must be under conditions that would insure the safety of each bank.

The first task of the supervisory officials is to see that only qualified individuals are allowed to organize banks, and then only when their banks are capitalized adequately and located where there is an economic need not met by existing banks. In carrying on this activity, regulatory agencies have been handicapped by the American "free-banking" philosophy and by the predominance of the small unit banks in the banking system; but, in spite of these handicaps, considerable progress has been achieved in keeping down the number of inadequately financed and poorly managed banks.

The second task of supervisory officials is to see that banks are operated according to the law and administrative regulations under the law. The banking code usually is complex and detailed because of the ease with which irresponsible groups may gain control over banks, because of the American "genius for bankruptcy," and because of the American tendency to correct (or try to correct) abuses by legislation. But just because a bank is being operated legally, it does not follow that it is being operated wisely. This is demonstrated by the fact that, while closures of banks for illegal operations have been few, closures for insolvency have been many.

The third task of supervisory officials is to see that banks are sound. These officials receive reports on banks' conditions, which are more complete and more informative than those given to the general public. They are required to audit or examine banks periodically and may make special examinations as may seem necessary. This procedure gives the supervisory authorities firsthand information on the legality of the banks' transactions and an opportunity to verify the existence of assets and to appraise the value of assets which the banks claim to possess. It permits the examiners to review the ability of officers of banks in carrying out previous suggestions and in operating their banks successfully.

The chief aim of bank supervision is normally identical with that of good management; but, at a particular time, management may be enmeshed in a local situation wherein potentially harmful practices are being followed. These practices may result from over-emphasis on dividends and earnings, from "carrying" some favored customer because of his position on the board of directors, and from other factors. Bank examiners and supervisory agencies raise practical questions as to the gathering of credit information on borrowers; collection practices; accounting reserves; sources of earnings; and adequacy of capital, fidelity insurance, and protective equipment.

Also, banks must secure the prior approval of supervisory authorities before changing their capitalization, opening or closing branches, and adding trust-banking functions. Care must be taken to follow the rules in regard to computation and maintenance of required reserves, computation of deposits on which insurance is paid semiannually, and the preparation of cash and noncash items for collection through the Federal Reserve System. Banks must abide by the restrictions in effect on lending and investing. However, not all the restrictions placed on banks are of a character that places the soundness of banks foremost, since some are of a monetary nature. Among these are (or have been) the high primary-reserve requirements and the high margin requirements on loans made for the purpose of purchasing and carrying stocks bought and sold on national exchanges, installment loans to consumers, and those made with real estate pledged as security.

Although bank supervisory agencies do not relish the responsibility, the final task which they must perform is to close any bank that continues to violate the law and to reorganize or close others whose capital has been impaired.

General Aspects of Supervisory Policies. Those who favor the use of bank examinations as a credit-control device stress the importance of raising banking standards during boom periods and lowering them during depressions. This approach recognizes that a given policy may be good for individual banks but harmful for the banking system as a whole. During a downswing in business, if individual banks call loans and liquidate investments to strengthen their own positions, it may accelerate the decline in business. To the extent that bank examiners urge banks to call substandard loans and sell substandard bonds, bank supervision may contribute to deflationary developments. The psychological effect of examiners' reports on bank management may be such as to discourage lending and investing.

Similarly, during an upswing in business, an individual bank may make loans and investments (which from the viewpoint of the individual bank are sound) that will accelerate the upswing in business. The "pat on the back" which examiners may give to a banker for operating such a "sound" bank may have an equally undesirable effect upon the bank's investing, lending, dividend, salary, and other policies. In general, bank supervisory leaders are alert to the dangers associated with the credit-expansion policies of banks and have been trying to check lending and investing by persuasion and by raising loans and investment standards. In addition, they have emphasized the need for retention of earnings to build up accounting reserves and other capital accounts as shock absorbers, the writing-down of real estate values, and the curtailment of "unproductive" loans.

The attitude of supervisory officials may have an important bearing upon the solvency of a bank. Since 1938 bank examiners have emphasized "normal value" rather than "market value" in appraising banks' loans and investments. Under the rules now in effect, this means that if a government bond is purchased at $100 (or more), it may be carried at that figure even though the market price falls to $96 (as happened in recent years). Other investments are appraised at market value; but banks' investments in this category are small compared to investments in government securities and others of "standard" quality, as noted in the preceding chapter. In the future, modern appraisal practices may mean that more banks, if not better banks, will be in operation; but even a functioning, "temporarily insolvent" bank is better than no bank.

Supervisory Agencies. For many years, governments have regulated and supervised banks in the United States; but questions remaining unanswered are: (1) should all commercial banks be placed under federal supervision and (2) which of the federal agencies should be dominant in supervision and regulation of commercial banks? Most students of the problem agree that at least those banks handling checking accounts should be supervised by the federal government. The power to coin money and to regulate its value is vested in Congress by the Constitution; therefore, since commercial banks create and destroy deposits, they should be supervised by the federal government. The banking business is national in scope and so lends itself best to federal control and supervision. Finally, banking disturbances are of national importance and can be dealt with most effectively by national action.

National control could be obtained by requiring all commercial banks (1) to secure national charters, which would make them members of the National Banking System, the Federal Reserve System, and the Federal Deposit Insurance System; (2) to insure their deposits with the Federal Deposit Insurance Corporation; or (3) to join the Federal Reserve System which also would force them to be members of the Federal Deposit Insurance Corporation. The second plan would permit banks to select or reject membership in the Federal Reserve System, and the third plan would permit banks to select either state or national charters.

1. Although the adoption of no one of these plans would clarify all the issues as to supervision and examination, the first plan (that of requiring national charters) would be the simplest procedure. It would have the advantage of making the office of the Comptroller of the Currency responsible for commercial bank supervision and examination. At present, it is responsible for the examination of more banking assets (in national banks) than the other two federal agencies which must share their examining and supervisory function with state authorities. Even under the plan requiring all commercial banks to have national charters, the Federal Deposit Insurance Corporation would be responsible for supervision and examination of insured noncommercial banks; and the Federal Reserve authorities still would have certain regulatory powers.

2. In order to avoid raising too many political issues and still place responsibility for examinations in the hands of a single agency, it has been suggested that the Federal Deposit Insurance Corporation be made solely responsible for examining and supervising all insured

banks. At the present time, it examines nonmember insured state banks periodically and makes special examinations of other banks. Through its insurance of deposits, the Federal Deposit Insurance Corporation is in contact with (1) over 96 per cent of the nation's commercial banks, holding over 99 per cent of all commercial-banks' deposits; and (2) almost 50 per cent of the mutual savings banks, holding almost 75 per cent of mutual savings-banks' deposits.

3. In its recommendations for the reorganization of the executive branch of the government, the "Hoover Commission" favored placing supervision and examination responsibilities under the control of the Board of Governors of the Federal Reserve System. This recommendation recognized not only the need for eliminating interagency friction but also the importance of avoiding examination policies that might intensify deflation or inflation. It was felt that this might best be avoided by centralizing responsibility for examinations with the Federal Reserve System, whereby credit policies and examining policies would be formulated by the same agency. If examining policy is to be used as a device of credit control, there is considerable justification for this proposal; but, if the primary function of bank supervision is to reassure depositors of the soundness of their banks, the examining and credit control functions should not be combined.

At present the Federal Deposit Insurance Corporation and the office of the Comptroller of the Currency have regional offices duplicating those of the Federal Reserve System. If either the Corporation or the Comptroller were to continue as the supervisory agency, this duplication would continue. By selecting the Federal Reserve System, duplication could be avoided and some savings would result. The Corporation could continue as the insurance and liquidation agency, and the supervisory and examining personnel of the Comptroller's office and the Corporation could be transferred to the Federal Reserve System.

SUMMARY

The concept of investing carries with it the idea of committing or laying out money for the purpose of obtaining an income or profit. Insofar as banks are concerned, investments represent earning assets, which must be safe to insure the bank's solvency and marketable to insure its liquidity. Federal government obligations represent a source of investments that is both safe and liquid, because among these issues may be found securities of any desired maturity and their liquidity has been assured by liberalization of Federal Reserve policy.

The classes of government obligations which may be owned by commercial banks include Treasury bills, certificates of indebtedness, Treasury notes, and Treasury bonds. Commercial banks may also invest in municipal securities—those issued by states and their political subdivisions; but because of their tax exemption quality such securities are in great demand and this is reflected in their price. The category "other securities" is of minor importance as an outlet for commercial banks' funds, first because of the problem of quality of such securities and second because the corporate bond market is now dominated by insurance companies and other institutional investors.

The size of a bank's investment department will depend, for the most part, on the size of the bank; but in all cases, the bank's board of directors is responsible for formulating and administering the bank's investment program. In addition to fulfilling the bank's needs for earning assets, which will depend on its size, the nature of its deposit liabilities, and its capital structure, a bank's investments must meet the standards set by regulatory agencies.

In most foreign countries, central banks have been nationalized; and, in many countries, commercial banking systems have also been nationalized. But, in the United States, the system wherein commercial banks operate as private institutions and Federal Reserve banks are privately owned has been retained. However, American banks are subject to considerable supervision and regulation. Responsibility for these functions is shared by states and the federal government. The three federal agencies among whom the supervisory and regulatory functions are divided are: (1) the Comptroller of the Currency, (2) the Federal Reserve System, and (3) the Federal Deposit Insurance Corporation.

QUESTIONS AND PROBLEMS

1. From a banker's viewpoint, what is the difference between a loan and an investment?
2. Identify the kinds of near money.
3. "Low interest rates have lessened the penalty for keeping funds idle." Explain.
4. How has the expansion in the federal debt contributed to liquidity?
5. What is meant by the "rights value" of government securities?
6. (a) Explain the popularity of federal government securities among

the investments of commercial banks; (b) What are the four types of government securities that bankers buy? (c) Are there any special advantages in holding "municipals"?

7. Explain the fact that corporate bonds comprise only four per cent of the investment portfolios of commercial banks.

8. (a) What should be the objectives of any bank's investment program? (b) What specific items should be included in the written investment program?

9. What provisions have been made for the regulation of commercial banks' investments? What standards have been set for banks' investments? What is meant by "regulated" and "nonregulated" investments?

10. Under what conditions are national banks permitted to own stock?

11. Why is the credit department of a commercial bank usually much larger than the investment department?

12. Give the arguments in favor of and opposed to placing the responsibility for supervision of commercial banks with the Board of Governors of the Federal Reserve System.

13. Analyze the following statement: "To attempt to use bank examinations for implementation of monetary policy would destroy the usefulness of bank examining procedures as a method of preventing the accumulation by banks of unsound or undesirable assets. Use of varying standards in evaluating assets would destroy the confidence of bankers and of officials of the Corporation in the results of bank examinations." (Reply of Federal Deposit Insurance Corporation in Joint Committee on the Economic Report, *Monetary Policy and the Management of the Public Debt* [Washington, D.C.: U.S. Government Printing Office, 1952], p. 953.)

Chapter	FOREIGN EXCHANGE AND
XVII	FINANCING FOREIGN
	TRANSACTIONS

AMONG the services provided by commercial banks are those arising out of foreign transactions. Businessmen and individuals who trade, travel, or make investments in foreign countries are dependent in part on the facilities supplied by commercial banks. Although the current amount of short-term credit lent to foreigners is below the average amounts outstanding during the 1920's, there has been some expansion in the volume of foreign trade financing by American banks since 1953. This growth in foreign financing is contributing to a more effective international money market. This chapter deals with the problems of foreign exchange from the viewpoint of American businessmen and others in the United States. International monetary principles and financial organizations are dealt with in Chapters XXV and XXVI.

FOREIGN EXCHANGE AND FOREIGN EXCHANGE INSTRUMENTS

Meaning of Foreign Exchange. When Americans make purchases or travel abroad, they need foreign exchange—money of foreign countries; and when foreigners make purchases or travel in the United States, they need dollar exchange, United States money. American commercial banks act as intermediaries for both groups— buying and selling money of foreign countries—which is usually in the form of demand deposits in banks. Title to bank deposits used as money in international transactions is transferred to a limited extent by personal checks but, more commonly, by bank drafts, cable transfers, and mail transfers.

Wire and Cable Transfers. A cable transfer is an order cabled, telephoned, or radioed by one party (usually a bank) to another party abroad (usually a bank located near the recipient of the funds) instructing him to pay a specified sum of money to the party named in the order (beneficiary). This is similar to wire transfers made in the United States by banks for their customers over the wire service of the Federal Reserve System or by an individual to a second individual or business firm through the facilities of Western Union. For illustration, a father in New York may arrange to have Western Union pay his son in Austin, Texas, a specified amount of money (assume $100) by paying for a telegram, fees, and amount of the wire transfer ($100). After the wire is sent, the transaction will be completed as soon as the son calls at the local Western Union office for his money (paid out of balances on hand).

Cable transfers are most commonly sent by one banker to another as principal, with the cable transfer company as agent; but the cable company may also act as principal in such transactions (as Western Union does in domestic transactions). Cable transfers are sent in code; and, to avoid fraud, key words are used for identification at the receiving end. The cost of sending a cable order is the price of the foreign money as quoted at the cable rate of exchange, plus the cost of the cablegram. For example, the cost of transferring £10 to London would be $31.70, assuming the cost of the cable to be $3.60 and the cable rate of exchange to be $2.81 for the English pound.

When transfers are made in terms of the United States dollar, as they sometimes are because of the strong position of the dollar in international exchange, instructions may be given to the paying bank or agent to make payment to the beneficiary for the equivalent in local currency at the "rate of the day," or to hold and wait for conversion instructions from the beneficiary. If payment is to be made in local currency, the equivalent would be found by dividing the number of dollars by the rate of exchange used in conversion (assume $2.81, if in English pounds). Although the time needed to transfer an order by cable is a matter of minutes, such transfers from the United States to Europe are usually completed the following day because of the difference in time.

Mail Transfers. A mail transfer is similar to a cable transfer in all respects except that the instructions are sent by mail rather than by cable, wire, or radio. The purpose in using a mail transfer rather than a cable transfer is to avoid the cost of the cablegram, which is paid by the buyer of the foreign exchange. Both cable and mail transfers are essentially cash transactions; and since an air mail letter can be delivered within one day, mail transfers are almost as fast as wire or cable transfers. The buyer of a cable, wire, or mail transfer receives no credit instrument but merely a confirmation of the transaction.

Settlement for Transfers. At one time, American banks kept large deposit accounts in foreign banks for use in paying funds to beneficiaries of mail and cable transfers; but, during periods of international financial uncertainty, fluctuating exchange rates, and controlled exchanges, American banks avoid keeping large balances with their foreign correspondent banks. On the other hand, foreign banks are glad to have dollar credits added to their accounts with American banks in exchange for the money paid to beneficiaries of mail and cable transfers because the dollar is always in demand and commands a high price in free or nonregulated markets. So, a popular modern practice for the settlement of a cable or mail transfer is for the foreign bank to accept credit to its account in its correspondent bank (assume in New York) in settlement for funds paid to the beneficiary of transfer which originated with its American correspondent bank. However, there are limits to the use of this method of settlement because foreign exchange authorities generally limit the size of deposits kept in foreign banks.

Banks that sell cable and mail transfers also buy similar foreign exchange transfers; and, by matching purchases and sales, they are able to handle a large number of orders with only a small volume of funds. Most banks prefer to have the aggregate of sales and purchases matched at the end of each business day. This same principle is applied to other types of foreign exchange transactions including purchase and sale of bank drafts, time bills, and forward exchange (see below).

Classes of Bank Drafts. Bills of exchange include chiefly trade and bank drafts. Trade drafts are those drawn on names other than banks and other financial institutions; and bank drafts are drawn on banks or other financial institutions. Trade and bank drafts are credit instruments which are payable either on demand or after the elapse of a definite period of time. In the latter case, there are two ways of figuring the time the draft is to run: (1) from the day the draft is drawn, and (2) from the day the draft is accepted.

Sight Drafts. Bank drafts are the most popular of the instruments used in meeting obligations abroad. These written orders are negotiable and have the same advantages in making payments in foreign trade as do checks in domestic trade. Generally, they are a more tangible and convenient means of payment than cable or mail transfers because they may be sent to any address designated by the creditor. The buyer of a sight draft must arrange for its purchase far enough in advance for it to reach the payee before his obligation comes due. To an American a sight draft may

seem strange because the amount is usually stated in foreign currency, the name of the bank is unfamiliar, and it may be
written in a foreign language.

Time Drafts.   A time draft is a written order by one party
on a second party to pay a specified sum of money to a third
party or his order on a specified future or determinable date. Time
drafts are also known as long bills or long exchange; and they may
be drawn either on a "date" or "sight" basis. Thus a 30-day date
draft would be payable 30 days after being drawn, but a 30-day
sight draft would be payable 30 days after having been presented
for acceptance. Therefore, the more common 30-, 60-, 90-, and
120-day sight drafts run from origin for a longer period of time
than similar date drafts (including mail transmission and the time
required to present a sight draft for acceptance plus the stated time
period). Since date bills "start running immediately," they are preferred by creditors; and, for the same reason, they are less popular
with debtors.

Exchange Rates.   The date of payment makes a difference in
prices (exchange rates) quoted for all types of exchange. The prices
for cable and mail transfers are the highest because settlement will
be made within hours or days. Sight and demand drafts are usually
clearinghouse items that take a day or two longer to collect than do
mail transfers, therefore the prices for them are somewhat lower;
and the prices of time drafts decline as their maturities lengthen.

The spread between rates of exchange for time and demand
drafts depends on what bankers' balances earn in the market wherein
the drafts are paid (the higher the interest rate, the greater is the
spread between prices quoted). In quoting the rate for cable exchange, the cost of transmission is not included because this item is
such a variable one that even the banker who sends it may not
know the exact price until transmission time (a night letter would
be cheapest).

Special Forms of Foreign Exchange.   In addition to the kinds
of foreign exchange most commonly provided by commercial banks,
other kinds are provided by institutions in the foreign exchange
market. These include the United States Post Office and the American Express Company, which provide postal and express money
orders.

Postal money orders may be expressed in terms of dollars or
in terms of certain foreign monetary units. In most cases the orders
are expressed in terms of the American dollar, which means that

the sender is not sure of the amount of foreign money that is being sent because the order in dollars involves a conversion rate that is unknown until the order is cashed. In making transfers to Great Britain, France, and certain other countries, "foreign currency orders" may be purchased at the conversion price for these countries. In a few cases the buyer sends the order directly to the payee; but, in most cases, the funds are transmitted between postal authorities. The sender receives a receipt, and the local post office sends the order to one of the money order exchange offices. The latter sends an advice (containing a list of all such orders with complete information as to payers, payees, and addresses of payees) to the foreign post office. Then the foreign post office notifies the payees where to call for their money. The United States usually has an adverse balance on postal money orders which is settled each week through banking channels.

In 1882 the American Express Company introduced a satisfactory method of making small payments at home and in foreign countries in the form of an express money order. Express money orders are issued through the offices of the company, banks, and other agents of the company. Orders may be cashed at banks and hotels as well as at the offices of the American Express Company. The company maintains offices in principal cities in this country and in certain foreign countries and has representatives or correspondents in other cities. Now, many metropolitan banks are selling their own money orders which are cheaper to service than bank drafts (cost analysis figures indicate that the cost of such bank money orders is about one half that of bank drafts).

Banks also offer a service, known as bank post-remittance, which assures the buyer that a definite amount of foreign money will be placed in the hands of the payee. The buyer pays all fees, and the bank's foreign branch or correspondent nearest the payee will deliver the appropriate sum in the payee's own currency. This device is popular in remitting to those abroad who have had no experience with banks and who, therefore, might not know what to do with a money order or bank draft. Bank drafts and other orders to pay are also originated by banks in order to meet their own obligations abroad. Many of the instruments appearing in foreign exchange are originated under letters of credit and/or the terms under which purchases or sales are financed. A seller of goods may draw directly on the buyer or his bank, giving rise to a trade or banker's bill of exchange. Travelers may obtain travelers' letters of credit which permit them to originate drafts and cash them in person at the current rate of exchange of the country wherein they are presented (see below).

FINANCING FOREIGN TRADE

Financing Exports. In financing trade the terms of sale are a matter of prior arrangement between buyers and sellers; and these terms depend on custom, credit standing of the buyer, exchange-control conditions, and whether the customer is old or new. Sales of American goods abroad (exports) are often made on the basis of drafts drawn by the American seller on the foreign buyer. Drafts may be drawn in dollars or foreign currency and may be either demand or time. Drafts are given to banks for collection and are usually accompanied by shipping and other documents with collection instructions. When payment is made abroad, the foreign bank correspondent remits the proceeds to the exporter's bank which, in turn, makes them available to the exporter. (Note the dotted line in the upper half of Chart 8 which graphically illustrates the steps followed in handling a foreign trade draft.)

Drafts may be handled by the exporter's bank in several ways including: (1) a discount basis whereby the exporter receives immediate credit from his bank minus the discount; (2) a cash advance or liquidation basis whereby, under a credit arrangement, the exporter receives a cash advance for all or a percentage of the amount from his bank; (3) a note basis whereby the exporter pledges the collection items as security for a loan made by his bank; or (4) an acceptance basis whereby one or more collection items are pledged as security for a time draft drawn on the collecting bank, which is accepted by the latter and then sold by the exporter in the bankers' acceptance market. This last method of financing is the one assumed in Chart 8.

By following the solid line at the bottom of Chart 8, it can be seen how the second draft, after acceptance by the bank on which it is drawn, was sold in the acceptance or bill market for cash. Before it matures, the foreign buyer will have remitted cash in payment for the trade bill and funds will be deposited in the exporter's bank and used to pay and cancel the bankers' acceptance. Any balance left after fees and commissions are deducted is paid to the American exporter.

Since the time period necessary for collecting and securing a remittance in dollar exchange for a foreign bill of exchange may

CHART 8

FINANCING AN EXPORT TRANSACTION BY BANKERS' ACCEPTANCES

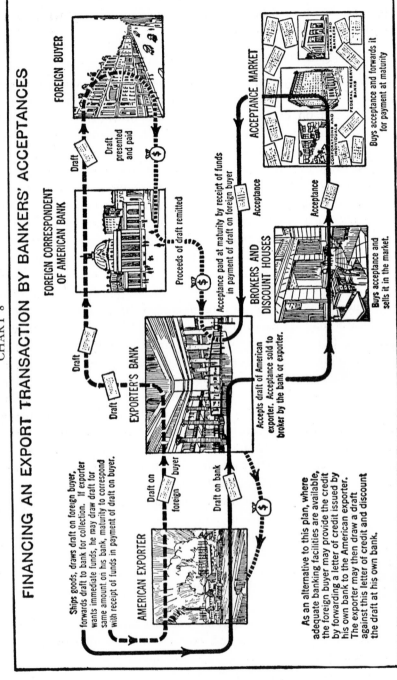

be months, the use of the second draft permits the exporter to have cash immediately at the low rate of interest (discount) that customarily prevails in the acceptance or commercial bill market. His bank charges a fee for accepting and usually there will be no refund of interest if the bill is paid in advance; therefore, the exporter may find the cost of financing about the same if he merely pledges the receipts from the trade bill as security for a loan from his bank.

An alternative to the use of a trade bill in financing an export of goods is to finance under provisions of a letter of credit issued by the buyer's bank. Under some circumstances, the American seller may insist that the letter of credit be issued by an American bank, or at least that the terms be guaranteed or confirmed by an American bank; and he may also insist that payment be in dollars which would mean that the buyer would assume the risk of exchange. (If the dollar exchange rate increases, the buyer would lose; but if it decreases, he would make a profit.) Since there is a well-developed foreign exchange market in New York for some foreign currencies, the foreign buyer may arrange for a futures contract in this market to provide him with the required number of dollars (see below).

The American exporter may lose sales by insisting on financing terms that are too burdensome; and, actually, many sales are made in international trade on the same terms as those used in the United States where the open-book account system prevails (as to Canadians, West Indians, Mexicans, and others). Many shipments abroad are made to branch offices and subsidiaries of American business firms wherein only accounting is involved, and other shipments are made on consignment to brokers and other specialists. At the other extreme are shipments which are made only after prepayment in whole or part for the goods shipped.

In selling to buyers in the Orient, shipments are sometimes made against an "authority to purchase." In this case, the foreign buyer makes arrangements for a bank in the United States to buy a draft drawn on him. Then, the American exporter draws the trade draft, attaches the shipping and other documents, and presents the trade draft through banking channels to the bank that issued the authority to purchase for payment. Although trade bills drawn on well-known names are usually discounted readily at banks, the time period may be unduly long or so uncertain as to impair their marketability (which accounts for the use of the authority to purchase in trade with the Far East).

Perhaps it is well to note here that a large percentage of American exports during and since World War II has been financed without the use of foreign exchange. Under provisions of military and economic grants and loans by the United States government, dollars have been made available to foreign governments so that they could buy goods in the United States. Abroad, the nonmilitary goods are sold by the foreign governments to their own citizens and some of the funds received are applied to meet the cost of goods and services sold to American military and other personnel abroad.

Financing Imports. All of the procedures used in financing exports may also be used in financing imports. Because of custom and the availability of expert services, most imports by Americans are financed under terms of letters of credit issued by American banks. To further clarify the use of letters of credit and bankers' acceptances, let us assume that a store in New York is buying cloth from a manufacturer in London, England. The letter of credit is issued by a New York bank, and it contains the following terms: (1) the time of the draft to be drawn is thirty days; (2) the expiration date of the terms is June 10, 1957; (3) the amount is to be approximately $10,000; and (4) the documents to be provided by the seller of the goods must include a commercial invoice, an ocean bill of lading, an insurance certificate, and a consular invoice.

A copy of the letter of credit[1] will be mailed to the seller in London; or, under certain circumstances, the terms may be cabled by the bank to its correspondent in London, and this correspondent will notify the seller in writing. On receipt, the letter of credit is examined by the seller; and, finding the terms in agreement with the sales contract, he proceeds to prepare the goods for shipment. He makes out a commercial invoice, secures a consular invoice from the American consul in London, insures the shipment with a marine insurance company, and obtains a bill of lading from the steamship company when he delivers the merchandise.[2] These and any other minor documents that may be necessary are then taken to the seller's bank, where a draft equal to the selling price of the goods is drawn, for example, $10,000.

---

[1] One copy of the letter of credit is retained in the files of the issuing bank, and a nonnegotiable copy is furnished the customer for his own record. In addition to the regular letter of credit, there is a revolving form—a circular letter of credit. For illustration, under a circular letter of credit, drafts may be drawn in amounts up to $x per month for a period of y months. It may be cumulative or noncumulative; that is, drafts are not drawn for the full $x in one month, they may or may not be drawn in excess of the amount at a later period.

[2] Other documents that may be required are a certificate or statement of origin, a certificate of quality and a weight certificate.

The dollar credit usually is sold to the seller's bank, and so the draft will be drawn in favor of the exporter's bank. Since the draft will have a term of thirty days after acceptance, and it may take the draft a week to be received in New York by mail, the amount paid the seller may be $9,975 (assuming a one fourth of 1 per cent discount on the face amount). The draft, with documents attached, will be sent by mail to a New York bank acting as correspondent for the London bank. When the draft and accompanying documents reach New York, they will be sent to the bank that issued the original letter of credit.

The bank issuing the letter of credit will check the documents to ascertain if the terms have been complied with. If the documents are correct, the bank will stamp the draft "accepted" and then date and sign it. (In case of a sight draft, the bank will pay it and immediately debit the account of the customer.) The accepting bank will retain the documentary set and then give it to the New York department store against a trust receipt. The department store will use the bill of lading to obtain possession of the goods as soon as they arrive.

On or before the maturity of the bankers' acceptance, the department store will pay the bank, which will remit or otherwise settle for the bankers' acceptance. The disposal of the bankers' acceptance in the interim between acceptance and payment depends upon instructions. Thus, the use of a letter of credit not only involves the guaranty of the bank but also permits the creation of a credit instrument that can be sold at a small discount in the "bill" market.

In effect, a bankers' acceptance is a predated certified check which permits the exporter to receive payment without waiting weeks or months for the goods to reach the importer and for remittance by the latter by mail or cable (depending on the terms for payment). The checklike quality is given a bankers' acceptance when the accepting bank places its credit behind this credit instrument by endorsing it on its face (acceptance), which makes the bank primarily responsible for it. The accepting bank charges the importer for this service at a rate which is most commonly 1½ per cent on an annual basis.

After acceptance, the exporter, the exporter's bank, or whoever has purchased the acceptance will either hold it until maturity or sell it in the acceptance market. In many cases, the accepting bank may act as the selling agent, selling the bankers' acceptance either directly to another bank or through the acceptance broker or dealer. The proceeds from the sale of the acceptance will be paid to the exporter or to the one who has acquired the time draft from him. When the acceptance comes due, the holder turns it over to the accepting bank for payment. As previously noted, by this time the importer will have received the goods, presumably sold them, and will have funds with the accepting bank to meet payment of the obligation.

OTHER USES OF ACCEPTANCE CREDIT

Domestic Shipments. American banks may be requested to finance domestic shipments of goods with the use of acceptance credit. Financing procedure involves the same general steps already noted. The bill of exchange is drawn by the seller under terms stated in the letter of credit, is secured by shipping and other documents, and then is sent to the accepting bank for its acceptance. The drawer of the accepted draft obtains funds immediately and economically by selling the accepted draft through a broker, or a bank, in the acceptance market. When the draft matures, the accepting bank pays the draft with funds provided by the purchaser of the goods.

Shipments between Foreign Countries. An American accepting bank may receive a request to finance a shipment of goods between a European seller and a South American buyer. The former is willing to sell goods to the latter, provided he arranges through his bank for the issuance of a letter of credit by a New York bank. If this is done, the financing proceeds as follows: The European exporter ships the goods to the buyer, draws a draft on the New York bank, and discounts it with his bank. The European bank forwards the draft to its New York correspondent bank to be presented to the American bank for acceptance. At maturity the American bank meets the draft with funds provided, through banking channels, by the importer located in South America.

Storage of Goods. In order to promote orderly marketing of goods, particularly agricultural staples, it is necessary to hold them from season to season. Owners may secure financial help from local banks under ordinary lines of credit or from the Commodity Credit Corporation, but it may be preferable to borrow in the acceptance market. The owners may arrange for a line of acceptance credit, permitting them to draw drafts on the accepting banks. After acceptance, the drafts are sold in the bill market; and the beneficiaries will have funds with which to purchase more staples or to finance other needs. The acceptance credit is secured by warehouse receipts, and these receipts are exchanged for trust receipts when the goods are removed from the warehouse. The bills of exchange are liquidated with funds received when the goods are sold.

Risks due to market fluctuations may be removed by requiring owners of the staples to sell futures contracts in the commodity market when the acceptance credit is given. If the price of the commodity falls, the loss is offset by the profit on the futures contract. When transactions are protected by this commodity-hedging operation, many banks will give acceptance credit to finance storage of staples for as much as 90 per cent of their market value. Similar problems arise in financing the storage of goods which may not be of American origin and which may be stored in a foreign country. Usually, accepting banks ask for satisfactory evidence of storage (warehouse receipts) and for letters of guarantee from actual takers of the credit.

Creating Dollar Exchange.   One important special use of acceptance credit is to make dollar exchange available to those buyers of American goods who are in poorly developed financial centers. By dollar exchange is meant New York drafts or other drafts drawn on banks in the United States. This type of financing gives rise to finance bills, a device for borrowing among banks which has been used widely abroad. Conditions under which member banks may finance with finance bills are limited by law and regulations of the Board of Governors of the Federal Reserve System. The purpose of using finance bills is to make credit of American banks available to banks in underdeveloped areas so that they may finance the purchase of American goods.

Normally, buyers of goods in most foreign financial centers are able to secure adequate dollar exchange from their local banks. But assume that steamships stop but once a month at some Central American port, that the one bank in the community keeps a balance of only $25,000 with its New York correspondent bank, and that there are no exchange dealers in the community. During the seasonal buying period, the steamship unloads $100,000 worth of goods sold by exporters in New York to the local merchants. There is an immediate need for $100,000 in New York drafts, which the local banker is unable to provide with his $25,000 balance in New York.

Assume that the Central American banker had previously opened a line of dollar acceptance credit with a New York bank. Under this credit agreement, he draws a thirty-day time draft for

$80,000, which he sends to New York to be accepted and then sold in the acceptance market. The proceeds from the sale will be credited to his deposit account in New York. In the meantime the Central American banker will have sold New York drafts to his customers for $100,000. He knows that the time draft will have been sold and that funds are available in New York to take up his sight drafts when presented. During the next thirty days, he can build up his deposit in New York so as to take up the time bill at maturity.

FINANCING FOREIGN TRAVEL

One function of banks and exchange dealers is to provide travelers abroad with acceptable means of payment for services, hotel accommodations, and goods. Two credit instruments have been created to finance travelers: namely, travelers' checks and travelers' letters of credit. Travelers' checks are printed blanks which may be purchased from banks, express companies, leading hotels, and other agencies, both here and abroad. The purchaser signs his name on each blank in the upper left-hand corner. The blanks, put up in book form, may be in denominations varying from $10 to $200. When checks are issued the agent collects the full value of the checks plus a small commission.

When a travelers' check is cashed at a bank, hotel, express company, or some other place, the traveler signs his name in the lower left-hand corner in order to make it negotiable. Travelers' checks may be secured in terms of dollars, sterling, francs, or other currencies. If they are in terms of dollars, they will be paid in foreign countries at the prevailing rate of exchange for sight drafts on New York. To avoid this risk of exchange, travelers' checks may be made up in terms of the currencies of the countries in which traveling is planned.

Similar principles are involved in the use of travelers' letters of credit and commercial letters of credit. The issuer (bank) makes it possible for the beneficiary (traveler) to purchase things in the foreign countries in which he is temporarily residing. The letter of credit is a printed form of letter addressed by a bank to its correspondents in foreign countries. It authorizes the beneficiary named in the letter to draw drafts on the issuer, which the correspondent banks are requested to honor. Since this letter of credit establishes the credit of the holder, it is similar to a commercial letter of credit. Because it is addressed to more than one bank, it is sometimes called a "circular letter of credit."[3] The drafts drawn under a travelers' letter of credit are negotiated in the presence of the correspondent banks that are asked to cash them. The drafts are unsecured (clean bills), and extra care is taken to see that fraud is not committed.

In order to clarify the use of the travelers' letter of credit, let us assume that Mr. White is planning to travel throughout western Europe, and, in addition to a small quantity of cash and travelers' checks, he wants to use a travelers' letter of credit. He goes to his local bank and arranges for one for $2,000 by depositing and/or assigning his account for $2,000, or depositing and assigning $2,000 worth of marketable securities, or simply signing a paper guaranteeing to pay the drafts as presented. The bank gives him a special form of letter of introduction on which he writes his signature. This is known as a "letter of identification" and is used in connection with the letter of credit. This, as well as the letter of credit, will be officially signed by his bank. Since all correspondents have received copies of the official signature, they will be able to determine whether or not the documents are authentic. Finally, Mr. White receives a list of the banks where he may negotiate drafts.

On arriving in London and desiring pound sterling for shopping and other needs, Mr. White checks the list of correspondents and notes the name of the Chase-Manhattan Bank. He checks the address and then goes to the West End Branch of the bank, which is located at 51 Berkeley Square. In order to obtain a draft for £50, he presents his letter of identification and letter of credit. On a blank provided by the bank, he draws a dollar draft for the equivalent of £50 (assume $140). The bank checks the documents to make certain that the time has not expired, that the letter has not been exhausted by previous withdrawals, and that the signatures are correct. If no further identification is necessary, the bank cashes the draft, provided it shows the number given in the letter of credit and the signature of Mr. White is authentic. Before returning the letter of credit to Mr. White the bank indicates in the space provided on the reverse side the amount of the draft, the date of negotiation, and the bank's own name. The bank charges a small fee for its services.

The Chase-Manhattan Bank then presents the draft through banking channels to the bank that issued the letter of credit and receives dollar credit in payment, probably at the head office in New

[3] Letters of credit addressed to one bank are known as "special letters of credit."

York. The New York office collects as it would for a personal check, through the local clearinghouse or, if drawn on an out-of-town bank, through the Federal Reserve System. The bank that issued the letter of credit debits Mr. White's account for the amount of the drafts, plus a small commission (usually one half of 1 per cent). This procedure is repeated in Paris, Brussels, Luxembourg, Rome, and other cities, until the total amount of credit is exhausted. The correspondent bank negotiating the draft which exhausts the credit takes up the letter and mails it to the issuing bank. In the meantime the issuing bank has been called upon to pay the drafts drawn at various places.

Both travelers' checks and travelers' letters of credit may be used to finance travel in the United States. Emphasis has been placed on the use of the travelers' letter of credit to finance travel, but this same document is also used to finance trade when buyers make their purchases in person. Thus a buyer from a New York department store may contact a seller of china in England and pay for a consignment of china by drawing a draft under a travelers' letter of credit.

FUNCTIONS OF FOREIGN EXCHANGE MARKETS

Foreign exchange markets have "transfer," "credit," and "hedging" functions. This means that banks and other specialists in the market (1) buy and sell different foreign exchange instruments, transferring dollars into foreign currency when they buy and transferring foreign currency into dollars when they sell; (2) make funds available to buyers and sellers of goods in international markets; and (3) buy and sell "futures" or forward contracts so that buyers and sellers may hedge against the risks of foreign exchange.

Transfer Function.   Normally, when an American sells goods to someone abroad, he expects to be paid ultimately in United States dollars; but he may receive a bank draft drawn on a foreign bank or an authority to draw a bill on the foreign buyer or his bank for a certain number of foreign monetary units. At the same time that the exporter is receiving foreign drafts or foreign credit instruments in payment, there are other Americans buying goods abroad who must have foreign drafts or other types of foreign credit instruments to complete their transactions. It is the need for a place where foreign exchange may be bought and sold that gives rise to exchange markets.

Credit Function.   When credit instruments are used, a grant of credit is involved. This means that the foreign exchange market has a credit function as well as a transfer function. The credit arrangements between foreign buyers and sellers include open-book accounts, promissory notes, or the right to draw bills on the buyers or their banks. The last, the most common method used in financing foreign trade, gives rise to a sight or time draft which is originated by the seller of the goods (exporter). When long-term bills are used, a market for them is needed; and so, the foreign exchange market overlaps the commercial bill market.

Hedging Function. In foreign trade there are hazards other than those associated with the credit standing of the buyers of goods —misunderstandings due to differences in languages, units of weights and measures, laws and trade practices, and currencies. A major hazard, not present in domestic trade, is the "risk of exchange." This refers to the fluctuations in the rate of exchange and means that this "price," as well as the price of the goods in question, must be considered in each foreign exchange transaction. And so, another function of the foreign exchange market is to provide the means for hedging against the risk of exchange. One method of hedging as practiced by banks consists of offsetting a sale or purchase at "spot" prices by a purchase or sale for future delivery,[4] thus practically eliminating the loss or gain resulting from price fluctuations.

Forward Exchange. Forward exchange may be defined as the purchase and/or sale of currencies for delivery at some time in the future with the rate of exchange being fixed at the time the contract is negotiated. Customarily this price is the same as the current price for the type of exchange that is to be delivered or purchased —cable or mail transfer or a demand draft. Banks and exchange dealers expect to make a profit; if they agree to purchase foreign exchange in the future, they quote the current price minus a discount; if they agree to sell foreign exchange in the future, they quote the current price plus a premium. The premium or discount for forward exchange depends on the demand for and supply of foreign currencies, the relative level of interest rates in the two financial markets, and the financial and political conditions in the two countries which influence the outlook for appreciation or depreciation of the currencies in terms of each other during the next few months.

[4] In the "spot" market for foreign exchange, sales are for immediate delivery and immediate payment, whether cable transfers, demand bills, or time bills are involved. In the "futures" or "forward" market, contracts calling for future delivery and future payment are bought and sold.

Usually the forward exchange transaction provides for the delivery or purchase of forward exchange on a fixed date (such as one month up to six months), but it may provide for purchase or sale of foreign exchange over a period of time at the customer's option. In the latter case, the option may never be used and so the date merely indicates when the option terminates. Banks and dealers customarily offset their purchases and sales of foreign exchange wherever possible. This so-called "marrying up" may not be complete, so banks and dealers may purchase or sell or arrange for "swaps" of forward exchange with other banks or dealers in the market in order to have each day's total purchases and sales equal.

The purpose of forward exchange transactions is to enable merchants, banks, and traders—once they are committed to make or receive payments in foreign currency—to eliminate the risks arising from the fluctuations of foreign exchange rates. If an exporter of goods has a thirty-day bill of exchange drawn on London, he may arrange for a thirty-day forward contract. Although the dollar value of the thirty-day "bill" may decline because of a decline in the rate of exchange, the exporter has a contract that permits him to deliver that amount of English money at a price agreed to at the time of the contract. Since the rate of exchange may move up as well as down, buyers of foreign goods may protect themselves by a forward or futures contract which calls for the future delivery of a cable or demand draft for a certain number of monetary units at the current exchange rate plus the premium being quoted on such futures contracts.

A bank may lend in the London market by purchasing a mail transfer and forwarding instructions that the funds are to be lent in London for 30 days (or a specified number of days) at the highest rate prevailing in that market. In order to bring home the funds in 30 days, the bank also arranges to sell the same amount of money plus interest in the forward exchange market. The difference in interest rates in the two markets must be enough to offset the costs including the discount on the forward exchange. One should not forget that in the forward or futures market the contracts calls for future delivery and future payment and no funds are transferred until a later date.

Speculation. Speculation in foreign exchange is the buying or selling of foreign exchange with the expectation or hope of making a profit from a change in the rate of exchange. Most speculation in foreign exchange is done by individuals, private bankers, brokerage houses, and foreign exchange dealers rather than by commercial bankers. If speculators expect a rise in exchange rates, they may take a long position in the market, purchasing or agreeing to purchase sight or cable exchange in the present with the expectation of selling it in the future at a higher price.

If speculators expect a decrease in the foreign exchange value of a currency, they may contract to deliver the currency at a future date at a given price, expecting to cover in the spot market for demand or cable at a lower price. For illustration, a speculator may agree to deliver £100,000 in thirty days at the current cable rate of $2.80½; and, if the rate goes below $2.80½, he may make a speculator's profit. During periods of international disturbances, there are opportunities for tremendous profits; in fact, they were so great during the early 1930's that international speculators and bankers were charged with creating conditions which made it impossible for certain countries to remain on the gold standard. At present the opportunities for making profits from speculation in foreign exchange are limited, and the risks are great because so much depends on what governments may or may not do. For the most part, speculation in exchange is done by the experts; and now the amounts involved are small compared to those involved prior to 1930.

Arbitrage. Arbitrage in foreign exchange is the operation wherein foreign exchange is bought and sold in the same or different markets simultaneously in order to make a profit from discrepancies in prices. In order to operate successfully between two or more markets, an arbitrager must be well informed as to current prices in these markets, must have branch offices or agents in these markets, and must be able to communicate orders to buy and sell for immediate execution. Usually, arbitraging is done by large banks with foreign exchange departments and by foreign exchange dealers. Sometimes, large investment houses and brokerage firms have divisions that arbitrage in foreign exchange and commodities as well as in securities.

Arbitraging differs from speculation in that arbitraging involves the making of a profit from differences in prices at a particular time, while speculation involves the attempt to profit from changes in prices over a period of time. If the calculations of the arbitragers are correct and the orders to buy and sell go through as scheduled, no risks are involved; but, in speculation, risks are always assumed by the speculators.

In arbitraging in the exchange markets, there may be two,

324 MONEY AND BANKING

three, or more exchange markets involved. Assuming no restrictions exist, a hypothetical illustration of two-point arbitrage is as follows: At a particular moment, if the sterling cable rate on New York is $2.80½, and the dollar rate in London is $2.80¼, there is a possibility of a ¼ point arbitrage profit. The New York operator may sell a £100,000 cable for $280,500, and to meet this obligation he instructs his agent or partner in London to obtain £100,000 by selling a cable on him for $280,250. The arbitrager has a gross profit of $250. This process may be repeated as long as there is any discrepancy in rates in different markets; but the fact that sterling exchange is being sold in New York will tend to lower its price, and the fact that dollar exchange is being bought in London will tend to raise its price. So the difference of ¼ point will be of short duration.

Although the margin of profit in arbitraging is small, the amounts dealt in are large. The financial success of such operations depends upon the speed with which they are performed, because purchases and sales tend to eliminate maladjustments in prices. The economic effect of arbitrage is to keep the major foreign exchange markets in alignment with each other. However, arbitrage operations are dependent on free markets, and these are lacking at the present time.

BANKS AND FOREIGN EXCHANGE MARKETS

Foreign Exchange Market. Although foreign exchange is bought and sold in every community in the United States, the foreign exchange market is thought of as the place where foreign exchange is bought and sold in large amounts. In the United States the principal foreign exchange market is in New York, where large commercial banks, foreign exchange dealers and brokers, subsidiaries and agents of foreign banks, some investment houses, and commodity and securities brokerage firms buy and sell foreign exchange to each other at wholesale prices. At the same time, commercial banks and others among the wholesale buyers and sellers act as retailers of foreign exchange instruments, dealing with businessmen and others at retail prices and in smaller amounts. Usually, retail transactions are made over the counter, while wholesale transactions are made over the telephone.

Profits on individual foreign exchange transactions are small, and so most of the foreign exchange business is in the hands of commercial banks and certain specialists who can obtain enough volume to make the business profitable. American banks have established correspondent relationships with other banks, and some have opened foreign branches and organized subsidiary foreign corporations and agencies. Correspondent banks, branches, and agencies are linked together by telephone, cable, telegraph, and/or wireless. If there were no restrictions on foreign exchange operations, the effect would be the creation of a world-wide foreign exchange market.

Foreign Exchange Departments of Commercial Banks. Many banks in seaport cities and in financial and manufacturing centers have organized foreign departments. These departments finance foreign trade and travel for their customers, and they trade in foreign exchange in both the "spot" and "forward" markets. They also assist their customers with general information about economic and legal conditions abroad and with specific information about foreign buyers and sellers.

The internal organization of a bank's foreign exchange department will vary from bank to bank, but there will be sections or divisions to service: (1) commercial customers, who finance with letters of credit; (2) travelers, who purchase travelers' checks and travelers' letters of credit; and (3) foreign correspondents and other customers who buy and sell securities for their own accounts. The department will also have sections or staff personnel responsible for the bank's (1) trading in exchange and making of futures contracts; (2) collecting foreign credit instruments; (3) paying when ordered by cable, mail, or over the counter (called "foreign tellers"); (4) receiving and sending cables, telegrams, and radiograms; and (5) keeping records of the balances of foreign correspondents and other customers, of the bank's deposits in foreign currencies abroad, and of the general assets and liabilities of the department.

Other Foreign Exchange Dealers. In addition to banks, there are other operators in the foreign exchange markets including the specialists. Some specialists act as agents for banks; while others purchase bills of exchange for their own accounts, taking title until the bills are sold to other exchange dealers. In such transactions they are acting as principals, being compensated for the risks assumed by the spread between the buying and selling prices.

Among the specialists in the foreign exchange market are the so-called "commercial bill brokers," who buy and sell bills of exchange that originate in exports of merchandise. They usually represent business firms that prefer to send their bills of exchange directly to New York instead of selling them to local banks. The commercial bill brokers may also buy and sell foreign exchange, arrange for foreign exchange contracts, and sometimes maintain foreign accounts. Most of their business is done with banks in New York and in foreign countries.

In New York there are also foreign agencies that buy and sell for the accounts of the foreign banks they represent. Several large private investment banking houses have foreign exchange divisions, and some of the stock and commodity brokerage houses have divisions that deal in certain parts of the foreign exchange market.

The Federal Reserve Act authorized the Federal Reserve banks to carry on a foreign exchange business; but for the most part these institutions have limited their activities to making a market for acceptances (bill market) and to acting as agents for the United States Treasury, the Stabilization Fund, foreign governments, and central banks. The Reserve banks have made little use of their power to initiate purchases of gold, cable transfers, bankers' acceptances, and bills of exchange; and they have left the development of a domestic foreign exchange market to member banks and to others. Because of their policy of buying all eligible bills offered, the Federal Reserve banks have contributed to the development of the credit function of the foreign exchange market.

SUMMARY

Foreign exchange consists of foreign currencies and credit instruments stated in foreign money. Foreign exchange instruments are most commonly classified as cable and mail transfers, sight drafts, and time drafts. The foreign exchange rate is the price of a unit of foreign money in terms of the dollar. Since there are many different rates, the rate of exchange for accounting purposes is usually the cable rate; but sometimes economists think of the *rate* as the price of sight bills of exchange. The prices paid for foreign money vary, with "cable" being the most expensive, and the longest time drafts being the cheapest. The prices of foreign currency will rise or fall together, but the spread among the different time drafts will depend upon maturity and the discount rate prevailing in the market.

Bankers extend acceptance credit to their customers by permitting them to draw drafts on their banks, which they accept. This makes the drafts a primary obligation of the accepting banks and readily negotiable in the bill or acceptance market. Member banks may accept drafts to finance exports, imports, domestic shipment of goods, storage of goods, and the creation of dollar exchange. Banks also sell travelers' checks and travelers' letters of credit. But much of the foreign export trade of the United States is financed with the use of trade drafts which are orders (time or demand) that are drawn on buyers by the sellers of goods.

Foreign exchange markets have "transfer," "credit," and "hedging" functions. How well the foreign exchange markets perform their functions depends, in part, on the activities of speculators and arbitragers in the market. Speculators buy and/or sell foreign exchange with the expectation of making a profit out of changes in prices over a period of time; while arbitragers buy and sell foreign exchange in order to make a profit from price discrepancies in the same or different markets at the same time. Most of the foreign exchange business is in the hands of large commercial banks and certain specialists in New York, although foreign exchange is bought and sold in every community in the United States.

QUESTIONS AND PROBLEMS

1. Distinguish between (*a*) cable and sight or demand exchange, (*b*) collection and payment items, and (*c*) postal and express money orders.

2. Account for the spread between sight and time rates of exchange. Is it always the same? Explain.

3. "The bankers' acceptance . . . makes possible the addition of the credit of a bank . . . to that of a purchaser or holder of merchandise." (C. H. Kreps, Jr., "Bankers' Acceptances," *Money Market Essays*, Federal Reserve Bank of New York [New York, 1952], p. 22.) Analyze this statement.

4. Explain how banks are compensated for issuing letters of credit. What risks do they assume? What is an "authority to purchase"?

5. What is the fundamental difference between a grant of acceptance credit and an ordinary bank loan? Does this difference break down when the accepting bank buys its own bills? Explain.

6. What factors in foreign trade explain the wide use of acceptance credit and bills of exchange? Do the merits of trade acceptances and bankers' acceptances justify their use in domestic trade? Why? May national banks make grants of acceptance credit to finance storage of goods at home or abroad?

7. Show how acceptance credit is used in financing an export of goods when there is no market for the foreign bill of exchange. Outline steps taken and give reasons for them. Use Chart 8.

8. The Federal Reserve Act authorizes member banks to accept drafts or bills of exchange drawn upon them to finance four broad categories of transactions. Identify them.

9. Explain how banks and other agencies finance foreign travel.
10. Identify the functions of the foreign exchange market.
11. Explain what is meant by speculation in foreign exchange. Who are the most active speculators? How does speculation differ from arbitrage?
12. Distinguish between the "spot" and "forward" exchange markets.

| Chapter | THE MONEY MARKET |
| XVIII | |

MONETARY and credit policies are made effective through changes in the amount, availability, and cost of loanable funds in the money and capital markets. In this chapter emphasis is on the different divisions of the money market. Since the open-market and discount operations of the Federal Reserve System are limited by law or policy to the money market, this chapter supplies an important background for the study of central bank policy discussed in later chapters.

THE MONEY MARKET AND RELATED MARKETS

The importance of a money market is due not only to a supply of short-term funds but also to a demand for these funds. While there is a supply of short-term funds and a demand for such funds in every community in the United States, money markets are usually thought of in terms of the larger financial centers where the regional, national, or international demands for and sources of funds meet. This means that the funds lent or invested in the New York money market have been placed there by banks, institutional investors, business firms, governments, and individuals from all corners of the free world. Likewise those who may borrow in the New York money market may be as different as to type and domicile as those who lend there.

Other Related Markets. The large money markets are related to and dependent on other markets such as the foreign exchange market and the stock and bond markets. In fact, these markets are so close to the money market that no one would be complete without the others. Furthermore, most of the large banks, dealers, and brokerage houses that participate in one of these markets also participate in one or more of the other markets.

The money market is also related to commodity markets such as the markets for cotton, coffee, corn, wheat, and other grains; and, while the insurance market is usually thought of as being most closely related to the capital market, it is also important to the money market. Markets for gold and silver, which operate within limits as permitted by governments, are also closely related to the money market; and now most of the transactions in gold are money transactions. All of these markets may be thought of as being related to the money market either as a source of demand for short-term funds or as a source of supply of short-term funds.

Divisions of the Money Market. The divisions of the money market include (1) the commercial bill market, composed primarily of bankers' acceptances, which is closely related to the foreign exchange market and commodity markets; (2) the commercial paper market wherein promissory notes of business concerns are sold; (3) the call loan market wherein dealers and brokers borrow to finance the purchase and sale of new securities as well as to finance trading in outstanding stocks, bonds, and other long-term obligations; (4) the federal funds market wherein bank reserve balances, United States Treasury deposits, and other claims against the Federal Reserve banks are bought either by member banks to adjust their reserve positions or by others who have obligations that must be paid in federal funds; and (5) the short-term government securities market.

General Characteristics of the Money Market. The first characteristic to note is that none of the divisions of the money market is organized as is the New York Stock Exchange, and there is no one place where trading takes place. Funds are lent or invested in the money market either directly or by open-market purchases. Now, the bulk of call loans are made directly by banks to dealers and brokers; but, in other divisions of the money market, funds are obtained by the sale of credit instruments to short-term investors.

Terms of purchases and sales of outstanding credit instruments are negotiated over the telephone, and generally the terms covering the original sale of an issue are negotiated between the seller and middlemen. The Federal Reserve banks act as agents for the federal government in placing short-term obligations, selling new Treasury bills to the highest bidders (with some concessions to the smaller bidders—up to $200,000). After the original distribution, trading is between a few specialized dealers on a negotiated basis (meaning that a certain amount of negotiation takes place before a sale can be effected).

Volume of Credit Instruments. The bulk of the credit instruments purchased and sold in the money market are United States government obligations—Treasury bills, certificates of indebtedness, and other government obligations which are approaching maturity. For illustration, at the beginning of 1956 the volume of outstanding Treasury bills, certificates of indebtedness, and Treasury notes maturing in less than a year was $59 billion, as compared to $2.5 billion in loans made to brokers and dealers, $2.3 billion of commercial and, sales-finance company paper, and $670,000,000 in dollar acceptances (commercial bills). No statistics are reported on federal funds.

Interest Rates. Interest rates in the money market fluctuate daily, but all tend to move up and down together. Usually, the range of interest rates from the lowest to the highest is as follows: Treasury bills, bankers' acceptances, commercial paper, and call loans. For reasons noted later, the rate on federal funds is customarily at or below the rediscount rate, which is usually above the Treasury bill rate and below the commercial paper rate.

COMMERCIAL BILL MARKET

The commercial bill market developed as a result of the need for better facilities to finance foreign and domestic trade.

Bankers' Acceptances. In 1913 those favoring banking reform in the United States were in general agreement as to the need for a commercial bill market. To fulfill this need the Federal Reserve Act permitted national banks to accept bills of exchange used to finance exports and imports of goods, domestic shipment of goods, shipment of goods between foreign countries, storage of certain staples, and creation of dollar exchange to finance trade with areas where financial institutions lacked adequate foreign exchange facilities. This Act opened a new source of income (commissions) for those banks desiring to make grants of acceptance credit to their customers.

In making grants of acceptance credit, commercial banks do not lend their funds, but they do assume liabilities. Therefore, they must use the same care in this type of financing as they use in lending on a straight loan basis. However, since no bank funds are involved immediately, there may be a temptation to resort to this type of lending after the bank has already committed all of its loanable funds. When reserves are plentiful, banks may prefer to lend; but when they are limited, the loan departments of banks may direct customers to their foreign exchange departments for additional funds. If a bank were to discount its own bills, this transaction would be classified as a direct loan. The law and the regulations of the Board of Governors under the law are carefully drawn so as to limit the total amount of acceptance credit that an individual bank may extend at one time and the terms of each transaction as to maximum maturity, purpose of financing, and required security.

Legal Regulations. The volume of acceptance credit that a member bank may have outstanding, at one time, is limited to 50 per cent of the accepting bank's capital and surplus; but a bank may apply and receive permission to accept an additional 50 per cent for general trade financing and another 50 per cent for the purpose of furnishing dollar exchange. Drafts or bills drawn for the last purpose are limited to those of maturities of not more than ninety days to run, exclusive of days of grace, while drafts drawn for agricultural purposes and secured at the time of acceptance by warehouse receipts or simular title documents may have maturities of six months' sight, exclusive of days of grace.

The rules pertaining to security include the following: If the amount a bank accepts for one name is in excess of 10 per cent of its capital and surplus, the excess credit must be secured by bills of lading, warehouse receipts, or some other form of title document or collateral giving adequate security. If the acceptances result from domestic financing of goods, they must be accompanied by shipping documents or warehouse receipts at the time of acceptance. Bills of exchange resulting from foreign trade need have no specific collateral, but they are usually accompanied by title documents at the time of acceptance.

Accepting Banks. National banks, state banks, three specialized acceptance banks, subsidiaries and agencies of foreign banking houses, private banks, and investment houses are represented in the list of leading acceptance bankers in the United States. While the Federal Reserve Act authorizes all member banks to accept time drafts, nearly two thirds of all acceptances outstanding are accounted for by ten banks (Guaranty, Chase-Manhattan, First National City, etc.) with the remainder accounted for largely by about ninety other banks. Most bankers' acceptances outstanding are created by New York banks and other institutions in New York, with those in San Francisco, Boston, Dallas, and Chicago following in that order. The specialized nature of acceptance credit and the need for foreign banking connections make it difficult for small banks to enter this field. Most bank acceptance credit is arranged for through foreign exchange departments of banks, even though the financing may be entirely domestic.

Accepting banks not only give acceptance credit and make possible the supply of bankers' acceptances but they are also the chief buyers of the accepted drafts. Their holdings are divided into two classes—"own bills" and "bills bought." Own bills represent the bills which the holding bank has accepted, and they must be reported as loans. Under acceptance credit, a bank lends only its credit standing and executes the credit by accepting drafts. When the drafts are sold in the acceptance market, the buyers of the drafts finance the transaction. But when the bank buys its own acceptances, it is lending the money to the customer. This situation is the same as that which exists when the bank lends directly to a borrower. Some banks follow the practice of selling bills to each other, which has reduced the volume of their bills to be classified as loans; but this practice is frowned upon by bill brokers whose function is to make a market for commercial bills.

Acceptance Dealers. There are about six dealers in the New York commercial bill market, and these dealers also buy and sell United States government obligations and other securities (the latter make up the greater part of the volume of their business). The dealer's profit on bankers' acceptances is the spread between his buying and selling prices (at present, one eighth of 1 per cent per year). Dealers sell acceptances immediately after purchasing them and hold only a small amount overnight. Their chief source of supply is accepting banks that have discounted their own bills at the dealers' buying rate, which are passed along to dealers with no profit to the banks. Usually, these banks expect to purchase an equal amount of acceptances from other banks at the dealers' selling rate. (This "swapping" of acceptances is sometimes made directly between two banks, thus saving the spread between the dealers' buying and selling rates.) Dealers also acquire bills from inland banks where no "swapping" is expected.

Purchases of Acceptances. Although accepting banks may prefer to hold their own bills, they may sell them and other bills acquired to meet the demand of their foreign correspondent banks. When such a bank acquires bills of other banks, it adds its own endorsement for which it charges a fee of from one sixteenth to one fourth of 1 per cent. These two-bank name bills are preferred by foreign investors who also acquire bills from dealers, sometimes through the facilities of the Federal Reserve Bank of New York, which purchases bills both for its own account and for the accounts of foreign central banks. Customarily dealers do not endorse their bills; but the Federal Reserve Bank of New York extends its guaranty on acceptances purchased for foreign central banks for which it charges a fee of a fraction of 1 per cent. Foreign banks regard bankers' acceptances as the preferred and traditional form in which to keep their dollar reserves.

Not only has the rate on bankers' acceptances usually been above the rate on Treasury bills but until recently the income thereon has been exempt from the federal withholding tax on foreign interest earnings in the United States. In 1955, the Internal Revenue Service ruled that foreign holders, who make up a large group of investors in acceptances, were taxable;[1] but the ruling exempts foreign central banks which are government-owned. With the increase in yield on acceptances, many American business corporations are purchasing them, particularly those of shorter maturities which are least attractive to foreign investors. At this time, as reported by the Federal Reserve authorities, the holdings of outstanding dollar acceptances is as follows: accepting banks, 29 per cent, of which the greater portion is their own bills; Federal Reserve banks, about 4 per cent, of which the greater portion is for foreign correspondents; and all others, 67 per cent, which is not broken down according to ownership.

Demand for Acceptance Credit. The volume of dollar acceptances outstanding depends as much on the demands of business firms and others as on the availability of such credits. Most businessmen who are eligible for acceptance credit are also eligible for direct bank loans and trade credit. It may be advantageous to use acceptance credit if the market rate thereon plus the commission is less than the interest rate on direct loans and no specific compensatory deposit balance is required. However, in the case of a direct loan, banks customarily permit loan customers to repay loans faster than anticipated when the loan agreement was signed, and they usually give a rebate on the interest taken in advance. Although acceptance credit customers may place funds in their banks before the maturity date of the acceptances, they rarely receive full, if any, rebates for doing so. Since the rebate practice is not standardized, some borrowers may regard acceptance credit as being more expensive than financing with direct loans (assuming the interest and other costs are equal).

---

[1] Hearings are being held on this ruling. Bankers are opposed to the tax since it entails additional bookkeeping expense. Bankers are also required to withhold taxes on income payable to foreign investors in United States government securities; but, in many cases, they avoid the paper work by sending them to the Federal Reserve banks for redemption when they mature, informing the Reserve banks that they are foreign owned, and shifting the responsibility for withholding the tax to the Federal Reserve banks. The situation is different for commercial bills because they are payable at the banks, and the banks must compute and withhold the tax.

In financing certain types of transactions, businessmen will use the methods specified by those with whom they deal; and sellers, in turn, will co-operate with their customers in working out acceptable sales terms. At the present time, of total acceptance credit outstanding, about 28 per cent is based on financing imports into the United States; 23 per cent on exports from the United States; 31 per cent on the storage or shipment of goods within the United States; 11 per cent on storage of goods between points in foreign countries; and 7 per cent on creation of dollar exchange.

COMMERCIAL PAPER MARKET

Nature of Open-Market Commercial Paper.   The oldest among the different divisions of the money market is that wherein issues of short-term notes of business firms and sales-finance companies are sold with or without the assistance of commercial paper houses. An issue of commercial paper is always in an even amount—such as $50,000, $100,000, or $1,000,000—and individual notes that make up an issue usually vary in amounts from $2,500 to $50,000, but they may be smaller or larger. Sometimes an issue of open-market commercial paper is secured by collateral held by a bank or trust company acting as trustee, but such issues are unusual.

Open-market commercial paper notes are drawn "payable to bearer" or "payable to ourselves" by the maker, who signs and endorses them in blank so that they are negotiable by delivery only. Usually the notes are payable at maturity at a designated bank or banks, are traded at a discount, have maturities varying from 30 to 270 days at the time of issue, and are single-name; if a second name appears, it is usually the endorsement of an officer or of someone closely connected with the business firm or finance company that is borrowing. Customarily the volume of this type of financing is substantially larger than the volume of financing in the commercial bill market.

Commercial Paper Dealers.   Originally commercial paper houses acted only as brokers for their clients in handling commercial paper, but now they usually buy issues outright at a discount and then resell the notes at the same price to investors. The commercial paper house remits in payment the amount received for the issue minus the commission which varies from one eighth to one half of 1 per cent. Some business firms are able to persuade the commercial paper house to take an issue on a straight discount basis, in which case the notes are offered to investors at a slightly higher price than that paid by the commercial paper house. At times, a commercial paper house will take an issue on consignment with payment delayed until the issue is sold. In other cases, the commercial paper house will make a down payment and then remit the remainder of the price when the issue is sold.

When a commercial paper house buys an issue outright, it assumes the risk of having acquired an issue that must be sold at a loss because of a sudden change in money rates in the market, or even worse, an issue that cannot be sold because investors shy away from it. If the commercial paper house is successful in selling an issue and the notes are not paid at maturity, the reputation of the house will tend to suffer. Although the commercial paper house does not guarantee the paper sold, it must investigate the borrower's credit position thoroughly. The paper is offered to investors with an option to return it within ten days or two weeks after purchase (the understanding being that it is to be returned only for adverse credit reasons).

Business Firm Borrowers. Business firms that borrow in the open market must meet high standards of liquidity as well as safety because, in this market, the relationship between investors and borrowers is impersonal and notes are not renewed when they come due. Most firms that borrow in the open market are subject to seasonal working capital needs and have strong commercial bank connections and large lines of credit that may be used in case of need. Most of these firms are fairly large, having net worth of from $1,000,000 to $5,000,000 in most cases. Open-market borrowers include firms engaged in manufacturing (particularly in fields such as textiles, grains, flour, fertilizers, metal products, meat packing, and so on), wholesalers (groceries, food products, hardware, paints, textiles, and leather goods), retailers (department and chain stores), and sales-finance companies. Now there are more than 500 concerns that are borrowing in the commercial paper market.

Short-term borrowers, who have a choice of borrowing directly from commercial banks or in the open market, may borrow in the open market for the following reasons: (1) to obtain more favorable interest rates, (2) to advertise their financial strength, (3) to secure larger loans than could be obtained directly from their banks, (4) to replace bank loans when their banks follow the policy of demanding an annual clean-up of loans, (5) to secure financial advice concerning the company's affairs, and/or (6) to broaden their source of funds and obtain better terms when borrowing from local banks.

Direct Placement by Sales-Finance Companies.   Sales-finance companies are among the most important borrowers in the commercial paper market. The growth in volume of installment credit and the amount of financing required has led five sales-finance companies to create their own sales organizations to place their issues of promissory notes. (This practice has been followed by the three largest companies for over fifteen years—General Motors Acceptance Corporation, C.I.T. Financial Corporation, and Commercial Credit Company; and for about five years for the two others—Associates Investment Company and General Electric Credit Corporation). The companies using the direct placement method of selling open-market paper hold nearly two thirds of all installment notes and other receivables held by sales-finance companies in the United States; and the volume of their paper placed directly exceeds that of all other borrowers in the market.

The characteristics of paper placed directly are similar to those of paper handled by dealers. The notes are drawn payable to bearer, they are unsecured, and the denominations are drawn to meet the demands of investors, with the minimum among the five companies ranging from $500 to $5,000 and maximums from $1,000,000 to $5,000,000. (Investors frequently make requests for paper by telephone.) The maturities of notes may be arranged so that they come due on any date specified by the purchaser (from 30 to 270 days). This flexibility of maturity is attractive to investors who want their funds returned on an exact date (for example, by business corporations on income tax dates). Part of the explanation of large sales-finance companies' borrowing in the open market is the legal limitations on banks' loans to one name. Assuming a 10 per cent lending limit for each member bank, it has been estimated that in 1954 a line of credit of $650,000,000 would have necessitated distribution among the 400 largest member banks.

Investors in Open-Market Commercial Paper.   Among the investors in open-market commercial paper are commercial banks, particularly small and middle-sized banks. Among the advantages of holding commercial paper are (1) earnings thereon are usually higher than on other money market obligations such as Treasury bills, commercial bills or bankers' acceptances, and brokers' loans; (2) liquidity is assured because notes are paid at maturity (the last loss having been in 1936 when the amount involved was but 0.0078 per cent of the total paper outstanding as of June of that year); (3) greater diversification of bank assets is offered because promises to pay may be acquired from firms in other areas and in other industries; (4) loanable funds may be kept more fully employed; (5) new outside business contacts may thereby be made which may become sources of future business; and (6) such paper is eligible for discount or as security for loans at Federal Reserve banks.

The market for open-market paper also includes industrial, public-utility, and railroad companies, trustees of pension funds, life insurance companies, and educational and other institutional investors. Many business firms acquire commercial paper in anticipation of tax payments and planned expenditures which they wish to fund.

LOANS TO BROKERS AND DEALERS

Borrowers. Bank loans secured by stocks and other collateral are made to brokerage firms, investment houses, and individuals in one sector of the money market commonly referred to as the "call loan market." Banks make loans to brokers who need funds in order to finance their customers who buy and sell on margin. The margin trader makes a payment equal to or in excess of the margin requirement (now 70 per cent of the market price) and the broker pays the difference because sales on stock exchanges are cash sales.

Investment bankers purchase new issues of securities, pay cash with funds borrowed, in large part, from commercial banks, and repay the loans when the securities being underwritten are sold to investors. Some individuals borrow directly from commercial banks in order to pay cash for securities being bought with the intent to sell when the market price increases. In all three cases, the loans which are made are protected by a pledge of the securities being purchased.

Call Loan Rate. Because the margin trader is usually unable to estimate when he will resell the securities purchased, the loan contract (demand note) is drawn so that it may be repaid at the option of the borrower or lender—that is, "on call." Sometimes loans made to brokers are evidenced by time notes that may run up to six months. The interest rate charged on demand loans is called the call loan rate, and it is subject to day-to-day adjustment (during 1929, the range was from 5 to 15 per cent). If either the borrower or the lender does not like the renewal rate established each morning, he may repay or call the loan. During the day, new funds may be lent or borrowed at the rate prevailing at that time.

Decline in Importance of the Call Loan Market. In the past, loans to brokers were impersonal, with loan transactions arranged through the money desk on the New York Stock Exchange (discontinued in 1946). Now, such loans are negotiated directly with banks; they are comparable to other customer loans, and they are seldom called in order for a bank to adjust its reserve position. For many years, economists criticized the United States commercial banking system for its dependence on call loans to security brokers and dealers for liquidity because such loans reflect prices and activity in the stock exchange and other securities markets. Now, in appraising the liquidity of the money market, attention should be focused on factors other than fluctuations in the volume of call loans because they are not used to adjust bank reserves as in the past.

MARKET FOR FEDERAL FUNDS

Federal Funds. Federal Reserve funds, or simply federal funds, are balances carried by banks, the United States Treasury, and others at the Federal Reserve banks. Although member banks are required to keep their legal reserves as deposits with their Federal Reserve banks, it does not follow that such funds are idle any more than are individual deposits in checking accounts at commercial banks.

Demand for Federal Funds. To avoid penalties, each member bank must match its reserve balances with reserve requirements throughout its reserve period (semimonthly for country banks and weekly for other banks). Some days a member bank may sell federal funds, because it has an excess of reserves, to other banks having a deficiency in reserves. Such transactions in federal funds among member banks are considered borrowing and lending; and, if the borrower is a national bank, it is subject to the rule that it can not be in debt to other than a Federal Reserve bank for more than its capital. The lender of federal funds, if a national bank, is also subject to the 10-per-cent rule applicable to an unsecured loan to one name.

The demand for federal funds may originate in the requirement of bond dealers or others when payment for securities bought must be made in federal funds. In fact, the market for federal funds began in 1920 when dealers found that they needed federal funds in their transactions with Federal Reserve banks. Sometimes the dealers found that their checks on their accounts at commercial banks were not acceptable to the Federal Reserve bank because they could not be collected until the next day (being classified as clearinghouse items); and so the dealers arranged with member banks for the transfer of member-bank reserve balances in payment (buying a wire, mail, or other form of transfer or Federal Reserve bank draft). Perhaps, other dealers had acquired federal funds through the sale of paper to the Federal Reserve banks. When buyers and sellers were brought together, the market for federal funds began; and today, this market is dominated by member banks both from the supply and the demand side.

Supply of Federal Funds. The supply of federal funds in the market may come from member banks' excess reserves, large bond dealers, and others having Federal Reserve bank drafts, wire transfers, United States Treasury drafts, and other orders on Federal Reserve banks for which immediate credit can be had at the local Federal Reserve bank. The supply of federal funds traced to member banks does not correspond to the amount of their excess reserves on hand. Some banks keep excess reserves in order to average up past deficiencies or to care for anticipated deficiencies before the end of their reserves periods, other banks may feel that the interest return on the amount of these funds does not justify placing them in the market, and other banks do not seem to realize that idle funds mean loss of income.

When veterans and other individuals receive government checks drawn on Federal Reserve banks, they customarily deposit them with their commercial banks without a second thought; but this is not true of large security dealers who receive them in payment for securities which have matured or for securities which the Federal Reserve System purchased from them in the open market. Such a check drawn on a Federal Reserve bank is the highest type of money that can be acquired because it can be applied immediately toward meeting a member bank's reserve requirements or obligations due a Federal Reserve bank.

If the market for federal funds is active, these funds may be offered for sale through a broker (such as Garvin, Bantel & Co., member of the New York Stock Exchange) or directly by the owner in the case of large bond dealers in United States government securities. Because the market for federal funds is not organized, it is difficult to estimate the volume of trading; but one New York Stock Exchange firm acts as broker in trades that total as much as $100 billion a year.

Interest Rate. The interest rate on federal funds varies according to the supply and demand, usually being the highest when the Federal Reserve System is following a tight money policy and not making additional amounts of Federal Reserve credit available by investing in the open market. Since member banks may adjust their reserve positions by borrowing at their Federal Reserve banks, the maximum rate on federal funds is usually set according to the local Federal Reserve bank's rediscount rate.

Major transactions in federal funds take place in New York; and, if the parties involved in a transaction are New York member banks, the purchaser either receives a check drawn on the Federal Reserve bank (a Federal Reserve bank draft) for the amount of federal funds purchased, or the seller advises the Federal Reserve bank to transfer the amount on its books from his reserve account to the reserve account of the buyer. The buyer will give the seller a clearinghouse check for the same amount plus interest at the agreed-on rate for one day (two or more if the transaction is made on Friday or the day before a holiday). From a physical viewpoint, this is the simplest transaction in the money market—no note, no collateral —only an exchange of checks or a transfer order for a check. If an out-of-town bank is involved in the transaction, it is just as simple because the transfer can be made through the facilities of the Federal Reserve wire transfer system without charge. Assuming funds are borrowed for but one day at the rate of 2 per cent, the interest per day on each $1,000,000 lent would be approximately $55.

THE SHORT-TERM GOVERNMENT SECURITIES MARKET

The characteristics of United States Treasury bills and certificates of indebtedness were discussed in Chapter XVI. While Treasury bills are issued on a discount basis and are payable at par, certificates of indebtedness are issued at par with the entire interest and principal being payable at maturity. Treasury bills mature in ninety-one days, while certificates of indebtedness have maturities of less than one year at the time of issue. New issues of Treasury bills are brought out each week, so there are always 13 issues outstanding. Sometimes the United States Treasury sells special issues of bills; at the present time there are three such issues outstanding. Holders of certificates have the privilege of exchanging them at maturity for new certificates on a par-for-par basis with interest adjustments made when necessary, and customarily this privilege is also given to holders of Treasury notes and bonds.

After the original distribution of Treasury bills and certificates of indebtedness, they are bought and sold in the money market. For many years, United States government bonds have been listed on the New York Stock Exchange; but trading in these bonds as well as all other government securities is primarily in the over-the-counter or over-the-telephone market by a relatively small group of securities dealers who specialize in government securities. Orders to purchase or sell are transmitted to the dealers in New York by telephone or wire from all sections of the United States and from some foreign countries (the principal market is in New York but there is a smaller one in Chicago).

The major investors in government securities are commercial banks which hold about 39 per cent of the marketable government debt, and about 63 per cent of their holdings are due or callable within five years. The Federal Reserve banks are second in importance among investors in marketable government securities, and their holdings are chiefly short-term obligations. Third among investors in government obligations are business corporations which invest temporary funds (such as funds accrued for taxes, dividends and other cash disbursements and proceeds of new long-term financing until used for capital outlays). Their holdings are chiefly in debt obligations due or callable within one year; and, in order to tap this market, the United States Treasury has made frequent use of tax anticipation notes, bills, and/or certificates that are surrendered to meet taxes when due.

The extent to which business corporations make temporary investments in government securities is illustrated by the following: at the end of 1955, General Motors Corporation held $1,328,583,800 in United States and foreign government securities in order to meet its United States and foreign government income tax obligations (reported as $1,383,309,272) plus other similar short-term investments of $833,966,763. The need for cash for the payment of income taxes and dividends is a recurring one which calls for peak cash outlays eight times each year (assuming dividend and corporate income taxes are paid quarterly). During the second quarter of 1956, General Motors made provisions for income tax payments of $234,-104,000; dividend payments on preferred stock of $3,232,075; and dividend payments on common stock of over $138,200,000.[2] Similar problems confront other corporations although the amounts involved may be smaller.

Rather than keeping large sums idle awaiting disbursement, corporations customarily invest these funds in the money market. Sometimes business firms borrow from commercial banks to supple-

---

[2] General Motors Corporation, *Shareholders' Quarterly* (June 30, 1956), pp. 10–11.

ment cash needed for peak outlays such as on income tax payment dates.

State and local governments, insurance companies, mutual savings banks, corporate pension funds, and savings and loan associations, as a group are more interested in the longer term marketable government securities than in those traded most actively in the money market. United States trust funds are invested chiefly in nonmarketable issues and the bulk of the $66 billion in government securities held by individuals are savings bonds (more than $50 billion).

A dealer in government securities may be an individual, a partnership or a corporation (including a bank), but the most common legal form is a partnership. The amount of dealers' own capital is relatively small and most of the funds which they use to acquire government securities are borrowed from commercial banks at rates which are lower than those on other types of loans (with the government securities used as collateral). The dealer's profit is chiefly from the spread between his buying and selling prices, one sixty-fourth to one thirty-second of 1 per cent ($156.25 to $312.50 per $1,000,000 par value), or less depending on maturity—lowest profits are on obligations having the shortest maturities. Although the dealer receives some income from securities held, the interest received is offset by the interest he must pay on funds borrowed to purchase the securities. A dealer may have capital gains or losses when he sells securities in his portfolio; therefore some dealers act only as brokers and others avoid large inventories particularly when lower prices of government securities are anticipated.

There are no published reports of purchases and sales of government securities in the over-the-counter market and there is no ticker tape to report prices; but, at the close of each business day, the large dealers issue quotation sheets showing their bid (buying) and ask (selling) prices. The spread between the two is usually an "outside market spread" with actual purchases and sales being negotiated during business hours at higher prices in case of dealer purchases and lower prices in case of dealer sales (conversely for the investor). There is frequent checking of prices over the telephone and when prices are quoted it usually means that they are in effect only while the telephone conversation is going on, unless the dealer specifically agrees that the bid or ask price will remain good for a specified period of time (for illustration, ten minutes).

Purchases and sales are customarily made by oral agreement

over the telephone with confirmation being dispatched by mail or hand delivery later in the day. Delivery and payment is made the regular way for government obligations—delivery and payment the next full business day (the "regular way" for government obligations differs for other securities, being four full business days after purchases of stock on the New York Stock Exchange). Checks are clearinghouse items (payable the next day), and if the seller is a bank it means that its Federal Reserve bank balance will not be credited for two days after the date of the sale. Therefore, sales terms may specify "regular delivery against federal funds" or "cash delivery against a clearinghouse check" with either of these giving the bank reserve funds in one day; or the payment terms may specify "cash delivery against federal funds" which provides the bank with reserve funds immediately.

The Federal Reserve System places orders for purchases and sales of government securities through dealers on whom the System relies to make a market in government securities with a minimum amount of support from the Federal Reserve System. At times, the System will enter into repurchase agreements with nonbank dealers (banks may borrow at the Federal Reserve banks) under which the System buys the securities, usually Treasury bills, and pays for them on the day of agreement. The repurchase agreement gives both parties the option of reversing the sale at any time (usually within fifteen days or less) at the same price for which the securities were sold or purchased plus interest. Such agreements are made during periods of financial strain (when interest rates are higher and prices lower) and may be renewed; but, if the securities are not repurchased and/or the repurchase agreement is not renewed, the securities involved are sold in the market or transferred to the Federal Reserve System Open Market Account.

SUMMARY

The money market is the center wherein the demand for and supply of short-term funds meet. The money market is closely related to and partially dependent upon other markets; and the importance of the New York money market which is national and international in scope of operations, is due in part to its being so closely related to large and well-organized markets for stock, bonds, commodities, and foreign exchange.

The divisions of the money market include the commercial bill market, the commercial paper market, the call loan market, the market for federal funds, and the market for short-term government obligations. Each of these markets has special characteristics; but, in general, their method of operation is by negotiation between parties before a sale is made. Money rates move up and down together, but the interest rate on Treasury bills is usually lowest and that on direct call loans highest. The bulk of the credit instruments bought and sold are issues of the United States government. Commercial bills, commercial paper, finance companies' promissory notes, and Treasury bills are sold on a discount basis with the par value paid at maturity and the other credit instruments are usually sold on a loan basis with principal and interest collected at maturity. The oldest among the different divisions of the money market is the one for commercial paper, and the newest is that for federal funds.

In order for the money market to be effective, it must have all the facilities needed to permit ready purchase and sale of credit instruments with practically no delay and a minimum spread between purchase and sale prices made through specialists who make the market a liquid one. Lenders in the money market are commercial banks, the Federal Reserve banks, investing institutions, business corporations, and wealthy individuals. The borrowers in the market include not only the United States government, business firms, and finance companies that sell their bills or promissory notes, but also brokers and dealers in securities and commodities.

QUESTIONS AND PROBLEMS

1. (a) What is meant by the money market? (b) Where do funds placed in the money market originate?

2. Identify: (a) the markets related to the money market, (b) the divisions of the money market, and (c) the general characteristics of the money market.

3. In terms of volume of transactions in the money market, what is the relative importance of the following: (a) short-term government obligations? (b) brokers' and dealers' loans? (c) commercial and sales-finance company paper? and (d) commercial bills?

4. What are the legal regulations applicable to the volume of acceptance credit that a member bank may have outstanding at one time?

5. Distinguish between "own bills" and "bills bought." Why are "own bills" classified as loans?

6. What is meant by "swapping" acceptances? Explain dealers' reaction to this practice.

7. Identify: (a) holders of outstanding dollar acceptances; and (b) "two-bank-name" bills.

8. Under what circumstances is financing with acceptance credit preferable to financing with direct bank loans?

9. Identify: (*a*) open-market commercial paper; (*b*) commercial paper dealers; (*c*) business firm borrowers in the commercial paper market; and (*d*) investors in the commercial paper market.

10. What relationship is there between the 10-per-cent rule and open-market financing by large sales-finance companies?

11. Identify: (*a*) call loans; (*b*) call loan market; (*c*) call loan rate: and (*d*) the relationship between liquidity of the banking system and call loans in the past and at the present time.

12. Identify: (*a*) federal funds; (*b*) demand for federal funds; (*c*) supply of federal funds; and (*d*) interest rate on federal funds.

13. Discuss: (*a*) "A check drawn on a Federal Reserve bank is the highest type of money that can be acquired"; and (*b*) "From a physical viewpoint, transactions in federal funds are the simplest in the money market."

14. Distinguish between Treasury bills and certificates of indebtedness as to (*a*) issuance; (*b*) provisions for interest payments; and (*c*) maturity.

15. (*a*) Identify the major investors in government securities. (*b*) Why do some business corporations invest temporary funds in government obligations?

16. "Funds in the money market may be thought of as the secondary reserves of banks and business firms all over the United States and to some extent of central banks and others in foreign countries." Analyze.

17. "Essentially, Federal funds represent the title to reserve balances with the Federal Reserve Banks." (H. C. Carr, "Federal Funds," *Money Market Essays* [New York: Federal Reserve Bank of New York, 1952], p. 13.) Why has a market developed in federal funds? What are the advantages to participating member banks?

18. "In addition to these transactions [open-market operations], the System also alternately released and absorbed reserves through repurchase agreements with Government security dealers, using this device more extensively [during December, 1955] than during any other month this year." (Federal Reserve Bank of New York, *Monthly Review of Credit and Business Conditions*, Vol. 38, No. 1, January, 1956, pp. 2–3.) Explain how these repurchase agreements may be used to affect member-bank reserves?

| Chapter XIX | THE ORGANIZATION OF THE FEDERAL RESERVE SYSTEM |

THE Federal Reserve System was created under provisions of an act signed by President Wilson on December 23, 1913. The preamble, or long title, of the Federal Reserve Act is: "An Act To provide for the establishment of Federal reserve banks, to furnish an elastic currency, to afford means of rediscounting commercial paper, to establish a more effective supervision of banking in the United States, and for other purposes."[1]

Today, if "other purposes" were to be given specific legislation, Congress would doubtless include "to foster orderly economic growth, a high level of employment, and a relatively stable general price level," because these goals have become the objectives of the Federal Reserve System. This chapter deals with the organization of the Federal Reserve System, which consists of the Board of Governors of the Federal Reserve System, the Federal Open Market Committee, the Federal Advisory Council, the twelve Federal Reserve banks and their branches, member banks, and special committees.

REGIONAL PLAN OF ORGANIZATION

The framers of our central-banking system believed that the economic interests of the United States could be cared for more rationally by regional banks than by one central bank. The one central bank plan, which is customary abroad, was opposed on economic, geographical, and political grounds. The United States had had experience with the one central bank plan (1791–1811 and 1816–36) and did not favor it because the American people are traditionally opposed to a great concentration of financial powers.

The Federal Reserve Act provided that there were to be no more than twelve or less than eight Federal Reserve banks and districts. The difficult task of dividing the United States into districts and selecting sites for Federal Reserve banks was given to an organization committee composed of three men—the Secretary of the

[1] Federal Reserve Act, approved December 23, 1913," 38 Statute, 251, ch. 6.

347

Treasury, the Comptroller of the Currency, and the Secretary of Agriculture.

Organization Committee. The Organization Committee held public hearings in eighteen cities; gave each national bank an opportunity to state by card ballot its choice of location for the Federal Reserve bank with which it desired to be connected; received petitions from clearinghouse associations, chambers of commerce, or other representatives of two hundred cities; and received requests from thirty-seven cities to be designated as the site of a Federal Reserve bank.

After three months of investigation the Organization Committee announced its decision to create the maximum number of banks and districts, with Reserve banks in each of the following cities: Boston, New York, Philadelphia, Cleveland, Richmond, Atlanta, Chicago, St. Louis, Minneapolis, Kansas City, Dallas, and San Francisco. (See Map 1.) The economic factors which guided the Organization Committee in its work were: (1) existing financial, mercantile, and industrial relations between areas and cities within the proposed Federal Reserve districts; (2) normal transportation and communication facilities; (3) prevailing business activities within a region; (4) probable ability of the Reserve bank to serve its district; and (5) equitable distribution of member banks among the districts, with particular care taken to see that the future member banks in the district would be able to subscribe the minimum required capital ($4,000,000) for each Reserve bank.

Federal Reserve Board. The members of the Federal Reserve Board, now the Board of Governors of the Federal Reserve System, took office on August 10, 1914. Its membership included two members of the Organization Committee (the Secretary of the Treasury and the Comptroller of the Currency) and five others appointed by the President with the consent of the United States Senate. Since 1914 the number of members on the Board has been changed twice, with the present make-up being provided for in the Banking Act of 1935. Now the Board is composed of seven members appointed by the President with the consent of the Senate. It is called the Board of Governors of the Federal Reserve System, but the older and shorter title is commonly used by the press.

Although the Board was authorized to adjust Federal Reserve district boundaries and to change the locations of Federal Reserve banks, no changes were made in the latter; and only minor ones were made in district boundaries. After the outbreak of World War I

MAP 1

FEDERAL RESERVE SYSTEM

Boundaries of Federal Reserve Districts and Their Branch Territories

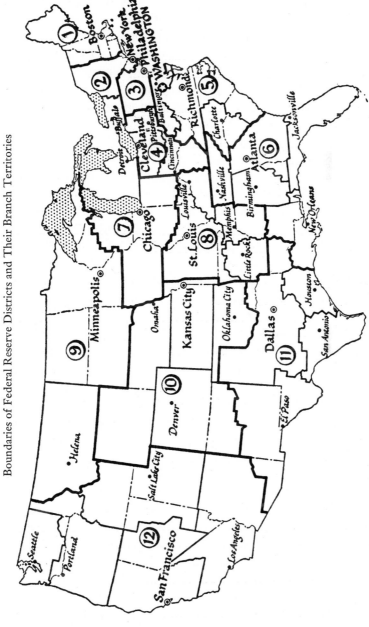

Source: *Federal Reserve Bulletin* (July, 1956).

the plans for organization of the Federal Reserve banks were hastened; and they were opened for business in November, 1914, just ten and one half months after the passage of the Federal Reserve Act.

Federal Advisory Council. The Federal Reserve Act also provided for a Federal Advisory Council, whose function, as the title implies, is purely advisory. Although the Council's advice and recommendations as to Federal Reserve bank operations, Federal Reserve policies, and general economic conditions are not binding on the Board of Governors, they are given consideration by the Board. The Council is composed of twelve members who are usually commercial bankers. They are selected by the boards of directors of the twelve Federal Reserve banks.

Member Banks. Membership in the Federal Reserve System is required of all national banks; and state banks, trust companies, mutual savings banks, and industrial banks may apply for membership. Technically, the desire for membership is indicated by an application, on a form that is provided by the Board of Governors, to buy an amount of capital stock of the district Federal Reserve bank equal to 6 per cent of the applying bank's paid-in capital stock and surplus. For a mutual savings bank, which has no capital stock, the amount equals six tenths of 1 per cent of its total deposit liabilities.[2] Before state-chartered banks may become member banks, the laws of the state under which they are incorporated have to authorize participation. One of the chief reasons why so few state-chartered banks applied for membership before 1917 was the delay on the part of states to give the necessary permission. But, during World War I, this situation was changed; and membership among state banks increased substantially.

CHANGES WITHIN THE FEDERAL RESERVE SYSTEM

Although only minor changes have been made in the framework of the Federal Reserve System, many important changes have taken place within the System. The most significant of these has been the concentration of power in the hands of the Board of Governors, which is responsible for all major decisions with the exception of investing, for which the Federal Open Market Committee is responsible.

The Federal Open Market Committee was provided for by Congress in 1933, but it had been functioning under regulations as to policy issued by the Federal Reserve Board in 1923. With minor

[2] For more complete details, see Board of Governors of the Federal Reserve System, *Regulation H.* Mutual savings banks and Morris-plan types of banks were first authorized by Congress to participate in the Federal Reserve System in 1933.

exceptions, its present membership and certain powers date from the passage of the Banking Act of 1935. Now the Committee consists of the members of the Board of Governors and five presidents of Federal Reserve banks, four of whom are elected annually. (The fifth is the President of the Federal Reserve Bank of New York, which has continuous representation on the Committee.)[3]

The most unusual aspect of the Federal Reserve System is the existence of twelve banks that have all the functions of central banks but whose major policies are determined for them by the Board of Governors and the Federal Open Market Committee in Washington (instead of by their own boards of directors as is the case with ordinary banks). Thus, in effect, the Federal Reserve banks are but individual units of a group central-banking system. The minor role currently played by these central banks in making policy decisions was not the original intention. But the United States of today is very different from that of 1913. Economic conditions within the country were revolutionized by the development of modern means of transportation and communication which shifted the emphasis away from regional problems to national problems. Equally important developments have taken place in the field of international finance. Following World War I, the United States emerged as one of the most important trade nations in the world, with New York as a leading financial center.

The economic collapse of 1929 resulted in a change in administration in Washington and ushered in a new philosophy of the role of the government in monetary and other economic affairs. So, today, we have twelve Federal Reserve banks performing all central banking functions—note issue, holding and creating bank reserves, and acting as fiscal agents for the national government—but carrying out decisions made, for the most part, by the Board of Governors of the Federal Reserve System and the Treasury Department in Washington.

The concentration of power on national credit and monetary policies in Washington has set the stage for a conflict between those in favor of greater governmental control of the Federal Reserve System and those in favor of "an independent Federal Reserve System." The issue flared in 1950, when there was a break between the Treasury and the Federal Reserve System over the question of stabilizing the

---

[3] The grouping of Federal Reserve banks for selecting the four members on the Open Market Committee is: Boston, Philadelphia, and Richmond; Chicago and Cleveland; Atlanta, Dallas, and St. Louis; and Minneapolis, Kansas City, and San Francisco.

price of government securities in the open market. During World War II, the federal government debt increased sharply; and the Federal Reserve System worked closely with the United States Treasury in stabilizing the price of government obligations. After the war, the Federal Reserve System opposed the free (unlimited) use of Federal Reserve credit to support government bond prices because of the inflationary effects of additional Federal Reserve bank credit on the economy as a whole. An "accord" was reached and announced on March 4, 1951, whereby the Federal Reserve System agreed to support an "orderly" market for government securities without any commitment as to interest rates (or security prices).

What the Federal Reserve System means by an "independent Federal Reserve System" is one independent of the executive branch of the government. Although the System is subject to legislative action by Congress, Congress should not make the System subordinate to the executive branch of the government. The Federal Reserve System should never be required to give primary consideration to financing the federal government and secondary consideration to the problems affecting the private sector of the economy. However, dividing control over money matters and credit matters may lead to situations wherein the Federal Reserve System and the Treasury would operate at cross-purposes with undesirable results. Today, a high degree of co-operation has been achieved between these two powerful agencies.

BOARD OF GOVERNORS OF THE FEDERAL RESERVE SYSTEM

Since 1936 the term of office for members of the Board of Governors of the Federal Reserve System has been fourteen years, with the terms arranged so as to have one term expiring every two years. This arrangement is expected to assure continuity of policies and a majority of experienced members. After serving a full term, a member may not be reappointed. It has been suggested that a shorter term with no restrictions as to reappointment would give the Board more enthusiastic and efficient members.

Although the members of the Board of Governors and its staff are often thought of as government employees, they are paid from funds secured from levies on the Federal Reserve banks. Geographic and economic representation on the Board is assured by the provision which requires the President to have "due regard to fair representation of the financial, agricultural, industrial and commercial interests and geographical divisions of the country" in his appointments. Each member is now called "Governor," and the President appoints one member as chairman and another as vice-chairman. The chairman and vice-chairman hold these offices for four years, but both may continue to be members of the Board after the expiration of their chairmanship terms. The chairman is the chief executive officer and spokesman of the Board of Governors, but he is subject to the Board's supervision.

Among the proposals to change the Federal Reserve System, one is to reduce the size of the Board (as proposed by the Hoover Commission). Those in favor of a board of three or five argue that better men would be attracted and that the board's decisions would be more prompt and better timed. Those opposed to this change contend that better decisions may be obtained by drawing on the wisdom of a larger group and that with a smaller board illness and absence of one member might delay decisions.

An even more sweeping proposal is to replace the Board of Governors and the Federal Open Market Committee with a governor who would have the deciding vote, two deputy governors, and advisory committees. The most important of the advisory committees would be made up of the twelve presidents of the Federal Reserve banks. Only after a conference with this committee could a major change in policy be initiated. The arguments in favor of and opposed to this proposal are the same as those in favor of and opposed to a smaller board.[4]

The Board of Governors of the Federal Reserve System is the directing agency of the System. It has many specific powers over the internal operations of Federal Reserve banks, including the power (1) to permit or require one Reserve bank to rediscount for a second Reserve bank; (2) to define the character of paper eligible for rediscount at the twelve Federal Reserve banks; (3) to prescribe the rules as to rediscounting; (4) to review and fix discount rates set by the Federal Reserve banks' directors; (5) to specify terms and conditions under which selective credit control regulations are to be administered; (6) to suspend reserve requirements of the Reserve banks for thirty days and to renew such suspension for fifteen-day periods (this power was used on one occasion, March 3, 1933, and it had no practical effect because the return flow of currency and gold to banks after the banking holiday was sufficient to keep the reserve

[4] Joint Committee on Economic Report, *Monetary Policy and Management of the Public Debt* (Washington, D.C.: U.S. Government Printing Office, 1952), Part 1, pp. 302-4.

ratio above the minimum required); (7) to examine the Federal Reserve banks; (8) to approve operating budgets including compensation of the chief officers and the salary classification for the staffs; (9) to approve the appointments of the president, vice-presidents, and the officers in charge of examinations and examiners; (10) to appoint Class C directors and designate one for each Federal Reserve bank as Federal Reserve agent and chairman of that Federal Reserve bank's board of directors, and a second Class C director as the deputy-chairman; (11) to permit or require the closing of branches and agencies; (12) to specify certain standards to be followed in dealing with member banks; and (13) to authorize and approve arrangements and relationships between Federal Reserve banks and foreign central banks and governments.[5]

The Board of Governors supervises and regulates the issue and retirement of Federal Reserve notes, a function which includes the formulation of rules and regulations for safeguarding all securities held as collateral for all Federal Reserve notes in circulation. The Board may withhold issues of Federal Reserve notes and impose interest charges on those in circulation. The Board acts as a clearinghouse for Federal Reserve banks and requires the Federal Reserve banks to act as clearinghouses for member banks. It has the authority to determine charges that may be made for the collection and payment of checks and drafts.

The Board of Governors has many powers pertaining to member banks, including among others (1) to pass on requests for admission of voluntary membership; (2) to limit, by regulation, the rate of interest which may be paid on time and savings deposits; (3) to expel a bank from membership in the Federal Reserve System; (4) to reduce or suspend a bank's discount privilege; (5) to regulate interlocking directorates; (6) to pass on requests of a state member bank to establish an out-of-town branch; (7) to pass on applications of national banks for authority to exercise tiust powers; (8) to grant authority to national banks to establish foreign branches; (9) to regulate the granting of acceptance credit; (10) to pass on requests of

---

[5] The regulations of the Board of Governors which are designated by letters of the alphabet and pertain to the activities of the Federal Reserve banks are: "A," discount for and advances to member banks; "B," open-market purchases of bills and bankers' acceptances; "E," purchase of warrants by Federal Reserve banks; "G," collection of noncash items; "J," check clearing and collection; "N," relations with foreign banks and bankers; "S," industrial loans by Reserve banks; and "V," financing of war production pursuant to the Defense Production Act of 1950.

member banks to accept drafts in excess of 50 per cent of their capital and surplus; (11) to increase or decrease reserve requirements within limits fixed by law; (12) to prescribe the conditions under which member banks' reserves may be deficient; (13) to supervise all international banking arrangements, including the formation of foreign branches, agencies, and correspondent agreements; (14) to examine state-member banks; (15) to remove any officer or director of any member bank "for continued violation of the law or unsound practices in conducting the business" of his bank; and (16) to require reports from member banks.[6]

In 1919, and on other occasions since that time, the Board of Governors has been given powers and responsibilities by Congress over the activities of financial institutions other than Federal Reserve banks and member banks. The first of these acts pertained to the chartering of bank corporations authorized to do a foreign banking business under the Federal Reserve Act as amended in 1919. The Board was made responsible for chartering, supervising, and examining these institutions. In 1933 Congress brought group banking under regulation by requiring any holding company owning or controlling any member bank to obtain a "voting permit" from the Board of Governors. Prior to giving the permit to vote the stock of the member bank, the bank holding company is required to agree to submit to periodic examinations, to file an annual report, and to meet certain standard requirements as to building up "surplus" by retaining earnings.

The greatest break with past regulatory policies came when the Board of Governors was authorized to regulate the use of credit by (1) brokers, dealers, and members of national securities exchanges; (2) advances of consumer credit by banks, other financial institutions, dealers, retailers, and others; and (3) the use of credit in new real

---

[6] The regulations of the Board of Governors which are designated by letters of the alphabet and pertain particularly to the activities of member banks are: "C," acceptance of drafts and bills of exchange by member banks; "D," required member bank reserves with Federal Reserve banks; "F," trust powers of national banks; "H," membership of state banking institutions in the Federal Reserve System; "I," changes in capital stock of Reserve banks (owned by member banks) and the issuance of new stock certificates; "L," interlocking bank directorates under the Clayton Act; "M," foreign branches of national banks and of corporations organized under provisions of Section 25 (a) of the Federal Reserve Act; "O," loans to executive officers of member banks; "Q," maximum rates of interest payable on time and savings deposits by member banks; "U," loans for the purpose of carrying stocks registered on national securities exchanges; "W," consumer credit; "V," financing of war production pursuant to the Defense Production Act of 1950; and "X," real estate credit.

estate construction (with the concurrence of the Administrator of the Housing and Home Finance Agency when the credit is to be used for construction of residential property).[7]

The chief divisions of the Board of Governors staff are: (1) Office of the Secretary, (2) Legal Division, (3) Division of Research and Statistics, (4) Division of Examinations, (5) Division of Bank Operations, (6) Office of the Controller, (7) Division of Personnel Administration, (8) Division of International Finance, (9) Office of Defense Loans, and (10) Division of Administrative Services.

FEDERAL OPEN MARKET COMMITTEE

The Federal Open Market Committee was created in recognition of the increased importance of Federal Reserve banks' investments. Control over the lending operations of the Federal Reserve banks was stressed originally because Reserve banks' lending was considered to be the most important means by which Federal Reserve bank credit would be obtained. This was in keeping with the emphasis then placed on the commercial aspect of banking. Prior to 1922, most of the open-market operations of Federal Reserve banks were in bankers' acceptances; and, when they did purchase other credit instruments in the open market, such purchases were in accordance with decisions made by each Federal Reserve bank's own directors and officers. The purchases were usually made to supplement the bank's income; and this need for supplementary income became important, during 1921 and 1922, when discounts and advances of the Federal Reserve banks fell sharply.

In May, 1922, the chief executive officers of the Federal Reserve banks appointed a committee for "the centralized execution of purchases and sales of government securities." Little in the way of policy decisions was involved. In March, 1923, the Federal Reserve Board, by resolution, created a "Federal Open Market Investment Committee" (the Federal Reserve banks of Boston, New York, Philadelphia, Chicago, and Cleveland were represented). The Board

---

[7] The regulations of the Board of Governors which are designated by letters of the alphabet and pertain, in whole or part, to the activities of institutions other than Federal Reserve banks and member banks are: "K," banking corporations authorized to do foreign banking business under the terms of Section 25 (a) of the Federal Reserve Act; "P," holding company affiliates—voting permits; "R," relationship of dealers in securities with Federal Reserve and member banks—generally forbidden to be directors and/or officers; "T," credit extended by brokers, dealers, and members of national securities exchanges; "W," consumer credit; "X," real estate credit (currently "W" and "X" are not in effect) and "Y," bank holding companies.

of Governors required this committee in its open-market operations to give primary consideration to the "accommodation of commerce and business" and to the effects of purchases and sales of securities on the general credit situation. A "System Open Market Account" was also created in which participation as to assets and income was allocated among the Federal Reserve banks. However, individual Reserve banks were permitted to maintain separate accounts of their own.

In March, 1930, an "Open Market Policy Conference," consisting of representatives of all Federal Reserve banks, was created; and the members of this "conference" became the members of the Federal Open Market Committee when it was provided for in the Banking Act of 1933.

In the Banking Act of 1935, concentration of responsibility for Federal Reserve banks' investments was made complete; and membership on the Committee was changed. Now the Federal Open Market Committee is made up of the members of the Board of Governors and the presidents of five of the Federal Reserve banks, including the president of the Federal Reserve Bank of New York. The new Open Market Committee required all securities held by Reserve banks to be transferred to the Federal Reserve System account; and subsequently all purchases and sales of government securities have been made according to the directions of the Committee, except during World War II when a special policy was followed in regard to Treasury bills.

Previous to June, 1955, the Federal Open Market Committee had an executive committee which carried out the decisions of the full Committee. Since improvements in transportation permit members to assemble on less than twenty-four hours notice, it was decided to discontinue the executive committee. Transactions in government securities are executed by the Federal Reserve Bank of New York (as agent), where a staff of economists and specialists is responsible for the daily operations of the System's open-market accounts.

As to the future composition of the Federal Open Market Committee, some favor the elimination of representation of Federal Reserve banks and making the Board of Governors responsible for all instruments of Federal Reserve policy; and others go to the opposite extreme favoring a return to the type of membership current before 1936. Greater co-ordination of credit policies would be achieved by placing exclusive responsibility for open-market operations, discount rates, and member-bank reserve requirements in the hands of either the Federal Open Market Committee or the Board of Governors.

THE FEDERAL RESERVE BANKS

The twelve Reserve banks are corporations having indeterminate charters issued by the federal government under a special chartering act. All their capital stock is owned by member banks, who must subscribe for capital stock equal to 6 per cent of their capital and surplus (one half paid in cash and the other half subject to call). The stock carries a provision for a maximum of 6 per cent cumulative dividend, which has been paid every year since 1916. This restriction on dividends was inserted so that the management of Reserve banks would not forget that the banks are to be operated as public and not as private institutions for profit. The income of the Reserve banks is used to cover the expenses of the Federal Reserve banks, the Board of Governors, and the Open Market Committee. After expenses and dividends are paid, the remainder is paid to the government or added to the "surplus," with the government receiving nine tenths at the present time.

Board of Directors. Provisions for management of the Reserve banks are similar to those of other large banking institutions. Each of these banks has a board of directors of nine members each having a term of office of three years. Six of the directors are selected by member banks (stockholders), and three are appointed by the Board of Governors of the Federal Reserve System (Class C directors). Three of the six directors selected by the member banks must be bankers (Class A directors), and three must represent industry (Class B directors). "Looking at the make-up of Reserve bank board of directors in another way, Class A directors represent lenders of funds, Class B directors represent borrowers, and Class C represent the interest of the general public."[8]

The board of directors of a Federal Reserve bank performs duties comparable to those of directors of any commercial banks, such as (1) adoption of bylaws under which the bank's general business is conducted; (2) selection of officers and their salaries, subject to approval by the Board of Governors; (3) appointment of an auditor in charge of internal auditing of the bank's books; (4) preparation of the annual budget, which is reviewed by the Board; and (5) supervision of the general functioning of the bank.

[8] Board of Governors of the Federal Reserve System, *The Federal Reserve System, Its Purposes and Functions* (Washington, D.C., 1947), pp. 53–54.

Directors of Federal Reserve banks also have functions peculiar to these banks, such as (1) election of a member and an alternate member of the Federal Open Market Committee as provided by law; (2) appointment of (*a*) a member to the Federal Advisory Council, (*b*) four of the seven directors including the chairman of branch offices, and (*c*) an industrial advisory committee to advise the bank on applications for industrial loans. The directors must make recommendations to the Board of Governors on applications for voting permits by holding companies and applications for trust powers by national banks. The board of directors or its executive committee must meet at least biweekly to pass upon discounts and advances, discount rates, and other matters requiring action. The board must keep itself informed as to the credit situation in its district, and this matter must be considered at each meeting.

Officers. The president is the chief executive officer of his bank and is responsible for its general functioning. All executive officers, except the auditor, are directly responsible to him. Although the president is not a member of the board of directors, he attends the meetings and participates in its discussions.

All Federal Reserve banks have a first vice-president, a variable number of other vice-presidents, and other officers in charge of departments and branches. There are officers in charge of discounts and collection of notes and other items; clearing of checks and transfer of funds; applying for Federal Reserve notes and providing the necessary collateral; fiscal agency functions for the government; bank examinations; collecting, analyzing, and distributing economic data; and personnel.

Federal Reserve Agent. One of the Class C directors is, at the same time, the chairman of the board of directors and the Federal Reserve agent. He presides at all meetings of the board and, in his absence, his place is taken by the deputy-chairman. The Federal Reserve agent is appointed by and is the official representative of the Board of Governors at his bank (as is the deputy-chairman). With the help of assistants, he administers duties in connection with the issuance of Federal Reserve notes and has such other powers as may be specified by the Board of Governors and by the board of directors of his bank.

Proposed Changes in Organization. Among the proposed changes pertaining to the organization of the Federal Reserve banks is one to transfer all Federal Reserve bank stock to the government and permit the Board of Governors to appoint both Class B and

Class C directors. Not much would be gained from such a change because credit policy is determined by the Board and the Federal Open Market Committee. Generally, directors do not act as representatives of their classes after they take office. In determining national credit policy, directors act only on discount rates which are subject to review and determination by the Board of Governors. The presidents of Federal Reserve banks, as members of the Federal Open Market Committee, act as individuals and not as agents of their boards of directors; although they may be influenced by the opinions of their boards.

BRANCHES AS AIDS TO MEMBER BANKS

Branches of Federal Reserve banks are offices of these banks that perform most of the functions of their parent banks. In effect, a branch bank is a miniature Federal Reserve bank, having a seven-man board of directors, of whom three are appointed by the Board of Governors and four by the parent bank. However, these directors serve in an advisory capacity and have no powers corresponding to those of directors of Federal Reserve banks.[9]

The deciding factors in placing branches are geographical and economic. Compact districts within easy reach of the district reserve city, such as districts 1 (Boston) and 3 (Philadelphia), have no branches; others have only one; but, in the South and West, where the districts are large, some Federal Reserve banks have three and four branches. Each branch is assigned a territory which includes banks that normally transact business with the city in which the branch is located. (See Map 1, p. 349.)

The specific activities of the branches depend upon rules and regulations of the Board and grants of power by the parent bank. Some of the branches carry on independently the same activities as those performed by the parent bank. During World War II the Federal Reserve banks increased the functions and powers of branches in order that they could give better service to member banks and the government. Now most of the branches have fiscal and certain other central-banking functions comparable to those of the head office.

By creating branches, the Federal Reserve authorities have given

[9] Twenty-five branches and two agencies have been established; but the Spokane branch of the San Francisco bank and the Havana, Cuba, agency of the Atlanta bank were discontinued in October, 1938, and the Savannah agency of the Atlanta bank was discontinued in 1945. An agency merely acts for a Federal Reserve bank in handling some routine functions such as making currency available to local banks.

member banks located in and near branch cities many of the advantages of a Federal Reserve city location. These advantages include: (1) faster clearing and collection of checks and other items; (2) reduction in vault cash needed since new currency can be obtained quickly; and (3) closer personal touch between member banks' officers and Federal Reserve banks' officers.

MEMBER BANKS

Member banks are national banks and those state-chartered banks which have met the requirements for and have been admitted to membership in the Federal Reserve System. After being admitted, a state member bank may withdraw after giving six months' notice (which requirement may be waived by the Board of Governors). The state member bank may also be expelled by the Board of Governors. Upon withdrawal, a member bank must surrender the Federal Reserve bank stock which it owns (being paid at par plus accrued dividends). Prior to 1952, a state-chartered bank's capital had to be equal to the amount required of a national bank similarly located. In 1952 Congress made membership easier by adopting about the same rules as those that apply to participation in Federal Deposit Insurance Corporation.

Since 1930, as a result of bank failures and bank mergers, there has been a decline in the total number of banks, including member banks; but now member banks' total assets are the highest in the history of the Federal Reserve System, both absolutely and relative to total commercial-bank assets. Member banks include about 4,780 national banks, 1,870 state-chartered banks (including three mutual savings banks). Deposits in member banks represent about 85 per cent of all commercial bank deposits, with national banks holding about 60 per cent and state-member banks about 40 per cent of member-bank deposits.

Being a member bank has certain peculiar characteristics that are justified on a broad social basis. Member banks provide the capital stock of their Federal Reserve banks on which they receive 6 per cent cumulative dividends, and they help to select six of their Federal Reserve banks' nine directors. A member bank's subscription to stock of its Federal Reserve bank is fixed at 6 per cent of the member bank's paid-in capital and surplus, and only one half of the subscription has been called. Because the Federal Reserve banks have the right of note issue, they could operate without any capital or deposits of member banks; therefore, about the only justification for calling upon member banks to buy all the shares subscribed for would be that it would give them more income (6 per cent is paid on their stock) and to make membership more attractive.

The amount of stock held by member banks is adjusted semi-annually. Stock certificates are not transferable and must be canceled if a bank ceases to be a member. There is no annual meeting of stockholders of Federal Reserve banks, and stockholder participation in management is limited to the election of six directors. As in most co-operative associations, each member has but one vote; but member banks are divided into three groups according to size, and each group elects one Class A director and one Class B director. Many of the proprietary rights that one associates with ownership are lacking in the relationship between member-bank stockholders and their Federal Reserve banks.

Member banks' legal reserves are kept with their Federal Reserve banks as checking accounts, and written or telegraphic orders on these deposit accounts are the preferred means of payment in financial circles in the United States. The Federal Reserve System also offers a nation-wide clearing and collection service at little or no cost which has improved the quality of checkbook money and other credit instruments. Currency in any available denomination may be obtained from Federal Reserve banks with these banks absorbing the shipping costs. The Federal Reserve banks also provide member banks with many advisory and safekeeping services as well as giving them the privilege of borrowing from them. While the wisdom of including many small banks in the Federal Reserve System has been questioned, the fact remains that, in order to be most effective, national credit policy must apply to all commercial banks. Because membership in the Federal Deposit Insurance Corporation is more attractive than membership in the Federal Reserve System, it has been proposed, as a method of increasing Federal Reserve membership, to make membership in the Federal Reserve System a prerequisite for membership in the Federal Deposit Insurance Corporation (rather than the other way around, as is true today).

Nonmember Banks. In explaining the existence of the large number of nonmember banks, it should be noted that, prior to 1952, many banks could not meet the capital requirements for membership.[10] Over one half of the deposits not held by member banks are those

[10] Now a state-chartered bank may be admitted to membership provided: (1) its capital stock and surplus are adequate in the opinion of the Board, and (2) it is approved for deposit insurance under the Federal Deposit Insurance Corporation Act. See *Federal Reserve Bulletin* (July, 1952), pp. 773–74.

of mutual savings banks for whom membership in the Federal Reserve System has few advantages (such as clearing and collection of checks and borrowing or rediscounting). Many nonmember commercial banks do not desire membership because more profitable banking may be carried on outside the System and they may obtain central banking services from their correspondent banks. Some of the nonmember commercial banks secure considerable revenue from exchange charges on checks forwarded to them for payment, while member banks must remit at par. But most important is the fact that nonmember banks' primary reserves need not be as large as those of member banks, and this is reflected in the earnings of nonmember banks.

State laws affecting nonmember banks' officers and directors are less restrictive, there being fewer restrictions on interlocking directorates, loans to officers, and number of directors. Finally, nonmember banks may be subject to fewer restrictions on loans and investments and less rigid examinations. However, some of these so-called advantages formerly enjoyed by nonmember banks have been eliminated by the standards set by the Federal Deposit Insurance Corporation, which has an important financial interest in the well-being of all insured banks. On the other hand, some of the privileges usually associated with membership in the Federal Reserve System have been extended to nonmember banks. These include (1) use of the clearing and collection services of the Federal Reserve System, provided the clearing nonmember banks keep funds on deposit with the Federal Reserve banks and remit at par for cash items collected, and (2) the privilege of obtaining funds from the Federal Reserve banks under special circumstances.

SUMMARY

The main divisions of the Federal Reserve System are the Board of Governors of the Federal Reserve System, the Federal Open Market Committee, the twelve Federal Reserve banks, and the member banks. The central banking part of the System consists of the Federal Reserve banks and their branches and the central banking authorities in Washington—the Board of Governors and the Federal Open Market Committee which are responsible for all major policy decisions. In effect, the central banking system of the United States is a group banking system with major policy authority vested in hands other than the directors and officers of the Federal Reserve banks.

QUESTIONS AND PROBLEMS

1. "The framers [of the Federal Reserve System] had as their purpose the strengthening of the existing banking structure without changing fundamentally the existing unit banking system." How did they achieve their objective?

2. Identify: (*a*) regional plan of organization of the Federal Reserve System, (*b*) Federal Reserve Board, (*c*) Federal Reserve districts, and (*d*) Federal Reserve banks.

3. What important changes have taken place in the organization of the Federal Reserve System since 1914? In the location of power over credit policies?

4. Summarize the powers and duties of the Board of Governors of the Federal Reserve System.

5. Identify the Federal Open Market Committee. What changes have been made in its composition and powers since 1922? Why have these changes been made?

6. Who owns the Federal Reserve banks? Who manages them? Should the Federal Reserve banks be nationalized? Why?

7. What are the functions of the office of the Federal Reserve agent? What other positions do the Federal Reserve agents hold?

8. What are Federal Reserve branch banks? Who owns and operates them?

9. What constitutes membership in the Federal Reserve System? What institutions are compulsory members? Voluntary members? What recent changes have been made in the requirement for membership? Why?

10. What justification would there be for requiring all United States commercial banks to be members of the Federal Reserve System?

11. "The System might be compared to a great pyramid with its base in the grass roots of our economy, and its apex in the Board of Governors. The breadth and strength of the pyramid is in its base, with the member banks and the Reserve Banks as elevations in the slope toward the top." (T. B. McCabe, "The Significance of Membership in the Federal Reserve System," *Federal Reserve Bulletin*, November, 1948, p. 1, 340.) Do you agree? Why?

12. "We recommend . . . that every effort be made to build up the quality and prestige of Federal Reserve officials; among these measures should be a reduction in the number of members of the Board of Governors from seven to not more than five and an increase in their compensation." (*Report of the Subcommittee on Monetary, Credit, and Fiscal Policies of the Joint Committee on the Economic Report Congress of the United States* [Washington, D.C.: U.S. Government Printing Office, 1950], p. 2.) Discuss. Might not shorter terms with the right to hold a second term be helpful?

Chapter XX | OPERATIONS OF THE FEDERAL RESERVE BANKS

THE TWELVE Federal Reserve banks are the institutions that carry out the policies of the Board of Governors of the Federal Reserve System, the Federal Open Market Committee, and the banks' own boards of directors and officers (which are referred to in the aggregate as the Federal Reserve authorities). In addition, these banks, in the capacity of fiscal agents, perform many services for the federal government, foreign governments and central banks, and others.

It is relatively easy for a board of directors or a committee to decide on what should be done, but the real burden falls upon those who are to carry out or administer these decisions or policies. (The truth of this statement is supported by the relatively high salaries paid to officers of the Federal Reserve banks as compared to those paid to members of the Board of Governors of the Federal Reserve System, and the salaries paid to officers of commercial banks as compared to the stipend of members of their boards of directors.)

In this chapter, the routine aspects of what Federal Reserve banks do are stressed; but it is difficult to distinguish between purely routine decisions and policy decisions. In practice, it is doubtful if they can be separated. Most of the employees of Federal Reserve banks, like those of commercial banks, are engaged in so-called routine activities rather than policy-forming activities.

ADVANCES AND DISCOUNTS OF FEDERAL RESERVE BANKS

The charters of the Federal Reserve banks, being banks, contain powers permitting them to lend and to invest under the provisions of the law and regulations of the Board of Governors of the Federal Reserve System and the Federal Open Market Committee.

The general rules covering the Federal Reserve banks' advances (loans) and discounts for member banks and Federal Intermediate Credit banks (see Chapter XXX) are found in Regulation

A of the Board of Governors of the Federal Reserve System.[1] Although the Board of Governors formulates general principles and specific rules to be followed, their application and interpretation call for judgment on the part of the members of the board of directors, loan committee, and officers of the Federal Reserve banks from whom credit is sought.

The Federal Reserve banks follow lending procedures which are similar to those followed by commercial banks; but the lending policies of Federal Reserve banks are unlike those of commercial banks because the Federal Reserve banks are not operated for profit as are privately owned and operated financial institutions. All loans made by Federal Reserve banks are secured by collateral which is usually in the form of government securities (but, it may be eligible paper or, under certain circumstances, other types of earning assets). When a commercial bank borrows from a Federal Reserve bank, it fills out an application form and signs a promissory note. The application for credit must be examined first by two officers of the Federal Reserve banks and later reviewed at the weekly meeting of the Federal Reserve bank's discount or loan committee and the bank's board of directors.

A commercial bank which borrows from its Federal Reserve bank receives its loan in the form of credit applied to its reserve (deposit) account; and interest is discounted (deducted from the principal) immediately at the rate in effect (this is where the term *discount rate* originates). Most loans (advances) are for but one or two days and, when the loan matures, the Federal Reserve bank deducts the principal from the borrowing bank's deposit account.

Since the Federal Reserve bank must be assured that the purpose for which the applicant desires funds is in keeping with the System's general credit policy, the borrower must provide the Federal Reserve bank with details as to its business (as do individuals and business firms when they borrow from their banks). Since the borrowing bank's promissory note is customarily secured by government securities, the problem is one of justifying the advance of Federal Reserve credit rather than one of determining the credit worthiness of the borrower.

A member bank may obtain Federal Reserve credit by offering eligible paper for discount (sale with recourse). Eligible paper is paper which the Federal Reserve Act and the regulations of the

---

[1] For a complete revision of Regulation A, see *Federal Reserve Bulletin* (January, 1955), pp. 8–14.

Board of Governors permit the Federal Reserve banks to rediscount. To be eligible for rediscounting, the paper must (1) be drawn for so-called industrial, agricultural, or commercial purposes; (2) have a maturity at the time of rediscount of not more than ninety days (except agricultural paper; and (3) carry the endorsement of a member bank. For illustration, the First National Bank may take a promissory note of a local firm from its loan portfolio that meets the qualifications as to purpose and time, endorse the note, fill out an application form, and send the paper and other supporting documents to its Federal Reserve bank. In acting upon the application, little consideration is given to the credit risk because the paper has been endorsed by the member bank; therefore, after checking on the eligibility of the paper for rediscount, the problem is one of justifying the advance of Federal Reserve credit.

There are drawbacks to the use of the rediscount method of obtaining Federal Reserve funds. First, many businessmen, farmers, and other borrowers object to having their promises to pay rediscounted by member banks; second, member banks are frequently unable to provide the financial statements and other information required by the Federal Reserve banks about the names on the paper submitted for rediscount; and third, member banks often want to borrow for only a few days (in order to build up their reserves or for other reasons) and eligible paper of the correct maturity (one, two, five, ten, or fifteen days) and the exact amount may not be available.

Now the rediscount method of obtaining Federal Reserve funds is seldom used by member banks. However, Federal Reserve banks rediscount bankers' acceptances but these transactions differ from negotiations for loans at the discount window of the Federal Reserve banks (see below). Most of the loans obtained by member banks from their Federal Reserve banks are made on the basis of promissory notes secured by United States government securities. However, in lieu of government securities, member banks may offer eligible paper and other earning assets as collateral. If other earning assets are used, the member bank is required to pay an interest rate on his loan at least one half of 1 per cent per annum higher than it would have to pay if United States government securities or eligible paper were used as collateral.

The provision for permitting member banks to use assets other than government securities and eligible paper as collateral for their promissory notes in obtaining funds from Federal Reserve banks was a depression measure of the early 1930's; and there is little or no need for this provision at the present time. Nevertheless, retention of this provision may mean that the Federal Reserve banks are able to guarantee the liquidity (but not the solvency) of any member bank. However, the current regulations of the Board of Governors state that the Federal Reserve banks *may* (not *must*) make advances and *may* discount, which means that any application for a loan or discount may be rejected. Furthermore, the Board of Governors may forbid Federal Reserve banks, and even member banks, to make additional loans under certain circumstances.

The law requires each Federal Reserve bank to keep itself informed as to the amount and character of the loans and investments of its member banks; as a result, the Federal Reserve banks' credit files pertaining to banks, business firms, and others are reported to be more complete than those of any other lender in their respective districts. This information is used not only in determining whether to grant or refuse advances or discounts but also in ascertaining whether or not undue use is being made of bank credit in speculation "in securities, real estate, or commodities or for any other purpose inconsistent with the maintenance of sound credit conditions." In acting upon a rediscount or loan application, a Federal Reserve bank must give attention not only to the purpose for which funds are sought but also to the probable effect of granting the credit on both the bank requesting it and the economy as a whole.

Profit and Need Theories of Member Bank Borrowing. The two general theories as to why member banks borrow at their Federal Reserve banks are the *profit* theory and the *need* theory. According to the *profit* theory, member banks borrow in order to make a profit from the interest rate differential (borrowing at a Federal Reserve bank at 2 per cent and lending at 4 per cent) or to obtain a tax advantage because interest payments are deductible as an expense in computing the bank's income tax. Although member banks obviously profit from borrowing at their Federal Reserve banks, borrowing to make a profit as the primary motive is out of keeping with the policies of the Federal Reserve System. The Federal Reserve banks may enforce the System's nonprofit policy in many ways such as raising the discount rate, applying moral suasion, requiring excess collateral for advances, and refusing to lend.

The more widely accepted explanation of borrowing by member banks is the *need* for reserve funds resulting from seasonal, emergency, and other developments such as currency withdrawals, unfavorable clearinghouse balances, and emergency or seasonal demands for commercial bank credit. At the time the Federal Reserve System was created there was a strong tradition against commercial-bank borrowing and so the Federal Reserve officials were confronted with the problem of educating member banks to use their privilege of borrowing at the Federal Reserve banks without abusing it. While banks dislike borrowing as a general rule, they do so for the same reason that individuals borrow—because of a shortage of cash. Most commonly, commercial banks need such funds to adjust their reserve positions at their Federal Reserve banks.

Since member banks may adjust their reserve positions in several ways (see Chapter XXI), presumably they borrow from their Federal Reserve banks because this is the least expensive way of building up their reserve (deposit) accounts. This means that the saving motive (profit) is present even though the member bank has a *need* for Federal Reserve funds. When a member bank grants a loan to one of its customers, it usually gives the borrower deposit credit and this new deposit necessitates an increase in the member bank's reserve account with its Federal Reserve bank. When the member bank's borrowing customer draws checks on his account which are deposited in other banks, the lending member bank tends to have an unfavorable clearinghouse balance, to lose reserves, and to be confronted with a need for borrowing at its Federal Reserve bank. Since the profit motive dominated the member bank in granting the loan to its customer, in practice it is difficult to separate the *profit* and *need* motives when it comes to administration of Federal Reserve banks' loan policies. In conclusion, it is suggested that member banks do borrow from their Federal Reserve banks both for profit and because of need. An analysis of the previous lending and investing activities of the member bank may indicate that the need was caused by excessive or speculative lending or investing to enlarge profits.

LOANS TO INSTITUTIONS OTHER THAN MEMBER BANKS

Making loans to institutions other than banks has always been an important part of the activities of certain foreign central banks, but lending of this type is a recent development on the United States. In 1913, the objective of Congress was to create bankers' banks, not institutions that would compete with existing commercial banks. However the collapse of banking in many sections of the country during the period 1931–34 made it difficult for many borrowers to obtain funds for business purposes; and, in order to help these borrowers, the Federal Reserve Act was amended in 1932, 1933, and 1934 so as to permit such loans.

Emergency Loans. The 1932 amendment to the Federal Reserve Act permitted Reserve banks to discount for "any individual, partnership, or corporation, notes, drafts, and bills of exchange of the kinds and maturities made eligible for discount for member banks and under other provisions of this Act. . . ." (The term "corporation" includes nonmember banks.) There was no intention on the part of Congress to permit Reserve banks to make copious use of this new power, for it was specified that they were to discount only after evidence had been obtained showing that the applicant was "unable to secure adequate credit accommodations from other banking institutions."

The Emergency Banking Act of March 9, 1933, contained a paragraph which authorized Reserve banks to make advances directly to individuals, partnerships, and corporations on the promissory notes of such individuals, partnerships, and corporations if secured by United States government obligations. Such advances may be made for periods up to ninety days, but it is not the practice to make such advances except in unusual or exigent circumstances. Since commercial and industrial borrowers with such collateral can readily obtain credit accommodations from ordinary commercial banking sources, this amendment is of minor importance to them; but it is of importance to nonmember banks because it permits them to secure advances from the Federal Reserve banks.

Industrial Advances. The Industrial Loan Act of June 19, 1934, as amended by the Act of August 23, 1935, authorized the Federal Reserve banks to make working capital loans for terms not to exceed five years to established commercial and industrial enterprises. Industrial lending by the Reserve banks is financed by the federal government with "profits" which resulted from the devaluation of the gold dollar (January 30, 1934). The amount allotted by Congress to each Federal Reserve bank was a sum equal to each bank's investment in the original stock of the Federal Deposit Insurance Corporation (the aggregate having been $139,299,557). Funds obtained from the Treasury are accounted for under "Surplus, Section 13b." These funds are transferred to and from the Treasury to individual Reserve banks as needed, but only a small part of the amount authorized has been used at any one time.

The Industrial Loan Act authorized the Federal Reserve banks to make direct loans and to join other banking institutions in making such loans if the borrower is unable to obtain financial assistance on reasonable terms from usual sources. To date, few such loans have been made and most of the Federal Reserve credit used has been due to commitments to discount or buy loans on demand or to accept them as the basis for loans. (The required terms are such that the Reserve bank cannot lose more than 80 per cent of the loan because the financial institution which originally made the loan must obligate itself for 20 per cent of any loss.) In discounting and making loans, advances, and commitments, each Federal Reserve bank has the assistance of an advisory committee of from three to five industrial leaders in its district.[2]

Loans to Foreign Banks. The statutory powers of the Federal Reserve banks permit them to operate generally in the international field of finance; but, generally speaking, little use has been made of some of these powers, such as purchase and sale of foreign bills of exchange. Nevertheless, the Reserve banks have dealt in gold and foreign exchange and have made loans with gold as collateral. Since January 30, 1934, transactions in gold have been subject to licensing requirements of the Treasury department, but this is not true of loans of Reserve banks wherein gold is used as collateral and such loans are the principal means whereby the Federal Reserve banks extend credit to foreign central banks for seasonal and other temporary requirements.

From 1924 to 1933, the Federal Reserve banks (particularly the Federal Reserve Bank of New York) participated in foreign transactions on their own accounts to promote foreign currency stabilization. Credit arrangements were made with foreign central banks or governments for the Federal Reserve Bank of New York to purchase foreign bills of exchange when their prices needed support in New York. The funds used were in the nature of short-term revolving credits with gold pledged as collateral. In addition, in 1925, the Federal Reserve System entered into an agreement to sell up to $200,000,000 in gold to the Bank of England in return for English money to be used for investment in sterling bills of exchange. Today, dollar credits are made available to foreign central banks and governments chiefly by the International Monetary Fund, the World Bank, and the United States Treasury with the Federal Reserve Bank of New York acting as the fiscal agent.

Discounts for Intermediate Credit Banks. The federal inter-

---

[2] For rates on loans and commitments, see table entitled "Federal Reserve Bank Rates on Industrial Loans and Commitments under Section 13*b* of the Federal Reserve Act" in current issue of the *Federal Reserve Bulletin.* For details as to the requirements set for this type of lending, see Regulation "S" of the Board of Governors of the Federal Reserve System.

mediate credit banks are government owned institutions which act as banks of rediscount for rural banks, production credit associations, and other lenders in the agricultural credit field (see Chapter XXX). In case of need, the federal intermediate credit banks usually borrow funds in the open market through the sale of their notes or debentures; but, under certain circumstances, they may find it more advantageous to discount their paper with the Federal Reserve banks. Paper presented to a Federal Reserve bank for discount must be eligible and have a maturity at the time of discount of less than nine months. In acting upon applications for discount, the Federal Reserve bank must have "due regard to the probable needs of its own member banks" who are to have priority in the receipt of Federal Reserve credit. Furthermore no Federal Reserve bank is permitted to rediscount any paper presented by a federal intermediate credit bank if the paper bears the endorsement of a nonmember state bank or trust company that is eligible for membership in the Federal Reserve System, and any paper discounted by a Federal Reserve bank for an intermediate credit bank must have the endorsement of such bank.

INVESTMENTS AND OPEN-MARKET LENDING

In addition to their power to make advances and to rediscount for member banks and other institutions, the Federal Reserve banks have broad powers which permit them to buy and sell certain types of securities in the open market at home and abroad. In these transactions, they may deal with bond houses, trust companies, commerical banks, individual dealers, and brokers of all types. In practice, the Federal Reserve banks do not "keep shop" where business firms, banks, and others drop in to negotiate purchases and sales of securities (see below for an exception).

In order to keep the assets of the Federal Reserve banks in liquid and safe form, their open-market operations are limited by law to the following four classes of securities:

(*a*) Cable transfers, bankers' acceptances, and bills of exchange arising out of commercial transactions and the financing of the storage of staples;

(*b*) Bonds, notes, Treasury bills, and certificates of indebtedness of the United States government and all securities guaranteed by it;

(*c*) Bills, notes, revenue bonds, and warrants with maturity of six months or less, issued in anticipation of taxes or assured revenues by the state, county, municipality, or other political subdivisions within the United States; and (*d*) Acceptances or debentures of federal intermediate credit banks, national agricultural credit corporations, and other agricultural institutions.

Among the four classes of credit instruments listed above, only the first two have been important in the open-market operations of the Federal Reserve System. Now the Federal Open Market Committee is responsible for all of the System's purchases and sales of government securities.

Under current regulations of the Federal Open Market Committee, each Federal Reserve bank must keep the Committee informed as to all purchases and sales in the open market other than in United States government securities. All acceptances and other bills purchased or sold must be eligible under Regulation B of the Board of Governors. In addition, each Federal Reserve bank must follow the directions of the Federal Open Market Committee when trading in foreign money and purchasing cable transfers for its own account. Individual Federal Reserve banks may also purchase eligible bills, notes, revenue bonds, and warrants of states and their political subdivisions under provisions of Regulation E of the Board of Governors of the Federal Reserve System.

Bills and Acceptances. The Federal Reserve banks may purchase bills and acceptances that (1) have been accepted by the drawee prior to purchase and are accompanied or secured by shipping documents, warehouse receipts, or similar documents conveying title, or bear a satisfactory bank endorsement; and (2) have a maturity not in excess of ninety days (except for agricultural purposes when the maximum maturity at the time of discount is six months). A bill of exchange is not eligible for purchase unless it has been endorsed by a member bank or is accompanied by a satisfactory statement of the financial condition of one or more of the parties thereto. Unless accepted or endorsed by a member bank, a bankers' acceptance is not eligible for purchase by a Federal Reserve bank until the acceptor has furnished the Reserve bank a satisfactory financial statement and agrees in writing to provide information on request concerning the transaction underlying the acceptance.

Two of the defects of the American banking system noted by the National Monetary Commission were the lack of commercial paper of a standard quality and the absence of a broad discount market. The Federal Reserve System has tried to correct these defects —the first by popularizing bankers' and trade acceptances, and the second by supporting the acceptance market.

From the beginning of the Federal Reserve System, the Federal Reserve banks have supported the market for bankers' acceptances by buying all eligible bills offered at their posted buying rates. This means that if the rate is 2 per cent and no one else will pay $9,950 for an eligible 91-day $10,000 bill, the Reserve banks will. The discount rates of Reserve banks are usually higher than the rates of other buyers; and, in effect, this means that the Federal Reserve banks are usually out of the market. Buying rates for the same time classes of bankers' acceptances are the same among the Federal Reserve banks; but they may be, and have been, different for short periods of time.

Bankers' acceptances are used primarily in private financing of foreign trade, and the buying rate for acceptances is given little publicity because "it does not ordinarily reflect judgment as to the general credit situation." Usually sales transactions are initiated by sellers, and the only way that the Federal Reserve banks encourage or discourage such sales is by lowering or raising the discount rate. In practice, this policy is passive rather than active, but all policies are subject to change, and early in 1955 the Federal Reserve Bank of New York purchased moderate amounts of acceptances from dealers at the direction of the Federal Open Market Committee. One of the reasons for this action was to broaden the market for bankers' acceptances and to develop a greater interest in this type of financing.

One means whereby the Federal Reserve banks may smooth out prices in the commercial bill market is by buying bills under repurchase agreements which are later reclaimed by the seller at the purchase price plus interest. The Federal Reserve Bank of New York also purchases bankers' acceptances as agent for foreign banks.

Government Securities. The Federal Open Market Committee uses the Federal Reserve Bank of New York as fiscal agent in carrying out its open-market operations in government securities. The over-the-counter (more accurately, the "over-the-telephone") market entails negotiations between buyers and sellers. Usually, the Federal Reserve Bank of New York deals through a limited number of dealers in order to minimize the number of transactions and to make its policies more effective. This means that banks and others do not sell their securities directly to the Federal Reserve Bank of New York (acting for the Federal Open Market Committee). During World War II, a different policy was used in regard to Treasury bills; this is discussed in Chapter XXII, where arrangements between the Treasury and the Federal Reserve System are examined.

In recent years, most of the open-market operations of the Federal Reserve System in government securities are in the "short-end" of the market—bills and certificates, notes, and bonds that are approaching maturity. The justification for this policy is that the monetary effects of a purchase or sale of short-term government securities will be felt most rapidly when the securities are owned by or will be purchased by commercial banks. Interest rate fluctuations on United States Treasury bills and other short-term obligations will be rapid, and these changes will affect the lending and investing policies of commercial banks. However, this policy of concentrating open-market operations in the short-end of the market is not a rigid one, being subject to change to meet changing circumstances. This happened in December, 1955, when the Federal Reserve System purchased newly issued certificates of indebtedness in order to help the United States Treasury at a time when the sale of the new issue was going badly. The Federal Reserve System is committed to helping in the maintenance of an orderly market for government securities; and at that time (December, 1955), there was a demand for more member-bank reserves to meet seasonal needs. Therefore two objectives were achieved by the purchase of certificates of indebtedness—an orderly market for government securities was maintained and new reserves were provided.

When the Federal Reserve System purchases government securities directly from the United States Treasury, the amount held at any one time may not exceed $5 billion. In the case of treasury bills, the Federal Reserve System may or may not place a bid for part of the weekly offering of the United States Treasury. If it does not bid or if the bid is too low, the Federal Reserve System will be paid in cash for its maturing obligations. Customarily, the Federal Reserve Bank of New York as agent is able to judge the market accurately enough to replenish its holdings of old bills with new bills. The other maturing government issues (certificates of indebtedness, notes, and bonds) are usually refunded by the Treasury. The Federal Reserve System may or may not accept the new securities offered in exchange for the maturing issue.

BANKERS FOR THE FEDERAL GOVERNMENT AND AGENCIES

The United States government has been by far the largest and most important single customer of the Federal Reserve banks. Since their existence, the Reserve banks have acted as both the commercial and the investment bankers for the government.

Depository Functions. The United States Treasury keeps its chief checking accounts with the Reserve banks; and, with minor exceptions, funds are transferred from ordinary banks to the Federal Reserve banks before they are spent. The receipts from taxpayers, from sales of government securities, and from other minor sources are deposited with the Reserve banks, their branches, or selected member banks designated as general or limited depositories. While the government finds it desirable to use the Federal Reserve banks as the chief medium through which to make disbursements, it has found it convenient to use other financial institutions to handle routine business not handled by the Treasury and to use member banks temporarily as special depositories.

The tax-and-loan accounts kept with banks are supervised by the Federal Reserve banks as fiscal agents of the government. The Reserve banks check on the collateral pledged as security for the balances in these accounts. The accounts are drawn on as needed and the funds are transferred to the Treasury checking accounts with the Federal Reserve banks. The amount to be withdrawn is usually prorated among the banks holding such accounts. To facilitate administration, banks are classified periodically according to the average amount of their tax-and-loan accounts, with banks being designated as Class A, B, and C banks for call purposes. Class A banks have the smallest average holdings of tax-and-loan accounts and Class C banks the largest average holdings, with Class B banks, holdings being between the two.

In recent years, during quarterly tax payment periods, the Treasury has permitted income and profit tax payments of $10,000 or more or some percentage thereof to be redeposited in these tax-and-loan accounts in order to minimize the immediate drain of funds from the depository banks. Such deposits are segregated as "X" balances and separate calls are made on them.

Services Relating to the Public Debt. Under instructions from the Treasury the Federal Reserve banks perform many functions pertaining to new marketable issues, savings bonds, and existing and maturing obligations. Other banks sell and redeem savings bonds, receive subscriptions for other government securities, hold Treasury tax-and-loan accounts, and accept tax payments (social security, withholding, and corporation income tax payments). A few banks (150) maintain facilities for receiving deposits and cashing checks at military and other government establishments, and several hundred other banks collect and pay Treasury funds in areas where there are no nearby Federal Reserve banks or branches.

Other fiscal agency functions of the Federal Reserve banks for the Treasury include:

1. The Federal Reserve banks distribute Treasury notices of new offerings, accept tenders or offers to buy, compute the average price, make allotments among the subscribers, deliver the securities, receive payment for the obligations, and credit the proceeds to the Treasury's account.

2. The Federal Reserve banks supply banks and other agents with savings bonds and notes, and handle special problems pertaining to outstanding savings bonds (reissue because of marriage, death, divorce, etc.). They also provide for safekeeping of Series E bonds if requested to do so by their owners. In the savings bond program, many of the 500,-000,000 individual savings bonds outstanding are owned by new investors. Any of these owners may apply to a Federal Reserve bank for information or some service. In addition, each Reserve bank is responsible for supervising hundreds of paying agents who are authorized to cash bonds for the owners on or before maturity. Special problems also arise because "F" and "G" bonds may be held by trust accounts. Since June, 1952, "J" and "K" bonds have been replacing "F" and "G" bonds, a new Series "E" bond has been replacing the old Series "E," and a new "H" bond has been added. (See Chapter XXIX.)

3. Federal Reserve banks pay coupons on existing bonds and mail interest checks to owners of registered bonds. On request, they exchange registered for nonregistered bonds (and vice versa) and also denominations (for illustration, five $1,000 bonds for one $5,000 bond, etc.). The Reserve banks will make "wire transfer" deliveries of securities, which means that locally held bonds sold in New York will be delivered to the local Federal Reserve bank and canceled; and a wire will be sent to the Federal Reserve Bank of New York to deliver similar securities out of stock. Since sales of government securities made by individual banks and other institutions may involve millions of dollars, the savings in time and expenses of delivery are important.

4. The Federal Reserve banks redeem securities as they mature or are called for payment and make conversions or exchanges in other securities. The Federal Reserve Bank of New York acts as fiscal agent for the Treasury in buying and selling government securities in the market in behalf of Social Security and other government investment accounts. The Bank also performs many other services for the Treasury in its purchase and sales of gold and dealings with foreign banks and governments.

Fiscal Agent for Government Agencies. The Federal Reserve banks act as depositories and fiscal agents for most of the government agencies. These include the institutions in Federal Farm Credit Administration and the Housing and Home Financing Agency which are considered in later chapters. Although not exclusively United States government agencies, the Federal Reserve banks act as fiscal agents for the "World Bank" and the International Monetary Fund.

THE FEDERAL RESERVE BANK OF NEW YORK

One of the chief factors favoring the decentralized central-banking system, as adopted, was the public's mistrust of big business. However, it was inevitable that one or more of the Federal Reserve banks would be of greater importance than the others. The Federal Reserve Bank of New York is located in the wealthiest city in the world, where the clearinghouse banks alone own more banking resources than all the banks in the United Kingdom. So it is not surprising to find that, during the history of the Federal Reserve System, the Federal Reserve Bank of New York's size and activities have reflected the fact that it is located in the most important commodities, foreign exchange, money, and capital markets of the United States. Its activities are more truly those of a central bank than are those of the other Federal Reserve banks. Since many of the fiscal operations of the United States government and the international transactions of the United States Treasury are centered in New York, the Federal Reserve Bank of New York has become the most important central bank in the world (even though policy decisions are made elsewhere).

The foreign exchange department of the Federal Reserve Bank of New York certifies to the Treasury the rate of exchange (used in administering customs duties); buys United States government securities for foreign banks and individuals, without any charge for the service; supports the British pound sterling (between $2.78 and $2.82); handles the in-and-out flow of dollar balances in wholesale lots, but has no retail letter-of-credit business; buys incoming gold and moves it to assay offices of the United States Treasury and debits the Treasury's general account; arranges for gold exports for the Treasury; tags and holds earmarked gold for foreign governments; and makes loans against such earmarked gold on request from the owners. (Loans on gold are usually seasonal and are also made on gold held abroad or in transit.)

The Federal Reserve Bank of New York operates the Stabilization Fund for the United States Treasury and administers Treasury regulations pertaining to assets and financial transactions with the government and nationals of Communist China and North Korea.

The Federal Reserve Bank of New York acts as depository and fiscal agent for both the International Bank for Reconstruction and Development and the International Monetary Fund. The Federal Reserve Bank of New York is also the depository through which foreign central banks transact most of their banking business in this country. It not only holds their earmarked gold[3] and some of their deposit accounts but also acts as their fiscal agent in the purchase and sale of United States government obligations and other liquid assets.

The Federal Reserve Bank of New York customarily shares its international business with other Reserve banks. For illustration, the item "foreign deposits" appears on statements of other Federal Reserve banks because these accounts are allocated among the other Reserve banks according to their "capital and surplus." Foreign loans on gold (now appearing under "other assets") are usually made in New York and allocated among the Federal Reserve banks. Most of the government securities owned by the Federal Reserve System are held by the Federal Reserve Bank of New York, as agent for the Federal Open Market Committee, and most of the System's securities transactions take place in New York.

FINANCIAL STATEMENTS AND OTHER STATISTICS

Statement of Condition of Federal Reserve Banks. The statement of condition of Federal Reserve banks, which appears as Table 14, is the combined statement of all the Federal Reserve banks and their twenty-four branches. After studying the preceding chapters, it is easy to identify each of the items that appear in this statement. Among the terms in use that are not listed on the statement is "Federal Reserve bank credit outstanding," which is equal to the "float" and all earning assets of the Federal Reserve banks (discounts and advances, industrial loans, and United States government securities).

"Bills purchased" sometimes appears on Federal Reserve banks' statements, indicating bankers' acceptances purchased by the Federal Reserve banks. A note appears on the statement of condition to the effect that the Federal Reserve banks had a contingent liability on acceptances purchased for foreign correspondents.

The "float" for which Federal Reserve credit has been given is included in Federal Reserve credit outstanding ("uncollected cash items" minus "deferred availability cash items"). The "reserve ratio"

---

[3] Labor costs involved in handling gold are about 30 cents for each 25-pound bar. In 1951 about 267,000 bars or $3.5 billion were involved.

TABLE 14
STATEMENT OF CONDITION OF FEDERAL RESERVE BANKS,
NOVEMBER 30, 1955
(In Thousands of Dollars)

ASSETS

Gold certificates..	20,138,351
Redemption fund for Federal Reserve notes...............	863,750
Total gold certificate reserves.....................	21,002,101
Federal Reserve notes of other banks.....................	227,338
Other cash..	325,148
Discounts and advances:	
For member banks...............................	618,329
For nonmember banks, etc............................	....
Industrial loans.....................................	704
Acceptances:	
Bought outright..............................	17,493
Held under repurchase agreement.....................	....
United States government securities:	
Bought outright:	
Bills...	1,269,846
Certificates:	
Special..	....
Other.......................................	2,520,076
Notes...	17,399,536
Bonds..	2,801,750
Total bought outright...........................	23,991,208
Held under repurchase agreement.....................	265,160
Total United States government securities...........	24,256,368
Total loans and securities......................	24,892,894
Due from foreign banks...............................	22
Uncollected cash items...............................	4,487,715
Bank premises.......................................	60,407
Other assets..	200,942
Total assets...............................	51,196,567

LIABILITIES

Federal Reserve notes...............................	26,629,284
Deposits:	
Member bank—reserve accounts.....................	18,474,149
United States Treasurer—general account..............	476,841
Foreign...	407,615
Other...	411,766
Total deposits...............................	19,770,371
Deferred availability cash items........................	3,604,599
Other liabilities and accrued dividends...................	20,280
Total liabilities..............................	50,024,534

CAPITAL ACCOUNTS

Capital paid in..	300,220
Surplus (Section 7).....................................	660,901
Surplus (Section 13 b).................................	27,543
Other capital accounts.................................	183,369
Total liabilities and capital accounts...............	51,196,567
Ratio of gold certificate reserves to deposit and Federal Reserve note liabilities combined (per cent)...............	45.3
Contingent liability on acceptances purchased for foreign correspondents......................................	27,234
Industrial loan commitments...........................	2,339

Source of statistics: *Federal Reserve Bulletin* (December, 1955) p. 1335.

appears as a footnote to the statement. The items "surplus (Section 7)" and "other capital accounts" indicate the volume of retained earnings being held by Reserve banks. "Surplus (Section 13b)" indicates government funds that have been advanced to the Federal Reserve banks to be used under the provisions of the Industrial Loan Act of 1934.

Earnings and Expenses of Federal Reserve Banks. Additional information on the relative importance of certain phases of the work of the Federal Reserve banks may be found in the summary statement of earnings and expenses. (See Table 15.)[4] While the expenses

TABLE 15

EARNINGS AND EXPENSES OF FEDERAL RESERVE BANKS IN 1955 AND 1954

ITEM	THOUSANDS OF DOLLARS	
	1955	1954
Current earnings...............................	412,488	438,486
Current expenses..............................	110,060	109,733
Current net earnings....................	302,428	328,753
Additions to current net earnings................	178	527*
Deductions from current net earnings............	443*	661
Net deductions.......................	265	134
Net earnings before payments to United States Treasury............................	302,163	328,619
Paid United States Treasury (interest on Federal Reserve notes)............................	251,741	276,289
Dividends...................................	17,712	16,442
Transferred to surplus (Sec. 7)................	32,710	35,888

Source: *Federal Reserve Bulletin* (January, 1956), p. 14.
* Includes $482,000 net profits in 1954 and $506 net losses in 1955 on sales of United States securities.

of Reserve banks have increased steadily throughout their history, earnings have fluctuated widely. They were at peak figures during the years 1918–20 and during and since World War II. In explaining these earnings, it should be noted that the chief lending power of the Federal Reserve banks is dependent not on their capital and deposits, as is true of individual banks, but chiefly on their power to create money (Federal Reserve notes). When the demand for Federal Reserve notes is the largest, the demand for Federal

[4] A more detailed report of earnings and expenses may be found in the *Federal Reserve Bulletin* (February, 1956), pp. 178–79.

Reserve credit tends to be the greatest. In addition, the Federal Reserve System makes more Federal Reserve credit available as member bank reserves; but the changes in the total amount of this Federal Reserve liability are less than those for Federal Reserve notes.

The distribution of Federal Reserve banks' net earnings reflects the public nature of these institutions; dividend payments are limited to 6 per cent on the stock held by member banks and, now, the remainder is being divided between the Reserve banks and the Treasury. In order to direct most of the net earnings to the United States Treasury, the Board of Governors is charging the Reserve

TABLE 16

ALLOCATION OF EARNINGS OF FEDERAL RESERVE
BANKS, 1914–54
(Chief Classes only, in Thousands of Dollars)

Current earnings.	$4,777,115
Current expenses.	1,636,462
Net earnings*.	3,090,836
Dividends paid.	352,589
Payments—United States Treasury†.	1,948,682
Transferred to surplus‡.	789,570

Source: *Forty-first Annual Report of the Board of Governors of the Federal Reserve System Covering Operations for the Year 1954* (Washington, D.C., 1955), p. 73.

* Net earnings before payments to the United States Treasury equals current earnings less current expenses, plus other additions and less other deductions.

† Combined payments under different laws and policies of the Federal Reserve System.

‡ Includes $139,299,557 used to buy stock of the Federal Deposit Insurance Corporation as required by the Banking Act of 1933, which was subsequently canceled, and this amount was paid to the United States Treasury by the Federal Deposit Insurance Corporation. Not included in amount paid to the Treasury.

banks interest on outstanding Federal Reserve notes not covered by gold certificates held by the Federal Reserve agents as collateral security for such notes. These charges are interest payments in name only; in reality, they are a device used by the Board of Governors to re-establish a practice required by law before January 1, 1934.

Prior to January 1, 1934, each Federal Reserve bank was permitted to carry net earnings, after dividends, to the "surplus account" until it equaled the bank's capitalization (which is twice the paid-in capital); and, thereafter, 10 per cent was to be retained by each Reserve bank, and 90 per cent was to be paid to the government. This provision of the law was repealed when the Federal Reserve banks were required to buy stock of the Federal Deposit Insurance Corporation in amounts equal to one half of their surplus as of January 1, 1933 (about $139,000,000). Subsequently, the Federal

Deposit Insurance Corporation paid this amount to the United States Treasury (an indirect contribution of the Federal Reserve System). When the surplus accounts were rebuilt, the Board used the "interest charge" as the means of diverting earnings to the Treasury.[5] A summary of the allocation of all earnings of the Federal Reserve banks from 1914 to 1954 appears as Table 16.

In the earnings of Federal Reserve banks for any one year, the predominance of the item "United States government securities" is not surprising since most of the earning assets are in this form.

TABLE 17

VOLUME OF OPERATIONS IN PRINCIPAL DEPARTMENTS OF FEDERAL RESERVE BANKS, 1954
(Numbers in Thousands, Amounts in Thousands of Dollars)

Item	Number of Pieces Handled*	Amounts Handled
Discounts and advances............................	10	22,871,449
Industrial loans....................................	.2	7,477
Commitments to make industrial loans...............	†	520
Currency received and counted......................	4,384,270	28,482,428
Coins received and counted........................	7,001,838	761,062
Checks handled:		
United States government checks..................	481,408	141,037,495
Postal money orders............................	354,368	5,943,178
All others‡.....................................	2,513,966	882,971,848
Collection items handled:		
United States government coupons paid.............	12,753	2,209,045
All others......................................	15,443	5,085,695
Issues, redemption, and exchanges of United States		
government securities............................	191,112	469,247,400
Transfer of funds.................................	1,808	1,038,100,606

Source: *Forty-first Annual Report of the Board of Governors of the Federal Reserve System Covering Operations for the Year 1954* (Washington, D.C., 1955), p. 69.
* Two or more checks, coupons, etc., handled as a single item are counted as one piece.
† Less than 50.
‡ Excludes checks drawn on Federal Reserve banks.

Under current earnings, the item "discounts and advances" is significant in indicating the extent to which banks have borrowed from the Federal Reserve banks. That these loans are for short periods of time is shown by the fact that "discounts and advances" handled during 1954 were about $22.9 billion (see Table 17), while the amount outstanding on November 30, 1955 was $618 million (see

[5] These contributions have been made since 1947, and the one made on January 5, 1956, brought the total to more than $2 billion.

Table 14). The year-end statements of some individual Reserve banks show no "discounts and advances."[6]

Volume of Operations. The statistics of the volume of operations of the principal departments of the Federal Reserve banks appear as Table 17. Most of the large items resulted from the clearing and collection of checks; the transfer of funds; the issue, redemption, and exchange of United States government securities; the handling of paper money and coins; and discounts and advances.

SUMMARY

Federal Reserve credit is made available to the economy primarily through the lending by Federal Reserve banks and open-market transactions of the Federal Reserve banks and the Federal Open Market Committee. Purchases of government securities by the Federal Open Market Committee (the Federal Reserve Bank of New York acts as fiscal agent) will increase the volume of reserves available to member banks. Conversely, sales of government securities by the Federal Open Market Committee will decrease the volume of reserves available to member banks. In the case of a purchase, a check of the Federal Reserve Bank of New York will be deposited by some member bank in a Federal Reserve bank; and, in the case of a sale, a check of some member bank will be collected by the Federal Reserve Bank of New York. In the first case, a member bank's reserve account will be credited; and in the second case, a member bank's reserve account will be debited. Similarly, when a Federal Reserve bank lends to a member bank, the latter customarily receives credit on the books of the lending Federal Reserve bank. When the loan is repaid, the Federal Reserve bank customarily debits the reserve account of the bank that is meeting its obligation.

The ways in which member-bank reserve accounts are affected by the investing and lending of the Federal Reserve System are reflected in the statement of condition of the Federal Reserve banks and the statement of the Federal Reserve banks' earnings and expenses. Of minor importance are the other ways in which Federal Reserve credit is made available to the economy—industrial and emergency loans to borrowers (other than member banks), discounting for acceptance dealers, and the Federal Reserve "float."

[6] This situation reflects "window dressing" by banks. Banks file their statements of condition as of June 30 and December 31 (a day earlier if the date falls on Sunday) with their supervisory agencies and publish them in newspapers. Since most banks are reluctant to have an item indicating that they have borrowed on their published statements, they plan to be out of debt on the reporting dates.

In addition to credit functions the Federal Reserve banks act as fiscal (that is, financial) agents for the United States Treasury. The Federal Reserve banks hold the most important of the checking accounts of the government and also supervise the "tax-and-loan" accounts in other banks (chiefly commercial banks). The Federal Reserve banks also help the United States Treasury in handling its government debt and also act as fiscal agents for United States government agencies, foreign governments, and central banks. Because of its location, the Federal Reserve Bank of New York has been given the responsibility for administering matters of policy which have been decided by the United States Treasury, the Board of Governors of the Federal Reserve System, and the Federal Open Market Committee. In addition to the services provided the United States Treasury, the Federal Reserve banks also provide the banks of the nation with currency and assist them in the clearing and collection of "cash" and "noncash" items. The public nature of the Federal Reserve banks is suggested by the allocation of their net earnings, with the bulk going to the United States Treasury.

QUESTIONS AND PROBLEMS

1. "A bank which wishes to borrow may do so in one of two ways: it may *rediscount* eligible paper with the Reserve Bank, or it may obtain a *direct advance* on its promissory note, which in turn is secured by either Government securities or eligible paper." (Madeline McWhinney, "Member Bank Borrowing from the Federal Reserve Banks," *Money Market Essays* [New York: Federal Reserve Bank of New York, 1952], p. 9.) Explain. Are there other ways in which Federal Reserve bank credit is made available to member banks?

2. How important is lending by Federal Reserve banks?

3. How did the Industrial Loan Act affect the operations of the Reserve banks? Has "direct" lending been important? Would a system of guaranteeing small capital loans by the Federal Reserve banks be practical?

4. To what classes of securities are open-market operations of the Federal Reserve banks limited? In practice, which ones have been most important in the portfolios of the Federal Reserve banks and in the System's open-market account?

5. Compare the Federal Reserve System open-market policies with reference to bankers' acceptances and government securities.

6. What services do Federal Reserve banks perform for the United States Treasury? For other governmental agencies?

7. The following questions are based on the Statement of Condition of Federal Reserve Banks (Table 14):

    a) What is the ratio of capital and surplus to deposits and notes? Is it too low? How does it compare to a similar ratio for member banks?

    b) What is the reserve ratio? How much excess reserves do the Reserve banks have?

    c) How much money is there in the 5 per cent redemption fund held against Federal Reserve notes? Is it enough? Why?

    d) What item or items show the amount of Federal Reserve credit in use?

    e) Identify "bills discounted."

    f) Are the types of government securities held significant? Why?

    g) Explain the existence of two surplus items.

    h) Identify "uncollected items" and "deferred availability items." Why are they not equal in amounts?

8. "The distribution of their [Federal Reserve banks'] net earnings reflects the public nature of these institutions." Explain.

9. "We recommend that Congress enact a franchise tax on the net earnings of the Federal Reserve System to replace the voluntary contributions now being made to the Treasury by the Board of Governors." (*Report of the Subcommittee on Monetary, Credit, and Fiscal Policies of the Joint Committee on the Economic Report Congress of the United States* [Washington, D.C.: U.S. Government Printing Office, 1950], p. 4.) What does this mean? Would it mean an important change in policy? Explain.

10. Explain the greater importance of the Federal Reserve Bank of New York. How do its functions compare to those of other Federal Reserve banks?

11. The earnings statement of the Federal Reserve banks indicates that their net earnings were less in 1955 than in 1954, while most commercial banks made more profits in 1955 than in 1954. The decline in the earnings of the Federal Reserve banks resulted from a decrease in income from government securities which was partly offset by an increase in earnings from discounts and advances. Are such changes to be expected? Why?

| Chapter XXI | MEMBER-BANK RESERVES AND TREASURY MONETARY POLICY |

THE ACTIONS of the Federal Reserve authorities and the United States Treasury will influence and be influenced by what is called the "tone of the money market"—a concept which is difficult to define but which includes the idea of quality or mood, such as *tight* when money is scarce and interest rates are high and *easy* when money is abundant and interest rates are low. An estimation of the money situation necessitates an appraisal of many complex factors and a starting point may be a discussion of member-bank reserves. This chapter deals with how the volume and availability of member-bank reserves are influenced by Federal Reserve action and the location of the United States Treasury's cash balances—whether deposited in member banks, in Federal Reserve banks, or kept in its own vaults.

MONETARY OBJECTIVES

While the Federal Reserve banks are important bankers' banks and service agencies for the federal government, they are also the institutions through which credit policies are made effective. The Federal Reserve banks can expand or contract member-bank reserves available for lending to business and financial communities in many ways.

Usually the effects of Federal Reserve policy are felt first in the money market. In establishing a policy or procedure to be followed by a Federal Reserve bank on its own account or as agent for the Federal Reserve System, the monetary authorities have to keep in mind that some temporary situations may demand action which if not offset will be harmful to the long-run objective of monetary policy. This objective is to promote the orderly growth of production so that the people of the United States may have a rising standard of living and, at the same time, will be able to meet their foreign economic, military, and political commitments.

The amount of money and credit made available in different

markets must be such that total monetary expenditures will be kept in balance with the increase in the volume of goods, services, and other things for which money is spent. One of the first indicators that the money supply is too abundant or is being spent too rapidly is a rise in general prices; conversely, one of the first indicators that the money supply is too scarce or is being spent too slowly is a decline in general prices.

The immediate objectives of monetary policy are the same as the economic or other objectives of a nation, which could be different under different circumstances, such as winning a war, stabilizing interest rates, or stimulating employment. It should not be assumed, when the monetary authorities are following a short-run policy which seems to reduce employment, that they have lost sight of the economic goal of helping businessmen, laborers, and the government in achieving greater output and a higher standard of living. Monetary procedures are designed to smooth the road taken by the economy by cutting down the hills and filling in the valleys so that travelling will be more comfortable and arrival at points along the way will not be delayed.

RESERVES AND THE BANKING SYSTEM

Member-bank reserves are credited balances or deposits at Federal Reserve banks. In preceding discussions, it has been noted that new bank reserves may result from imports of gold, issues of new currency (coins and silver certificates) by the United States Treasury, and creation of new Federal Reserve bank credit. Since the volume of new Federal Reserve credit can be increased or decreased so easily, the amount outstanding can be manipulated to offset other changes which would be detrimental to the well-being of the economy considered in terms of long-run developments.

The volume of Federal Reserve credit in use is measured by the amount of earning assets of Federal Reserve banks including United States government securities, loans, advances, and discounts, and float (the difference between uncollected items and deferred availability items on the statement of condition of the Federal Reserve banks). There is a tendency for the amount of member-bank reserves to increase or decrease as the amount of Federal Reserve credit increases or decreases. However, this tendency may be offset by other developments such as a decrease or increase in gold stock; and it may be augmented if Federal Reserve credit and the gold stock increase or decrease at the same time.

The amount of member-bank reserves would also tend to be increased by an expansion in Treasury currency outstanding, such as new issues of silver certificates. However one should not conclude that member-bank reserves will always increase if there is an increase in the volume of Federal Reserve credit, gold stock, and Treasury currency outstanding (nor conversely that member-bank reserves will always decrease if they decrease) because others compete with member banks for new reserves.

Uses of Reserves. The general public, the United States Treasury, foreign central banks and governments, nonmember clearing banks, and others may want to hold Federal Reserve credit, gold, and Treasury currency. When the general public expands its holding of currency, commercial banks must obtain coins and paper money from the Federal Reserve banks; this means that commercial banks' checking or reserve deposits will be debited and that there will be a dollar-for-dollar loss in member-bank reserves. (Currency in circulation is currency outside the United States Treasury and the Federal Reserve banks; therefore, the amount of currency in circulation increases as soon as currency has been shipped by the Federal Reserve banks.)

When the United States Treasury increases its holdings of currency, gold, or deposits in checking accounts at the Federal Reserve banks, it deprives the commercial banks of reserve funds. When foreign governments and central banks and certain United States government banks and agencies, which have deposits with Federal Reserve banks, collect checks drawn on commercial banks, settlement usually entails crediting their accounts at the Federal Reserve banks and debiting the accounts of the member banks on which the checks are drawn. Likewise, when a clearing nonmember bank's account at its Federal Reserve bank is being credited with a cash item, the account of a member bank is being debited. Of course, the cash item may be drawn on a second clearing nonmember bank, in which case the total nonmember banks' reserves would be unchanged; but our interest is in changes that affect the location of reserves among different groups as a unit.

In conclusion, assuming that the volume of total reserves is fixed, the amount of reserves acquired by the public, the Treasury, and depositors (other than member banks) of Federal Reserve banks, member banks lose; and conversely, the amount of reserves released by the public, the Treasury, and depositors (other than member banks) of Federal Reserve banks, member banks acquire. Each

Friday, many newspapers publish a box score of what happened, during the preceding week, to the components of Federal Reserve credit (investments, loans, and float), the gold stock, Treasury currency outstanding (issues of the United States Treasury irrespective

TABLE 18

MEMBER-BANK RESERVES, RESERVE BANK CREDIT, AND RELATED ITEMS
(In Millions of Dollars)

ITEM	WEEKLY AVERAGES OF DAILY FIGURES		
	Week Ending June 8, 1955	Changes from Week Ending	
		June 1, 1955	June 9, 1954
Reserve bank credit:			
United States government securities			
Bought outright—System account..............	23,683	+ 83	−1,277
Held under repurchase agreement..............	—	− 3	—
Acceptances—Bought outright..................	16	+ 3	+ 16
Loans, discounts, and advances			
Member bank borrowings....................	463	− 82	+ 316
Other....................................	70	+ 3	+ 45
Float....................................	812	+ 40	+ 142
Total Reserve bank credit.................	25,004	+ 43	− 758
Gold stock......................................	21,675	+ 1	− 249
Treasury currency outstanding...................	5,602	+ 1	+ 44
	51,720	+ 43	− 963
Currency in circulation.........................	30,059	+ 98	+ 131
Treasury cash holdings.........................	835	+ 12	+ 12
Treasury deposits with Federal Reserve banks........	440	−142	+ 98
Foreign deposits with Federal Reserve banks.........	387	− 13	− 162
Other deposits with Federal Reserve banks...........	416	− 62	+ 58
Other Federal Reserve accounts (net)..............	935	− 1	+ 58
	33,072	−108	+ 194
Member bank reserve balances....................	18,648	+152	−1,157
Required reserves (estimated)..................	18,028	− 40	− 857
Excess reserves (estimated)...................	620	+192	− 300

Source of statistics: Mimeographed release of the Board of Governors of the Federal Reserve System, dated June 9, 1955.

of their location), the amount of currency in circulation, and other items appearing in Table 18 with a summary of the effects of the changes on the reserve position of member banks.

RESERVES AND INDIVIDUAL BANKS

Member banks' legal reserve balances are their checking accounts at their Federal Reserve banks. The Reserve banks give their member banks immediate credit for some cash items and deferred credit of one or two days for other cash items. This means that member banks may be receiving credit for some cash items that may take several days or even weeks to collect. In other words, member-bank reserves are *credit* balances, not *collected* balances, at their Federal Reserve banks.

Excess and Required Reserves. Normally, banks in general do not keep excessive amounts of reserves; but, even with careful planning, large unexpected deposits or withdrawals may cause an "excess" or a "deficient" reserve situation for individual banks. However, what one bank loses a second bank gains if other things remain the same; and so, the overall situation may not change materially. With about 7,000 banks involved, and with each bank being careful to have enough reserves, an "excess" reserve situation is the normal one. When the amount of excess reserves falls to about 3 per cent of the total, now around $600,000,000, the amount is considered to be low (see Table 18). Today, member banks do not fear minor reserve deficiencies at a particular time because of the current system of computing required reserves.

Central reserve city and reserve city banks are required to compute their reserve balances for a weekly period, beginning on Thursday, and country banks compute their reserve balances on the fifteenth day and the last day of the month. As noted previously, banks keep a daily record, computing their reserve needs on the basis of total time deposits and net demand deposits on hand when the banks are open at the beginning of the day and their reserve positions at the end of each day. Any surplus or deficiency is carried over to the next day. Although there is nothing to prevent a bank from having a temporary deficiency in reserves, the average must be maintained in order to meet the required percentages, or the offending bank is subject to penalties. (The penalty is assessed on the deficiency at a rate of 2 per cent per annum above the Federal Reserve bank rate applicable to discounts on ninety-day commercial paper for member banks in effect the first day in which the deficiency occurred. Notice is sent to the directors of the offending bank; and, if the deficiency continues, the action taken may result in the loss of charter by a national bank or loss of membership in the Federal Reserve System by a state-chartered member bank.)

Adjustment of Reserve Position. An individual member bank may build up its reserve position by (1) purchasing the excess reserves of another member bank, (2) presenting eligible paper for rediscount to its Federal Reserve bank, (3) borrowing from its Federal Reserve bank on its own promissory note, or (4) selling certain assets in its portfolio. The amount of excess cash reserves held by an individual bank ordinarily determines the additional amount the bank may lend or invest. In the analysis of bank lending, this is estimated to be the amount of total reserves minus the legal required reserves.

When a member bank finds it necessary to borrow at its Federal Reserve bank, the amount of the member bank's reserves is increased; but the bank must repay its loan. So reserves created in this way are soon destroyed, first, because member banks do not like to be in debt and, second, because Federal Reserve banks prefer to lend for but a short period of time.

Free Reserves. Some individual member banks may have excess reserves while others may be borrowing at their Federal Reserve banks. So a more accurate measure of the reserve positions of member banks as a whole may be obtained by subtracting the average required reserves from total average reserves (giving average excess reserves) and then deducting the average volume of borrowing from the Federal Reserve banks for the same period (giving free reserves). This emphasis on free reserves helps to explain why there may be a tight money situation even though statistics indicate that there are unused member-bank reserves available for lending (see Chart 9).

FEDERAL RESERVE CREDIT AND THE MONEY MARKET

The Federal Reserve System may take the initiative in ironing out any disturbance in the money market by purchasing more or fewer Treasury bills and other government obligations. The resulting changes in the volume of securities held by the System are often made merely to offset the influence of other forces which alter the volume of bank reserves in an undesired way. For illustration, a rise in the volume of currency in circulation during the Christmas shopping season may be offset by purchases of government securities by the Federal Reserve System; and conversely, a decline in the volume of currency in January may be offset by selling government securities or not replacing those which mature.

Similar practices may be followed to offset an increase or decrease in the volume of float, a rise or fall in the Treasury's balance at the Federal Reserve banks, an increase or decrease in the gold stock, and so on for other changes. Since the United States economy is growing in terms of real goods and services, there is a secular or long-run need for more member-bank reserves.

If the increase in the gold supply does not match this secular demand for more reserve money, new investments in securities by the Federal Reserve System must provide the new reserves if monetary needs are to be met properly. Therefore, smoothing out the weekly, seasonal and other changes in the demand for new reserves by an

CHART 9

Member Bank Reserve Positions, 1955
(Monthly Averages of Daily Figures)

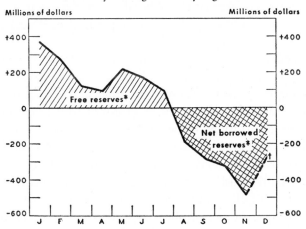

* Represents excess reserves minus borrowings from Federal Reserve banks.
† The December average is based on three weeks of preliminary figures plus estimates for the last nine days.
Source: Federal Reserve Bank of New York, *Monthly Review of Credit and Business Conditions*, Vol. 38, No. 1 (January, 1956), p. 2.

increase or decrease in the volume of investments does not necessarily indicate a change in the policy of the Federal Reserve System.

The Federal Reserve System's policy may be one of "restraint," which would mean that member-bank reserves may be made available less freely. Then the Federal Open Market Committee would be a "reluctant" buyer of government securities and a more willing or active seller of government securities. Conversely, the Federal Reserve System's policy may be one of "easy" money, which would mean that member-bank reserves may be made available more freely and the Federal Open Market Committee would be a more willing buyer of government securities and a less willing or active seller of government securities. The Federal Reserve System's credit policy may be one of "neutrality," which would mean that no action would be taken on making member-bank reserves more or less freely available.

Since a policy of restraint, easy money, or neutrality is customarily accompanied by a day-to-day policy of increasing or decreasing the volume of Federal Reserve credit in order to eliminate the day-to-day and week-to-week fluctuations in member-bank reserves, it is difficult to interpret the significance of an expansion or contraction in the volume of government securities owned by the Federal Reserve System as of one time. Sometimes, when the United States Treasury offers new securities, the Federal Reserve System finds it necessary or desirable to support the market by buying government securities (generally criticized when the effects seem out of step with the broader objectives of Federal Reserve policy).

The Federal Reserve System may be confronted with a problem of helping a member bank adjust its reserve position because of some temporary factor such as an adverse clearinghouse balance due to a large deposit withdrawal. A group of banks may be similarly affected—for illustration, those in New York by a flow of funds to banks in other parts of the country. In this area, as in the case of an individual bank, the Federal Reserve System may want to provide the member banks with additional credit, even though the aggregate reserve position of all member banks may be satisfactory. The device used may be one of permitting banks needing reserves to borrow reserves temporarily from the appropriate Federal Reserve bank or to sell securities to a Federal Reserve bank under a repurchase agreement. Reserves are never denied a bank needing them, even though a Federal Reserve bank is under no obligation to lend. (Applications for funds are subject to critical analysis under all circumstances.)

In deciding on short-term policies, the Federal Reserve Bank of New York as agent for the Federal Open Market Committee watches the reserve positions of member banks and particularly those of New York City banks. The Bank follows clearings and wire transfers, public and private financing in the securities markets, and the plans of the United States Treasury pertaining to calls on Treasury tax-and-loan accounts in special depositories. In addition, the Bank is in almost continuous contact over the telephone with government securities dealers in New York and by telephone or wire with other Federal Reserve banks.

There is one way in which Federal Reserve credit in use may be changed without involving rediscount or open-market operations. As noted earlier the Federal Reserve banks give member banks credit for cash items in process of collection according to a time schedule. In effect, the Reserve banks are discounting checks. The amount of "float" (checks credited prior to collection) is an important source of Federal Reserve credit because of the increase in volume of such items being collected through the Federal Reserve System. The statistics published in the *Federal Reserve Bulletin* indicate that it is second in importance only to Federal Reserve credit made available by the Federal Reserve System's investments in United States government securities. Weekly changes may be several hundred million dollars, reflecting the tendency for businessmen and individuals to pay by check on certain days of the week or month.[1] Other events that cause the weekly or semimonthly changes in the "float" to vary are transportation delays and bank holidays. Although the "float" is an important source of Federal Reserve credit, it is not an instrument of policy, in fact, its existences complicates the problem of control of member-bank reserves.

TREASURY FUNDS

The Federal Reserve banks are the fiscal agents of the United States Treasury in handling its deposits and administering its debt. These fiscal agency functions are carried out under regulations of the Treasury. In this respect the relations of the Federal Reserve banks to the Treasury are similar to their relations to the Board of Governors. Any policy aspect associated with management of government funds or the government's debt will be reflected in the regulations and instructions of the Treasury. Since officers of Federal Reserve banks are in close contact with money markets, they are in a position to advise the Treasury and thus influence Treasury policy although final responsibility rests with the Treasury.

Treasury Balances and the Money Market. The way the Treasury handles its cash balances has an effect upon the money market. The Treasury has funds in its own vaults, in the Federal Reserve banks, and in about 11,000 special depositories, chiefly commercial banks. With minor exceptions, Treasury checks are drawn on funds in the twelve Federal Reserve banks; therefore deposits in commercial banks must be transferred to the Reserve banks before they are spent.

[1] From December 1, 1954, to December 31, 1955, the volume of float, reported as averages of daily figures for the week, varied from $627,000,000 for August 10 to $1,875 billion, a record high level, for December 28 (in some areas, airports were "fogged in" delaying air mail delivery). Since the figure reported is for the week ending on certain days and the first report date in each month usually includes days in the preceding month, the peak during the month is the third report date which tends to confirm the trade practice of end-of-the-month billing with cash remittances permitted by mail in ten days.

The amount of funds involved in some quarterly income tax payments is in excess of all member-banks' reserves. If the checks drawn in payment of income taxes are deposited in Federal Reserve banks and settled for by crediting the United States Treasury account at the Federal Reserve banks and debiting the reserve accounts of member banks, the latter would lose all of their reserves at the Reserve banks temporarily. Fortunately, methods of handling Treasury receipts have been developed so as not to disturb the reserve or money positions of member banks. Although billions of dollars are handled each quarterly income tax payment period, there is hardly a ripple in the level of interest rates in the money market.

The United States Treasury follows the policy of leaving tax and loan receipts with commercial banks until they are to be transferred to the Federal Reserve banks for spending. When the Treasury receives checks for $10,000 or more in payment of income taxes, it immediately deposits that amount or some percentage thereof in the banks on which they were drawn. (A small bank that is *not* a special depository would seldom have a check of that size drawn on it.) These deposits of the Treasury are segregated and called "X" balances. Throughout the year, a commercial bank will also be accepting receipts from businessmen and others in payment of withholding taxes, savings bonds, or other government securities. Sometimes a bank may buy new bills or other government securities on its own account for which it settles on its books by crediting a tax-and-loan account of the government.

Eventually, the funds in the tax-and-loan accounts in commercial banks must be transferred to the Federal Reserve banks. Usually these transfers are announced in advance by the United States Treasury which specifies the percentage of the "X" balances or other deposits to be called for each class of banks. Calls are made less frequently on the smaller banks (Class A) and most frequently on the largest banks (Class C). Since the Treasury is paying out money at the rate of $6 billion each month, the transfer from United States Treasury deposits in commercial banks to the Federal Reserve banks is rapid. By careful management of expenditures (such as arranging maturities of debts so that they correspond to receipts), Treasury deposits in banks tend to average around $4 billion and those in the Federal Reserve banks between $500,-000,000 and $600,000,000. (The United States Treasury also has other cash items, such as Treasury-owned gold.) During the middle of January, 1956, the cash balances of the Treasury dropped to around $1.5 billion plus $500,000,000 in Treasury-owned gold. This situation was corrected after the January 15 tax receipts started to flow in; otherwise, the Treasury would have been in difficulty because its power to borrow is limited. Now the debt ceiling is $278 billion (reverting to $275 billion on June 30, 1957).

By speeding up the flow of funds from the tax-and-loan accounts to the Federal Reserve banks and then holding unusually large balances at the Reserve banks, the Treasury may exert a restraining influence on the money market. Conversely, the Treasury may exert a stimulating influence on the money market by permitting its checking accounts at the Reserve banks to drop to an abnormally low figure.

Treasury Cash and Monetary Policy. Under certain conditions, the United States Treasury may prefer to withhold funds entirely from the central and commercial banking systems. Historically, this practice was provided for in the Act of 1840 when an Independent United States Treasury System was established. Treasury cash holdings may be in the form of circulating money as well as silver and gold not represented by certificates (excluding gold held as reserves for United States notes and Treasury notes of 1890); but free gold is most important.

As a matter of policy, the United States Treasury may either monetize gold by issuing gold certificates or keep it idle as "inactive" gold. Most of the profits from devaluation of the dollar were kept idle from 1934 to 1947; and, at the present time, about $500,000,000 is being kept in the Treasury's inactive gold account. In December, 1936, the Treasury not only kept gold imports inactive but also paid for gold imports by borrowing or withdrawing money from the "tax-and-loan" accounts with special depositories. In 1947, when Congress required the Treasury to use the remaining gold profits to meet, in part, the United States' International Monetary Fund quota, it resulted in a sharp decline in Treasury cash and a temporary increase in Treasury deposits.

In case of a sudden foreign demand for gold the $500,000,000 "inactive" gold held as Treasury cash may be drawn on to offset the deflationary effects of gold exports—simply by depositing gold credits with the Federal Reserve banks and spending the Federal Reserve bank credit. Since New York is the financial market through which most of the world's trade is financed, fluctuations in foreign balances may be extreme; and the Treasury's "inactive" gold may be used to neutralize the effects of these fluctuations on the New York money market.

The Treasury also holds the nation's silver reserves and, under the law, it has certain powers which it may use to influence member-bank reserves. Owners of domestically mined silver have the privilege of delivering this silver to the Treasury at a price of 90.5 cents per ounce, and the Treasury is required to print silver certificates to match the cost of the silver bought. The question of policy arises with reference to the "free" silver that exists. The Treasury may or may not "monetize" the difference between the cost (90.5 cents) and $1.29 per fine ounce. However, this aspect of the silver policy is relatively unimportant because the amount of domestically mined silver is small. In addition, the Treasury may or may not buy other silver under provisions of the Silver Purchase Act of 1934; but, if it does, it has no discretion about issuing silver certificates in sums necessary to pay for the silver purchased. However, the Treasury may or may not monetize the "free" silver (resulting from the difference between the cost price and the coinage price of $1.29 per fine ounce). Since World War II, very little silver, other than that domestically mined, has been purchased by the Treasury.

CHANGES IN LEGAL RESERVE REQUIREMENTS

One remaining aspect of member-bank reserves is that pertaining to the availability of these reserves. For illustration, if the volume of member-bank reserves is doubled over a period of time, the inflationary potential of this increase can be neutralized if the required reserve percentages are doubled. If the average reserve percentage requirement for member banks' net demand deposits is 10 per cent, the increase in the volume of the money supply may be ten-fold if no allowance is made for the cash drain. With $10 billion in reserves, the volume of net demand deposits may be $100 billion. If the volume of member-bank reserve balances increase to $20 billion and the reserve requirement is increased to 20 per cent, the volume of net demand deposits may still be but $100 billion. Under some circumstances, the percentage reserve requirements may be reduced; in this case, banks would have more resources available for lending and investing even though the total of member-bank reserves remains the same.

What actually follows a change in the required legal reserve percentage depends on the reserve position of each member bank. If reserve requirements are increased, the lending and investing practices of banks having ample excess reserves may not be affected; some banks may borrow at their Federal Reserves or sell assets, and others may not renew their customers' loans when they come due. Usually, there is some increase in Federal Reserve credit when member banks' reserve requirements are increased either because of borrowing by member banks or purchases of government securities by the System.

Some commercial banks have complained about higher reserve requirements because the increase results in the Federal Reserve banks having relatively more earning assets while commercial banks have relatively less.[2] Although this may be true, the reallocation of earning assets between the Federal Reserve banks and commercial banks is merely the result of the overall objectives of the Federal Reserve System to do two things at the same time, to serve the broader objectives of monetary policy and to provide individual banks or groups or banks with reserves when they have a clearly established temporary need for them.

The current level of legal required reserve percentages were established in the summer of 1954 (see Table 11 Chapter XIV), and whether or not they are to be changed presumably depends on the effectiveness of general devices of credit control. During the late 1930's, changes in reserve requirements were linked to the excess reserve position of member banks; but, at the present time, excess reserves are practically nonexistent.

During and immediately following World War II, little or no use was made of general credit control devices (see Chapter XXII) and more reliance was placed on changes in member-bank reserve requirements as a credit control device. In 1948, under temporary legislation, the Board of Governors of the Federal Reserve System was permitted to increase reserve requirements above the previous statutory limits.[3] Since 1951, there has been wider use of general credit control devices and fewer changes have been made in required reserve percentages of member banks.

Although the present legal-reserve requirements are almost

[2] On the other hand, Senator Paul Douglas (Illinois) asked the Board of Governors why it had not increased member-bank reserve requirements during 1955 in order to tighten money market conditions instead of using a combination of open-market operations and successive increases in the discount rate. See *New York Times*, January 21, 1956, p. 27.

[3] The increases for demand deposits were from 20 to 26 per cent for central reserve city banks, from 20 to 22 per cent for reserve city banks, and from 14 to 16 per cent for country banks; and, on time deposits, from 6 to 7½ per cent for all banks. Until June 30, 1949, those on demand deposits could have been raised to 30, 24, and 18 per cent, respectively. The emergency powers were not renewed by Congress. So, the maximum legal limits reverted to the levels of August, 1948—6 per cent for total time deposits and 26, 20, and 14 per cent for net demand deposits.

twice those in effect from 1917 to 1935, they are comparable to those in existence before the creation of the Federal Reserve System. Under the old National Bank Act, required reserves for central reserve city, reserve city, and country banks were, respectively, as follows: 25 per cent, 25 per cent, and 15 per cent, applicable to both demand and time deposits. The old reserve requirements were more favorable to banks, other than central reserve city banks, in that part of their reserves could be kept with correspondent banks as bankers' balances on which interest was paid. However, central reserve city banks were required to keep all of their reserves in the form of lawful money (gold coins, gold certificates, and all currency except national bank notes) and other banks were required to hold their vault reserves in similar currency.

Present member-bank reserve requirements are superior to those under the old National Banking System because new member-bank reserves may be borrowed in case of need, and reserve requirements may be changed for all or any group of banks or types of deposits by rulings of the Board of Governors if conditions justify a change. The power of the Board of Governors to influence the volume of bank credit by changing member-bank reserve requirements is limited to the percentages specified in the law. However, the Board has the power to suspend all reserve requirements during an emergency; and the limits of these percentages may be changed by Congress (as they were on a temporary basis in a special session of Congress in 1948).

PROPOSALS FOR CHANGES IN RESERVES

Secondary Reserve Requirements. In the preceding pages, primary-reserve requirements, which necessitate keeping bank resources uninvested, were emphasized; but, at various times, the United States has had experience with a reserve requirement that necessitated keeping assets in some designated form of earning assets. The Louisiana Banking Act of 1842 provided for 100-per-cent backing for notes and deposits, one third in specie and two thirds in short-term paper, thus combining the cash-reserve and earning-asset types of reserve requirements.

In recent years, some state laws have permitted state-chartered banks to use earning assets (generally, United States government and state and municipal obligations) as part of their reserves for both time and demand deposits (Colorado, Connecticut, Florida, Idaho, Massachusetts, Nebraska, Pennsylvania, South Dakota, Vermont, and Wisconsin); and other states have permitted the use of earning assets as reserves only for time deposits (California, Georgia, Maryland, Michigan, and Ohio). State chartered banks that are members of the Federal Reserve System must meet the reserve requirements appropriate for other member banks similarly classified (country, reserve city, or central reserve city).

In anticipation of inflationary developments, it was proposed during and since World War II that all member banks be required to meet secondary-reserve requirements in addition to cash-reserve requirements. This secondary-reserve requirement would be a fractional one, perhaps 10 or 15 per cent of total deposits, added to the existing cash-reserve requirement. It would mean that commercial banks would be required to invest a fixed percentage of total deposits in government securities.[4]

Among the arguments in favor of a secondary-reserve requirement in the form of treasury bills and other short-term government obligations are that it would (1) save interest on the public debt, (2) expedite the growth of the short-term money market, (3) reduce fluctuations in the market price of government securities, and (4) increase the Federal Reserve System's control over commercial banks' lending powers. From the viewpoint of monetary control, the last of these arguments is most significant; because, if heavy reliance is to be placed on monetary control, the conditions under which it may be applied should permit control to be as effective as possible.

At the present time, it is common practice for commercial banks to reduce their holdings of government securities during periods of tight money so as to increase their loans to business and other borrowers. If the volume of such switching was to be reduced by a secondary-reserve requirement, it would be necessary for banks to scrutinize applications for loans more carefully and to reject or curtail those of marginal and other applicants. However, if the minimum secondary reserve required did not absorb all of commercial banks' surplus funds, they could switch from investments in securities to loans. Therefore, in order to be most effective as a control device, the secondary-reserve percentage would have to be a variable or flexible one.

The monetary authorities may use moral suasion to prevent banks from switching from securities to loans (as in Canada during the first part of 1956, when banks were persuaded to increase their holdings of treasury bills to 15 per cent in addition to their

---

[4] See Joint Committee on Economic Report, *Monetary Policy and the Management of the Public Debt* (Washington, D.C.: U.S. Government Printing Office, 1952), Part I, pp. 171–73 and 477–82; and Part II, pp. 726–28.

primary reserves of 8 per cent) but, in the United States, where banking is less centralized than in most foreign countries, this device would tend to be less effective. A secondary-reserve requirement would force commercial banks to meet a specified liquidity position as determined by the monetary authorities; but the weakness of this device is that it would make no allowances for variations in the nature of different banks' deposits, investments, and loans.

In preference to establishing a secondary-reserve requirement, the practice of switching from investments to loans could be curtailed if the United States government were to replace its short-term obligations with long-term bonds. Then, commercial banks would be more reluctant to sell their long-term bonds in the face of large capital losses (the locked-in theory). Another practice that would improve the environment for more effective monetary management would be for the United States government to plan its receipts and expenditures so that there would be a surplus during boom times and to use the surplus to retire the government's short-term debt. The one fact that stands out is, that in order for monetary policy to be effective, Congress must see to it that the United States Treasury is in a strong position when obligations mature during business booms (see also Chapter XXIII).

Supplementary-Reserve Requirements. To check the expansion in bank credit during inflationary periods, it has been proposed that banks be required to keep supplementary cash reserves against either an increase in their deposits or an increase in their loans and investments.[5] If applied to deposits, the supplementary reserves would be kept only on the deposits above the level fixed at the time the plan was adopted. If deposits were to increase by $1,000, it would mean that in addition to the customary reserve of $200 the bank would be required to keep a supplementary reserve of another 20 per cent, or $200. If the plan were applied to loans, the supplementary reserves would be kept only on the loans above the level fixed at the time the plan was adopted. Thus, if a bank were to increase its lending by $1,000, it would be required to meet not only the existing cash-reserve requirement of 20 per cent on its demand deposits but also a second cash-reserve requirement of possibly 20 per cent ($200) on its new loans. Since lending banks are primarily responsible for an increase in bank deposits, requiring supplementary reserves for loans would place the burden on the banks extending the credit.

---

[5] *Ibid.*, Part I, pp. 173–76 and 482–84; and Part II, pp. 728–29.

Assets as a Base for Reserve Requirements. Since minimum-reserve requirements are being used as a device of credit control rather than as a means of protecting depositors, maintaining minimum-cash reserves against classes of assets rather than against deposits would be justifiable. The impact of such a plan would depend upon the size of the cash reserve required and upon the classification of assets. Requiring reserves against assets would tend to increase the cost of borrowing where the reserve requirements are the highest. The percentages would need to be larger than those against deposits because the volume of loans and investments is smaller than the volume of deposits. The adoption of this plan would penalize those individual banks which are lending the most freely. Since banking difficulties are traced to unwise or careless lending and banking practices, the asset-reserve plan would tend to penalize the least conservative types of banks. All of the proposals suggested in this section have been used, in whole or in part, abroad in conjunction with other devices of credit control. (In a different category is the proposal to eliminate the classification of member banks as "central reserve city," "reserve city," and "country.")

100-Per-Cent-Reserve Plan. Although the Federal Reserve authorities have requested powers to increase substantially member-bank reserve requirements, their requests for new powers have been modest compared to those favoring the minimum reserves proposed for demand deposits in the 100-per-cent-reserve plan. While the reserve powers favored by the Federal Reserve authorities would be subject to administrative change, those favored by the advocates of the 100-per-cent-reserve plan would be permanent. The most practical of the 100-per-cent-reserve-plan proposals is the one which would require all commercial banks to hold reserves equal to 100 per cent of their demand deposits, either as cash in their vaults or as deposit accounts with their Federal Reserve banks. In effect, this would mean that banks handling demand deposits would be required to shift enough earning assets from their portfolios to the Federal Reserve banks so that their cash and/or Federal Reserve balances would be 100 per cent of net demand deposits. At the same time, the banks would continue to hold fractional reserves against their time deposits.[6]

[6] See Irving Fisher, *100% Money* (New York: Adelphia Co., 1935); F. D. Graham, "Reserve Money and the 100 Per Cent Proposal," *American Economic Review*, Vol. XXVI, No. 3 (September, 1936), pp. 428–40; Frederick Soddy, *The Role of Money* (New York: Harcourt, Brace & Co., 1935); and W. E. Spahr, *Fallacies of Professor Fisher's 100% Money Proposal* (New York: Farrar & Rinehart, Inc., 1938).

One of the most serious objections to this plan is the effect that it would have on banks' earnings. That banks could offset these losses, by reducing expenses and increasing service charges, is debatable. A decrease in loan and investment operations would reduce the need for personnel so employed. In well-managed banks, checking accounts already are paying their own way; and, where the volume is great enough, service charges provide a substantial profit. In general, bankers are opposed to the 100-per-cent-reserve plan because it would mean loss of jobs to key officers and probably a sharp reduction in the market price of bank stock.

The 100-per-cent-reserve plan would mean a transfer of most of the earning assets of commercial banks to the Federal Reserve banks, leaving commercial banks with only those earning assets acquired with time deposits and capital provided by owners. If the plan were adopted, there would be a temptation to reclassify demand deposits as time deposits, but whether depositors would cooperate is a question. Any movement of this nature could be checked by the Board of Governors by tightening the regulations in regard to savings-deposit withdrawals, by requiring "notice" in all cases, and by lengthening the notice period from thirty to sixty days for both time- and savings-deposit withdrawals.

The effect of the 100-per-cent-reserve plan on the total volume of hand-to-hand money and deposit currency would be to freeze it near the level existing at the time of adoption of the plan. There would be no change in processing checks; but, after collection, all the cash would be held as a reserve and the bank would have no new funds to lend or invest. Depositors would notice no change in banks' handling of deposit currency other than a probable increase in service charges.

The burden of the 100-per-cent-reserve plan would tend to fall on borrowers, who would have greater difficulty in securing funds from commercial banks. The proceeds of loans would be taken in the form of deposit currency, but the banking system would have to match these new deposits with cash reserves rather than to hold a fractional reserve. The funds used in lending would have to be provided by savings depositors and the owners of the bank. This would mean that commercial banks would have to compete, under less favorable conditions, with other lenders, with the effect of deteriorating their position while improving the position of other institutions (savings banks, insurance companies, investment banks, sales-finance companies, personal-loan companies, agricultural banks, and others). It may be concluded that, from the viewpoint of both borrowers and commercial banks, the effects of the 100-per-cent-reserve system would be unfavorable.

Commercial bank lending and investing has a monetary aspect, and it is this monetary aspect that is stressed by those favoring the 100-per-cent-reserve plan. Under the plan, the expansion of means of payment (recognized as an instrument of inflation) would not take place; and, during depressions, contraction in the means of payment (recognized as an instrument of deflation) would not take place. If currency were hoarded, the volume of deposit currency would decrease and the volume of hand-to-hand money (outside of banks) would increase; but there would be no change in the total means of payment. To be sure, there would be changes in velocity of money and deposit currency, but the inflationary and deflationary changes in the volume of means of payment would not be added to these changes.

Under the 100-per-cent-reserve plan, long-run changes in demand for currency would be met by open-market operations of the Federal Reserve banks. Under the most rigid of the proposals for 100-per-cent money, the Federal Reserve System would be required annually to add to the monetary supply an amount fixed by law in terms of the normal annual increase in physical volume of trade, production, and other weighted factors. This would mean that the Federal Reserve banks would increase their earning assets by lending and investing just enough to keep the total amount of paper money and deposit currency expanding by a fixed percentage of the existing amount of the total means of payment. Others in favor of the 100-per-cent plan would give the Federal Reserve authorities, or others made responsible for administering the plan, more discretionary authority.

EXPERIENCES ABROAD

Until twenty years ago only a relatively small number of the countries of the world required their commercial banks to maintain minimum percentage reserve balances against deposits. However, in some countries (as in the United Kingdom), commercial banks customarily maintained such balances with the central banks; and, in other countries (as in Canada), commercial banks could keep required reserves either as vault cash or as deposits with their central banks. During and since World War II, many countries have made provisions not only for requiring minimum reserves against deposits but also for making such minimum-reserve requirements variable (in about twenty-six countries in addition to the United States). Some countries have also added a secondary-reserve requirement in the form of cash and government securities or some other form of bank assets, such as special types of loan paper and investments, that the monetary authorities wish to promote.

Several conclusions are suggested by the current trend in requiring reserves abroad: (1) It seems to be standard practice in countries with well-developed banking systems to require by law or custom the keeping of minimum reserves with the central bank (except Spain, Argentina, and Japan, where the central bank has the power to require reserves but has not used it). (2) About twenty-six foreign countries have provided for and are using the variable minimum-cash-reserve requirement to check inflationary developments. (3) The provision for use of special-reserve requirements including government securities and other special assets is becoming less popular, which indicates a trend away from selective credit controls and a shift to monetary controls of a more general character. (4) Changes in minimum-reserve requirements seem to be most frequent in countries wherein money market conditions do not permit open-market operations to be used as effectively as in the United States. (5) The use of changes in bank-reserve requirements is a powerful instrument of credit control that may be used in conjunction with other devices of control—rediscount rate changes and open-market operations. (6) Where countries are dependent on foreign trade, frequent changes in reserve requirements may be made because of large seasonal swings in cash balances. (7) Selling government securities or letting them run off (not replacing them as they mature) to obtain additional reserves disturbs the money market. (8) Changes in banks' reserve requirements create different problems for different individual banks; therefore advance notice may be given when changes are to be made so that reserves may be built up gradually to meet the new requirements.

SUMMARY

In the United States, central bank and Treasury monetary policy have been directed at influencing the volume and availability of member-bank-reserve balances. Originally, minimum reserves were required to protect depositors; but, now, they are used as an instrument for influencing the quantity of bank credit. Sources of new bank reserves are Treasury currency outstanding, gold, and

Federal Reserve credit. Member banks must compete with the public, the Treasury, foreign central banks, and others for new reserve funds. In managing its cash funds the United States Treasury may contribute to maintenance of a stable money market. The Board of Governors has used its power to change member-bank reserve requirements to offset the inflationary and deflationary effects of changes in the gold stock. Because of the size of the public debt and the postwar inflation, interest has been aroused in devices that might be used to reduce the impact of increases in banks' loans and investments on the volume of money. Among the suggestions that have been made are: (1) higher primary-reserve requirements, (2) secondary-reserve requirements, (3) supplementary cash-reserve requirements against increases in deposits or loans and investments, (4) reserves based on assets rather than on deposits, and (5) 100-per-cent-reserve plan.

QUESTIONS AND PROBLEMS

1. Identify "excess" reserves and "required" reserves.
2. What are the three sources of new reserve money? Explain how new reserve money may be used.
3. Explain how an individual bank may adjust its reserve position.
4. Why may the volume of "free" reserves be a better indicator of credit conditions in the money market than "excess" reserves or the total volume of Federal Reserve credit?
5. What are the items in the Federal Reserve banks' statement that measure the amount of Federal Reserve credit in use?
6. What is your reaction to the use of uncollected items (Federal Reserve float) as reserves for member banks? How may this situation be corrected, if it is undesirable?
7. How do increases in Treasury cash and deposits in the Federal Reserve banks tend to cause member bank reserves to fall?
8. In what ways may the Treasury use its "deposits" as an instrument of monetary policy?
9. What is meant by Treasury "cash holdings"? How may they be used as an instrument of credit policy? Illustrate.
10. What relationship has there been between changes in the gold stock and changes in member-bank-reserve requirements?
11. Analyze: (a) secondary-reserve proposals, (b) supplementary-reserve plans, (c) the proposal to base reserves on assets, and (d) the 100-per-cent-reserve plan.
12. Analyze: The "Federal Reserve sells U.S. securities in move to stiffen the money market" (*New York Times*, January 13, 1956, p. 33).

What factors tend to ease the money market at this time of the year? Why?

13. Analyze: "float climbed very sharply during the statement week ended December 21, . . ." Federal Reserve Bank of New York, *Monthly Review of Credit and Business Conditions*, January, 1956, p. 2.

14. "That the levels of member bank borrowings and of excess reserves did not fluctuate more widely in response to the large and often erratic swings in reserve pressures was largely a result of extensive security transactions by the Federal Reserve System." Explain. Federal Reserve Bank of New York, *Monthly Review of Credit and Business Conditions*, January, 1956, p. 2.

15. Analyze: "The Federal Reserve apparently ran off Treasury bills on January 26 and then bought bills in the market early in the calendar week to keep the month-end decline in float from tightening too much the reserve position of member banks. On the average, however, free reserves were minus $555 million, a larger deficiency than in recent weeks." (Aubrey G. Lanston & Co., Inc., *Letter*, dated February 3, 1956).

16. Analyze: "Reserves not supplied by these instruments [open-market operations and lowering reserve requirements] are available at the initiative of individual member banks through borrowing at the Reserve banks. When reserve funds are obtained this way, however, banks are obligated to repay and tend to restrict their credit extensions in order to do so." (Richard Youngdahl, "Monetary Policy in Recent Years," *American Economic Review*, Vol. XLV [May, 1955], No. 2, p. 402.)

Chapter XXII | CREDIT AND MONETARY POLICY

IN THE Federal Reserve Act, and in other laws, Congress gave many specific directives to the Federal Reserve authorities concerning the use of credit control devices; but the general purposes of the Federal Reserve System's credit operations are most authoritatively stated in the annual reports of the Board of Governors of the Federal Reserve System. In the report for 1945 the following appeared:

It is the Board's belief that the implicit predominant purpose of Federal Reserve policy is to contribute, insofar as the limitations of monetary and credit policy permit, to an economic environment favorable to the highest possible degree of sustained production and employment. Traditionally this over-all policy has been followed by easing credit conditions when deflationary factors prevailed and, conversely, by restrictive measures when inflationary forces threatened.[1]

REVIEW OF CREDIT POLICY

Instruments of Credit Policy. The so-called instruments of Federal Reserve credit policy refer to the specific things that the Federal Reserve authorities may do to influence the money supply and its use by the economy. They have included changes in (1) discount rates on Federal Reserve banks' loans and advances, lowering them to encourage borrowing by member banks and raising them to discourage borrowing; (2) the volume of investments of Federal Reserve banks, increasing investments to place more reserve funds at the disposal of banks and decreasing them to reduce such funds; (3) the legal reserve requirements for member banks, lowering reserve requirements to make more of the assets of member banks available for lending and raising them to make fewer assets available for lending; (4) "down payments" and time payment period requirements for certain consumer-goods purchases, reducing and

[1] *Thirty-second Annual Report of the Board of Governors of the Federal Reserve System Covering Operations for the Year 1945* (Washington, D.C.: U.S. Government Printing Office, 1946), p. 1.

lengthening them respectively to encourage consumer buying and increasing and shortening them respectively to discourage such purchases; (5) margin requirements, lowering them to encourage the use of credit for purchases of stocks and raising them to discourage such purchases; (6) "down payments" and time payment period requirements for new real estate construction loans, reducing and lengthening them respectively to encourage, and increasing and shortening them respectively to discourage the use of credit for this purpose, and (7) moral suasion, using persuasion to encourage or discourage bank lending and investing.

Classification of Instruments. Instruments of Federal Reserve credit policy are classified as "general" and "selective." General instruments or devices are those which affect the overall volume of credit in use, and selective instruments affect the amount of credit used in special segments of the economy. Rediscount rates, open-market investments, and reserve requirements are commonly classified as general instruments of credit control because they influence the volume of credit and the price (interest rate) paid for the use of credit.

Requiring a minimum down payment on purchases of consumer goods, real estate, and securities, and placing a limit on the time period for which consumer credit and real estate credit may be advanced are called "selective" instruments of credit control. They cover advances of credit in special segments of the economy.

Moral Suasion. Moral suasion may be classified as both a general and a selective device of credit control. If the Federal Reserve authorities notify member banks that the general economic situation calls for more restraint in lending and investing, it would be considered a general device of credit control. On the other hand, if the communication is one calling attention to the sharp increase in the volume of consumer credit, it would be considered a selective device of credit control. Moral suasion may be directed at a group of banks or a single bank if the situation seems to warrant doing so.

Moral suasion may be made effective by withholding discounting privileges from the offending bank (or banks) because the law states that each Federal Reserve bank must give attention to the probable effects of new Federal Reserve credit upon the maintenance of sound credit conditions "both as to the individual institution and the economy generally." The standards set for the classification of bank assets may be changed so as to discourage certain types of lending. In extreme cases, the Board of Governors of the Federal Reserve System has the power (1) to remove any officer or director of any member bank for continued violation of the law or for following unsound practices in conducting the affairs of his bank, and (2) to expel a member bank from membership (in case of a national bank, this would lead to forfeiture of its charter). There is also some evidence that moral suasion has been used by the Federal Open Market Committee to influence securities dealers' purchases and sales of government securities.

Sometimes the federal government places its influence behind moral suasion as illustrated by the use made of the authority given by the President, under provisions of the Production Act of 1950, to the Board of Governors to encourage financial institutions to organize and supervise programs of voluntary restraint. The purpose was to persuade banks to make only essential loans so as to implement the financing of the defense program.[2]

Selective Devices. The conditions recognized as essential for successful administration of selective credit controls are (1) areas which can be reasonably defined, such as consumer credit, stock market credit, and real estate credit; (2) use of credit contracts, or collateral for credit, which can be easily identified, such as mortgages, stocks, installment sales, and loans; and (3) businesses wherein trade practices are specialized and standardized so that participants can be regulated, such as banks, sales-finance companies, real estate dealers, brokers and dealers in stocks, etc.

DISCOUNT POLICY

The oldest among the devices of credit control is to increase or decrease the discount rate so as to make borrowing from the Federal Reserve banks more or less expensive. Thus, during inflationary periods, the orthodox policy would be for the Reserve banks to raise their discount rates; and, during deflationary periods, to lower them.

Presumably, business profits will be reduced when interest rates are increased and increased when interest rates are reduced. However, changes in rediscount rates tend to have greater significance because of their anticipated effects on the availability of funds and the anticipated changes in general business conditions than because of their effects on the actual cost of borrowed funds. If business is expanding and the outlook for profits is favorable, high interest

[2] The principles and the program for voluntary credit restraint were worked out by representatives of the American Bankers Association, Investment Bankers Association of America, and Life Insurance Association of America, in consultation with the Board of Governors.

rates may not deter businessmen from borrowing; and conversely, if business is depressed and the outlook for profits is bleak, low interest rates may not induce businessmen to borrow.

Advantages of Discount Policy. The discount mechanism is well-suited to supplying individual member banks with new reserves when there is a temporary or seasonal need for them. In contrast, open-market purchases of government securities by the Federal Reserve System increase the total Federal Reserve credit outstanding, and banks not in need of new federal funds may participate in the credit expansion more fully than those in need of them. During periods of financial stress, reserves can be supplied directly and efficiently to banks in difficulty; and, when they come to the Federal Reserve banks for loans, negotiations may be such as to promote the broader aspects of credit policy. In addition, the discount mechanism provides a device for "disciplining" member-bank borrowers (the same type of disciplinary action that other prospective borrowers must face).

The discount mechanism is more flexible than other methods of credit control because there may be differences in the rediscount or discount rates to member banks among the Federal Reserve banks. However, the mobility of funds may make maintenance of different discount rates among the Reserve banks impractical when there is an active demand for funds; banks in low interest-rate districts may borrow through the federal funds market in order to lend in the high interest-rate districts. In addition to discount rates applicable to member banks, there are other discount rates which may and do vary among the Federal Reserve banks.

Changing discount rates is a simple and easily understood technique of making known the views of the monetary authorities on the economic and credit situation. Expectations of changes in discount rates, and the actual changes when made, will have varying effects on market psychology. Sometimes, the change in rates is discounted in advance, being viewed merely as bringing the discount rate in line with market rates (confirming past events); at other times, the money market is caught by surprise with considerable psychological effect (either bearish or bullish depending on circumstances). Often commercial banks wait until a change in the discount rate is announced before changing their interest rates on customers' loans. In some cases, the escalator clause in term-loan agreements provides for an automatic change in the interest rate on term loans with changes in the Federal Reserve banks' discount rate on loans to member banks. The interest rate on outstanding call loans may be changed at any time, but changes are usually made at the beginning of the business day.

Tradition against Borrowing. While following a restrictive credit policy, the Federal Reserve authorities are aided by a tradition against member-bank borrowing. Before the existence of the Federal Reserve System, most commercial bankers considered it to be a sign of weakness to have the item "rediscounts and bills payable" appear on their bank statements. So, member banks are more willing to lend and invest when their indebtedness to the Reserve banks is small and less likely to do so when their indebtedness is large. Inasmuch as member banks are reluctant to remain in debt, reserves borrowed from their Federal Reserve banks are usually extinguished promptly when the need for them passes.

The tradition against borrowing has continued, but it is complicated by the fact that sensitiveness to indebtedness is not the same among different banks and is not the same among all banks during different phases of the business cycle. The aversion toward borrowing is greatest among New York banks which, because of their contacts with the money market, are in the best position to avoid all except very short-term indebtedness at their Reserve bank. Other city banks are second in their avoidance of borrowing; while country banks are least reluctant to borrow. Customarily, the interest rate charged by commercial banks is higher than the rediscount rate; this increases the temptation to rediscount or borrow.

During the upswing in business, the need for liquidity is less pressing, borrowing becomes profitable, banks are less sensitive to indebtedness, loan demands of commercial banks' customers are large, and there may be a greater spread between market rates and the discount rate. During the downswing in business, the need for liquidity is greater, borrowing is less profitable, and banks are more sensitive to indebtedness. Although Federal Reserve officials have encouraged seasonal and war-emergency borrowing by member banks, they have discouraged continuous borrowing by individual member banks.

Different Rates. The discount-rate policy may entail the use of more than one rate at a particular time. What is considered to be "the discount rate" is the one applicable to discounts and advances to member banks secured by government obligations and eligible paper. A second rate, which must be at least one half of 1 per cent above the discount rate, is applicable to other short-term loans to member banks.

Since Federal Reserve banks are no longer strictly bankers' banks, there are other interest rates applicable to emergency advances to individuals, partnerships and corporations (including nonmember banks); and interest, fees, and commissions are added when lending under provisions of the Industrial Loan Act of 1934 as amended. To the individual borrower, the interest rate charged is important; but this rate may be ignored in discussing discount policy which purports to influence the credit and money supply generally.

OPEN-MARKET POLICY

Co-ordination of Discount and Open-Market Policies. During the early history of open-market policy, investing and disinvesting by the Federal Reserve banks were used to supplement and, in many cases, to lead the way for the use of discount-rate changes. By merely using open-market policy to provide a volume of reserves just sufficient to care for secular growth and seasonal requirements (the amount of purchases and sales of government securities would depend on the season of the year as well as the behavior of noncontrollable reserve factors discussed in Chapter XXI), the Federal Reserve authorities exert pressure on the market to make a decision as to the direction in which the wind is blowing (toward more or less inflation). If the Reserve authorities feel that a business expansion is proceeding too rapidly, some of the System's holdings of government securities may be sold or permitted to mature without replacement. If the funds received in payment are withheld from the commercial banking system, member banks will be short of reserves and will be inclined to borrow at their Federal Reserve banks to replenish them. If the demand for loanable funds is strong, the market rates will increase. The next step is to raise the discount rate in order to bring it in line with the market rates.

These techniques would be used in reverse if the Federal Reserve authorities felt a down turn in business activity to be imminent. After making open-market provisions for growth and seasonal needs, the Federal Reserve authorities would wait to see if the volume of discounting would fall as demands for funds subsided. If this occurred, there would be greater ease in the money market, lower market rates, and a downward adjustment in the Federal Reserve discount rate.

In 1923, 1925–26, 1928–29, the Open Market Committee sold government securities and the Federal Reserve banks raised their discount rates. The reduction in the supply of Federal Reserve credit, resulting from the liquidation of investments, was offset in part by an increase in the amount of discounting at the Reserve banks at the higher rates in effect. The opposite policies were followed in 1924, 1927, and 1930–33. From September, 1929, to December, 1933, the Federal Reserve banks purchased more than $2 billion in government securities in order to check deflation. At that time the amounts seemed large, and they did aid in creating an easier money situation. However, additional purchases would have been helpful; but the Federal Reserve note collateral and reserve requirements then in effect were such as to check further expansion.

Open-Market Policy without Discount Policy. From 1933 to 1942 the investments of Federal Reserve banks remained around $2.5 billion (rising slightly above this figure in 1937, when member banks' reserve requirements were increased, and then declining slightly until 1939). Discount rates were kept very low because the recovery from the business depression was not complete until the beginning of defense and war spending in the early 1940's.

Prior to the outbreak of World War II the effect of the influx of gold was offset, in part, by a decline in Federal Reserve banks' investments. However, the near panic that hit the market with the outbreak of the war in Europe (September, 1939) was followed by buying bonds; and, by the end of the year, total holdings of government securities reached about $2.5 billion. During World War II, Federal Reserve policy was dominated by the Treasury's and economy's need for money and credit. The greater portion of the new Federal Reserve credit was used to meet the public demand for new currency. Beginning in 1942, the volume of Federal Reserve credit resulting from Federal Reserve banks' investments increased sharply, reaching $24 billion at the end of 1945.

Special War Policies. In the government-securities market (which is only one segment of the money market), there are many rates of interest, chiefly because of the variation in maturities, presence or lack of tax exemption, and eligibility or noneligibility as a commercial bank investment. In handling their purchases of government securities during the war, the Federal Reserve System adopted two unique policies. One was to permit member and nonmember banks to sell Treasury bills at any time to the Federal Reserve banks at a discount of three eights of 1 per cent, which meant that Federal

Reserve bank credit was on "tap" insofar as the supply of Treasury bills permitted. The second was the adoption of a "pattern of interest rates" for government securities; in other words, prices of different classes of government securities were pegged.

The pattern of interest rates agreed on ranged from three eighths of 1 per cent on ninety-one-day Treasury bills, seven eighths of 1 per cent on certificates of indebtedness of one-year maturity, 2 per cent on eight- to ten-year bonds, to 2½ per cent on those of longest maturities. These measures were adopted to "facilitate war financing and to stabilize the market for government securities." During wartime, investors are reluctant to buy government bonds because they expect the first bond issue to be followed by others bearing higher interest rates and that bond prices will fall as the war continues. This attitude was not dispelled entirely by the practice of pegging interest rates because many investors did not expect the policy to succeed. Therefore these investors bought short-term government obligations; if they had not done so, the entire burden of making a market for short-term government obligations would have fallen on the Federal Reserve System from the beginning of the war.

Before the end of the war most of the United States Treasury bills had been acquired by the Federal Reserve System. When the mechanics are considered, the purchase of all bills offered by Federal Reserve banks had the advantage of placing credit in the hands of individual banks in need of reserves and not forcing them to borrow. While the traditional type of open-market operation does increase the supply of Federal Reserve credit in use, it does not follow that the new bank reserves will be acquired by the banks which need them most for reserve purposes.

The principles involved in purchasing Treasury bills were the same as those involved in purchasing bankers' acceptances; namely, establishment by Federal Reserve banks of uniform discount or buying rates with the initiative for selling left to banks. The revolutionary nature of this war-financing measure was due to the volume of Federal Reserve credit that could be created (while bankers' acceptances outstanding amounted to millions of dollars, Treasury bills amounted to billions of dollars) and the relatively high price paid for Treasury bills.

While the Federal Reserve banks' discount rates on bankers' acceptances are ordinarily above the market (that is, buying prices are ordinarily below the market), just the opposite policy was followed in regard to Treasury bills. This meant that the United States Treasury (and not the Federal Reserve authorities) was in a position to control the member-bank reserve situation by controlling the volume of Treasury bills. In July, 1947, when the policy of purchasing new Treasury bills was abandoned, it was stated that "only about 1.5 billion dollars of the nearly 16 billion total of Treasury bills outstanding are held outside the Federal Reserve Banks."[3] The Federal Reserve System also purchased substantial amounts of the other securities, chiefly certificates of indebtedness and short-term Treasury notes.

The Federal Reserve policy of stabilizing the price of government securities during World War II was a success (the average rate of interest on government securities actually declined as the war continued). Although an effort was made to sell the new securities to investors other than commercial banks, the United States Treasury's emphasis on short-term obligations, pegged prices, and redeemable issues actually encouraged monetization of the national debt (purchase by commercial banks). Once the Federal Reserve System had embarked on a program of stabilizing government securities prices, it was difficult to stop (its position was like that of the boy who had a bear by the tail).

PROBLEMS OF PUBLIC DEBT MANAGEMENT

After the end of World War II the shift from war to peacetime financing was slow. With the removal of direct price control in 1946, commodity prices increased sharply. The amount of the national debt had increased from $50 billion to more than $280 billion. Most of the government obligations had been purchased at low yields (interest rates) prevailing during the war. Because a sharp rise in interest rates would have meant a sharp fall in the market price of outstanding marketable issues, perhaps it is not surprising that the Federal Reserve System continued the policy of maintaining relatively stable prices for government securities for some time. Consequently, such anti-inflationary steps that were taken were often offset by the need for buying government securities in order to maintain their prices.

In 1946 the Board of Governors raised margin requirements to 100 per cent, eliminated the one-half-of-1-per-cent preferential rate on advances secured by short-term government securities, and in-

---

[3] *Thirty-fourth Annual Report of the Board of Governors of the Federal Reserve System Covering Operations for the Year 1947* (Washington, D.C.: U.S. Government Printing Office, 1948), p. 93.

creased the rediscount rates on bankers' acceptances. In July, 1947, the Federal Open Market Committee eliminated the three-eighths-of-1-per-cent buying rate on Treasury bills and worked toward the abandonment of the policy of stabilizing the prices of all United States government securities.

Late in 1947, trouble developed in the long-term government bond market when banks and institutional investors began selling these securities in fairly large amounts. So, again the System bought government bonds in order to support the market, when the traditional credit policy called for the opposite action. However, the System offset, in part, these purchases of bonds by reducing its holdings of other government obligations, particularly Treasury bills.

Late in the summer of 1948 the President called Congress into special session to take action on bills proposed to check inflation. Authority was granted to raise member-bank reserve requirements. The ironical aspect of this situation was the fact that the Federal Open Market Committee was increasing the System's holdings of government securities—the most inflationary measure—in the midst of all the anti-inflationary clamor. The increase in member-bank reserve requirements was counterbalanced by further investments by the Federal Open Market Committee.

The picture changed so rapidly that by the spring of 1949 the business situation warranted adoption of a policy of easy credit. Therefore emergency measures were allowed to elapse and reserve requirements were reduced. The United States Treasury and the Federal Reserve System came to an agreement on two points: (1) the open-market purchases and sales of government securities would be made according to the needs of general business and the credit situation; and (2) the Federal Reserve System would assist in "maintaining orderly conditions in the security market rather than a fixed pattern of rates on United States government securities." What these general statements meant no one knew for certain. Did they mean that "maintaining orderly conditions in the government securities market . . ." was to take precedence over preventing inflation? The interpretation of this statement of policies was to be tested after Korea.

Following the outbreak of war in Korea, the Federal Reserve authorities raised buying rates on acceptances and the discount rates from $1\frac{1}{2}$ to $1\frac{3}{4}$ per cent, and asked for the co-operation of supervisory agencies in restraining credit. But these measures were merely expressions of what the System desired—tighter money market conditions. The real issue to be solved, if it was capable of solution, was in the System's freedom to contract its holdings of government securities so as to reduce the volume of Federal Reserve credit in use even if the prices of government bonds fell below par.

During the last part of 1950, the picture was confused because the Federal Reserve System was tightening money-market interest rates at a time when the Treasury was refunding maturing obligations. If there had been an agreement between the System and the Treasury on interest rates before the securities were offered, the new issues would not have been offered at yield rates below the market. The System acquired most of the new securities ($8 billion), but sold about $7 billion from its portfolio of short-term government securities and bonds at lower prices (higher yields). Although this was an unprofitable transaction for the Federal Reserve System, it had the effect of increasing money rates in the market (an anti-inflationary development). It also stressed the need for co-operation between the Treasury and the Federal Reserve System on matters of policy and this resulted in the so-called "Treasury-Federal Reserve Accord."

Treasury-Federal Reserve Accord.   On March 4, 1951, a joint announcement by the Secretary of the Treasury, the Chairman of the Board of Governors, and the Chairman of the Federal Open Market Committee was released to the press:

The Treasury and the Federal Reserve System have reached full accord with respect to debt management and monetary policies to be pursued in furthering their common purpose to assure the successful financing of the Government's requirements and, at the same time, to minimize monetization of the public debt.

In this accord there was no commitment by the Federal Reserve System to support the government bond market at fixed prices. The policy adopted was to maintain an "orderly" market for government securities (preventing a sharp increase or decrease in prices), to discourage sales to the System, and to develop a self-sustaining market. The specific items agreed upon included the need for (1) refinancing certain long-term bonds with a new nonmarketable issue, (2) reducing or discontinuing purchases by the Federal Reserve System of short-term securities so that the short-term market rate may adjust to a position where it will be advantageous for banks to borrow from the Federal Reserve banks, (3) maintaining for a time the rediscount rate at 1¾ per cent, and (4) working together by the two agencies (the Federal Reserve System and the Treasury) on a new program for obtaining new funds for defense mobilization purposes. Later, the prices of government bonds did drop below par, but there was no panic selling. Now member banks are borrowing more freely from the Federal Reserve banks, indicating a preference for borrowing over selling government securities at a loss in the market (the locked-in theory of the effect of higher interest rates).

CURRENT MONETARY POLICY

Since the spring of 1952, there has been a return to monetary policy which has been redirected toward keeping the economy stable at a higher level of employment without price inflation. From the spring of 1952 to the spring of 1953, the monetary authorities were confronted with a high level of business with inflation as a potential threat. This period was followed by a leveling off of business and a threat of deflation, and this in turn was followed by a revival of business activity which again reached a boom and inflationary level in 1955. So within the last few years the monetary authorities have been forced to follow a restrictive credit policy from mid-1952 to mid-1953 and again from the spring of 1955 to date, with the intervening period having been one of credit ease.

Today the monetary authorities are relying chiefly on general devices of credit control in order to achieve the objective of monetary policy. As indicated earlier, this objective is to keep monetary expenditures in balance with the flow of things so as to facilitate the normal growth of the economy without booms and depressions. If there is a threat of overexpansion, inflationary spending is discouraged by reducing the rate of increase of the money supply. By a combination of open-market operations and rediscount policy, the Federal Reserve System may create a tight or an easy money situation. The question is, how do these changes affect the economy as a whole?

Effects of Credit Restraint on Lending. The response of commercial banks to a situation of money restraint may be to borrow from the Federal Reserve banks and/or to sell their government and other securities in order to obtain funds to finance an increase in loan demands. When banks sell securities, expansion in the credit and money supply due to more commercial bank lending is offset, at least in part, by the decline in commercial banks' holdings of securities. For commercial banks to sell or to forego buying government securities tends to reduce the price of these securities, and bank management may have to choose between sustaining a capital loss if they sell securities and foregoing higher income that would result from lending at higher interest rates.

All financial markets are affected by the leveling off of the volume of loanable funds provided by commercial banks, first the money market and then generally all capital markets. A tight money situation may be thought of in terms of higher interest rates and/or lower prices for fixed income securities. Lower prices of United States government obligations, and those of state and local governments and private corporations, affect both lenders and borrowers. Lenders will be faced with capital losses on their investments if they sell their securities and so they may hold them and postpone new lending and investing (the locked-in theory). Some borrowers, such as cities, states, public utility companies, and others, may postpone new issues of bonds until the market becomes more favorable.

Some financial institutions operate with loans from commercial banks as well as with savings, and, if the loans are obtainable only at higher costs or not at all, the lending activities of these institutions must be restricted. If they turn to open-market financing, they may find a scarcity of funds because commercial banks use this market chiefly as an outlet for their surplus loanable funds, and there would tend to be little or no surplus during a period of credit restraint. In negotiating with their over-the-counter borrowers, commercial banks may be required to ration their funds, turn away marginal applicants for loans, raise the over-the-counter interest rate on loans, and enforce their compensatory-balance rules more rigidly.

During a period of credit restraint, consumers as well as businessmen will be faced with higher interest costs and higher loan standards when trying to arrange for credit. Prospective homeowners will tend to have greater difficulty in arranging for nonconventional real estate loans (Veterans' Administration and Federal Housing Administration guaranteed or insured loans) than for conventional loans because the interest rate on nonconventional loans is fixed by regulation and the law and cannot be adjusted upward as can the interest rate on conventional loans. Generally, banks attempt to satisfy the credit demands of their regular customers even if they have to liquidate investments to do so. But, if the prices of government and other securities fall sharply, the banks may not only retain their investments but may even add to their portfolios by buying more securities at bargain prices.

Effects of Credit Restraint on Expenditures. Restraint on the expansion of bank credit reduces the rate of increase of the money supply, and higher interest costs together with the inability to obtain all of the credit sought tend to decrease the amount of expenditures. Because higher interest rates reduce the capitalized value of all existing assets, especially fixed-income securities, some individuals may postpone consumption and investment expenditures in order to build up their deposit balances. Fear of future difficulties in obtaining credit tends to increase the demand for liquid assets and, if there is expectation of more stable prices from monetary policy, individuals tend to build up their savings without fear of depreciation in their purchasing power. On the other hand, some spending units may reduce their cash balances relative to expenditures, thus increasing the turnover or velocity of money.

Effects of Easing Credit. When the demand for funds is declining or is stationary, the Federal Reserve System may take action to encourage the continued growth of the economy by reducing the cost of borrowing, making new reserves available to member banks by investing in government securities, and releasing existing member-bank reserves by reducing reserve requirements. The commercial banks may use part of the increase in reserves or freed reserves to reduce their indebtedness at the Federal Reserve banks and then use the remainder to increase their loans and investments. When interest rates fall, the capitalized value of assets increases, and there is a general improvement in the liquidity of the economy. Commercial banks and other lenders are more active in seeking new loans and investments, and some credit will be extended and some expenditures will be made that would not have taken place during periods of tight credit. The availability of funds on more liberal terms will encourage financing by state and local governments, corporations, consumers, and homeowners. So the overall effects of an easy-money policy on borrowing, the money supply, and the amount of spending tend to be the opposite of those previously noted as resulting from a tight money policy.

SUMMARY

The objective of the Federal Reserve System's credit policy has been the creation of an "economic environment favorable to the highest possible degree of sustained employment." Except during war periods, this policy called for easing credit conditions during periods of depression and restricting credit conditions during periods of inflation. The two major devices of credit control are changes in the rate at which Federal Reserve credit may be obtained and changes in the volume of investments by Federal Reserve banks. Supplementary devices are changes in member-bank reserve requirements, margin requirements for security transactions, down payment and length of credit terms involved in sales contracts or consumer loans made on the instalment plan, and (from 1950–52) down payments and time-payment periods for new real estate construction loans.

The traditional credit policy of the Federal Reserve System has been sidetracked during wars when the major objective is to assure the United States Treasury of all the funds needed for war financing. As a result of commitments to keep down the interest rates paid on government obligations, the Federal Reserve System became enmeshed in a post-World War II debt management policy from which it had difficulty in freeing itself. In order to check inflationary developments in the private segments of the economy, higher interest rates and less Federal Reserve credit were desirable; but there cannot be higher interest rates in the private segments of the money and capital markets without having higher interest rates on government securities.

Treasury debt and monetary policies may be helpful in preventing monetary fluctuations. But, faced with a national debt of $275 billion, the extent to which prices of different government issues may be affected by Treasury action is limited. The Treasury-Federal Reserve Accord of March, 1951, did free the Federal Reserve System from any responsibility it may have had for pegging the prices of government securities. While most wars are thought of as being temporary, the "cold" war may last for generations. Thus, policies that may be adaptable to a situation such as that prevailing from 1941 to 1945 are not equally adaptable to the current situation.

Since 1951, the Federal Reserve System has given an extraordinary demonstration of how monetary policy may be used to stabilize the economy without sacrificing the normal growth of a nation such as ours. While changes in interest rates and the availability of credit may not counteract cyclical movements in expenditures completely, they have been powerful factors in preventing cumulative movements in one direction or the other. The effects on expenditures and on the liquidity of consumers and business firms have been of the contracyclical type; but, if a recession were to become a depression, fiscal policy may have to be used more aggressively.

QUESTIONS AND PROBLEMS

1. Distinguish between "selective" and "general" instruments of Federal Reserve credit policy. In what category would you place each of the following: (a) discount rate changes, (b) purchase and sale of gov-

ernment securities, (c) changes in legal-reserve requirements for member banks, (d) regulation of consumer credit, (e) changes in margin requirements for security transactions, (f) regulation of real estate construction loans, (g) moral suasion? Why?

2. Summarize the advantages claimed for discount policy.

3. How and why may the "tradition against borrowing" influence the effectiveness of the discount policy of the Federal Reserve System? What is meant by the discount rate? Are there other rates applicable when borrowers obtain funds over the counter from the Federal Reserve banks?

4. What is meant by the co-ordination of discount and open-market policies? Illustrate.

5. What type of open-market policy was followed during World War II with reference to Treasury bills? What were its advantages and disadvantages?

6. Why was a pattern of interest rates for government securities maintained during World War II? What were its ill effects? Why was there a delay in abandoning it?

7. What was the Treasury-Federal Reserve System "accord" of March 4, 1951? Why is it important?

8. Explain how a Federal Reserve policy of credit restraint affects the volume of loanable funds and the money supply. The amount of borrowing and expenditures? Savings?

9. How do higher interest rates affect the liquidity of the economy?

10. What is meant by the "locked-in" theory?

11. How does easing of credit tend to influence (a) lending? (b) the money supply? (c) expenditures? and (d) the liquidity of the economy?

12. "A central bank should endeavor to reduce as much as possible fluctuations in business. It should try to stimulate business at a time when confidence is weakening, and act as a restraining factor when there is danger of the development of boom conditions." (G. F. Towers, "Bank of Canada," radio address, December 1, 1938.) Do you agree? How successful have the Federal Reserve authorities been in following such policies during the last ten years?

13. "Readjustment to postwar conditions entailed carrying over some of the reserve banking practices adopted to meet the war emergency. . . . In the Government securities market, because of the sheer size of the war accumulated public debt, the dominant focus continued to be the maintenance of orderliness and stability, and this pattern persisted into the first year of the current defense emergency." (M. S. Szymczak, *Reserve Banking in a Dynamic Economy*, mimeographed copy of a speech delivered before the Fifty-first Annual Convention of the National Association of Supervisors of State Banks, September 24, 1952, p. 3.) Analyze this statement.

14. Is the following statement equally applicable to the American Bank-

ing System? "By buying securities, or adding to its assets in any way whatever, the central bank increases the reserves of other banks, because the cheques which it issues in payment for such securities, etc., are deposited in banks, and swell the deposits of the receiving banks at the Bank of Canada when the cheques are presented to the Bank of Canada for payment." (G. F. Towers, *Bank of Canada*, radio address, December 1, 1938.)

Chapter XXIII

FISCAL POLICY

Fiscal policy refers to the use of the federal government's taxing, borrowing, spending, and other powers not only to carry on its normal business but also to maintain a high level of employment. The factors that have given rise to fiscal policy are the growth in the size of the national budget and the national debt. Since Congress has powers over revenues and appropriations, the basic responsibility for fiscal policy rests with this legislative body. However, the President is responsible for presenting to Congress, for such action as is deemed necessary, an annual budget and semiannual reports on the economic state of the nation; and numerous govermental departments and agencies are involved in planning. Therefore fiscal policy is the joint responsibility of both the legislative and executive branches of the government (hereinafter referred to merely as the government). Fiscal policy is a common sense recognition of the fact that governmental financial activities do have inflationary and deflationary effects on the economy.

The elements in fiscal policy are (1) taxation, both as to amount and incidence; (2) expenditures, both for investment and consumption purposes; (3) debt management, not only as to volume and ownership but also as to how the types and amounts of debt are to be manipulated so as to affect the amount of money and the propensity to consume; and (4) the location of United States Treasury balances so as to influence the amount of member-bank reserves and the supply of money and credit (see also Chapter XXI).

BACKGROUND FOR FISCAL POLICY

Employment Act of 1946. The passage of the Employment Act of 1946 represents the culmination of the development of the philosophy concerning the role of the government in economic affairs. The statement of economic policy contained in this Act, which is applicable to all agencies of the federal government including the Federal Reserve authorities and Federal Reserve banks, is as follows:[1]

[1] U.S.C. §1021, 60 Stat. 23.

The Congress hereby declares that it is the continuing policy and responsibility of the Federal Government to use all practicable means consistent with its needs and obligations and other essential considerations of national policy, with the assistance and cooperation of industry, agriculture, labor, and State and local governments, to coordinate and utilize all its plans, functions, and resources for the purpose of creating and maintaining, in a manner calculated to foster and promote free competitive enterprise and the general welfare, conditions under which there will be afforded useful employment opportunities, including self-employment, for those able, willing, and seeking to work, and to promote maximum employment, production, and purchasing power.

National Income Statistics. In order to have a measurement of the general welfare, the Office of Business Economics within the Bureau of Foreign and Domestic Commerce, United States Department of Commerce, has developed the work on national income statistics (initiated in 1932 in response to Senate Resolution No. 220 of the 72nd Congress). These statistics are published in the *Survey of Current Business;* and, periodically, as in 1947, 1951, and 1954, in more complete form as a supplement called *National Income, A Supplement to the Survey of Current Business.*

Statistics of national output are presented from two principal points of view: (1) as a summation of the market value of final products produced by the economy, and (2) as a summation of costs incurred in producing these products (again in terms of dollar figures). The total of these two sums will be equal, and they are ordinarily presented in the form of a balance sheet. (See Table 19.) As a measure of progress, from year to year and from decade to decade, two adjustments are desirable—allowances for changes in prices and in population. If the national income has increased by twofold because general prices have been inflated by 100 per cent, there has been no real gain; and, if the increase in national income in terms of real income has not increased in proportion to the increase in population, there has been a per capita loss.

Even after making allowances for changes in general prices and population, national income statistics are but aggregates and need to be broken down into component parts to show sources of income and nature of expenditures. Since national economic policy is "to foster and promote free competitive enterprise," the allocation of income between the private and the public segments of the economy is important.

Goods and services produced at home may be consumed abroad, and goods and services produced abroad may be consumed in the United States. If there is an excess of imports over exports, the

United States gains in terms of real income; or conversely, if exports exceed imports, it loses in terms of real income. Because the United States has a growing economy, the distribution of private expenditures between consumption and investments is significant.

TABLE 19

NATIONAL INCOME AND PRODUCT ACCOUNT, 1955

(In Millions of dollars)

Compensation of employees:		Personal consumption expenditures.253,971
Wages and salaries............210,354		
Supplements................. 12,838		Gross private domestic investment. 60,557
Income of unincorporated enter-		Net foreign investment.......... −470
prises and inventory valuation		
adjustment.................. 39,019		Government purchases of goods
		and services................. 76,802
Rental income of persons........ 10,076		
Corporate profits and inventory		
valuation adjustment:		
Corporate profits before tax:		
Corporate profits tax liability. 21,533		
Corporate profits after tax:		
Dividends............... 11,218		
Undistributed profits...... 9,915		
Inventory valuation adjustment.. −1,738		
Net interest.................... 10,833		
National income...............324,048		
Indirect business tax and nontax		
liability..................... 32,521		
Business transfer payments....... 1,430		
Statistical discrepancy.......... 1,820		
Less: Subsidies minus current sur-		
plus of government enterprises.. 297		
Charges against net national prod-		
uct.......................359,522		
Capital consumption allowances... 31,338		
Charges against gross national		*Gross national product.......*390,860
product...............390,860		

Source: *Survey of Current Business* (July, 1956), p. 8.

National Product or the Flow of Goods and Services. The gross national product is the market value of the output of goods and services before deductions are made for depreciation charges and other allowances for business and institutional consumption of durable capital goods. The gross national product measures the money or market value of the national output of goods and services; and, after allowances for price changes, it provides an index of the physical volume of goods and services produced. The major components of the gross national product are (1) personal consumption expenditures; (2) gross private domestic investment; (3) federal, state, and local government expenditures; and (4) net foreign investment (which is very small).[2]

National Income or Earnings from Production. National income is defined as the aggregate earnings of labor and property which result from the current production of goods and services of the national economy. The statistics of national income by distributive shares (see Table 19) are inclusive of taxes on earnings, which means that they cannot be accepted as an indication of the well-being of the recipients.

The classes of distributive shares do not correspond to those in classical economics—wages, interest, rent, and profits. Among the distributive shares, "employees' compensation" is the most important. Other classes of distributive shares are "proprietors' and rental income," "net interest," and "corporate profits and income" plus or minus a figure to show the change in the value of inventories.

A reconciliation between national income and gross national product necessitates the inclusion of allowances for capital depreciation, indirect business taxes, and other allowances. When all of these bookkeeping items are added to "national income," the aggregate is "gross national income" which is equal to "gross national product."

Personal Income or Receipts of Consumers. Personal income includes the current income received by persons from all sources. It differs from national income because it excludes income earned during a certain period which is not paid out (social security payments which have consistently exceeded benefit payments, giving the government a cash surplus) and includes income paid out but not earned during a certain period (government interest and transfer payments).[3]

[2] Although "net foreign investments" were small, there was a net export surplus of about $4.1 billion, which was financed by the United States government grants and private remittances (accounted for respectively under "government" and "personal consumption" expenditure). "Net foreign investments" indicates for the year that receipts and payments on current accounts were practically in balance, as indicated in the balance-of-payments statement of the United States. See Chapter XXV.

[3] Transfer payments include benefits from social security, direct relief, military pensions, aid to veterans, state bonuses, and such minor business transfer payments as corporations' gifts to nonprofit institutions, consumers' bad debts, prizes, and other unilateral transfers.

Disposable Personal Income. Disposable personal income is the total of all personal income after taxes are deducted. This income may be spent for consumption or saved. If saved, the owner has the choice of improving his liquid position by building up his cash balances, retiring a debt, or investing. In effect, the owner may spend this income for consumption or for investments, or he may withdraw his income from the income stream.

Since an expenditure is usually followed by successive expenditures by others during a year, the withholding of income, or conversely the spending of income, has many secondary effects which will lead to a change in the volume of payments in excess of the original decrease or increase. The secondary effects are ordinarily explained in terms of the "multiplier" principle and the "acceleration" principle.

The multiplier principle indicates the approximate effects throughout the year that an increase in private or public expenditures will have in raising national income through its effects on consumption expenditures. This may be several fold, depending on the marginal propensity to consume. If only one half of each dollar of income is being spent on consumption (the rest being hoarded), then the multiplier effect is two; but if 80 per cent of each new income dollar is spent the multiplier effect will be five.

The increase in consumption expenditures may have a subsequent effect on investments, called the "acceleration principle." This effect will depend upon the nature of the demand for additional consumption. If there are unused productive resources in the industry where the new consumption expenditures occur, the effect of new capital expenditures may be zero; but, if the consumption expenditures induce new capital expenditures, then the amount of new investments may be great.

Although the multiplier and acceleration principles are customarily described in terms of the expansionary effects of new income expenditures on the economy, these principles are equally applicable to the withholding of new income expenditures. There would be a multiple contraction of national income and an added loss of any induced investments. In terms of the income equation of exchange (see Chapter III), the concepts of the multiplier and acceleration principles are included in the concept of the income-velocity of money.

According to Lord Keynes' "fundamental psychological law," there is a natural tendency for men "to increase their consumption as their incomes increase, but not by as much as the increase in their income."[4] Conversely, if income is falling, there is a tendency to decrease consumption but not by as much as the decrease in income. This may not be true in the United States for a number of reasons. While it is true that American consumers purchase more than is necessary to sustain life and that they may forego outlays for many things if they expect a recession, this picture is inaccurate. In reality, American consumers' desire for a higher standard of living is so strong that they are ready to go into debt and spend their savings to achieve it. Often personal consumption expenditures are in excess of disposable personal income (personal income after taxes).

The position of American consumers has been strengthened by the creation of both private and public unemployment, sickness, and other benefit and pension plans. Furthermore, a greater stability of family income has resulted from two or more members of families being employed and from greater stability of employment due to seniority rules, year-round employment (guaranteed annual wage), and better business management (giving consumers steadier incomes).

Much of modern personal savings is traced to contracts that run for long periods of time (purchases of life insurance and homes) and periodic savings plans (participation in "bond-a-month" plans, purchases of shares of savings and loan associations, Christmas savings clubs), which may take precedence over additional spending for consumption. This means that savings may be more stable than anticipated in the Keynesian theory and spending for consumption may be less passive than assumed in the "fundamental psychological law."

Finally, the "fundamental law" stresses personal savings and does not include those of corporations and other business institutions that are financing expansion with retained earnings (an important source of savings in the American economy). There are aspects of business finance, such as accounting and dividend policies, which help to explain why changes in total savings, including personal savings, are not closely correlated with changes in national income.

Because business planning now covers anticipated spending over a period of years, short-term factors have less influence than in the past. Improvements in inventory management have lessened short-term business fluctuations to such a degree that so-called inventory booms and recessions are mild. The rapid growth of technological research is providing industry with new ideas for development—in

[4] J. M. Keynes, *The General Theory of Employment, Interest and Money* (New York: Harcourt, Brace and Company, 1935), p. 96.

fact, the chemists and physicists have stated that we have hardly "scratched the surface" in some fields of science. Instead of being faced with a situation wherein there are no outlets for savings (the mature economy thesis), there may be such a demand for funds as to require not only savings but also new bank credit in order to meet the needs of the economy.

Savings and Investments. Over the long-run, savings will tend to equal investments; but over the short-run, there may be considerable disparity between them. Acceptance of the "fundamental psychological law" principle would suggest that the responsibility for investing, and therefore the maintenance of the flow of income, rests with the wealthier classes. Bank credit could be expanded to offset the loss of income due to hoarding (uninvested savings); but, to be effective, the credit would have to be used. If, for any reason, bank credit is not used, the fall in national income may continue. But all demands, including the demand for cash balances, have a saturation point; and so the problem is one of being sure that the cash-balance demand is more than met so that enough new bank credit will be spent to offset the non-investment of savings.

Importance of Liquid Assets. Liquid assets include money and near money, those assets that may be converted into money for spending with little loss or delay. At times, the volume of liquid assets has been considerably larger than national income. The importance of liquid assets as a source of spending, both actual and potential, was demonstrated by the spending of accumulated cash balances following World War II. Because consumers use their credit as well as their liquid assets, the total of consumer spending is not so closely related to consumer income as was assumed in the past (see also Chapter III).

Among the factors which tend to increase the stability of the American economy are built-in or automatic stabilizers—both public and private—which increase the number of dollars placed in or left in the hands of businessmen, farmers, and consumers during recessions and which decrease the number of dollars in their hands during periods of business boom. Since the different techniques considered in the remainder of this chapter are not fully developed, Congress may have to enact new laws to supplement existing ones in order to prevent major depressions in the future.

In order to expedite any desirable legislation, the Council of Economic Advisors has been created. This Council reports on general economic conditions through the President to a joint committee of Congress. The joint committee has its own staff to help members in evaluating the reports and recommendations as presented by the President.

FISCAL POLICY AND THE NATIONAL BUDGET

Compensatory Fiscal Policy. Fiscal policy may be thought of as being similar in principle to central bank policy—as an instrument to check booms or depressions by decreasing or increasing income-creating activities. During the downswing in the business cycle and during depressions, governmental spending will be increased, taxes will be lowered, debt retirement will be retarded or stopped, and new funds will be borrowed from commercial banks. During the boom phase of the business cycle, governmental spending will be decreased, taxes will be raised, debt retirement will be accelerated, and borrowing will be curtailed or stopped.

From a budgetary viewpoint, compensatory action is reflected in the size of the government's deficit or surplus. During the downswing in business, corrective measures will be reflected in an increase in the size of the deficit (or at least a reduction in the size of the surplus); during the upswing, corrective measures will be reflected in an increase in the size of the surplus (or at least a reduction in the size of the deficit). Unless a surplus is assumed, compensatory spending would be an expediency rather than a policy. The only exception would be in the case of a mature economy wherein a secular deficiency exists.

A budgetary deficit may result from a decline in tax income or a rise in government expenditures or both; and, conversely, a budgetary surplus may result from a rise in tax income or a decline in government expenditures or both. A compensatory budgetary policy may stress either fluctuating tax income, which would reduce the danger of misinvesting, or fluctuating governmental spending, which would increase the danger of misinvesting. While the first would be easier to administer, the second would be more adaptable to financing certain basic social needs. In practice, both are involved in fiscal policy.

Importance of Government Spending. In a modern economy government expenditures account for a considerable percentage of the total national income (about one sixth, in the United States). If this spending is financed by taxation and by borrowing savings that otherwise would have been spent for consumption or invested by owners, there may be no net increase in money expenditures (or perhaps even a decrease because of the lag between collection of revenues and expenditures by the government).

The effectiveness of any stabilization measure depends upon its timing. If action is taken soon enough, inflationary or deflationary developments will be checked before they set off the chain reaction known as the "spirals of inflation and deflation." Since there is more fear of deflation than of inflation (traced to the depression of the early 1930's and the slow recovery that followed), anti deflationary rather than anti-inflationary measures have been stressed. Members of Congress and government officials are always subjected to group and individual pressure to spend from both outside and within the government. So, it is easier to "go along" with anti deflationary policy than an anti-inflationary one. In short, it is "good politics." When major emphasis is on contracyclical spending policies by the government, the danger of misspending is great.

In approaching the problem of contracyclical spending, there seems to be a preference for spending for investment rather than for consumption. Perhaps this is short-sighted because the elimination of idleness, disease, and squalor may be much more desirable than new roads, dams, buildings, and so on. The problem of timing most public expenditures to coincide with the need of promoting economic stability is difficult because the nature and purposes of most of such expenditures make them ill-adapted to prompt change. Some emergency expenditures may not be postponed until a recession develops (for illustration, those for war and defense). On the other hand, certain public works plans may be kept "on the shelf" until a recession occurs; but, if public works are justifiable economically, even the wisdom of these postponements may be questioned. (For illustration, how much justification was there for postponing construction of public schools and some veterans' emergency housing projects following World War II?)

Since the United States is a democracy, to what extent may the blueprints for the next depression be permitted to stand in the way of the construction of new roads, public buildings, harbors, and dams? Floods do not wait for depressions and neither do democracies. If additional public works are to be planned as an anti deflationary measure, there is danger that the spending aspects will be stressed with little regard to the economic needs for such expenditures. Many public projects are of such a nature that it takes months and years for completion.

While the use of public works as a device for stablizing the economy seems attractive on paper, it would be less flexible and would tend to be more wasteful than other devices. If the sphere of governmental enterprise were enlarged to include public ownership of railroads and public utilities (which would be socialism), the fields for public outlays would be greater. The merit of replacing private ownership with governmental ownership is questionable, and the wisdom of delaying improvements until a depression occurs would be questionable even in a socialistic economy.

However, there are certain types of government expenditures that will increase during periods of recession and decrease during periods of prosperity. An automatic stabilizer is one wherein spending increases or decreases without delay; these include unemployment insurance and price-support programs for certain farm crops. By extending compensatory government spending to include payments to all of those who lose income during a recession, greater stability of national income would be achieved.

With the exception of the "built-in" or automatic budgetary stabilizers, increasing government expenditures to counteract a recession is objected to because it is difficult to increase such expenditures wisely, to time them correctly, and to administer them efficiently because of politics. Short of communism or socialism, it is doubtful if a policy of compensatory spending in amounts sufficient to eliminate all cyclical losses of income could be followed.

Contracyclical Tax Policy. Contracyclical tax policy stresses both the amount of taxes levied and their incidence (where the tax burden falls). The amount of tax receipts will fluctuate cyclically if use is made of a progressive personal income tax collected on a pay-as-you-go basis. Assuming a fixed tax rate schedule, the relative amount of disposable personal income will be less during a business boom and more during a business recession because tax receipts will rise even faster than the increase in national income and will fall more rapidly than the decline in national income. Generally, corporate income and other business taxes are not progressive but proportional; these will also rise during boom periods and decline during recessions.

Fixed tax rates for both individuals and corporations could be selected so as (1) to balance the budget when labor is just short of full employment, (2) to provide a surplus when labor is fully employed, and (3) to permit a deficit when employment falls below a certain percentage. Thus a budgetary "deficit" or "surplus" would result from fluctuations in tax income, and the budget would be balanced over the business cycle (called a "stablized budget policy" by the Committee on Economic Development).[5] If the "deficit" is financed by borrowing new bank credit from commercial banks, the results will be less deflationary. Then, if the government "carries on" during boom years and collects and uses a surplus to retire that part of the national debt held by commercial banks, the results will be less inflationary.

If Congress would enact the necessary legislation, even greater flexibility could be given to the tax program. Tax schedules could be worked out in advance, and the administration could be given the responsibility for placing either higher or lower schedules in effect (depending upon economic conditions). Changes in the tax program may involve the introduction of new taxes during boom periods and their removal during recessions or adjustments of rates on existing taxes. Placing corporate income taxes on a pay-as-you-go basis would facilitate the "timing" of tax policies to coincide with the changes in corporate income and therefore in national income. Because of the size of the tax budget, a flexible tax system has much to recommend it as a contracyclical policy.

In administering a tax program, just as in governmental compensatory spending, there may be faulty practices. Congress may change the tax system in the wrong direction—a reduction during a boom when the government has a surplus or an increase during a recession when the government has a deficit—which would handicap the program designed to stabilize the economy. Sometimes, tax reduction may be poor fiscal policy but good politics. In tax policy, there is also a decision as to whose taxes are to be reduced or increased. While some may contend that corporations' taxes should be lowered to stimulate investment, others may contend that the taxes of those in the lower income brackets should be lowered to stimulate consumption.

Importance of Consumption. The chief source of national income is personal consumption expenditures. Over a period of time, people spend differently for different things. This means that each subdivision of consumer expenditures will vary in magnitude during different phases of the business cycle. However, the expenditures for nondurable goods are not only the largest but also the most stable in terms of physical quantities. Spending for consumer durable goods is cyclically most variable, which suggests the reason for selecting it as a target for selective controls.

[5] Committee on Economic Development, *Taxes and the Budgets: A Program for Prosperity in a Free Economy* (New York: 1947), pp. 28–34.

Theoretically, a high-consumption economy, one in which practically all income is spent for consumption, is more stable than one in which consumption spending is relatively small. Thus, long-run stability in the economy could be promoted by encouraging consumption and discouraging saving. Policies which would tend to have this effect include: (1) establishment of an even more progressive income-tax schedule; (2) removal of excise and retail sales taxes (common at the state level and not uncommon at the city level of government); (3) enlargement of social security benefits, veterans' and other pension plans; and (4) expansion of home relief and subsidized housing projects. The creation of a high-consumption economy would mean less private investment; and, in terms of economic progress, the social price would be a heavy one.

In the field of private investment, government policies may be directed toward increasing or decreasing loans and investments by use or nonuse of guarantees. At present, the government is guaranteeing loans through different agencies; and, although this has not been a flexible program, it could be made flexible by withholding the guarantees on new loans and investments during periods of prosperity and using guarantees during depressions. As provided for in Articles of Agreement for the World Bank, the use of the guarantee principle has been extended to international investments.

Since 1930 the United States government has not only created many direct-lending institutions but has also strengthened and enlarged the activities of those in existence. It is unfortunate that so little has been done to direct their lending and investing activities along contracyclical lines because, if a contracyclical program is to be most effective, the scope of the lending operations of these institutions necessitates co-ordination with monetary and fiscal policies. Some progress has been made along this line, as illustrated by shortening maturities and increasing down payment requirements for houses financed with mortgages guaranteed by the Veterans' Administration and the Federal Housing Administration in July, 1955, and then reversing these requirements in January, 1956.

FISCAL POLICY AND THE NATIONAL DEBT

Part of the opposition to financing with a budgetary deficit is traced to the fear of a national debt of huge proportions—"a burden transferred from the present generation to future generations." The idea that a high national debt means heavy interest costs and therefore an oppressing tax burden is deeply imbedded in the minds of businessmen, politicians, and the general public. Insofar as the debt is held by the inhabitants of a country, interest payments are not lost by the domestic economy. But interest payments on the national debt do cause a redistribution of income among individuals within a nation —from the taxpayers to the owners of government securities.

New-Financing Problem. When a deficit is to be financed with an issue of government securities, the method of financing may be planned so as to minimize or maximize the effects on (1) the money supply, (2) consumer spending, and/or (3) production. When new funds are to be obtained, the questions which must be answered by debt managers are: From whom to borrow? What is the volume of borrowing to be? Who is to own the government debt? If the only objective is to acquire funds cheaply, the answer may be to borrow where the interest rate is the lowest; but if the broader objective of fiscal policy is the guide, the answer will depend, in part, on conditions other than those in the financial markets. At the same time, some thought must be given to the whole debt structure—avoidance of an unmanageable debt—and safeguarding the future ability of the government to borrow at reasonable rates.

If the economy is in a business recession, new issues may be planned so as to have the greatest appeal to commercial banks and the least appeal to individuals and savings institutions. Not only would this provide the Treasury with funds but it would also increase the money supply. Federal Reserve banks' purchases of government securities would have the same primary effects and, in addition, would have potential secondary effects due to the expansion in the supply of member-bank reserves. Since funds would not be obtained from consumers and producers, spending by these groups would not be discouraged.

If the economy is in a business boom, new financing may be planned so as to appeal to consumers and institutional investors other than commercial banks, thereby absorbing savings in the hands of these groups. The interest rate, maturity, provisions for redemption, and the call feature would have to be planned to make the issue attractive. The problem is one of channeling purchasing power away from the private sector of the economy to the government without resulting in inflation and monetization of the debt.

Refinancing Problem. Since World War II, the government's need for additional loanable funds has been small relative to the total national debt; therefore, the problem of debt management has been one of refinancing. Some of the problems present when new financing is planned are also present in refinancing. During a recession the objective should be to contribute to business recovery; therefore new issues should be made attractive to commercial banks (usually short-term securities) rather than to individuals and institutional investors. If the securities are purchased by commercial banks, it would result in an increase in the liquidity of the economy and an expansion in the money supply. During boom periods, the opposite approach would be in order—appeal to individual and institutional investors other than commercial banks (usually by offering long-term securities).

Savings Bonds. For certain issues, the terms may be drawn so as to give the owners privileges that would tend to contribute to contracyclical spending. Now, Series E savings bonds may be re-deemed at purchase price plus allowable accrued interest. Presumably, redemption is most likely to take place when there is unemployment, thereby placing additional spending power in the hands of consumers. In selling Series E bonds, the government has emphasized not only the importance of its needs for funds but also the anti-inflationary aspect of purchasing savings bonds rather than spending for goods.

Treasury Trust Funds. United States government agencies and departments are among the important owners of the national debt (about 19 per cent of the total, of which the major portion is in various social security trust funds). Most of the trust funds are invested in special nonmarketable issues, but the others may be used to influence financial markets directly and the economy as a whole indirectly. During 1946–47, when the objectives of credit policy were to check inflation and to stabilize the price of government bonds, the trust funds sold long-term securities to insurance companies and other institutional investors, thereby tending to check the rise in prices of long-term obligations (lowering market yields).[6] The United States Treasury sold special issues in the trust funds and used the proceeds to retire short-term government securities held chiefly by commercial banks and the Federal Reserve banks. Previously the banking system had acquired these short-term obligations from insurance companies and other institutional investors.

By changing the maturities of issues from short-term to long-term, debt managers prevented an inflationary increase in the money supply caused by an expansion in bank credit and also avoided an increase in the national debt. By keeping down money rates, greater liquidity of assets was avoided (the lower the money rates, the higher the capitalized value and the more marketable are assets of

[6] See *Federal Reserve Bulletin*, November, 1947, p. 1349.

all kinds). The effect of a decrease in liquidity of money market and other assets cannot be computed accurately; but the changes which accompanied the United States Treasury's use of trust funds were in the right direction because they tended to reduce the money supply by absorbing investment funds of institutional investors, keeping interest rates up, and reducing liquidity.

Short-Term Adjustments. The management of the Treasury debt may be used to influence member-bank reserves and the money supply in order to reduce seasonal or unusual disturbing factors as well as cyclical and long-run factors. When quarterly corporate income taxes become due, there is danger that collection of checks given in payment will deplete member-bank reserve accounts at the Federal Reserve banks (member banks' accounts on which the checks are drawn are debited and the United States Treasury account is credited). Now the Treasury not only follows a policy of re-depositing an equal amount with the banks on which large checks are drawn but also offers tax anticipation notes and bills months prior to the quarterly income tax dates. Corporations and individuals may purchase these notes and bills in advance of the income tax payment date and present them in payment of income taxes. Since expenditures by the government outrun receipts during the first half of the fiscal year, the United States Treasury's need to borrow in anticipation of tax receipts seems to be an annual one.

Use of "Surplus" to Reduce Bank Credit. By reducing its expenditures, by increasing taxes, or by doing both, the government would tend to reduce money expenditures and inflationary pressure on the economy. Since tax obligations are usually met by checks, the supply of deposit currency and member-bank reserve balances will be reduced; and Treasury balances with Federal Reserve banks will be increased. Since most of this tax revenue is spent for goods and services and to meet interest payments and maturing government obligations, the loss of reserves and deposits may be only temporary. If the volume of bank lending is increased, this increase in bank credit may offset the decrease in "disposable income" due to taxation. So, the anti-inflationary effects of higher taxes may be nullified, unless the Federal Reserve banks enter the picture and "mop up" excess reserves by reducing the volume of Federal Reserve credit available.

A government surplus may be used (1) to reduce the volume of government obligations held by Federal Reserve banks, thereby decreasing the volume of Federal Reserve credit; (2) to reduce the holdings of government obligations of commercial banks, thereby decreasing their earning assets and replacing them with cash reserves; or (3) to reduce the volume of government obligations in the hands of investors (other than commercial banks), thereby increasing investors' deposits and increasing cash reserves of member banks (assuming that recipients of government checks would deposit them with commercial banks). The most deflationary of these uses of a government surplus would be the first—reducing the volume of Federal Reserve credit, which would decrease member-bank reserves. But the effects of this anti-inflationary measure would be nullified if the Federal Open Market Committee were to purchase other government securities for the System's account (which suggests the need to co-ordinate policies).

Existing Treasury cash balances may be used to retire federal debt when funds are available. Beginning on March 1, 1946, the Treasury inaugurated a debt "pay off" program when it used cash balances obtained from the "Victory loan," to retire debts held chiefly by banks. The Treasury also used the cash surplus of the fiscal years 1947, 1948, and 1951 for this purpose. In 1953, in order to keep below the national debt limit, the Treasury also used $500,000,000 in free gold in its vaults in order to retire that amount of Treasury notes held by the Federal Reserve System.

SUMMARY

Fiscal policy refers to the use of the federal government's taxing, borrowing, spending, and other powers not only to carry on its activities but also to maintain a high level of employment. The techniques of fiscal policy include deficit financing, preferably with new money during depressions, and debt retirement, with surplus funds during boom periods after making allowance for the growth factor in the economy. Compensatory financing works both ways, except in the case of a mature economy when there would be a need for offsetting a secular deficiency in private spending.

In adopting taxation policies, there are problems relative to the amount and incidence of taxes as well as their timing. As a result, there is general approval of the reliance on progressive personal income taxes and proportional income taxes on business firms at rates fixed so as to create a deficit during depressions and a surplus during business booms.

In adopting expenditure policies, the normal needs of the government are recognized; but, in addition, there are built-in stabilizers that will increase the government's disbursements to the unemployed, farmers, and others during business recessions and will decrease these disbursements during business booms.

Debt management involves problems such as from whom to borrow, in what form, and on what terms. The objective is to change the amount and to manipulate the ownership of the federal debt so as to influence the money supply and the propensity to consume and/or to invest. In management of United States Treasury balances, the objective is to help in stabilizing money market conditions by influencing member-bank reserve balances. In the last analysis, the purpose behind fiscal policy is to stabilize the flow of money payments so as to maintain a high level of employment. Perhaps the main criticism that can be made of the administration of fiscal policy and debt management as instruments of economic stabilization is that they have not been used more extensively.

QUESTIONS AND PROBLEMS

1. Identify the employment theory of credit policy. Analyze the statement of economic policy contained in the Employment Act of 1946.
2. Identify: (*a*) gross national product, (*b*) gross national income, (*c*) national income, and (*d*) disposable personal income.
3. In view of Keynes' "fundamental psychological law," explain why changes in total savings are not closely correlated with changes in national income.
4. "Every dollar of a given national income must be used if the yearly income is not to fall by the unused amount multiplied by its annual velocity, except as new money is added to the system." (H. Gordon Hayes, *Spending, Savings, and Employment* [New York: Alfred A. Knopf, 1948], p. 24.) Analyze this statement.
5. Explain this statement: "From a budgetary viewpoint, compensatory action by the government is reflected in the size of the government's deficit or surplus."
6. What is meant by provisions in governmental budgets for "built in" or "automatic" stabilizers? Illustrate.
7. Explain why a fiscal policy of financing expenditures by deficit financing with commercial bank credit must have central bank support.
8. How may the Treasury's management of the federal debt best contribute to a contracyclical policy by influencing the amount of the ownership of the debt? Why? How may interest rates, maturities, and other techniques be used to influence policies?
9. To what extent are the Treasury's debt management policies dependent upon the support of the Federal Reserve System? Explain.
10. What is meant by Treasury trust funds or government investment accounts? How may they be used to influence the money supply?

11. "We recommend that Federal fiscal policies be such as not only to avoid aggravating economic instability but also to make a positive and important contribution to stabilization, at the same time promoting equity and incentives in taxation and economy in expenditures. A policy based on the principle of an annually balanced budget regardless of fluctuations in the national income does not meet these tests. . . ." (Subcommittee of the Joint Committee on the Economic Report, *Monetary, Credit, and Fiscal Policies* [Washington, D.C.; U.S. Government Printing Office, 1950], pp. 11–12.) Analyze.

12. On January 17, 1956, the terms of United States government insured and guaranteed housing mortgages were relaxed when the Veterans' Administration and Federal Housing Administration announced extension of maturities from 25 to 30 years (reversing the action taken in July, 1955). Why was this done?

13. "A variety of objectives have guided the use of these tools [various forms of government obligations, manipulation of the government securities market, and powers of compulsion]. Most economists have urged the debt authority to use them primarily as weapons for the control of inflation." (M. A. Robinson, "Federal Debt Management: Civil War, World War I and World War II," *American Economic Review*, Vol. XLV, No. 2 [May, 1955], p. 388. How may these tools be used to prevent deflation as well as inflation? Note other objectives.

Chapter XXIV

ECONOMIC STABILIZATION

CENTRAL bank policy as well as fiscal policy has been directed toward stabilizing monetary expenditures so as to keep them in balance with the growing needs of the economy at a high level of employment without inflating or deflating general prices. This chapter deals with the problems of full employment and stable prices, interest rate theories, interest rate changes and credit policy, co-ordination of fiscal and monetary policies, and inflation.

FULL EMPLOYMENT AND STABLE PRICES

One of the weaknesses of the declaration of economic policy found in the Employment Act of 1946 is that it contains no specific mention of a policy to prevent inflation. As a result, an interpretation of this statement as a directive might lead to the erroneous conclusion that the Federal Reserve System is to promote expansion of employment and production regardless of the means employed. When this directive was being formulated, it was predicted that there would be a decline in governmental expenditures with the end of the war, which would reduce the national income by some $50 billion and lead to the unemployment of from 10,000,000 to 15,000,000. The Federal Reserve Bank of Philadelphia was among the few that predicted that inflation would follow the war (which was like a voice crying in the wilderness).

Although the Employment Act of 1946 stresses expansionary policies, this does not mean that credit policies which lead to inflation, with its injurious effects on real income and on redistribution of wealth and income, are to be tolerated. If the long-run interpretation of the economic directive is accepted, the employment theory is in keeping with the traditional policy of central banking, namely, to provide stable prices at a high level of employment.

The Federal Reserve System and other agencies are jointly responsible for initiating and following policies that interpret the phrase "to foster and promote free competitive enterprise and the general welfare" to mean to foster and promote a free economy wherein the real income in the hands of the public is increased. The concept of a free economy is antithetical to that of a communistic, socialistic, or any other type of regimented state. When there is maximum employment (for "those able, willing, and seeking to work") and maximum production, then additional supplies of money income created by spending new bank credit would merely cause inflation and would not increase real income (purchasing power).[1]

The reasons for curbing inflation have been given in earlier chapters, but it is well to note here how inflation prevents attainment of the objectives stated in the Employment Act of 1946. Rising prices encourage speculation by consumers and businessmen—buying goods in excess of present needs in anticipation of future needs and as protection against still higher prices. Speculation—holding goods for higher prices—may replace rather than promote production. The reasoning is, if profits can be made by speculation, why work? Inflationary conditions also foster strikes and breed inefficiency in both labor and management. Easy money-profits make economy in operations seem unimportant and unnecessary.

During inflationary periods, conditions of maladjustment or distortion occur among and within different segments of the economy. Industries selling goods and services which are fairly stable in price (railroads and utilities) are adversely affected. The relationships between costs and receipts and between income and expenditures are variously affected—some favorably and others unfavorably. Statements of net profits, after taxes, give a distorted picture of the situation because replacement costs of capital are greater as a result of higher prices. "General welfare" is not served by the redistribution of wealth and income that takes place among classes and individuals during rising prices. Commendable as direct price control, rationing, wage control, and allocations of scarce materials may seem, they are hardly compatible with the directive "to foster and promote free competitive enterprise."

It is now recognized that banking, monetary, fiscal, and business-cycle problems are inseparably interwoven. In the Employment Act of 1946, Congress rejected the principle that booms and depressions were part of the inevitable course of things and accepted

[1] So long as there is unemployment, *employment* will change in proportion as the quantity of money; when there is full employment, *prices* will change in the same proportion as the quantity of money." (J. M. Keynes, *The General Theory of Employment, Interest, and Money* [New York: Harcourt, Brace & Co., 1936], p. 296.)

the principle that the government should do something to prevent them. This law provided for an Economic Council of three advisers to the President, whose duty it is to analyze economic conditions and to recommend appropriate action. Reports and recommendations are to be made to a joint committee of seven men from each house of Congress, which is set up to study the periodic reports of the Economic Council and to devise appropriate legislation. In addition, Congress has set up its own board of experts in order to assist this joint committee.

At any one time, there are at work in the economy a number of inflationary and deflationary factors which tend to increase or decrease the national income. Since any type of spending is inflationary and any type of nonspending is deflationary, and since there are millions of spending and/or nonspending units, how accurately can the future of business conditions be forecast? Behind each spending or nonspending decision of businessmen is the expectation of profits; and behind each individual consumer's decision are such factors as current and expected future needs, size of income, need for cash balances, and profitable outlets for savings.

Within the powers of the monetary and fiscal authorities to control economic conditions, the question of goals of monetary and fiscal action still remains. The ideal would be the achievement of full employment of productive resources at a fairly stable price level without destruction of free markets and private enterprise. As has been indicated, there is a need for a directive to the monetary authorities to stabilize the general price level.

By "full employment" is meant employment of a higher percentage of the labor force (about 95 per cent of those able and willing to work). Specifically, it means that jobs at prevailing wages will not be lacking for practically all qualified workers who want jobs. The concept behind the "full employment" theory is that mass unemployment, as it existed in 1932–33, may be prevented.

Some contend that full employment is not compatible with stable general prices. Their reasoning is that full employment means the use of resources under conditions which will increase marginal costs to a level where higher prices are necessary if marginal revenue is to cover marginal cost. Among the factors pointed out are: the decline in the efficiency of labor at or near full employment, the danger of wage rates increasing more rapidly than production, the presence of monopolists who fix production and prices at levels which will bring the largest net return, and the undercapacity of fixed plants and equipment. In general, this line of reasoning is in keeping with the concept of production under conditions of increasing per unit costs (conditions wherein unit costs increase with increased production). If the marginal cost curve does rise steeply as full employment and boom conditions approach, it would be difficult to achieve and maintain full employment without price inflation. However there are many factors that suggest that a linear or even a decreasing per unit cost curve is more typical of the American economy than the so-called U shaped curve for marginal and total per unit costs. By using new processes, machines, and managerial and labor techniques, output may be increased with a reduction in per unit costs.

There is no agreement on the concept of full employment of plant and equipment; and, during World War II, it was found that plant and equipment may be expanded within wide limits by adopting two or three working shifts per day and keeping plants in operation over week ends and on holidays. The labor force was expanded beyond the concept of full employment by using the services of women, workers beyond the age of 65, and high-school and college students on a part-time basis. So, during boom periods, the total per unit cost curve may be fairly flat.

The factors remaining to be considered are those of labor-management relations and monopolies. Collective bargaining by powerful unions may result in wage rates being increased more rapidly than production, with the higher costs being passed along to consumers in the form of higher prices by oligopolists (those having partial control over a commodity price).[2] A general increase in wage rates is likely to cause a greater use of machinery, thereby increasing the productivity of labor; but, if a wage increase is not matched by an increase in prices, labor's share in national income will be more favorable. A large wage increase could depress employment; but, in general, it would tend to arouse expectations of increased expenditures for consumption and investment and of price inflation resulting from increased spending.

The cost approach to an explanation of general prices ignores the fact that both demand and supply are factors in influencing prices

[2] Under oligopoly there are a few sellers acting to some extent as a group because each seller would be influenced by and would influence the action of others. When one raises or lowers prices, similar price changes are usually made by others in the industry. Oligopoly price is largely established by custom and by open or tacit agreement, and the change in output may not respond rapidly to shifts in marginal cost curves.

and the price level. By use of monetary and fiscal policies, the demand for goods and services may be dampened during boom periods and encouraged during periods of falling prices; this would have a stabilizing effect on both production and prices. Greater stability in national income would tend to stifle the creation of monopolies and to lessen the clamour for governmental protection (tariffs, fair-trade laws, farm-price supports, and other "protective" measures) which may appear at any time but most successfully during depressions. The escalator and other clauses in modern labor union contracts have been inserted to protect labor union members from the effects of higher prices on one hand and from a decrease in employment and wages on the other hand.

If there were stable prices and a continuing high level of employment, the picture could change radically. The conclusion that full employment and stable prices are incompatible is based on a cost theory that may not be applicable to a dynamic and expanding economy such as that of the United States. To attempt to solve a problem of unemployment growing out of action by labor monopolies through monetary action would mean a race between high prices and higher wages and would result in constant industrial warfare and inflation. Monetary policy should only be used to create effective demand when there is chronic or cyclical unemployment.

Another approach might be to remove decisions as to business spending from the hands of private management and place them in the hands of governmental agencies. This would be socialism. If carried to the degree prevalent in certain countries, there would be no serious problem of unemployment; and, if combined with government price-fixing, there would be no general price fluctuations. These alternatives suggest the amount of turmoil in the world today—the struggle between competitive and noncompetitive forces within nations and among nations.

INTEREST RATE THEORIES

Background for Interest Rate Theory. Economic development is commonly considered in terms of income, output, wealth, and the labor force. The increase in real income (goods and services) has been the center of attention in economic literature; but, at the same time, there has been a corresponding growth in financial transactions. For illustration, in the flow-of-fund system of accounts, there are four entries when a buyer pays cash for goods (a purchase of goods, a sale of goods, a decrease in cash for the buyer, and an increase in cash for the seller). Some transactions are entirely financial in character, such as the repayment of a debt in cash or the purchase of securities with cash; conversely, there are barter transactions which are nonfinancial in character.

The development of the United States economy has been closely associated with an increase in debt in some sectors and a corresponding increase in financial assets elsewhere. While the accumulation of debt has been a part of the growth process, it does not follow that there has been a constant ratio between the expansion in debt and the increase in national income or wealth. Some spending is entirely self-financed—as corporate investments made out of retained earnings and individual consumption from income—but, over the long run, the trend has been away from self-financing. This development suggests the increasing importance of financial intermediaries whose function is to issue their own debt instruments in exchange for the surplus funds of spending units and then to invest these loanable funds among other spending units whose debts they absorb (see Chapters XXVII–XXXI). However, no current discussion of interest rate theory can have much meaning unless there is some understanding of the extent to which both savings and investments have passed beyond the control of individuals to institutions.

Interest Rate. The interest rate is the price paid for the use of loanable funds. There are many interest rates; but pure interest is the payment for use of funds exclusive of administrative costs of making and collecting the loan, risks involved, and any additional charges. After these adjustments are made, the factors determining the rate of interest are those which create the demand for and the supply of loanable funds. In the explanation of demand is found the answer to the question of why interest may be paid, and in the explanation of supply is found the answer to the question of why interest must be paid.

Demand for Loanable Funds. The demand for loanable funds may be either a producer's demand or a consumer's demand for credit. The government's demand may fall into either category, depending on the purpose for which the funds are borrowed. Consumer credits include those indicated in bank statements as such, real estate loans on homes, and perhaps most of the credit represented by government securities (depending on the viewpoint with reference to defense and war spending in particular).

Many consumer loans are made to finance the purchase of

goods, the production of which involves time-consuming processes (automobiles, houses, tanks, airplanes, roads, etc.). In this respect, they are similar to producers' credit which is also used directly in financing time-consuming processes. In the case of consumers' credit the responsibility rests with the consumer; while in the case of producers' credit, it rests with the producer. If the automobile manufacturer finances a sale, it is producers' credit; but if the consumer finances a sale, it is consumers' credit. In effect, there may be little difference regardless of which label is applied.

In case of the demand for loanable funds for production, there is general agreement—the demand is dependent on anticipated profits from the planned investment. On the side of demand for loanable funds, the rate of interest is influenced by marginal borrowers (those who would not borrow if the interest rate were higher). It is anticipated return, as based on the expected marginal efficiency of capital (the net yield from the last capital good), that determines the actions of businessmen. This means that many mistakes will be made. In addition, anticipations are subject to sudden changes; and prevailing pessimism or optimism may have effects on the demand for loanable funds entirely divorced from the prevailing interest rate.

The anticipated "break-even" point in planning production involves much more than the cost of borrowed funds. In fact, the effect of a fall in interest rates may be insignificant compared to the effect of an increase in taxes and/or costs of labor and materials. Changes in methods of production, volume of sales, and/or managerial policies are more important than interest rates in explaining anticipated and real profits.

Many capital improvements are financed with replacement funds (depreciation and other accounting reserves), and often expansion of output is financed with retained earnings. Thus, much of modern capital formation is planned and financed without borrowing in the capital market. When the economy as a whole is considered, the interest rate may have but limited applicability as an equalizer of the demand for and the supply of capital. Therefore, too much should not be expected of reductions or increases in interest rates as a device for stimulating or discouraging capital formation.

Liquidity-Preference Theory. One theory explains interest rates in terms of the demand for money (not capital or loanable funds). Interest is defined as the reward for parting with liquidity, or for not hoarding. Since there are many rates in the market, the more like money a credit instrument is, the less liquidity is surrendered and the smaller is the reward (interest rate). The explanation for holding cash balances in excess of transaction and other normal needs is that the owner prefers to hold idle cash balances rather than investments. So, the interest rate is the price "which equilibrates the desire to hold wealth in the form of cash with the available quantity of cash."[3]

As already noted, savings may or may not be invested. If the parting with liquidity is the explanation for interest, then the interest rate for short-term credit instruments should be less than for long-term (less for Treasury bills than for government bonds). During the years since 1933, this has generally been true; but there were times during the 1920's when the yields on long-term government bonds were lower than on short-term obligations.[4] Although the liquidity-preference theory is an explanation for interest, it is not the complete answer. There are many demands for loanable funds which may be arranged in a sequence of decreasing attractiveness (called the "demand schedule of loanable funds"). One of the demands for loanable funds is the demand for cash balances.

Time-Preference Theory. The time-preference theory is based on the psychological law that consumption, in the present, is preferred to that in the future. Interest is the payment to equate present and future values. If the interest rate is 4 per cent, $104 a year hence is equal to $100 today. Thus the interest rate will be determined by the time-preference of the marginal savers on the supply side.

Currently, a large part of individuals' savings is on a contract basis and seemingly not related to any time-preference or any other theory of interest. Many individuals are under contract to pay premiums on life insurance policies periodically, many buy savings bonds on pay-roll deduction plans, others purchase stock under employee-ownership plans, and most individuals purchase homes and many other durable consumer goods on the installment-payment plan. In addition, many individuals are under contracts to make periodic contributions to government and private pension plans, others make periodic payments into savings accounts in savings and other banks, and some purchase stock or shares of credit unions and savings and loan associations.

The institutionalization of savings means that the amount that individuals save will be about the same whether interest rates are

[3] J. M. Keynes, *op. cit.*, p. 167.
[4] See tables in Board of Governors of the Federal Reserve System, *Banking and Monetary Statistics* (Washington, D.C., 1943), pp. 460 and 468–69.

high or low. In order to achieve the same purpose in saving, the rate of savings may be less when interest rates are high than when interest rates are low. For illustration, in order to arrive at a fixed amount of dollars at the end of a specified period of time, the rate of savings would have to increase with a decline in interest rates because growth in principal under compound interest is less when the rate is 3 or 4 per cent than when it is 5 or 6 per cent. When dividends on life insurance policies are applied to premium payments, savings tend to decline when interest rates and earnings of these companies increase and to increase when their interest rates and earnings decline.

Business firms as well as individuals save; and, although most of the savings of business firms are used in their own operations, some savings may be used to acquire ownership interests in other firms, some may be placed with banks and institutional investors, and some may be lent directly to the government, to other business firms, or to individuals (the concept of lending is used here to include investing). Of course, not all savings come within the institutional or business pattern; and the question that remains to be answered is the extent to which the supply of loanable funds can be explained on the basis of the price paid for the use of savings (presumably increasing when interest rates are high and decreasing when they are low).

Loanable-Fund Theory. The loanable-fund theory explains the interest rate in terms of supply of and demand for loanable funds. This means that both money (as in the liquidity-preference theory) and savings (as in the time-preference theory) are considered to be loanable funds. While savings are stressed, interest centers on bank credit which is divorced from the limiting factors that explain savings. As a result of the operation of the banking system, interest rates in the money market are determined primarily by actions taken by the Treasury and the Federal Reserve System. This is illustrated by the "pattern of interest rates" maintained for government securities during and after World War II.

When there is a policy of matching an increase in demand for loanable funds with an increase in supply of loanable funds, the interest rate plays but a minor role in keeping savings and investments in equilibrium. Instead, savings plus bank credit are kept in equilibrium with investments. While this brief statement may account for the market rate of interest, this rate may be out of line with the natural rate of interest (used here to mean the one that would prevent the price level from rising or falling under conditions of full employment).

INTEREST RATE CHANGES AND CREDIT POLICY

Monetary policy involves the amount, availability, use, and price of bank credit. If price is a factor, an increase in the interest rate should reduce the amount of bank credit in use. Because so much of the current supply of loanable funds reaches the market through banks and other institutional intermediaries, changes in the level of interest rates may be more important to these lenders than to borrowers. In other words, interest rate changes may have more effect on the supply of loanable funds than on the demand for loanable funds. In discussing monetary policy, it was noted that higher interest rates result in less liquidity of assets and lower capitalized value. It was also pointed out that higher interest rates would tend to make lenders less inclined to sell their bonds at a loss (the locked-in theory) and to increase emphasis on regaining liquidity which would cause the volume of funds available for lending to decline.

However, if progressively higher interest rates are anticipated, an increase in interest rates may encourage bankers to sell their government securities before capital losses become greater. In addition, bankers may reason that higher returns obtainable in other parts of the capital and money markets justify shifting funds out of government securities. But, it must be remembered that the volume of acceptable paper is small relative to the volume of government securities. However, one effect of anticipated higher interest rates has been to increase banks' holdings of short-term government securities on which potential capital losses are minor compared to potential capital losses on long-term obligations.

Insurance companies, as well as banks, are sensitive to capital losses due to the fall in prices of government securities; but, because insurance companies have an inflow of cash in the form of premium payments in excess of their benefit payments on matured policies, they are in a position to meet current commitments without liquidating their investments. However, shifts in insurance companies' investments do take place; and these shifts are influenced by interest rate changes. Higher interest rates are expected to be contracylical in their effects by inducing institutional lenders to keep their government securities. If government securities are retained by insurance companies, banks, and other lenders, new real estate and other loan commitments must necessarily be reduced.

It is assumed in interest-rate theory that higher interest rates encourage individuals to save and invest more. Since individuals and businessmen have at their disposal not only current income but also liquid assets, the most important effect of higher interest rates may be due to the anticipated effect of higher interest rates on commodity prices. For illustration, if the public believes that higher interest rates are an indication that general prices are to be stabilized or reduced, there may be a reduction in spending traced to sources other than current savings. The consensus of opinion among economists, bankers, and other financial leaders is that interest rate changes may be used to stabilize business because of the effects of these changes on business psychology, on expectations as to future business conditions, and on lending activities of commercial banks and others.[5]

If increasing interest rates may be used to check inflation, the preceding analysis should justify the assumption that reducing interest rates may be used to check deflation. But, as noted above, the results may be due more to the effect on consumer and business spending than to the decrease in the cost of borrowed funds. If lower interest rates lead to expectations of higher prices and better business conditions, there may be an increase in the flow of monetary expenditures because of freer spending of both cash balances and current income. If the reduction in interest rates is accompanied by lower reserve requirements, more of the existing bank assets will be available for lending and investing.

Open-market purchases by the Federal Open Market Committee could be used to supplement deposits and member-bank reserve funds, thus adding to the volume of funds available for spending. Lowering down payments on real estate and consumer loans (if they are being regulated) would permit the use of more credit in these fields of selective credit control. In order to encourage production, the market rate may be kept artificially low (below the natural rate)

[5] Professor James W. Bell comments: "A curiously illogical argument has become popular among Keynesian theorists, viz., that small increases (one fourth to one half per cent) in interest rates are not effective in fighting inflation, but that large increases (2 to 4 per cent or 5 to 10 per cent) will cause chaos and disaster in the money markets and will precipitate deflation."

After explaining the origin and history of these arguments, Professor Bell adds:

"These arguments are not consistent. Either small increases have some effect in curbing inflation or large increases will not cause collapse (unless we assume that the collapse is due to a breakdown in confidence in the integrity of the monetary unit). . . . Rate changes have effect on the demand for funds and even greater effect on the supply of funds. . . ." Joint Committee on Economic Report, *Monetary Policy and the Management of the Public Debt* (Washington, D.C.: U.S. Government Printing Office, 1952), p. 1015.

until full employment is reached (presumably the increase in flow of goods and services would offset the increase in the flow of money payments without inflation resulting).

Since the United States government is the largest debtor, it has a special interest in low interest rates. As stated by the Secretary of the Treasury,[6] "It would be a serious error to conclude that the Treasury Department believes that holding down interest cost of the public debt should be the sole or major goal of debt management." But the Secretary also added, "I cannot conclude that the interest burden on the public debt is of negligible importance," with which no one disagrees. At the same time that there is a need for keeping down the "interest cost" burden to the taxpayers, there is a greater need for keeping down the costs of other expenditures of the federal government inflated by higher prices. It would be poor economy to save $500,000,000 by the first and add $5 billion to the latter. This is merely a statement of possible conditions and does not mean that the Treasury has necessarily failed to integrate its debt management and monetary-credit policies to contribute toward "healthy economic growth and reasonable stability in the value of the dollar."

CO-ORDINATION OF FISCAL AND MONETARY POLICY

Fiscal and monetary measures must be co-ordinated in order to achieve and/or to maintain full employment. The fact that the fiscal measures work through income and the monetary measures work through the money supply means that there must be agreement on interest-rate policies and consultation on and co-ordination of fiscal and monetary measures. It would be foolish to apply a restrictive policy to the private sector of the economy when governmental lending agencies and the United States Treasury are following the opposite policy. Conversely, the same may be said about foregoing essential governmental expenditures for schools and other public projects while the private sector of the economy has been on a "spending spree" (which has been generally true since World War II).

Fiscal Policy versus Bank Policy. During the Great Depression the United States emphasized fiscal policy rather than central bank policy. In Great Britain, emphasis remained on monetary policy. As a result the latter escaped the increase in government debt which accompanied the recovery program in the United States. The criticism of the Federal Reserve easy-money policy was that (1) Federal

[6] *Ibid.,* pp. 104–5.

Reserve System's action drove down interest rates only in the money market, and, therefore, special agencies had to be created to secure lower interest rates in the urban and rural mortgage fields; and (2) lower interest rates alone were not sufficient to encourage borrowing. The first criticism is applicable to the unit-banking system and not to central bank policy; the second has been recognized as the chief advantage of fiscal policy over central bank policy. Since the United States used fiscal and monetary policies at the same time, it is not known whether monetary policy, without fiscal policy, would have been adequate if it had been followed more rigorously.

While there is doubt as to the central bank's ability to stimulate production during depressions, there is no doubt as to the central bank's ability to dampen inflation. Since depressions are considered to be the result of excessive use of credit during inflations, central bank action can be most effective in preventing depressions by preventing the excesses that breed depressions. In the past, changes in credit policy have often been delayed. Rediscount rates have been increased, and the volume of Federal Reserve investments has been reduced only after inflation was well advanced.

When used wisely, central bank credit measures have many advantages over fiscal measures. In general, credit devices are impersonal. They operate through the market mechanism and are unhampered by political pressure. Exceptions to these statements are certain credit policies classified as selective—Regulations W and X, which are at this writing not in effect.

Central bank credit devices are flexible and can be changed quickly to counteract economic changes. Therefore, they may be more effective than fiscal policy because their timing may be more precise. The difficulties and delays inherent in tax and spending programs have already been indicated. In general, the more impersonal and less disturbing the control policy is to the market, the more effective the control policy will be in the long run. However, as indicated by the long-run record, there is need for better administration of monetary policy as well as better administration of fiscal policy.

The discussion in this and the preceding chapters, where credit control and management of Treasury cash balances and the national debt were considered, emphasizes the need for co-ordination of monetary and fiscal policies. This need is widely recognized and is the basis for the recommendation for creation of a "National Monetary and Credit Council" by the "Hoover Commission" (officially, the Commission on Organization of the Executive Branch of the Government).[7] This proposed council would be similar to the National Advisory Council on International Monetary and Fiscal Problems, which is concerned with foreign lending. It has been recommended that the new Council be composed of the Secretary of the Treasury as chairman, the Chairman of the Board of Governors of the Federal Reserve System, the Director of the Bureau of the Budget, and a representative of the Federal Farm Credit Administration and/or Housing and Home Financing Agency.

In 1950 the subcommittee of the Joint Committee on the Economic Report recognized the need for co-ordination of monetary and fiscal policies as indicated by the following: "We recommend the creation of a National Monetary Council which would include the Secretary of the Treasury, the Chairman of the Board of Governors of the Federal Reserve System, the Comptroller of the Currency, the Chairman of the Federal Deposit Insurance Corporation, and the heads of the other principal Federal agencies that lend and guarantee loans. This Council should be established by legislative action, should be required to make periodic reports to Congress, and should be headed by the Chairman of the Council of Economic Advisors. Its purpose should be purely consultative and advisory, and it should not have directive power over its members."[8]

PROBLEM OF INFLATION

Present indications are that the current century will go down in history as one of inflation. Those who make this prediction are thinking of "secular," "long-run," or "creeping" inflation. The forces at work in the present-day economy, which give cognizance to this point of view, are summarized below:

1. No modern government will permit the development of a serious depression. Therefore, no government will hesitate to operate with a large deficit in order to check a depression by providing new money income. Many depression measures will become deeply imbedded in the political economy and will be continued during periods of prosperity.

2. Certain cost factors will continue to push up prices. These include such things as wage contracts, which are tied to the cost-of-living index (escalator clause), and agricultural price-support programs, which

[7] The Commission on Organization of the Executive Branch of the Government, *Treasury Department, A Report to Congress* (Washington, D.C.: U.S. Government Printing Office, March, 1949), p. 9.

[8] Subcommittee of the Joint Committee on the Economic Report, *Monetary, Credit, and Fiscal Policies* (Washington, D.C.: U.S. Government Printing Office, 1950), p. 4.

are tied to the concept of parity prices (meaning the cost of things that farmers buy).

3. The easy-money policy will be continued because of the size of the national debt. While there may be some increases in money rates, when the real pinch comes central banks will not be permitted to interfere seriously with financing deficits through the use of commercial bank credit.

4. International tensions will continue for a long time. This means continuing large expenditures for past and future wars and more expenditures for an increasing number of veterans.

5. Foreign investments and foreign economic and military aid by the United States are expected to continue. Such practices are inflationary because they create money income in the United States which is not offset by a flow of goods and services.

6. Increases in life expectancy are expected to continue, and this means more old-age pension payments. Over the next ten years, the population of the United States is expected to increase 19 per cent but the 65-and-over age group is expected to increase more than 30 per cent. When pension payments are in excess of cash receipts, the effects will tend to be inflationary.

7. Finally, the mere fact that inflation is expected leads people to do things that cause inflation. People spend more freely; and, in order to do so, they borrow more freely. People are looking for hedges against inflation—such as owning stock and real estate. This increase in spending tends to increase prices. Other hedges against inflation are inflationary in that they tend to place more money income in the hands of consumers and/or producers when prices are increasing.

Each time there is an increase in general prices one may expect a renewed demand for purchasing-power savings bonds, more generous depreciation allowances when computing business income for tax purposes, retirement incomes computed in terms of purchasing power, and wage rate and salary adjustments linked to changes in the general price level.

Offsetting these inflationary factors are certain anti-inflationary forces which are listed below:

1. The productive capacity of the United States was large at the end of World War II, and it has subsequently been expanded. Since 1945, capital expenditures have been more than $250 billion and annual expenditures for new plants and equipment are double those of ten years ago. Temporarily, these capital expenditures are inflationary; but, sooner or later, they will taper off, and there will be less inflationary pressure on the economy. As the projects are completed, the flow of goods and services should increase, thereby exerting further anti-inflationary pressures.

2. Foreign output is increasing, and this will mean less dependence on the United States for economic and military aid. In addition,

it may mean more foreign goods for American markets, which will tend to keep down prices.

3. Higher prices tend to check inflationary expenditures—many potential buyers are "priced out of the market." Of course, it is probable that these potential buyers may be replaced by new buyers who have gained from inflation.

4. Monetary control will be used to check inflation. It has been demonstrated that the Federal Reserve System can check inflation if it is permitted to use all of its control measures. Since the agreement with the United States Treasury (the "accord" of March, 1951), the Federal Reserve authorities have made freer use of their powers to curb inflation.

5. Fiscal policy will be used to check inflationary developments and Congressmen are displaying an understanding of basic needs for stabilization of general prices to a degree not matched by many in the academic profession. There is a general understanding of the fact that inflation produces inequities in the distribution of real income among different classes and most Congressmen seem to be aware of this fact. Almost daily, they are faced with demands for wage increases, higher salaries, larger depreciation allowances, purchasing-power savings bonds, increases in pensions and social security payments, higher postal rates, and other increased outlays because of higher prices. So, more Congressmen are willing to go along with proposals for the continuance of high tax rates in the face of anticipated budgetary surpluses, are more reluctant to approve higher debt ceilings, and are less willing to appropriate larger amounts which are not matched by legislative changes which would increase revenues.

6. Many question the argument that a policy of rising prices means a greater demand for output because consumers will anticipate higher prices by increased spending before the prices increase. Surveys of consumers' attitudes toward price changes indicate a negative correlation between expectation of price inflation and an attitude that it is a good time to buy. Only when prices are stable and considered to be right are people inclined to think that it is a good time to buy (with anticipation of seasonal sales and discounts in some lines).

7. To an increasing extent, the thesis that rising prices increase production is being questioned. Rising prices encourage all types of hoarding—material and labor—in anticipation of future needs and may cause less than full use to be made of materials and trained personnel such as engineers, chemists, and others (a common complaint made by recent college graduates). On the other hand if all available staff members were to be put on the assembly line, it may mean a decrease in future production because it would entail foregoing technological improvements, advances in product design, and other changes associated with a dynamic society.

SUMMARY

In general, the employment theory is in keeping with the traditional central-bank policy, namely, to provide stable prices at a high level of employment. While some contend that full employment is incompatible with stable prices, the arguments used to support this claim are based on concepts which may not be applicable to an economy such as that of the United States. The concept of increasing per-unit-cost and the U-shaped curve, may not be valid in the United States wherein there is evidence of a linear or even a decreasing per-unit-cost curve. Stable prices and full employment are not necessarily incompatible in the United States, provided all of the devices of monetary and fiscal control are used.

The factors determining the interest rate are those which create the demand for and supply of loanable funds (governments and consumers, as well as producers, are important in determining the volume of demand for loanable funds). In the case of loanable funds to be used for production, usually the demand is dependent on anticipated profits from planned investments; however, many capital improvements are financed with replacement funds and often expansion of output is financed with retained earnings. Therefore, much of modern capital formation is planned and financed without borrowing in the capital market.

The loanable-funds theory explains the interest rate in terms of the supply of and demand for loanable funds which include both money (as in the liquidity-preference theory) and savings (as in the time-preference theory). The level of interest rates in the money market is influenced primarily by actions of the Federal Reserve System. Because of the role played by banks and other institutional intermediaries, changes in interest rates may have more effect on the supply of loanable funds than on the demand for such funds.

Although interest-rate theory assumes that higher interest rates encourage individuals to save and to invest more, the most important effect of higher interest rates may be due to the anticipated effect on prices. Generally, interest-rate changes may be used to stabilize business because of the effects of these changes on business psychology, anticipated future business conditions, and lending practices of banks and others.

In order to achieve stable prices and full employment, fiscal and monetary measures must be co-ordinated. When used wisely, central-bank measures may have advantages over fiscal measures because they are impersonal and operate through the market mechanism unhampered by political pressure. In addition, monetary devices are flexible in that they may be changed quickly in response to economic changes. In order to facilitate co-ordination of fiscal and monetary policy, the establishment of a National Monetary and Credit Council has been proposed. While there are many forces at work in our economy that tend to lead to creeping inflation, there are other factors that tend to offset the inflationary factors; but whether or not they will do so depends on how well and how courageously the devices of fiscal and credit control are used by the United States Treasury and the Federal Reserve System.

QUESTIONS AND PROBLEMS

1. "Speculation may replace rather than promote production." Explain.
2. Identify: (*a*) full-employment, (*b*) oligopoly, and (*c*) interest rate.
3. Identify: (*a*) liquidity-preference theory, (*b*) time-preference theory, and (*c*) loanable-funds theory.
4. "A large part of individuals' savings is on a contract basis." Explain.
5. What advantages does monetary policy have over fiscal policy?
6. Analyze the case for and against the prospects of "secular," "long-run," or "creeping" inflation.
7. "Appropriate credit policies are essential to the success of a stabilization program. Market demand is generated by the extension of credit and the use of past savings, as well as by the use of current income. Credit policies affect market demand primarily through their impact on credit extension, and they also may affect the volume of saving out of current income and the form in which savings are held." (Council of Economic Advisers, *The Midyear* 1952 *Economic Review* [Washington, D.C.: U.S. Government Printing Office, 1952], p. 94.) Analyze.
8. In describing the Shanghai market under hyperinflation (1947–48), a student writes: "The interest [rate] was likely to be the premium for compensating the depreciation of the paper money." (Pao-Chung Ma Yang, "The Shanghai Market under Hyperinflation," *Current Economic Comment*, Vol. 13, No. 4 [November, 1951], p. 51.) With the increase in loanable funds, why did not the interest rate decline? Does this mean that the concept of supply and demand is not applicable during periods of hyperinflation?
9. "Fiscal policy operates in the medium and long term rather than in the short term. . . . The customary monetary techniques may serve as a short-term adjuster of the supply of funds, of liquidity and of the interest rate. For example, if it is desired to check expansion the check must act quickly." (W. M. Scammel, "The Changing Aims of Fiscal Policy," *Westminster Bank Review*, May, 1950, p. 8.) Does this suggest the need for using both monetary and fiscal policy?
10. Governmental "measures designed to fight depression . . . are easy to initiate, politically popular and exceedingly tenacious of life. . . . By contrast, policies designed to fight inflation and achieve a tolerable stability of prices seem inherently slow in getting started, while

their political popularity is likely to vary inversely with their economic effectiveness." (B. C. Gardner, *Address to the Shareholders of the Bank of Montreal* [Montreal, December, 1951], pp. 12–13.) Do the experiences of the United States since 1933 support the above quotation? Illustrate, with specific references to United States fiscal and monetary policies.

11. "We should reject any theory which implicitly holds that prosperity is a form of economic sin for which we must make atonement in the form of depression. We should maintain the highest level of economic activity possible without inflation." Elmer Wood, "Recent Economic Policies," *The Journal of Finance* (September, 1955), p. 325. Discuss.

12. In commenting on new wage increases and their effects, Mr. D. J. Roberts of the National Provincial Bank stated "An intensive campaign needs to be undertaken to explain . . . that increases of money wages, unaccompanied by increases in productivity, must have the effect of raising prices and the cost of living, and undermining the stability of our economy." (D. J. Roberts, Chairman, National Provincial Bank Limited, *One Hundred and Twenty-Third Report of the Directors and Balance Sheet 31st December, 1955,* n.p.) Analyze.

Chapter XXV | INTERNATIONAL MONE-TARY PRINCIPLES

In the United States, domestic factors are more important in influencing monetary policies than is the case in most foreign countries. This is due to our productive capacity, large international reserves, and output chiefly for domestic markets. On the other hand, most foreign countries are faced with the problem of improving their balance-of-payments positions and building up international reserves. In some countries, international transactions make up as much as one third of their total economic activities (United Kingdom, Belgium, the Netherlands, Norway, and so on), and their problem of making international payments, particularly dollar payments, is a serious one. Over the last fifteen years, deficits in their balance of payments have been financed to a large extent by grants and loans from the United States government.

BALANCE OF INTERNATIONAL PAYMENTS

The "balance of international payments" for the United States is a systematic record of all economic transactions between residents of the United States and all foreigners (or residents of all other countries) for a period of time. The concept of "foreigners" or residents of other countries includes the central government and all local governments, business firms, nonprofit organizations, and individuals living in the country permanently. (Hereinafter, all of these will be referred to as foreigners.) Like other accounting systems, changes in items within the balance-of-international-payments statement reflect not only economic changes at home but also those abroad (see Table 20).

Items in the balance-of-payments statement appear either as credit or debit items; but only net movements for unilateral transfers, capital, and monetary gold appear in Table 20. Credit items are claims that we have against foreigners that tend to bring money to the United States; debit items are claims that foreigners have against us that tend to take money away from the United States.

TABLE 20

BALANCE OF PAYMENTS OF THE UNITED STATES, 1955

(Amounts in Millions of Dollars)

Item	Credit Items	Debit Items	Balance
Military transfers under grants, net, total..........	2,134		
Other goods and services:			
Military transactions.......................	202	2,804	
Merchandise (adjusted) excluding military......	14,264	11,516	
Transportation...........................	1,336	1,202	
Travel..................................	645	1,155	
Miscellaneous services.....................	956	734	
Income on investments.....................	2,512	512	
Total (goods and services)	22,049	17,923	+4,126
Unilateral transfers (net):			
Private.................................	....	456	
Government:			
Military supplies and services..............	....	2,134	
Other grants............................	....	1,865	
Pensions and other transfers................	....	141	
Total (net)...........................	....	4,596	−4,596
Capital and monetary gold:			
Investment:			
United States capital (net):			
Private.............................	....	1,153	
Government.........................	....	302	
United States (net)...................	....	1,455	−1,455
Foreign capital (net):			
Long-term...........................	344	....	
Transactions in United States government securities...........................	529	....	
Short-term...........................	700	....	
Other short-term liabilities..............	....	−140	
Foreign (net)	1,573	−140	+1,433
Gold.....................................	41		+41
Errors and omissions........................	451		+451

Source of statistics: *Survey of Current Business* (June, 1956), p. 24.

Each time a foreigner purchases a commodity, service, security, or gold in the United States, he owes money in the United States (which would appear as a credit item). Conversely, each time a resident of the United States makes a purchase in a foreign country, he owes money to someone outside of the United States (which would appear as a debit item).

Current Transactions. On the credit side of the United States balance-of-payments statement classified as "current transactions" are:

(1) exports of goods and services including transportation, insurance, governmental, military, and tourists; (2) payments by foreigners of interest, dividends, and other forms of investment income to Americans; (3) "donations" by foreigners to Americans including governmental, personal, institutional, and any other grants or one-way transfers (unilateral transfers); and (4) all other miscellaneous items giving Americans current claims against foreigners.

On the debit side of the United States balance-of-payments statement, classified as "current transactions," are: (1) imports of goods and services, including those for transportation, insurance, governmental, military, and American tourists; (2) payments by Americans of interest, dividends, or other forms of investment income to foreigners; (3) "donations" to foreigners by Americans, including governmental, personal, institutional, and any other unilateral transfers; and (4) all other miscellaneous items giving foreigners current claims against Americans.

Movements of Capital and Monetary Gold. On the credit side of the United States balance-of-payments statement, classified as "capital and monetary gold movements," are: (1) imports of long-term capital (exports of bonds and other long-term credit instruments, stock certificates, and other items indicating the shift of capital funds from foreigners to Americans); (2) imports of short-term capital funds (exports of short-term credit instruments or any other evidence that foreigners are increasing their short-term investments in the United States); and (3) exports of monetary gold from the United States. Foreigners must pay for their bonds, stock certificates, and gold; and so, when credit instruments and gold are exported, these items appear as "credit" items.

On the debit side of the United States balance-of-payments statement, classified as "capital and monetary gold movements," are: (1) exports of long-term capital (imports of bonds, other long-term credit instruments, stock certificates, and other items indicating the shift of capital funds from the United States to foreigners); (2) exports of short-term capital funds (imports of short-term credit instruments, etc.); and (3) imports of monetary gold. Since Americans must pay for these bonds, stocks, and gold, these items appear as debits.

In 1955, foreigners had a deficit of $4.1 billion in the total goods and services account. In Table 20 under unilateral (one-way) transfers, appears a favorable receipts balance of $4.6 billion, most of which represents military supplies and services and other grants of the United States government. The data under capital and monetary gold indicate that the net foreign investments by United States residents for the year were about the same as those of foreigners in the United States (chiefly in the form of international reserves). Foreigners also acquired $41,000,000 of monetary gold from the United States.

The "errors and omissions" item is explained chiefly in terms of lack of information covering prices at which transactions take place and the absence of statistical information on other transactions that cross national boundaries, legally or illegally. This item tends to be largest during times of financial disturbance because of an increase in unrecorded capital movements.

Balance of International Payment Items and Cash Transfers. The transactions that enter the "debit" side of the balance of international-payments statement of the United States give the basic economic reasons why there is a demand for foreign exchange—foreigners usually expect to be paid in their own currency for their goods, services, securities, etc. Likewise, those items that appear on the "credit" side of the balance-of-payments statement give the basic economic reasons why there is a supply of foreign exchange—Americans have foreign exchange instruments given for goods, services, and so on which they want to convert into dollars. (See also Chapter XVII.) But there are some items that appear on the balance-of-payments statement that are one-way or unilateral transfers, and there may be changes in other items that involve no cash transfers, across national boundaries. But the international accounting practice requires that these items be entered on both sides of the balance-of-payments statement.

During a year the volume of cash transfers will be many times the amount indicated under "investments." Actually, the foreign exchange business involves daily, in and out, transfers of funds. Banks and other dealers in foreign exchange use funds in arbitrage transactions, speculation in foreign exchange, and short-term capital movements. The amount of funds actually tied up at any one time may be small, but the turnover of funds is rapid. The volume of business done by a merchant is not measured by the change in his inventories at the end of the year as compared to the beginning of the year. Likewise, the volume of business done by foreign exchange merchants in the capital markets is not measured by changes in the net investment position of the United States as portrayed by the balance-of-payments statement. But, considered from the viewpoint of the United States as a whole, the net changes are important as an index of the change in the international position of the United States.

In presenting the balance-of-payments statement, accounting terminology is used, but this does not mean that each item is accounted for at the same time as a "credit" and a "debit." The accounting practice followed is similar to that used in keeping records of cash receipts and payments in a personal checking account. It is

CHART 10

UNITED STATES BALANCE OF PAYMENTS, 1955

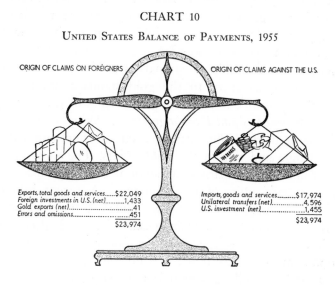

| ORIGIN OF CLAIMS ON FOREIGNERS | ORIGIN OF CLAIMS AGAINST THE U.S. |

Exports, total goods and services......$22,049	Imports, goods and services.........$17,974
Foreign investments in U.S. (net)..........1,433	Unilateral transfers (net)..............4,596
Gold exports (net)...............................41	U.S. investment (net).................1,455
Errors and omissions.........................451	
$23,974	$23,974

more accurate to think of the balance-of-international-payments statement as a "balance-scale," as illustrated in Chart 10. In order for the scales to balance, every addition on one side must be offset by an equal addition of real things on the other side. When a Kansas farmer's wheat crop is sold abroad, this export will be matched by an import of some kind—goods, services, promises-to-pay, or "thank you" notes for governmental or other donations. How these seemingly unrelated items are brought into balance is explained in the sections that follow.

GOLD AS THE REGULATOR OF THE BALANCE OF PAYMENTS

Normal operation of foreign exchange—the mechanism for paying debts between buyers and sellers in different countries—has not been permitted for many years. In a "free" world, changes in gold and gold reserves are of interest to all countries; and, for this reason, this subject is considered in this section. As indicated in an earlier chapter, gold is still the standard of value in international trade, and it is the only completely acceptable kind of money in the world today.

Gold may be added to the scales when needed in order to balance the total of all items. Actually, monetary gold movements involve more than balancing international payments because such movements may affect the respective economics of the two countries through their effects on interest rates, price levels, and international movements of goods, services, and capital. These effects would be greater if the economies in question were not regulated; but, whether regulated or not, the principles are applicable if and when countries are on the gold standard. Since the "free nations" through their acceptance of the International Monetary Fund Agreement are committed to a return to the gold standard, these principles are of great significance in suggesting the "rules of the game."

Gold Movements and Exchange Rates. When countries are on the gold standard, the sight rates of exchange fluctuate around the par of exchange and within the gold points. The mint par of exchange is found by comparing the amount of fine gold in the two-standard monetary units of two countries. A recent issue of the International Monetary Fund's "Schedule of Par Value" gives the weights of monetary units in grams of pure gold; the United States gold dollar, 0.888671; and the English pound sterling, 2.44828. When one compares these units, it is obvious that the pound is the equivalent of 2.80 dollars, which is the par of exchange between the two monetary units expressed in terms of dollars.

When countries are on the gold standard, the extreme fluctuations of the demand rate are fixed by the gold-export and gold-import points. The gold points are found by adding the cost of exporting gold to the par of exchange to get the export point and by subtracting the cost of importing gold from the par of exchange to get the import point. The cost of moving gold includes the cost of preparing for shipment, insuring, mint charges, and loss of interest on the sum while in transit. Since most gold is shipped by air, some of these costs are unimportant.

Theoretically, every individual who has a foreign obligation to meet may want to compare the total cost of acquiring and shipping gold to the rate quoted for foreign exchange in the foreign exchange market. If the amount of the obligation is £1,000, the mint price of the gold would be $2,800 plus a $7.00 handling charge made by the United States Treasury. When freight, insurance, and other charges are added, the total cost in making payment by remitting gold may be $2,820 or more. If an exchange rate or price of $2.82 or less per pound sterling can be obtained in the exchange market, it would be less expensive to purchase foreign exchange drafts and to mail them in payment of obligations. In practice, gold shipments are usually initiated only in large amounts by banks, bullion dealers, and other specialists because, as noted above, the use of gold in payment by individuals would not be economical.

If one assumes that bills of exchange drawn in terms of dollars on New York are selling at a premium in London, English bankers may profit from this situation by shipping gold to New York and immediately selling dollar exchange drawn on New York. The price of the bills must be enough to justify the purchase of gold plus the cost of shipping it. The effect of the increase in the supply of bills is to keep the price of exchange from going above par plus the cost of shipping gold (the gold-export point).

American bankers in New York may initiate gold movements because they are faced with a gold-import-point situation. Bills of exchange drawn in terms of the pound sterling will be selling at a discount in New York. Rather than take a loss, American bankers may withhold offerings of new bills of exchange from the market and cable their correspondent banks in London to purchase gold for them and debit their balances in payment. If their estimates of the situation are correct, they will realize more (even after deducting costs of importing gold) than they would have received if they had created and sold new bills of exchange. The effect is to keep the price of bills of exchange on London from falling below the gold-import point in New York. If one assumes just the opposite of the above, then American bankers would be arranging for gold exports and London bankers would be arranging for gold imports.

The international gold standard gives international bankers an option of substituting gold for bills of exchange in international financial transactions, and it is the use of this option that keeps the exchange rates from fluctuating much below or above the par of exchange. Normally, it is cheaper to use credit instruments than gold; but there are important exceptions.

Gold Movements and Interest Rates. Behind the exchange rate situation causing the pound sterling rate of exchange on London in New York to be high or low (and conversely, the dollar exchange rate on New York in London to be low or high) are all the international factors that cause the demand for foreign exchange to be great or small relative to its supply. The factor considered here is that of capital movements.

Again we may assume that bills of exchange drawn in terms of dollars on New York are selling at a premium in London, with just the opposite situation in New York with reference to the price of pound sterling bills of exchange. The reason for this situation may be that international bankers find that lending funds is relatively more profitable in New York than in London. Therefore, London bankers not only buy dollar exchange but also ship gold to New York in order to increase their supply of loanable funds; and New York bankers not only sell sterling exchange but also import gold in order to increase their supply of loanable funds.

Gold, as the regulator of the balance of payments, should check this movement of capital. The loss of gold will be reflected in the decreased supply of credit and currency available for use in the London money market. This reduction in the supply of money and credit will tend to be followed by higher interest rates in the London market. Just the opposite developments should be taking place in the New York money market where the increase in the supply of loanable funds will tend to lower interest rates. As a result of gold flow, the London money market becomes relatively more attractive and the New York money market relatively less attractive (thereby eliminating the original reason for the gold movement).

This analysis assumes that the original movement of capital from London to New York was caused by a desire for more favorable investments. While this reason for capital movements may be thought of as the normal one, international capital movements may be motivated by fear—fear of deprecation and/or fear of confiscation. At different times the fear of depreciation has led to large shifts of capital funds away from different countries. From 1939 to 1941, it was fear of both depreciation and confiscation that led to the shift of capital funds out of western Europe.

Gold Movements and Price Levels. When countries are on the gold standard, a third automatic factor which tends to bring about equilibrium between countries is the effect of gold movements on imports and exports of goods. If there is a loss of gold due to imports of goods and services in excess of exports, gold, as the regulator of the balance of payments, should check imports and stimulate exports. The loss of gold should lead to restrictive credit policies, a decrease in the supply of money and credit, a decline in money income, and a lower domestic price level. With less money to spend, the domestic demand for goods will tend to decrease, which means that fewer foreign goods will be imported. As a result, domestic and foreign producers will be looking for markets in foreign countries. If they are successful, there will be an increase in exports and a further decrease in imports (because the foreign producers are finding markets elsewhere). These movements—decrease in imports and increase in exports—will tend to bring into balance the relationship between the exports and imports of goods.

Under different circumstances, American exports of goods and services in excess of American imports of goods and services will tend to increase imports of gold. The increase in the supply of gold will tend to be followed by an increase in the supply of money and credit, an increase in money incomes, and higher price level. Because the American market will be a more favorable one for domestic and foreign sellers and a less favorable one for foreign buyers, exports will tend to decline and imports will tend to increase. Once more, by influencing exports and imports of goods, gold will help to secure equilibrium in the balance-of-payments statement. If the corrective movement goes too far, gold will flow away from the country of high prices; and, ultimately, this will set in motion the opposite of the effects already considered.

The effects of gold imports and exports upon domestic economy are not automatic but depend upon the behavior of the aggregate of individuals who control the community's power of investing and spending. Their behavior may modify the velocity of the circulation of money and credit so as to offset the effects of imports or exports of gold. On the other hand, their behavior may intensify these effects.

Central banks may intervene to offset the loss of gold by increasing the volume of reserve credit or may neutralize the effects of gold imports by decreasing the volume of reserve credit. Thus, when a country has a large supply of gold, it may insulate itself against many of the depressing effects which normally accompany the loss of gold. On the other hand, many of the inflationary effects of gold imports may be offset by central-bank and government control over bank reserves.

FLEXIBLE OR FLOATING EXCHANGE RATES

When countries are on the gold standard, there is no wide fluctuation in exchange rates. Demand bills rise or fall in price, depending upon the supply and demand; but the fluctuations are confined to the limits set by the gold points. The norm around which rates fluctuate is the par of exchange. When countries leave the gold standard, exchange transactions continue to mean the purchase and sale of credit instruments denominated in foreign currencies. Gold movements are no longer effective in keeping the demand rate of exchange within the gold points because international bankers no longer are in a position to obtain gold at the old fixed price. Assuming that two countries are on paper standards, is there a norm around which the exchange rate will fluctuate? One answer is found in the concept of a purchasing power par of international exchange.

The Purchasing Power Parity Theory. The purchasing power parity theory of international exchange is that the basic exchange rates depend on the relative purchasing power of the two currencies in their respective countries. The price at which bills of exchange are bought or sold in the exchange market may be above or below the purchasing power par. In fact the deviation from the market rate of exchange may be considerably above or below the purchasing power parity for many reasons at a particular time. But the idea that the rate of exchange (the value of a foreign currency unit in terms of the dollar) depends in part on prices at home and abroad is valid at all times when there is freedom to buy and sell things without restrictions in the respective countries.

The price of any particular security or commodity, bought and sold in different markets, will tend to be the same at any particular time. When the price of American Telephone and Telegraph Company stock is around £54 in London, the price in New York will be around $151, when the exchange rate is $2.80. If there are no barriers to trade (natural or artificial), the price of wheat will be £1 in Liverpool when the price is $2.80 in New York. In each case the price reflects the purchasing power of the currency unit in which it is expressed.

If prices rise in the United Kingdom and remain stationary in the United States, the pound sterling will have less purchasing power not only in the United Kingdom but also in the United States, where fewer American dollars and fewer commodities will be exchanged for it. There would be no demand for sterling bills of exchange at the old rate; consequently, the rate of exchange would fall. When the new exchange rate falls to the point where it reflects the lower purchasing power of the pound sterling, a measure of stability will be achieved.

In practice international arbitragers in commodities, gold, securities, and bills of exchange buy and sell in order to make profits from differences in prices in different markets at the same time. The purchasing power parity theory is but an application of these principles to the determination of exchange rates of the respective currencies in terms of purchasing power as measured by price index numbers.

Purchasing Power Par. The formula for determining the purchasing power par between two countries, both of which have price index numbers using the same base year, is as follows:

$$\frac{\text{Index number–Country A}}{\text{Index number–Country B}} \times \text{old par of exchange} = \text{purchasing power par.}$$

For example, if the United States and Great Britain have paper standards, and the index number of prices in the United States is 120 and that of Great Britain is 160, the purchasing power par is computed as follows:

$$\frac{120}{160} \times \$2.80 = \$2.10.$$

If the purchasing power par is $2.10 and the market rate of exchange is $2.00, it obviously would be to the advantage of American buyers to purchase goods in England, where the equivalent of $2.00 would buy $2.10 worth of goods. An increase in purchases abroad would tend to bring the actual exchange rate and the purchasing power par together. The adjustment would be a three-way process: (1) Buying abroad would make it necessary for merchants to go into the exchange market and to purchase exchange, and the rate of exchange would tend to increase. (2) Buying goods abroad would tend to increase prices in that market. (3) A decrease in purchase of goods in the United States would tend to lower prices of goods in the domestic market. The first movement would tend to increase the exchange rate, and the last two movements would tend to lower the purchasing power par. For example, should prices go up two points in England and down two points in the United States, the new purchasing power par would be:

$$\frac{118}{162} \times \$2.80 = \$2.04.$$

Assume also that, in the meantime, the exchange rate would increase 4 cents (from $2.00 to $2.04); the exchange rate and the purchasing power par would thus be brought together.

If the exchange rate is above the purchasing power par, just the opposite of these movements would tend to take place. That is, goods would tend to be purchased more freely in the United States and less freely abroad, the rate of dollar exchange would tend to rise, domestic prices would tend to increase, and foreign prices would tend to decrease. In computing the purchasing power par, the most satisfactory results are secured when only prices of goods bought and sold in international markets are considered. When sheltered goods are considered, differences in purchasing power of money in two markets may be great. Further deviations of the exchange rate away from the purchasing power par norm may result from capital movements, domestic price control, and other restrictions placed on the markets. In a free economy operating on a paper standard the adjustments which tend to take place are those which involve individual prices rather than the general price level—as would be the case when on the gold standard.

Flexible Exchange Rates and the Balance of Payments. While the preceding discussion has emphasized the relationship between the purchasing power parity of exchange and the market rate, the mechanism whereby exchange rate fluctuations tend to keep the balance-of-payments statement in equilibrium is of primary interest. It was noted that, when on the gold standard, exchange rate fluctuations are minor, being limited by gold movements; on leaving the gold standard, this limiting factor is removed and a country's exchange rate may fluctuate widely.

If foreign goods and services are being imported excessively by Americans, exchange rates will tend to increase; and this will mean that higher prices (when converted into dollars) will have to be paid for foreign goods, thereby checking imports. Foreign exchange rates are ratios; and so, like a teeterboard movement, the price of the dollar is low in foreign markets if the foreign exchange rates are high in New York. This means that American goods may be purchased more cheaply (in terms of foreign currencies), which will stimulate American exports. Thus, by discouraging imports and encouraging exports, fluctuations in foreign exchange rates will tend to curtail American imports and to stimulate American exports, thus bringing into equilibrium the relationship between exports and imports.

Conversely, if American goods and services were being exported excessively, the fluctuations in exchange rates would tend to correct this situation. The price of American dollars in foreign markets would be high, and the price of foreign currencies in New York would be low. The first would discourage foreign purchases of American goods, and the second would encourage the purchase of foreign goods by Americans. This would tend to bring into balance the relationship between exports and imports by reducing the former and by increasing the latter.

If there are free foreign exchange markets, fluctuations in exchange rates become a major factor in bringing about equilibrium in the balance of payments. Under the gold standard, a fall in the rate of exchange or price of the pound sterling to the gold-import point would have only a minor influence on the international credits and debits of Great Britain; but, under a paper standard (assuming free exchange markets), a decline of 25 per cent would tend to increase sharply the export or credit items and to decrease sharply the import or debit items. Thus an equilibrium rate of exchange would be established without involving gold movements; and, as already noted, this rate would correspond roughly to the purchasing power parity of the two units involved.

CONTROLLED EXCHANGES AND PAPER STANDARDS

In practice, few countries permit exchange rates to bring about equilibrium between the inflow and outflow of goods and services because fluctuating exchange rates tend to create as well as to correct situations which are in disequilibrium. If the price of pound sterling is falling, speculators are encouraged to sell bills of exchange on London, bankers are encouraged to shift funds away from London, foreign buyers of English goods and services will tend to wait for lower prices, and English importers will tend to enlarge their purchases from abroad in order to avoid higher prices (in terms of the pound sterling). All of these capital and goods movements will tend to accelerate the fall in the price of the pound sterling.

Orderly exchange markets are necessary; but, in adopting foreign exchange-control measures, countries may have objectives other than the elimination of disturbing effects of fluctuating exchange rates. For illustration, if nations are buying heavily abroad, it is desirable to keep their exchange rates above the purchasing power par norm in order to get the most goods and services from what they have to spend. But, in order to sell, they may want to keep their exchange rates below the purchasing power par norm—in fact, they may try to do both at the same time by introducing a multiple-exchange system, with one rate for one purpose and a second rate for a second purpose.

Foreign Exchange Control. Foreign exchange control means the detailed control over the exchange markets and complete, or almost complete, suppression of free dealings in exchange. This form of control was inititated in Germany in 1931. It was adopted by most warring countries at the outbreak of World War II and has been continued to date in many countries. Usually, it is introduced in order to support a foreign exchange value of a currency at a level above its international purchasing power. In addition to a government monopoly of the exchange market, direct exchange control usually includes a licensing system for the import and export of goods, control of foreign assets of nationals, regulation of foreign investments, and specifications of the amount of funds that individuals may take out of the economy.

Having a monopoly of the supply of foreign exchange, the control authority must decide on its apportionment for commodity imports, debt service, tourist expenditures, and other items. The next type of decision involves the distribution of the funds among different countries. This power permits all types of international favoritism, often in violation of most-favored-nation clauses in existing treaties.[1] For example, applicants for exchange who want to buy American goods may be refused, while applicants who want to buy French goods may be sold exchange.

Further complications arise because of the question of the distribution of available exchange among different commodities. These decisions make it possible to favor certain industries at the expense of others, to favor industry at the expense of agriculture, and to bring about a redistribution of national income among the domestic classes. For example, manufacturers of chemicals may be permitted to buy abroad, while manufacturers of cloth may be forced into bankruptcy because they cannot secure raw materials from abroad. Finally, the exchange authority must allot exchange among competing business firms, a source of one of the most vicious types of abuse in exchange regulation. For example, Firm A is permitted to buy exchange and therefore raw materials abroad; but Firm B is denied foreign exchange and is forced to get along with inferior domestic substitutes, to change the nature of its business, or to liquidate.

---

[1] The most-favored-nation clause contained in trade agreements provides for the extension of the benefits of liberalization of trade restrictions and lower import duties to all countries with whom trade agreements have been signed. This places all on the same trade basis.

Thus, arbitrary administrative decisions are substituted for the old system of free exchange in which price serves as the mechanism of allotment. In the system of free exchange, if the total demand for foreign exchange for all purposes is greater than the total supply, its price rises until supply and demand are balanced; therefore, there is no problem of discriminating among buyers in different fields and among individuals in the same field. "The less urgent needs are excluded by price, and there is no direct interference in the process of production and trade. Vested interests do not grow up which are dependent on the continuance of an artificial system of control and allocation and which accordingly resist any attempt to change that system."[2]

The control agency controls not only the use of foreign exchange but also the supply. Exports are the most important source of supply, and the owners of the resulting bills of exchange are required to sell all or part of them to the exchange authorities at a rate fixed by the control agency. Exchange is then available to finance governmental payments abroad and to sell to importers and to others. If the plan in operation permits the exporter to retain a part of his foreign exchange, he may use it to buy goods abroad, or he may sell it to an importer at a negotiated price, usually above the official buying price in the free market.

In addition to the seizure of bills of exchange resulting from exports, foreign exchange holdings of the exchange authorities may be increased by requiring all persons to report and to surrender title to all bank balances abroad, all foreign securities, and other foreign assets, including even real estate in certain countries. Imports of foreign currency may be tolerated; but, since some currencies (such as the American dollar) are widely hoarded abroad, the exchange-control authorities may prefer to have it exchanged for domestic money at the port of entry. Domestic currency may be taken out of the country by tourists, but limits are placed on the amount that may be imported.

As short-term capital movements are the most dynamic among the items in the balance of payments, exchange control was first introduced in many countries in order to prevent these short-term debt transfers from causing exchange disturbances. Governments commonly decreed that nationals must pay their interest and prin-

---

[2] League of Nations, Committee composed of members of the Economic and Financial Committee, *Report on Exchange Control* (Geneva: League of Nations, 1938), p. 39.

cipal charges into a fund at the central bank. These payments were made in domestic currency calculated at the debtor country's official exchange rate. The coupons of foreign bondholders were then presented to the central bank for payment. In some cases, arrangements have been made for payment of principal; but the conditions under which these funds can be utilized vary greatly. Usually, these "blocked balances" or bank accounts may be used to purchase goods within the country where they are held and may be sold to tourists for expenditures within the boundaries of the country.

Usually, no international banker will place funds in an exchange-control country where he knows restrictions will be placed on their withdrawal. So in order to have normal capital movements, confidence in the future of exchange-control countries must be re-established. Experience suggests that this may not be expected so long as these countries follow any policy of exchange control which prevents the creditor from receiving, in free exchange, interest, dividends, and installment or other payments on principal. Therefore, exchange control tends to restrict international lending and to shrink the total volume of transactions involved in the balance-of-international-payments statement (unless offset by governmental lending).

While the United States (with relatively free exchange) has suffered from exchange control practices of foreign countries, evidence supports the conclusion that exchange-control countries are the chief losers. As noted, they tend to suffer from loss of the use of private foreign capital; and both their imports and exports tend to decrease while production tends to decline. "In consequence, the total national income in a country resorting to exchange-control is likely to be lower than it would have been had it allowed its currency to fall to the equilibrium level." Temporarily, exchange-control countries may rely upon "grants" and "loans" by the United States; but the long-run policy calls for the abolition of exchange control.

The restrictions on movements of capital funds and currency may be evaded in various ways, and such funds do flow illegally to markets wherein they may be used most profitably. Unfortunately such flights of capital, chiefly to the United States, have deprived the home countries of resources needed for reconstruction and development. Although the United States may discourage the influx of such funds by keeping interest rates below those of foreign countries, much of this foreign money has been invested in stocks wherein the yield rate and capital appreciation are much higher than interest rates.

The philosophy of the International Monetary Fund Agreement is that "restrictions are to be regarded as temporary devices to be removed as soon as conditions permit."[3] In general terms, there has been a tendency toward relaxation of restrictions with Canada having abolished its entire exchange control system and the United Kingdom, The Netherlands, and other countries having liberalized theirs to some degree.

Since Canada adopted a flexible or floating rate of exchange in 1950, the arguments in favor of this system have been reconsidered. While it is recognized that some international trade may be discouraged by a free-rate system, it is argued that fluctuations will be small when the balance of payments is in equilibrium and forward exchange markets may be used to protect buyers and sellers from losses due to exchange rate fluctuations. If the balance of payments is in disequilibrium, the exchange market provides not only a self-correcting mechanism but also information on which the trend of the market may be judged.

Advocates of the flexible or floating exchange rate argue that events since World War II do not support the argument that fixed rates help the flow of trade. In 1949, they point out, traders, bankers, and others were kept in suspense for months waiting for a change in the pegged rate of exchange of the United Kingdom and other countries in terms of gold or the United States dollar. With each recurrent balance-of-payments crisis, trade and international payments are disrupted by rumors of devaluation of the pound sterling or whatever currency is involved. Instead of discouraging speculation and capital movements, the pegged exchange rate system actually invites them.

Perhaps, flexible exchange rates would encourage speculators to shift funds to markets wherein rates have fallen (expecting the rate to rise again); but it is also possible that more funds will be withdrawn in the expectation that exchange rates will fall further. One thing is certain, pegged rates do encourage equilibrating movements in response to changes in interest rates (see below).

Methods of Trade Control. Parallel to restrictions on exchange markets are restrictions placed on foreign trade by countries whose governments limit the purchase of goods by import quotas, licensing

[3] International Monetary Fund, *Third Annual Report on Exchange Restrictions* (Washington, D.C., 1950), p. 1.

systems, and protective tariffs. In addition, governments have made discriminatory bilateral agreements which have practically closed certain markets to other countries. Among these agreements were the prewar "barter" and "clearing" agreements that Germany made with her satellite countries and the postwar agreements between Russia and the nations in her sphere of influence—the Molotov Plan for eastern Europe. Another agreement, less sweeping in nature, was the Anglo-Russian exchange of grain and other Soviet products for English manufactured goods. Under agreements of the latter type, individuals as well as governments may participate. Buyers in each country pay for the goods purchased by remitting to their central bank or some other governmental agency. From the funds received, each control agency pays exporters in their own country for the goods shipped to the other country. Thus, goods are purchased and sold without the use of foreign exchange, settlement being made by domestic drafts. Final settlement of any balance between the two countries is made by the two exchange authorities according to prior arrangements.

A major problem inherent in clearing agreements is that of arriving at the correct exchange rate to be used. Often, in the past, trade was carried on at artificially high prices; and this tying together of the economies of two countries at an artificially high price level tended to deprive these countries of freedom of action in dealing with other countries operating at the international price level. Since trade with the larger country was relatively more important to the smaller country, the economy of the smaller country was more seriously affected and the shock to it was greater when other markets had to be found.

INTERNATIONAL ASPECTS OF UNITED STATES MONETARY POLICIES

Although the monetary problems of the United States are of such a nature as to require the attention of monetary management to be directed more to domestic than to international financial problems, what the United States does or does not do is of vital importance to foreign nations.

Trade and Prices. Usually there is some interrelationship in cyclical movements in business activity among all countries of the free world; and, the position of the United States in international trade and finance is such that if it is able to achieve greater domestic stability other countries will feel this stabilizing effect. Insofar as the United States is able to maintain stable prices and a growing economy, it will be promoting stability in prices and economic conditions in the rest of the free world.

Capital Movements. As long as the international flow of capital is restricted by exchange control, fluctuations in interest rates within the United States can not have much direct effect on capital movements to and from the United States. Low interest rates in the United States may not encourage Americans to seek capital outlets abroad; and high interest rates in the United States may not openly and legally encourage the flow of capital to the United States. As long as there is a lack of confidence in foreign currencies, the capital flows that do take place may not reflect interest-rate differentials.

The flow of funds between the United States and Canada is unrestricted, and the capital flows between these two countries are very important. However, these capital flows are influenced not only by real and anticipated differences in interest rates and profit yields but also by actual and prospective changes in the exchange rates (at times, the latter is more important than the former). From March, 1952, until October, 1955, the Canadian dollar was bought and sold at a premium in the United States chiefly because of the capital flow to Canada; and when the price or exchange rate started to decline in January, 1955, finally going to a discount in October, one reason given was that interest rates or yields on investments were relatively more attractive in the United States.

The United Kingdom has liberalized its exchange restrictions and has restored a free gold market in London (March, 1954); and these steps, along with the expectation that the United Kingdom would provide for free convertibility of the pound sterling into American dollars, have encouraged a flow of funds from New York to London in order to take advantage of the interest rate differential on short-term funds. In May, 1954, the central bank discount rate was reduced to check the accumulation of "hot money" in the London market; but toward the end of the year this interest rate change was reversed to attract funds to London. These developments indicate how monetary policy may be used to influence short-term capital movements (the first such experience since World War II involving the London, New York, and other markets).

Greater Dependence on Monetary Policy. The successful use of monetary policy in the United States since 1951 may have had some influence on the fiscal and monetary policies of other countries. Abroad, as in the United States, there is now less dependence on fiscal policy and more on monetary policy. In fact, in West Germany flexible monetary policies have been used since 1950; and some attribute West Germany's rapid recovery to this fact.

In most countries having highly developed capital markets, the two most widely used credit-control devices are the discount rate and open-market operations (in Austria, Belgium, and Germany). In other countries, the greatest dependence seems to have been on open-market operations (in Canada, India, The Netherlands, and the United Kingdom). Dependence on changes in reserve requirements seems to be greatest in less industrialized countries (in Australia, Ceylon, Colombia, Mexico, Peru, and New Zealand). Where government regulations are most typical of the economy, there seems to be some preference for selective or direct-control devices (in Denmark, France, Finland, Japan, Norway, Phillippine Islands, and Sweden).

Of course, any instrument of credit control in use may be supplemented by others; and today there seems to be a tendency for more countries to shift to increased use of general credit control devices—changes in discount rates, open-market operations, and reserve requirements. Moral suasion is also used; and its use is most successful where the banking system is highly centralized (as in Canada, the United Kingdom, and Italy) and the personal influence of the monetary authorities on a few key bankers has been able to obtain the desired results.

During the period since World War II, the international monetary problem has been one of preventing inflation rather than deflation. In many countries, there has been a fear that monetary action taken to stabilize prices might handicap the development of national resources. To an increasing extent, the fact that economic growth and stable prices are not incompatible is being recognized and that therefore countries may enjoy record peaks in prosperity without inflationary pressures on their international foreign exchange reserves or on their domestic prices.

SUMMARY

The balance of international payments of a given country is a systematic record of all economic transactions between residents of that country and those of all other countries for a given period of time. The balance-of-payments statement may be thought of as a balance-scale with every addition on one side necessitating an addition on the other to keep it in equilibrium. Gold, as the regulator of the balance of payments, may be added to the scales when needed to balance the total of all items. However, gold movements involve more than balancing international payments because they affect national economies by their effects on interest rates, price levels, and international movements of goods and services. When countries are on a gold standard, the norm around which exchange rates fluctuate is the par of exchange. When two countries are on inconvertible paper standards, the norm around which exchange rates tend to fluctuate is known as the "purchasing power par."

When operating on paper standards, most countries have controlled exchanges—that is, detailed control over exchange markets and almost, if not complete, suppression of free dealing in exchange. Restrictions on exchange markets are usually paralleled by restrictions on foreign trade. Thus, foreign trade, foreign investment, and even foreign travel have been placed in a strait jacket by devious devices. The United States, which has the most at stake, has been the leader in the movement to eliminate these restrictive trade and foreign exchange-control practices, which are deeply embedded because of prewar, war, and postwar emphasis on economic nationalism. One of the reasons for creating the International Monetary Fund was to have an international agency "to assist in the establishment of a multilateral system of payments in respect to current transactions between members and in the elimination of foreign exchange restrictions which hamper the growth of world trade."[4]

QUESTIONS AND PROBLEMS

1. What is meant by the "balance of international payments"? Identify the chief classes of items involved.

2. When operating on the international gold standard, how does gold tend to operate as the regulator of goods and services items in the balance-of-payments statement?

3. "Thus the cost of transmitting specie is the limit to the premium on bills." (William S. Jevons, *Money and the Mechanism of Exchange* [New York: D. Appleton & Co., 1875], p. 303.) Why? Is it also the limit on the discount on bills? What bills (sight, time, or cable)?

4. When countries are operating on the international gold standard, how does gold act as the regulator of the volume of capital items in the balance-of-payments statement?

5. Explain why the market rate of exchange tends to fluctuate around

[4] International Monetary Fund, *Articles of Agreement* (Washington, D.C., 1944), p. 1.

the purchasing power par of exchange when a country is operating on an inconvertible paper money standard and has a free exchange market.

6. What are the specific administrative problems confronting exchange-control authorities when foreign exchange is sold?

7. Present the arguments in favor of exchange-control practices. If these practices are beneficial to the country in question, why should they be subjected to criticism?

8. "In the short run at least, the large fluctuations that can occur in capital movements are likely to have a determining influence on the exchange rates . . . The flow of interest-bearing capital, as shown by recent experience, is highly sensitive to international differences in interest rates, . . ." (Bank of Montreal, *Business Review*, July 21, 1955, n.p.). Do you agree with the above statement? Why?

9. May United States monetary policies be directed so as to help foreign countries in solving their international financial problems? How?

10. Analyze: "On the two-way street of foreign investment, the heavier traffic is coming this way . . . In recent years, a heavy proportion of this foreign money has been going into American corporate stocks. By the end of 1954, the total had reached a record $5,254,-000,000." (*New York Times*, October 1, 1955, p. 23.)

| Chapter | INTERNATIONAL FINANCIAL |
| XXVI | ORGANIZATIONS |

IN THE hierarchy of finance the International Monetary Fund deals primarily with governments, central banks, and agencies such as foreign exchange stabilization funds. The International Bank for Reconstruction and Development makes loans based on government credit to member countries or to institutions within member countries when guaranteed by their governments. The International Finance Corporation, a subsidiary of the International Bank for Reconstruction and Development, encourages the flow of international funds into productive private enterprises. The Bank for International Settlements was created in 1930 to help solve the foreign exchange problems of that time. The Export-Import Bank of Washington was created in 1934 to help finance imports and exports of the United States. However, in the lower echelons of finance, where the ordinary foreign exchange transactions take place, most financing is handled by commercial banks, subsidiaries of commercial banks, and certain specialists (see also Chapter XVII).

BACKGROUND FOR INTERNATIONAL FINANCIAL ORGANIZATIONS

Currency Depreciation. Throughout modern times international monetary chaos and depreciated currencies have been associated with wars and their aftermath, with one major exception—the Great Depression following the abandonment of the gold standard in 1931 by the United Kingdom and subsequently by other nations. As used here "depreciation" means a loss in exchange value of one currency unit in terms of foreign currency units (for illustration, a loss in value of the United States dollar in terms of the pound sterling, the franc, etc.). During the depression of the 1930's, many countries adopted the policy of depreciating their currency units; and among the advantages sought therefrom were an increase in exports and a decrease in unemployment (a policy referred to as exporting unemployment).

The main disadvantage of a policy of depreciation is that it encourages similar action by other countries which, in an effort to recapture their lost markets, will lower the cost of their money (exchange rates). Once started, competition in depreciation seems to follow and to continue until all countries have devalued their monetary units. At any time a new wave of depreciation may be started if one major country further reduces the international value of its currency.

Any advantage gained from depreciation is usually temporary because prices in the depreciator's market tend to rise if for no other reason than the increase in international demand for its goods. The reduction in purchasing power of the depreciator's currency in foreign markets where raw materials and other goods are purchased will also contribute to higher domestic costs and prices. If this country is a debtor country, it will mean that the burden of its international debts will be increased; if it is a creditor country, depreciation will cancel a portion of its foreign credits in terms of real income.

Retaliation by other nations against depreciator nations may take forms other than competitive depreciation. These measures include: (1) raising tariffs to offset any trade advantage gained by the depreciator country; (2) establishing quotas to limit imports in order to assure domestic producers a certain percentage of the domestic market; (3) licensing imports; (4) entering into bilateral barter agreements whereby goods are exchanged for goods rather than money; and (5) making trade agreements with other countries which block out the depreciator's goods from their markets.

Exchange Control.   When goods are purchased abroad, they are usually paid for in foreign money; and, by allocating foreign exchange available, a country may direct or control its imports. Gradually the control of foreign exchange was linked to import control by requiring would-be importers to obtain import licenses before applying for foreign exchange.

In order for the government to have foreign exchange to sell, exporters and others are required to sell their foreign exchange to the government in whole or part at the official price. If there are foreign deposits in the banks in the exchange-control country, these funds may be blocked and the banks may not honor checks drawn on them except to buy things permitted by the government. Foreign investors and others having assets in exchange control countries may be unable to liquidate them and withdraw their money except as permitted by the exchange control country.

Once the foregoing methods of international economic warfare have been perfected, as they were during the 1930's, they may be applied against nations other than those who have depreciated their currencies (such as enemy countries during war, and a strong competitor such as the United States since World War II). When limits are placed on the use of foreign deposits and other international reserves, they may or may not be applied uniformly. There may be differentiation with respect to the ownership of deposits (as between residents and nonresidents, and/or foreign central banks and other nonresidents); to the purposes for which the deposits are to be used (as current transactions and capital transfers, and travel and other purposes); and to origin of the deposits (between old and new and/or between prewar and postwar).

Stabilization Funds. Not all of the international financial developments during the 1930's were of the type which handicapped and suppressed international trade, travel, and investments. Some countries created stabilization funds which sought to minimize government interference in the exchange markets and to maintain free foreign exchange markets. For illustration, when the United Kingdom abandoned the gold standard in 1931, it created an Exchange Equalization Account to stabilize the value of the pound sterling. Unlike the English Equalization Account, the American Stabilization Fund, provided for in the Gold Reserve Act of 1934, was used very little because of the strong international position of the dollar, the stress on domestic recovery, the link to gold, and the greater degree of economic and political stability in the United States as compared to some foreign countries.

Tripartite Agreement. Some degree of exchange stability resulted from the Tripartite Agreement of 1936 among the United States, the United Kingdom, and France, which was later joined by the Bank for International Settlements, Belgium, Holland, and Switzerland. The participants in this Agreement contracted to sell gold to each other at fixed prices which were to be unchanged unless twenty-four hours' prior notice was given. Thus the monetary unit of each country was fixed in terms of gold, subject of course to change (a principle which is found in the International Monetary Fund Agreement wherein prior approval of the Fund is required if the change is to be more than 10 per cent of the gold price of the currency unit). When World War II started in 1939, the Tripartite Agreement became of secondary importance when economic controls replaced free markets in order to enhance the war effect.

Bretton Woods Twins. In approaching the postwar monetary problems, it was apparent that fairly stable exchange rates and free exchange markets were requisites if international trade, investments, and travel were to be financed with the minimum of risks. Attainment of these requisites would relieve merchants, bankers, and others from the fear that their receipts may be reduced by depreciation of foreign currency units and that their funds may be "blocked" and will have to be spent according to the dictates of a foreign government. By their nature, these problems are international in their effects and require international co-operation for their solution.

In July, 1944, at Bretton Woods, New Hampshire, representatives of forty-four nations met and approved the Articles of Agreement for the International Monetary Fund and the Articles of Agreement for the International Bank for Reconstruction and Development (World Bank). The actions of these representatives were not binding on their governments,[1] and the governments of several of the original forty-four nations have taken no action on the Agreements. However, in addition to those at Bretton Woods, others have approved; and, at the present time, there are fifty-eight members. Both the Fund and the World Bank are co-operative ventures, being owned, controlled and operated by and in the interest of members. Each member nation appoints a governor and an alternate to the Fund and a governor and an alternate to the Bank. Generally, the governors have been finance ministers or central bank presidents of their respective countries.

INTERNATIONAL MONETARY FUND

Purposes. The purposes of the International Monetary Fund are: (1) to promote international monetary co-operation through a permanent institution which provides the machinery for consultation and collaboration on international monetary problems; (2) to facilitate the expansion and balanced growth of international trade,

---

[1] The United States was the first country to take action on the agreements. The Bretton Woods Agreements Act, was approved by the President on July 31, 1945 (59 Stat. 512). The Bretton Woods Conference provided that, when the governments representing 65 per cent of the total subscriptions accepted and signed the Articles of Agreement, they would be effective. Action was required before the end of 1945; and on December 27, 1945, all but seven of the original forty-four nations had signed the Articles of Agreement; and, subsequently, three of the seven have been admitted. The only important nonacceptor was Russia.

thereby contributing to high levels of employment and real income; (3) to promote exchange stability and to avoid competitive exchange depreciation; (4) to assist in the establishment of a multilateral system of payments in respect to current transactions, thereby eliminating foreign exchange restrictions that hamper the growth of trade; (5) to provide members with resources with which to correct temporary maladjustments in their balances of payments; and (6) to shorten the duration and to lessen the disequilibrium in the international balance of payments.

Quotas. The International Monetary Fund is financed by participating countries, with each country's contribution fixed according to the relative importance of its prewar national income and international trade. The amount of capital has varied according to membership, but at the present time it is about $9 billion. Although the contributions are measured in dollars, they were made in gold and credits of the participating countries.[2]

Management. The Fund is managed by a board of governors (one from each member nation) and twelve or more (now fourteen) executive directors and their alternates. The executive board meets two or three times each week to consider problems brought before the Fund. The success of the Fund depends upon adherence to its regulations by all members, which is a matter of member co-operation and a problem in public relations.

Policies are carried out by a managing director and his staff. Voting power of member countries depends, in part, on the size of their quotas (that of the United States being about 30 per cent of the total). Decisions do not always depend upon a majority; for example, a change in quotas requires a fourth-fifths vote, which gives the United States a veto power. It also provides that, in important questions relating to "loans," a country's voting power increases on a sliding scale as the loans or "sales" of its currency increase, with a corresponding decrease in the voting power of borrowing countries.

Par of Exchange. One of the first functions of the Fund was that of fixing the par value of the currency of each member nation, with the latter's co-operation, in terms of gold or the United States dollar. In 1946 these par values were announced for thirty-two countries and a number of nonmetropolitan areas. At the requests of the members concerned, the selection of par values of some members

---

[2] The Bretton Woods Agreements Act authorized the Secretary of the Treasury to borrow a total of $4.125 billion to finance the Fund and the Bank. Since this sum was in addition to the $1.8 billion in the Stabilization Fund which was used to pay part of the United States subscriptions to the Fund, the amount authorized by Congress was $5.925 billion. *Ibid.*, Sec. 7 (*a*) and (*b*).

was postponed. Acceptance of par values permitted the Fund to begin operations on March 1, 1947.

The International Monetary Fund Agreement recognizes that changes in exchange rates may be necessary and provides the procedure whereby such changes may be made. No change may be made except on a member's own proposal, and members agree not to propose any change except to correct a fundamental disequilibrium in the balance of payments.

Member countries, after consultation with the Fund but without the latter's concurrence, may increase or decrease the par values of their currencies by 10 per cent from those initially established. A proposed change of more than 10 per cent must be either concurred in or objected to by the Fund within seventy-two hours after a member makes the request, and over thirty such changes have been made since the Fund began operations. There is a special arrangement that permits the Fund to make a uniform proportionate change in the par value of all currencies in terms of gold. This change must have the approval of each country which has a quota equal to more than one tenth of the total (that is, the United States and Great Britain). Since this change would mean a change in the value of domestic currency in terms of gold, a country may refuse to accept it, provided the Fund is notified within seventy-two hours.

The Fund has recognized that under certain circumstances fluctuating rates are desirable and has permitted certain countries to establish "free" markets (where the exchange rate is not pegged to gold). In principle, the Fund is opposed to floating exchange rates and regards these departures from the par rate of exchange as temporary, as by Canada in 1950.

Exchange Control. The Articles of Agreement of the International Monetary Fund provide for the elimination of restrictions on payments or transfers for current transactions except those that the Fund may approve (as in the case of "scarce" currencies). However, there are provisions in the Articles of Agreement whereby the member countries might place restrictions on current transactions during the postwar transitional period from war economy to a peace economy.

Beginning in 1950 the Fund has issued an annual report on "exchange restrictions" still in force. In 1952, as required in the Articles of Agreement, the Fund commenced consultations with member countries on the further retention of exchange restrictions. Because of the "cold war" and the war in Korea, the peace economy visualized in 1944 has not materialized. Nevertheless, there has been considerable development toward currency convertibility (as used here to mean that a holder of any national currency is free to exchange it at the existing rate of exchange into any other currency).

Now, and in the future, member countries may exercise such controls as are necessary to regulate international capital movements; and they may also impose limitations on the freedom of operations in scarce currencies. For illustration, if the demand for dollars in the Fund were to become so great as to threaten the Fund's ability to supply them, the Fund could formally declare the dollar to be a "scarce" currency. Then, after consultation with the Fund, member countries could impose limitations on the freedom of exchange operations in the dollar.

Transactions. Ordinary transactions in foreign exchange are effected through private agencies, which means that foreign exchange principles and practices have not been changed fundamentally. Only when there is a shortage of foreign currency does the market come to the central authorities for help, and then the latter may apply to the Fund. The Fund deals only with or through central banks, exchange stabilization funds, or similar agencies.

The Fund has been called a huge "central bank for central banks," but this is a misnomer because lending is not its chief function; and the ideal situation would be one wherein the foreign exchange markets function so smoothly that there would be no need for using the Fund's resources. The Fund is not expected to be the source of any funds other than those needed to offset temporary disequilibriums in the balance of payments. The Fund may be compared to a pool of dollars, pounds, francs, etc., contributed by all members to finance certain current needs. Thus, France may add French francs and withdraw dollars with which to buy goods in the United States. Similarly, other countries may add their currencies to the pool and withdraw dollars for making purchases in the United States; and the United States may add dollars to the pool and withdraw francs to buy goods in France. After allowing for changes due to profits or losses, this means that the form of assets (insofar as the currencies involved) will change; but total assets will not change. So, the total amount of borrowings from the Fund would be much less than the total capital of $9 billion because a member country may not be a net creditor and a net debtor at the same time. This means that the capital should not be considered as the amount of possible loans that could be made by the Fund.

The original concept was one of automatic accessibility of members to the resources of the Fund. Thus, when a country applies for a certain type of foreign exchange, it will be provided by the Fund if the latter has not given notice that its holding of this currency has become scarce, or if the transaction would not increase the amount of the applicant's currency in the Fund by more than 25 per cent of its total quota during the preceding twelve months,[3] or by more than 200 per cent of its total quota. The Fund's resources are to be used to care for temporary disequilibriums in the exchange markets. So the Fund has wisely taken the position that its resources are not to be used if they might become frozen.

At the annual meeting of the Board of Governors in 1955, the managing director of the International Monetary Fund reported that the Fund has had transactions exceeding $1 billion with twenty-seven member countries. Currently, the Fund is under commitment to lend the United Kingdom 1.3 billion dollars. The Fund is in a very liquid position due in part to the restrictions on borrowing and a requirement that qualified members whose currencies in the Fund are equal to or above 75 per cent of their quotas must make an annual cleanup in whole or part of their borrowing by repurchasing a part of their currencies in the Fund (with gold or foreign exchange). Their ability to repurchase is measured by their monetary-reserve positions at the end of the year. In general, participating countries have been able to increase their gold and dollar exchange holdings substantially in recent years. Another provision that would tend to increase the gold assets of the Fund is the requirement that, if there are no disadvantages in doing so, members must reacquire their currencies from the Fund with gold payments.

Charges. The charges (in effect, interest rates) made against members are arranged so as to discourage the continuous use of the Fund as a source of foreign exchange. The rates charged increase with the time and with the amount borrowed, estimated in terms of the member's quota (being nil for three months if the amount does not place the applicant above 150 per cent of its quota). They are increased on the longer term credits in order to encourage members to repay their "loans" more promptly, and either kept low or made without charge on the short-term credits in order to encourage members to use the resources of the Fund more freely.

---

[3] This rule applies only if the applicant's currency in the Fund is above 75 per cent of its quota, or if the transaction would bring it above 75 per cent of its quota.

Gold Policy. The gold policy of the Fund is one of maintaining a single price for gold. It permits transactions by members above or below par value at a margin equal to (1) one fourth of 1 per cent plus certain handling charges or (2) 1 per cent which includes all charges.

Work of the Fund. Because of its nature, the Fund is subject to careful analysis both in the United States and abroad. In general, there is no quarrel with its aims; and doubts expressed as to its successful operation have been abated because of the way the Fund has been administered. Foreign exchange transactions are but exchanges of one national currency for another; and it was this aspect of the Fund that has been criticized in the United States, where bankers claimed that the United States quota of $2.75 billion would be withdrawn and replaced by paper currencies of questionable value. The fact that the Fund has been husbanding its dollar resources so as to perform its primary function has caused it to be criticized bitterly abroad. (In other words, those who supplied most of the money in demand feel that the Fund's resources should be used cautiously and those who want these funds feel that the Fund should be more generous.)

In managing the Fund, the administrators must distinguish between a short-run disturbance and a long-run disequilibrium in the balance-of-payments position of a country. Perhaps no one appreciates better than staff members of the Fund how their problem of maintaining liquidity of the Fund's resources has been eased by the Marshall Plan, the Mutual Security Program, and other contributions of the United States government. To date, most of the demands on the Fund have been for American dollars with which to buy American goods. These loans are in addition to the help provided by the United States government in the form of gifts, grants, and loans (likewise taken primarily in the form of American goods).

The influence of the International Monetary Fund has come primarily from the work of its staff in improving monetary practices within member countries. Although the Fund regards internal monetary stability, relaxation of exchange restrictions, simplification of multiple exchange rates, and adoption of more realistic exchange rates as basic for the proper functioning of the Fund, it has not interfered unduly with the monetary management systems of European and other countries. Gradually, more countries have come to appreciate that the Fund is trying to improve the stability of currency systems and the underlying economic conditions that make possible the functioning of an international money system. In order to aid convertibility, the Fund is encouraging greater use of the Fund's resources as a substitute for exchange control.

Currency Convertibility. Prior to the advent of the Great Depression, currency convertibility meant the right to convert currency freely into gold at a fixed rate (now lacking even in the United States). What is now meant by currency convertibility in international finance is the right to exchange money of one country for that of any other country at the prevailing rate of foreign exchange (which may be either a fixed or a floating rate in terms of any other currency).

Today convertibility is regarded as indispensable to the achievement of a multilateral trade system based on the concept of free enterprise wherein the forces of demand and supply determine prices. This concept of currency convertibility is linked to questions of tariffs and other methods of import restriction. Fortunately the United States and other nations among those having "hard" currencies have been the leaders in reducing trade restrictions. These changes make convertibility by the "soft" currency countries easier by permitting sales abroad in larger amounts to obtain gold and other international reserves.

Ironically, some of the soft currency countries have suggested that more rapid convertibility may be achieved if exchange convertibility is accompanied with restrictions on imports (the opposite of what the Fund aims to achieve by greater convertibility—to maximize world output, to check government interference in free markets, and to minimize red tape in international trade). As the matter now stands, the issue of convertibility is one that is seriously dividing the free world.

Recent Developments. Since 1953 the restrictions on foreign trade and foreign payments have been relaxed throughout the free world. This movement has taken the form of fewer quantitative restrictions on imports of goods and greater freedom in the use of currency in foreign countries. The output of goods has increased, more goods have been sold in foreign markets, and the aggregate holdings of gold and dollar reserves have increased. These increases in cash and near-cash holdings in the United States have been followed by liberalization of restrictions on buying in the United States (to date, concentrated largely on raw materials with restrictions continued on foodstuffs and manufactured goods).

There has also been some relaxation of restrictions on invisible trade or service items—remittances of interest, dividends, profits, insurance premiums, rentals, and travel allowances. Some restrictions have been eased on capital movements such as the withdrawal of funds resulting from the sale of securities held by nonresidents. Little progress has been made in the elimination of multiple exchange rates —one price for money to be spent by tourists and other prices for other uses of money acquired.

Those countries whose balance-of-payments trends have been favorable in recent years have made the most progress toward the development of multilateral trade practices, wider convertibility of currency, and freer international financial practices. Nevertheless, the movement toward multilateral trade and convertibility of currency has been much slower than anticipated.

INTERNATIONAL BANK FOR RECONSTRUCTION AND DEVELOPMENT

Primarily at the request of the American representatives at Bretton Woods, provisions were made for a world bank—the International Bank for Reconstruction and Development. Perhaps the American economists realized that there would be a greater need for long-term funds for reconstruction and development than for short-term funds to iron out disturbances in the foreign exchange markets.

The management of the International Bank for Reconstruction and Development consists of a board of governors (the same as for the International Monetary Fund), executive directors and their alternates, a president, and a vice-president. The Bank has an authorized capital of $10 billion, of which about 85 per cent has been allotted to present members ($3.175 billion to the United States). Only one fifth of the subscription has been called, and most of the loanable funds have been obtained by the sale of bonds.

The World Bank may (1) lend funds directly, (2) guarantee loans made by others, and (3) participate in loans made by others. The borrower must be the government of a member nation or a political subdivision thereof, or a private business enterprise in the territory of a member nation. When the borrower is not the member government, the loan must be guaranteed by the member government, the central bank, or some other agency acceptable to the World Bank. This means that government credit lies behind loans made or guaranteed by the Bank. In addition, the government whose credit is pledged is a member and therefore part owner and manager of the World Bank. Later, the Bank may sell the credit instruments to private bankers and thus free its resources for more lending. The initiative for investing in foreign countries may be taken by private banking firms, with the World Bank improving the investment status of the credit instruments involved by guaranteeing the credit instruments.

Funds borrowed through the Bank will affect the balance of international transactions of the nations involved. Technically, while the World Bank is the lender when dollars are borrowed, the economy of the United States is affected by the economic effects on the balance of international payments. Therefore, before dollars are lent the United States director must approve the loan.

As the title of the World Bank, "International Bank for Reconstruction and Development," suggests, its function is to help in the reconstruction of war-devastated areas and in the economic growth of underdeveloped countries. When the United States government assumed major responsibility for giving aid for reconstruction, most of the activities of the Bank were diverted to helping underdeveloped countries.

While the World Bank has abundant resources with which to work, its lending activities have been small compared to the contributions of the United States government. In 1944, it was assumed that the chief requisite for the economic growth of underdeveloped areas was capital; but, in its operations, the Bank found that "know how" (to use capital productively) was equally important. In the opinion of the Bank the development problem requires for its solution "a combination of technical and financial aid." Within recent years, both the Fund and the Bank have been helping to train senior officials as a part of their basic programs of strengthening the economies of underdeveloped nations.

The demand for loans has been chiefly for United States dollars which, if made freely, would mean an additional strain on the already fully employed productive capacity of the United States economy. Dollars, whether provided by the World Bank, the Fund, or the United States government as "gifts" or "credits" to foreigners, must be balanced by shipments of goods and services to foreign countries. This suggests the need for broadening the activities of the World Bank to include lending currencies other than dollars. Now, the financially stronger countries such as the United Kingdom, The Netherlands, and Switzerland are permitting the World Bank to raise money in their currencies for lending to borrowers throughout the world. To use this method, the Bank must have the consent of the members whose currencies are involved, and more than twenty countries have given their consent.

International Finance Corporation.   Late in 1955, the International Bank for Reconstruction and Development made provisions for a subsidiary corporation to supplement its normal lending operations. This subsidiary, the International Finance Corporation, has an authorized capital of $100,000,000; and membership therein is open to members of the Fund and the World Bank.[4] The purpose of the International Finance Corporation is to stimulate the flow of private capital into underdeveloped areas. Its resources are to be used to finance productive *private* enterprises (those of the Bank are limited to public and publicly guaranteed enterprises) in association with private lenders. The International Finance Corporation is not to undertake any private financing for which private capital can be obtained on reasonable terms, nor is it to make its resources available on bargain terms. Furthermore, the Corporation is not to own any capital stock or to assume responsibility for managing any private enterprise.

REGIONAL MONETARY ORGANIZATIONS

In conflict with the primary function of the International Monetary Fund, which has been to build up an international monetary and trade system, three regional trade areas have been formed—Russia and her satellite nations, the European Payments Union, and the sterling area. The last two are considered in this section.

European Payments Union.   The European Payments Union, established July 1, 1950, is a system of multilateral settlements under which the current transactions of sixteen member countries (or the monetary areas they represent) are paid. The central bank of each member country makes monthly reports on its net deficit or surplus on current transactions with each other member country to the Bank for International Settlements (see below). The net position of each country is computed by offsetting each country's total net surplus or deficit. If the balance is unfavorable, that amount is owed to the Union; but, if the balance is favorable, the Union owes that amount to the member country. In effect, this is identical to the daily clearings of checks and other items through local clearinghouses; but, unlike the functioning of a clearinghouse, there are no provisions

---

[4] The charter of the International Finance Corporation went into effect on July 20, 1956, with 31 members and capital subscriptions of $73,366,000. Currently, twenty other countries have indicated their intention of becoming members.

for the immediate cash settlement of balances. Instead, each country is given a "cumulative position" (a sort of overdraft credit) equal to 15 per cent of its visible and invisible trade with other members in 1949.

After the first clearing, some members had "credits" due from the Union and others had "debts" owed to the Union. No payments were to be made until a country had more credits or debits than one fifth of its quota. When the cumulative surplus of any country exceeds one fifth of its quota, half of the excess is settled in gold or dollars by a transfer from the Union to the member. If a member's cumulative deficit exceeds one fifth of its quota, the debtor has to settle in gold or dollars. As in the case of the International Monetary Fund, the Union deals only with central banks, and no changes in foreign exchange practices were made at the lower levels.

The weakness of the European Payments Union plan is that it forces the strong, prudent member countries to assume the burdens of the improvident, inflationary, and financially weak member countries. In June, 1955, EPU decided that effective August 1, 75 per cent of all balances were to be settled in gold and only 25 per cent in credit. However, quotas were doubled and so the credit facilities or total credit obligations remained the same. If general convertibility of currencies were provided for, there would be no need for the European Payments Union; but liquidating EPU may be difficult because such organizations acquire secondary functions and vested interests are created which may cause them to be continued after elimination of the need for their primary functions.

In 1955, plans were made for the future replacement of the European Payments Union in the event that one half of the member countries make their currencies convertible. The new system would be made up of two parts, one dealing with intra-European payments to be known as the Multilateral System of Settlements and the other dealing with credit facilities to be known as the European Fund.

In the Multilateral System of Settlements each member would agree (1) to stabilize its currency within certain limits, (2) to make its currency available on a temporary basis within certain mutually agreed upon limits, and (3) to settle its net debt in dollars each month. Gold, the United States dollar, or some other convertible currency unit would be used as the standard of valuation. Central banks would make currency available to one another either by the exchange of currency or as overdraft credit. A uniform rate of interest would be charged by the lender and repayment could be made in the lender's currency. The monthly settlement would be, as previously, through the Bank for International Settlements. The European Fund would take over the credit duties of the European Payments Union without provisions for automatic credits.

Sterling Area. The sterling area includes the United Kingdom, the British dominions and colonies, and other countries which have linked their currency to the English pound sterling. Generally, within the sterling area currencies are freely exchangeable. Sterling balances held by monetary authorities are also convertible into dollars under about the same restrictions as those applicable to dollar balances of the United Kingdom. This means that the United Kingdom may be called upon, as the banker for the sterling area, to pay dollars for balance-of-payments deficits of other nations in the sterling area. The $10.8 billion in sterling balances represents about 30 per cent of the gold and foreign exchange of the free world outside of the United Kingdom and the United States.

The nations in the sterling area account for about 25 per cent of total world trade; therefore, the growth of more multilateral trade as well as international convertibility of currencies over wider areas depends chiefly upon what the United Kingdom may do. To be sure, there are risks associated with international convertibility of the pound sterling which are not insurmountable; and of course, there are disadvantages to any delay in convertibility. In the United Kingdom, there is strong emotional resistance to the elimination of all exchange control practices traced to (1) the deflation of the 1920's when the gold standard was restored, (2) the success achieved by the monetary authorities in managing the nation's domestic and international financial problems, and (3) the depletion of reserves during the premature attempt to undertake convertibility in 1947.

AMERICAN FOREIGN POLICY AFTER WORLD WAR II

Following World War II, the industrial capacity of European countries was in need of repair because of destruction and obsolescence; and financial resources were needed for food, working capital, and industrial equipment. The problem was one of placing American goods and services at the disposal of European nations as was done through lend-lease arrangements during the war.

Marshall Plan. In June, 1947, General George C. Marshall, Secretary of State, urged the United States to do all in its power to assist in the return of normal economic health in the world "without which there can be no political stability and no assured peace . . ."

After suggesting the need for co-operation in drafting a plan for European recovery, he indicated that the role of the United States was to support such a program insofar as it was practical to do so. Some time after (September, 1947), the *Report of the Committee of European Economic Cooperation*, which contained a recovery plan as suggested by General Marshall, was signed in Paris. In April, 1948, the United States Congress passed the Foreign Assistance Act and created an American agency, the Economic Cooperation Administration (ECA) to administer it. The United States government provided Western Europe and certain nations of Asia and Africa with materials and financial assistance to aid them in (1) promoting industrial and agricultural production, (2) furthering the restoration and/or maintenance of "sound currencies, budgets, and finances," and (3) facilitating and stimulating the growth of international trade. Through other legislation, Congress made provisions for special aid to Turkey, Greece, and China. Another part of the Marshall Plan was designed to finance technical assistance and to exchange "know-how" so as to improve industrial production.

Mutual Security Program. The Mutual Security Program was established in October, 1951, to continue the Marshall Plan and technical-assistance programs with emphasis on mutual security. In authorizing the use of United States government funds, Congress is providing military, economic, and technical assistance to strengthen the free world. The scope of the activities of the Mutual Security Agency (its forerunner was the Mutual Security Organization which replaced ECA) is broader than those of preceding agencies in that it includes not only military and economic aid but also health programs, educational missions, and other projects of broad social significance.

BANK FOR INTERNATIONAL SETTLEMENTS

The Bank for International Settlements completed its twenty-fifth year of operations in 1955, having been established on May 20, 1930, in Basle, Switzerland. The Bank for International Settlements (BIS) is a "bank for central banks" organized to promote co-operation among central banks and to provide trust and agency services in regard to international financial settlements entrusted to it under agreements with parties concerned. (Under this provision, BIS is doing certain work in connection with the European Payments Union and the European Coal and Steel Community.)

One objective in the original plan for BIS was to bring together the presidents or governors of the central banks of the seven leading countries responsible for financing and organizing the Bank (Belgium, France, Germany, Italy, Japan, the United Kingdom, and the United States). Each of the seven countries was allotted an equal amount of the Bank's stock which the central banks could purchase or sell to others. The capital was guaranteed by the original subscribers—the five European central banks and two private banking groups acting in the place of the central banks in Japan and the United States (J. P. Morgan and Company, the First National Bank of New York, and the First National Bank of Chicago). Other central banks were given the privilege of subscribing, but few did so because of the chaotic international conditions during the early 1930's. The charter of BIS was revised in 1950 and subsequently all European central banks, except the Bank of Spain and the State Bank of USSR, have purchased stock. The shares held by the Japanese banking group were repurchased by the central banks that were founder members, most of whom retained their stock. All of the American-held stock was sold in the United States market and most of it has been resold to Europeans. The rights to representation and to vote are not linked to ownership and so the status of BIS as a central bank for central banks is assured (about three fourths of the outstanding stock is owned by central banks).

Compared to the World Bank and the Fund, the authorized capital of the Bank for International Settlements is small, 500,000,000 Swiss gold francs of which about one fourth has been paid in (equal to 41,000,000 current United States gold dollars). As indicative of the American international policy at that time, the Federal Reserve Bank of New York was not permitted to participate officially in this plan for international co-operation; and the United States has never taken the seats on the board of directors that the original sales of shares in the United States permits. However, the Federal Reserve Bank of New York acts as the correspondent bank for BIS in the United States. The Bank for International Settlements is managed by a board of directors composed of the presidents or governors of the five founding European central banks, a second director appointed by each, and three elected directors from among the presidents or governors of other central banks (at present, The Netherlands, Sweden, Switzerland, and their nominees).

The powers of the Bank for International Settlements are less restrictive than are those of the Fund or the World Bank. They include the rights to (1) buy and sell goods and gold bullion, bills of exchange, Treasury bills, and other securities for its own account or for the account of central banks; (2) make secured advances to or borrow from central banks; (3) act as depository and correspondent for central banks and arrange for the latter to act in similar capacities for it; (4) carry on credit operations for banks and others, in any market, provided that the central bank in the country where the money market is located does not object; and (5) enter into special agreements with central banks to facilitate the settlement of international transactions among them. However, the Bank for International Settlements may not (1) issue notes payable at sight to bearer, (2) "accept" bills of exchange, or (3) make advances to governments.

The Bank for International Settlements acted as trustee and reparation agent in the collection of German reparations until these payments were ended by the Hoover International Debt Moratorium (June 20, 1931). During the spring and summer of 1931 the Bank made loans and organized lending syndicates to meet the international crisis of that period; but, when England left the gold standard in September, 1931, the Bank ceased making international loans to keep currencies tied to gold. During the trying months of the international economic crisis, the Bank was a rallying place for the officials of the central banks of the world and served as "a common center of contact, counsel, and collaboration." During World War II, the Bank's activities were almost suspended and its place in the postwar world was in doubt; and, in its final declaration, the Bretton Woods Conference recommended that BIS be liquidated. After World War II, BIS worked on troublesome postwar problems and soon found a place for itself, chiefly as a central bank for European central banks. The Bank has continued to work for stable exchanges and for better international monetary, credit, and trade conditions. Its annual report has come to be one of the most important documents of its kind, eagerly awaited by government officials, bankers, economists, and others.

EXPORT-IMPORT BANK OF WASHINGTON

One of the most profitable of federal government agencies is the Export-Import Bank of Washington. Its capital stock is held by the Treasury; and in addition, it may borrow from the Treasury. The Export-Import Bank is authorized to make loans and guarantees to facilitate the export and import trade of the United States. In the light of current conditions, it is interesting to note that the original Export-Import Bank was created (1934) to finance trade with Russia. In carrying out its functions the Bank is directed by Congress to supplement and encourage private capital (and not to compete with it) and to make loans for specific purposes that offer reasonable assurance of repayment.

The Export-Import Bank is prepared to aid in financing both imports and exports of products and the purchase of engineering and other technical services in the United States. Most of its experience has been with the financing of exports, for which it offers: (1) credits for the benefit of individual exporters in the United States; and (2) a line of credit to a foreign government, foreign bank, or foreign firm to facilitate the purchase of specific goods (material and equipment) and services in the United States.

The Export-Import Bank is managed by a board of directors of which the Secretary of State, or someone appointed by him, is the chairman. The National Advisory Council on International Monetary and Financial Problems acts as an advisory council for the Export-Import Bank. This council (NAC) co-ordinates all foreign government lending; but loans made by the Export-Import Bank must "offer reasonable assurance of repayment," which may or may not mean its lending is political in nature.

SUMMARY

The main event that caused the various international financial organizations to be created was the Great Depression which lead to the abandonment of the gold standard, currency depreciation, economic restrictions on world trade, instability in foreign exchange, and a sharp reduction in foreign trade. On the national front, stabilization funds were created to stabilize the foreign value of domestic currencies; and, on the international front, the Tripartite Agreement was signed. The latter went into an eclipse with the onset of World War II. In 1944, the Bretton Woods twins—the International Monetary Fund and the International Bank for Reconstruction and Development—were born. The purposes of the Fund are to promote international monetary co-operation, to aid international trade, to promote exchange stability, to eliminate foreign exchange restrictions by establishing a multilateral system of payments, to provide members with resources to correct temporary maladjustments in their balances of payments, and to correct the disequilibrium in the international balance of payments.

As the title of the World Bank, "International Bank for Reconstruction and Development," suggests, its function is to help in the reconstruction of war-devastated areas and in the economic growth of underdeveloped countries by making long-term funds available. However, it was soon found that the ability to use capital productively was lacking in many cases; and the Bank (together with agencies of the United States government) has been supplying "know how" along with financial aid. Although the World Bank has abundant resources, its lending activities have been small compared to the contributions of the United States government as "gifts" or "credits" to foreign countries.

Recently, the World Bank organized a subsidiary corporation to supplement its normal lending operations. The purpose of this subsidiary, the International Finance Corporation, is to stimulate the flow of private capital into underdeveloped areas, and its resources are to be used to finance productive private enterprises in association with private lenders, as distinguished from those of the Bank which are used for public or publicly-guaranteed enterprises.

Three regional organizations have developed: (1) Russia and her satellite nations, (2) the European Payments Union, and (3) the sterling area. The European Payments Union is a system of multilateral settlements under which current transactions of sixteen member countries are settled, thereby encouraging international trade. The sterling area organization includes those countries which have linked their currencies to the English pound sterling. Within the area, currencies are freely exchangeable, and sterling balances held by monetary authorities are also convertible into dollars under about the same restrictions as those applicable to dollar balances of the United Kingdom.

The United States, through various agencies, has given military and economic aid to many countries. Among the most important plans under which more than $50 billion has been given away are Lend Lease, United Nations Relief and Rehabilitation Administration, Marshall Plan, and Mutual Security Program.

The Bank for International Settlements was established in 1930 as a bank for central banks, and now it is functioning as a central bank for European central banks. BIS has continued through the years to work for stable exchanges and for better international monetary credit and trade conditions. As its title suggests, the Export-Import Bank of Washington is authorized to make loans and guarantes to facilitate the export and import trade of the United States.

Since United States public funds are involved in the functioning of several of these international organizations, the National Advisory

Council on International Monetary and Financial Problems was created in order to co-ordinate the policies of the representatives of the United States in the Fund and the World Bank with the agencies of the United States government in lending and other matters. Since most of the funds used by the Fund and the World Bank are provided by the United States, the need for co-ordinating policies is fully appreciated (except perhaps by some foreign countries). It must be remembered that when dollars are borrowed they are ordinarily spent in the United States; and, in terms of the balance of payments, this means that the United States is providing goods and services.

QUESTIONS AND PROBLEMS

1. What are the purposes of the International Monetary Fund?
2. "The Fund may be compared to a pool of dollars, pounds, francs, etc. . . ." Explain.
3. What is meant by "borrowing" from the Fund? What provisions in the Articles of Agreement would tend to limit indebtedness of each member?
4. Compare the Fund and the World Bank as to organization and management.
5. How do the functions of the International Bank for Reconstruction and Development differ from those of the International Finance Corporation?
6. Explain the justification for the provision that necessitates the prior approval of a country's representative on the Board of Governors whose currency is being borrowed from the International Monetary Fund? From the World Bank? What United States group advises the American representative when dollars are requested?
7. Describe the Bank for International Settlements. How do its current activities compare to those anticipated in 1930? What role has the United States played in the development of the Bank for International Settlements?
8. What are the functions of the Export-Import Bank? How does it duplicate the work of the World Bank? Explain.
9. Identify the European Payments Union. If provisions are made for convertibility of the currencies of member nations, how will it operate in the future?
10. What is the sterling area? Why is it important? To what extent may Great Britain hold the key to more rapid currency convertibility in the free world?
11. "What is often described in financial terms as 'dollar shortage' is in reality a symptom of the present inadequacy of production in many parts of the World in relation to the continuing great need for goods resulting from the War." (International Monetary Fund, *An-*

nual Report of the Executive Director for the Fiscal Year Ended April 3o, 1948 [Washington, D.C., 1948], p. 9.) To what extent has the United States aided in the solution of this problem? Was President Eisenhower justified in requesting the placement of foreign aid on a long-term basis?

12. "A brief glimpse of a . . . conflict over the future pattern of international trade . . . was revealed in the resumed discussion of the International Monetary Fund's annual report . . . [when the French Governor urged] expansion of regional trading facilities such as the European Payments Union and greater Fund support for their activities." ("World Fund Lifts Veil on Trade War," *New York Times*, September 10, 1952, p. 7.) Does this suggest that regional trade unions may be trying to solve their payment problems by creating trading areas closed to the dollar area? Are payment problems regional or world-wide?

Chapter XXVII | CAPITAL MARKETS AND INVESTMENT BANKING

SAVINGS are the amount of income or earnings not spent for consumers' goods and services during a given period of time. Although individual savings may be hoarded, there are many types of savings institutions which provide a safe outlet for such funds. Therefore, hoarding is uncommon in the United States, except during times when there is a loss of confidence in financial institutions. In a high savings economy, it is important to have savings and investing institutions in order to assure the flow of savings into investments.

Capital funds are necessary to the establishment, maintenance, and growth of modern industry. Capital funds are customarily referred to as (1) short-term or working capital, and (2) long-term or fixed capital. When short-term assets are needed, the enterprise seeks working capital in the money market; and when long-term assets are needed, the enterprise seeks long-term or investment capital in the capital market.

THE CAPITAL MARKET

One of the most significant characteristics of the capital market is the degree to which it is dominated, on the supply side, by institutions. Most of the savings of individuals flow indirectly into the capital market through the medium of life insurance companies, commercial banks' time and savings departments, mutual savings banks, savings and loan associations, investment companies, trust companies and trust departments of commercial banks, public and private pension funds, fire and casualty insurance companies, foreign monetary authorities, philanthropic foundations, and educational institutions. Decisions pertaining to investments are transferred thereby from the individual savers to institutions.

During World War II the capital market was dominated on the demand side by defense and war needs of the federal government. The latter did not depend exclusively on institutions for funds but raised more than $50 billion by sales of savings bonds directly to individual investors. However, by the end of the war, government securities represented the most important investments of savings and similar financial institutions. But most significant of all was the increase in commercial banks' holdings of government securities.

Since World War II, private institutions have been dominant in the demand for new loanable funds (savings and bank credit). The capital needs of corporations have been met, in part, by retained earnings and, in part, by funds raised in the capital market. Because interest payments may be deducted before computing the corporate income-tax base and dividend payments may not, debt obligations (bonds, debentures, and notes) are the preferred instruments of corporate financing. Since World War II, noncorporate debts have also increased sharply, particularly real estate mortgage debts. For the most part, investments of savings institutions are limited to debt obligations; and, since these institutions dominate the capital market, perhaps it is fortunate that the federal government tax structure encourages the use of these instruments of long-term financing. But, is it sound financing?

The investment activities of savings and other financial institutions are determined primarily by their functions, the laws under which they operate, and the resources at their disposal. All are confronted by the need for earnings, safety of principal, and liquidity. Life insurance companies have been most active among the various institutional investors, other than commercial banks, in meeting the postwar private demands for long-term funds. This is due in part to: (1) the more liberal laws under which they operate; (2) the fact that their contracts (insurance policies) are for longer periods of time than are those of other institutions, which permits them to stress long-term investments; (3) the semicompulsory nature of their savings contracts which assure them a steady stream of funds (savings); and (4) the rapid growth in life insurance and retirement or pension plans. As a result, they are in a position to meet cash needs from current collections (premium payments).

INVESTMENT BANKING AND SECURITIES MARKETS

Definition of Investment Banking. Sometimes the term "investment banking" is used to include all financing activities that pertain to the raising and lending of long-term credit. Used this broadly, all of the financing institutions that provide long-term or investment funds would be classified as "investment banks." However, there are differences among financing institutions other than the type of credit which they provide. For illustration, accepting demand deposits and making loans to the general public have been recognized as the functions that distinguish commercial banks from other types of financial institutions. Mortgage bankers sell their promises to pay and use these funds along with their own capital to make loans secured by mortgage liens on real property. Savings banks accept time deposits from the general public and invest them in real estate mortgages, bonds, and other credit instruments.

The economic function of investment houses is to provide long-term or fixed-capital funds for business and governmental enterprises. They do this by gathering "other people's money" (savings) through the sale of stocks, bonds, notes, and other instruments. On one side of the capital market are the borrowers (governments, public utility companies, railroad and industrial companies); and on the other side are those that have funds to invest (individuals, insurance companies, and other financial institutions including commercial banks). It is the task of the investment banker to service both the borrowers and the lenders. It is the purchase of securities from issuers and their resale to investors, the underwriting and distribution functions, that distinguish investment banking from other types of banking.

In addition to purchasing issues of new bonds and stocks outright and selling them publicly or privately, investment bankers also aid corporations in selling securities to insurance companies and institutional investors, advise business firms about recapitalization, act as agents in negotiating mergers and acquisitions of corporations, purchase large blocks of securities outright from estates and investing institutions and arrange for their resale, and maintain trading departments.

Commercial Banks as Underwriters. Since 1929, there have been several fundamental changes in the capital market. The Banking Act of 1933, as amended, forced commercial banks to withdraw from the business of dealing in securities ("one who as a merchant buys securities and sells them to customers with a view to the gains and profits that may be derived therefrom"), except domestic government issues and those of the International Bank for Reconstruction and Development. In addition, commercial banks were required to dispose of their interests in investment houses or companies that carried on a general investment banking business.

In 1930, commercial banks' investment affiliates retailed over one half of all new securities distributed; and it seemed that they were destined to dominate the security business in the same way that foreign exchange departments of commercial banks had come to dominate the foreign exchange markets. During the 1930–33 depression the dangers of the commercial investment banking tie became apparent. The loss of reputation of investment bankers in general not only hurt the investment affiliate companies but also threatened the lives of the parent commercial banks. The failure of the large Bank of the United States in 1931 was traced directly to its investment affiliate situation.

The Banking Act of 1933 gave member banks one year in which to dispose of their investment affiliates.[1] Since restrictions were to be placed on the investment-banking activities of commercial banks, their spokesmen asked Congress to place restrictions upon the deposit-banking business of investment-banking houses, which seemed reasonable enough. So, the Banking Act of 1933 contains provisions which forced the investment houses either to qualify as commercial banks and give up underwriting of securities or to give up their deposit-banking business.

When J. P. Morgan & Co. gave up its investment-banking business in order to keep its deposit-banking business, the world's foremost investment banker withdrew from the investment field. Morgan, Stanley & Co. was formed in 1935 by some of the former partners of J. P. Morgan & Co. and the grandson of J. P. Morgan. The firm was incorporated, and it assumed most of the investment business formerly held by the elder Morgan's firm. Upon the liquidation of the National City Company, an affiliate of the National City Bank of New York, the world's leading distributor disappeared. Now commercial banks are active participants in purchasing agreements involving government securities or government guaranteed securities and also take orders to buy and sell stocks and bonds for their customers as agents. Investment bankers are permitted to perform all their former functions except that of accepting deposits.

Investment Houses. The term "investment house" is not well defined, and one hears it applied to the small bond dealer as well as

[1] Section 20 of the Banking Act of June 16, 1933 (48 Stat. 188) as amended reads in part as follows: "After one year from the date of the enactment of this Act, no member bank shall be affiliated in any manner . . . with any corporation, association, business, trust, or similar organization engaged principally in the issue, flotation, underwriting, public sale, or distribution at wholesale or retail or through syndicate participation of stocks, bonds, debentures, notes, or other securities. . . ."

to the large underwriting and distributing houses having branch offices and representatives covering the United States. Although the main offices of investment firms or houses are concentrated in or near Wall Street (New York) and La Salle Street (Chicago), the market for securities is nation-wide in scope.

The risks assumed by investment houses are similar to those assumed by merchants generally, chiefly loss in value of inventories. Usually, investment houses purchase securities outright from issuers, but they may act as agents or as underwriters of an issue to be sold by the issuer. The average unit transaction is large, and the margin of profit is small.

The investment banker may have a "market" clause in contracts for purchase of stocks or bonds which may be used if the market turns unfavorable. The market for securities is extremely sensitive to adverse news—political, economic, and/or psychological. Relative to the dollar value of securities handled, the amount of capital of investment houses is small. Investment houses depend heavily on borrowed funds obtained from commercial banks, and their combined capital accounts probably amount to no more than $500,000,000. This fact explains why they spread the risk among a large number of houses by forming temporary partnerships (called "syndicates") to handle each large issue. For this reason, it is said that investment houses are "gregarious."

In the investment-banking process the position of the investment house as owner of securities and as a source of capital funds is temporary. While the investment house may "get out from under" a financing project, this is not true of the general investor. Someone must assume the risks of the venture, and this risk ultimately falls upon the investor.

From 1929 to 1933, capital values shrank approximately 50 per cent; and, although both creditors and equity holders were involved, the burden fell most heavily on the latter. Most of these losses were due to the decline in general prices and the business depression, but investment bankers received much of the blame. Part of this criticism was justified because investors were not provided with adequate information about the risks they were assuming. This situation explains why Congress passed "the truth in advertising act" (Securities Act of 1933). The justification for the existence of the investment banker, like that of any specialist, is that he can do certain things better than others can do them. By knowing investment conditions better and by having contacts with prospective investors, the investment banker is able to raise capital funds more successfully for governments and business corporations.

FUNCTIONS OF INVESTMENT BANKERS

The general function of investment bankers is to merchandise securities, which includes investigating, underwriting, and distributing. The investigation of the applicant for credit is the first task of the investment banker. Although he seldom buys the securities to hold as an investment, he wants to make a profit and, at the same time, to establish a reputation for sound merchandising. He realizes that the maxim "a commodity which is well bought is half sold" applies equally as well to security selling as to any other type of merchandising. In order to remain in business, the investment banker must have satisfied clients who will buy the bank's new offerings.

Investigation. In order to determine the investment quality of a proposed issue, the investment banker makes a thorough analysis of the credit worthiness of the applicant with emphasis on both short-term and long-term factors. With the aid of accountants, business analysts, economists, and lawyers, the investment banker checks the prospective issuer as to the following: (1) earnings and earning prospects, (2) condition and efficiency of equipment and plant, (3) anticipated uses of new funds, (4) capital structure, (5) corporate powers, and (6) financial statements. The investment banker must then estimate the reaction of the market to the proposed issue and determine how the terms can be drawn so as to make the issue command the best price (in case of bonds, the interest rate, maturity, call features, conversion features, timing of offering, price to the investment banker, and price to the public).

The cost of investigation is considerable, therefore the investment banker customarily obtains an option to underwrite the issue before making more than the briefest type of investigation. The amount of work necessary declines as the investment quality of the issue increases. Consequently, little investigation is done for securities to be offered by governments and for other securities of such standard quality as to be sold to the highest bidder. In the latter case, the analysts estimate the market price of similar securities so as to arrive at a bid price (submitted in writing just before the closing hour) for the new issue.

Underwriting. In investment banking the word "underwriting" is used to describe: (1) transactions wherein investment houses purchase an issue outright from the issuers, and (2) transactions wherein investment houses guarantee the sale of an issue by agreeing to buy it if others fail to do so. If a group of investment houses purchases a $10,000,000 issue and pays for it on a specific day, it merely purchases the issue; but it is called an "underwriting operation." The terms "purchasing syndicate" and "underwriting syndicate" are often used interchangeably, and both terms customarily appear on the prospectus issued by the group. The second type of transaction is usually referred to by investment bankers as "stand-by underwriting." It appears when investment houses agree to purchase an issue of stock or convertible bonds of a well-established corporation if stockholders of the corporation fail to do so.

One or two investment houses may agree to purchase an issue but, usually, many investment houses participate, with the number varying with the size of the issue, the resources of the investment houses, the risk-nature of the issue, and conditions of the market. Usually, each syndicate member agrees to buy a fixed amount of the issue, thus assuring a broad market for the securities. Sometimes the size of the public offering is such as to justify the use of hundreds of investment houses in the distribution process. For illustration, when the common stock of the Ford Motor Company was sold to the public in 1956 seven syndicate managers and 2,000 other members of the underwriting syndicate shared in selling more than 10,000,000 shares to the public.

A typical originating house will have several issues in different stages of processing, the ideal situation being one in which there will be a steady stream of issues from the issuers through investment-banking channels into the hands of investors. The originating house is usually the syndicate manager, handling the details and signing the purchase contract with the issuer, thus binding the members of the syndicate. The responsibilities, rights, and privileges of each member of the purchasing syndicate are covered in the syndicate agreement.

If a corporation is to sell bonds or long-term notes of more than $1,000,000 publicly in interstate commerce, it must select a trust company or bank which meets the standards (disinterested and qualified) set for trustees by Congress in the Trust Indenture Act of 1939. The trustee holds the contract that is drawn to show the rights and privileges of bondholders and the responsibilities of the issuing corporation, and it is the function of the trustee to see that the debtor performs its duties and meets its obligations. The proposed issue must be registered with the Securities and Exchange Commission in accordance with the requirements of the Securities Act of 1933, which provides for many exceptions (such as obligations of the national, state, and local governments, railroad securities, and those which are to be sold privately).

Distribution. Issues are purchased by investment houses for resale, and the syndicate agreement may provide that the entire issue is to be prorated among the members of the purchasing syndicate. This is the usual practice in handling issues of states and political subdivisions (called "municipal issues") and the highest quality issues in the corporate field (such as equipment trust obligations of railroads and bonds and notes of communications companies and others in the public utility field). In handling some corporate issues, other investment houses in addition to the members of the purchasing syndicate may be invited to participate as brokers in the distribution of the securities in order to get more selling pressure behind the issue.

In recent years, considerable use has been made of the "best effort" method of distributing new issues. When this method is used, the investment bankers do not buy the issue but agree to do their best to sell the securities to investors. The investment bankers may sign (1) a group agreement, which may be as detailed as the syndicate agreement signed by members of a purchasing or underwriting syndicate, and (2) a selling agreement between the investment bankers and the issuer. If securities are unsold, the investment bankers are under no obligation to the issuer; and the issuer benefits only to the extent that his selling costs are reduced through the services of investment bankers.

When an issue of common stock or of securities convertible into common stock of an established company is to be sold, the new securities are customarily offered to old stockholders; but, in many cases, investment bankers agree to purchase the unsold portion at a stipulated price. In return, they receive a small fee for the risks they assume even though the entire issue may be sold by the issuer to old stockholders (see below).

METHODS OF SELLING NEW ISSUES

When a government or private corporation wishes to raise funds by the sale of new securities, it may (1) sell the bonds, notes, or shares to investors with or without the assistance of investment bankers; (2) sell the issue to a few large investors, who hold the securities and do not offer them for resale (called private placement);

(3) invite bids and sell the issue to the highest bidder (competitive bidding); (4) sell the issue after negotiation to investment bankers, or (5) arrange to sell the bonds or shares through investment bankers on a "best effort basis." Normally, the offering is made under the plan most advantageous to the issuer; but, in some cases, the issuer has no choice because of state laws, regulations of the Interstate Commerce Commission, regulations of the Securities and Exchange Commission, and/or the common law pre-emptive right of old common shareholders to buy new common stock or other investment instruments (preferred stock, bonds, notes, etc.) convertible into common stock.

Direct Sale of Securities by Issuers to Investors. When small firms are raising funds to start a business or to enlarge an existing one, they often sell securities directly to investors. Usually, the issues are too small to warrant the assistance of investment houses, which are more interested in handling the issues of large and well-established borrowers. This is true because the costs of investigating and selling are large and the profit margins are small. During the 1920's, it was a common practice for investment bankers to sell speculative securities to wealthy individuals whose names appeared on the investment bankers' "preferred customer" list. In many cases, large profits were made by those who sold their securities before the stock market collapse late in 1929, but most of those who held their securities suffered large losses.

During the 1920's, some public-utility companies experimented with customer-ownership plans, which meant that they sold their securities (stocks and bonds) to the users of their services. Other companies experimented with employee-ownership plans wherein their securities were sold to employees. Because of the heavy losses taken by investors from 1929 to 1933, little use was made of either customer-ownership or employee-ownership plans of raising new capital until after World War II. Now, many large companies offer shares of stock to employees under various retirement, pension, or personnel plans, but raising new capital is not the primary motive. At the present time, one of the attractive features associated with working for many large corporations is the fact that their officers and employees are given the opportunity to acquire stock under option, employee-ownership, bonus, and other plans.

When an established company offers new shares of stock (or bonds that may be converted into common stock), the current procedure is for the company to make the offering directly to the old stockholders. The reason for this practice is to protect the board of directors from legal action that otherwise might follow if the old stockholders can prove losses as a result of the dilution of their equity in the company. Therefore, old stockholders are given "rights" to buy the new stock (or bonds convertible into stock), which they may use, sell, or permit to lapse. The world's largest private business corporation—the American Telephone and Telegraph Company—has financed most of its post-World War II capital needs by selling debentures, convertible into common stock to its stockholders.[2]

The largest borrower of all, the United States Treasury, with the assistance of the Federal Reserve banks offers its own securities to investors. While the history of the United States provides many illustrations of the dependence of the Treasury on investment bankers, this dependence no longer exists. After United States government securities are distributed through the Federal Reserve banks, the chief reliance for making a market for them is placed on bond dealers, commercial banks, business corporations, insurance companies, and other institutional investors.

Private Placement of Issues. Sometimes issuers of new securities sell the issues to one or a few large investors and thereby avoid not only the costs entailed in public distribution but also registration with the Securities and Exchange Commission (when securities would have been subject to registration if offered to the general public). Theoretically, both issuers and investors should profit from the direct placement of issues, the former from a higher net price and the latter from a lower purchase price (that is, a wholesale rather than a retail price). However, comparing yields on privately placed securities to those sold publicly indicates that the borrower pays more when he borrows privately than when he borrows publicly. As compared to issues sold publicly, privately placed securities usually have longer maturities and their call prices and other secondary terms are usually less favorable to the investor. These factors help to explain their higher interest rates.

Factors in the higher price (lower interest rate) at which publicly offered issues are sold are traced in part to the value of special services of investment bankers who are more objective in

[2] Stockholders of record September 14, 1956, were offered one share of American Telephone and Telegraph Company common stock for each ten shares held at a price of $100 per share (total of $580,000,000 for 5,800,000 new shares of common stock). This was the second largest issue ever registered with the Securities and Exchange Commission. The largest issue was 10,200,000 shares of Ford Motor Company stock sold for $657,000,000 in 1955; and the third largest was 4,380,000 shares of General Motors Corporation common stock that raised $438,000,000 in 1955.

appraising the credit status of the borrower and are able to time and shape offerings so as to command the best market price. Nevertheless, issuers are often willing to forego a more favorable price for their securities in order to (1) obtain funds sooner by private placement, (2) avoid the costs of registration, and (3) evade the publicity associated with public offerings.

Competitive Bidding. Where the credit risks are small and the securities involved are of standard quality requiring little credit investigation, the issue may be sold to the highest bidder. Syndicates— investment houses in association and informal agreement with each other—submit sealed bids to be opened at a previously arranged day and hour. In general, this method of selling is required by state laws for issues of state and local governments, and, in some states, for issues of public utility companies.

For many years the Interstate Commerce Commission has required that equipment trust certificates and certain issues of railroad companies be sold to the highest bidder. Since 1941 the Securities and Exchange Commission has required the issues of registered public-utility holding companies and their subsidiaries to be disposed of in this way (with the Commission granting exemptions in cases where unusual circumstances are present). The growing practice of issuer-disposal of securities by competitive bidding has had far-reaching effects on the investment houses in the market, tending to weaken the position of the older houses (which have had banker-borrower relationships with large corporations for many years) and to strengthen that of the newer ones.

Negotiation with Investment Houses. The oldest method of placement is by negotiation between the investment banker and the issuer. At one time, this was about the only method of placing issues, including those of the federal government, state and local governments, and private corporations. Today, it is customary for issuers to request investment houses that have handled their underwriting in the past to handle their new financing (unless competitive bidding is required by state laws or by regulations of federal agencies). While an investment house usually finds new customers (issuers) through promoters, finders, and their own officials and agents, some borrowers bring their needs directly to the attention of the investment house. The volume of financing for new customers is relatively small compared to that for old customers.

Formerly, it was customary for commercial banks to suggest that borrowers refinance their loans of a nonseasonal nature through investment houses; now, commercial banks are financing more of their customers' fixed-capital needs by using "term" loans and by having several banks and insurance companies participate in large loans. These changes mean that the customers of commercial banks have become less dependent on investment houses for fixed capital.

Best Effort Basis. In some cases, investment bankers will agree to handle a new security issue on a best effort basis. This means that the investment bankers are acting as agents for the issuer who retains all of the risks associated with the inability of the investment bankers to sell the securities. In some cases, the "best effort basis" of handling an issue will be combined with a purchasing agreement covering a given number of bonds, notes, or shares and the sale of the remainder of the issue on a best effort basis.

LIFE INSURANCE COMPANIES

Life insurance companies issue many kinds of policies (contracts) in which they agree to make certain cash payments—lump sum or installments—to the beneficiaries in the event of death, on reaching a certain age, in case of disability, or for other reasons. There are about 1,060 life insurance companies in the United States with combined assets of about $90.4 billion. Customarily, the insured make payments periodically as prescribed in the contract; and these payments or premiums are usually arranged so that the same amount is paid annually.

Insurance seeks to protect the individual by spreading the economic risk, and insurance companies amass large funds for this purpose. While the savings function of insurance companies is secondary, they hold the largest pool of savings among the private noncommercial-banking institutions in the United States. Life insurance companies assets are growing, and their cash collections are greatly in excess of current payments because of two important factors: the increase in volume of insurance and the improvement in health together with increased life expectancy. Therefore, the liquidity need of life insurance companies is small, and they may invest in long-term securities with yields as high as obtainable within reasonable limits as to safety. To be sure, some of their assets must be in cash and short-term securities in order to meet legal requirements and short-term demands for funds, but their emphasis is on keeping funds fully invested in long-term obligations or other assets. At the present time the amount of total life insurance contracts is at a record of more than $372 billion.

Life insurance companies operate under state charters and are regulated by insurance commissioners of the respective states in which they do business. In general, state laws restrict life insurance companies' investments to debts obligations—high-grade bonds and real estate mortgages. Some state laws permit the purchase of a limited amount of stocks and the placement of from 10 to 20 per cent of their funds in rental housing projects and certain types of commercial and industrial property.

While insurance companies are buying securities offered by investment houses at retail prices, they are also competing with them in the wholesale market. In some cases, they are the highest bidders for issues sold by this method (to the highest competitive bidder). They may also act as members of purchasing syndicates; and, in many cases, they negotiate successfully with issuers (borrowers). The competitive position of insurance companies for issues has been strengthened by (1) the rapid growth of their assets; (2) the increase in "competitive bidding" for issues; and (3) the Securities Act of 1933, which has encouraged private placement of securities by exempting such securities from registration.

During World War II, life insurance companies purchased United States government securities in quantities greatly in excess of their secondary reserve needs because they were the only investments available in large volume; but, since that time, they have shifted their investments more fully to real estate mortgages and securities of business and industry. At the end of 1955, the assets of United States life insurance companies ($90.4 billion) were invested as follows: (1) securities of business and industry, 43.9 per cent; (2) mortgages, 32.6 per cent; (3) United States government securities, 9.5 per cent; (4) other government bonds, 3.4 per cent; (5) policy loans, 3.6 per cent; (6) real estate, 2.9 per cent; and (7) miscellaneous assets, 4.1 per cent.

The yield advantage of corporate securities over government securities is considerable, but corporate securities are less marketable and entail higher administrative costs and greater risks. However, the yield advantage seemingly outweighs the disadvantages of holding corporate securities; and, at the end of 1955, life insurance companies' investments in the securities of business and industry totalled between $39 billion and $40 billion, of which almost $4 billion was invested in railroad bonds, almost $14 billion in public utility bonds, over $18 billion in industrial and miscellaneous bonds, and $3.6 billion in stocks.

Life insurance companies are among the chief lenders in the real estate mortgage market; but, in this market, they must compete more actively with commercial banks, mutual savings banks, and savings and loan associations than in the market for industrial securities. At the end of 1955, life insurance companies' investments in mortgages amounted to over $29.4 billion. The cost of mortgage lending is high (varying with the length of time mortgages remain outstanding because origination costs must be amortized over this period), including service fees paid to correspondents, agents or mortgage companies, office expenses, and other variables; and, for noninsured and nonguaranteed mortgages, the risks of default are great. Higher overhead costs and salaries paid to personnel have tended to reduce the net yield differential between mortgage loans and investments in industrial securities.

INVESTMENT COMPANIES

Investors in the capital market include, in addition to those already considered (Federal Reserve banks, commercial banks, business corporations, and life insurance companies), trust institutions (see Chapter XXVIII), savings banks and savings and loan associations (see Chapter XXIX), banks and credit agencies operating in the farm credit field (see Chapter XXX), credit unions and other specialists in the consumer financing field (see Chapter XXXI), nonprofit organizations (such as nonprofit private schools and hospitals, charitable and welfare organizations, labor unions, and social and athletic clubs), and financial institutions not otherwise classified. Among the last are investment companies.

Investment companies are financial institutions which raise funds in the capital market mainly by the sale of shares (stock or trust certificates) to individual investors and invest the funds thus raised chiefly in marketable corporate securities. They are agencies through which funds of participating investors are combined and invested in diversified securities so as to prevent loss of principal (the law of averages which assumes gains on some securities will offset losses on others).

In the general management type of investment company, expert management is offered; and, in the fixed trust type of company, management is of the routine type with expertness limited to selection of original securities. Between these two types of companies are other types which have features of both the general management and fixed trust companies. In all cases, the objective is to provide individual investors with safe and profitable employment of funds and to relieve investors of the burden of direct responsibility of management of their savings.

The various type of investment companies or trusts may be classified as follows: (1) the unit or fixed or semifixed type of trust; (2) "face amount" companies; (3) general management, closed-end companies; and (4) general management, open-end companies.

1. The unit type of trust is organized for a definite period of time (20 to 25 years) under terms of a trust indenture, a contract of custodianship or agency or similar legal instrument. The promoters select the securities, a bank or trust company acts as trustee (see Chapter XXVIII), and the investors (certificate holders) are the beneficial owners of the property left in trust. Funds are invested at the beginning of the trust period and management (trustees) may be given little or no power of substitution of new investments for the original ones. (In some cases, management may be provided with a supplementary list of securities in which it may reinvest.) A modification of the unit trust is the periodic payment plan wherein investors make payments for certificates to the trustee bank in installments over a period of 10 to 15 years. Generally, these payments are made in relatively small amounts which means that costs (sales, loading charges and others) are high.

2. A few large investment companies are classified as "face-amount" companies. These companies sell face-value certificates on the installment plan whereby they are committed to pay the holders either a stated sum on a specified future date or to pay a cash-surrender-value prior to maturity provided the holders meet all the terms of the contract. In effect, the investment certificates are unsecured promises to pay. (During the first years, when the investors' equity in the plan is small, lapses on payments tend to be high.)

3. Most important among the trusts are the management type of investment companies, of which the oldest are the closed-end type. The closed-end type of company usually has a fixed amount of capital, and its shares are usually listed on a stock exchange. In addition to the diversification of risk represented by their portfolios, the officers are expected to provide skilled management in purchasing and selling securities. Like many other corporations, they finance in part with bonds and notes as well as with stock. This means that the element of leverage is present.

4. The open-end general management trust company is similar to the closed-end company, except that new shares may be sold at

any time. Generally, they issue a single class of shares and are called "mutual" companies. The shares are purchased at market value plus a "loading" charge, and they are redeemable at market value minus a "loading" charge. Market values are calculated twice daily, and the initial selling costs average 7 per cent. Today, they are the most popular of all management companies. Some are organized as corporations and others as common law trusts (often called "Massachusetts Trusts").

The Investment Company Act of 1940 also distinguishes between diversified and nondiversified companies. A diversified company is a management company having at least 75 per cent of its assets in cash, government securities, securities of other investment companies, and other securities. The holdings of any one issuer may not exceed 10 per cent of the outstanding securities of the issuer, or five per cent of the total assets of the investment company. The Investment Company Act of 1940 requires investment companies to register with the Securities and Exchange Commission which is responsible for supervising these companies in order to assure the public honest management, cheaper selling costs of new securities, sounder capital structures, and greater publicity as to their affairs.

Among the different types of investment companies, the mutual investment companies are now the most important, having assets of about $8 billion in 1956 as compared to $1 billion at the end of 1940. New sales are running about three times redemptions of stock. The typical investor in the shares of mutual companies is almost 50 years old with an annual income in the $5,000 to $7,000 bracket.

SECONDARY MARKETS FOR SECURITIES

Investment involves a long-term commitment of funds. Bonds are issued for long periods of time, and stock certificates have no maturity dates (except for stock of investment companies organized for a specific number of years, and preferred stock issued for a definite period of time). Because most individuals hold a particular stock or bond for no more than a few years, so-called "secondary" markets have been developed. These markets are provided in part by investment bankers, dealers, and brokers who operate in the over-the-counter market or on securities exchanges. Investment bankers may maintain a trading department to peg prices of their issues during the period of distribution, to dispose of bonds their clients have traded in for new issues, and to buy and sell securities. Dealers buy and sell securities for their own account; brokers execute orders to buy and sell securities for principals; and stock exchanges are associations of brokers and dealers.

Over-the-Counter Market. The expression "over the counter" is a loose term applied to the activities of dealers, brokers, bankers, and others in buying and selling unlisted securities. The Securities Exchange Act of 1934 defined the over-the-counter market to include all transactions in securities which take place otherwise than upon a national exchange. In buying or selling a stock or bond that is traded in in the over-the-counter market, it is more convenient and usually more profitable to deal through the medium of a broker or to buy from or sell to a dealer. Those who specialize in this type of business often have private wire systems to other brokers' and dealers' offices, which greatly facilitate the purchase and sale of unlisted securities.

The shares of most banks and insurance companies and the stock of many public utility, railroad, and industrial companies are bought and sold in the over-the-counter market. There is also an enormous over-the-counter bond market, where there is trading in private securities and in federal, state, and local government securities. There are 100,000 securities not listed on security exchanges as compared to 6,000 that are. Finally, the primary distribution of the underwriting houses usually takes place in the over-the-counter markets.

The Maloney Act of 1938 (which added Section 15 to the Securities Exchange Act of 1934) provides for organization of over-the-counter brokers into self-regulatory associations under supervision of the Securities and Exchange Commission. In August, 1939, the National Association of Securities Dealers, Inc., was registered with the Securities and Exchange Commission. It now has more than 2,800 members. Its chief activity has been to raise business standards of all over-the-counter brokers and dealers and to devise a uniform business practice code. It may take, and has taken, disciplinary action against members for violation of the Association's rules. Facts concerning violations by different firms are brought to the attention of the Association by the Securities and Exchange Commission for whatever action the Association may find desirable. An "aggrieved party of disciplinary action" may request a review from the Securities and Exchange Commission, as provided by law.

Security Exchanges. Brokers and dealers who are members of security exchanges provide the best-known secondary market for securities. In a broad sense a security exchange is the meeting place for buyers and sellers of securities. A more modern and correct definition is: "A security exchange is an unincorporated association or incorporated company, the members of which trade in securities for others and themselves."

Securities exchanges whose business is predominantly interstate are, since 1934, under the general regulation of the Securities and Exchange Commission and are called "national securities exchanges." At the present time, there are fifteen exchanges registered with the Securities and Exchange Commission and four that are exempt from registration. New York, Chicago, and San Francisco have two each. The largest, and by far the most important, exchange is the New York Stock Exchange, where stocks and bonds of national and international importance are bought and sold.

The New York Stock Exchange. The New York Stock Exchange is a voluntary organization—an association—and, as such, is subject to internal regulation. Membership is now in the process of being reduced from 1,375 to 1,325 and admission is dependent upon getting a member to retire in the applicant's favor, a favorable vote (two-thirds) of the committee on admission, and satisfaction of certain other requirements, including payment of an initiation fee. Annual dues, which are payable quarterly, may not exceed $1,000. Obtaining a "seat" on an exchange was first used literally; but now it refers merely to membership, which carries with it the privilege of buying and selling on the exchange.

Individuals or firms having seats on the New York Stock Exchange (since May 1, 1953, corporations may be members) are classified according to their activities as follows: (1) inactive members who rarely go near the exchange but retain their membership as an investment or for social or noneconomic reasons; (2) "wire houses," who execute orders that are received locally and by wire from branch offices and correspondents in American and foreign cities; (3) commission brokers, who buy and sell for their firms' clients; (4) floor brokers, who are not affiliated with stock exchange firms but execute orders for other members, particularly commission brokers; (5) specialists, who are assigned by the Exchange to one or more stocks and act as floor brokers for other brokers and as traders for themselves; (6) floor traders, who buy and sell for their own accounts; (7) odd-lot dealers and brokers, who buy and sell lots of less than 100 shares to commission brokers and others; and (8) bond dealers and brokers, who deal in bonds for their own accounts and for customers.

The general public makes purchases or sales on the stock exchange through commission brokers. A prospective buyer or seller merely goes to any broker's office or branch (of which there are several in every city of any size) and places his order to buy or sell. In the case of buying, if he has not already made credit arrangements with the broker, he must deposit cash or acceptable securities. The order will be executed, and the securities will be delivered within a reasonable time. It is, of course, taken for granted that the brokerage house has a member on the floor of the exchange or a correspondent relationship with some member of the exchange on which the order is to be executed.

FEDERAL REGULATION OF SECURITIES MARKETS

The Securities and Exchange Commission was created in 1934 to assume the responsibility for supervision of the Securities Act of 1933 (previously under the administration of the Federal Trade Commission) and the Securities Exchange Act of 1934. Subsequent legislation has made the Commission responsible for the Public Utility Holding Company Act of 1935, Trust Indenture Act of 1939, Investment Company Act of 1940, and Investment Advisors Act of 1940. Under provisions of Chapter X of the National Bankruptcy Act, as amended in 1938, the Commission serves as advisor to the United States district courts in connection with reorganization procedures for debtor corporations (in which there is a substantial public interest).

The Securities and Exchange Commission consists of five members and a supporting staff of experts—accountants, engineers, lawyers, security analysts, and others. The general objective of the laws which it administers is to protect investors and the public against malpractices in financial or securities markets. To this end, use has been made of (1) registration and licensing requirements for security dealers and brokers, (2) registration of specific issues, and (3) civil and criminal prosecution for malpractices.

The laws provide for (1) public disclosure of pertinent facts about new issues and those listed on national securities exchanges; (2) regulation of trading in securities on exchanges and in the over-the-counter market; (3) simplification of the financial structures of utility systems, their reorganization, and regulation of holding companies involved; (4) better trust indentures under which bonds and debentures are sold to the general public; and (5) supervision of the activities of investment companies and investment advisors. In enforcing the laws and the regulations under the laws, the Commission prefers to function through the pertinent investment and other associations and state enforcing agencies. The Commission maintains regional offices and has its own staff of investigators which may report willful violations of the law to the attorney-general for criminal prosecution of the offenders.

Among the various trade and other associations working with the Securities and Exchange Commission are: (1) Investment Bankers Association of America; (2) the New York Stock Exchange and other national exchanges; (3) the National Association of Investment Companies; (4) the National Better Business Bureau, Inc.; and (5) local Better Business Bureaus.

SUMMARY

The capital market, wherein the demands for and supply of long-term funds meet, is dominated on the supply side by institutional investors. The intermediaries in this market are the investment bankers who underwrite and distribute securities. An original issue of securities may be sold directly to investors (private placement); to the highest bidder (competitive bidding); or through investment bankers, who may purchase the issue outright for resale, guarantee the sale of the issue, or take the issue for sale on a best-effort basis.

By placing issues directly with investors, the issuers avoid the costs entailed in public distribution through the facilities of investment houses and in registration of issues with the Securities and Exchange Commission (required of most publicly offered private issues). When credit risks are small and the securities are of standard quality requiring little credit investigation, the issue may be sold by competitive bidding (required of some securities such as issues of state and local governments, public-utility companies, and certain issues of railroad companies).

Life insurance companies, the most important single group of investors in the capital market, are both customers and competitors of investment bankers in bidding for issues of securities. The competitive position of these companies has been strengthened by (1) the rapid growth of their assets, (2) the increase in competitive bidding, and (3) the provision in the Securities Act of 1933 which has encouraged private placement by exempting such issues from registration. At the present time, life insurance companies are absorbing most of the new industrial offerings of bonds and, to a lesser extent, those of public-utility, communications, and railroad companies which have better established public markets. Life insurance companies are also active lenders in the real estate mortgage field and are also important investors in government securities (federal, state, and local).

Investment companies sell their securities to investors and reinvest these funds in other securities. Their main purpose is to provide small investors with diversification of risks. These companies may be organized as unit type trusts, face-value companies, or management companies of which there are two types, open-end and closed-end companies. At the present time, the general management companies of the open-end type are the most popular.

The secondary markets for securities include the over-the-counter market and security exchanges, of which the New York Stock Exchange is the most important. The individuals and firms having "seats" on this stock exchange are divided into seven categories according to their activities, and it is through the commission brokers that the general public makes purchases and sales of securities listed thereon.

The various laws and regulations that have been adopted to protect investors and the general public against malpractices in financial and securities markets are administered by the Securities and Exchange Commission created in 1934. To this objective, use has been made of (1) registration and licensing requirements for security dealers and brokers, (2) registration of specific issues, and (3) civil and criminal prosecution for malpractice.

QUESTIONS AND PROBLEMS

1. Identify: (*a*) the capital market, (*b*) investment banking, and (*c*) investment houses.
2. What is the current status of commercial bankers as underwriters and distributors of new (*a*) industrial issues, (*b*) municipal securities, and (*c*) government securities?
3. Distinguish among (*a*) direct sale of securities by the issuer, (*b*) competitive bidding, (*c*) direct placement, and (*d*) negotiation with investment houses.
4. What are the functions of investment bankers? Explain each.
5. Distinguish between underwriting and stand-by underwriting.
6. Explain the statement: "The machinery for distribution of new securities is complex; but it is fundamentally only merchandising on a broad scale."
7. Explain the reasons why life insurance companies have been most

active among institutional investors in providing long-term funds to industry since World War II. How important are they as a source of new capital?

8. Distinguish between (*a*) primary and secondary markets for securities, (*b*) broker and dealer, and (*c*) auction and negotiated trading.

9. "Costly Furniture: Exchange Seat is sold at $95,000, up $5,000" (*New York Times*, January 7, 1956, p. 22). What does this quotation mean?

10. What are the chief types of investment companies or trusts? What are the weaknesses of each? The strong features of each? Which type is the most important? Why?

11. Summarize the duties and responsibilities of the Securities and Exchange Commission.

12. Dr. Sumner H. Slichter said: "The investment opportunities created by technological research will in most years exceed the supply of investment-seeking funds provided by corporate and personal savings and pension funds. Part of these investment opportunities will be financed by credit." (*New York Times*, April 29, 1952, p. 39.) Analyze. Compare to the concept of a "mature" economy found in Chapter XXIII.

Chapter XXVIII

TRUSTS AND TRUST
BANKING

T RUST COMPANIES include specialized institutions and trust departments of commercial banks that perform trust and agency functions for the general public and corporations. Investment services performed for an individual by a trust company may continue not only during the life of the individual but also after his death. Formerly, the services of trust companies were demanded almost exclusively by corporations and wealthy individuals; but, now, they are managing pension funds in which many small savers participate.

Trust companies are permitted to combine the assets of small trusts, to invest them as a unit, and to issue participation certificates in each trust. As a result, small trusts may be serviced more efficiently; and a more stable income may be assured. Therefore, trust companies are accepting a larger number of relatively small trusts than they did in the past.

TRUST INSTITUTIONS IN THE UNITED STATES

Early History. Trust institutions include all trust departments of banks as well as fiduciary or trust companies engaged exclusively in the trust business. The word "fiduciary" is derived from the Latin word *fiducia,* which means "trust" or "confidence." It is practically synonymous in meaning with the Anglo-Saxon word "trust," which is more commonly used.

Lawyers and others have served as trustees and agents for individuals and associations for hundreds of years, but the incorporation of trust companies and the grants of trust powers to banks are recent and distinctly American developments. Insurance companies were the first corporations permitted by law to perform trust functions; but, until after the Civil War, their trust business was a minor activity. The first company to do an exclusive trust business was not organized until 1853. Later, as the trust business developed, many insurance companies reorganized into trust companies; and new trust companies were formed with charters broad enough to permit them to carry on most types of banking.

Trust Companies. Since 1900 the trust business has been closely allied to banking, and the modern trust company is one of the best illustrations of the results of the integration movement in banking. Because of the very nature of the trust business, trust companies are responsible for the investment and safety of large sums of money. In addition, they provide many agency services to corporations and others; and, as a result, they are in daily contact with many business institutions. It was reasonable to expect them to accept commercial and savings deposits from their clients, to make loans, to clear and collect checks, and to perform other banking functions.

Trust Departments of Commercial Banks. With trust companies entering the commercial banking field, it was logical for commercial banks to enter the field of trust banking. The Federal Reserve Act of 1913 authorized national banks to carry on a trust business. At the present time about 1,760 national banks hold permits to exercise unlimited or restricted trust powers, which are being used by all except 250 of these banks. Some trust companies do no general deposit-banking business, but many of these are subsidiaries of large banks which prefer to carry on their trust business under this legal form rather than as separate departments within their banks.

The Federal Reserve Act, as amended, permits national banks to act (1) as trustees for individuals and others; (2) as executors and administrators of estates that are being liquidated under provisions of the intestacy laws or of wills; (3) as registrars of stocks and bonds for corporations; (4) as guardians of estates; (5) as assignees and receivers; (6) as committees of estates of incompetents; and (7) in other fiduciary capacities in which state banks, trust companies, or other corporations with which national banks compete may act. In order to perform any trust functions, a national bank must obtain permission of the Board of Governors of the Federal Reserve System; and, after a state bank becomes a member of the Federal Reserve System, it must obtain permission of the Board of Governors to exercise new trust powers and meet the standards set for trust banking for national banks. Nonmember insured banks must obtain approval of the Federal Deposit Insurance Corporation in order to perform new trust functions.

In passing upon applications for permission to exercise one or more trust powers, the Board of Governors considers such questions as the following: (1) Does the community need the kind of trust service applied for? (2) Does the bank have sufficient capital and surplus? (3) Are its officers and legal counsel competent and qualified to supervise a trust business?

Meaning of a Trust. A trust is the relationship which exists where legal title to property has been given to one person (the trustee) by a second person (the trustor) for the benefit of a third party (the beneficiary). This means that the trustee receives title to property left in trust, but someone else receives the income minus the fees and commissions taken by the trustee for the management of the property. The trustee may be an individual, a properly authorized trust institution, or both, as in the case of co-trustees. Any type of property may be placed in a trust.

Agency Services. Trust companies serve in various capacities as agencies for individuals and corporations. An "agency" is defined as the legal relationship which exists where one person, called an "agent," is employed and authorized by another, called the "principal," to represent and act for the latter in his business or contractual dealings with third persons. The main difference between an agency and a trust relationship is that the trustee holds legal title, whereas the agent does not. Authority to act is derived from a simple request or agreement to perform certain definite acts. It may be in the form of a letter or general or special power of attorney, which usually can be revoked at any time.

Classes of Trusts. When the beneficiary (or beneficiaries) of a trust is an individual (or individuals), it is called a personal trust. If the beneficiary of a trust is an educational, religious, or similar institution, it is called a public trust. There are also certain types of long-term business trusts. When a trust is created as a result of a voluntary agreement between living trustors and a trustee, it is called a voluntary trust. If the terms of the trust agreement become effective during the life of the trustor, it is called a living trust; but, if the terms do not become effective until after the death of the trustor and the terms are contained in his will, it is a testamentary trust. Court trusts are those which are arranged by the court having jurisdiction in such cases when there are no voluntary trust agreements that are applicable (see Table 21).

A trust may be created to provide an income for the support of dependents, for the maintenance of educational institutions, for equipment and supervision of public parks and playgrounds, or for the support of almost any project. Since property left in trust to finance public and quasi-public institutions (educational, charitable, religious, medical, and the like) is exempt from inheritance taxes, many wealthy men have created trust organizations to which they have given the bulk of their estates (as illustrated by the Cullen, Ford, and Rockefeller Foundations).

Business corporations have been encouraged to create tax-free

TABLE 21

FIDUCIARY ACTIVITIES OF NATIONAL BANKS, DECEMBER 31, 1954

[Dollar Figures in Millions]

		Liabilities
Number of personal accounts		
Living trusts	106,647	$ 8,270.7
Court accounts	100,510	4,342.6
Agency, custodian, etc.	82,032	30,737.6
	Total	$43,350.9*
Number of corporate accounts		
Bond issues	8,011	
Paying agents	24,609	
Depositories and miscellaneous	6,506	
Number of Accounts—acting as		
Transfer agents	3,508	
Registrars	3,773	
Total number accounts administered	335,596	
Bond and debenture issues outstanding where banks act as trustees		$19,485.7
Trust departments' gross earnings for year		$ 100.8

Source of statistics: *Ninety-second Annual Report of the Comptroller of the Currency* (Washington, D.C., 1955), pp. 122–23.
* Other liabilities not identified were $4,587.8 million.

foundations by the federal income tax law which provides that a corporation may deduct five per cent of its net income if it is to be used for charitable and other public purposes (more than five per cent in one year if the excess is absorbed in the next two years). It has been estimated that there are more than 7,400 charitable foundations in the United States of which 1,200 have been established by business corporations.

Tax-free foundations, whose assets are in excess of $7 billion, are organized either as nonprofit corporations or as trusts. Nonprofit corporations are created in the same way as business corporations except that they have members rather than stockholders. The members, who are often from the founding company or family, elect the directors, and they in turn select the officers. A foundation organized as a trust is formed by use of an irrevocable trust agreement; and it is managed by a board of trustees selected by the company, individual, or family establishing the trust. Any vacancy on the board of trustees, because of death or resignation, is filled by the remaining members of the board of trustees. Public trusts include not only strictly charitable institutions but also those created to finance research, education, and other projects. Among the foundations, the Ford Foundation has been in the news frequently in recent years, having attracted attention because of its size ($2.5 billion), the sale of part of its original assets to the general public, and large gifts which it has made to private educational institutions and hospitals.

Considered from a broad economic viewpoint, the original primary function of a trust company is to conserve wealth. The desire on the part of individuals to conserve part of their wealth for their own and their heirs' benefit was one of the primary reasons for the development of corporate fiduciaries in the United States. The old adage, "Three generations from shirt sleeves to shirt sleeves," has been dealt a severe blow by using the services of trust companies—the spendthrift son or daughter may be prevented from wasting the principal of an estate. When a person has a large estate, he may desire to keep it intact; but, because of the rule against perpetuities, he can do this only to a limited extent if the beneficiary is an individual or individuals.

Life of a Trust. At an early date, English courts took the position that it would be harmful for society to hinder the alienation of property, since this would tend to (1) undermine commerce; (2) keep property in the hands of the wealthy after they had lost their ability to care for it; and (3) create the basis for the formation of a social caste, with a resulting curtailment of opportunities for individuals. The common law makes a personal trust void if the vesting of the title is postponed for a longer time than "a life or lives in being and twenty-one years." Under the New York State code, it may not extend beyond two lives in being and the minority of a third life. However public trusts, those created to finance education, health, and so on, may be established in perpetuity.

MANAGEMENT OF PERSONAL TRUSTS

In many large trust institutions the fiduciary work is divided into two divisions—personal and corporate. This arrangement permits the trust institution to give more personal attention to the needs of individuals and allows greater specialization in handling corporate accounts. The executive committee of the Trust Division of the American Bankers Association drew up the following principles to serve as a guide to administration of personal trusts:[1]

[1] Board of Governors of the Federal Reserve System, *Trust Powers of National Banks, Regulation F* (Washington, D.C., 1940), pp. 31–32.

SECTION 1. *Personal trusts.*—In the administration of its personal trust business, a trust institution should strive at all times to render unexceptionable business and financial service, but it should also be careful to render equally good personal service to beneficiaries. The first duty of a trust institution is to carry out the wishes of the creator of a trust as expressed in the trust instrument. Sympathetic, tactful, personal relationships with immediate beneficiaries are essential to the performance of this duty, keeping in mind also the interests of ultimate beneficiaries. It should be the policy of trust institutions that all personal trusts should be under the direct supervision of and that beneficiaries should be brought into direct contact with the administrative or senior officers of the trust department.

SECTION 2. *Confidential relationships.*—Personal trust service is of a confidential nature and the confidences reposed in a trust department by a customer should never be revealed except when required by law.

SECTION 3. *Fundamental duties of trustees.*—It is the duty of a trustee to administer a trust solely in the interest of the beneficiaries without permitting the intrusion of interests of the trustee or third parties that may in any way conflict with the interests of the trust; to keep and render accurate accounts with respect to the administration of the trust; to acquaint the beneficiaries with all material facts in connection with the trust; and, in administering the trust, to exercise the care a prudent man familiar with such matters would exercise as trustee of the property of others, adhering to the rule that the trustee is primarily a conserver.

The chief types of personal trust and agency functions that trustees are asked to assume are to serve as executors or administrators of estates, trustees under wills of deceased persons or under agreements or deeds of trust; guardians of property of minors and incompetent persons; and fiscal agencies, attorneys in fact, and depositories in various capacities.

Executors and Administrators. Individuals or trust companies may be appointed to take charge of the settlement of estates under wills (called "executors") or by orders of the court having probate jurisdiction (called "administrators"). In both cases the duties of a trust company or individual trustee are practically the same. They include the receipt of property, payments of all claims against the estate, and the division of the remainder among the heirs according to the law or the terms of the will. The authority of the executor is derived from the will, and the authority of the administrator is derived from the intestacy law. However, the administrators or executors cannot take possession of the property until authorized to do so by the court having probate jurisdiction. (Probate means officially proving a will. Under probate the will is certified by the court to be the deceased's last will and testament, and the executor is empowered to act under the terms of the will and the laws of the state controlling the duties and functions of executors.) In the past, the maker of a will usually named an individual as executor; but, at the present time, there is a growing tendency to name a trust company or a trust department of a bank as executor. Because of the nature of the trust activities involved, the duties of executors and administrators are temporary; but the one who serves as executor or administrator may also be asked to act as trustee.

Trustees. The maker of a will may want his heirs to enjoy the income of an estate but may not want them to take over its management. In that case, he may select a trust institution to manage his estate after all the debts and other obligations are paid. A trustor may wish to place a part of his property beyond his own control in order to assure his family a certain income in the event of business losses. He may do this through a trust agreement in order to provide a separate income for his wife and children. Although the beneficiaries of trusts are usually third parties, the trustor may make himself the beneficiary until his death, specifying that after his death the benefits shall go to others, as indicated in the trust agreement or will.

Guardians and Conservators. In the case of the death of parents (natural guardians), the protection of minors and their property is assumed by the state. A guardian may be appointed by will, by deed, or by the probate court. A trust company may serve as the guardian of a minor's property and, in some states, of his person. The guardianship ends when the ward reaches legal age. The principal duties of the guardian of an estate are: (1) to accept the property of the ward, (2) to make investments according to law, (3) to keep accurate records of receipts and expenditures, (4) to render a final accounting when the guardianship terminates, and (5) upon the decree of the court to deliver the property to the beneficiary.

Habitual drunkards, idiots, and insane persons are incompetent and, therefore, wards of the state. The courts, upon proper application, appoint guardians of their persons and property. The duties of the conservator (sometimes called "committee") of the estate are similar to those of a guardian. The life of the trust varies according to the needs of the case.

Fiscal Agents, Attorneys in Fact, and Depositories. Trust companies act as agents for clients in the purchase and sale of securities and may be retained to rent, sell, repair, and manage real property.

If one is to be absent for an extended period, a trust company may be employed to manage his personal business. In general, a trust company may serve an individual in the same fiscal capacities that one individual may serve a second (as custodian, managing agent, investment counselor, salesman, etc.). Escrow depository is one of the more complicated agency services offered by trust companies. They accept property on deposit which is to be delivered to another upon the fulfillment of specified conditions. It is a useful device in business transactions where the parties are separated by long distances, in real estate transfers where property is in dispute, in connection with alimony payments, and whenever the first party of a contract does not trust the second party or vice versa.

Advantages of Using Corporate Trustees. Although most trust functions may be performed by individuals, trust companies may be better equipped to perform certain specific services. The advantages of the trust companies over individual trustees may be summarized as follows:

1. Trust companies offer continuous administration, which the individual cannot do. Whereas the life of an individual is short, trust companies have perpetual charters. If an individual trustee dies or resigns, a successor must be appointed. This is usually costly, for it involves a complete accounting on the part of the former trustee or his estate, the cost of which is charged against the trust fund.
2. Trust companies offer continuous service at their place of business, but an individual trustee is not always at his home or office; moreover, his residence may be changed many times during the the life of the trust. Many annoyances to beneficiaries and losses because of delay may result from these conditions.
3. Trust companies are more responsible than individual trustees, having had more experience with investments and being more impartial than individuals. Banks are subject to periodic examinations by the government, and their capital resources are large. Trust companies are not, however, responsible for losses of trust funds unless fraud or negligence can be proved.
4. Trust companies have available expert services in the investment, accounting, taxation, and legal fields and have more experience in handling estates, circumstances which make the cost of administration less than is usually the case under management of an individual trustee.

Objections to Corporate Trustees. The chief objection to corporate trustees is that they are impersonal in their treatment of beneficiaries and trust funds. Although banks' public relations have improved, many people still regard them as being too impersonal.

Many assume that corporate trustees' primary consideration is to keep within the law and to avoid future claims against them for illegal operations, which means that their activities are too passive and too routine in nature. Even when they have been granted broad discretionary powers, banks sometimes hesitate to take necessary action, seemingly preferring the safer legal policy of doing nothing. The chief critics of the trust work of banks are their chief competitors, lawyers. During the 1930–33 depression, trust companies, along with all other banking institutions, lost prestige but gained a great deal of experience. Since 1933 the trust business of banks, especially national banks, has increased rapidly.

SEGREGATION OF TRUST BUSINESS FROM OTHER ACTIVITIES OF BANKS

All national banks and most state banks are required by law to separate their trust work from other departments in the bank. All the books and records are kept "distinct from other records of the bank." There is no mingling of assets of the trust department with those of the commercial, savings, or other departments of the bank. The only exception is when trust funds are held by a bank awaiting investment or distribution. In some states these funds may be used by the bank under authorization of its board of directors, provided that (1) adequate collateral is deposited as security, (2) the deposits are preferred claims on the assets of the banks, and (3) interest is paid on deposits. In addition, many state laws require banks acting in a fiduciary capacity to deposit some of their own securities with state officers in order to protect trusts from losses due to fraud, etc.

Each individual trust must be segregated from others being handled by the department; and an institution having 1,000 trusts will have to keep 1,000 investment, earnings, disbursements, and other bookkeeping records. The separation of records explains the most noticeable equipment in a trust department, that is, filing cabinets.

The bank's board of directors is directly responsible for general supervision of the trust department—investments, policies, and disposition of trust investments. The board of directors or committee of the board must approve the acceptance of all fiduciary accounts and the closing-out or relinquishment of all old accounts. All trust funds are invested by a trust committee composed of three or more members who must be experienced officers or directors of the bank. The investment committee must review, at least annually, the assets held in, or for, each fiduciary account. It must "determine their safety and current value and the advisability of retaining or disposing of them; and a report of all such reviews, together with the action taken as a result thereof, shall be noted in the minutes of the trust investment committee."

Ordinary bank statements do not contain reports of the assets in the trust departments, since the properties involved are held in trust for the beneficiaries as provided in the trust agreements and by law. The banking business of other departments may be suspended without seriously involving the work of the trust division of the bank. If an individual trustee dies or is incapacitated, the probate judge appoints a new trustee, and this principle applies to the "death" of a corporate trustee.

In case of liquidation of a bank the trust work may be continued, with legal permission, by organizing the trust department into a trust company, by a reorganized bank, or by a transfer of the trusts to another trust company. Therefore, bank failures do not mean that the trusts must be liquidated or that the beneficiaries lose their rights to trust funds. Trustees are not insurers or guarantors of trusts left with them for management; but they are expected to act in "good faith" and in the sole interests of the beneficiaries and to exercise ordinary care, prudence, and skill in making or "liquidating" investments of trust funds (the "prudent-man" theory).

INVESTMENT OF TRUST FUNDS

The future of trust institutions depends, to a considerable extent, upon their success in keeping down expenses and keeping up income from trust estates. Careful cost analysis often shows that a bank's profits from trust services are more apparent than real. While it is desirable for a trustee to secure a high rate of return on investment of trust funds, safety of principal must be the major consideration. In order to avoid any suspicion of self-dealing, banks usually separate the organization for the investment of trust funds from the investment department of the bank.

The creator of a trust may give definite instructions as to the character of investments, or he may leave it entirely to the discretion of the trustee. Unless otherwise specified in the trust agreement, the trustee must limit his investments to the so-called "legal" securities. These are determined by law; but, if the state has no legal list, the investments must be approved by the surrogate's court. The "legal" lists include first mortgages on real property, government bonds, and the high-grade bonds of public utilities, railroads, and a few industrial corporations. Since 1933 the fear of inflation has led many trustees to seek permission to buy high-grade common and preferred stocks, and some states have made statutory provisions for such investments. Similar purchases may be authorized, or even required, by voluntary trust agreements.

In general, trust bankers favor the repeal of the "legal list" requirement for trust investments and favor the adoption of the prudent-man principle. Now, more than thirty states permit trust companies to operate under the prudent-man rule in whole or part. Some states specifically permit trust funds to be invested in shares of investment companies registered under the Investment Company Act of 1940; others permit a percentage of trust funds to be invested in specified types of preferred and common stock.

Trust companies may be held liable for losses suffered through failure to follow state laws or instructions found in trust agreements, but they are not liable if the loss is due to an error in judgment. At the end of 1954, trust departments of national banks were administering investments of $27.5 billion which were distributed as follows: bonds, 65.27 per cent; stocks, 23.25 per cent; real estate mortgages, 4.23 per cent; real estate, 3.32 per cent; and miscellaneous, 3.93 per cent.[2]

Common Trust Funds. Prior to the authorization of common trust funds, each trust was required to be invested separately; therefore those who were responsible for administering small trusts were at a disadvantage from the standpoint of diversification, liquidity, unit cost of administering, and earnings as compared to results obtainable in the administration of large trusts. For example, assume that Smith left $500 in trust with a trust company, the income to be used to buy current periodicals for his fraternity or school library. Originally, this sum had to be invested separately, and little diversification was possible. Now, in an effort to correct this situation, all states except Iowa have authorized banks to invest small accounts collectively, issuing participating certificates to each trust account (similar privileges have been given to national banks offering competing fiduciary services).

The Board of Governors of the Federal Reserve System regulates common or co-mingled trust funds managed by national banks; and, in order to qualify their common trust funds for tax exemption under rulings of the Internal Revenue Service, other banks must con-

[2] *Ninety-second Annual Report of the Comptroller of the Currency* (Washington, D.C., 1955), p. 124.

form to Regulation F of the Board of Governors. The amount that may be invested in a common trust fund by any one trust is limited either to $100,000 or to 10 per cent of the value of the assets of the common trust fund, whichever is less. Once legally obtained, participation in a common trust fund does not have to be withdrawn if the amount becomes more than 10 per cent of the value of the assets in the fund.

To an increasing extent, banks are being requested to administer employee-benefit funds of various types including pension, thrift, welfare, profit-sharing, and bonus plans set up for the exclusive benefit of employees or their beneficiaries. The problem of investing funds paid in periodically is similar to that inherent in the investment of small trusts; and so, in 1955, the Board of Governors of the Federal Reserve System changed Regulation F to permit collective investment of funds of two or more such trusts. However, such collective investment must be authorized by the instruments creating the trusts or by court orders. Such trusts must be managed according to the rules and regulations of the Board of Governors in order to be exempt from federal income taxation as provided for in the Internal Revenue Code (see Section 401 (a)).[3] Annually, the employer receives a report on his individual participation in the combined trusts' investment as well as an annual report on the combined trusts as a group.

The first of the annual surveys of common trust funds by the Federal Reserve System revealed that there were 198 common trust funds in 1955, operated by 162 banks with combined assets of $1.857 billion. Of these common trust funds, 138 were classified as diversified discretionary funds wherein investment is left to the discretion of the trustee; 42 were classified as diversified legal funds wherein investment is limited to the "legal" list; and 18 were classified as special funds wherein investments are limited by law or discretion to one class of securities, such as common stock.

The size of the common trust funds varied from the smallest, $145,000, to the largest almost $100,000,000. A number of banks operated more than one common trust fund, the largest for one bank having been four (two diversified legal and two diversified discretionary) as a result of the merger of two banks. The assets of the common trust funds were divided as follows: common stock, 48.7 per cent; bonds, notes, and certificates, 38.2 per cent; pre-

---

[3] *Federal Reserve Bulletin* (May, 1955), p. 501.

ferred stock, 11.5 per cent; other investments, 1.1 per cent; and principal held as cash, 0.5 per cent.[4]

In addition to the common trust funds managed by banks, there are other trust funds that are so large that no collective investment is necessary. It has been estimated that the volume of employee pension and welfare funds alone which are administered by banks is in excess of $12.5 billion. About 60 per cent of the banks which handle such funds are in New York State.

Regulation of Banks' Trust Business. All books and accounts of member banks must be kept in forms approved by supervisory authorities. Assets of each trust account must be examined by the bank's investment trust committee, and audited annually by a special committee of the bank's board of directors. Examiners give special attention to the auditing, examining, and investing work of the trustees. In addition to following intelligent investment policies, trustees are expected to provide physical safeguards such as vaults and safe storage places for all assets of trusts; and fire, burglary, fidelity, and other types of insurance as may be deemed necessary. Under the leadership of the Trust Division of the American Bankers Association, standard rules and practices have been adopted.

Steps must be taken to insure the administration of each fund in accordance with the wishes of the creator (trustor) and/or the law as interpreted by the court. Administration may be difficult when the trustee is given discretionary powers as to the distribution of income from or principal of a trust. In some cases, the trustee is permitted to use his discretion in paying money to or spending it for the beneficiary, or in refraining to do so. Trustees are frequently required to interpret clauses in trust agreements, such as "a proper education for my son," "a nice car," "adequate support of my family," and so on (often using the principal as well as the income from property left in trust). In cases wherein the beneficiaries of income from a trust are not to inherit the principal when the trust is liquidated, there is a conflict of interests between the two groups of beneficiaries that may result in legal action against the trustee.

Commissions and Fees. The trust company is compensated for managing the trust by receiving a percentage of the income during the life of the trust and a percentage of the principal. The charges are fixed by law or, in some states, by the probate courts. For trusts, charges may consist of annual fees on income, annual commissions

[4] *Federal Reserve Bulletin* (August, 1956), pp. 800–805.

on principal, and commissions collected on the principal when a trust is terminated. If annual commissions are collected on principal, they are deducted from the commissions collected on termination of the trust. There are no commissions on principal allowed on perpetual trusts under the law of New York State, where the only fee permitted is 5 per cent of the income accruing to the trust annually. Under the same state law, if the corpus of the trust is less than $100,000, only one commission on principal and only one on income are permitted annually. Since some trusts are administered by two trustees, this means that there is usually an equal division between the trust company and the co-trustee. If the corpus is above $100,000, two or more fees and/or commissions may be collected.

In most states, fees and commissions are authorized in detail by law. For illustration, fees and commissions for executors, administrators, guardians, and committees for incompetents for New York State are:

1. Annual income fees:
   5 per cent on first $2,000 of income; 2½ per cent on the next $20,-000 of income; 1½ per cent on the next $28,000 of income; and 2 per cent on the balance of income over $50,000.
2. Principal commission and fees:
   5 per cent on the first $2,000 of principal; 2½ per cent on the next $20,000 of principal; and 2 per cent on the remaining principal balance.

Normally, one half of the principal fees is taken upon receipt of the trust, and the other one half is taken upon the distribution to the residuary legatees. The commissions on voluntary trusts are fixed by trust agreements but are about the same as those allowed by law. Because of heavy taxes, creators of trusts are creating them for longer periods of time. This has tended to give stability to the trust business and has popularized the pay-as-you-go schedule for commissions on principal as well as on income.

Statutory provisions are also made for fees and commissions for acting as fiscal agents, such as serving as custodian for securities and supervising investments (however, most agency fees are negotiated). Periodic statements of transactions affecting investment accounts are also required. The principal may arrange for additional services, such as a periodic review of the investment account as to quality with suggestions on changes to be made at the discretion of the principal.

Dominance of Large Banks. The amount of clerical and other work in connection with trust banking is large. The overhead is so great that the small banks are in no position to handle any trust business except pension funds and life insurance trusts, which require relatively little management. Therefore, trust banking is largely confined to the metropolitan centers and the wealthier states. Almost 35 per cent of the assets of individual trusts administered by national banks are in New York State and of the $27.5 billion investments under the administration of national banks' trust departments, $26.2 billion is managed by banks with capital stock of more than $500,-000. Many trust departments of smaller banks may be operated at a loss because contacts made through the trust departments may bring new business to other divisions of the banks. But ill will which so often follows the settling of estates and the administering of trusts may more than offset the expected advantages from the trust business. Many banks in the United States prefer to leave the trust business to individual trustees or to specialists in the field.

Trusts vary in size from a few hundred dollars to millions of dollars. Most of the income from individual trusts is being used for the benefit of women and children—support of homes, education, care of parents, and the like. A recent survey made by the Trust Division of the American Bankers Association shows that more than 63 per cent of the trusts administered by its members produced an annual income of less than $3,000 and about 34 per cent produced less than $750 (the average for this group being $261). At the other extreme are 4.4 per cent of the trusts reported which had an annual income of over $25,000.[5] Although these statistics cover only living trusts, insurance trusts, and testamentary trusts, they do indicate the extent to which trust services of banks are available to all income groups.

Trust institutions are managing more property at the present time than at any other time in history. This reflects, in addition to the great expansion in money incomes, fundamental changes in American life. An increase in life expectancy has led to the creation of many living trusts to give financial security to the beneficiaries during old age. In addition, the investment, legal, tax, and other problems associated with the management of estates have increased in complexity. Many of those who have accumulated moderate estates

[5] "National Survey of the Size of Trusts," *Banking* (February, 1956), pp. 56, *passim.*

have had previous financial reverses and are desirous of guarding against repetition. High income, estate, and inheritance taxes make the accumulation and preservation of estates more difficult.

TRUST AND AGENCY SERVICES FOR CORPORATIONS

The need for corporate trust and agency services is confined to large centers of population; and, for this reason, many small banks limit their trust business to agency and fiduciary services for individuals. In administering corporate trusts and agency services, banks are expected to follow the same administrative principles considered under personal trusteeship. "Promptness, accuracy, and protection are fundamental requirements of efficient corporate trust service. The terms of the trust instrument should be carried out with scrupulous care and with particular attention to the duties imposed therein upon the trustee for the protection of the security-holders."[6]

Corporate trust business includes all fiduciary services given to corporations, educational institutions, fraternal organizations, hospitals, and religious institutions. The most important types of corporate fiduciary services rendered by banks are: (1) to act as trustee under a corporate mortgage; (2) to act as trustee under reorganization plans, receiverships, etc.; (3) to serve as transfer agent, registrar, paying agent, etc.; (4) to serve as fiscal agent, attorney in fact, and depository in various capacities; and (5) to help societies and institutions in various ways, including the management of pension trusts (see Table 21).

Trustee under Corporate Mortgage. Corporations borrowing for long periods may desire amounts too large to be provided by one lender. Through the medium of an investment banker, bonds are sold to investors in convenient denominations, usually $500 or $1,000. A single mortgage or indenture agreement is usually drawn up and made payable to a bank or a trust company.[7] This mortgage or indenture agreement contains provisions to protect the bondholders. The corporation conveys to the trustee, under certain conditions, title to all or part of its property. This mortgage or indenture agreement is held in trust by the trustee for the benefit of the holders of the bonds which the corporation has issued thereunder.

---

[6] Board of Governors of the Federal Reserve System, *op. cit.,* p. 32.

[7] An indenture trustee "shall mean a trustee under a mortgage, deed of trust, or indenture, pursuant to which there are securities outstanding, other than voting-trust certificates, constituting claims against a debtor or claims secured by a lien upon any of its property." (Art. II, sec. 106, chap. x, of the National Bankruptcy Act.)

Prior to 1939, trust companies were not bond trustees in the true sense of the word but merely agents of the bondholders.[8] They rarely took action on their own initiative, being guided by the traditional attitude, which was opposed to taking positive action. Even when trustees were given discretion to act, they rarely did so. As a result, bondholders did not have the protection which the word "trustee" denotes. However, trust companies were faithful in performing their routine functions in connection with their trust under corporate mortgages.[9]

One purpose of the Trust Indenture Act of 1939 was "to bring all indenture trustees up to a high level of diligence and loyalty and to place them in a better position to protect security holders. The means adopted is a requirement that bonds, notes, debentures, and similar debt securities exceeding $1,000,000 in principal amount may not be offered for sale to the public unless they are issued under a trust indenture which conforms to specific statutory standards and has been duly qualified with the [Securities and Exchange] Commission."[10] Now the trustee is expected to take action to protect bondholders in the event of default on payment of interest, principal, or some other part of the indenture agreement.

Trustees under Reorganization Plans, Receiverships, etc. The work of trust institutions in reorganizations is usually passive. They accept the securities deposited with them by one or more of the reorganization committees. After the committees and the courts have worked out an acceptable plan for reorganization, the depository issues the reorganization certificates authorized by them.[11] Under requirements of the National Bankruptcy Act of 1938, the Securities and Exchange Commission must serve as advisor to the United States district courts in connection with the proceedings for reorganization of debtor corporations in which there is "a substantial public interest."

[8] See Securities and Exchange Commission, *Report on the Study and Investigation of the Work, Activities, and Functions of Protective and Reorganization Committee* (Washington, D.C.: U.S. Government Printing Office, 1937), Part I, "Strategy and Techniques of Protective and Reorganization Committee."

[9] See Trust Indenture Act of 1939 (76th Cong., 1st sess., *Public Law 253*). This act gave the Securities and Exchange Commission the power to approve or disapprove of trust indentures under which securities are issued.

[10] *Tenth Annual Report of the Securities and Exchange Commission (Fiscal Year Ended June 30, 1944)* (Washington, D.C.: U.S. Government Printing Office, 1945), p. 5.

[11] Note new provisions for corporate reorganization in chapter x of the National Bankruptcy Act (75th Cong., 2d sess., *Public Law 696*).

Transfer Agents, Registrars, Paying Agents, etc. Stockholders are the owners of a corporation's capital stock. The names of the owners and the number of shares held by each are shown on the books of the corporation. If title is transferred to a second party, transfer of the certificate is not sufficient; the title must be passed on the books of the corporation. This transfer of title may be made by the corporation or by some trust institution appointed as the transfer agent. If a stock is actively traded in on a stock exchange, trust institutions commonly serve as transfer agents, since they are able to transfer titles to stock rapidly and skillfully; but some of the larger corporations, such as the American Telephone and Telegraph Company, have their own transfer offices in New York City.

In order to prevent fraud in the form of illegal issues of stock, the New York Stock Exchange now requires, as a prerequisite for listing stocks, the appointment of a transfer agent and a registrar, both to be located in the Borough of Manhattan, City of New York. The registrar must be a trust institution. The registrar checks upon the transfer work of the transfer agent; and he receives both the canceled certificate of stock, or a registered bond, and the new stock certificate or bond issued in its place. The canceled certificate is examined to see if it is genuine and if the new certificate is drawn to represent the proper number of shares. Proper entries are made in the registration records; and the registrar's certificate is signed, and then returned to the transfer agent. Bonds may be registered in the same way as stock certificates and the same procedures for transfer of title are followed. Usually, no new bond is issued when ownership changes but the name of the new owner is placed on the bond and in the books of the transfer agent.

Trust companies also serve as payment agents for private corporations, state and local governments, and other debtors. If a trust institution serves as paying agent, the debtor deposits funds with it prior to the interest, dividend, or maturity dates of the obligations.

Fiscal Agents, Attorneys in Fact, and Depositories. Trust institutions also serve corporations in many of the special agency capacities in which they serve individuals. They act as liquidating agents for corporations which have decided to discontinue business, as escrow depositories, as managers of real property, as custodians of securities, and in other capacities.

Agents for Institutions. Trust companies serve as trustees and agents for many types of foundations, educational institutions, hospitals, religious organizations, and other institutions. The community trust is a recent development in this field, the first having been created in 1914 in Cleveland, Ohio. Under a community trust, gifts and bequests are received by one or more trust companies, which, with the help of an advisory board of citizens, expends the funds for public purposes. The community trust in New York is the largest in this country. Among the most important of the new agency functions is that of administering pension funds.

Title Search and Mortgage Insurance. Trust companies buy and sell real estate mortgages and act as middlemen in arranging real estate transactions. As large investors in real estate mortgages, they accumulate considerable knowledge about titles and values of real property. Some state-chartered banks operate a special department which insures the title and, sometimes, the repayment of principal and payment of interest on real estate mortgages. When institutions make a specialty of such a business, they are called "title and mortgage insurance companies." They charge fees and accumulate reserves to cover contingent liabilities; but, normally, the number of bad loans insured is small and losses are nominal. Because of the severity of the 1930–33 depression in real estate, most large companies in this business were unable to meet their obligations and were liquidated or reorganized. This same type of insurance is now written by the Federal Housing Administration.

National banks are not permitted to carry on a title and mortgage insurance business. However, small national banks are permitted to act as mortgage brokers or agents for others. In addition, they may act as agents for fire, life, or other insurance companies. They may also sell insurance and collect premiums, for which work they receive fees and commissions. All national banks are specifically prohibited from guaranteeing or insuring titles, from paying premiums, and from vouching for accuracy of statements.

SUMMARY

Trust institutions have as their primary functions the protection of private property against waste and loss and the supervision of the transfer of income or title to property (such as from trustor to the beneficiary or of securities bought and sold in the open market). In the capacity of trustee, the trust company takes title to and manages property left in trust by the creator of the trust as provided for by a trust agreement, a will, and/or the law. Trust companies also perform many agency services for individuals, corporations, governments, societies, and institutions.

Individuals as well as corporations may act as trustees; and, in the administration of estates, often provisions are made for co-trustees—an individual and a corporation, thereby combining the advantages of having both kinds of trustees. In investing funds left in trust and distributing the income therefrom, the trustee is required to give primary attention to the wishes of the trustor. Assuming that the trust agreement does not specify the types of investments, in some states, the trust must be invested in securities classified as legal investments for trust funds by the state governments; but, in an increasing number of states, the trustees are permitted to invest in securities in which a prudent man would invest under like circumstances.

Services performed for business corporations include acting as trustee under a corporate mortgage, trustee under reorganization plans, transfer agent, registrar, and paying agent. Trust companies also administer funds contributed to educational institutions, research foundations, hospitals, community trusts, and pension and similar plans. Trust companies may be held liable for losses due to failure to adhere to instructions in the trust agreement, requirements in the state law, or actions of an imprudent nature. The chief reason why individuals and business firms select trust companies to manage their property is the ability of such institutions to do a better job than can individuals.

QUESTIONS AND PROBLEMS

1. What is meant by a "trust"? How does the receipt of title to property by a trustee differ from a bank's receipt of title when a time or demand deposits is made?
2. What is the proper trust business for banks, as stated by the Trust Division of the American Bankers Association?
3. Distinguish between (a) corporate and individual trusts, (b) corporate and individual trustees, and (c) living and court trusts.
4. What are the principles laid down by the American Bankers Association to guide in the administration of personal trusts? Are they sound?
5. Identify the following: (a) executors, (b) administrators, (c) guardians, (d) conservators, (e) fiscal agents, and (f) depositories.
6. What trust and agency services do trust institutions supply corporations? Explain.
7. In what respects is a corporate trustee superior and inferior to an individual trustee in the performance of fiduciary services?
8. By transferring 90 per cent of the Ford Company stock to the Ford Foundation, inheritance taxes at the death of Henry and Edsel Ford

were avoided which would have necessitated sale of 60 per cent of the stock and would have weakened the Ford family's control of the company. Analyze.

9. Assume that a college graduate wants to endow a "Chair of Finance" in memory of his parents. How may this be done through the facilities offered by a trust company?

10. What is the significance of the following quotation from an editorial in a metropolitan newspaper? "The dead hand of obsolescence can never smother or destroy memorial funds left with the New York Community Trust, because the seventeen financial institutions serving as trustees of this great association are empowered to redirect the application of such funds if the purposes for which they were established become out-moded."

11. As stated by Selden B. Daume, president of Detroit Wabeek Bank and Trust Company, on the merger of Detroit Trust (formerly the largest independent trust company in the United States without bank affiliations) and the Wabeek State Bank, " ' In reality a bank is a feeder for a trust company and a trust company is a feeder for a bank.' " (Merrill Lynch, Pierce, Fenner & Beane, *Investor's Reader*, December 14, 1955, p. 16.) Analyze.

| Chapter XXIX | # URBAN MORTGAGE CREDIT AND SAVINGS INSTITUTIONS |

THE ECONOMIC growth of the United States is dependent to a considerable extent upon an increase in expenditures by consumers for goods and services. These expenditures include those for homes. When mortgage credit is cheap and abundant, real estate developments are encouraged; conversely, when mortgage credit is expensive and scarce, real estate developments are discouraged. Because of the complexity of the housing and mortgage markets, the influence of monetary and fiscal policies is not always clear; but there is no doubt as to the effects of these policies even though there may be some delay before a change from easy to tight money conditions (or vice versa) becomes evident in the mortgage market and in the construction and sale of urban residential property.

The volume of home building and home improvement is dependent in large part upon funds provided by intermediaries such as mutual savings banks, life insurance companies, savings and loan associations, and savings departments of commercial banks. The flow of savings into financing homes and other types of urban residential property has been encouraged by the Federal Home Loan Bank System, Federal Housing Administration, and Public Housing Administration.

TYPES OF LENDERS

The mortgage banking field includes (1) investment bankers who finance the construction of large buildings by underwriting issues of securities; (2) mortgage companies that buy and sell mortgages; (3) savings and loan associations which technically sell their stock to individuals and use funds acquired in this way to make loans to homeowners; (4) banks that accept savings deposits and lend to homeowners; (5) institutions created by the federal government that acquire and hold mortgages and sell their securities in the open market; and (6) others, including life insurance companies and individuals.

Investment Bankers. At one time issues of mortgage bonds were sold through the facilities of investment bankers to raise funds to finance the construction of hotels, office buildings, and other large structures; but such issues are almost unknown at the present time. Customarily, when such structures are to be built, the business is incorporated, stock is sold to owners, and any additional funds needed to finance the building are borrowed from life insurance companies and other lenders.

In Massachusetts and in certain sections of the Midwest, land-trust certificates are sometimes issued to finance major improvements. The trust certificates are sold to investors, title to the property is held by a trust company (trustee), the propery is leased under arrangements whereby the lessee pays rent sufficient to pay interest and to retire the certificates which are usually arranged to mature in series. The lessee also contracts to insure, maintain, and otherwise protect the property to which he takes title when the trust certificates are retired.

Mortgage Companies. The term "mortgage company" has been used broadly to include lenders who are specialists in financing purchases of real property. More specifically, the term is used to mean institutions and individuals that purchase mortgages and sell them to investors. Sometimes such mortgages are deposited with trustees, and investors buy participation therein; in other cases, mortgages are purchased with funds borrowed from commercial banks before being resold. In effect, the mortgages are warehoused until they can be sold to insurance companies and other permanent investors. In many instances, the mortgage company does not even take title to mortgages but merely acts as an agent or broker for more permanent investors. At one time, mortgage companies sometimes guaranteed the title and principal payments (by endorsement) of the mortgages which they handled; but this practice has generally been discontinued because of losses incurred during the 1930's and the advent of Federal Housing Administration and other federal insuring and guaranteeing agencies.

Currently, the chief function of mortgage companies is to make loans and service them for mortgage investors, many of whom are located in the capital markets. Therefore capital market conditions tend to have considerable effect on the volume of lending and particularly on the volume of federally underwritten mortgage loans.

Savings and Loan Associations. Savings and loan associations sell their shares over the counter to individuals, banks, and others;

and the funds thus acquired are either lent to homeowners and others or invested in government and other securities. Technically, these associations do not accept deposits; but they do accept savings in payment for shares. In effect, they operate as institutions of deposit and are so treated later in this chapter. Savings and loan associations are interested chiefly in conventional mortgage loans which tend to have a more local market than do those insured or guaranteed by federal agencies.

Savings Banks. Savings banks operate as institutions of deposit, acquiring funds from depositors and then lending or investing them preferably in home mortgages. Savings banks include mutual and stock savings banks and the savings departments of commercial banks and trust companies (see below).

Federal Banks and Agencies. The federal banks and agencies which are, or have been, participants in the urban home financing market include: the Home Owners' Loan Corporation, the eleven regional federal home loan banks, the Federal National Mortgage Association, Federal Housing Administration, Veterans' Administration, and Public Housing Administration. Generally, the federal government has used three methods of helping homeowners: (1) strengthening existing home financing institutions by providing them with central banking facilities and insurance of their savings accounts, (2) insuring or guaranteeing mortgage loans, and (3) subsidizing public housing projects. To avoid repetition, these banks and agencies are considered later in this chapter, as are miscellaneous lenders including individuals, who purchase home mortgages as investments, and life insurance companies which are among the most important lenders in the urban mortgage credit field.

HOME MORTGAGES

The amount of long-term credit needed to purchase homes is relatively large compared to the income and assets of most purchasers. When the average individual buys a home, he usually makes a down payment, pledges the property as security for a loan, and signs a contract to meet interest and principal payments, to pay taxes and special assessments, to insure the property, and to maintain it in good physical condition.

Real Estate Mortgages. Technically, a mortgage is a conditional conveyance or transfer of title to property by the mortgagor (borrower) to the mortgagee (lender) with the conditional aspect of the transfer removed if the debt is not paid as promised in the mortgage note. Today, a real estate mortgage is generally considered to be a lien upon the mortgaged property; and, if the debtor fails to meet the terms of his contract, the lender may take court action to protect his interest. Following judicial hearings, the court may render a judgment for the debt and direct the sale of the property at public auction (called a foreclosure sale). Usually, the lender attends the sale and bids for the property; but, if the property sells for less than the mortgage claim, he may seize nonexempt property of the debtor to satisfy the unpaid balance.

Second Mortgages. The bulk of real estate mortgages outstanding are first mortgages; but, under certain circumstances, second mortgages are used. For illustration, a seller may finance the sale of his $15,000 house on which there is a first mortgage of $10,000 to a buyer having but $1,000 for a down payment by taking a second mortgage for $4,000. If the seller is unwilling to take a second mortgage for part of his equity, the buyer may arrange to have another party buy a second mortgage to obtain the cash for the seller's equity. Sometimes building contractors accept second mortgages, which they usually sell to buyers of second mortgages at a generous discount. Generally, national and state-chartered banks and most institutional investors are not permitted to invest in second mortgages.

Installment Payments. Other things being equal, the soundness of a mortgage is increased if provisions are made for repayment of the principal on the installment plan. In the past, when banks made first mortgage loans maturing in five years in amount not in excess of 50 per cent of the appraised value of the property, the terms rarely called for periodic payments on the principal. It was understood that borrowers would be repaying the loans represented by second mortgages; and, usually, when first mortgages came due, they were extended to suit the convenience of the homeowners.

The more modern practice in home mortgage lending is to increase the amount of the first mortgage loan, thereby reducing the need for a second mortgage. The policy of making larger first mortgage loans has been accompanied by requiring repayment of the principal on the installment plan, careful appraisal of the pledged property, and emphasis on the income and credit standing of the mortgagor. In some cases, the willingness of institutions to lend is dependent upon the insurance or guarantee of the mortgage note by the Federal Housing Administration, the Veterans' Administration, or some other agency or third party. All of the periodic payments (interest, principal, taxes, and insurance) are often combined so that the property owner is making monthly payments in much the same manner as he would if he were paying rent.

Small Down Payments and Long Maturities. The two aspects of modern home-mortgage lending which have been most criticized are (1) the small down payment required relative to the high loan value given to property being financed; and (2) the length of the mortgage loan. In some cases, 100 per cent loans are arranged which means that the debtor makes no down payment except the costs involved in making the loan (about 50 per cent of the Veterans' Administration loans made during certain years have required no down payments).

Other things being the same, a small down payment means a larger loan and larger monthly payments, but this increase in monthly payments may be avoided by lengthening the loan period (assume from 25 to 30 years). The conditions under which Veterans' Administration loans are made are not typical, but the maturities of some mortgage loans have been lengthened from 25 to 30 years which has resulted in the monthly repayment charges on such loans being reduced almost 10 per cent. The soundness of small or no down-payment mortgage loans depends upon the income of the debtor and this factor is being stressed to an increasing extent in all types of mortgage lending. Lengthening the maturities of loans and reducing down payments have contributed to the increase in the amount of mortgage debt outstanding.

Volume of Mortgage Lending. The total volume of mortgage debt outstanding in the United States is more than $133.6 billion. Of this amount, $9.3 billion is on farm property (see Chapter XXX), $33.2 billion is on apartment buildings and commercial property, and $91.1 billion is on family houses (defined as 1- to 4-family houses). Among the chief holders of mortgages are banks and other financial institutions ($102.5 billion), selected federal agencies ($3.2 billion), and individuals and others ($28 billion). While repayments are reducing the volume of mortgage debt, these reductions are being offset by new mortgages on new and on old property (mortgages often being rewritten for larger amounts when property is resold). The volume of mortgage debt on all property has increased from an estimated figure of $35.5 billion in 1945 to $133.6 billion at the present time. Since other types of mortgage loans are discussed elsewhere in this book, only those on urban residential property are stressed here.

All types of financial institutions are participating in the expansion of residential mortgage debt—savings and loan associations, life insurance companies (some of which have found it convenient to "warehouse" some of their mortgages with commercial banks in order to obtain funds for current lending), mutual savings banks, and commercial banks. At the present time, holdings of residential loans are estimated to be (1) $32.0 billion for savings and loan associations, (2) $31.0 billion for life insurance companies, (3) $16.1 billion for mutual savings banks, (4) $16.2 billion for commercial banks, and (5) $4.2 billion for others including individuals.

Of the $91.1 billion of mortgage debt outstanding on residential property, about $40.2 billion is underwritten by government agencies ($14.7 billion insured by the Federal Housing Administration and $25.5 guaranteed by the Veterans' Administration). The remainder of residential mortgage debt, $50.9 billion, is in the form of conventional mortgages; and almost one half of these mortgage loans ($24.9 billion) are held by savings and loan associations. The nonconventional loans are more popular with institutions that operate more fully in the national mortgage market (such as insurance companies, the Federal National Mortgage Association, and some mutual savings and commercial banks).

Influence of Monetary and Credit Policy. As suggested previously, the volume of mortgage lending may be influenced by changes in terms of contracts such as length of loan period, down payment, and interest rate. From the viewpoint of monetary management, the volume of mortgage lending may be influenced by the use of general and selective devices of credit control. The Board of Governors of the Federal Reserve System expressed its concern over the situation in the mortgage credit field in the fall of 1955, and frowned on the warehousing of mortgages by commercial banks for life insurance companies and other mortgage lenders (temporary loans were made by banks upon packages of mortgages pledged as collateral).

Because many of the mortgages outstanding are financed by commercial banks, insurance companies, and other institutions that invest in the capital market, the flow of funds into the mortgage market is affected by interest rates in the capital market. After all costs of lending and investing are considered, a fixed rate of 4 or $4\frac{1}{2}$ per cent on nonconventional mortgages may be less attractive than yields on long-term government securities during periods of credit restraint. Therefore, the flow of insurance funds and those of other investors into the mortgage market may be dried up in response to a tighter monetary policy; and, conversely, the flow of funds into the mortgage market may be increased in response to an easy monetary policy.

Investors are reluctant to create capital losses when money rates are high and, if they regard the situation as temporary, they may do little switching of investments. Although there may be no net rate differential between home mortgages and government securities, terms that permit prepayment tend to make mortgages a less attractive investment.

MUTUAL SAVINGS BANKS

Definition. "Mutual savings banks are defined as banks without capital stock transacting a savings bank business, the net earnings of which inure to the benefit of their depositors after payment of obligations or any advances by organizers." Depositors are paid "dividends" or interest at a fixed rate; and earnings, above the amount necessary to pay expenses and dividend charges, are retained for banking purposes and are accounted for in the surplus. As a result of conservative management, most mutual associations have large surplus accounts.

The idea of the mutual savings bank was imported from the United Kingdom, where these institutions are known as "trustee" savings banks because they are managed by boards of trustees. The savings-bank movement owes its origin to humanitarians who wanted to help the poor to help themselves. The basic principle on which the mutual savings bank movement is founded is that depositors provide the funds and are the beneficiaries of the operations of mutual savings banks.

Management. Management of a mutual savings bank is in the hands of a board of trustees; each member holds office for life unless he resigns or is removed by his colleagues on the board. The officers of a mutual savings bank are selected by the board of trustees. In a large savings bank there are a president, one or more vice-presidents, a secretary, a treasurer, an auditor, a counsel, and many assistant or junior officers. In a small bank the major part of the work is performed by a secretary-treasurer, and the offices of president and vice-president are primarily honorary. The clerical work is carried on by tellers, bookkeepers, clerks, messengers, and assistants.

Location in the Northeast. Mutual savings banks have been organized in seventeen states, but most of the banks are located in New England and the Middle Atlantic states. Owing to mergers, suspensions, and reorganizations, the number of mutual savings banks has declined from 634 in 1914 to 528, but the decrease in number of banks has been offset by the opening of approximately 310 branches. The three most important savings bank states are New York, Massachusetts, and Connecticut. The 129 mutual savings banks in New York hold about 60 per cent of all mutual savings bank deposits, and of the 15 largest savings banks in the nation, 14 are in New York. Massachusetts has 189 mutual savings banks, Connecticut has 71, and only Maine, New Hampshire, and New Jersey have more than eight mutual savings banks.

Deposit Insurance. Mutual savings banks have total deposits of $28.9 billion of which over $21.2 billion are insured by the Federal Deposit Insurance Corporation. All of the mutual savings banks in New York and Pennsylvania (seven) are participating in the Federal Deposit Insurance Corporation plan. (Pennsylvania ranks fourth in terms of amount of deposits among mutual savings bank states.) The mutual savings banks of Massachusetts have their own deposit-insurance fund. Of the seventy-one mutual savings banks in Connecticut, sixty-six operate their own insurance plan, but the five largest banks, which hold more than one half of the total mutual savings banks' deposits in the state, have insured their deposits with the Federal Deposit Insurance Corporation.

Assets and Liabilities. Unlike commercial banks, mutual savings banks carry on a highly specialized business stressing time and savings deposits and investment in long-term obligations. The form in which mutual savings banks' funds may be invested is regulated by laws which have as their purpose protection of deposits. A "legal list" of securities is composed by the state legislature or some delegated administrative agency, such as a state banking board. The tendency is to limit investments to real estate mortgages and to government, railroad, and public-utility bonds. Real estate mortgages normally make up more than one half of the assets of mutual savings banks; and, at the end of 1955, $17.5 billion was invested in mortgages, as compared to $8.5 billion invested in United States government securities and $4 billion in other securities. Although mutual savings banks have no capital stock, they hold surplus and reserve accounts which amounted to $2.8 billion at the end of 1955 compared to total deposits of $28.2 billion (approximately a ten to one deposit—net worth ratio).

Income and Allocation. In 1955, 63.3 per cent of the income of insured mutual savings banks was derived from loans, 17.8 per cent from government obligations, 11.7 per cent from other securities, 3.3 per cent from other current sources, and the remainder from recoveries on loans and investments. During 1955, the income of insured mutual savings banks was allocated as follows: interest and dividends on deposits, 63.4 per cent; salaries and wages, 8.9 per cent; other recurring and current expenses, 9.8 per cent; charge-offs and so on, 6.6 per cent; income taxes, 1.1 per cent; and additions to capital accounts, 10.3 per cent. Although these percentages include only those for insured mutual savings banks, it may be assumed that they are typical of all mutual savings banks.

Limitations on Individual Deposits. Most mutual savings banks permit depositors to open accounts with $1.00 or more, and the state legislature usually provides for the maximum amount of an individual balance kept with one bank (most commonly $10,000). There are no rules against keeping deposits with more than one savings bank or dividing an account among different members of a family in order to circumvent the maximum-deposit rule. The maximum-deposit rule has been attacked on numerous occasions; but the primary reasons for its continuance are: (1) savings banks are for small depositors; (2) the dangers of disturbances resulting from withdrawals of a few large deposits are eliminated; (3) smaller reserves are necessary when a given volume of deposits is divided among, say, 15,000 depositors than would be the case with 500 depositors.

Participation in Central Banking Systems. Three mutual savings banks are members of the Federal Reserve System (two in Indiana and one in Wisconsin), and twenty-five are members of the Federal Home Loan Bank System. (See last section of this chapter.) The mutual savings banks of New York have organized their own "central bank," the Savings Bank Trust Company, which is a member of the Federal Reserve System. The mutual savings banks in New York State keep reserve balances with the Savings Bank Trust Company as well as with commercial banks. The Savings Bank Trust Company has an excellent research division to assist mutual savings banks in planning their loan and investment programs, and it has been instrumental in bringing about changes in the "legal list" of investments for mutual savings banks.

Guaranty Savings Banks. A peculiar modification of the mutual savings bank developed in New Hampshire. Known as "guaranty savings banks," these institutions have special deposits which are virtually capital stock. After the customary interest is paid to general depositors, the surplus goes to the special depositors. The charters of the banks usually require that special deposits must equal 10 per cent of the total deposits. The special deposits constitute a guaranty fund to protect the earnings and assets of general depositors. There are only eight of these banks in New Hampshire, and they represent an insignificant part of the savings-bank resources of the country. Most of the savings banks in New Hampshire are of the customary mutual type. The savings banks in New Hampshire hold over one half of the total deposits in that state.

Mutual savings banks have an excellent record, and few have failed. However, since World War I, they have become relatively less important because commercial banks have opened savings departments not only in states not served by mutual savings banks but also in mutual savings bank states. Although the savings bank movement had its origin in poverty and charity, it has outgrown its humble beginnings. The largest mutual savings bank, the Bowery Savings Bank of New York, has assets of more than $1 billion. In form, mutual savings banks still have their original type of organization; but their present size and the wealth of many of their depositors have made nominal their charitable and benevolent purposes, as suggested by some of their titles (for illustration, Philadelphia Savings Fund Society, Emigrant Industrial Savings Bank, and Dime Savings Bank).

SAVINGS DEPOSITS IN COMMERCIAL BANKS

At the end of 1955, the volume of time and savings deposits in all banks in the United States was $78.8 billion of which 60 per cent (about $50 billion) was in insured commercial banks. The larger amount of time deposits in commercial banks, as compared to mutual savings banks, is due chiefly to the fact that there are commercial banks in all states. In communities wherein there are both types of institutions, commercial banks may have a competitive advantage over mutual savings banks because of the greater variety of services offered and the lack of restrictions on the size of individual accounts. On the other hand, the lower operating costs of mutual savings banks make it possible for them to pay a higher interest rate on savings deposits than commercial banks can pay; and, as a result, the relative importance of time deposits in commercial banks is declining (from about 62 per cent at the end of 1954 to 60 per cent at the end of 1955).

Problem of Segregation. When savings deposits are accepted by commercial banks, the funds are mingled with other assets of the bank. Since the very nature of commercial banking requires that more risks be assumed than in the case of savings banking, time deposits are subject to more risks when left with commercial banks than with mutual savings banks (part of these risks may be shifted from depositors to the Federal Deposit Insurance Corporation). The savings depositors do not benefit from the risks associated with commercial banking, since they are not commercial borrowers and do not have the privilege of using their deposits as a means of payment.

During the seventy years from 1865 to 1934, 75 per cent of the total losses due to bank failures were taken by depositors with accounts of $5,000 or less.[1] Many bankers now regard the Federal Deposit Insurance Corporation as the solution to the problem of the need for protection of the small time and demand deposits; but a more equitable solution is the proposal for the complete segregation of the two types of banking, even though they may be carried on by the same bank.

Segregation of savings deposits would require: (1) the complete legal separation of the savings department from the rest of the bank, (2) allocation of a proportionate share of the bank's capital and surplus to this department, and (3) investment of savings deposits in assets similar to those purchased by mutual savings banks. Small banks vigorously oppose the plan to segregate the savings account business because they consider the costs to be prohibitive. Without question, the costs would be increased; but not so much as would be the case if two separate institutions conducted the commercial and savings bank business. Segregation of time deposits as proposed would still keep the advantages of combining several banking functions under the same management, in the same institution, and under the same roof. The added protection which would be given to savings depositors is of primary importance.

Limitations on Real Estate Mortgage Investments. National banks' investments in real estate mortgages may be 60 per cent of their time and savings deposits, or an amount equal to 100 per cent of their capital stock and surplus, whichever is the greater. Since guaranteed mortgages are excluded in computing the volume of real estate mortgages that member banks may hold, some commercial banks may have all of their time and savings deposits invested in real

---

[1] "Losses to Depositors in Suspended Commercial Banks, 1865–1934," *Annual Report of the Federal Deposit Insurance Corporation, for the Year Ended December 31, 1934* (Washington, D.C., 1935), pp. 73–110.

estate mortgages. (Of the residential real estate loans made by insured commercial banks at the end of 1955, $4.5 billion were insured by FHA, $3.7 billion were guaranteed by VA, and $7.5 billion were conventional loans.)

Commercial banks are also subject to the following restrictions on conventional loans: (1) the amount of any loan with a maturity of not more than five years is limited to 50 per cent of the appraised value of the real estate offered; (2) if provisions are made for liquidating the loan in installments, the loan value may be increased to 60 per cent and maturity to ten years provided the installment payments will amortize 40 per cent or more of the principal; (3) the loan value may be increased to $66\frac{2}{3}$ per cent and the maximum maturity extended to twenty years, provided the entire loan is amortized in twenty years. However, the loan limits on residential property do not apply to those insured or guaranteed by a federal agency. Commercial banks may also make construction loans to finance residential and farm buildings (classified as commercial loans), but the maximum permissible maturity is nine months.

POSTAL SAVINGS, SAVINGS BONDS, AND SCHOOL SAVINGS

Postal Savings System. The United States Postal Savings System, authorized in 1910, is managed by a board of trustees consisting of the Secretary of the Treasury, the Postmaster General, and the Attorney General.[2] During 1910 and 1911 the arguments used in favor of establishing the United States Postal Savings System were: (1) savings bank facilities were not being provided by private enterprise and could not be so provided because of the prohibitive expense of operating banks in some communities, (2) the thrifty needed greater protection against losses and inconveniences arising from bank failures; (3) hoarded funds would be brought back into circulation; (4) existing banks had nothing to fear from government competition because they had the advantages of established clientele, higher interest rates, and higher maximum limits on individual deposits; (5) it would aid the development of thrift; and (6) postal savings deposits would be transferred to banks as soon as they reached the limit fixed by law.[3]

[2] The Division of Postal Savings Banking and Investments in the "Bureau of the Third Assistant Postmaster General" has supervision over all the revenues and financial operations of the Postal Savings System. This division also supervises the sale of United States savings bonds and savings stamps at post offices.

[3] See American Bankers Association, *Postal Savings System of the United States* (New York: American Bankers Association, 1937), chap. II.

The proponents of the bill which originally provided for the Postal Savings System argued that the system would not be in competition with banks because the latter were (1) paying higher interest rates on deposits (from 3 to 4 per cent whereas only 2 per cent would be paid on postal deposits) and (2) accepting deposits in excess of the maximum on postal savings accounts (then $500). Most of the arguments in favor of the Postal Savings System are not applicable to present circumstances, and there is considerable interest in banking circles in the liquidation of the Postal Savings System.

Anyone over the age of ten may open a savings account at any post office that is authorized to accept deposits (about 8,000) but only one account may be kept at the same or different post offices at any one time. Instead of passbooks, deposits are evidenced by nontransferable certificates or vouchers issued in denominations of $1.00 up to and including $500. The maximum balance allowed one person is $2,500, exclusive of accumulated interest; but an additional noninterest-bearing balance of $1,000 may be left with the post office for safekeeping. The interest rate is fixed at 2 per cent but may not exceed the rate prescribed by the Board of Governors of the Federal Reserve System.[4]

In recent years, the volume of savings in the Postal Savings System has declined progressively relative to total savings. The reasons given for this development include: (1) limitations are placed on the amount in one account; (2) joint accounts are not permitted, which means that funds are frozen pending the settlement of a depositor's estate; (3) checks are not accepted for deposit; and (4) savings bonds are being purchased by those who otherwise might have placed their savings in the Postal Savings System. However, there are still about 3,000,000 investors with deposits of about $2 billion in the Postal Savings System.

At the present time, there are some thoughtful students who argue that the Postal Savings System should be retained because (1) it provides a source of funds with which to buy government securities, (2) it may be needed as a haven for savings in case of another depression, and (3) it is considered to be a preferred de-

---

[4] When the state banking commissioner of New York, of New Jersey, and of Mississippi reduced the interest rate of state banks to 1 per cent, the Federal Reserve System reduced rates on postal and other time deposits in those states to 1 per cent. Interest is not compounded, but certificates may be surrendered each year after having earned a full year's interest and reinvested in postal savings certificates.

pository by many individuals. In keeping with the attitude of bankers, the Hoover Report on the Organization of the Executive Branch of the National Government (1949) concluded that the Postal Savings System is no longer needed.

Actually, the procedures for issuance and redemption of certificates, maintenance of accounts, and reissuance of certificates each year are both inconvenient and expensive. The Division of Audits and General Accounting Office of the federal government have criticized the Postal Savings System as being inefficient and wasteful. The "charges" made against the Postal Savings System for "general overhead" have been criticized as being inadequate and the allocation of current expenses do not include all costs (such as handling mail matter of the Postal Savings System which is transmitted free of postage). With the advent of the Federal Deposit Insurance Corporation's insurance coverage for smaller deposits and the offering of United States savings bonds, small savers are given the same amount of protection as provided in the Postal Savings System.

United States Savings Bonds. The United States Savings Bond Division of the Office of the Secretary of the Treasury has been responsible for promoting the sale of United States savings bonds. In 1952, provisions were made by the Treasury to replace Series E, F, and G bonds with new Series E, J, and K bonds, respectively, and a new Series H bond was added. Offices of the United States Savings Bond Division are maintained in every state and the District of Columbia, but sales are made through approximately 60,000 issuing agencies. Today some 45,000,000 investors own savings bonds having a maturity value of $58.2 billion.

In 1952 the yield on all the new savings bonds was increased, and the adjustments made in the redemption schedule increased their conversion value during the earlier years. The yield on new Series E bonds was raised from 2.9 to 3 per cent, if held to maturity, by reducing the maturity period from 10 years to 9 years and 8 months. Series E bonds are not transferable, but they may be redeemed at the option of the owner during each half year at progressively increasing redemption values (reflecting the interest earned).

The new Series H bonds involve semiannual payments of interest by check with the interest graduated in amount to correspond to the new Series E bonds. After they have been outstanding six months and after notice of one month, the H bonds are redeemable at par. The denominations of the new E bonds vary from $25 to $10,000; and H bonds are in denominations of $500, $1,000, and $10,000. The new J and K series are similar to the old F and G bonds, paying 2¾ per cent instead of 2½ per cent if held to their twelve-year maturity. The Series F and G bonds are designed for larger savers than are the Series E and H bonds.

School Savings Banks. Banks and savings and loan associations have co-operated with the public schools in forming habits of thrift and saving among the younger groups by sponsoring school savings banks. School banks have been established in a number of places to receive deposits from the school children. These deposits are later placed with banks or savings and loan associations. Prior to the transfer of deposits to banks, school savings are administered customarily by pupils; but, thereafter, quoting the distracted employee of a bank, "it is our headache." Although the turnover of some individual deposits is rapid, the total balances are from two to three times the amount deposited annually. Some institutions automatically reclassify school savings deposits, after they reach a certain amount, as ordinary savings accounts. In addition to inculcating thrift habits, the school savings bank movement will sooner or later bring pupils into direct contact with banks. As every parent of a pupil-depositor knows, this stimulates a healthy interest in such institutions. Now 529 banks are serving 4,150,000 school savers in 10,000 schools with accumulated balances totaling $145,250,000.

SAVINGS AND LOAN ASSOCIATIONS

In the United States in 1831 the first building and loan association was founded in a suburb of Philadelphia. Savings or building and loan associations are organized to make loans to homeowners and to conduct a savings business. Technically, they do not accept deposits; but, when they issue passbooks in which savings accounts are recorded, they do practically the same thing as banks do when they accept savings deposits. Savings accounts in a savings and loan association are payments for stock of the association. Thus, savers using the facilities of these associations are not creditors (as is true of depositors in banks) but are "equity" holders or part owners of their associations.

Many of the early savings and loan associations were organized on a temporary basis, being dissolved when all members desirous of doing so had obtained their loans; and the nonborrowing members were paid off in cash and the others surrendered their stock in payment of their loans. The terminating type of association was followed by the serial type which permitted continuous operation by taking in new members at various times (for example, at the beginning of each year). Now most associations are organized on the permanent plan wherein new members may join at any time and may subscribe for as many shares as they wish.

Most state as well as federal savings and loan associations may now sell different types of shares, classified as follows: (1) installment thrift shares, for which the subscriber makes uniform periodic payments called "dues"; (2) optional savings shares, calling for such payments as the subscriber can make conveniently; (3) prepaid shares, which are sold at an estimated present value and on which dividends are applied, making them shares fully paid at maturity; and (4) income or fully-paid shares, which are paid in a lump sum at the time of purchase and on which dividends are paid in cash when declared.

Although savings and loan associations are among the most important home-financing institutions in the United States, they are among the least known, since (1) they deal with a "small man's business," (2) they are local in nature and until recently were of only local interest, (3) they are mutual and controlled by investors, and (4) they limit their activities chiefly to advancing thrift and financial homeownership. Now, in addition to having their own insurance corporation (see below), they have their own central banking system, which includes eleven regional or central banks, a Home Loan Bank Board, and an Advisory Council.

Savings and loan associations are incorporated under either state or national law. Those incorporated under national law must have the word "federal" in their titles. State associations have different names in different states—including "building and loan associations," "co-operative banks," "homestead associations," and "savings institutions." About one fourth of the associations have federal charters and their combined assets represent slightly over one half of the total assets of all savings and loan associations in the nation. During the period since World War II the assets of savings and loan associations have increased more rapidly than those of other savings institutions because of their more aggressive campaign for new accounts, the higher rate of return, and the increased demand for mortgage credit. In mid-1956, assets of savings and loan associations were $39 billion, distributed approximately as follows: 84 per cent in mortgages, 6 per cent in government obligations, 5 per cent in cash, and 5 per cent in other assets.

FEDERAL HOME LOAN BANK SYSTEM

Home Loan Bank Board. The Federal Home Loan Bank Board was created by authority of the Federal Home Loan Bank Act of 1932 to provide a central banking system for savings and home-financing institutions. The System includes a Home Loan Bank Board, which serves also as the board of trustees of the Federal Savings and Loan Insurance Corporation. The Board consists of three members who are appointed by the President with the advice and consent of the Senate. The expenses of the Board are paid by assessments against the regional federal home loan banks and from funds obtained from charges against the other agencies under its supervision and from examination fees collected from institutions examined by the Board's examining division.

Advisory Council. The Federal Savings and Loan Advisory Council consists of one member elected by each of the eleven boards of directors of the federal home loan banks and six appointed by the Home Loan Bank Board. Its duties are similar to those of the advisory council of the Federal Reserve System.

Federal Home Loan Banks. The Federal Home Loan Bank System has eleven (originally twelve) regional federal home loan banks located in New York, Boston, Pittsburgh, Greensboro, Cincinnati, Indianapolis, Chicago, Des Moines, Little Rock, Topeka, and San Francisco (see Map 2). The capital stock of the banks is owned by member institutions;[4] but, like the federal land banks, most of the funds they lend are raised through public sale of bonds, debentures, and/or other obligations. A federal home loan bank may accept deposits from member institutions and from other federal home loan banks. They make short-term loans to member institutions

---

[4] Originally, part of the stock of the federal home loan banks was owned by the federal government; but this was gradually repurchased by the Banks, and the government's holdings of stock were retired on July 1, 1951. In case of an emergency the federal home loan banks may request the Secretary of the Treasury, at his discretion, to purchase the banks' obligations in an amount limited to $1 billion at any one time.

The mutualization of the federal home loan banks was hastened by an Act of Congress, approved June 27, 1950, which required each member institution to increase its holdings of stock in its federal home loan bank in amount from 1 to 2 per cent of the aggregate of the unpaid principal of home-mortgage loans, home-purchase contracts, or similar obligations owned by the institution, but in no case less than $500.

(as do Federal Reserve banks to member banks) and long-term loans to member institutions (as federal land banks do to national farm loan associations). So these banks have a dual role in strengthening existing home-financing institutions—serving as both bankers' banks and as a normal source of long-term credit to supplement local home mortgage funds. Each bank is managed by a board of twelve directors (except San Francisco bank which has fifteen directors), four

MAP 2

FEDERAL HOME LOAN BANK DISTRICTS

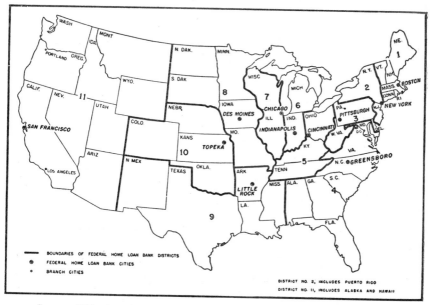

Source: *Fifth Annual Report Housing and Home Finance Agency* (Washington, D.C.: U.S. Government Printing Office, 1952), p. 170.

of whom are appointed by the Home Loan Bank Board for terms of four years each, and eight of whom are elected by member institutions for terms of two years each. The board of directors select a president who must be approved by the Federal Home Loan Bank Board.

Member Institutions. Federal savings and loan associations are required to be members of the Federal Home Loan Bank System. In addition, membership includes state-chartered building and loan associations, insurance companies, and mutual savings banks. Federal savings and loan associations are supervised by the Federal Home Loan Bank Board, and the state associations are supervised by state authorities (in some states by the superintendent or commissioner of banking and in others by separate agencies). The Board must approve applications for new federal charters and for the establishment of branch offices.

Federal Savings and Loan Insurance Corporation. In Title IV of the National Housing Act, Congress made provisions for insurance

CHART 11

FEDERAL HOME LOAN BANK SYSTEM

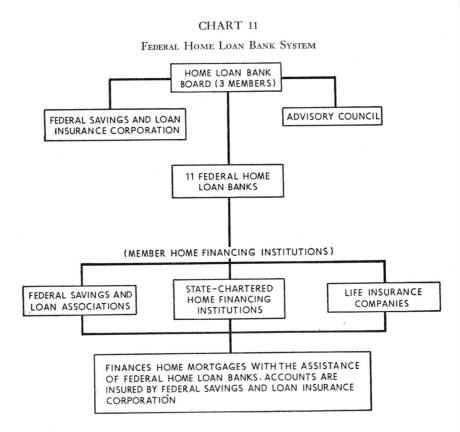

of accounts in all federal savings and loan associations and participating state-chartered associations. The insurance agency, the Federal Savings and Loan Insurance Corporation, is owned by the government; but the law now provides that the capital stock held by the government is to be retired out of earnings (as was done for the Federal Deposit Insurance Corporation). Of the original capital stock of $100,000,000 about one half has been retired. The Corporation has accumulated reserves in excess of $180,000,000 and may borrow from the United States Treasury up to a total of $750,000,000 outstanding at any one time.

All federal savings and loan associations must, and qualified state savings and loan associations may, insure their accounts with the Federal Savings and Loan Insurance Corporation. Individuals who have accounts in insured savings and loan associations have the same type of protection as do depositors in insured commercial banks—$10,000 per investor in each insured savings and loan association. The insurance premium is one twelfth of 1 per cent on the association's share accounts and credit obligations.

In case of failure of an association the beneficiary receives either a new insured account in a solvent institution or is paid in cash. The Corporation may act to prevent the default and liquidation of an insured association (its powers being similar to those of the Federal Deposit Insurance Corporation). The Home Loan Bank Board acts as the board of trustees for the Federal Savings and Loan Insurance Corporation and while the Home Owners' Loan Corporation was in operation, it also acted as its board of directors.

HOUSING AND HOME FINANCE AGENCY

The Housing and Home Finance Agency was established in 1947 to co-ordinate and assume responsibility for the principal urban housing programs in which the federal government had an interest (formerly it included the Federal Home Loan Bank System). Now, the chief federal agencies supervised by the Housing and Home Finance Agency are the Federal Housing Administration, the Public Housing Administration, and the Federal National Mortgage Association. The National Housing Council advises the Administrator of the Agency on general policies and practices with the view of promoting the long-run housing objectives of the government and preventing overlapping of activities and functions among institutions.

Federal Housing Administration. A discussion of mortgage lending would be incomplete without particular reference to the Federal Housing Administration. FHA was created by the National Housing Act of 1934 and was designed to insure mortgagees against losses from default. The protection provided by FHA has been for institutional lenders, not individuals (an important factor in explaining the predominance of institutional lenders in the home financing field).

The Federal Housing Administration, following a plan similar to that employed by insurance companies, has accumulated reserve funds (seven in all) to meet claims when borrowers default on their payments. The most important of these funds is the Mutual Mortgage Insurance Fund which was created to carry the insurance on residences (1- to 4-family units). As the title implies, this fund is mutual and, as a result, a home purchaser may receive a rebate when his loan is amortized. The funds were initially provided by the federal government, but some have been repaid.

Customarily, the payment for insurance is made by the borrower and amounts to one half of 1 per cent. However, in the case of repair and improvement loans (Title I), the cost of insurance is borne by the lender. In the event of default, repair and improvement loans are paid in cash, and home loans are paid in debentures.

In addition to the insurance program previously discussed, the activities of the Federal Housing Administration have included the insurance of large housing projects, group housing units, co-operative housing units, and war and military housing units. FHA has also insured mortgages issued when certain permanent government housing units were sold to private investors. The activities of FHA have been felt in aspects of the housing industry other than the insurance of loans. For illustration, FHA has made a major contribution to the housing industry by setting and enforcing building standards for units financed with FHA mortgages. It has also made a major contribution in the field of urban mortgage credit by encouraging the flow of private funds into urban mortgage loans.

Since 1945, nonfarm mortgage debt has risen from $30.8 billion to $105.6 billion; and the debt on housing units for four families or less has increased from $18.5 billion to $75.9 billion (much faster than the increase in gross national product, but perhaps not alarming because the volume of home mortgage debt was relatively small in 1945).

Veterans' Administration Loans.   Although the Veterans' Administration is not a part of the Federal Housing Administration, it is appropriate to note that it co-operates with and supplements the work of FHA. The Servicemen's Readjustment Act of 1944 as amended authorized the Veterans' Administration to guarantee institutional loans made to eligible ex-servicemen for purposes such as purchase of farms and livestock, business property within the United States, and homes. The Veterans' Administration may guarantee real estate loans up to 60 per cent of the loan or $7,500, whichever is less. In addition, the Veterans' Administration is also authorized to make direct loans to veterans.

Federal National Mortgage Association.   The Federal National Mortgage Association was organized in 1938 by the Reconstruction Finance Corporation to provide a national rediscount or secondary market for insured mortgages. In 1954, it received the charter under which it is now functioning. Most of the funds used by the association (popularly known as "Fannie May") are acquired by the sale of notes or debentures to the general public (restricted in amount to ten times the association's total capitalization and surplus). Borrowers must subscribe to common stock of the association in an amount equal to 3 per cent of the amount of unpaid balance of the mortgages they sell to the association. Such mortgages must be insured by the Veterans' Administration or the Federal Housing Administration. Mortgages bought by the association from banks, mortgage companies, savings and loan associations, and other organizations are usually resold to permanent investors as quickly as possible.

At different times, the Federal National Mortgage Association has been authorized by Congress and the President to give special assistance to some specified type of mortgages until a more permanent market could be made for them. Since 1938, the association has purchased about $5 billion of mortgages, of which about one half have been liquidated through repayment by borrowers or resale to investors. Although the operations of the association are designed so that it will eventually be privately owned and operated, the United States Treasury owns $93,000,000 of its preferred stock.

Public Housing Administration. The agency now known as the Public Housing Administration was originally established in 1937 to administer the low-rent housing projects authorized in the United States Housing Act of 1937, and it was placed within the Housing and Home Finance Agency in 1947. The functions of the Public Housing Administration are: (1) to give financial assistance to local public housing authorities in slum clearance and construction of rental housing for low-income families; and (2) to assume responsibility for war housing and other public housing projects (many of which were converted into low-rent housing after the wartime need had passed).

The low-rent housing projects constructed under the United States Housing Act program are administered by local housing authorities, organized under state enabling acts as public corporations. They are managed by boards appointed by the chief executive of the cities in which the housing authorities are located, and each board if responsible for the construction and management of the buildings. Members serve without pay, employing experts and others to administer the projects. The management must keep uniform accounting records and must make periodic reports to state and national housing authorities. Financial assistance by Public Housing Administration is given in the form of capital loans at low interest rates and annual subsidies. The financial assistance of local governments most commonly takes the form of making the housing projects exempt from local property taxes.

SUMMARY

The volume of expenditures for housing and other forms of real property in urban areas is an important factor in determining the well-being of the economy. If these expenditures are too low, it may cause a recession or depression; if too large, it may cause a business boom, inflation, and creation of conditions that may lead to a depression. Funds used to finance urban real estate developments come from lenders of all types but particularly institutional investors.

The United States government has assisted in developing the housing industry by creating and operating certain government agencies. Three methods have been used: (1) strengthening private home-financing institutions by creating the Federal Home Loan Bank System, which includes eleven regional federal home loan banks and the Federal Savings and Loan Insurance Corporation; (2) underwriting home mortgages, as by the Federal Housing Administration and the Veterans' Administration, in order to make mortgages more attractive to institutional investors; and (3) subsidizing public housing projects, as by the Public Housing Administration.

In general, the government has stressed the use of private credit in the financing of homes; and the actual amount of public funds committed, relative to the volume of urban mortgages outstanding, has been small. Private home-financing institutions have assumed most of the financial responsibility for the different federal banks and agencies (mutualization of the Home Loan Bank System is now complete; and mutualization of the Federal Housing Administration and Federal National Mortgage Association Funds is in process). The chief beneficiaries of the direct and indirect aid given by the government have been homeowners—which is as it should be.

In addition to the institutions in the mortgage credit field sponsored by the government, there are other institutions which are important lenders. The most important of these are: (1) mutual savings banks, which invest the major portion of their savings deposits in real estate mortgages; (2) savings and loan associations, which invest more than 80 per cent of their funds in mortgages; and (3) life insurance companies (see Chapter XXVII). While the federal savings and loan associations are required to be members of the Federal Home

Loan Bank System, state-chartered savings and loan associations, mutual savings banks, and life insurance companies may be members of the System.

The eleven federal home loan banks are the regional central banks of the Federal Home Loan Bank System which is the central banking system for savings and home-financing institutions. The Federal Savings and Loan Insurance Corporation insures the accounts of federal and qualified state-chartered savings and loan associations. The deposits of most of the mutual savings banks are insured either by the Federal Deposit Insurance Corporation or by deposit insurance corporations organized by mutual savings banks in some states.

The Public Housing Administration has been helpful in providing emergency housing, chiefly for veterans (as on or abutting most college and university campuses); but its more permanent role is to assist local housing authorities in the elimination of slum dwellings and replacing them with low-rent housing projects.

QUESTIONS AND PROBLEMS

1. Identify: (*a*) mortgage companies, (*b*) savings and loan associations, (*c*) Home Owners' Loan Corporation, and (*d*) Federal National Mortgage Association.
2. Compare the financing of hotels, large office buildings, and apartment houses during the 1920's to their financing at the present time.
3. Distinguish between (*a*) a first and a second mortgage, and (*b*) conventional and nonconventional mortgages.
4. Summarize present-day standard terms for most home mortgages.
5. To what extent is the income of the borrower, as compared to the appraised value of the property pledged, the determining factor in justifying current mortgage lending practices?
6. What was the origin of the mutual savings bank movement? How important are the savings deposits in these institutions? How do you account for the geographical distribution of mutual savings banks? In what sense are these banks mutual? Not mutual?
7. Describe the organization and functions of savings and loan associations.
8. Analyze: "Banks alone have the capacity to create demand deposits and currency . . . , but only savings and loan associations can create savings and loan shares; both 'create credit,' both transmit loanable funds, both enable spending units to diversify their portfolios." (J. G. Gurley and E. S. Shaw, "Financial Aspects of Economic Development," *American Economic Review*, Vol. XLV, No. 4 [September, 1955], p. 521.)
9. Identify the Federal Savings and Loan Insurance Corporation. Compare to the Federal Deposit Insurance Corporation as to ownership,

insurance fees, and methods of settling claims against suspended institutions.

10. Describe the organization of the Federal Home Loan Bank System. Has this system achieved a place in the home-financing field corresponding to that of the Federal Reserve System in the commercial banking field? Has the Federal Housing Administration helped the Federal Home Loan Bank System?

11. Federal Housing Administration insures mortgages on the assumption that the mortgages will bear a reasonable relation to long-term stabilized value. Other aspects of the federal government housing program aim to reduce the costs of constructing new homes and to keep down rents. What is the solution of this dilemma?

12. Explain the purpose, organization, management, and financing of the Public Housing Administration.

13. Do you agree that housing credit is not only a financial but also a social problem? Why?

Chapter	AGRICULTURAL CREDIT
XXX	INSTITUTIONS

IN GENERAL, farmers have about the same sources of credit as do small business firms; but, in addition, they have other facilities created with governmental aid. There are certain reasons given to justify this favoritism. The hazards of farming are great because of the uncertainty of weather, the inelasticity of the supply of farm products, and the large number of small producing units which makes voluntary crop control difficult. As a business unit, the average farm is small which means that farmers are denied direct access to the money and capital markets (just as small business firms are).

Traditionally, farming has been a way of life, the farm having been not only a place of business but also a home; and the resulting mixture of business finance and home or personal finance complicated the problem of lending. In case of foreclosure, the farmer lost both his business and his home. Although this situation still exists in many parts of the country, an increasing number of farms are becoming solely a place of business with those who operate them living in towns and commuting to work as do most other businessmen. Farming has also become more specialized which means that farms, as family units, have become less self-sustaining.

Advances in the art of farm management and contributions of science have made it possible for fewer farmers to raise larger crops on less acreage; as a result, emphasis has shifted from creating new financing facilities for farmers to finding new uses for farm products and supporting farm commodity prices. Because of governmental support of farm commodity prices, the mechanization of farms, and other factors, the aggregate short-term and intermediate-term debt of farmers now exceeds their mortgage debt. On January 1, 1956, the real estate debt on farm property was $9 billion, and all other farm debts were $9.8 billion including nonrecourse loans of $1.9 billion held or guaranteed by the Commodity Credit Corporation. Since the total assets of farmers amounted to $170.1 billion, their proprietary equity was $151.3 billion (making agriculture technically the most solvent major industry in the United States).[1]

This chapter deals chiefly with the institutions created over the last forty years to lend directly to farmers. Although started with government funds, most of them are now functioning with little or no governmental aid. In fact, many of them have invested in government securities and are now net creditors rather than debtors of the federal government. Although the average farmer is an individualist, co-operative banks and mutual associations predominate in the federal farm credit system. Unlike home financing, little use has been made of the government-guarantee principle in the field of agricultural credit. Instead, the federal government has inaugurated a program of price support for farm products linked to the cost of farming, which is even more significant than insurance of farm loans would be.

FARM MORTGAGE DEBT

Private Lenders. Farmers require credit for long-term, intermediate-term, and short-term needs, corresponding in time to those of industry and commerce. In the agricultural field, long-term credit is associated with the purchase of farms. Part of this need for long-term credit is due to state laws which require equal division of property among children of deceased persons. In many cases, this means either that some member or members of the new generation will mortgage the home place to pay off the other heirs not remaining on the farm, or that the farm will be sold to some outsider who will have to borrow in order to finance the purchase. If the mortgage is amortized during the new owner's life, the mortgage creating and repaying process will start over again at his death. Therefore, there will be a farm-mortgage-debt problem in the United States as long as we have antiprimogeniture laws that prevent the first male child from inheriting all land.

Throughout the history of the United States, individuals have been the chief holders of farm-mortgage debt. When a farmer retires and sells his farm, he may accept a first or second mortgage as part of the price. In addition to retired farmers, investors in farm mortgages include wealthy individuals who acquire mortgages directly from borrowers or through mortgage brokers.

Mortgage Companies. Mortgage companies operate in both the

---

[1] See also *Federal Reserve Bulletin* (August, 1956), pp. 823–32.

farm- and urban-mortgage fields through branch offices and local correspondents who investigate to determine whether or not mortgages should be purchased for resale. Sometimes, mortgage companies hold mortgages acquired and pledge them as security for loans or for issues of securities. Loans made by mortgage companies are usually for five years or less; and, during this period, the borrower usually strengthens his financial position by increasing his equity in the farm so that he may refinance elsewhere for a longer period of time.

Short-term financing of long-term credit needs tends to be expensive due to renewal fees and high interest rates; but, if the policy of long-term lenders is to make loans for but a fraction of the appraised value of farms, the farmer-borrowers may have no choice except to borrow on a short-term basis until their equity is sufficient to make them eligible for long-term mortgage contracts. Today, mortgage companies usually act as brokers or dealers in farm mortgages for insurance companies and other large lenders. After a mortgage company sells a farm mortgage, the mortgage holder may contract with the company to administer the mortgage loan agreement, collect interest and principal payments, and so on.

Federal Land Banks. Now, the federal land banks and other federal agencies are less prominent in the farm-mortgage market than during the depression of the 1930's, when they were about the only source of new farm mortgage credit. During this period, they absorbed many of the farm mortgages which were held by other lending institutions. The influence of federal land banks has been great not only because they provided farmers with long-term credit but also because of their effect on mortgage-lending practices. When the federal land banks were established, they pioneered in the use of amortized farm mortgages. Largely through their influence, more modern principles of mortgage lending were gradually adopted throughout the farm-mortgage credit field—small down payments, higher loan values, careful appraisals, emphasis on farm income, and periodic equal payments that include principal, interest, insurance, and other charges. (Federal land banks are discussed more fully under the subsection entitled *Federal Land Bank System,* later in this chapter.)

On January 1, 1955, individuals and others held 41.1 per cent of the total farm mortgages; life insurance companies, 25.1 per cent; federal land banks, 15.5 per cent; commercial banks, 14.8 per cent; Farmers Home Administration, 3.3 per cent; and Federal Farm Mortgage Corporation, 0.2 per cent.

Insurance Companies. As holders of farm mortgages, life insurance companies are second only to individuals and miscellaneous lenders, including mortgage companies (see Table 22). Life insurance companies lend directly to farmers through local offices or agents and buy farm mortgages from brokers and mortgage companies. Generally, insurance companies use the same terms in mortgage-loan contracts as those noted above; however, they are usually able to

TABLE 22

FARM MORTGAGE DEBT OUTSTANDING, BY LENDERS IN THE UNITED STATES
(January 1, Selected Years, 1940–56)

LENDER	AMOUNT OUTSTANDING (In Millions of Dollars)				PERCENTAGE CHANGE*	
	1940	1950	1955	1956	1940–56	1955–56
Total......................	6,586	5,579	8,176	8,960 †	36	10
Federal land banks‡...................	2,010	906	1,267	1,480	−26	17
Federal Farm Mortgage Corporation‡§..	713	59	13	0	......	......
Farmers Home Adm.‖.................	32	189	271	278	770	3
Life insurance companies‡.............	984	1,172	2,052	2,270 †	131	11
Insured commercial banks.............	534	879	1,136	1,270	138	12
Individuals and miscellaneous¶.........	2,313	2,374	3,437	3,662 †	58	7

Source: *Federal Reserve Bulletin* (August, 1956), p. 830.
* Computed from unrounded data.
† Preliminary.
‡ Includes regular mortgages, purchase-money mortgages, and sales contracts.
§ Loans were made for the Corporation by the Land Bank Commissioner. Authority to make new loans expired July 1, 1947. On June 30, 1955, loans of the Federal Farm Mortgage Corporation were sold to the twelve federal land banks.
‖ For 1940 tenant-purchase loans only. The period 1945–56 includes tenant-purchase; farm-enlargement; farm-development; project-liquidation loans; beginning July 1950, farm-housing loans; beginning 1955, building-improvement loans; and beginning Jan. 1, 1956, direct soil and water loans to individuals. Data also include similar loans from State Corporation trust funds.
¶ Estimates of farm mortgage debt held by individual and miscellaneous lenders for 1951 and later years should be regarded only as general indicators of trend.

make larger loans and to lend relatively more in terms of appraisal value than are federal land banks whose loans are restricted by law to a specified percentage of the appraised value of the property as well as to the amount they may lend to one farmer.

Commercial Banks. Although rural commercial banks have always been prominent in the farm-mortgage field, they lost their dominant position during the depression of the 1930's. Currently, they are increasing their lending activities in the farm-mortgage field wherein there is little suggestion of credit being overextended as is the case in the urban-mortgage field. Although there has been an increase in the amount of farm-mortgage debt, this increase has been more than offset by the increase in the value of farm land and other farm assets.

Commercial banks have many advantages over other lenders in the farm-mortgage field because of their location, ability to serve, and existing contacts with farmers. Rural commercial banks are faced with less competition from large urban banks, savings banks, and savings and loan associations in the farm-mortgage field than are urban banks in the urban-mortgage field; and now rural banks hold about the same amount of farm-mortgage debt as is held by the federal land banks.

FARMERS' NON-REAL-ESTATE DEBT

The farmer's need for credit to finance working capital assets is similar to that of any other businessman but his need may be greater because he must finance the storage of his products as well as their production. Crops are seasonal in nature and their market prices tend to be lowest at the time they are harvested. Weather and growing conditions change rapidly; so a farmer's land is subject to drought, unseasonal frosts, heavy rainfalls, and other disasters that may destroy crops. With little or nothing to sell, a farmer's ability to repay loans is impaired. When weather conditions are favorable, bumper crops depress farm prices; this has an adverse effect on a farmer's ability to discharge his obligations. Consumers and the government have an interest in the normal flow of goods from the farm to the market; and the price-support program for certain basic farm products was developed out of this need to finance the storage of bumper crops to be sold at a later date (the age-old idea of storing crops during the seven fat years for use during the seven lean years).

Commodity Credit Corporation. While the current price-support program for certain farm products may seem to have degenerated into something other than that for which it was intended, the purpose is to encourage farmers to plant wheat, cotton, corn, and other crops by accepting loan contracts at crop-planting time. If a farmer meets the terms as to acreage, uses of idle land, and so on, he may sign a contract that gives him the option at marketing time of placing his crop under loan at the contract price or selling it in the commodity market. If the loan price is higher than the market price at the time of harvesting, he would place the crop under loan with the Commodity Credit Corporation (usually through or by the local bank, and, in the latter case, the loan is guaranteed by the Commodity Credit Corporation). The loan is without recourse and if the farmer does *not* repay it on or before maturity, title to the commodity passes to the Commodity Credit Corporation. The volume of Commodity

Credit Corporation loans (see Table 23) is influenced by a number of factors, the two most important of which are the current and anticipated market price of the price-supported commodity and the loan price as contained in the loan contract as drawn at the time of planting.

Banks and Federally-Sponsored Agencies. Farmers go into debt to finance planting and harvesting crops, to purchase livestock, to make improvements on farm buildings, to purchase consumer goods, and to finance other personal and business needs. However, the greatest change in farmers' indebtedness has resulted from the mechaniza-

TABLE 23

FARMERS' NON-REAL-ESTATE DEBT IN THE UNITED STATES
(January 1, Selected Years, 1940–56; in Billions of Dollars)

Type of Debt	1940	1950	1955	1956
Price-support loans made or guaranteed by Commodity Credit Corporation*.............................	.4	1.7	2.2	1.9
Other loans by banks and Federally sponsored agencies...	1.5	2.8	4.0	4.4
Loans and book credits by miscellaneous lenders †........	1.5	2.4	3.3	3.5
Total, excluding Commodity Credit Corporation loans..................................	3.0	5.2	7.3	7.9
Total, including Commodity Credit Corporation loans..................................	3.4	6.9	9.5	9.8

Source: *Federal Reserve Bulletin* (August, 1956), p. 831.
  * Although these are nonrecourse loans, they are treated as debts. Borrowers must either pay them in cash or deliver the commodities on which they are based.
  † Estimate based on fragmentary data.

tion of farms. Now it is not unusual for a corn-belt farmer to have as much as $100,000 invested in a farm venture, of which $20,000 may be in machinery and equipment. When cash loans are needed, farmers borrow from rural banks, production credit associations, and miscellaneous lenders. Loans may be secured by chattel mortgages on cattle or other livestock and other types of tangible personal property.

Miscellaneous Lenders. Farmers have the same sources of store and installment credit as those open to other consumers and businessmen. Thus, sales credit for automobiles, tractors, trucks, radios, television sets, and so on is just as available to farmers as to other individuals. Included among the miscellaneous lenders are the specialists in the farm credit field which include livestock loan companies. These companies lend to cattle breeders and other stockmen on their promissory notes, which they endorse and sell to commercial banks or to the federal intermediate credit banks (see below). Loans may be for small or fairly large amounts (such as $500,000). The maturities of notes vary according to the purposes for which loans are made, being from three to six months when funds are to be used for fattening cattle and sheep (hogs are seldom financed because the loans would be too speculative) and up to three years when used for breeding purposes. The livestock companies' gross profit is the difference between the interest rates on farmers' promissory notes and the rates at which the paper is discounted by the institutions which buy it. In some areas, there are produce dealers, factors, and merchants who finance farm production. They make loans secured by liens on anticipated crops and/or assets of the borrower. When crops are sold, the loans are repaid plus interest and fees or commissions.

On January 1, 1955, individuals and others held 45.2 per cent of the non-real-estate debt of farmers; commercial banks, 40.2 per cent; production credit associations, 7.9 per cent; Farmers Home Administration, 5.9 per cent; and the federal intermediate credit banks, 0.8 per cent.

FARM CREDIT ADMINISTRATION

The Farm Credit Administration is an independent agency in the executive branch of the government. Laws and policies are administered by a governor and his staff under general supervision of a Federal Farm Credit Board. This Board consists of thirteen members, one appointed by the Secretary of Agriculture and the other twelve by the President of the United States with the advice and consent of the Senate. There is one member from each farm credit district, and the appointments are made by the President only after consideration is given to nominations by national farm loan associations, production credit associations, and marketing, purchasing, and service co-operatives. Board members are part-time employees; but they select the Governor of Farm Credit Administration (FCA) who must be approved by the President as long as the government has any capital invested in the System. The Federal Farm Credit Board is required to make reports to Congress, to make recommendations as to changes in the Farm Credit System, and generally to direct, supervise, and control Farm Credit Administration.

The Farm Credit System, supervised by the Federal Farm Credit Board, consists of twelve federal land banks, twelve federal intermediate credit banks, twelve production credit corporations, thirteen banks for co-operatives, 1,100 national farm loan associations, 500 production credit associations, and the Federal Farm Mortgage Corporation. The purpose of the Farm Credit System is to give agriculture a complete and co-ordinated credit system by providing short-term, intermediate, and long-term credit (see Chart 12). The office of the Governor of FCA in Washington has (1) an examination division to make the required annual examinations of banks, corporations, and production credit associations supervised by FCA, and to examine the national farm loan associations when so directed by the Governor of the Farm Credit Administration; (2) a legal division;

CHART 12

FARM CREDIT ADMINISTRATION

(Permanent Agencies)

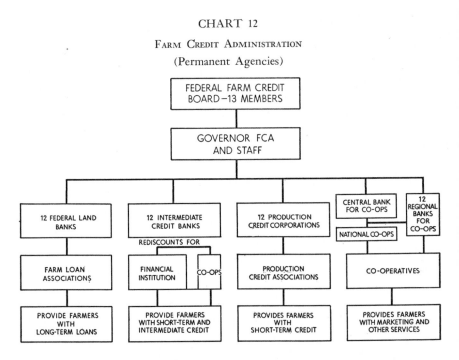

(3) three credit service divisions (a) for the twelve federal land banks and the 1,100 national farm loan associations; (b) for twelve intermediate credit banks, twelve production credit corporations, and 500 production credit associations; and (c) co-operative bank service for the thirteen banks for co-operatives; and (4) other divisions which emphasize general services for the System (such as finance and accounts, personnel, etc.).

Originally, rural mortgage credit was emphasized, and the first agencies provided for were the twelve federal land banks and local farm loan associations (organized and operated by groups of farmers with funds obtained from the federal land banks). As the need for other types of credit became more pressing, instead of enlarging the powers of the federal land banks to permit them to make nonmortgage loans, other agencies were created. Now each federal land bank city is the site of a federal intermediate credit bank (1923), a production credit corporation (1933), and a bank for co-operatives (1933) as well as the original federal land bank (1916).

The activities of the four institutions in each district farm credit city are under a single board of directors (Farm Credit Board) and a general agent who acts as joint officer of the four units. The general agent and his staff are responsible for accounting, informational, legal, and statistical activities and certain personnel and physical facilities of all units. In addition, each district farm credit unit has its own officers; and the farm credit board acts as the board of directors for each. However, most of the day-to-day activities are administered by the general agent, who along with the four presidents of the regional institutions acts as an advisory council for each farm credit board.

The Farm Credit Act of 1953 provided for greater farmer control over regional banks by permitting the national farm loan associations to elect two directors, the production credit associations to elect two directors, and the co-operatives borrowing from banks for co-operatives to elect one director.

FEDERAL LAND BANK SYSTEM

Throughout much of the history of the United States, there has been a demand for banks created chiefly to aid farmers. When Congress provided for the creation of the Federal Reserve System in 1913, the agitation which followed for creation of a similar central banking system for agriculture resulted in the passage of the Federal Farm Loan Act of 1916.

The structural arrangement for the Federal Farm Loan System was very similar to that for the Federal Reserve System; (1) a Federal Farm Loan Board, (2) twelve federal land banks operating within twelve districts, with district lines drawn to achieve diversified agricultural activities within each district (see Map 3), and (3) ownership by member institutions, the national farm loan associations.

Federal Land Banks. Most of the original capital for the federal land banks was provided by the federal government, but now all of the capital of the banks is owned by the national farm loan associations. Relative to the volume of loans made by these banks, their capital is small because the system was planned so that the federal land banks could tap the capital market and borrow at low interest rates and lend these funds to farmers at a higher interest rate (but no more than 1 per cent higher). The mortgages acquired by the banks can be used as collateral for new bond issues, and the funds thus obtained can be used to acquire more mortgages. The process can be repeated over and over by each federal land bank as long as the bank's debts do not exceed its capital and surplus more than twenty times. Now, mortgage loans are being made chiefly with funds raised by the sale of consolidated federal farm loan bonds to the public (being

MAP 3

FARM CREDIT ADMINISTRATION

DISTRICT BOUNDARIES AND LOCATION OF DISTRICT UNITS

Source: *Fourteenth Annual Report of the Farm Credit Administration, 1946–47* (Washington, D.C.: U.S. Government Printing Office, 1947), p. iv.

consolidated, the bonds are the individual and joint responsibility of the twelve federal land banks).[2] During the interim between bond sales, the federal land banks sometimes borrow from commercial banks.

The Federal Land Bank System makes it possible for farmers to share in the benefits of the low rates prevailing in the investment market. The spread between the interest rate paid on bonds by the federal land banks and that charged by these banks on farm mortgages may not exceed 1 per cent. For example, if federal land banks borrow at a rate of 3 per cent, the most they may charge farmers who borrow through a farm loan association is 4 per cent (which is the prevailing

[2] In order to simplify the procedure for open-market financing, the Farm Credit Act of 1955 (Public Law 247, 84th Congress) permits the issuance of consolidated federal land bank debentures which are unsecured promises to pay.

rate, with certain special exceptions). The maximum rate which federal land banks may pay on their bonds is fixed by law at 5 per cent, which automatically fixes the maximum rate that farmers may be charged at 6 per cent.

National Farm Loan Associations. The national farm loan associations are the member institutions in the Federal Land Bank System. Borrowers from a federal land bank must be members of national farm loan associations. Individual membership is contingent on securing approval of an application for a mortgage loan and continues as long as the farmer remains in debt. Since loans are repaid on the installment plan, membership may be for twenty years (and, due to extensions authorized, it may be longer).

A farmer-borrower must buy stock in his association equal to 5 per cent of his loan; and the association, in turn, must buy an equal amount of stock in its district federal land bank. The association endorses and becomes liable for all loans made to its members. Through its loan committee and board of directors, it must approve the application for a loan; and this automatically includes subscription for the association's stock. The land bank's appraiser appraises the land subject to the mortgage lien (the loan committee having made its own appraisal). If the loan application is approved, the transaction will be completed when the association has issued stock to the farmer-member and has endorsed the mortgage note to the federal land bank. This bank will issue its stock to the farm loan association, which will hold it as security for the loan and will send a bank draft for 95 per cent of the mortgage to the farmer through the farm loan association. New members may be taken in at any time, but the membership is usually fairly steady. The minimum number of members is ten, but there is no maximum.

Types of Loans. Loans may be made for no less than $100 and for no more than $200,000 to any one borrower for purposes such as purchasing land for agricultural uses; repairing and improving farms; purchasing equipment, fertilizer, and livestock; acquiring funds for general agricultural uses; and refinancing real estate mortgages. In no case, may a loan exceed 65 per cent of the appraised normal agricultural value of the farm offered as security. The loans are long-term, are amortized, and bear interest rates of from 4 to 5 per cent at the present time. Deferment of principal payments may be permitted under certain conditions.

The national farm loan associations illustrate three important features of the Federal Farm Credit System: (1) placement of a local institution between the regional or central bank and the borrower, (2) co-operative financing, and (3) mutual ownership of the federal agency by private member institutions.

Joint-Stock Land Banks. In addition to providing for the federal land banks and farm loan associations, the Federal Farm Loan Act of 1916 contained a section that provided for the organization of joint-stock land banks by private interests. Under this "free banking" provision of the law, any ten or more natural persons were permitted to organize a joint-stock land bank. The Act gave existing mortgage companies an opportunity to recharter as national institutions, but few did so, and so most federal joint-stock banks were new institutions. The Federal Farm Board issued charters to eighty-eight joint-stock land banks, but careless loan practices and fraud hurt the system. In 1933 these banks were prohibited from making new loans; since that time, their activities have been confined to liquidation of assets. The last of these banks surrendered its charter on April 26, 1951. The Treasurer of the United States holds a balance of $187,-000 for payment of valid claims on their bonds and certain other obligations which have not been presented.

Federal Farm Mortgage Corporation. The Federal Farm Mortgage Corporation was established in 1933 with direct financial aid of $200,000,000 from the government. Most of the funds used by the Corporation were raised by the public sale of government-guaranteed securities. During the 1930's, loans made on its behalf made it possible for thousands of farmers to save their farms. On June 30, 1955, the federal land banks purchased all of the Corporation's remaining assets except cash, accounts receivable, and mineral rights. Now, the only function of the Corporation is to dispose of its mineral rights and any that remain on September 5, 1957, are to be transferred to the Secretary of the Interior for administration. The total amount of dividends paid to the United States Treasury by the Corporation was $133,000,000.

INTERMEDIATE AND SHORT-TERM LENDERS

Federal Intermediate Credit Banks. The Agricultural Credits Act of 1923 provided for the creation of twelve federal intermediate credit banks, one in each farm credit district. These banks are wholly owned by the federal government, but most of the funds for lending are acquired by the sale of short-term consolidated trust debentures which are the joint and several liability of the twelve federal intermediate credit banks. Individual banks may borrow from other federal intermediate credit banks, Federal Reserve banks, and commercial banks.

The federal intermediate credit banks do not lend directly to farmers and stockmen or otherwise conduct a general banking business. Their function is to rediscount agricultural paper and to make loans to existing farm lending institutions operating in the short-term and intermediate credit fields, including production credit associations, agricultural credit corporations, livestock companies, state and national banks, banks for co-operatives, and certain farmers' co-operative marketing and production associations.

The type of paper which the federal intermediate credit banks may discount or accept as security for loans may have maturities up to three years, but most of their funds are used for periods of less than one year. Without prior approval of the Governor of FCA, the interest rate on their loans and discounts may not exceed by more than 1 per cent the rate on their preceding issue of debentures; thus borrowers are assured the advantage of low interest rates in the money market. The annual volume of credit provided by the twelve intermediate credit banks through intermediaries (production credit associations, marketing associations, and so on) for the use of farmers is now about $2 billion.

Production Credit Corporations. The Farm Credit Act of 1933 authorized the establishment of twelve production credit corporations (one for each federal land bank city), whose chief function is to help organize, finance, and supervise local production credit associations. At the present time, their chief function is that of supervision because the associations are now functioning with but a small amount of government funds. Of the original capital of the production credit corporations ($120,000,000 supplied by the government) $90,000,000 has been liquidated.

Production Credit Associations. The production credit associations are co-operative organizations that now number about 500 and have approximately 465,000 farmer and rancher shareholders. The associations are incorporated under federal law, and they may issue two classes of stock (nonvoting Class A stock which represents the investment of the district production credit corporation and members and voting Class B stock which represents the investment of member-borrowers). Today many of the associations have retired all of their government-owned stock, as required by the Farm Credit Act of 1953, and are completely mutualized.

Borrowers are required to invest 5 per cent of their loan credit in Class B stock of their associations and each Class B shareholder has one vote irrespective of the number of shares held. It is not uncommon for co-operatively minded shareholders to stay in debt for the minimum amount ($50) in order to be voting shareholders. Shareholders elect the board of directors which, in turn, selects the officers and staff members.

The production credit associations make loans to farmers and ranchers for general agricultural purposes; and the loans are usually secured by first liens on crops, equipment, or livestock. Loans, based on a budgetary plan, provide for complete financing throughout the year or season: and those made to finance purchases of equipment, breeding stock, and other items of a semicapital nature may be carried over in part to the second year or even a third year.

Usually, loans made by production credit associations are disbursed as needed, with interest being computed on the length of time each loan dollar is outstanding. Interest rates vary, depending somewhat on the rates charged associations by the intermediate credit banks (from which the associations borrow most of their working-capital funds). An inspection fee and other direct expenses incurred in making a loan must be paid by the borrower. Interest charges of most associations are usually more favorable than those of local commercial banks. For the year ending June 30, 1955, loans amounted to more than $1.3 billion. During the history of the production credit associations, losses on loans have been small—slightly more than one tenth of 1 per cent of total cash advances.

Banks for Co-operatives.   The Central Bank for Co-operatives and the twelve district banks were organized under authority of the Farm Credit Act of 1933. The banks were created to provide farmers' co-operatives with a permanent source of credit. In addition, the Co-operative Bank System assumed responsibility for assisting farmers in the co-operative movement by research and other services. The co-operative farm marketing movement has a three-point program: (1) to increase farmers' profits, (2) to eliminate or reduce the middlemen's profit, and (3) to lower prices and to increase the volume of sales to consumers.

The funds lent by the banks for co-operatives are obtained from (1) sales of consolidated collateral trust debentures, which are the joint and several obligations of the thirteen banks for co-operatives; (2) loans from the federal intermediate credit banks and from commercial banks; and (3) sales of stock to the federal government and farmers' co-operatives. All of the original capital stock of the banks for co-operatives was subscribed for by the government. In the Farm Credit Act of 1955, Congress provided for eventual retirement of the capital stock of the thirteen banks for co-operatives now owned by the United States government. When the objectives of the plan are realized, the Central Bank for Co-operatives will be owned by district banks for co-operatives and the district banks will be owned by the co-operatives that use the banks.

To be eligible for loans from the banks for co-operatives, co-operative associations must (1) operate for the mutual benefit of members, (2) do most of their business with members, (3) limit dividends to 8 per cent a year, (4) limit voting privileges so that no one has more than one vote, and (5) arrange ownership so that 90 per cent of the voting rights are held by producers. In addition, the association must be engaged in marketing farm products, purchasing farm supplies, and/or furnishing business service to farms.

The banks for co-operatives are making commodity loans, working-capital loans, and facility loans to more than 2,000 co-operatives. Commodity loans are short-term and usually secured by first liens on approved farm products or farm supplies. Working-capital loans are made to supplement capital advanced by members of co-operative associations. They may be secured or unsecured and may be made on a short- or medium-term basis. These loans may be made for such periods as conditions seem to justify, but most of them are retired at the end of the marketing season for which they were made.

Facility loans are made to marketing associations to help finance the purchase or lease of physical property required in handling, storing, processing, and/or merchandising agricultural products. The loans are secured by mortgages on the property being financed. Most loans are made for ten years or less and are repaid in installments. The Central Bank for Co-operatives may lend to the district banks, but most of its loans are made to national and large regional co-operative associations.

Farmers' Co-operatives. Among the co-operative types of farm organizations, the marketing associations are the most popular. These associations number about 7,000, and their membership is estimated at more than 4,000,000. In addition, there are more than 3,000 purchasing associations having 2,500,000 members, and 8,500 various types of production associations with about 650,000 members. Among the other types of co-operative associations are those in the financial field which include the 1,200 national farm loan associations, 500 production credit associations, and 13 banks for co-operatives. There are also 500 rural credit unions, 1,800 farmers' mutual fire insurance companies, 33,000 mutual telephone companies, 950 electric power and light associations, 2,300 soil conservation associations, and 50 rural health co-operative associations. Since many farmers belong to several associations, the total membership is several times the number of farmers in the United States.

EMERGENCY LOANS AND FARMERS HOME ADMINISTRATION

During local and regional emergencies, the United States government has come to the assistance of those in distress at home as well as abroad. Since 1918, direct government loans have been made to farmers to provide funds to meet emergency seed, feed, and other needs. More than $500,000,000 has been lent, of which more than 80 per cent has been repaid. In addition, Farm Security Administration and its predecessor, the Resettlement Administration, made rehabilitation loans to over a million farmers totaling more than $1 billion.

In an attempt to centralize the emergency lending agencies in the agricultural field, Congress provided for Farmers Home Administration in 1946. Farmers Home Administration also supervises loans made through its offices, usually located in county seat towns, to farmers who cannot get needed credit elsewhere under reasonable conditions and at adequate terms. Applications for loans are reviewed by a committee of three, at least two of whom must be farmers. The committee passes upon the eligibility of the applicant, certifies as to the value of the farm, and reviews the borrower's progress.

Farmers Home Administration is responsible for supervising "operating" loans, farm-ownership loans, soil and water conservation loans, and emergency and special livestock loans. The agency may insure loans made by private lenders to farmers for purposes similar to those for which direct loans are made. Operating loans are made to farmers who are operating farms no larger than family-type units. Such loans have maturities of from one to seven years, depending on the use made of the funds.

Farm-ownership loans are made to encourage farm tenants, sharecroppers, and others to become farm owners and to help existing landowners to improve or enlarge their farms so as to make them efficient family-type farms. The water-facility loans are authorized for seventeen western states and are made for purposes such as construction of wells, ponds, windmills, and irrigation projects.

The Secretary of Agriculture has designated Farmers Home Administration to administer flood and production-disaster loan programs.

Veterans having farming experience are eligible for all types of Farmers Home Administration loans. Only a relatively small percentage of advances made by private agencies has been insured by Farmers Home Administration. In 1955, this agency was authorized to handle insured farm mortgages on a basis whereby the agency holds and services the mortgages and collects the loans. The government-guaranteed loans are made by banks which receive a return of 3½ per cent on them. In order to make such loans more attractive, the Department of Agriculture also reduced the time that such loans must be held by the lender (from ten to five years).

Other governmental agencies in the agricultural field which have primary functions other than financial are not discussed here (Rural Electrification Administration, Soil Conservation Service, Federal Crop Insurance Corporation, and Production and Marketing Administration).

SUMMARY

The credit requirements of agriculture correspond in time to those of industry and commerce—long-term, intermediate, and short-term. The need for long-term credit is associated with the purchase of farms. The farm-mortgage-debt problem in the United States is linked to our antiprimogeniture laws which, in most cases, necessitate refinancing of farms each generation. The holders of farm mortgages, ranked in order of their importance, are: individuals and miscellaneous lenders including mortgage companies, life insurance companies, federal land banks, commercial banks, Farmers Home Administration, and the Federal Farm Mortgage Corporation.

The non-real-estate debt of farmers includes intermediate and short-term debt, and the lenders include both private and federal agencies as well as miscellaneous lenders, who supply retail and installment credit, and specialists such as livestock loan companies. The Farm Credit Administration includes twelve federal land banks, twelve production credit corporations, Central Bank for Co-operatives, and twelve regional banks for co-operatives. All of these institutions aid in financing farmers through their member institutions. In creating and administering the institutions within the Farm Credit Administration, emphasis has been on co-operative financing and going to the grass-roots level in determining whether or not loans are to be made.

QUESTIONS AND PROBLEMS

1. In agricultural credit, "personal and business finances are combined." Is this true to the same degree today as it was in the past? Explain.

2. "Of the approximately 14,000 commercial banks in the United States, over 90 per cent extend credit to farmers." (Federal Reserve Bank of St. Louis, *Monthly Review*, December, 1955, p. 134.) What type of credit is granted? Does the volume of bank lending to farmers reflect seasonal, cyclical, and/or trend factors?

3. "Despite a step-up in surplus disposal activities, stocks of commodities owned and under price support loan to CCC have increased each year since 1952." (Federal Reserve Bank of Chicago, *Business Conditions*, January, 1956, p. 12.) Explain.

4. Identify the different divisions of the Farm Credit Administration. How has the administration of regional problems of FCA been centralized in each of the federal farm credit cities?

5. Describe the Federal Farm Loan System as provided by Congress in 1916. What changes have been made in its structural organization? Why was emphasis shifted away from the development of a joint-stock land bank system?

6. Identify the national farm loan associations as to membership, source of loanable funds, type of lending, and source of earnings. Compare to the production credit associations.

7. Are production credit associations more dependent on federal intermediate credit banks for funds than on the production credit corporation? Why? Are there other agencies dependent on the intermediate credit banks for help? Explain.

8. "The principal function of the Cooperative Farm Credit System . . . is to provide channels through which farmers can tap available investment funds in the money markets." *Annual Report of the Farm Credit Administration 1953–54* (Washington, D.C.: U.S. Government Printing Office, 1955), p. 1. Explain how this objective is achieved in the (*a*) Federal Land Bank System, (*b*) Intermediate Credit Bank System, (*c*) Production Credit System, and (*d*) Cooperative Bank System.

9. What is meant by the "mutualization" of the four different farm credit systems that are contained in the Farm Credit Administration. To what extent has this mutualization been achieved in each case? Explain.

10. Identify Farmers Home Administration. What are its functions?

<table>
<tr><td>

Chapter

XXXI

</td><td>

CONSUMER CREDIT AND
CONSUMER FINANCING
INSTITUTIONS

</td></tr>
</table>

WHEN considered from the viewpoint of the economy as a whole, consumer credit enlarges buying power, broadens the market for consumer goods, and permits mass production of goods. One criticism of consumer credit is that it may leave less purchasing power for future buying. However, new buyers using new consumer credit may enter the market; therefore, the effect of consumer debt on total spending depends on whether old debt is paid off more or less rapidly than new debt is contracted. (According to a survey made in 1955, consumer installment debt was being contracted at the rate of six dollars per month for each five dollars paid off.) One thing seems assured, once a person has established a certain standard of living he will go into debt to maintain it. The continued prosperity of the United States depends, in part, on a steady growth in consumption; and for this reason, monetary authorities, economists, businessmen, and others are giving increased attention to consumer finance.

Expansion in the durable goods industry depends upon a wide market for its products; and, during the 1920's, the automobile industry was the leader in popularizing the purchase of goods on the installment plan. Many of the early automobile sales-finance companies were organized or acquired by manufacturers to provide the automobile dealers and their customers with credit. Gradually, installment credit provisions were made not only for other durable consumer goods but also for nondurable goods and services.

It has been said that "the only thing that cannot be paid on the installment plan is the installment payment." Today the things that can be purchased on a buy-now-pay-later basis include: maternity care, dancing lessons, college educations, trips around the world, wedding receptions, and funerals. With previously issued credit cards, one can obtain gasoline, tires, and automobile repairs; train, bus, and airplane tickets; meals; and hotel accommodations. In general, experiences with granting consumer credit have been good, with the protection given being primarily the integrity of the consumer rather than the things pledged as security.

COMPOSITION OF CONSUMER CREDIT

The composition of consumer credit outstanding at any one time is classified in the *Federal Reserve Bulletin* as (1) installment credit, which is divided into sales credit and loan credit; and (2) noninstallment credit, which includes single-payment loans, charge accounts, and service credit (credit extended by professional people, public utility companies, and others). By definition, real estate loans for housing are excluded, but loans made for the repair and

TABLE 24

CONSUMER CREDIT STATISTICS FOR SELECTED YEARS

(In Millions of Dollars, Amounts Estimated)

END OF YEAR	TOTAL CONSUMER CREDIT	INSTALLMENT CREDIT					NONINSTALLMENT CREDIT			
		Total	Automobile Paper	Other Paper	Repair and Modernization*	Personal Loans	Total	Single Payment	Charge Accounts	Sales Credit
1940	8,338	5,514	2,071	1,827	371	1,245	2,824	800	1,471	553
1945	5,665	2,462	455	816	182	1,009	3,203	746	1,612	845
1950	20,813	14,490	6,342	4,337	1,006	2,805	6,323	1,821	3,006	1,496
1956†	37,093	28,890	15,077	6,247	1,663	5,903	8,203	3,099	3,231	1,873

Source of statistics: *Federal Reserve Bulletin* (November, 1955), p. 1262, and (August, 1956), p. 878.
* Includes only repair and modernization loans held by financial institutions; such loans held by retail outlets are included in other consumer goods paper.
† June 30.

modernization of homes which are insured by Federal Housing Administration are included (see Table 24).

Installment Credit. Consumer installment credit is of two types—installment-loan credit and installment-sales credit. Installment-loan credit consists of cash advances to consumers which are repayable on the installment plan. Installment-sales credit is credit extended to consumers by vendors which involves future payments on the installment plan. For illustration, if an individual borrows funds, repayable in installments, from his bank in order to pay cash for an automobile, he is using installment-loan credit; but, if he arranges with his automobile dealer for a down payment and credit terms that involve periodic payments, he is using installment-sales credit.

Most of the consumer installment loans are relatively small loans to individuals which are payable in weekly, semimonthly, or monthly installments. In addition to using their own resources, many of the cash-lending institutions borrow from commercial banks to obtain funds to lend to customers.

Installment-sales credit is sometimes classified according to the goods sold and sometimes according to the type or class of vendor. When the amount of credit is large and the resources of the vendor are small, as is often true in the case of automobile dealers, the installment-sales contracts may be sold to sales-finance companies, banks, and other financial institutions. Many of the sales-finance companies also borrow funds from commercial banks either over the counter or, more commonly, through sales of promissory notes in the open market.

Financing with installment-loan and installment-sales credit has been attacked periodically, the common charge being that "people have mortgaged their future to live in the present." Since most installment credit is granted to facilitate the purchase of durable goods, people are paying for goods while they are enjoying them, thus following a "pay-as-you-go" plan. (The assumption is that sound financing principles, as discussed below, are being followed.)

Installment Financing Principles. Before World War II the National Association of Finance Companies had taken numerous steps to standardize business practices. During the war, further standardization resulted from the regulation of consumer credit by the Board of Governors of the Federal Reserve System (Regulation W). The standard terms are based upon the following principles: (1) The buyer must have sufficient equity in the property to make him feel that he is a purchaser rather than a renter. (2) At all times the remaining salable value of the property, regarded as a used article, must be greater than the unpaid portion of the price. (3) At all times the unpaid portion of the price should be small enough to encourage the buyer to complete the payments rather than to lose his investment in the property.

The question of how long the payment (repayment) period will be is involved in all types of installment credit. In the case of installment-sales credit, the size of the down payment is also involved. Ordinarily, the longer credit is outstanding and the smaller the down payment, the greater is the credit risk.

Charge Accounts. Many purchases made "on credit" are evidenced by book accounts. Since credit terms are usually for 30 days, the annual volume of business carried on in this way is many times larger than that suggested by the amount of credit "on the books" at a particular time. Banks, sales-finance companies, and other financing institutions may assist the vendors in financing these credits by making unsecured loans or loans secured by the "accounts receivable."

Retailers make extensive efforts to promote sales through the use of charge accounts; and, in some cities, merchants have made arrangements for banks to factor their charge accounts (buy them outright and assume responsibility for collection). Some retailers use a system of revolving credit in which the customer pays a fixed amount each month and is permitted to buy up to a certain maximum, usually six times the monthly payment. The customer pays a service charge of one per cent of the unpaid balance each month. If purchases exceed the maximum amount authorized, the customer is billed for one-fourth of the excess each month together with the regular monthly payment.

Service Credit. Service credit, evidenced by book accounts, includes charges made for services such as those of public utilities, doctors, dentists, and automobile-repair firms. Sometimes the vendors of these services call upon banks, sales-finance companies, and other financing institutions for assistance in financing these credits. These loans may be either unsecured or secured by the "accounts receivable" or other assets of the borrowers.

Single-Payment Loans. Many consumer single-payment loans are made by banks, pawnbrokers, and other financial institutions. Such loans are due at the end of a stated period rather than being payable in equal periodic payments over a period of time. This type of lending is common among pawnbrokers and "salary buyers" as well as among banks.

Repair and Modernization Loans Insured by Federal Housing Administration. The repair and modernization loans insured by FHA under Title I of the National Housing Act are made to eligible borrowers for alterations, repair or improvement of existing structures, new buildings for nonresidential purposes, and new structures to be used in whole or part for residential purposes. The qualified lenders who finance customers under Title I must bear 10 per cent of the loss on each loan and the Federal Housing Administration will bear 90 per cent of all losses provided they do not exceed 10 per cent of the lender's portfolio. Although these loans are reported separately, they are made by all consumer financing agencies which finance under provisions of Title I of the National Housing Act.

CONSUMER LOANS AND CASH-LENDING INSTITUTIONS

Forty years ago it was difficult to arrange for an emergency personal loan on a businesslike basis. Lending to finance purchases of automobiles and other consumer goods was shunned by banks on the assumption that it was in violation of the thrift principle on which banking was built. The need for borrowing or going into debt to finance consumption was regarded, in general, as a sign of shiftlessness. But, in spite of this attitude, consumers were going into debt to retailers and others for goods and services and were borrowing from pawnbrokers, unlicensed lenders, loan sharks, charitable societies, and friends to finance major and minor household and other personal needs. The right to borrow in order to finance the operation of a business has long been recognized, but the right to borrow to finance the operation of a home is a relatively new concept.

New Attitudes Toward Consumer Loan Credit. Studies made by the Russell Sage Foundation contributed to a change in the attitude toward consumer loans—the poor must be offered loans at fair rates in order to prevent their being exploited by loan sharks. (The usury laws did not prevent consumers from seeking loans but forced them to deal with unscrupulous lenders.) The federal and state governments, instead of permitting commercial banks to adjust their interest rates so as to compensate for the greater risks and higher costs involved in extending certain types of credit, permitted the organization and operation of credit institutions which are allowed to lend at higher rates than those applicable to commercial banks.

The organization of Morris Plan banks and remedial loan companies, beginning in 1910, did not satisfy the objectives of the Russell Sage Foundation which was then engaged in writing a model small-loan law. In 1911, this model law was used as the basis for the Massachusetts small-loan law, the first of its kind. This law provided for the organization of small-loan companies whose interest rates, although regulated, were exempt from usury restrictions. In addition they were carefully regulated as to maximum amount of loans and the basis for computing interest and other charges.

A second approach to the problem of consumer credit emphasized co-operative or mutual lending. Mr. Edward A. Filene of Boston, through the Twentieth Century Fund, set up the Credit National Extension Bureau in 1921 to aid the credit union movement. Since that time most states have passed laws permitting credit unions to be chartered; and, in 1934, the national government authorized groups to charter credit unions under federal law.

Characteristics of Consumer Loans. Most consumer loans are for small amounts and are payable in equal weekly, semimonthly, or monthly installments. Because of their size and the method of re-payment, the cost of administering consumer loans is high. This means that a higher interest rate must be charged to offset the added costs. The borrowers, unlike business firms, are relatively unknown, and their earning capacity may not be increased as a result of the loan. Frequently, a loan is renewed in whole or part, which means that the credit status of the borrower is deteriorating.

In general, three types of loans are made: (1) unsecured loans endorsed by two names (co-makers' loans); (2) loans secured by chattel mortgages, wage assignments, insurance policies, and other acceptable collateral; and (3) unsecured loans based upon promises to pay of husband and wife. The chief requisites for consumer credit, even though some loans are secured, are good character and a steady income on the part of the borrower.

With certain exceptions, consumer loans do not increase the ability of the borrower to repay; and so payments must be made from his normal income, and this is done most conveniently on the installment plan. If a borrower returns repeatedly for loans, it means that he is managing his affairs poorly, he is not a good risk, and his application for a loan should be reduced or refused. For this reason, agencies in this field are forced to make special efforts to secure new borrowers by advertising, one of the chief costs of carrying on a small-loan business.

The methods used in analyzing credit risks vary; but, as a rule, the basic information is secured from the applicant. He fills in an application blank which calls for his name, age, marital status, number of dependents, residence (place and length of time), weekly earnings, other income, rent (amount and to whom paid), insurance (amount and beneficiary), real estate (value, title status, encumbrances, and location), and credit references. When the lender requires the signature of co-makers, similar but less extensive information is demanded of them. The lending agency usually verifies the data on the information sheet. Special attention is given to answers as to place of employment, length of employment, amount of salary, rent, residence in one place, ownership of real estate and automobiles, and personal habits which have a bearing upon personal finance. General stability of an applicant's record is probably the best barometer of his credit worthiness.

Commercial Banks. Although commercial banks entered the personal-loan field during the 1920's, it was not until the 1930's that they began to make a sizeable amount of consumer loans. The interest of banks in installment credit was stimulated by their experiences with homeowners who borrowed under Title I of the National Housing Act of 1934. These repair and modernization loans made by banks are insured by FHA; and, to date, the losses on more than 18,000,000 such loans, with a value of $8.5 billion, have been less than 1 per cent.

Now, the personal-loan departments of commercial banks are foremost among the lenders in the personal-finance field, being dominant not only in making single-payment loans but also those repayable on the installment plan and second only to sales-finance companies as holders of installment paper. Commercial banks' small-loan departments now hold almost 30 per cent of the total volume of consumer credit outstanding.

Prior to 1930, probably less than 200 banks operated small-loan departments;[1] but now practically all commercial banks have some provisions for making installment cash loans and/or for purchasing installment sales notes. Among the cash-lending agencies in the consumer-finance field, interest rates charged by banks are usually the lowest. Now certain banks are offering loans at a 3½ per cent discount rate plus a charge for a life insurance policy to protect the bank during the loan period.[2]

In most states the interest rates charged by personal-loan departments of commercial banks are subject to general bank statutes and not to special legislation, as is true of small-loan companies and other "licensed lenders." New York State is an exception—an amendment to the banking code, passed in 1936, permits banks to charge a rate that will yield 1 per cent per month (12 per cent per year). This law permitted New York banks to broaden the scope of their activities so as to compete more favorably with other agencies in the field. When loans are made by personal-loan departments of com-

---

[1] Frieda Baird, "Commercial Bank Activity in Consumer Installment Financing," *Federal Reserve Bulletin*, March, 1947, pp. 264–69.

[2] The formula for computing the yield on loans discounted in advance and payable in installments is:

$$I = \frac{2PC}{N+1}$$

in which I is the annual yield or effective interest rate, P is the number of payment periods in the year, C is the discount rate expressed as a percentage of the net proceeds of the loan and not the quoted rate, N is the number of equal periodic payments on the note. If a $100 note payable in 12 equal periodic payments is discounted at 3½ per cent, the effective rate or yield would be

$$\frac{2 \times 12 \times 0.0362694}{12 + 1} = 0.0669666.$$

mercial banks, borrowers may be requested to open special accounts in which periodic deposits are made (sometimes in a different bank). The best accepted practice is to make this periodic deposit compulsory; and, generally, this practice is followed wherever the state law does not interfere (since 1936, it is not permitted in New York State). In some cases the borrower receives interest on these deposits. Among the consumer loans made by commercial banks, the majority are secured by stocks, bonds, savings-account passbooks, and/or insurance policies; but co-maker and other loans are made on an unsecured basis. Currently, the volume of single-payment loans is much greater than installment loans.

Personal-Finance Companies. Personal-finance companies or small-loan companies operate under provisions of the Uniform Small Loan Law adopted, with various modifications, by more than forty states. These companies are exempt from usury laws applicable to other lenders, but the interest rates they may charge and the maximum amounts they may lend are fixed by law. Their lending practices are subject to detailed regulation. For some years, the maximum loan permitted was $300; but, in most states, this amount has been increased generally to $500 in recognition of inflation that has taken place during the last 20 years.

The maximum interest rate on unpaid loan balances is fixed at from 2½ to 3½ per cent per month, or less in some states.[3] The only fee is one to cover actual filing costs. In order to protect borrowers, lenders are required to give a written statement of pertinent information, such as the amount, security, rate of interest, and maturity. Lenders must permit borrowers to repay their loans in whole or in part at any time, and the interest is computed to the exact date of payment. The lender must give a receipt for all payments; and, when the loan is paid, all pledges and paper must be returned.

Small-loan companies make loans based upon chattel mortgages, wage assignments, and, to some extent, the unsecured note of husband and wife, provided the borrower is a good credit risk and has been employed at one place for a number of years. The first type—a note secured by a chattel mortgage, which usually covers household furniture—is the most common way in which loans are made (about 60 per cent). The chattel mortgage is rarely

[3] This does not mean that the annual charge on a $100 loan would be from $30 to $42 per year. Because of the installment repayments and computing of interest on unpaid balances, the cost of a loan would be $22.75 at a 3½ per cent rate payable in twelve equal monthly payments (assuming no other fees are charged).

filed—which may effect its legality; but this policy permits the personal-finance companies to use their most successful advertising slogan—"strictly confidential and private loans."

Normally, the market value of the chattel given as security for personal loans would not cover the loss; and the chief advantage of this type of security is psychological—the borrower prefers to make every effort rather than go through the humiliating experience of giving up his furniture. The personal-finance companies seldom take such a step; and so, in effect, most of their loans are character loans signed by husband and wife.

The cost of credit investigation, collection of delinquent loans, and absorption of losses on bad debts make total operating costs of personal-finance companies higher than those of other types of licensed institutions. The success of companies operating under small-loan laws depends upon careful analysis of applicants and unremitting follow-up until accounts are paid. In comparing interest charges to those of other types of companies, the following facts should be recognized: (1) the rates charged are usually computed on unpaid balances of principal for the actual time the money is borrowed; (2) there are no fees, fines, or other charges;[4] and (3) the interest is computed on a loan basis rather than on a discount basis.

Where small-loan companies have been operated properly, they have made a real contribution by replacing many illegal lenders that had dominated this market for loanable funds. Among cash-lending institutions, the personal-finance or small-loan companies are second in importance only to commercial banks.

Now there are about 5,400 personal-finance companies. About one third of these companies are members of the American Association of Personal Finance Companies, and many are members of state associations. Many of the large companies operate separate corporations in different states and branches within states, thus combining the principles of group and branch banking.

Credit Unions. A credit union is a co-operative association "organized for the purpose of promoting thrift among its members and creating a source of credit for provident or productive purposes." Today, there are more than 8,000 credit unions, which operate under federal or state charters. Most credit unions are incorporated and accumulate funds by selling shares to members. From this pool

[4] Monthly rates are based on the assumption that the regular installment will be paid on or before the third day of the month. If the account is delinquent, a greater amount will be charged to interest, which is computed from the last date of payment.

of funds, loans are made to members at an interest rate that may not exceed 1 per cent per month on the unpaid balance. The responsibility for operating each credit union rests upon its directors and officers selected by its members. Most loans are based on unsecured promises to pay, but some unions require the signature of two co-makers.

Most of the credit unions now in operation have come into existence since 1930. In 1934 Congress passed the Federal Credit Union Act, which makes it possible to organize these thrift and personal-loan co-operatives in any state and in the District of Columbia. The field of membership for each federal credit union is specifically described in its charter, and most state-chartering laws have similar specifications. The credit union movement has made its greatest progress among employees of specific concerns or offices, railroads, municipal employees, and teachers' associations. Charters are granted to groups having a common bond of association or occupation—factory, store, or office. In some cases the common bond may be religious, fraternal, social, or community.

Credit unions appeal to persons who ordinarily have no bank accounts. Savings in amounts as small as 25 cents per month are encouraged. A member must own at least one share of stock with a par value of $5.00, which may be purchased on the installment plan. Credit unions are co-operative and are mutually owned and managed. Costs of funds are reasonable; interest rates are limited; and loans are made promptly. The cost of operation is low because there are no large salaries to pay (most of the work is done by members without pay), and usually the overhead is nominal (rent, heat, and light are donated by the organization around which the credit union is formed).

In 1948, responsibility for the examination and supervision of federal credit unions was transferred from the Federal Deposit Insurance Corporation to the Bureau of Federal Credit Unions (now in Social Security Administration an agency in the Department of Health, Education and Welfare). Credit unions are examined periodically by the supervisory agency—once a year by the Bureau of Federal Credit Unions, which is followed by a written report to the credit union concerned. Wide use is made of standard accounting forms and procedures.

Industrial or Morris Plan Banks' Loans. Industrial banks are financial institutions which specialize in small personal loans. They obtain their funds from sales of stock and from either the acceptance of deposits or the sale of "deposit" or "investment" certificates. The 700 industrial banks are organized under general banking laws, special legislation, or general incorporation laws. Arthur J. Morris, an attorney from Norfolk, Virginia, is given credit for establishing the first industrial bank in the United States and for developing the Morris Plan of banking.

In 1910 the first industrial bank, the Fidelity Savings and Trust Company, was established in Morris' home town. The parent company, the Industrial Finance Corporation, provides Morris Plan banks with copyright forms, literature, and loan plans; and it gives financial advice and the use of its name. It may provide Morris Plan banks with part of their capital, but most of their stock is locally owned. These banks vary widely in size, corporate structure, and type of business. Originally, these industrial banks specialized in co-maker loans repayable on the installment plan. A discount of 6 per cent plus a fee of 2 per cent is customarily deducted in advance on small loans. This means that the actual interest paid is more than it would be on a 6-per-cent-per-annum basis. Within recent years, Morris Plan banks have extended their operations to other fields; and many of them are now being operated as ordinary commercial banks.

Industrial Loan Companies.   Industrial loan companies operate in much the same way as industrial banks, except that they do not accept deposits. Now separate statistics are reported for these institutions; but, originally, statistics were reported with those of industrial banks.

Remedial Loan Associations.   Remedial loan associations are credit agencies originally established along philanthropic lines. Although they were among the pioneers in the field of consumer credit, they now number less than thirty. In organizing remedial loan associations, capital funds are subscribed by public-minded citizens; and, in order to lessen the profit motive, dividends are limited to from 6 to 8 per cent by the charters of most of these associations. The Provident Loan Society, located in New York City, is the largest among the remedial loan associations. It has 17 offices spread throughout the city and does a pawnbrokerage business, being one of the city's 130 licensed pawnbrokers. Some of the remedial loan associations are now operating under provisions of the small-loan law.

Pawnbrokers.   A pawnbroker is one who lends money on the security of personal property pledged in his keeping. There are two types of pawnbrokers: those who make secured loans and those who purchase the property offered as security on agreement to re-sell to the borrower within a designated time. Pawnshops are pa-tronized by two types of individuals: (1) those who are not poor but are financially embarrassed because of ill health, accident, scarcity of work, business needs, or requests from relatives; and (2) the traditionally poor. About one fourth of all pawnbrokers' loans have been for business purposes and the remainder for household or per-sonal use. The transactions require less red tape than loans from other institutions in this field. It has been estimated that normally 85 per cent of the pledges are redeemed. Greatest profits have been made on large loans and in selling unredeemed pledges. The average-size loan is estimated to be less than $10, but the total amount of loans made by pawnbrokers may be as high as $200 million annually.

Almost anything may be pawned, but jewelry is the most ac-ceptable pledge. Most state laws prohibit the taking of goods from minors, intoxicated persons, servants, and apprentices. In order to check on stolen goods a register must be kept in which the property pledged is described. Some states require a description of the person who pledges the property. The pawn ticket, the pawner's only receipt, shows the length of time allowed for redemption and usually the interest rate. Rates vary from 24 to 120 per cent per annum, with 36 per cent being considered typical.

Unlicensed Lenders. In spite of hostile public opinion the amount of business done by unlicensed lenders remains at a high figure, even though it has been reduced in recent years. Although many attempts have been made to eliminate lending at usurious rates, the practice persists. Part of this situation is due to the statutory provisions for lending at nonusurious rates and their interpretation by the courts. Even some legal lending agencies, such as commercial banks, are in doubt as to the legality of contracts at the legal rate of discount plus service fees when loans are repaid over the life of the contract.

The unlicensed lender makes loans on whatever security he can obtain—wage assignments, chattel mortgages on automobiles, or pledged articles left on deposit. In some cases, he accepts notes signed by two co-makers. In order to avoid charges of usury the loan may be disguised in some way. When signing the contract, the borrower may agree to pay a larger sum than he borrows. For example, if he pledges to pay $60 of his next month's salary for

$50 at the time of the contract, which may have only fifteen days to run, the borrower pays $10 for the use of $50 for fifteen days, that is, 480 per cent interest on an annual basis. Usual charges made by "salary buyers" are from 20 to 40 per cent per month (240 to 480 per cent per year).

Salaried men and small wage earners are not the only ones to borrow from unlicensed lenders. Prosecution of usurious lenders in New York revealed that small merchants were frequently paying more than 100 per cent per year for their borrowed funds. Most of the illegal loan business is done by individuals operating in single offices, but a number of chain organizations have been created.

Interest Rates on Consumer Loans. Although the legal rates on consumer loans do not lend themselves to comparison because of the different types of loans made and the misleading manner in which lending institutions quote the interest rate, the fact is that many borrowers are paying too much for loans which they secure. Licensed agencies have suffered only small losses because of delinquent payment, justifying the faith of the sponsors of credit unions, industrial banks, and other small-loan institutions in the honesty and integrity of the workingman, small householder, and professional man of limited income.

SALES-FINANCE COMPANIES

Sales-finance companies are specialists that purchase installment-sales credit contracts and/or make loans based on assigned accounts. They finance the sales of specific goods in the retail and wholesale markets. Some companies make cash loans, thus operating like other cash-lending institutions. The growth of sales-finance companies is closely linked to the growth of the automobile industry and several of these companies have been connected with automobile manufacturers.

There are more than 1,500 sales-finance companies operating in the United States. The origin of these companies varies, the earliest having been specialists that purchased or discounted commercial receivables, including "accounts," "notes," "bills" and acceptances. Some of the first automobile sales-finance companies were organized to finance dealers in need of cash to pay manufacturers when cars were delivered. From financing automobiles at the wholesale level, it was but natural for them to expand their operations to financing sales at retail. Generally, the automobile sales-finance companies have severed their relations with the manufacturers, and are now financing paper on its merits.

Sales-finance companies range in size from local units to those that are national in scope of operations. The latter have branches in key cities throughout the United States, operating a national financing business through these branch offices. Finance companies do not accept deposits; and so they operate with their own capital and borrowed funds, obtained by direct loans from banks and by the sale of promissory notes in the money market. In general, finance companies have good credit ratings and are able to borrow at banks at low interest rates. The larger companies act as their own brokers in selling their promissory notes, which may be unsecured or secured by collateral deposited with a trustee (called "collateral trust notes").

Some finance companies finance installment sales resulting from the purchase of producers' rather than consumers' goods (for illustration, refrigeration systems and automatic fire extinguisher systems). In addition, they may make loans to dealers, merchants, and others. These business loans are of two major types: (1) those to dealers in motor vehicles and other durable goods, and (2) those to business firms on pledges of receivables.

Installment-Sales Credit Arrangements. Buyers of automobiles and other durable goods customarily apply for the privilege of purchasing goods on the installment plan and support their applications with statements of their financial positions (income, etc.) and give references as requested. If such an application is accepted (following investigation by the finance company) and a sale is made, the purchaser makes a down payment in cash and/or trades in his used car as a down payment. The buyer agrees to make monthly payments for the remainder of the purchase price according to the terms of the contract (twelve to twenty-four months in some cases). Unless included in the down payment, interest charges, filing fees, and insurance costs are included in the monthly payments. In terms of simple interest, the interest charge is usually 12 per cent on the average of all unpaid balances.

The purchaser's note may be discounted by the finance company or bank at a rate determined by market conditions, maturity, recourse arrangements, and so on. The dealer or finance company will hold a conditional bill of sale, lease, or chattel mortgage signed by the purchaser until all payments have been made. A default on any one of the installments means that the balance of the payments are due and payable immediately at the option of the finance company or bank.

In order to protect its equity in case of repossession of the automobile, the finance company or bank insists on installment payments being large enough to offset depreciation. The lender will also be protected by adequate insurance for collision, fire, theft, and so on; and, in some cases, the lender will demand the endorsement of the dealer on the note which is discounted (giving the lender recourse against the dealer). Sometimes a repurchase agreement will be negotiated whereby the finance company (or bank) may require the dealer to buy the repossessed car for the unpaid balance, but the finance company (or bank) loses if the car cannot be repossessed. In order to increase their business, some finance companies assume all the credit risks by waiving endorsements or repurchase contracts (called nonrecourse companies).

Criticism of Sales-Finance Companies. Some sales-finance companies have been criticized because of excessive financing charges, misleading advertising of interest rates, and "kickbacks" to dealers. The task of regulation is difficult because of the many variations in installment-sales credit. One method of attack is to limit the interest on installment-sales credit to 1 per cent per month on unpaid balances. There is need for giving the buyer information as to the total costs of financing and for requiring the seller to itemize charges and to make refunds to buyers on interest and insurance charges when contracts are paid before maturity.

Criticism of Installment Sales. There are many criticisms of installment sales in general. The buyer often pays an excessive price for an inferior article, such as jewelry or a second-hand car, because he thinks in terms of small weekly or monthly payments rather than the total cost. In installment selling, emphasis tends to be on the sale of luxury items, thus shifting demand away from more important markets without increasing total demand. Service charges, often hidden, are excessive which tends to offset some of the advantages claimed for mass production of goods. Unwittingly, people are encouraged to extend their total debts beyond their ability to pay, causing distress when goods are repossessed or when obligations cannot be met without serious personal sacrifice.

Advantages of Installment-Sales Credit. In answer to the criticisms of installment-sales credit, there are arguments in its favor. Individuals are enabled to purchase goods which they could not otherwise own. The losses on installment-sales credit have been small, which suggests moderation in its use by most consumers. The economies due to mass production permit sales at lower prices which more than offset the costs of financing.

REGULATION OF CONSUMER CREDIT

Interest Rates. The oldest objective of regulation of consumer credit is that of preventing exploitation of borrowers by establishing maximum interest rates. Even today, irrespective of general credit conditions, the welfare aspect of consumer-credit regulation directed at the prevention of extortion is always present. During the Middle Ages, the Church banned the taking of interest; and, in modern times, most governments have enacted so-called usury laws that place a limit on the interest rate that may be charged. Compared to businessmen, the applicants for consumer loans are relatively unknown and the administrative costs and risks assumed in making these loans are relatively high. Too often the low ceiling on interest rates prevented legitimate agencies from making small loans; and, as a result, borrowers were forced to depend on illegal lenders. Today there are agencies specifically authorized to lend at rates above the legal rates applicable to other lenders.

Economic Control. A newer type of consumer-credit regulation is that illustrated by Regulation W of the Board of Governors of the Federal Reserve System. This type of economic control pertains to down payments and length of time that installment and other credit contracts may be outstanding. One purpose of this type of economic regulation may be to direct production away from the creation of durable consumer goods (as it was before and during World War II), which might be achieved more efficiently by direct control of the strategic materials involved because credit control will not necessarily decrease purchases by cash customers.

The primary purpose of economic control of consumer credit is to ease inflationary pressure in the segment of the economy which is covered by regulation. The credit terms specified by the Board of Governors in regard to down payments and length of life of the credit contracts are more rigid than those specified by the lending agencies. If they were not, they would not be effective; and, if they were not effective, there would be no political pressure to have them removed. Since commercial banks are not only the most prominent among the institutions in the consumer-credit field but also a chief source of loans to others who finance consumers' credit needs, the volume of consumer credit may be influenced by general credit-control devices of monetary authorities.

Since the amount of consumer credit outstanding has reached such large figures (now in excess of $40 billion), there is some fear that a decrease in the amount of consumer credit will have adverse effects on the economy. When compared to the amount of disposable income, the amount of consumer credit is only 2 per cent above the amount outstanding before World War II (now 12.2 per cent of disposable personal income). After allowances are made for financing automobile purchases, the volume of consumer credit is actually lower, relative to disposable personal income, than it was in 1939. Nevertheless, the volume of consumer spending during 1955 and 1956 caused inflationary pressure on the economy; and, without the increased use of consumer credit the amount of spending would have been less.

Direct Devices of Credit Control.   The volume of consumer credit in use at any one time may be influenced by the use of direct devices of credit control, as illustrated by Regulation W of the Board of Governors of the Federal Reserve System. When consumers are required to increase the amount of down payments and make larger installment payments over a shorter period of time, the effect is to reduce the amount of installment sales credit outstanding. In the case of installment loan credit, the same result may be obtained by requiring larger monthly installment payments and shortening the loan period.

The use of Regulation W and similar types of economic regulation is unpopular with automobile dealers and other sellers of durable consumer goods which are customarily sold on the installment plan. Nevertheless, Regulation W was used at different times during and since World War II, when specifically authorized by Congress. Since 1951, the Federal Reserve System has had considerable success with general credit control devices and, since May, 1952, the Regulation W type of control device has not been used. However if the Board of Governors had had the power to fix the terms of sale (down payment, monthly-installment payments, and maximum maturity) for automobiles in the fall of 1955, there is no doubt but that it would have been used in order to achieve greater economic stability.

Moral Suasion.   Moral suasion has been used by different Federal Reserve banks during boom years to reduce the amount of consumer financing by member banks. In 1955, the three federal bank examining agencies (Comptroller of the Currency, Federal Reserve System, and Federal Deposit Insurance Corporation) began close examination of consumer-credit policies of commercial banks under their supervision. A special questionnaire was added to the forms for reporting the results of bank examinations to bring out individual bank's consumer-lending practices with emphasis on automobile financing. This information was checked to see if a bank was getting out of line with accepted banking practices. The procedure had excellent psychological effects in that it advertised the anxiety of the federal government concerning the inflationary effects of the growing volume of consumer debt.

General Devices of Credit Control. The general devices of credit control now favored by the monetary authorities are those which tend to reduce the availability of member-bank reserves and the volume of loanable funds. Not only are commercial banks the chief direct lenders in the consumer-credit field but they are also a source of funds used by other consumer-financing institutions and retailers who finance their own receivables. So, a general tightening of credit conditions tends to reduce the amount of consumer credit available, to tighten credit terms, and to bring about a reduction in lending and in sales. The opposite of the foregoing would tend to increase consumer borrowing and credit sales during periods of business recession.

SUMMARY

Post-Keynesian economic theory recognizes that consumer spending is a dynamic factor in explaining changes in national income; therefore economists are giving more attention to consumer finance and the sources and uses of consumer credit. Today, there are two broad classes of consumer-credit regulation: (1) the traditional one which has as its purpose the prevention of extortion of the borrower, and (2) the more modern type of regulation which has as its purpose the prevention of too much spending and expansion of debts when they would be injurious to the economy.

Perhaps the most important development in consumer financing has been the rapid increase in the number of banks making consumer loans and purchasing installment contracts. In seeking outlets for loanable funds, banks have captured much of the small-loan and discount business formerly done by personal-loan companies, industrial banks, and discount or finance companies. The aggressiveness of banks, their lower rates, and the prestige of dealing with banks has permitted them to secure the "cream" of the small-loan and discount business.

The chief problem of commercial banks is to keep down collection costs so as to show a profit on the smaller margin on which they are forced to operate. The most equitable and simplest solution would be to permit all banks whose deposits are insured by the Federal Deposit Insurance Corporation to charge 1 per cent per month on the unpaid balance of all loans made for less than $500.

The loss of some sales-finance business to commercial banks is forcing some of the sales-finance companies to finance small-loan transactions that were formerly handled by small-loan companies; in addition, some of these companies have gone into the cash-lending business either directly or indirectly through subsidiaries; others are stressing the financing of mercantile credit (trade credit between business firms). The personal-finance and small-loan companies are extending their activities to include the financing of installment purchases in order to compensate for relative losses in volume of loans. For legal and competitive reasons their activities are confined to smaller loans and discounts.

Credit unions are among the most rapidly growing of the specialized consumer-financing institutions, and they seem to have a secure place in the small-loan business. However, there is little privacy in connection with their lending and many individuals prefer to borrow elsewhere.

QUESTIONS AND PROBLEMS

1. Analyze: Most of those having installment debts who responded to a questionnaire on consumer attitudes and intentions, conducted by the survey Research Center of the University of Michigan, "replied that indebtedness did not lead to postponement of purchases." (Federal Reserve Bank of Kansas City, *Monthly Review*, February, 1956, p. 11.)

2. "The spotlight has focused on automobile and homebuilding industries as primary sources of weakness in 1956" (First National City Bank of New York, *Monthly Letter*, February, 1956, p. 13). Why?

3. Analyze: "The development of consumer installment credit has been highly beneficial to our economy. However, it sometimes accentuates movements in the buying of consumer durable goods . . . [and] this is a good time for Congress and the Executive branch to study the problem" ("Letter of Transmittal" accompanying the President's

Economic Report to Congress dated January 24, 1956). What device of consumer credit control would you suggest? Why?

4. Distinguish between (a) consumer credit and nonconsumer credit, (b) consumer installment credit and consumer noninstallment credit, and (c) consumer installment-sales credit and consumer-installment-loan credit.

5. Identify: (a) installment-sales financing principles and (b) installment-sales credit arrangements.

6. How do sales-finance companies aid in financing the sales of automobiles at the wholesale level? At the retail level? Has the use of sales credit had much effect on the development of the automobile industry? Explain.

7. Analyze: Thirty-five years ago commercial banks failed to meet the rising demand for consumer credit and almost "before we knew it, there developed a full-fledged industry outside the commercial banking field, rendering helpful service to borrowers who were not welcomed at most commercial banks." (James K. Vardaman, Jr., "Human Trust Certificates," a speech before the 8th District Group, Georgia Bankers Association, October 19, 1955.) What is the current situation?

8. Compare the lending practices of industrial or Morris Plan banks and personal-finance companies as to security, interest payments, and repayment plan. What is the relative importance of each of the cash-lending institutions?

9. A wife's signature on a note is considered to be a valuable addition because "there seems to be a higher degree of pride among women in meeting their obligations . . ." (American Bankers Association, *Banking*, November, 1948, p. 118.) Are there other reasons for desiring wives' signatures on personal notes?

10. "Because it is not directly susceptible to control, as is bank credit, consumer credit has on several occasions shown a tendency to expand excessively at times of potential inflation." (*New York Times*, February 3, 1956, p. 22.) Do you agree? Why?

Chapter XXXII

FOREIGN BANKING SYSTEMS

THIS chapter deals with the banking systems of selected countries. In the free economies abroad, most of the banking problems are similar to those faced by bankers in the United States. In European countries, emphasis on reconstruction and development has been necessarily greater than in the United States; and European governments are directing the lending and investing activities of banks more minutely.

CANADIAN BANKING SYSTEM

Of all foreign banking systems the one of greatest interest to most students of money and banking in the United States is that of Canada. The Canadian banking system is a branch-banking system, and a Canadian commercial bank is best defined as "a bank of branches." Head offices neither lend money nor accept deposits but operate branch offices that do their banking business.[1] In Canada there are 11 chartered banks that operate over 3,000 branches (in addition, they have about 150 foreign branches).

The Canadian banking system, in one sense, dates from the formation of the Confederation in 1867. In that year the dominion government was given control of banking and currency, and the banks were authorized to continue doing business under a temporary federal act. The first general Bank Act was passed in 1871; however, before that date, banks had been chartered by the provinces. The oldest of these banks is the Bank of Montreal (1817), which is still in existence and is operating more than 500 branch offices.

The charters of the early Canadian banks were very similar to that of the first Bank of the United States, containing in some cases the same essential clauses and even the same phraseology. The Dominion Bank Act of 1871 reflected this influence, and so it is "gen-

---

[1] For a description of the work of a head office, see "The Head Office of a Bank," *Monthly Review* (The Bank of Nova Scotia, Toronto), April, 1949.

erally agreed that the Canadian banking system is a direct descendant
of the first Bank of the United States. . . ."[2] The Bank Act of 1871
gave the commercial banks charters for but ten years, and ever since
the unique policy of giving decennial charters and renewals has
been followed (delayed twice: 1910–13 and 1933–34). This policy
forces the legislature to appraise its banking system every ten years
and has brought about periodic improvements. One of these revisions
led to the provision for a central bank in 1934.

The Bank of Canada. The Bank of Canada, the central bank of
Canada, has a monopoly of bank-note issue. It is owned by the
dominion government and serves as its fiscal agent, acting as depository and taking charge of public debt operations. The Bank of
Canada also holds reserve deposits of the chartered banks (mostly
commercial banks). In addition to carrying on all the customary
central banking activities, the Bank of Canada also owns and operates
a subsidiary corporation, the Industrial Development Bank, which is
a source of capital funds when such funds cannot be obtained elsewhere. The Bank of Canada began operations on March 11, 1935,
and rapidly assumed an important place in Canadian banking. The
head office is in Ottawa and, subject to governmental approval,
the Bank may establish branches at home or abroad (none has been
established but the Bank does operate nine agencies in different sections of Canada).

The board of directors of the Bank of Canada is appointed by
the government; and, with the approval of the government, the
board selects the chief executive officers—governor, deputy-governor, and assistant deputy-governor. The executive committee,
which consists of the governor, deputy-governor, and a director
selected by the board, meets weekly and exercises the powers of
the board of directors, but submits all decisions to the board for
review. However, the governor (or in his absence, the deputy-
governor) may veto any decision made by the board or the executive committee, but this veto is subject to review by the Minister
of Finance.

Although modified somewhat during wars, the objectives of
the Bank of Canada are basically the same as those provided in
the preamble of the Bank of Canada Act of 1934, which is as
follows:

[2] *Report of the Royal Commission on Banking and Currency in Canada*
(Ottawa: J. O. Patenaude, Printer to the King's Most Excellent Majesty, 1933),
p. 15.

To regulate credit and currency in the best interests of the economic life of the nation, to control and protect the external value of the national monetary unit and to mitigate by its influence fluctuations in the general level of production, trade, prices, and employment, so far as may be possible within the scope of monetary action.

Practically all of the earning assets of the Bank of Canada are in the form of investments in Dominion and provincial governments' short-term and other securities. The Bank may make advances to Canadian banks on any of these securities as collateral. The device of credit control most frequently used is the purchase and sale of government securities, that is, open-market operations. In the Bank Act of 1954, provisions were made for variable reserve requirements; and chartered banks were required to maintain an average minimum cash ratio which may be varied between 8 and 12 per cent by the Bank of Canada. However, an increase in reserve requirements may not be more than 1 per cent in any one month and the banks must be given a month's notice before a change is made.

The Dominion and provincial governments and savings banks may keep deposits with the Bank of Canada; however, 75 per cent of the deposits in the Bank of Canada are those of the chartered banks. But, like central banks the world over, the lending power of the Bank of Canada is due primarily to its right of note issue.

Chartered Banks. A "chartered" bank in Canada is a commercial bank operating under the provisions of the Dominion Bank Act as amended. There are eleven privately owned chartered banks in Canada which carry on commercial banking activities similar to those performed by American commercial banks. The par value of their stock is fixed by law at $10 per share, but the equity per share is more than double that amount. Stockholders elect directors annually, and the banks are managed by officers selected by the directors; but the shareholders are required to select two auditors, responsible to them, who must make an independent audit of the bank each year. These auditors must be selected from a list provided by the Minister of Finance, and they must be from different firms. After July 1, 1959, a person is ineligible to be elected or appointed a director if he has reached the age of 75 years.

The chartered banks are supervised by the Minister of Finance through the office of the Inspector-General of Banks. Banks must submit monthly statements of condition to the government, and the inspector-general examines each bank annually, and he may examine its books at any time. Current loans must be shown on financial statements "less provisions for estimated loss," and securities must be carried at a figure "not exceeding market value." Each bank maintains its own examination department which is responsible for examining each branch at least once a year.

The minimum subscribed capital for chartered banks is $500,-000 (ten times the minimum in the United States), one half of which must be paid in before business may commence. Actually, each bank's capital is many times this minimum, and most of the banks have a surplus equal to or in excess of the paid-in capital. As in most banking systems, the right of note issue was originally granted to the Canadian banks; and, as in the case of the first Bank of the United States, the maximum issue was fixed at an amount equal to each bank's total paid-in capital.[3] The bank notes of the chartered banks have been retired, but the law still permits the chartered banks to issue notes outside of Canada in amounts limited to 10 per cent of each bank's paid-in capital (through foreign banking offices and under provisions of the laws of the governments where the branches are domiciled).

The chartered banks are permitted to engage in "such business generally as appertains to the business of banking." They receive both demand and time deposits, the latter being defined as subject to fifteen days' notice of withdrawal. No charge for collection of checks and other items for services, or because of "activity," may be made against a checking account except upon expressed agreement between the customer and his bank. Collection and certain commission charges are regulated by law; and in this detail, as in many others, Canadian banks are subject to greater regulation than those in the United States. Checks are cleared rapidly and efficiently through regional clearing centers which have been organized by the Canadian Bankers' Association. The results of these daily clearings are reported by telegraph to the Bank of Canada and are settled each day by crediting and debiting clearing balances kept there for this purpose by the chartered banks.

Loans are made by local managers, but investments are usually made by the head office. The branch manager may make individual loans up to a maximum fixed for him by the head office. The amount

[3] By 1908 the elasticity of Canadian bank note circulation had just about reached its limit. The law was changed in 1908 to permit a bank to issue notes in excess of its paid-in capital during the crop-harvesting season. This provision gave desirable elasticity to the note-issue system. See James Holladay, "The Currency of Canada," *American Economic Review*, Vol. XXIV, No. 2 (June, 1934), pp. 266–78.

depends upon the ability of individual managers, the collateral offered for the loans, and the size of the branch. Requests for loans above this maximum are passed upon by a district supervisor or the head office. Loan policies are similar to those in the United States, large loans being made under lines of credit. Much of the work of the head office is given over to supervising bank loans. Although investments are in large amounts, they consist chiefly of government securities and require little attention. There are restrictions on the amount of credit which may be extended to an officer of a bank and on the circumstances under which a loan may be made to a director of a bank or to any firm or corporation in which he is interested. The volume of such loans appears as a separate item on the monthly statement as published by the Minister of Finance.

Part of the success of the Canadian banking system has been due to the restrictions placed upon real estate mortgage lending; however a break with the tradition against mortgage lending came in 1953 when the National Housing Act permitted chartered banks to make home mortgage loans insured under provisions of this Act. Liquidity of such loans was assured when the Bank Act of 1954 permitted the Bank of Canada to make advances to chartered banks secured by insured mortgages in good standing.

There are general restrictions placed upon lending on the security of merchandise, goods, and wares, except as specified in the law. In order to facilitate the business of the borrowers, the banks merely receive an assignment of the merchandise or grain pledged as security for the loans. The legal result is that the banks become preferred general creditors. The scope of this part of the law (Section 88) has been enlarged with each revision of the Canadian Bank Act by redefining terms (as in 1954 when "livestock" was defined to include poultry, and "fisherman" was defined to include partnerships and corporations). In order to facilitate making small personal loans, the banks were authorized to use chattel mortgages or their equivalent in making loans secured by motor vehicles and household property. Banks have also been empowered to make loans on security of natural gas and oil in the ground and rights of ownership thereof.

In general, the investment operations of chartered banks are unrestricted; and many of these banks act as middlemen in marketing securities. However, their underwriting activities are limited to obligations of governments, those guaranteed by the government, and those of certain public utility companies.

Canadian Bankers' Association. The Canadian Bankers' Association, organized in 1890 as a voluntary association, was incorporated by an act of Parliament in 1900 "to effect greater co-operation among the banks in the issue of notes, in credit and control and in various aspects of bank activities." All banks to which the Dominion Bank Act is applicable must be members. The Canadian Bankers' Association performs many co-operative services for banks, and it sponsors the important educational program conducted by Canadian banks. This program is similar to that of the American Institute of Banking. However, most of the success in training the well-managed staffs, for which Canadian banks are famous, is due to the existence of the branch-banking system and the opportunity it offers the management to shift personnel from position to position according to individual administrative records. The personnel of a branch may be small or large—may number two or three or several hundred.

Noncommercial Banks in Canada. In addition to the chartered banks, there are more than one hundred investment banks that act both as brokers and as dealers. They have formed the Investment Bankers' Association of Canada. In the Dominion, there are seven different stock exchanges, the two oldest and most important being the Montreal Stock Exchange and the Toronto Stock Exchange.

In Canada the trust business is separated from the commercial banking business, but many trust companies are closely allied to banks. The trust companies accept savings deposits, act as executors, trustees, and administrators, and serve in other fiduciary capacities. They also perform many agency and trust services for corporations as well as for individuals. These functions are similar to those of trust institutions in the United States, and their loan activities are similar to those of the mortgage loan companies. There are about thirty trust companies in Canada, the largest of which are located in Montreal, Quebec, and Toronto.

In Canada, most of the specialized savings institutions are government-owned. The postal savings system began operations in 1868 and now has more than 1,500 offices which accept individual deposits in any one year in amounts not to exceed $1,500 per person and up to a maximum of $5,000 per account, exclusive of interest.

The governments of Ontario and Alberta operate provincial savings banks which may be illustrated by describing that of Ontario. This bank has twenty-one branches throughout the province, and it has approximately 100,000 individual savings accounts. It accepts deposits which are payable on demand without notice, and it permits depositors to write checks against their accounts. The bank also handles money orders, travelers' checks, and foreign exchange. The bank makes no loans of any kind; and, inasmuch as the bank is a branch of the government, its surplus funds are turned over to the Treasury of the Province of Ontario. In Alberta the provincial Treasury receives savings deposits and issues demand savings certificates. The Quebec savings banks are similar to chartered banks in that they carry on commercial as well as savings banking, and their charters are subject to decennial revision.

A system of People's Banks (*Caisses Populaires*) was introduced in the province of Quebec by Commander Desjardins. These institutions are similar to the People's Banks of Italy and France. Loans, made only to members, may be secured by first mortgages on real property, by bonds, or by tangible personal property. There are more than 250 People's Banks, located chiefly in Quebec, which are the oldest co-operative credit banks in North America.

Mortgage loans are made by trust companies, savings institutions, building and loan associations, and two mortgage companies. A number of rural lending institutions have been set up to finance farmers' needs for credit, and many of these institutions are financed by the provincial governments. In Canada, small-loan companies operate under special legislation that permits them to make installment loans not exceeding $500 for fifteen months at an interest rate up to 1½ per cent per month on outstanding monthly balances, with lower rates on a sliding scale for longer term loans.

Currency and Gold Reserves. When the Bank of Canada began operations in 1935, it assumed responsibility for retiring Dominion notes. Gold coins have not been struck in Canada since 1919; but there are provisions for a subsidary coinage system similar to that of the United States–$1, 50-, 25-, and 10-cent silver coins; 5-cent nickel coins; and 1-cent bronze coins. Subsidiary coins have limited legal tender: silver coins in one payment up to $10, nickel coins up to $5, and bronze coins up to 25 cents. Most of the gold mined in Canada is being delivered to the Bank of Canada (acting as agent for the Department of Finance), and most of it is being held in the form of bars of approximately 400 fine ounces for monetary purposes. The rest is being sold to manufacturers and others for nonmonetary purposes.

On April 30, 1940, the gold reserves of the Bank of Canada were transferred to the Foreign Exchange Control Board; and the requirement that the Bank keep a reserve of gold equal to no less than 25 per cent of its note and deposit liabilities was temporarily suspended. On December 14, 1951, exchange control over the Canadian dollar was abandoned; and the foreign exchange value of the Canadian dollar was permitted to "seek its own level."

BRITISH BANKING SYSTEM

Like the Canadian Banking System, the British (or more commonly the English) Banking System is a branch banking system. Instead of being called "chartered" banks, the English commercial banks are known as "joint-stock" banks. Like all modern banking systems the English Banking System has a central bank, the Bank of England. But, instead of being relatively a newcomer, the Bank of England is the oldest bank in England. Its charter dates from 1694.

Bank of England. The Bank of England is the central bank for the United Kingdom. It has a monopoly of bank-note issue in England and Wales, manages the national debt, and holds part of the reserves of the joint-stock banks. Although the Bank of England was nationalized by the Labour government in 1946, government ownership has caused no change in the Bank's policies since it was already functioning as a government agency. The Bank of England is managed by a court of directors, consisting of a governor, deputy-governor, and sixteen directors appointed by the Queen. In general, the bank's policies are decided by the court of directors; but the "Treasury may from time to time give such directions to the Bank as, after consultation with the Governor of the Bank, it thinks necessary in the public interest."

The Bank of England has two departments—the note-issue department and the banking department. The note-issue department may be compared to the Federal Reserve Agents division of each Federal Reserve bank. It issues Bank of England notes to the banking department and holds government securities, gold bullion, and coins which are pledged as collateral.

The maximum amount of bank notes secured by government debt (and a small amount of coins other than gold coins) that the Bank of England may issue is fixed by law. However, the Treasury may increase or decrease this amount for a six-month period subject to three renewals (total time period would be two years), after which the matter must be presented to Parliament. The Bank of England may issue bank notes in excess of the "fiduciary" amount authorized by the government, provided the notes are covered unit for unit in gold coin or bullion. Today, most of the monetary gold stock of Great Britain is held by the government in the foreign exchange Equalization Fund; and there is relatively little gold being used directly to support the bank notes issued by the Bank of England.

The Bank of England is not required to keep a reserve against its demand deposit liabilities; and, since 1931, it has not been required to convert its obligations into gold coin or gold bullion. The banking department counts the Bank of England bank notes as an asset and uses them to meet its obligations. These notes are also used by commercial and other banks for the same purpose. In practice, all kinds of English money are interchangeable for Bank of England notes which are not freely convertible into gold coin or gold bullion.

The Bank of England is required by law to manage "British stocks and bonds outstanding" (except those on the registers of the Post Office Savings Department, and those of the trustee savings banks and the Bank of Ireland). These fiscal agency functions include payment of bonds that have matured or have been called for redemption, exchanges for other issues, and transfers of titles from old to new owners. It also acts as registrar of loans guaranteed by the government, local authorities, and public boards, and for the bonds of certain colonial and dominion governments. Prior to 1931 the Bank of England used rediscount rate changes and open-market operations as devices of credit control. Because of the small number of banks and the close relationship between them and the Bank of England, moral suasion has been effective in Great Britain.

Customarily, the joint-stock banks do not borrow from the Bank of England; instead, they adjust their reserve positions through the bill market by calling loans to bill brokers or by selling bills in the market. If more of the resources of the Bank of England were to be used, the increase would result from the Bank's open-market purchases of bills or the Bank's advances to bill brokers. This means that about thirty specialists, chiefly discount companies and private firms, are the "buffers" between the Bank of England and the joint-stock banks. Today, most of the trading in the bill market is in Treasury bills rather than in bankers' and trade acceptances.

In addition to being the central bank for the English Banking System, the Bank of England has some ordinary commercial bank characteristics which date back to the time when central banks were also ordinary commercial banks. Although the Riksbank of Sweden is older, the Bank of England was the first to recognize and accept the responsibilities of a central bank. Gradually, it assumed its current role as the bank of issue, custodian of reserves, "lender of the last resort," regulator of the money supply, bank for settlement of clearing balances, and government banker, agent, and advisor.

Joint-Stock Companies. With the exception of the Bank of England, English banks have been organized under the Companies Act, that is, a general incorporation act. Now thirteen incorporated banks with more than 8,000 branches carry on most of the banking in England. The Big Five—namely, Midland, Barclays, Lloyds, Westminster, and National Provincial—hold about 85 per cent of the resources of the English chartered banks.

The checking system is widely developed in England, giving the desirable quality of elasticity to her currency and credit system. There are a few local clearinghouses; but, for the most part, checks are cleared through London. The branch banks send their checks to their head offices in London, and the head offices clear through the London Clearing House. There are three divisions: city (financial district), metropolitan London, and country. Settlements of clearing balances are made by checks drawn on the Bank of England.

There are two classes of deposits—"current accounts" (demand) and "deposit accounts" (subject to seven days' notice). The Bank of England pays no interest on deposits; other banks rarely pay interest on current accounts. The rate paid on time deposits is tied by London Clearing House agreement to the Bank of England's discount rate (normally 2 per cent below, but when the bank rate was 2 per cent, is was fixed at ½ of 1 per cent). The discount houses, trustee (savings) banks, and other agencies normally pay a slightly higher rate than the London Clearing House members. The practice of tying the interest rate on deposits to the rediscount rate of the central bank makes the rate changes of the Bank of England far more significant than similar rate changes of the Federal Reserve banks in the United States.

In granting credit the emphasis placed on short-term commercial loans was so great in the past that English bankers were accused of neglecting industry. Although English bankers prefer to have advances cleared up yearly, many loans have been extended for long periods of time. One system of extending credit which has been popular for years in England is that of lending under lines of credit that permit customers to overdraw their checking accounts. This method of lending has the advantage of permitting customers to use credit only when it is needed. There is no need to secure in advance funds which will lie idle during part of the loan period or a part of which may not be used at all. The interest rate on overdrafts is slightly higher than that on other types of loans (and fees may be charged).

Prior to 1947 the banks made up their monthly bank statements on different days. In practice, this meant that the banks were withdrawing funds from the money market on different days in order to show a stronger cash position. Staggered reports permitted the banks, individually, to show a much larger cash ratio than if all had reported on the same day. Among the recommendations of the Committee on Finance & Industry (the Macmillan Committee) was one that this "window-dressing" practice be given up at once.[4] However, the London Clearing House banks did not agree to this until 1947. Now all banks make monthly reports on the same dates.

For years the item, "cash in hands and balance with the Bank of England," was from 10 to 12 per cent of total assets; but, after the adoption of uniform reporting dates, the cash ratio was 8.7 per cent. This figure was in keeping with the 8 per cent agreed on by the Bank of England and other banks "after consultation." Even though there is no statutory minimum reserve requirement for joint-stock banks, the Bank of England has brought about a similar situation by informal action.[5]

With the exception of forbidding note issue, no specific restrictions are placed on English banking. There are no special or general banking laws, and the banks have the same legal status as any other joint-stock company. Clause 4 of the Bank of England Act of 1946 came in for considerable speculation because of its potential effects on policies of commercial banks. This clause empowered the Bank of England to "request information from or make recommendations to bankers" and, with the authorization of the Treasury, to "issue directions to any banker for the purpose of securing that effect is given to any such request or recommendation." This clause may be used to implement any policy that is now established by custom, or it may be used to direct banking resources into new channels.

[4] Committee on Finance & Industry, *Report Presented to Parliament by the Financial Secretary to the Treasury by Command of His Majesty June 1951* (London: Printed and Published by His Majesty's Stationary Office, 1951), p. 157.

[5] In order to augment the resources of the Bank of England, the Macmillan Committee recommended that the joint-stock banks keep larger balances with it. This is in keeping with the erroneous concept that central banks' strength depends upon primary deposits when, in fact, the note-issue privilege is far more important.

Since the initiative will come from the Bank and not from the Treasury, it has been suggested that this clause will make no fundamental difference in bank policy, since in the past no individual English bank was in a position to take lightly a suggestion of the Bank of England. On the other hand, it seems unlikely that a court (governors and directors) appointed by the government would not be willing to "initiate" action.

Other Financial Institutions. Since London has been a leading financial center for several hundred years, many of the leading banking houses of the world have branches or subsidary corporations in London. These include the largest American commercial banks and investment houses[6] as well as branches of colonial and dominion banks. Other English financial institutions include trustee savings banks, postal savings banks, trust companies, and merchant bankers.[7] Although there are specialists in the money market, there has been a tendency for English commercial banks and other institutions to broaden their activities.

In addition to the savings accounts in the commercial banks, English depositors keep large sums in the postal savings banks and the 370 trustee (savings) banks which operate branch offices. In recent years, balances with the trustee banks have increased while those in the Post Office Savings Bank have declined. There are two kinds of accounts in the trustee banks, ordinary accounts and special investment accounts. The latter bear a higher interest rate ($\frac{1}{4}$ and $\frac{1}{2}$ per cent more than the traditional $2\frac{1}{2}$ per cent on ordinary deposits), but the amount that may be accepted from one customer is limited (now £1,000 as compared to the £3,000 in ordinary accounts with trustee savings banks and the Post Office Savings Bank). Savings banks are in a better competitive position to attract savings than is the Post Office Savings Bank because they offer many special services (such as receiving payments of gas and electricity bills, safe depository services, etc.). In addition, savings certificates are sold to those who prefer these instruments to savings accounts. Since interest paid thereon is exempt from taxation, savings certificates are popular

[6] American banks, brokers, and investment houses having branches or subsidiaries in London include Bache & Co.; Baker, Weeks, and Harden; Bankers Trust Company; Bank of America National Trust and Savings Association; Calvin Bullock, Ltd.; Chase-Manhattan Bank of New York; Guaranty Trust Company of New York; International Banking Corporation; and First National City Bank of New York.

[7] Many of the merchant banking houses are of foreign origin, for example: J. Henry Schroeder & Co. (1804); Hambros Bank, Ltd. (1839); Kleinwort Sons & Co. (1830); Lazard Brothers & Co., Ltd. (1877); and Seligman Brothers (1864).

with those in the higher income brackets. This tax exemption is also applicable to defense bonds. The postal savings system is much older (1861) and relatively more important in England than in the United States. In the United Kingdom, as in the United States, there has been a growth in employee pension plans with an increasing percentage of employees being subjected to "contractual savings." And, as in the United States, there has been an increase in sales of consumer goods on the installment plan. In the United Kingdom, school savings groups include approximately one third of the school population.

The problem of mortgage credit has been a minor one in England and Wales because of the inheritance system and the concentration in ownership of real property. As a result of this situation, real estate collateral is considered among the highest types that may be offered as security for loans; and most of the agricultural and other mortgage needs have been cared for without specialized agricultural mortgage institutions. In 1928 the Agricultural Mortgage Corporation, Limited, was established.

FRENCH BANKING SYSTEM

Prior to World War II, the French Banking System was unique in that the Bank of France was not only the central bank but also the most important commercial bank in France, combining central and ordinary commercial banking functions. It was this dual role of the Bank of France that justified the operation of over 650 branches and agencies through which the Bank brought its services directly to the general public. The Bank of France competed actively with other banks for ordinary deposits, transfer (*giro*) accounts, and loans; but, in recent years, the Bank of France has become mainly a central bank.

There are 278 deposit banks in France which is dominated largely by the big six which operate thousands of branches throughout the country in much the same manner as do the large English banks. In addition, there are 39 investment banking houses (*banques d'affaires*), a number of foreign and colonial banks, specialized banking houses, and public and semipublic institutions.

In 1945, in a sweeping reform law, the French government provided for reorganization of the French Banking System. First the government purchased the stock of the Bank of France and of four large commercial banks. Then, these banks were placed under the management of directors selected, for the most part, by the government. As a second step, remaining banks were required to register as banks of deposit, as business banks (*banques d'affaires*), or as long-term or intermediate credit banks. After self-classification, each bank was given one year in which to adjust its business to standards as provided for its class. Then, all banks were to be subject to regulation as provided for in other sections of the law. The standards set for deposit banks limited their underwriting and other investment-banking activities, and the standards set for business banks limited their deposit-banking business. The other classes of banks are specialized institutions which, for the most part, had been operating under special statutes (savings, agricultural, mortgage, people's banks, etc.).

Now there are three separate authorities responsible for the regulation of the banking system. (1) In 1945, a National Credit Council was created to advise the government and to take general responsibility for credit policy (sort of national monetary and credit control council such as has been recommended for the United States). The Minister of Finance is the president of the Council, the Governor of the Bank of France is the vice-president, and all of the economic departments of the government are represented. There are 38 members, and their function is to make general studies and recommendations. (2) In 1941, the law provided for a Banking Control Commission of five members which is a supervisory agency, authorized to impose penalities if its requirements are not met. (3) The Bank of France, in its capacity as a central bank, is largely responsible for carrying out the policies of the National Credit Council.

Bank of France. The Bank of France (*Banque de France*) has a monopoly of note issue (acquired completely in 1848), which is more important in France wherein the use of checks is of less importance than in English-speaking countries. The Bank of France was established by Napoleon in 1800 without a charter; but, three years later, its organization and powers were laid down by law. Throughout most of its history, the Bank was owned privately and managed conservatively, having suspended specie payments only twice prior to 1914 (1848–50 and 1870–77).

During World War I the heavy commitments of the Bank of France to war financing caused inflation in general prices. Between the two World Wars, France continued to have currency and other financial problems; and the French franc decreased to less than one tenth of its prewar value. World War II increased France's financial burdens by increasing its outlays for war, occupation costs of the German army, and postwar reconstruction. Many of these expenditures were financed by increasing the volume of Bank of France notes, which was one of the factors causing the value of the France franc to decline to about one fourth of a cent (compared to 2 cents at the time of "liberation" by General Eisenhower's Armies).

On December 2, 1945, the government nationalized the Bank of France, acquiring title to all stock in exchange for bonds. The chief administrative officers have been appointed by the nominal head of the government (the Emperor or President of France) throughout the history of the Bank. Now, as before nationalization, the President of France appoints the governor and two deputy-governors. The three officials plus two *censors* and twelve *conseillers* (directors) make up the membership of the General Council. Seven of the directors are appointed by the Minister of Finance on nomination by cabinet members to represent various groups, one is elected by the staff of the Bank, and four are ex officio members representing certain public credit institutions. The Minister of Finance is represented on the General Council (board of directors) at its weekly meetings by two *censors* (auditors) who have no vote.

Since World War II, in carrying out its credit policies, the Bank of France has used open-market operations and changes in the rediscount rate, but major dependence has been on various selective or direct control devices. These consist of requirements that commercial banks hold a certain amount of their resources in short-term government paper and refer requests for large loans to the Bank of France for approval. In addition, limits (ceilings) were placed on the amount of rediscounting with the Bank of France, except for certain types of paper. At times, use has been made of a secondary ceiling to cover supplementary borrowing, but at a penalty rate, at the Bank of France. For a long period of time, the commercial banks did not need to borrow from the Bank of France; and this handicapped its functioning as a central bank.

Deposit Banks (Establissements de Crédit). About the middle of the last century a number of chartered banks appeared, including three of the most important banks of deposit in France—*Crédit Industriel et Commercial*, 1853; *Crédit Lyonnais*, 1853; and *Société Générale*, 1864. Now there are six large incorporated banks of deposit that are national in scope of operation, having about 300 branch offices in Paris and more than 4,000 in the provinces. The four large banks which have been nationalized now do about two thirds of the commercial banking business in France.[8] One of the two large banks which has not been nationalized is technically a Paris bank (*Crédit Industriel et Commercial*), but it holds an investment interest in groups of regional banks; and the other (*Crédit Commerciel de France*) has a less complete coverage of branches than the other large banks. The 22 regional banks include 12 which are associated with the *Crédit Industriel et Commercial*.

In addition to the national and regional branch-banking systems, there are local provincial banks, some of which have branch offices. In Paris, there are also many small banks that operate as unit banks, but their interests are not confined to Paris even though they have no branches. In the provinces, as in Paris, there is a tendency for the smaller banks to be absorbed by larger banks or to die out with the passage of time because their survival depends upon personal relations which may be discontinued after the death of certain individuals. Nevertheless, there is a demand for personal services that family concerns provide most satisfactorily.

Paris, being one of the important money markets of the world, is the locale of a number of subsidiaries, branches, and offices of colonial and Franco-foreign banks and of foreign banks. Among the foreign banks, there are fifteen which are incorporated outside of France (such as branches of the Chase-Manhattan Bank of New York, Midland Bank, Ltd., and the Guaranty Trust Company of New York), and eleven others are French companies under foreign control (such as Morgan et Cie. and First National Bank of New York, France).

Prior to 1946, banks of deposit were subject to no general banking regulations and were free to develop banking along various lines except note issue, which was a monopoly of the Bank of France. There were no legal ties (as in the United States) or formal ties (as in Great Britain) between the Bank of France and the deposit banks. At the end of World War II, the earning assets of the commercial banks were largely in the form of government securities; but now treasury bills and other short-term securities comprise only

---

[8] The four banks are the Crédit Lyonnais, Société Générale, Comptoir Nationale d'Escompte, and Banque Nationale pour le Commerce et l'Industrie. The other two members of the Big Six were exempt because their business was not national in scope. The Crédit Industriel et Commerciel does have national coverage through its affiliates in the provinces (twelve regional banks and their branches). The Crédit Commerciel de France deposit business is more regional in nature.

15 per cent of total assets, with over two thirds of total assets being in commercial discounts, loans, and overdrafts.

Business Banks. The business banks (*Banques d'Affaires*) are most similar to investment houses in the United States, their chief function being to help finance the capital needs of new and old business firms. Some of the early investment bankers were of Swiss Protestant antecedents, such as Hottinguer, Mallet, Mirabaud, and Vernes; others were of Jewish origin, such as Oppenheim and Rothschild. These *hautes banques* (higher banking houses) carried on investment-banking, foreign-exchange, arbitrage, and deposit-banking activities. Their scope of activities was even broader than that of American private banks, such as the old J. P. Morgan & Co. and Kuhn, Loeb & Co. These French banking houses owned most of the stock of the Bank of France before 1936; and, due to directorship, investments, and close family connections, they controlled most of the French economy, as well as having "interests" throughout the world.

In addition to the *hautes banques,* the "aristocracy of French banking," there were smaller and less influential private banks in Paris (bringing the number of such banks to more than fifty, of which six were incorporated). Today, these banks are classified as *banques d'affaires* (business banks). The business banks (*banques d'affaires*) accept deposits; but they differ from other banks in their extensive participation in promotion of new industrial enterprises and underwriting of existing corporations, often holding blocks of shares and maintaining a close relationship with the corporations concerned. These banks have no branches and use the large deposit banks to market securities; therefore, they often have a large ownership-interest in the deposit banks (*establissements de crédit*) so as to be sure of their co-operation in merchandising securities.

In addition to the large business banks in Paris, there are private security houses or brokerage firms and various types of specialists including two bullion brokers, discount houses that operate in the money market either as brokers or dealers (the most important is the *Campagnie Parisienne de Réescompte* which is the official broker for the Bank of France), and eight banks that make intermediate and long-term loans.

Under provisions of the banking act of 1945, the *banques d'affaires* were required to register either as investment or business banks; but they were permitted to accept deposits under limited circumstances. Demand deposits may be accepted only from a limited range of customers and other deposits that are accepted must be for a period of at least two years. Their deposit-banking business tends to be linked more or less directly to their function of providing investment funds.

Savings Banks. Unlike other French banks, savings institutions have been subject to regulation under special law since 1835. Some of the savings banks are privately owned and controlled, while others are operated by local governments or by the national government. Savings banks include the ordinary savings banks (*Caisses d'Épargne Ordinaires*) and the postal savings system (*Caisse Nationale d'Épargne*). Among the ordinary savings banks, those operated by municipalities differ from others chiefly in the way the directors are chosen—being appointed by the local government. The others are managed by self-perpetuating boards (as in the case of mutual savings banks in the United States). These ordinary savings banks, numbering 550, operate over 2,200 branch offices.

The postal savings system, established in 1881, was modeled after that of Great Britain. Every post office is authorized to accept deposits and to transfer accounts from one post office to a second. In addition, the post offices operate a system of transferring funds between communities, accepting accounts on which checks may be drawn or, more frequently, used to make transfers on written instructions. Deposits of savings banks are invested by the *Caisse des Dépôts et Consignations*, which is a government agency created to manage insurance, trust, savings, and pension funds.

Agricultural Credits. In the agricultural field, co-operative financing has been promoted by the state. At present, there are local co-operatives, regional co-operatives, and *Caisse Nationale des Crédit Agricole* (a government institution) and independent co-operative associations. Loans are usually for short terms; and funds are obtained by the sale of stock to members, from depositors, and by borrowing from the appropriate regional office (which in turn borrows from the national office). The agricultural credit system resembles a pyramid with more than 6,000 local associations, affiliated with 98 regional associations which, in turn, are assisted by the national association—a state institution with broad powers over the system.

Mortgage Banking. In France, there are about forty-five mortgage banks and kindred institutions. The method of raising funds employed by one of these mortgage banks, the *Crédit Foncier de France*, has been used as a model by numerous governments in creating mortgage banks. This institution, established in 1852, obtains loanable funds by selling bonds to the general public. These funds are lent to homeowners and others; but, in recent years, lending to local governments has been emphasized. The amount of funds that this bank may have outstanding at one time is limited to fifty times its capital (as compared to twenty for federal land banks and home loan banks in the United States). The bank's operations are national in scope; and all of its activities are under the supervision of the government, which appoints the governor and two deputy governors.

Since most of the French farmers have owned their land for years, there is little need for farm mortgage credit. (French families are small, and estate settlements cause little demand for additional credit.) Residential mortgage loans are more frequent; but, because of the stationary population, the demands for new credit are small. War-damaged buildings are being rebuilt with assistance from the government (through municipal and departmental institutions). And so, mortgage banking is less widely developed in France than in most other countries.

People's Banks. The *banques populaires*, or people's banks, were created to provide credit for small businesses either by loans or by guarantees of loans made by others. Although the people's-bank movement has been heavily subsidized and closely supervised by the government, the record of these banks has been unsatisfactory. Since the people's banks tend to lend to those who cannot get credit accommodations from other lenders, their record reflects the emphasis on social policy rather than a lack of sound bank management.

Pawnbrokering. In France the pawnbrokerage business may be carried on only by special institutions of a public character (municipal institutions), and these institutions are regulated by law. Accounts are audited by the Treasury; and funds are provided by endowments, gifts, and sometimes by the municipalities. Interest rates vary from 1 to 14 per cent, and profits are either retained in the business or given to charitable institutions.

SUMMARY

The banking system of the United States has influenced and has been influenced by the banking systems of other countries. At the central banking level, the United States has twelve central banks while most other countries have but one; but, because of the concentration of policy decisions in the hands of the Board of Governors of the Federal Reserve System and the Federal Open Market Committee, this difference is chiefly technical. Most of the central banks established prior to the establishment of the Federal Reserve System originated as ordinary commercial banks with ordinary commercial-banking functions as well as central-banking functions; but the newer central banks have been patterned after that of the United States, that is, they have been created as banks of issue, bankers' banks, and bankers for their governments. In recent years the older central banks have been emphasizing their central-banking functions to an increasing extent and have been curtailing their commercial-banking functions; as a result, the activities of central banks the world over are not too different from those of the Federal Reserve banks in the United States except that most foreign central banks are owned by their governments.

The greatest difference between the organization of commercial banks in the United States and in foreign countries is the operation of large numbers of branch offices. In most foreign countries, most of the commercial banking is done by fewer than ten banks with their hundreds or thousands of branches. When computed on a per capita basis, the people in most foreign countries are served better, in terms of the number of banking offices, than are the people of the United States. Abroad, as in the United States, banking is generally subject to detailed regulation (the most important exception being the United Kingdom where tradition is a determining factor). Credit-control policies are determined by central banks and governments, with perhaps the latter being more important abroad than in the United States.

With the possible exception of France, no foreign country has achieved the complexity and completeness in the noncommercial banking field as that found in the United States. In most foreign countries, there is a tendency to expand existing sources of credit available to homeowners, farmers, and consumers rather than to create new credit-granting institutions. The more complex noncommercial banking systems in the United States are due, in part, to legal restrictions on commercial banking, the local nature of most commercial banks, and the complexity of American laws due to the existence of forty-nine legislative bodies. In the United States, local or state groups are continually experimenting with some new type of bank or association arising out of some special need (some of these have been adopted later by the national government).

The commercial banks in the United States hold over one half of the commercial banking resources of the world, and the noncommercial banking institutions hold an even larger percentage of the world's investment banking resources. In comparing the banking facilities of the United States to those of foreign countries, the dominant position of the United States must be kept in mind. For example, the New York City banks alone hold more assets than do all of the banks in England, and the two largest banks in the United States have more assets than all of the commercial banks in Canada.

QUESTIONS AND PROBLEMS

1. Justify this statement: "The Canadian banking system is a direct descendant of the first Bank of the United States. . . ." Why did not the American system develop along similar lines?

2. Explain and give advantages of the decennial chartering and renewal policy in Canada.

3. In what way does Canadian banking reflect the influence of British and American banking practices and organization?

4. "In short, it is difficult to think of any other business in Canada that is under more close and continuing inspection and control than is the business of banking" (Bank of Montreal, *Business Review*, July 22, 1954, n.p.). Justify this statement by summarizing provisions for supervision and regulation of Canadian banks.

5. What divisions in the Federal Reserve banks tend to correspond to those of the banking and issue departments of the Bank of England?

6. Distinguish between the "fiduciary" and the "covered" issues of the Bank of England. In what way is the English bank note-issue system inferior to the provisions for the issuance of Federal Reserve notes? Explain. Is the Banking Department justified in counting the Bank of England notes as reserves?

7. Describe the "overdraft" system of lending. Compare to the type of bank lending common in the United States. What are the advantages of the first to the borrower? Are banks justified when they charge a higher rate for overdraft loans than for other types, assuming that other things are the same? Explain.

8. "About thirty specialists . . . are the 'buffers' between the Bank of England and the joint-stock banks." Explain.

9. Would you expect the type of credit control suggested by the following to be effective? "The chancellor sent a letter to the Governor of the Bank of England expressing the view that it was the duty of the banks 'to reduce the amount of bank credit below what they would be glad to give in less difficult times,' and stating that he

looked for 'a positive and significant reduction in their advances over the next few months.' " (Midland Bank Limited, *Midland Bank Review*, November, 1955, p. 12). Why?

10. "The Bank of France is the greatest and in many respects the strongest of the banks of the world, and its development exhibits many of the most interesting phases of banking history outside of Great Britain." (C. A. Conant, *A History of Modern Banks of Issue* [5th ed.; New York: G. P. Putnam's Sons, 1915], p. 38.) Is the first part of this statement, first made in 1902, still true?

11. Summarize the provisions made for the reform of the French banking system at the end of 1945.

INDEX

635

Finance
  instruments of long-term, 197–202
  instruments of short-term, 202–4
Financing
  exports, 311–14
  foreign trade, 311–14
  foreign travel, 318–20
  imports, 314–16
  shipments between countries, 316
  storage of goods, 316–17
First Bank of the United States, 153–55
Fiscal policy, 426–41
  background for, 426–33
  bank policy versus, 455–56
  compensatory, 433
  co-ordination of monetary and, 455–57
  national budget and, 433–37
  national debt and, 437–41
"Float," 84, 224, 379–81, 394–95
Flow of bank funds, 265
Flow of funds system of accounts, 25,
    46–47
Foreign banking systems, 613–34
  reserves of, 405–6
Foreign branches of American banks,
    185–86
Foreign exchange, 306
  arbitrage in, 323–24
  controlled, 475–80
  credit instruments of, 306–11
  foreign trade financing, 311–16
  meaning of, 306
  par value of, 468
  purchasing power par of, 473–74
  purchasing power parity theory of,
    472–73
  rates of, 109, 309
    spread between, 309
  risks of, 321
  special forms of, 309–11
  speculation in, 322–23
Foreign exchange control, 486–87
Foreign exchange dealers, 325–26
Foreign exchange departments of com-
    mercial banks, 325
Foreign exchange markets, 324–25
  banks and, 324–26
  "forward," 325
  functions of, 320–24
  "spot," 325
Foreign trade financing, 311–16
Foreign travel financing, 318–20
Forward exchange, 321–22
Fractional reserve plan, control of
    money and, 65
France, banking system of, 625–31
Free coinage, 113, 130
Free reserves, 392
Free silver, 397–98

Full-bodied money, 97, 127, 129–30
  trend away from, 131, 132
Full Employment Act of 1946, 444–48
  stable prices and, 444–48
Fundamental Psychological Law, 430–31
"Futures," 321–22

G

General purchasing power, 4
Gold, 3 (*see also* Gold standard; etc.)
  banks, 137 n.
  bars, 101
  coinage prohibited, 101, 142
  coins, 101, 131–32
  earmarked, 104–5
  export-import points, 109, 468–69
  Federal Reserve credit and, 103–4
  government ownership of, 101–2
  "inactive," 144, 397
  mining, 116–17
  monetary and nonmonetary demands
    for, 117–20
  money, 100–105
  movements, 468–71
  payments suspended, 139–40
  production of, 116–17
  qualities of, 116–17
  regulator of balance of payments,
    110–12, 464–71
  regulator of the currency, 112–13
  underrated, 130
Gold Bill of 1834, 131–32
Gold bullion standard, 113, 139–45
Gold Certificate Fund, 85
Gold certificates, 3, 4, 92, 101, 137–38
  transfer of, 86
Gold coin standard, 113, 135–39
Gold credits, 3
Gold dollar, 4, 17–18, 100, 108
  devaluation of the, 142–43
Gold drafts, 113–14
Gold exchange standard, 113–14
  restricted, 114–15
Gold imports and exports, 110–12
  sterilization of, 144, 397–98
Gold purchase plan, 141
Gold Reserve Act of 1934, 142, 143–44
Gold reserves (*see* Reserves)
Gold standard, 108–24, 135–39
  adoption of, 115–16
  international, 108–12
  "limping" or "peg-leg," 135–36
  types of, 113–15
  why the, 115–20
Gold standard mechanism, 112–13
Gold stock of the United States, 102–3
Gold transactions regulated by the
    Treasury, 143–44, 397–98